AGENCY AND PARTNERSHIP

Cases, Materials and Problems

CONTEMPORARY LEGAL EDUCATION SERIES

CONTEMPORARY LEGAL EDUCATION SERIES

Agency and Partnership

CASES, MATERIALS AND PROBLEMS

J. DENNIS HYNES

Professor of Law
University of Colorado

THE BOBBS-MERRILL COMPANY, INC.
A SUBSIDIARY OF HOWARD W. SAMS & CO., INC.
PUBLISHERS • INDIANAPOLIS • KANSAS CITY • NEW YORK

To My Family

Preface

This casebook is designed for coverage of the law of agency and partnership in a course offering less classroom time than the customary 45 classroom hours. In general, however, the format remains traditional, with the exception of the following three features. First, most chapters begin with a series of questions raising some of the legal issues in the chapter and usually posed both in the abstract and in concrete (through fact situations) terms. Second, there are fewer cases and substantially more text in this book than in many casebooks. Third, there are problems at the end of nearly all chapters.

The purpose of beginning a chapter with questions is to get the reader thinking about what a common sense and fair solution to the problem posed would be before what others have done with such matters influences his train of thought. This may enhance the prospect of approaching the law critically since the reader will have thought about it on his own first, and of observing the legal process in action, including the underlying bases on which it seems to operate, from a different perspective.

As mentioned, there are relatively few cases in these materials, and substantial amounts of text. The reason I did this is that, for the reason noted above, this casebook attempts to cover the subjects of agency and partnership in considerably fewer pages than the other casebooks in the area, of which there are five.* To rely solely—or even mainly—on cases seemed a less productive use of space under these limitations. In addition, the textual nature of the materials provides the instructor with the opportunity to rely more heavily than usual on student self-education and thus to move through the materials more rapidly by, for example, assigning a chapter or even an entire section and pausing only on several of the problems at the end of the chapters in order to explore the extent to which the basic principles and their limitations have been understood.

Nevertheless, a balance must be struck. Agency is a common law subject, and there is no better way to get an impression of the common law than to observe courts using and talking about it in

---

* Since this was written, a sixth casebook has been published, authored by Professor Henn of Cornell Law School. It too is planned for course treatment of less than three hours. I have not yet carefully read the book, but welcome the interest of someone else in making possible a more concise treatment of agency and partnership law.

the process of resolving disputes. I thus have included at least several court opinions in the presentation of each major topic and, with partially the same objective in mind, have included citations to most of the problems which have been drawn from cases, as will be discussed below.

The text contains many questions in addition to a description of the law. These are designed to stimulate the reader to think about some of the law raised earlier in case or textual form. Since this is a casebook, not a hornbook or treatise, I did not make an effort to answer all questions, engage in complete analysis of all problems, and so forth. Also, the questions set forth in this book are just a beginning. There remain many interesting and subtle points to be thought of and explored.

The purpose of including problems at the end of nearly all chapters is to encourage the reader to work with the legal principles set forth in each chapter in varying contexts, which should reinforce an understanding of the principles and their limitations. Also, this gives the reader the opportunity to work with the law the way a lawyer does after having done some preliminary research. No attempt is made in the problems to follow the order of the presentation of materials in the chapters.

The problems are drawn mainly (but not exclusively) from actual cases, usually with citations to the cases at the end of the problem. I have done this for two reasons. The first is that it makes things more realistic. One knows that this is a situation that actually happened and that the law involved was sufficiently unclear and the issue sufficiently important that people were willing to spend time and money in taking it to an appellate court. The second reason is that usually the reader, having thought about the problem, can look up the case and see how one group of lawyers who have become judges resolved it. This doesn't always supply "the answer," of course, but it does provide another and frequently helpful perspective. Occasionally I have altered the facts of a particular case, with the objective of raising additional issues.

A brief comment about the practical nature of the subject matter of this book may be useful. The law of agency deals basically with the legal consequences of people acting on behalf of other people or organizations. In order to assess the importance of this area of the law, consider how many people in this country today are truly self-employed and self-sufficient. Not necessarily the small manufacturer, because usually he hires employees and thus is not self-sufficient; not the lawyer who is a sole practitioner and does his own typing and filing, for he performs services for others and thus is subject to their direction and control. Perhaps the farmer with a very small operation is a good example, but he must run an operation so small as to not need to hire workers or use members of his family. The shop-keeper may be another example, but how many shops are run entirely by the owner with no other help? And even the entirely self-employed and self-sufficient have to deal with the agents of others in their business and personal matters.

The universality of the operation of the law of agency is there-fore apparent. The materials to follow will introduce the main concepts underlying the law of agency, with the three party nature of most transactions, involving differing rights and duties among the various parties, presenting an added dimension of complexity.

The law of business organizations, including partnerships, carries a different focus. It deals with the problems created when people choose to operate a business concern in a man-ner and form created or tolerated by the state. Many of the problems are internal: who receives what, who owes what to whom, who makes the decisions. In one form—the corpora-tion—the internal and regulatory problems are sufficiently com-plex to justify several courses in the law school curriculum. The problems raised by doing business in the partnership form are of a different order, both because much of partnership law is based on agency law and because the scope of state regulation and the level of organizational formality are less pronounced than for the corporate form of doing business. A treatment of partnership law thus fits naturally into a course on agency, and is the subject of Part IV of these materials. The introductory materials to Chapter 12 contain some statistics and comments on the widespread use of partnerships today by people in busi-ness.

With respect to matters of form, all textual omissions, whether of a few words, a paragraph, or several pages, are indicated by an ellipsis. No ellipsis is indicated where the omission consists of footnotes or of citations to cases or articles. Footnotes which have been retained carry their original numbers. Footnotes by the author are identified by asterisks.

Acknowledgments

Permission of the following copyright owners to reprint extracts from their publications is gratefully acknowledged: The American Law Institute and West Publishing Company, publishers of the Restatement (Second) of Agency and the Uniform Commercial Code (1962 Official Text); West Publishing Company, publisher of the Uniform Partnership Act, the Uniform Limited Partnership Act and Prosser on Torts (4th ed.); The Joint Committee on Continuing Legal Education of the American Law Institute and the American Bar Association, publishers of Mulder and Volz, The Drafting of Partnership Agreements; Harvard University Press, publisher of Harvard Legal Essays; and the Yale Law Journal.

Grateful acknowledgment for their valuable assistance in the preparation of these materials is also made to my colleagues on the faculty of the University of Colorado School of Law, especially Clifford Calhoun, Homer Clark, Frederic Kirgis, Alfred McDonnell, Courtland Peterson, Arthur Travers and James B. White, all of whom read and commented on portions of the manuscript, to student assistants Jon Harnish, Kent Williamson, Mark Levy and Randy Nelson, and to Mrs. Dorothy Westcott, an exceptionally able typist.

Summary Table of Contents

Table of Contents

Table of Cases

Principal cases and the pages on which they appear are in italics.
Noted and cited cases and their page references are in roman.

Restatement (Second) of Agency Citations

References are to page numbers

Uniform Partnership Act Citations

References are to page numbers

PART I

DEFINING THE AGENCY
RELATIONSHIP

Chapter 1

THE ELEMENTS OF AN AGENCY RELATIONSHIP

A. THE GENERAL DEFINITION

As was mentioned in the Preface, an effort has been made in this casebook to begin each chapter with questions about aspects of the law which you will encounter in the chapter before you are exposed to the principles which already have been formulated by the courts and others. We commence below with that effort.

Most of us have some idea of what constitutes an agency relationship, and who is and who isn't an agent. Using this, and common sense, ask yourself which of the following fact situations, if any, involve an agency relationship, and why. A commonly recognized definition of the agency relationship will be set forth shortly.

Suppose that Smith's friend, Fred Jones, asks to borrow Smith's power lawnmower for the afternoon. Smith says, "Sure, Fred, but don't run it at full throttle. The blade is a little loose." Jones agrees and uses the mower. He forgets about the warning and instructions, however, and the blade flies off, injuring a passerby. Is Jones the agent of Smith, raising the possibility, as will be developed below, that Smith could be held liable for the negligence of Jones?

Suppose that the situation is changed so that the blade flew off while Jones was mowing Smith's lawn. Smith had neither knowledge of nor requested Jones' act, which was prompted by Smith's past favors to Jones including permission to use the lawnmower whenever he wished, coupled with the warning about the blade. Jones simply had gone into Smith's garage and taken the mower, hoping to surprise Smith when he came home at the end of the day. Does this variation weaken or strengthen an argument for liability based on an agency relationship?

Finally, suppose that Jones had agreed to mow Smith's lawn in return for the use of the mower, that Smith knew about this and had given the instructions and warning, and the accident had happened while Jones was mowing Smith's lawn. Now is the argument stronger or weaker that Jones is an agent of Smith?

To shift away for a moment from liability for physical injury to contractual questions, consider the following: Sam Peters agrees with Joe Adams to act as trustee for Adams' children. Peters enters into this relationship and holds title to various items of property for the children, investing for them, distributing income to them, and so forth. Is Peters the agent of the Adams' children? Of Joe Adams? Would it make any difference in your response if Joe Adams had drafted an elaborate trust instrument, retaining detailed control over the type of investments Peters made, over when and under what circumstances income was distributed, over who would be the beneficiaries, over what income Peters would get from this, and so forth? If so, why? What if Adams designated himself as beneficiary during his lifetime, with the income going to him until his death and then to his children?

The RESTATEMENT (SECOND) OF AGENCY § 1 (1958) (referred to throughout these materials as "Restatement" or sometimes "Restatement of Agency")* defines the agency relationship as follows:

§ 1.   Agency; Principal; Agent.

(1)   Agency is the fiduciary relation which results from the manifestation of consent by one person to another that the other shall act on his behalf and subject to his control, and consent by the other so to act.

---

* The Restatement (Second) of Agency is a three-volume work which was published in 1958 under the auspices of the American Law Institute ("ALI"), a voluntary, nonofficial association of practicing lawyers, judges and law teachers. The first two volumes contain the text of the Restatement, including the sections (of which there are 528), explanatory comments to the sections, and illustrations of the principles stated in the sections. The third volume is the Appendix, which contains annotations of court decisions referring to particular sections and, with respect to some sections only, brief memoranda of law written by the principal draftsman of the Restatement (called the "Reporter").

The first edition of the Restatement of Agency was published in 1933. It was the second of the many restatements of the law published by the ALI. The section numbers of the second edition correspond to those of the first edition, and the annotations in the Appendix to the second edition summarize court decisions made while the first edition of the Restatement was outstanding.

The Restatement of Agency is an important source of agency law for lawyers, courts and commentators. In part this is because there has existed no major treatise on the law of agency since the late Professor Floyd Mechem's two-volume work in 1914, and in part the heavy reliance on the Restatement doubtless reflects the careful analytical and taxonomical work of its authors. This casebook will cite to and quote from the Restatement on a frequent basis. This does not mean, however, that the Restatement should be treated with undue veneration. There are many questions in this book directed toward aspects of the doctrinal analysis contained in the Restatement. You should be encouraged to critically analyze Restatement doctrine, both as a result of pursuing the questions raised in the book and by asking and pursuing your own questions.

(2) The one for whom action is to be taken is the principal.

(3) The one who is to act is the agent.

This definition has enjoyed widespread acceptance. This is not to say, however, that it is consistently applied in all decision making, as the following materials will demonstrate.

Using the Restatement definition, return to the questions asked above. Do the elements of an agency relationship set forth in section 1 assist in supplying the answers to the questions for you?

B. THE ELEMENTS OF A MASTER-SERVANT RELATIONSHIP

The definition of an agency relationship quoted above from section 1 of the Restatement normally serves as a starting point for analysis of contractual issues arising from an agency relationship. Special problems are involved, however, in trying to define the circumstances where vicarious tort liability is imposed. As will be explained below, words of art ("master" and "servant") are used by the Restatement in delineating such circumstances. A master-servant relationship is a type of agency relationship.

VICARIOUS LIABILITY

It is accepted tort law that one is liable for the damages occasioned when he directs or participates in the commission of a tort by someone else. Thus, if an employer directs his employee to physically restrain an innocent customer or to arrange a display containing dangerous objects in an obviously negligent manner, or participates in this, and someone is injured as a result, his liability to the injured person is clear. See § 212 of the Restatement.

But the above is not *vicarious* liability, is it? *Webster's International Dictionary, Second Edition,* defines "vicarious" as "of or pertaining to a vicar, substitute or deputy" and notes that it is derived from the Latin word "vicarius," meaning the place or office of one person as assumed by another. What the law is talking about, therefore, is some form of substitute liability for the employer. (It is technically more accurate to describe vicarious liability as liability *in addition* to the liability of the employee, who remains personally liable for his torts.)*

---

* See RESTATEMENT (SECOND) OF AGENCY § 343 (1958); Seavey, *Liability of an Agent in Tort,* 1 So. L. Q. 16 (1916), *reprinted in* W. SEAVEY, STUDIES IN AGENCY 1-27 (1949); United States v. Hull, 195 F.2d 64 (1st Cir. 1952).

The personal liability to an injured party of an agent for his affirmative acts of wrongdoing has never been seriously questioned. See Lane v. Cotton,

Suppose, for example, that the employee described above re-
strained the customer or negligently arranged the display and
someone was injured, but the employer was absent, knew nothing of this, and had instructed his employee to the contrary.
Could you reasonably argue that the employer should be held
liable for the harm caused? What sort of argument would you
make?

JONES v. HART
Court of King's Bench
2 Salk. 441, 90 Eng. Rep. 1255 (1698)

A servant to a pawn-broker took in goods, and the party came
and tendered the money to the servant, who said he had lost the
goods. Upon this, action of trover was brought against the master;
and the question was, whether it would lie or not?

HOLT C.J. The action well lies in this case: If the servants of
A. with his cart run against another cart, wherein is a pipe of
wine, and overturn the cart and spoil the wine, an action lieth
against A. So where a carter's servant runs his cart over a boy,
action lies against the master for the damage done by this negligence: and so it is if a smith's man pricks a horse in shoeing, the
master is liable. For whoever employs another, is answerable for
him, and undertakes for his care to all that make use of him.

The act of a servant is the act of his master, where he acts by
authority of the master.

NOTES

1.   Chief Justice Holt's statement that "whoever employs another, is answerable for him, . . ." is commonly cited as the

---

12 Mod. 472, 88 Eng. Rep. 1458 (1701), and the authorities cited in the
paragraph immediately above.   A more troubling question involves the
personal liability of an agent where he did no affirmative act but simply
failed to perform a duty he owed to his principal, such as a failure to repair
certain property of his principal contrary to his agreement with his principal, and a person was injured as a result. A well known and frequently
quoted case held an agent not liable under such circumstances, based on
both common law and civil law principles. Delaney v. Rochereau & Co., 34
La. Ann. 1123, 1128, 44 Am. Rep. 456, 457-58 (1882), saying, "At common
law, an agent is personally responsible to third parties for doing something
which he ought not to have done, but not for not doing something which
he ought to have done, the agent, in the latter case, being liable to his
principal only. . . . No man increases or diminishes his obligations to
strangers by becoming an agent." The "increases" aspect of this view is
criticized by Seavey in the article cited above, principally by stressing the
control which an agent may have under some circumstances because of his
agency status (such as being in control of property), which should increase
his obligation to strangers under such circumstances.

beginning of the modern law of vicarious liability. Note that *Jones v. Hart* was decided almost 300 years ago and that the court talked of imposing strict liability on masters, in that they would be subject to liability for the negligence of their servants without any inquiry into the nature of their conduct toward their servants or the injured third party. This form of vicarious liability is usually referred to as *respondeat superior* liability. The question whether this strict tort liability can be justified and if so, in what terms, is the main topic of Chapter 2. For criticism of the manner in which *Jones v. Hart* has been interpreted and applied by commentators and courts, considering its apparent contractual context, see T. BATY, VICARIOUS LIABILITY 23-25 (1916).

2. What did Chief Justice Holt mean by the qualification "where he acts by authority of the master"? Would the pawnbroker have had a good defense if he had instructed his servant to "be careful and never misplace" goods received in the shop?

3. The words "master" and "servant" used by Chief Justice Holt are passé today in ordinary speech, but as noted above retain significance in the law as terms of art used by most (but not all) courts to describe the two parties to this common form of vicarious liability. The term "servant" nevertheless does carry its old connotation of an unfortunate doing menial work and subject to arbitrary command, a connotation which, as will be seen in the materials to follow, does not fit some jobs that fall into the servant classification. The Restatement of Agency seeks to avoid the problem of calling "ship captains and managers of great corporations" servants by calling them "superior servants." *See* § 220, comment a.

4. It is clear from *Jones v. Hart* that an employer-employee relationship raises immediately the possibility of vicarious liability for the employer. Should, however, the existence of an employment relationship automatically result in vicarious liability for an employer in all cases in which an employee commits a tort while acting on his employer's behalf? We can draw from *Jones v. Hart* the obvious case, where a deliveryman operating his employer's truck (translating "cart" into 20th century terms) negligently injures someone while on his route. But suppose the employee is a salesman rather than a deliveryman; he operates in a four-state territory, drives his own car, and the act of negligent driving takes place 500 miles away from the main place of business. Or suppose the employee is a lawyer who works full-time on a salaried basis for his employer and negligently causes

an accident while driving directly to a bank in order to represent
the employer at a routine closing of a loan.

At this stage you have in front of you only *Jones v. Hart* and
the general definition of an agency relationship contained in
section 1 of the Restatement. Would you hold the employer liable
for the act of the salesman or the lawyer? Why or why not? What
distinctions are there between these two variations and the facts
in *Jones v. Hart?* Are they significant?

The Restatement Definition

After you have given these variations some thought, consider
the following quotations from the Restatement of Agency. Ask
yourself whether or not the distinction made by the Restatement
makes sense, and what reasoning you think underlies it.

§ 2. Master; Servant; Independent Contractor.

(1) A master is a principal who employs an agent to perform service in his affairs and who controls or has the right to
control the physical conduct of the other in the performance
of the service.

(2) A servant is an agent employed by a master to perform
service in his affairs whose physical conduct in the performance
of the service is controlled or is subject to the right to control
by the master.

(3) An independent contractor is a person who contracts
with another to do something for him but who is not controlled by the other nor subject to the other's right to control
with respect to his physical conduct in the performance of the
undertaking. He may or may not be an agent.

Comment:

. . . .

b. Servant contrasted with independent contractor. The word
"servant" is used in contrast with "independent contractor." The
latter term includes all persons who contract to do something for
another but who are not servants in doing the work undertaken.
An agent who is not a servant is, therefore, an independent contractor when he contracts to act on account of the principal.
Thus, a broker who contracts to sell goods for his principal is an
independent contractor as distinguished from a servant. Although,
under some circumstances, the principal is bound by the broker's
unauthorized contracts and representations, the principal is not
liable to third persons for tangible harm resulting from his
unauthorized physical conduct within the scope of the employment, as the principal would be for similar conduct by a servant;

nor does the principal have the duties or immunities of a master towards the broker. Although an agent who contracts to act and who is not a servant is therefore an independent contractor, not all independent contractors are agents. Thus, one who contracts for a stipulated price to build a house for another and who re- serves [is subject to?—*Ed.*] no direction over the conduct of the work is an independent contractor; but he is not an agent, since he is not a fiduciary, has no power to make the one employing him a party to a transaction, and is subject to no control over his conduct.

§ 250. Non-liability for Physical Harm by Non-Servant Agents.

A principal is not liable for physical harm caused by the negligent physical conduct of a non-servant agent during the performance of the principal's business, if he neither intended nor authorized the result nor the manner of performance, unless he was under a duty to have the act performed with due care.

Comment:

a. A principal employing another to achieve a result but not controlling or having the right to control the details of his phys- ical movements is not responsible for incidental negligence while such person is conducting the authorized transaction. . . .

The term "master" is included within the broader term "prin- cipal"; the same is true with the terms servant and agent. We thus can use the language of sections 1 and 2 of the Restatement to broadly establish the boundaries of the relationship giving rise to vicarious liability. The decision whether or not such a relationship exists in a particular case normally is made by the trier of fact. "If the inference is clear that there is, or is not, a master and servant relation, it is made by the court; other- wise the jury determines the question after instruction by the court as to the matters of fact to be considered." Restatement § 220, Comment *c*. The problems concerning the limits of this tort liability and its underlying rationale are explored in Part II, *infra*.

As you read through the materials to follow, you will notice that the words "employer" and "employee" are frequently used today in place of master and servant. This is accurate most of the time, but you now should be alert to the fact that one can employ a nonservant, usually referred to in agency law as an "independent contractor." The scope of the independent con- tractor exclusion from vicarious liability is covered in Part II

(Chapter 3). Note, however, that this term is not appropriate when talking about regular employees, as the Restatement itself acknowledges in its use of the term "non-servant agent" in section 250.

5.   The activity involved in *Jones v. Hart* was the running of a pawnshop, an income generating activity. *Respondeat superior* liability is not limited to such activities, however. The doctrine applies whenever one becomes a "servant" of another. An individual hired out of an employment office to mow the lawn and clean the windows of the home of Mrs. Means is the servant of Mrs. Means despite the fact that he is not part of an income-generating activity of his employer. This is reflected in the unqualified language of the Restatement definitions quoted above. It is instructive to test this fact against the various rationalizations and applications of *respondeat superior* liability that you will see in the materials in Part II, *infra*.

C.   IS CONSIDERATION NECESSARY?

As mentioned above, it is clear from *Jones v. Hart* that an employment relationship raises immediately the possibility of vicarious liability for the employer. Is, however, an employer-employee relationship *the* threshold to *respondeat superior* liability? In other words, does one expose himself to the risk of vicarious liability only by the act of hiring someone else to work for him? Should this be the law, if it is not?

Assume, for example, that you had driven three friends to your summer cabin in order to show off your freshly stocked private pond that you recently had constructed. Assume further that you left your car with the keys in it 500 feet down the road and walked in with one of the three friends in order to check that the road was safe. After you ascertained that it was in good condition, your accompanying friend said to you, "I'll drive in the others." You said nothing in return. Your friend, unfortunately, drove rather badly and turned the car over, seriously injuring one of the other occupants.

It is obvious that your friend is liable for his own negligence, assuming there is no guest statute in the jurisdiction. The interesting question is, are *you* liable? You didn't pay him anything to drive the car in for you. He volunteered to do it.

Would it make any difference if you had expressly assented to his statement? If you had asked him to go get the others and drive the car up? If you had told him to drive carefully?

Does the following case aid you in answering the above questions?

***

HEIMS v. HANKE

Supreme Court of Wisconsin
5 Wis. 2d 465, 93 N.W.2d 455 (1958)

Action for ~~personal injuries sustained when~~ plaintiff slipped and fell on a ~~patch of ice~~ on a sidewalk. The case was tried by the court without a jury, and . . . ~~judgment~~ was entered for the ~~plaintiff. Defendant appeals.~~

The accident occurred about 11 a.m. on April 3, 1954, when the temperature was below freezing. A few minutes before the accident, defendant had finished washing his car at the street curb across the sidewalk from a house which he owned. His sixteen-year-old nephew, William Hanke, helped him as an unpaid volunteer. Defendant washed the street side of the car and William the side next to the curb. Water was obtained by the pailful from a faucet on the outside of the house across the sidewalk. The court found on sufficient evidence that defendant several times requested or directed William to get more water, and William did so, and that in carrying the water from the faucet to the automobile some of it was spilled on the sidewalk, where it froze. After the car washing was finished and defendant and William had left and the water had frozen, plaintiff walked along the sidewalk in an easterly direction, failed to see the ice, and slipped and fell on it.

WINGERT, J. Appellant contends that there was no evidence of actionable negligence on his part, that William's negligence, if any, could not properly be imputed to defendant, that no nuisance was established, that plaintiff's negligence was the sole cause of the accident, and that the trial court erred in excluding certain evidence.

1. *Defendant's negligence.* The finding that the icy condition of the sidewalk was caused by the negligence of the defendant is supported by sufficient evidence.

The court could properly find that William, the nephew, was negligent in spilling water on the sidewalk in freezing weather and doing nothing to prevent the formation of ice or to remove or sand it, or to warn pedestrians of it. While the day was not too cold for washing a car barehanded, the car was in the bright sunlight while the sidewalk where the water was spilled was then or soon would be in the shade of the house. The court could well infer that one in the exercise of ordinary care would have foreseen the formation of a slippery condition and would have done something to protect users of the sidewalk.

It was also permissible to conclude from the evidence that defendant was liable for injuries resulting from William's negligence, on the principle *respondeat superior*. Probably William was defendant's servant in carrying the water. A servant is one employed to perform service for another in his affairs and who, with respect to his physical conduct in the performance of the service, is subject to the other's control or right to control. Restatement, 1 Agency (2d), p. 485, sec. 220. The evidence permits the inference that William was in that category, although he was an unpaid volunteer. One volunteering service without any agreement for or expectation of reward may be a servant of the one accepting such services. Restatement, 1 Agency (2d), p. 497, sec. 225. The illustration given in comment *a* under that section is pertinent:

"A, a social guest at P's house, not skilled in repairing, volunteers to assist P in the repair of P's house. During the execution of such repair, A negligently drops a board upon a person passing upon the street. A may be found to be a servant of P."

If William was not the employee or servant of the defendant in the strict sense, he was certainly defendant's agent in fetching water from the faucet, although he received no compensation. Restatement, 1 Agency (2d), pp. 7, 85, secs. 1(1) and 16; *Krzysko v. Gaudynski*, 207 Wis. 608, 615, 242 N. W. 186. A principal is subject to liability for physical harm to the person of another caused by the negligence of an agent who is not a servant, where the principal is under a duty to have care used to protect others and he confides the performance of the duty to the agent. Restatement, 1 Agency (2d), pp. 551, 463, secs. 251(a) and 214; *Schmidt v. Leary*, 213 Wis. 587, 590, 252 N. W. 151.

When defendant sent his agent to carry water across the sidewalk in freezing weather, he was under a duty to have care used to protect users of the sidewalk from ice, and since he confided the performance of that duty to William, he was responsible for William's negligence in the premises.

. . . .

Since the finding of negligence attributable to defendant is sustainable, there is no need to consider whether the condition constituted a nuisance.

. . . .*

Judgment affirmed.

---

* The omitted material contains, among other matters, language dealing with the scope of liability of a doctor who subsequently aggravates the

NOTES

1. Biedenbach v. Teague, 194 Pa. Super. 245, 166 A.2d 320 (1960), is a case which involved a fact situation very similar to that first presented above dealing with the friend volunteering to drive the car up to the cabin, and the owner saying nothing. The defendant was held liable for the negligent driving of his friend. (As an aside, articulate what other agency problem the case involved besides whether or not a paid relationship is necessary to vicarious liability.) Try to determine for yourself the rationale behind imposing vicarious liability in these circumstances. Note, incidentally, that it is not necessary that the parties intend their relationship be principal-agent (or master-servant, to be more precise in the physical harm context of the *Heims* and *Biedenbach* cases in order for it to be such in the eyes of the law.

2. Does it make any difference if the person who is gratuitously aiding the defendant acts for his own motives and not with a primary intention to help the defendant? Suppose, for example, that a car is stalled in traffic and another driver, Jones, gets out of his own car and assists in pushing the stalled car to the curb under the directions—limited as they are—of the owner of the stalled car. Is Jones the servant of the owner of the stalled car if his purpose is to remove an obstruction to his own progress down the street? Should this make any difference? See RESTATE-MENT § 225, Comment *b*, stating (without explanation) that it does. Why?

Suppose, on the other hand, that Jones intends to aid the owner of the stalled car, but the owner has not asked him to help. Would the owner be liable if Jones was negligent and somehow caused a loss?

3. As we have seen, *respondeat superior* liability is imposed on a master whether or not he acted with due care toward the injured third party, so long as his servant acted without due care. This does not mean that we ignore all inquiries into the master's due care, however. The alternative holding of the *Heims* case provides a useful antidote to that temptation.

The court in *Heims* cites to sections 214 and 251(a) of the Restatement. Section 214 would not seem directly relevant to the situation before the court. It sets forth the nondelegable duty concept, which is briefly covered in Chapter 3, *infra,* and states

---

plaintiff's injuries due to malpractice. Such language was overturned by the Wisconsin Supreme Court in *Butzow v. Wausau Memorial Hosp.,* 51 Wis.2d 281, 187 N.W.2d 349 (1971). The agency aspect of the *Heims* case was not relevant to or discussed in the *Butzow* case.

that a principal under certain circumstances cannot delegate to another his duty of due care to others. The circumstances under which this happens are vague and ill-defined, as is reflected in the language of section 214. An example of this is the nondelegable duty of care imposed upon common carriers and innkeepers, as well as some duties imposed by statute, which are held to be nondelegable.

Section 251(a), which cross-refers to section 214, also involves the nondelegable duty concept, although the black-letter language of the section reads more broadly ("Liability for Physical Harm Caused by a Servant or a Non-servant Agent. A principal is subject to liability for physical harm . . . caused by the negligence of a servant or a non-servant agent (a) in the performance of an act which the principal is under a duty to have performed with care; . . ."). Perhaps this language is what drew the attention of the court. If it is taken literally, however, and applied to circumstances between strangers as in *Heims,* it would seem to envelop completely the law of *respondeat superior* that we will cover in the next four chapters. As we go through this material, ask yourself if a broadened interpretation of the nondelegable duty concept would supply a superior analytical tool for treatment and resolution of these problems.

D. NONEMPLOYMENT AGENCY RELATIONSHIPS

i. *The Joint Enterprise Relationship*

HOWARD v. ZIMMERMAN
Supreme Court of Kansas
120 Kan. 77, 242 P. 131 (1926)

BURCH, J. The action was one for damages resulting from the death of plaintiff's wife, who was killed through negligent operation of an automobile, in the rear seat of which defendant was riding. Plaintiff recovered, and defendant appeals.

Defendant is a minor, and lives at Sterling. He and Orville Higbee were in the habit of taking automobile journeys together for pleasure. On a Sunday evening they agreed they would go to defendant's father and together ask him for one of his cars to take two girls automobile riding. They did so, permission to use the car was granted, and the four young persons went to Hutchinson. Defendant drove from Sterling to Nickerson. At Nickerson Higbee took the driver's seat and drove to Hutchinson. On the way home defendant drove from Hutchinson to Nickerson, and Higbee drove from Nickerson to the place where the accident occurred. When Higbee was driving defendant sat in the rear seat.

The road from Nickerson to Sterling is paved. Plaintiff lived on a farm west of Nickerson. His family consisted of his wife and a boy 9 years old. On the evening in question they attended church in Nickerson, going in a buggy drawn by a single horse. Two miles west of Nickerson a north and south highway crosses the paved road. On the way home, and near the intersection, plaintiff noted the lights of an automobile approaching behind him. His horse and the left wheels of the buggy were on the pavement, and the right wheels were off the pavement on the north side. When plaintiff saw the lights he pulled the horse off the pavement and as far to the right as he could without getting into the ditch. The approaching car was the Zimmerman car. It struck the buggy, completely demolished it, killed plaintiff's wife outright, and injured the little boy. . . .

The court instructed the jury that, in order to render defendant liable for Higbee's negligent operation of the car, it was necessary that the two should have been engaged in a common purpose or enterprise and should have had joint control of the automobile at the time of the accident; and if the jury believed the two were out for a common purpose and had joint control and equal control of the automobile at the time of the accident, it would make no difference which one was driving. The jury found that Higbee was negligent in that he was driving too fast, and returned the following finding:

"Did the defendant have any control or the right to control Orville Higbee as to the manner in which he would operate said car while the same was being driven by Orville Higbee, or did the said Orville Higbee have any control or the right to control the manner in which said car was being driven while the same was being operated by the defendant? A. Yes."

Defendant contends that, since the evidence was undisputed, the court submitted to the jury a question of law. If so, defendant may not complain because he requested the court to give an instruction which left to the jury the question whether defendant and Higbee were engaged in a joint enterprise and were in equal control of the car. Besides that, defendant's brief contains an argument based on the evidence, directed to the proposition that defendant did not in fact have joint control with Higbee of the automobile at the time of the accident.

The term "joint enterprise" is not helpfully elucidated by definition. An enterprise is simply a project or undertaking, and a joint enterprise is simply one participated in by associates acting together. The basis of liability of one associate in a joint enterprise for the tort of another is equal privilege to control the method and means of accomplishing the common design. If the means employed be an instrumentality negligent use of which inflicts injury, the associate whom the law regards as participating in the conduct of the actor must have had equal control over its use. This control, however, need not have extended to actual manipulation at the time injury was inflicted. It is sufficient that, at the beginning of the enterprise, or as it progressed, or at any time before the tortious event, he possessed equal authority to prescribe conditions of use.

con

In this instance, the enterprise was a joint one. The two boys together borrowed an automobile to take two girls riding. The girls were guests, but neither boy was guest of the other, or a mere passenger while the other was driving. Each one had equal authority to say whether they should go southeast to Hutchinson or northwest to Ellenwood, and whether one should drive to Hutchinson, and the other from Hutchinson back to Sterling, or alternate more frequently at the wheel. Each one had equal authority to decide how much time should be spent at Hutchinson and when they should get back to Sterling. Each one had equal authority over manipulation of the instrumentality by which the undertaking was to be accomplished, and, as a matter necessarily involved, had equal authority with respect to speed.

This appears to be the more important of the joint control.

Doesn't seem to follow

. . . .

The judgment of the district court is affirmed.

All the Justices concurring.

NOTES

1. Consider the consequences of this case. You and some friends are driving in a borrowed car to a neighboring state on a hunting trip, sharing expenses. The driver negligently drives into and kills or seriously injures someone. A damage award of $175,-000 is recovered. Would you, as a passenger in that car on that trip, be required to pay all or part of that judgment if you were joined in the suit? If *Howard v. Zimmerman* is still good law in Kansas (and a look at Shepard's Citations through June 1973 shows no citations to cases overruling, distinguishing or criticizing the *Zimmerman* case, for whatever that is worth), the answer would be obvious to the Supreme Court of Kansas, wouldn't it? Would your automobile insurance policy cover you in such a situation? Incidentally, would you be entitled to contribution from your fellow joint enterprisers? Indemnity from the driver?*

If just a passenger seems distinguishable from Howard v Zimmerman

---

* **Indemnity, which involves shifting the entire loss from one party to another, is to be distinguished from contribution, which involves distributing**

Should the risk of loss fall on the passengers in such situations? Such an allocation clearly increases the number of pockets available to the party injured in the other vehicle. But is that a justification for holding the passengers liable?

2. Would it make any difference if the car was owned by one of the passengers, rather than borrowed for the trip? If it was owned by the person driving at the time? *See* Bonney v. San Antonio Transit Company, 160 Tex. 11, 325 S.W.2d 117 (1959); Manley v. Horton, 414 S.W.2d 254 (Mo. 1967) (indicating that it does).

3. Suppose the defendant in the *Zimmerman* case had shouted "Slow down!" to Higbee some time before Higbee drove into the plaintiff, and Higbee had ignored him. Would the outcome of the case have been different?

4. Assume that you are about to enroll your child in a co-operative nursery school, which also involves joining a car pool. Would the *Zimmerman* case be of concern to you?

5. In trying to determine what elements are important in this area, consider Shook v. Beals, 96 Cal. App. 2d 963, 217 P.2d 56, 18 A.L.R.2d 919 (1950), where five persons jointly leased an airplane to take a fishing trip. The rental price was divided equally between four of them; the fifth member (Beals) arranged for the rental and flew the plane (he was the only one of the five who knew how to fly an airplane). Beals negligently overshot a runway and damaged the plane. The owner of the plane sued all five for the damage to the plane ($9000), on the theory that they were all joint venturers and thus each, legally, had the right of control over the plane and the pilot.

Judgment in full based on a jury verdict for plaintiff was affirmed by the appellate court. Again, consider the contribution and indemnity rights, if any, flowing from such a result. *See* 1 F. HARPER & F. JAMES, THE LAW OF TORTS § 10.2 (1956), and Prosser at 305-313, indicating that indemnity would lie against the actual wrong-doer. Contribution between the fellow joint enterprisers apparently would be available in some jurisdictions, Harper & James, *Id.* at 716, and would seem a logical by-product of legislation directed toward overturning the common-law refusal to allow contribution among joint tortfeasors. See the Commissioners' Prefatory Note and § 1 of the Uniform Contribution Among Tortfeasors Act, 9 U.L.A. 230, 233 (1957), containing language sufficiently broad to resolve any question about contribution among those held vicariously liable for the tort

---

a loss among tortfeasors by requiring each to pay his proportionate share. See W. PROSSER, LAW OF TORTS 310 (4th ed. 1971) (referred to hereafter as PROSSER).

of a third person. One could argue that it should not be necessary to rely on the Uniform Act, since the rationale for the common-law refusal to allow contribution among joint tortfeasors does not apply under this circumstance in any event. Also, the contribution and indemnity rights between partners recognized in sections 18 and 40 of the Uniform Partnership Act would seem analogous.

6. The consequences of holding a passenger liable on joint enterprise grounds can be so drastic that some courts including, it seems, most of the recent decisions, have defined the elements of a joint enterprise relationship more narrowly than the court did in the *Zimmerman* case. The standards set forth by the Supreme Court of Washington in the case of Carboneau v. Peterson, 1 Wash. 2d 347, 374, 95 P.2d 1043, 1054 (1939), which are frequently quoted, read as follows:

> Briefly stated, a joint adventure arises out of, and must have its origin in, a contract, express or implied, in which the parties thereto agree to enter into an undertaking in the performance of which they have a common purpose and in the objects or purposes of which they have a community of interest, and, further, a contract in which each of the parties has an equal right to a voice in the manner of its performance and an equal right of control over the agencies used in the performance. Thus, we note (1) a contract, (2) a common purpose, (3) a community of interest, (4) equal right to a voice, accompanied by an equal right of control.

Despite some doubt which may have been created by the language in the *Zimmerman* opinion, the application of these (or similar) standards to the facts of a particular case customarily is left to the jury, if there exists sufficient evidence to sustain a jury verdict for either party.

The subsequent history of the *Carboneau* test in Washington is interesting. It was used in the case of Manos v. James, 7 Wash. 2d 695, 110 P.2d 887 (1941), *noted in* 21 B.U.L. REV. 566 (1941), where the court held that an agreement between strangers who chanced to meet in Spokane and agreed to drive together to Seattle, one for a vacation and the other to work, sharing expenses of food, gas and oil on the ride, constituted a joint adventure. Several years later, in Poutre v. Saunders, 19 Wash. 2d 561, 143 P.2d 554 (1943), *noted in* 19 WASH. L. REV. 42 (1944), the *Manos* decision was expressly overruled. The majority opinion in the *Poutre* case held that thereafter in Washington parties would not be held to have entered into a joint venture relationship unless they are in a business relationship or the contract between the parties by its terms specifically provides for the right of control. The majority (5-4) opinion stated that it will infer a right of control "as a matter of law" if the relationship is of a business nature but refuses to do so, and requires control "as a matter of fact," like the control reserved over a chauffeur, in a nonbusiness venture. The *Zimmerman* case would thus have been decided differently if it had arisen in Washington, at least after *Poutre v. Saunders,* wouldn't it?

Social
Non-Social

7. With respect to terminology, you will notice that the *Carboneau* court referred to the relationship as a "joint adventure." The *Zimmerman* court called it joint enterprise. "Joint venture" is another variation. Although, as you know, the terms are sometimes used indiscriminately, "joint enterprise" usually refers to a nonbusiness relationship. And the term "joint venture" or "adventure" usually is used to describe business relationships, where the parties have a joint interest in a business undertaking, an understanding as to the sharing of its profits and losses, and a right of joint control. *See* Connor v. Great Western Sav. & Loan Ass'n, 69 Cal. 2d 850, 447 P.2d 609, 73 Cal. Rptr. 369 (1968), where the court held that Great Western was not involved in a joint venture with a developer of a large tract development despite considerable participation in and control of the project by Great Western, on the ground that, "Although the profits of each were dependent on the overall success of the development, neither was to share in the profits or losses that the other might realize or suffer. Although each received substantial payments . . ., neither had an interest in the payments received by the other."

8. A passenger's liability to third parties, while it could be drastic, is not the only consequence that you can think of which may arise from a joint enterprise relationship, is it? Suppose the passenger is injured and wants to sue his negligent driver.* If a passenger is liable to a third party for the driver's negligence, on the ground that the driver's negligence is "imputed" to a fellow joint enterpriser, does it follow that the negligence is also imputed when the passenger is suing the driver? Several cases have so held. *See* PROSSER at 480 n.7. Can you justify such a result? PROSSER, *id.* at n.11, cites a number of cases in support of the statement that most courts, including most of the recent cases,

---

* In some jurisdictions legislation exists which denies the passengers in a car a cause of action against the driver unless the driver has been guilty of gross negligence or intentional wrongdoing. These statutes are usually called "guest statutes." They apparently do not apply to parties in a joint enterprise relationship, however. *See* 10 A.L.R.3d 1092 (1966), stating the general rule that a joint enterprise relationship takes the people involved outside of the operation of a guest statute. What is the reason for this?

refuse to impute negligence in this situation. Does this make better sense to you?

9. Or suppose that both drivers were negligent (which apparently is frequently the case in automobile accidents) and the injured passenger sues the driver of the other car, not wishing to sue his own driver due perhaps to the problem raised above in note 8, or because of friendship, or because his driver is judgment proof. Again, will the negligence of the driver of his car be imputed to him? Should it be? It is under this circumstance, as a defendant's doctrine, that the concept of joint enterprise is most frequently applied today. PROSSER at 476. 2 RESTATEMENT (SECOND) OF TORTS § 491(1) (1965) states that negligence is imputed in this circumstance. *See* Pierson v. Edstrom, 286 Minn. 164, 174 N.W.2d 712 (1970), for a move away from this position.

10. One more variant on the theme: assume that a vehicle with two passengers collides with a bridge support as a result of the negligence of its driver. Assume further that all courts would agree that a joint enterprise was involved among the three persons. One of the passengers is seriously injured and wants to sue the other passenger on vicarious liability grounds. Assess the probable success of his lawsuit. Does the material on pages 23-24 *infra,* help you in resolving this question?

11. PROSSER indicates that there is a judicial trend in favor of limiting the joint enterprise doctrine to business ventures (at 479); this is clearly what he would like to see happen. Do you agree?

12. Note in the *Zimmerman* case that the person held liable was a minor. Not all jurisdictions resolve the question of a minor's vicarious liability so easily. *See, e.g.,* Bell v. Green, 423 S.W.2d 724 (Mo. En Banc 1968) (reasoning that agency relationships, with the right of control which such relationships establish, are derived only from contract and thus a minor cannot be held to vicarious liability); *criticized in* 34 Mo. L. REV. 288 (1969). *See also,* P. MECHEM, OUTLINES OF AGENCY §§ 419-20 (4th ed. 1952) (noting and sharply criticizing the rule of no vicarious liability for minors, and stating that the relationship of master and servant need not rest on a legally enforceable contract). *See also,* H. CLARK, THE LAW OF DOMESTIC RELATIONS 231-32 (1968) (noting a divergence of opinion), and Seavey, *The Rationale of Agency,* 29 YALE L. REV. 859, 863 (1920), reprinted in W. SEAVEY, STUDIES IN AGENCY 65, 70 (1949) (stating that agency is not based on contract. "It is rather the result of a grant of power by the principal and the assumption of a fiduciary obligation by the agent. . . . [T]he mutual obligations are created by the fiduciary character of the relationship . . .").

ii. The Partnership Relationship

1. A partnership is defined in section 6(1) of the Uniform Partnership Act (referred to hereafter as UPA), which is adopted in most states and is set forth in full in Appendix A, as "an association of two or more persons to carry on as co-owners a business for profit." Partnership law has its own unique features, which are the subject of Part IV, *infra*. It does, however, incorporate much of agency law, as is expressly acknowledged in section 4(3) of the UPA ("The law of agency shall apply under this act").

The questions of exposure by the partners to contractual liability, and termination of that exposure, are raised in Chapters 6 and 7, *infra*. With respect to tort liability, sections 13-15 of the UPA establish joint and several liability of all partners for "any wrongful act or omission of any partner acting in the ordinary course of the business of the partnership. . . ."

2. After reading the material above on joint enterprise liability, the fact that partners are liable for each other's torts made in the ordinary course of business comes as no surprise to you, does it?

3. Questions concerning what kind of activities fit within the "ordinary course of the business" of a partnership are related to the scope of employment materials, and will be included briefly with those materials in Chapter 5.

4. Is there a distinction between business joint ventures and partnerships? *See* 2 R. ROWLEY, ROWLEY ON PARTNERSHIP §§ 52.1-52.62 (2d ed. 1960), which, among other things, distinguishes joint ventures from partnerships on the ground that a joint venture is usually, but not necessarily, limited to a single transaction, while a partnership is ordinarily formed for the transaction of a general business of a particular kind. (§ 52.14)

The distinction between joint ventures and partnerships is said to have legal significance in some jurisdictions. The contractual and tort liability of members of a joint venture may be more limited than that of partners in some, but not all, jurisdictions. The boundaries of this distinction are vague and may be drawn on the basis of the continuing nature of a partnership as opposed to the limited nature of a joint venture. *See id.* §§ 52.55-52.58. *See also* the distinction between general and special agents in Chapter 7 of these materials.

Another distinction concerns corporations. In some jurisdictions it is doubtful whether a corporation can become a partner in a partnership, on the reasoning that it would be surrendering control over its affairs to the other partners and thus the act of becoming a partner would be ultra vires. It may, however, be permitted to do so by statute or by a provision in its charter, if such provision is not expressly or impliedly prohibited by statute. This restriction is not applied to corporate joint ventures in some of the jurisdictions restricting corporate partnership, even though the element of mutual control also exists in a joint venture relationship, apparently on the reasoning that a joint venture is of limited scope. This distinction carries less importance than it once did, due to modern legislation which has largely eliminated ultra vires as a ground for invalidating corporate acts. *See* A. BROMBERG, CRANE AND BROMBERG ON PARTNERSHIP 55 (1968), citing to the Model Business Corporation Act and a collection of statutes.

See also, Mechem, *The Law of Joint Adventures,* 15 MINN. L. REV. 644 (1931), arguing there is no distinct legal concept of joint venture.

---

iii.   *The Unincorporated Association Relationship*

Unincorporated associations are formed, usually, for some sort of nonprofit continuous operation, such as clubs, fraternal societies, labor unions, farmer co-ops, and so forth. The forming of such associations raises a variety of contractual and tort liability problems.

---

a.   Liability of the Members

The usual rule is that membership alone in an unincorporated association does not render one vicariously liable for the torts committed by its officers, members or employees. The member must have participated in, authorized or ratified the tortious acts before he is liable for them. *See generally,* 1 R. ROWLEY, ROWLEY ON PARTNERSHIP § 6.8, B.2 (2d ed. 1960). The same rule applies with respect to liability for contracts made by the association. Azzolina v. Sons of Italy, 119 Conn. 681, 179 A. 201 (1935); Cousin v. Taylor, 115 Ore. 472, 239 P. 96, 41 A.L.R. 750 (1925). Note, however, that if a particular association is organized for profit it may be held to be a partnership, with the contract and tort liability consequences for the members then being considerably broader.

---

b.   Liability of the Association
I.   *In General*

Unincorporated associations were not recognized as entities by the common law and thus were not suable. This has been changed by statute in some jurisdictions, with the question of the personal liability of members of such organizations sometimes remaining unresolved. *See* Lyons v. American Legion Post No. 650 Realty Co., Inc., 172 Ohio St. 331, 333, 175 N.E.2d 733, 735, 92 A.L.R.2d 492, 496 (1961), construing such a statute to the effect that individual members actively participating in the event giving rise to the injury (a fish fry), and who knew or should have known of the defective condition of the instrumentality causing harm (an unsafe heating system) remained personally liable (would this, incidentally, be vicarious liability?), despite language in an Ohio statute that, "A money judgment against such unincorporated association shall be enforced only against the association as an entity and shall not be enforceable against the property of an individual member of such association." The plaintiffs in the *Lyons* case had not joined the association itself as a party, and the court held that the statute did not take away rights previously existing at common law.

II. *To Its Members*

Suppose a member of an association (a labor union) is injured on the union premises due to negligent maintenance of the premises which he did not participate in nor authorize. Can he successfully sue his association and recover? *See* Marshall v. International Longshoreman's Union, 57 Cal. 2d 781, 22 Cal. Rptr. 211, 371 P.2d 987 (1962), holding yes, and that "reality is apt to be sacrificed to theoretical formalism" if the concepts of partnership are applied to voluntary organizations like labor unions, "which act normally through elected officers and in which the individual members have little or no authority in the day-to-day operations of the association's affairs. . . ." *Accord,* White v. Cox, 95 Cal. Rptr. 259, 17 Cal. App. 3d 824 (1971). The court held that a condominium owner and member has a cause of action against the nonprofit unincorporated association of owners of the condominium for a personal injury sustained due to negligently maintained premises. The question concerning what assets the member could execute against if liability insurance was inadequate or nonexistent was not addressed by the court.

The opinion in *Marshall* noted substantial authority against its position. The basis of the contrary authority, which holds the group immune from liability to one of its members for the tortious actions of another of its members or of an employee of the group, is that each member is a principal and agent of every **other member, and thus the wrongdoer, whether a member** or an employee, is an agent of the plaintiff as well as the other mem-

bers for the purpose of determining group liability. See 14 A.L.
R.2d 470. This concept is also applied to members of a partnership for similar reasons, and is reflected in § 13 of the UPA.
This explains the "concepts of partnership" language used in the
Marshall opinion. See A. BROMBERG, CRANE AND BROMBERG ON
PARTNERSHIP 315 n.31 (1968). See, however, Smith v. Hensley,
354 S.W.2d 744, 98 A.L.R.2d 340 (Ky. 1962), for a move away
from this doctrine in the partnership area in a case involving
suit by a partner against his firm for damage to his truck which
was loaned to the firm. The damage was caused by the negligence
of an employee of the firm. The court thus was not forced to
confront the precise language of § 13 of the UPA. See also,
Crane, *Liability of Unincorporated Association for Tortious Injury to a Member,* 16 VAND. L. REV. 319 (1963). It should be
emphasized that in any event the actual wrongdoer remains personally liable to the injured party.

III. *For the Actions of Its Affiliates and Chapters*

This application of vicarious liability, which normally depends on control or ratification, is raised in an unusual context
by NAACP v. Overstreet, 384 U.S. 118 (1966), *noted in* 52
A.B.A.J. 674 (1966) *and* 13 How. L. J. 193 (1967). The Sa-
vannah branch of the NAACP organized picketing against a
local market, urging that it be boycotted. Apparently violence
resulted and the NAACP was sued by the market owner, together
with its local branch (for what tort? *See* Note, *Reason by Analogy: Agency Principles Justify Conspirators' Liability,* 12 STAN. L.
REV. 476 (1960)). The NAACP was held liable at the state
level, with damages assessed at $85,793, of which $50,000 constituted punitive damages. A writ of certiorari to review the state
court decision was granted by the United States Supreme Court.
Subsequently, however, the writ was dismissed by the Court as
improvidently granted.

Justice Douglas and three others dissented, urging reversal of
the Georgia decision on the ground that the relationship between the NAACP and its affiliate did not establish that the
NAACP was vicariously liable for the acts of its branch or the
acting officer of the branch. Justice Douglas pointed to the
absence of evidence showing power to control, past control,
authorization of the demonstrations or ratification of the activities of the branch by the NAACP. He urged the Court to
review what normally would be a routine question of state law
because of the First Amendment implications of the case. He
recommended that the Court draw an analogy from the existing

treatment of labor unions, which apparently at one time were the object of frequent damage suits under the vicarious liability concept and now are exempt from liability for acts of their agents and affiliates by virtue of § 6 of the Norris-LaGuardia Act, "except upon clear proof of actual participation in, or actual authorization of, such acts, or of ratification of such acts after actual knowledge thereof." Quoted *id.* at 124-25.

---

iv. *Three Unusual Examples of Vicarious Tort Liability*

a. Vicarious Liability by Estoppel

This section raises the question whether one can be vicariously liable for the torts of another in the absence of an agency relationship between the two. The response would seem to be obviously no, based on our prior understanding that agency is a consensual relationship. But consider Manning v. Leavitt Co., 90 N.H. 167, 5 A.2d 667, 122 A.L.R. 249 (1939). Leavitt Department Store leased a portion of its premises to one Chierney for his use as a beauty parlor, retaining no control over the parlor or its operations. The store did, however, permit Chierney to use its name in his advertising, and the parlor was advertised as "Leavitt's Beauty Salon." Plaintiff went to the Salon for a permanent wave and was injured by the negligent operation of the machine used for that purpose. She sued the Leavitt Company on *respondeat superior* grounds. Apparently she testified that she believed she was dealing with the Leavitt Company. The court upheld a jury verdict for her on the ground of estoppel, reasoning that she was entitled to rely on the presumption that the store would employ skilled personnel and on the fact that she would have a responsible party to answer for negligence. *See also,* Hannon v. Siegel-Cooper Co., 167 N.Y. 244, 60 N.E. 597 (1901) ; Rhone v. Try Me Cab Co., 65 F.2d 834 (D.C. Cir. 1933).

Suppose plaintiff instead had been shopping several blocks away and was struck and injured through the negligent operation of a stationwagon prominently marked "Leavitt's Beauty Salon." Assume that the stationwagon was used by Chierney as a business vehicle to obtain supplies, give permanents to customers at home, and so forth. Would the plaintiff still have a valid cause of action against Leavitt Department Store? The answer to this question is no, isn't it? Do you see why? Suppose she had been hit by the stationwagon just as she was about to enter the Leavitt Department Store to do some shopping, or to patronize the beauty salon. Could you make out a case on her behalf in either of these situations?

b.   The "Family Car" Doctrine

Although vicarious liability almost always arises out of a relationship or apparent relationship between persons (or between a person and an entity), and while the family involves relationships among its members, the common law, as a general matter, has not chosen to base vicarious liability on family relationships.* Thus, parents are not liable for their children's negligent or intentional torts, in the absence of their own negligence like, for example, handing a loaded gun to a young child or negligently supervising their child after receiving notice that a situation exists where control should be asserted over the child's behavior. Some states have legislated exceptions to this exclusion from vicarious liability, most frequently by imposing liability on parents for the delinquent acts of their children, covering vandalism and similar misconduct, whether or not the parent was aware of the child's misbehavior and had an opportunity to correct it.

The common law in some states has also carved out an exception, usually called the family car doctrine, to the above principle. The owner of a car "who permits members of his household to drive it for their own pleasure or convenience is regarded as making such a family purpose his 'business,' so that the driver is treated as his servant" (Prosser at 483), with the result that the owner is vicariously liable for the damage caused by the driver. Based on what you have read and studied to date, can such liability legitimately be explained on the basis of agency law, or is the family car doctrine, which Prosser indicates has been accepted in about half of the American courts, based upon a legal fiction? If it is based on fiction, why was this done?

---

c.   Owner Consent Legislation

A similar result for car owners has been reached by "owner consent" statutes, which make the owner liable for the negligence of any person, whether a member of his family or not, who is driving the car with his express or implied consent. Apparently about a dozen states have enacted such legislation. *See* Prosser at 486.

---

* One major exception to this statement was the old common-law rule that a husband was liable for the torts of his wife. This was usually explained on the grounds of the husband's control of his wife's property, his authority over her, and the fact that a wife was incapable of being sued alone. Prosser at 870. This common-law rule is now "almost entirely abrogated by statute" and is a matter of "purely historical interest." *Id.* at 870, 871.

The apparent intent of this legislation and the family car doctrine is to increase the chance that victims in automobile accidents will obtain recourse against solvent drivers. This is accomplished by expanding vicarious liability. The omnibus clause in a liability insurance policy, which provides insurance coverage for the named insured and "any other person using such automobile with the permission of the named insured," achieves the same result, although not through vicarious liability. Apparently almost all automobile liability policies today contain such a clause. *See* C. GREGORY & H. KALVEN, CASES AND MATERIALS ON TORTS 640 (2d ed. 1969).

Would omnibus clause coverage be required in all owner consent states? Do you see why it would not be? If omnibus clause coverage had been in existence in Kansas in the 1920's, and Zimmerman's father had had such coverage, do you think it would have affected the result in the *Zimmerman* case?

The search by the plaintiff's lawyer for a solvent defendant, and the unavailability of traditional vicarious liability when a relationship is based on mere ownership, extends beyond the automobile, of course. Note the following quotation from the Colorado Trial Lawyer's Association newsletter, *Trial Talk* 2 (Oct. 1970):

"AVIATION INSURANCE FOR RENTER-PILOTS

"We have received a very important communication from CTL member, L. B. Ullstrom, calling attention to a need for legislative action. The text of his letter is as follows:

"In several cases I have found, when bringing a suit on behalf of a widow and children against the pilot for the death of the father who was a passenger in an aircraft crash, that there may be significant damages and an excellent liability case against the pilot, but he is dead and has no insurance nor estate. The case against the operator or owner of the aircraft may be weak. The Colorado State Supreme Court has not yet held the owner of an aircraft per se liable for the pilot's negligence in Colorado (contra, in some states such as Florida, Iowa and Texas). The owner or fixed base operator (F.B.O.) frequently purchases insurance to cover his liability for maintenance, etc., but the insurance policy *excludes* renter pilots to whom the operator rents the aircraft. Yet, when a pilot inquires of an operator whether the aircraft is insured, he may be reassured that it is, but without the details that the policy covers liability for the owner-operator and perhaps hull coverage on the aircraft, but no liability to the passengers for

the pilot who is going to do the flying. I think you will find
this is different from automobile insurance issued in Colorado.

Thus, may I suggest that an effort be made to require a
change in the insurance laws in Colorado requiring the insurance policies to cover the pilot, whether renting or not, as
well as the owner or operator. Another alternative is to make
the owner vicariously liable for the consensual operation of the
aircraft."

E.   AGENCY DISTINGUISHED FROM OTHER RELATIONS

The above title is taken from topic 4, section 14, of the
Restatement of Agency. Subsections 14 A to 14 O discuss specific
relations which resemble agency but, depending sometimes on
the facts, are not held to be agency relationships. For example,
the distinction between an agent and a trustee is contained in
subsection 14 B. It is there pointed out that, while a trustee
holds a legal or equitable title on his beneficiary's behalf, he is
not normally subject to the beneficiary's control, and thus an
agency relationship, with the unique powers possessed by the
agent, does not exist. The same is true of guardians, executors
and receivers, who act on behalf of persons but are not subject
to their control. Also, a trust may be created without the consent
of the beneficiary (or the trustee, for that matter), whereas an
agency relationship is created only by agreement between the
principal and the agent. Agents and trustees are both fiduciaries,
of course (defined in section 13 as a person having a duty, created
by his undertaking, to act primarily for the benefit of another
in matters connected with his undertaking). It is possible, however, for an "agent-trustee" to exist, which occurs when the
beneficiary does have control.

The agency status of a board of directors of a corporation is
covered in subsection 14 C, stating that the board of directors,
although they act on behalf of others and are fiduciaries owing
duties of loyalty and care to the corporation itself, nevertheless
are not agents of the corporation, since they control the corporation and are not controlled by it, nor are they agents of the
shareholders, since the shareholders do not control them except
indirectly through elections at the end of a term of office. The
Restatement also notes that an individual director "has still
less resemblance to an agent" since he has no power to act on
his own. He may, however, be appointed by the Board to an
agency position, such as executive officer.

Subsections 14 J and 14 K, distinguishing the agent from the
buyer or supplier, are hard reading, but serve as a useful intro-

duction to what has proved to be a difficult problem of analysis. And subsection 14 M contains, in the Reporter's Notes in Volume 3, a note on the question whether majority ownership of the stock of a corporation in itself makes the corporation the agent of the stockholder. The Note concludes that normally it does not, in recognition of the privilege of limited liability. It does describe circumstances, however, where a corporation, including a corporation that is a subsidiary of another corporation, can be classified as an agent of its controlling stockholder with resulting contractual and vicarious tort liability for the stockholder if there is evidence of actual control. The Note states, "It is an accepted principle of agency that the term 'agent' includes both natural persons and corporations . . . . [likewise the terms principal, master and servant], notwithstanding the anthropomorphic sound of the titles. It follows that a corporation can be an agent for another corporation." *See also,* Berkey v. Third Ave. Ry. Co., 244 N.Y. 84, 155 N.E. 58, 50 A.L.R. 599 (1926).

PROBLEMS

The following problems will put to use some of the principles described in this chapter. You will notice that some of them involve questions of contractual liability, although most of the illustrations in this chapter have been based on vicarious tort liability. Problems involving nonphysical harm are included because they also raise complex and recurring questions concerning the existence of an agency relationship.

Assume for the purposes of these problems that once an agency relationship is established, the acting party in the problem can bind his principal to the contract involved or the principal will be vicariously liable for the tortious conduct of the acting party. We will cover vicarious tort liability in more detail in Part II, and the creation, scope and termination of contractual powers in the agency relationship in Part III.

As you go through these problems, and the problems generally in this casebook, analyze the facts first from the perspective of the lawyer of the aggrieved party, asking what arguments would you make, referring specifically to the law and policy discussions contained in the preceding materials, what facts would you stress, and so forth, and then do the same from the perspective of the defending lawyer. Then put on yet another hat, that of judge acting without a jury, and decide the case.

As was mentioned in the Preface and as you will observe below, citations to cases follow most of the problems which were drawn from actual cases, for reasons described in the Preface. I strongly encourage the student reader to take the time, which sometimes may be of considerable length, to carefully think through the problem on his own *before* consulting the reports, however. The learning value of proceeding in this manner, in particular going through the exercise of formulating your own analysis of a fact situation, otherwise is considerably weakened.

1.   In September, 1934 (in the days, we can assume, before owner consent laws and omnibus clause coverage), Miss Doty, a teacher of Latin at the Soda Springs (Idaho) High School, volunteered her car for use in transporting the high school football team to a game in Paris, Idaho. She had the day previously asked the coach of the team, Russell Garst, a teacher of Mathematics at the school, if he had all the cars necessary for the trip. He had said he needed one more and she told him that he could use her car if he drove it. She was not promised compensation for the use of her car and did not receive any. The coach filled the car with gas and charged the bill to the school district. Unfortunately, on the way back from the game the coach negligently caused an accident, severely injuring Richard Gorton, one of the players on the football team and a passenger in the car. Gorton sued Miss Doty.

a.   Analyze these facts in the manner suggested above. Then, for the view of one group of judges on this, *see* Gorton v. Doty, 57 Idaho 792, 69 P.2d 136 (1937), *noted in* 13 Wash. L. Rev. 56 (1938) (the opinions in this case are relatively long and involved, and the court was divided). Then consult, and try to rationalize with the *Gorton* case, a case decided by the same court two years later, Colwell v. Bothwell, 60 Idaho 107, 89 P.2d 193 (1939), where a member of the school's basketball team for girls borrowed her father's car upon her request to drive the team to a game and negligently caused an accident on the return trip. One of the injured passengers sued the father.

b.   Would your analysis change if Miss Doty had also said to Garst, "Oh, would you please pick up a Latin book for me from a teacher at Paris High whom I will call and have meet you after the game?"

c.   Suppose instead of the above facts that Miss Doty had been interested in selling her car; Garst had presented himself as a prospective purchaser, and Miss Doty let him drive it, but had specified only him. Would this variation alter your analysis made above?

2.   Thayer called Adams, a stockbroker who deals in unlisted securities, and gave him an order for the purchase of 30 shares of a particular company at a stated price of $1000. Adams bought the stock on two separate occasions at a price several points below

the price set by Thayer. He sent a bill to Thayer for the prices he had agreed to pay, with no commission charged. Adams had borrowed money to pay for his purchase of the stock and pledged the stock as security. Thayer refused to take or pay for the stock. Adams sued for the price and was met at trial with the defense of Statute of Frauds. (The UNIFORM COMMERCIAL CODE § 8-319 makes, with some qualifications, a contract for the sale of securities unenforceable in the absence of a writing meeting certain requirements.) Adams is obviously in trouble if the transaction is classified as a sale. The statute is not applicable if the transaction is one of agency. (Why isn't it applicable?)

a. Advance and evaluate the arguments that can be made on behalf of Thayer and Adams in the manner suggested in the introduction to these problems.

b. Would Adams' case be stronger or weaker if the more traditional brokerage transaction had been entered into, where the broker is instructed to "get me the best deal you can," and the compensation for the broker is a commission? Does it make any difference who holds title to the stocks?

c. Would your answer vary if the transaction was on margin, where a partial payment is made by the customer and the securities are carried by the broker to protect him for the balance, with the customer's credit added? *See,* with respect to the first situation above, F. C. Adams, Inc. v. Elmer F. Thayer Estate, 85 N.H. 177, 155 A. 687 (1931), *aff'd on rehearing,* 85 N.H. 177, 156 A. 697 (1931), *exception to denial of petition for new trial overruled,* 86 N.H. 555, 171 A. 771 (1934), *noted in* 45 HARV. L. REV. 739 (1932). *See also,* Stott v. Greengos, 95 N.J. Super. 96, 230 A.2d 154 (1967); Lindsey v. Stein Bros. & Boyce, Inc., 222 Tenn. 149, 433 S.W.2d 669 (1968).

d. Suppose instead that the broker had acted for both parties in making the sale. What would be his agency status under this circumstance? Would it make any difference whether the broker took a more active role in the negotiations than just bringing the parties together? *See* RESTATEMENT § 391, comments a, b and d; § 392; § 14 L; R. KEETON, INSURANCE LAW § 2.5(c) (1971).

3. In 1964 Voss was appointed the "loan correspondent" of the Prudential Insurance Company with authority to submit applications for and close real estate mortgage loans located in the state of Iowa. The contract between them read in part as follows:

Whereas the party of the first part desires to submit to the insurance company applications for loans upon the security of mortgages on lands located in the state of Iowa, and the insurance company is willing to receive such applications, and make loans where said applications are approved, . . . [providing for credits to Voss's account, after an application is accepted along with the borrower's notes, plus the abstracts of title, of the amounts which were advanced by Voss to close the loans. Voss agreed to purchase from Prudential all loans which contained errors and to pay to Prudential all amounts in excess of one-half of the value of the security. The following language was also part of the contract:]

It is further mutually understood and agreed that in all transactions arising out of the performance of this agreement, the party of the first part is acting and will act as agent of the borrower in negotiating said loans, and in no instance is acting or shall be authorized to act as agent for the said insurance company.

This relationship continued for a number of years, with occasional letters from Prudential in the files calling Voss's attention to such matters as commission charges for securing loans, and exhorting him to exercise unusual care "in connection with all applications where the loan per acre is in excess of $50.00."

In February, 1971, Rose and George Argotsinger, who had an $18,000 mortgage outstanding to the Burlington Savings Bank, contacted Voss about obtaining a new mortgage on their property. Voss prepared on their behalf an application to Prudential for a loan of $24,000, it being intended that the proceeds of this loan would be used in part for the payment of the $18,000 mortgage held by Burlington Bank. The Argotsingers executed to Prudential a note for $24,000, dated February 14, 1971, and a mortgage on the land. Voss forged and recorded a release of Burlington's $18,000 mortgage and furnished Prudential an abstract of title showing the release. This was unknown to the Argotsingers. Prudential then loaned the $24,000, of which Voss appropriated $18,000, remitting the balance to the Argotsingers. Burlington's mortgage was not paid, of course, and it foreclosed. In the foreclosure proceedings the court cancelled the Prudential mortgage except for $5,557.76, for which amount personal judgment was rendered against the Argotsingers. Prudential appeals, contending that the Argotsingers should be responsible for the full amount of the mortgage to them. What result?

4. Sam Jones rented his home to four single, adult women, each of whom signed the one year lease, and moved to a new location 2000 miles away. The lease contained a standard renewal clause, giving the tenants the option to renew for an additional one year period. Approximately two months before the lease was to expire Jones discovered an individual who wanted

to rent his house in whom he had a great deal of confidence. One Saturday morning Jones called at his house and got one of the women. He asked her if they intended to renew. The woman answered, "No. We're moving out." Jones then signed a lease with his new tenant. A week later he got a notice of renewal in the mail from two of the other women. Could you make a successful argument on his behalf that he had been released from the option to renew? What other facts, if any, would you want to ascertain?

5. By arrangement with an insurance company, an employer handles group life and medical insurance for his employees, including enrolling employees into the plan of the insurance company, terminating and reinstating insurance, reporting details of coverage and premiums paid to the company, remitting premiums, and issuing to the employees certificates of insurance provided by the insurer. This is done under the broad direction of the insurance company. Unfortunately, the employer, through a good faith mistake, erroneously determined the eligibility of one of his new employees to qualify under the plan and enrolled the employee in the plan prematurely. Thereafter the employee suffered a loss which normally would be covered by the insurance. The insurance company refused to pay the claim on the ground that the employee was ineligible. The loss is a serious one, and you have been retained by the employee to prosecute his claim for him. What legal analysis would you make of his position? Would you expect him to succeed in an action against the insurance company? What arguments would you expect from the insurance company? *Compare* Note, 1968 DUKE L. J. 824 *with* R. KEETON, INSURANCE LAW § 2.8 (b) (1971).

In formulating arguments on the above fact situation, and other situations involving similar problems, consider whether it might be possible for a person to be an agent of one of two parties to a transaction with respect to one aspect of the transaction (say, receiving payments) and the agent of the other party with respect to a different aspect of the transaction (sending notices, for example). See W. SEAVEY, LAW OF AGENCY 23-24 (1964). To the extent that this reasonably can be concluded with respect to a particular fact situation or, alternatively, that it can be concluded that a person is the agent of one or the other of the parties to a transaction in all respects, but not both paries, it is possible to avoid the generalization (sometimes called the "dual agency" or "double employment rule") that an agent does not have the capacity to represent both parties to a transaction in the absence of full knowledge and consent by both parties. The rationale underlying this is stated to be that "no man can serve two masters" and give to each of them his undivided allegiance and support. See P. MECHEM, OUTLINES OF THE LAW OF AGENCY §§ 501-505 (4th ed. 1952). See § 391, Comment *g* of the Restatement for discussion and cross-references to other sections with respect to the legal consequences for or options available to the principals in a double employment situation.

PART II

TORT LIABILITY ASPECTS OF AN AGENCY RELATIONSHIP

The previous materials described, in basic terms, the broad circumstances under which the law will impose vicarious tort liability on a party who did not direct or participate in the tortious conduct. The next four chapters involve a more complete treatment of the consequences and limitations of this widespread instance of strict tort liability. We will begin with a description of some of the better known attempts to justify or explain the imposition of this type of liability by a fault oriented legal system.

Chapter 2

SOME JUSTIFICATIONS FOR (OR EXPLANATIONS OF) VICARIOUS TORT LIABILITY

This chapter contains as complete a presentation as the limitations of these materials make practicable of some of the writings on the continuously frustrating questions of loss allocation. You should be forewarned that there is no widely accepted resolution of these problems. It seemed preferable, therefore, to expose you as fully as possible to the thoughtful efforts of some intelligent people to rationalize vicarious tort liability, and then let you make up your own mind.

A. APPROACH OF JUSTICE HOLMES

Any student of torts realizes that the fault principle is fundamental to that subject. Departures from personal fault as a basis for tort liability usually have been viewed with suspicion and accepted with misgivings. Consider, for example, the reaction of Justice Holmes to the doctrine of vicarious liability established in *Jones v. Hart, supra* page 6:

> I assume that common-sense is opposed to making one man pay for another man's wrong, unless he actually has brought the wrong to pass according to the ordinary canons of legal responsibility,—unless, that is to say, he has induced the immediate wrong-doer to do acts of which the wrong, or, at least, wrong, was the natural consequence under the circumstances known to the defendant. . . .* I therefore assume that common sense is opposed to the fundamental theory of agency, although I have no doubt that the possible explanations of its various rules which I suggested at the beginning of this chapter,** together with the fact that the most flagrant of them

---

* The omitted material contains Holmes's brief, conclusory objections to the agency doctrines involving the undisclosed principal and ratification. These doctrines are covered in Chapters 6 and 10, *infra*.

** Holmes there referred to adherence by courts to formulas, such as "the master and servant are considered as one person" or "the act of the servant is the act of the master" *(qui facit per alium facit per se)*, which originated

now-a-days often presents itself as a seemingly wholesome check on the indifference and negligence of great corporations, have done much to reconcile men's minds to that theory. [Holmes, *Agency*, 5 HARV. L. REV. 1, 14 (1891), *reprinted in* O. W. HOLMES, COLLECTED LEGAL PAPERS 101-102 (1920).]

The fact, however, that the doctrine of vicarious liability operates as a "wholesome check" on great corporations would not justify applying it to the many small businessmen still remaining in this country, nor to nonbusiness masters like Mrs. Means (*see* p. 10 *supra*), would it?

B. THE ENTREPRENEUR THEORY

Professor Warren Seavey, one of the principal architects of modern agency law,* stated his own position on the legitimacy of vicarious tort liability in an essay published in 1934, from which the following excerpt is taken:

> Perhaps the strongest reason which can be given for the imposition of "absolute" liability applies even more strongly in the case of vicarious liability, that is, the fact that one who is responsible for all consequences is more apt to take precautions to prevent injurious consequences from arising. If the law requires a perfect score in result, the actor is more likely to strive for that than if the law requires only the ordinary precautions to be taken; the cases where, either *de jure* or *de facto*, an actor is made absolutely liable for consequences indicate that this reason plays a very large part. The extent to which the law of torts has a preventative func-

---

in Roman law with respect to historical vicarious liability relationships, such as master and slave. He concluded that these formulas had through time acquired an independent standing of their own and supplied the basis for decision-making (without rethinking) even when the agent was a free person. This explanation was challenged by Wigmore, *Responsibility for Tortious Acts*, 7 HARV. L. REV. 315, 383 (1894). Wigmore stated that the principle of vicarious liability, which he traced to German law, had receded in England between the time of the Norman Conquest and the end of the Seventeenth Century to the point that generally the liability of the master was limited to acts commanded or assented to by him. It then was expanded to its present breadth under the influence of Lord Holt and others in response to increasing commercial activity, according to Wigmore.

* Professor Seavey was the Reporter for both editions of the Restatement of Agency (as noted earlier, the first edition was published in 1933; the second in 1958). He authored a short hornbook on the law of agency in 1964, and wrote a number of articles on the subject, most of which are reprinted in the book W. SEAVEY, STUDIES IN AGENCY (1949). Professor Seavey died in 1966 at the age of eighty-eight.

tion is of course debatable, and it is doubtful if reliable statistics can be obtained as to its effect upon the ordinary individual. To me, however, it seems fairly obvious that the likelihood of personal liability plays a very important part in our affairs. . . .

2)   Another reason for liability without fault in many cases is the difficulty of proving negligence. This reason is particularly cogent in imposing liability upon a master. Whether an employee was unfit at the time of the accident or whether there was improper supervision would ordinarily have to be proved by the testimony of fellow workers. Truthful testimony in such cases is difficult to obtain from the members of a well-disciplined organization. Aside from self-interest, which is obvious, only disgruntled fellow-workers are likely to subject themselves to the name commonly applied to a "tattle tale" within the organization . . .

Another reason not frequently acknowledged specifically by the courts is the "long purse" cynicism of Baty [more popularly known as the "deep pocket" theory, which are the words that Baty actually used—*Ed.*]. The bald statement that the master should pay because he can pay may have little more #3 than class appeal, although it is in conformity with the spirit of our times to believe that if one is successful enough either to operate a business or to employ servants, in addition to the income taxes taking off the upper layers of soft living, he should pay for the misfortunes caused others by his business or household. This, of itself, may not be a sufficiently strong reason; the liability of a master for the negligence of his domestic servants is less obvious than that of one employing his servants in business. To-day, however, we realize that the loss from accident usually falls upon the community as a whole, and that a cause of action is not money in pocket. As a result, we are beginning to wonder if the theory back of the Workmen's Compensation Act cannot be extended at least to certain types of accidents with financial security obtained through the use of insurance. The business enterprise, until it becomes insolvent, can shift losses imposed upon it because of harm to third persons to the consumers who ultimately pay, and it is

#3   not unjust to have the burden of misfortune shared by those who benefit from the work in the course of which liability occurs. It is this which is leading to the extension of absolute liability.

The lack of injustice to the employer becomes clearer if the business is of sufficient size so that there may be actuarial experience with regard to the number of negligent acts performed by employees. In large enterprises, recurring harms, while regarded individually as accidents, are not such when considered as a unit and with reference to the entire business, since their number is predictable with a fair degree of accuracy. Without insurance, the burden upon an individual employer conducting a small business might be too great; one victim might be substituted for another. But with insurance this hardship disappears. The injured person is, perhaps, in the majority of cases, one who is unprotected by insurance against harm. Sporadic and desultory inquiries lead me to believe that while many business-men insure their businesses against liability and losses, comparatively few persons have anything like adequate protection against accidental harm to themselves. The injured persons themselves are, however, consumers, and since the consumer pays, the imposition of liability upon employers is an indirect method of requiring the consumer class to provide its own insurance. It must be admitted that this argument leads to liability of the business organization, irrespective of fault by the employee, but we may as well recognize that we are rapidly approaching a time when the present methods of finding for the plaintiff will be replaced by some more rational method of imposing liability.

Finally, in the situations most frequently occurring, that is, those in which a corporation or other business organization is a defendant, it is reasonably obvious that the doctrine of *respondeat superior* is practically a necessity. Without this, the members of the organization, normally free in any event from personal liability, would be released as to the funds contributed, not only for the harms caused by the physical negligence of servants, but also for the wrongs done by the deceit and other similar torts of the directors and other corporate executives. To permit a group of persons so to organize that without personal liability they can secure the profits resulting both from the lawful and the unlawful conduct of those in charge of the organization without having the assets subject to liability for the harm caused by the unlawful conduct, is so shocking that it would seem to be unnecessary to do more than to state the alternatives. Whether or not the rule of *respondeat superior* was sustainable as a matter of justice when it originated, it is reasonably clear that in the modern world we cannot get along without it. [Seavey, *Speculations as to "Respondeat Superior,"* HARV. LEGAL ESSAYS 433, 447, 449-51 (1934), *reprinted in* W. SEAVEY, STUDIES IN AGENCY 147-153 (1949).]

C. THE GENERAL DETERRENCE THEORY

Another theory supporting the doctrine of vicarious liability is advanced by Professor Calabresi in *Some Thoughts on Risk Distribution and the Law of Torts*, 70 YALE L. J. 499 (1961). This article, which grounds the problem in economics, advances the thesis that the doctrine of vicarious liability is justified by the "resource allocation" or "general deterrence" theory. The next several pages contain a broad summary of this theory. The summary is no substitute, however, for a careful reading of the article itself, which contains a lengthy and intelligent discussion of a new approach (and its limitations) to loss allocation in torts.

The Theory

Briefly, the theory states as its fundamental postulate that

[B]y and large people know what is best for themselves. If people want television sets, society should produce television sets; if they want licorice drops, then licorice drops should be made. And, the theory continues, in order for people to know what they really want they must know the relative costs of producing different goods. The function of prices is to reflect the actual costs of competing goods, and thus to enable the buyer to cast an informed vote in making his purchases. [70 YALE L.J. 502.]

Calabresi defines "cost" to include the full cost of the goods to society—"their cost, whether in terms of the physical components of the item or of the expense of accidents associated with its production and use." (p. 503.) (You should note that this definition of cost contains a value judgment. It is doubtful that all cost accountants and economists would agree that "cost" includes the expense of accidents associated with the production and use of goods. *See also* Morris's statement on this in Part D *infra*.)

As an example of the above, Calabresi posits two different societies, in one of which (State *A*) all accident costs are borne by the state and come out of general taxes; in the other (State *B*) accident costs are charged to the doer. An individual in State *B* wants to buy a second car, which would cost $200, plus an additional $200 for insurance. The cost of train fares, taxis and alternative forms of entertainment to driving comes to $250. He decides to forego buying a second car by contrasting the $400 to the $250. In State *A* the cost would merely be $200, since the individual would have to pay the general taxes in any event. The individual in State *A* would probably buy the second car. Thus cars would be overproduced in State *A* relative to their true cost.

Calabresi states that it is not necessary to imagine people sitting around thinking about relative prices in order for the theory to make sense. His appeal apparently is to common sense. One can assume that the demand for cars would increase if the expense of owning one was considerably reduced, and vice versa. He states as an example of this the fact that, with the coming of compulsory liability insurance in New York, "the bottom has fallen out of the jalopy market in that state" (p. 503 n.16).

Underlying Rationale of the Theory

The underlying rationale of the resource allocation theory seems to be two-fold. First, as explained above, people are able to cast an informed vote in making their purchases, which is a good in itself and is consistent with and indeed enhances a free enterprise system. Second, accident losses are reduced because of the "general deterrence" provided by applying the theory. This second reason behind the theory is developed with much more precision in Calabresi's later writings. The following passage, taken from Calabresi, *Fault, Accidents and the Wonderful World of Blum and Kalven,* 75 YALE L. J. 216, 223 (1965), may clarify the general deterrence rationale.

> Specifically, the thesis holds that although, for instance, we may not want the *safest* possible product, we do want the manufacturer to choose a means of production which may be somewhat more expensive in terms of materials used if this expense is made up by savings in accident costs. Similarly, although we do not wish to abandon cars altogether (they give us more pleasure than they cost us—despite accident costs), we may, if we are made to pay for car-caused accidents, drive less, or less at night, or less when we are of accident-prone ages, or with more safety devices, than if we are not made to pay for accident costs when we decide to use a car. I call this thesis general deterrence, because it seeks to diminish accident costs not by directly attacking specific occasions of danger, but (like workmen's compensation) by making more expensive those activities which are accident prone and thereby making more attractive their safer substitutes.

An example of the general deterrence effect of having activities bear their "actual" costs can be drawn from the apparent collapse of the jalopy market in New York after compulsory liability insurance was adopted in that state. The bottom fell out of the market doubtless because insurance was so expensive for youthful drivers that many chose not to buy and drive jalopies. The law presumably thus reduced the total number of accidents by forcing youthful drivers to bear more of the cost of their activity. "Safer substitutes" had been made "more attractive," with the result that fewer accidents would be caused by this age group because fewer of its number would be driving.

Allocation Among the Parties Involved

Calabresi notes in the previously quoted *Risk Distribution* article that

> [T]he theory requires that among the several parties engaged in an enterprise the loss should be placed on the party which is most likely to cause the burden to be reflected in the price of whatever the enterprise sells.

But which is that party? Is it the worker who has been injured, or his employer; is it the depositor whose check is forged, or the bank; is it the pedestrian, or the driver of the car that hit him? Here, traditional economic *theory* is of little help. For in the economist's world it often makes no difference whether, for example, the cost of an injury is put on a worker or on his employer. In terms of "pure" resource-allocation-loss-distribution theory, if the injury were put on the worker he could insure, and he could demand higher wages to pay the cost of that insurance. Alternatively, although he might not insure, he would still demand higher wages as compensation for the risk. On the other hand, the employer would lower wages if he were suddenly charged with the risk of injury to his workmen. Either way, the theory goes, the cost would find its way into wages and into prices.

This "pure theory" loss-distribution argument, which was used in discussions of workmen's compensation some fifty years ago to explain why compensation would not save workers money, is in fact inaccurate. It presupposes an all knowing, all rational economic world which does not exist. In the first place, even if such a world did exist, *some* risks would still be assignable to the activity which caused them by only one party. Thus, a pedestrian—even if tempted to buy accident insurance because of the risk of being hit by a car—would not be able to make this part of the price of cars. As a result, car buyers would have no reason not to buy cars, even though their purchases raised the cost of pedestrian auto insurance.[24] In

---

24 In effect such a result would amount to a decision that automobile accidents are more a true cost of walking and of living generally, than of automobile driving. Actually they are probably a cost of both.

I have not, in this article, attempted to probe what influences our decision that a particular "cost" is caused by one activity rather than another. Clearly this is an important question. Indeed, it is the next step in any thorough analysis of risk distribution. At this stage of analysis, however, when we have not yet examined the need and the effect of charging activities with those costs which all would agree they cause, that step seems

fact, they would be in the same situation as [the consumer in State *A—Ed.*] for whom the real cost of a car is not reflected in its purchase price. Were the risk of accident put instead on the car owner as driver, this added cost would be reflected in the real expense of owning a car and would affect purchases. Secondly, in the real world not all parties evaluate losses equally, or are equally likely to insure. Before workmen's compensation the individual worker simply did not evaluate the risk of injury to be as great as it actually was. He took his chances; and even if he did not wish to take his chances, the fact that other workmen took a chance forced him to do the same, or to starve. The result—apart from some individual tragedies —was that wages and prices in certain industries simply did not reflect the losses those industries caused. Finally, insurance may cost one party less than it costs another. If that is so, the proper party to bear the risk is the party whose insurance costs are lower. For only then are the true costs of injuries, and not some false costs of more expensive insurance, reflected in price.

There are, naturally, some situations where the pure loss-distribution theory applies, and where it actually does not matter who bears the loss initially. Some, though by no means all, independent contractor cases and some product liability cases involving commercial buyers and sellers may be examples. But whenever one party is in fact in a better position to allocate the cost of the particular loss to the appropriate activity or merchandise, allocation of resources requires that party to bear the original burden of the loss. [70 YALE L. J. 505-507.]

Limitations on the Theory

Calabresi recognizes as limitations on the theory the unequal distribution of income in our society and the existence of monopoly power in some industries, but argues against the significance of these limitations. He states that redistribution of income— if any is desired—should be met honestly through the tax mechanism, not indirectly through artificially subsidizing goods and services the poor are in need of. He acknowledges that political realities frequently dictate otherwise, and that subsidization of certain goods and services (such as municipal bus service) may be necessary.

---

somewhat far removed. [Calabresi deals with that step in the article mentioned above, Calabresi, *Fault, Accidents and the Wonderful World of Blum and Kalven,* 75 YALE L. J. 216, 230-233 (1965). It is not pertinent to our immediate concern, however, and will be covered in the sections to come dealing with the problems of borrowed servants and of defining the independent contractor.—*Ed.*]

All this is really no more than saying that there are other things which count more in our society than allocation of resources and that we will gladly forego the best allocation of resources if by doing so some more important policy is served. It does not mean, however, that resource allocation should not be an important consideration in deciding what should be done. [70 YALE L. J. 504 n.17.]

Also, he argues that the importance of the monopoly power limitation is diminished by the fact that generally in our economy similar degrees of monopoly power are enjoyed by industries which produce goods that compete with each other, *i.e.*, steel and aluminum are both oligopolistic industries and they compete with each other. Assuming that one has a higher accident rate than the other, charging them with accident costs theoretically should influence their relative prices and result in enhanced consumer choice and thus a proper allocation of resources.

Another question which can be raised about the theory is whether large businesses producing several products actually allocate costs precisely enough that accident costs would be assessed to the particular product which caused them. Calabresi covers this point in 70 YALE L. J. 514 n.41, as follows:

> This is as good a place as any to call attention to another reason why the resource allocation justification cannot be pushed to extremes. Many companies which produce several goods allocate costs to these separate goods somewhat arbitrarily. It could well be that under such a system accident costs caused essentially by one item might be charged to several and reflected in the prices of each. Such a system would result in some misallocation of resources. Much needless time could be spent in analyzing whether placing of accident costs on specific industries helped or hindered this misallocation. The very fact that the firms involved do not find it worth their while to allocate the costs more precisely indicates, however, that the misallocation cannot be too significant. If, then, we are concerned only with avoiding major misallocations in tort law, this imperfection need not trouble us unduly.

Application to Respondeat Superior Concept

Calabresi concludes that the *respondeat superior* form of vicarious liability fits the resource allocation theory very well. A "failure to show injury costs [through abandoning *respondeat superior* liability, for example] means that the prices of the goods the industry sells understate their true costs, and that too much is produced in that industry compared to those which are less accident prone." (p. 544.) Also, "[T]he master is the best insurer, both in the sense of being able to obtain insurance at the lower rates and in the sense of being most aware of the risk. Consequently, he is the best primary risk spreader." (p. 543.)

D. THE SPECIFIC DETERRENCE THEORY

C. Robert Morris, Jr., *Enterprise Liability and the Actuarial Process—The Insignificance of Foresight,* 70 YALE L. J. 554, 555 (1961), observes that "[T]he justice of enterprise liability is now unquestioned, though the proper scope of such liability is still a matter of concern. The entrepreneur theory* is an important cornerstone of this modern view." Enterprise liability "causes little business dislocation," and there is no competitive disadvantage since all competitors are subject to the same liability and thus have to set aside a reserve or purchase insurance. Morris's approach to the policy underlying enterprise liability differs sharply from Calabresi, however, as the following excerpt illustrates.

Dean Smith stated that the function of enterprise liability is "[T]o include in the costs of operation inevitable losses to third persons incident to carrying on an enterprise." His idea was seconded by many, including Talbot Smith, who observed that "business must pay its passage." But what losses are properly considered "incident to carrying on an enterprise"? What costs are part of a business' "passage"?

The language used implies an analogy to other business expenses. As businesses must pay for capital, material, and labor, so must they pay for the lives, bodies, and property they inadvertently consume. This analogy to economic principles, however, conceals value judgments, similar to those involved in other branches of the law, which dictate the extent to which businesses should pay for the capital, material, and labor intentionally devoted to an enterprise. Technology requires the barest union of labor and materials. While capital goods are necessary, "capital" is not. All that is required is some technique

---

* The entrepreneur theory was broadly described in Seavey's discussion of the rationale behind vicarious liability, Part B *supra,* at pages 38-40. Dean Young B. Smith of Columbia Law School first advanced this rationale in the article, *Frolic and Detour,* 23 COLUM. L. REV. 444, 716 (1923). Smith justified the existence of respondeat superior liability on the ground that, ". . . it is socially more expedient to spread or distribute among a large group of the community the losses which experience has taught are inevitable in the carrying on of industry, than to cast the loss upon a few; . . . the master should be made responsible not merely because he is better able to pay, but because he is best able to effectuate the spreading (by means of insurance) and the distribution (by enhanced price) of such losses." *Id.* at 716.

to feed and maintain the labor force which creates capital goods, given the fact that the product of that labor will not be immediately useful for consumption. Labor, furthermore, need only be paid enough to continue working. These are the technological minima; and they are completely unsatisfactory on nontechnological grounds. Hence, we embrace a market economy, including capitalistic methods of obtaining capital goods, instead of forced labor or collective economic organization. But the economic forces of even this market economy lead to undesirable results, and for humanitarian reasons (though not without some economic justification) we have mitigated the rigors of a free market economy with minimum wage laws, wages and hours laws, child labor laws, etc. And it is upon these same nontechnological and humanitarian grounds that we approve of enterprise liability. In other words, those losses which enterprise liability seeks to repair are not losses which need be repaired to assure the maintenance of production. Moreover, though these losses have some economic effect, since their immediate victims are removed from the ranks of consumers, their repair is no more important to the operation of a market economy than is the repair of losses from natural causes. These repairs are made, then, for humanitarian and moral reasons rather than for technological or economic ones. [70 YALE L. J. 583-84.]

In addition, Morris takes the position that an important justification for such liability is that it can reduce losses by placing the economic burden of damages caused by negligent employees on the master. He will be more careful to hire safety conscious employees and to supervise and discipline careless ones. In other words, enterprise liability has "managerial as well as financial functions. That is, not only could the entrepreneur insure and spread the risk, but he could also seek to minimize the loss or prevent it altogether." (70 YALE L. J. 554.)

The availability of insurance reduces the economic impact of vicarious liability on the master and thus would appear to damage the above thesis. It can be argued, however, that the incentive to reduce losses remains for at least some enterprises because a carelessly run business, if it is large enough, may find itself faced with cancellation of coverage or with coverage being made conditional upon compliance with certain safety requirements set by the insurance company, in addition to the virtual certainty of higher premiums; and the self-insurer obviously will be interested in reducing the amount of reserves it must set aside in order to meet claims.

An example supporting "managerial economics" (or "specific deterrence" or "risk prevention") can be drawn from James & Dickinson, *Accident Proneness and Accident Law*, 63 HARV. L. REV. 769 (1950). The authors cite the actual experience of a large trucking company as an example to support their thesis both that some people are accident prone and that steps can be taken to minimize the damage done by such people. The company, which employed many drivers and covered several million miles a year, analyzed the accident records of all its drivers, discovered that some were accident prone, shifted them to departments with low accident potential and filled their places with drivers whose records were kept under careful scrutiny. At the end of seven years, during which time the total mileage had increased slightly, the company found that by shifting one-eighth of the drivers it had decreased its accidents by 78 per cent. Presumably the risk of vicarious liability supplied at least part of the incentive for the company to take this action. Literature describing other examples of sharp reductions (41% to 70%) in accidents by retraining, by individual attention to high-accident employees, and hiring on the basis of "estheto-kinetic co-ordination scores" is cited in footnote 34 of the article.

For other literature on this topic, see P. ATIYAH, VICARIOUS LIABILITY IN THE LAW OF TORTS 12-28 (1967); T. BATY, VICARIOUS LIABILITY (1916); James, *Vicarious Liability*, 28 TUL. L. REV. 161 (1954); Douglas, *Vicarious Liability and Administration of Risk I and II*, 38 YALE L. J. 584, 720 (1929); Laski, *The Basis of Vicarious Liability*, 26 YALE L. J. 105 (1916).

E. A JUSTIFICATION FOR THE JUSTIFICATIONS

By now, some law students would confess that they are tired of reading about theory (or policy; the "why" behind the law) and want to "get to the law; that's what I'm going to have to practice." That approach overlooks the fact that every legal rule reflects a policy decision. Granted, judges usually do not refer to policy (other than the policy of stare decisis and that usually through action) in their opinions. This does not mean, however, that the fundamental principles upon which a court is proceeding are not important to the case before them. Most judges simply bypass any inquiry into them and instead seek the relieving certainty of precedent. Someone else has done the basic job for them. And that person may have decided on the basis of an intuitive reaction—perhaps the *Jones v. Hart* case is an example of this—rather than attempting to reason from existing doctrine.

One cannot conclude, however, that mere exposure to existing precedent will suffice. How do you answer—or recognize, for that matter—the inevitable new and only slightly related problem that comes up? It is crucial to the imaginative use of precedent that you recognize that seemingly dissimilar doctrine may rest on the same or similar basic policy, and that seemingly similar doctrines may not (*see,* for example, the notes on imputed negligence following *Howard v. Zimmerman,* pp. 16-20 *supra*). Also, an argument directed toward policy can be instrumental in persuading a court to overturn prior cases standing against your client's position. As an example of this, *see Weber v. Stokely-Van Camp,* p. 53 F *infra.*

Consider in this context the following language from Holmes, *The Path of the Law,* 10 HARV. L. REV. 457, 465-66, 474 (1897), reprinted in O. W. HOLMES, COLLECTED LEGAL PAPERS 180-81, 195 (1920):

> The danger of which I speak is not the admission that the principles governing other phenomena also govern the law, but the notion that a given system, ours, for instance, can be worked out like mathematics from some general axioms of conduct. This is the natural error of the schools, but it is not confined to them. I once heard a very eminent judge say that he never let a decision go until he was absolutely sure that it was right. So judicial dissent often is blamed, as if it meant simply that one side or the other were not doing their sums right, and, if they would take more trouble, agreement inevitably would come.

> This mode of thinking is entirely natural. The training of lawyers is a training in logic. The processes of analogy, discrimination, and deduction are those in which they are most at home. The language of judicial decision is mainly the language of logic. And the logical method and form flatter that longing for certainty and for repose which is in every human mind. But certainty generally is illusion, and repose is not the destiny of man. Behind the logical form lies a judgment as to the relative worth and importance of competing legislative grounds, often an inarticulate and unconscious judgment, it is true, and yet the very root and nerve of the whole proceeding.

> . . . .
> . . . I look forward to a time when the part played by history in the explanation of dogma shall be very small, and instead of ingenious research we shall spend our energy on a study of the ends sought to be attained and the reasons for desiring them.

Finally, the study of law can prove deadly boring if you let history do your creative and critical thinking for you, and your study consists merely of memorizing various rules and precedents without attempting to understand the reasoning behind the rules and critically analyzing such reasoning in terms of the realities of existing society.

GENERAL QUESTIONS

1. *Indemnification of the Master.* Can a master who is held vicariously liable for a loss caused by the negligence of his servant obtain indemnification from the servant? Would that make sense to you? What arguments for and against granting the master this right can you think of? Are the preceding materials in this chapter of any aid to you in responding to this question?

The state of the law in this country and in England is that the master does have a right of indemnification against his servant. *See* Fireman's Fund Am. Ins. Co. v. Turner, 260 Ore. 30, 488 P.2d 429 (1971), a recent case containing a lengthy discussion of the policy behind the right of indemnification. The court upheld a claim of indemnification made by the employer's insurer against an employee who was driving his own car on company business when he negligently caused a loss to a third party. The injured person sued both the employer and employee and obtained a judgment against them. The liability insurer of the employer paid the judgment and, acting under a subrogation clause in the policy, brought suit against the employee for indemnification. The employee had his own automobile insurance; apparently his insurance company handled the defense in the indemnification suit.

The theory of the defense was that the rule granting an employer indemnification against an employee was out of date; that it was inevitable that an employee driving many miles each year on the job would have an accident; that the employer had insurance coverage, which is sufficient protection for it; that the accident involved "mere inadvertent negligence," not drinking or gross negligence, and thus "the employer should not, as a matter of public policy, be entitled to pass the economic loss off on to the employee when it is foreseeable at the outset."

The trial court agreed with the above argument and entered judgment in favor of the defendant. This was reversed unanimously on appeal on the ground that "the 'fault concept'—that all persons should be held responsible for the consequences of their wrongful acts, including 'inadvertent negligence,'—while subject to criticism, is still firmly established as the foundation of tort liability." The Oregon Supreme Court stated, with this as a premise and citing the Restatement of Restitution § 96, that it is not contrary to public policy to permit the employer, who is held liable without fault on his part, to obtain indemnity from the person at fault. The court noted that some of the cases upholding indemnification did so on the alternative ground of breach by the employee of an implied term of the employment contract to perform his duties with reasonable care. It observed that no cases have abolished the rule of indemnity, although the United States Supreme Court declined to create such a rule when faced with the question in a case under the Federal Tort Claims Act. United States v. Gilman, 347 U.S. 507 (1954). *See* Seavey, *"Liberal Construction," and the Tort Liability of the Federal Government*, 67 HARV. L. REV. 994 (1954) (commenting on the lower court decision); Note, 63 YALE L. J. 570 (1954).

A leading English case, after lengthy consideration, reached the same result as the *Turner* court. *See* Lister v. Romford Ice and Cold Storage Co. Ltd., [1957] A.C. 555 (H.L.) (upholding, with several dissents, indemnification on the basis of breach of an implied term in the employment contract to use due care). *See also*, W. PROSSER, LAW OF TORTS 311 (4th ed. 1971); Restatement of Agency § 401, Comment *d*.

Does the widespread use of the omnibus clause (see p. 27 *supra*) affect the employer's right to indemnity from his employee, at least in automobile accident cases? Since the driver is himself an insured party under the omnibus clause, the injured party could either proceed directly against him and be assured of a solvent defendant or, if he sued the employer, then one could argue that indemnification of the insurance company as in the *Turner* case (which did not involve an omnibus clause) would not make sense since the company also insured the driver and would be proceeding against itself.

The master's right of indemnification has been sharply criticized. *See* Steffen, *The Employer's "Indemnity" Action*, 25 U. CHI. L. REV. 465 (1958); Williams, *Vicarious Liability and the Master's Indemnity*, 20 MODERN L. REV. 220, 437 (1957). Both of these articles were inspired by the *Lister* case. For literature in support of the case, see Jolowicz, *The Right to Indemnity Between Master and Servant*, [1956] CAMB. L. J. 101; Sandford & McMullin, *Master and Servant: Employer's Claim Against Negligent Employee*, 33 N.Z.L.J. 252 (1957).

Professor Steffen argued that it is unfair and unjust to hold an employee liable for mere inadvertence so long as he was rendering faithful service to his employer. Professor Williams argued that it would misallocate costs to put the loss on to the employee; losses occasioned by unintended accidents instead should be left on the business and passed on to the persons who choose to benefit from the business: the customers. Arguments along these lines were rejected by the Oregon court in the *Turner* case.

Both the *Turner* and *Lister* cases involved income generating enterprises. Consider, in evaluating the soundness of the right to indemnity, the fact that *respondeat superior* liability extends beyond such enterprises.

Finally, as a variant on the above, can an employer collect damages from an employee who has caused him a loss but not as a result of liability to third parties? Suppose, for example, that a truck driver, driving negligently, damages the company truck or a waiter negligently drops a platter of expensive dishes. Is the employee (assuming no express contractual provision) liable under the common law to the employer for such losses? Would you call the employer's right of action against the employee, assuming he has one, a right of indemnification?

2.   *The Fellow Servant Rule.* One long standing limitation on an employer's vicarious liability for the torts of his employees is that he is not liable when the injured party is another one of his employees. This limitation is known as the "fellow servant" rule. The employee injured under circumstances where his employer was not negligent toward him was left with a cause of action against the employee at fault and whatever personal resources (like medical insurance) he had available to him.

[handwritten margin note: workmen's compensation has pretty much made this obsolete]

The law of workmen's compensation has made this limitation obsolete for many employees. *See* Chapter 3, part D, *infra,* which briefly covers workmen's compensation and the common law duties an employer not under workmen's compensation owes to his employees.

What do you think was the reasoning behind the fellow servant rule? For one view, *see* Posner, *A Theory of Negligence,* 1 J. LEGAL STUDIES 29, 44-46 (1972).

3.   *Imputed Contributory Negligence.* The preceding materials, in discussing vicarious liability, are talking about imputed negligence. Under what circumstances does the master-servant relationship have a bearing on imputed contributory negligence? You will recall that this topic was raised in a different context in the notes following *Howard v. Zimmerman,* pp. 16-20 *supra.*

The widely adopted rule is that a master is barred from recovery against a third person who negligently caused a loss to the master if his servant has been negligent in the accident giving rise to the loss. Restatement of Agency § 317. Does this make sense?

The first part of this chapter summarized the elaborate arguments and painstaking efforts that have been made to explain the imputed negligence involved in vicarious liability. In reviewing these writings, are they equally persuasive (or unpersuasive) with the matter of contributory negligence in mind?

At least one court thought that the above rule did not make sense. In Weber v. Stokely-Van Camp, 274 Minn. 482, 144 N.W. 2d 540 (1966), the "both ways" test (if the employee's negligence is imputed to his employer, so is his contributory negligence) set forth above in the Restatement and in earlier Minnesota cases was rejected. The court held that an employer who was injured while riding with his employee could recover against the negligent driver of the other vehicle even though his employee was contributorily negligent. The "both ways" test was criticized as illogical and unfair mainly for relying on the deep pocket theory as the underlying policy of vicarious liability and then noting that the theory of making a solvent defendant available does not apply to the employer's suit. Thus the court concluded that the "both ways" test should be rejected.

A casenote on the *Weber* case in 39 U. COLO. L. REV. 170 (1966) points out that even if imputed contributory negligence blocks his suit against the third party, the master can still sue his servant for his personal and property losses. In most instances involving automobile losses, the servant will be covered under the omnibus clause of the master's liability insurance policy (*see* p. 27 *supra*), and the prevailing view is that the master, even though he is the named insured, can recover for damage caused him by the negligence of the driver. *See* 7 APPLEMAN, INSURANCE LAW AND PRACTICE § 4409 at n.86 (1962). One problem which has been raised is that such a construction of the omnibus clause (which, in most policies and in the standard policy form, does not expressly exclude coverage for injury to or death of the named insured, *id.* at n.91.5) might turn the policy into a personal accident policy for the named insured. Appleman states that a few courts are persuaded by this but most are not; instead, they view the question from the perspective of the driver, who is faced with liability regardless of who the injured party is.

Suppose, on the other hand, that a servant is hurt in an accident caused in part by his master's contributory negligence. Is the servant's cause of action blocked by imputation? Assume, for example, that a taxi driver is hurt in a collision with someone who was driving negligently. Assume further that the brakes of the cab were negligently maintained in the shop and failed at a critical moment with no previous warning to the driver, contributing to the accident. We have seen, with the *Weber* case to the contrary, that the law will impute contributory negligence up to the master. Will it also impute down to the servant?

4. *Limitation to Losses Caused by Tortious Behavior.* Another limitation on the doctrine of vicarious liability is that the doctrine is limited to the tortious acts of servants. Why? Why not also include the nontortious harms committed by servants in the course of their employment so long, at least, as they are predictably recurring losses caused by the enterprise? Consider the policy arguments noted above in the first part of this chapter. Do you see any distinction that rationally can be drawn between negligently and nonnegligently caused harms? What would be the response of the advocates of the entrepreneur and general deterrence theories to this limitation?

For an interesting discussion supporting the existing status of the law, see C. MORRIS, TORTS 254-55 (1953). Morris takes the position, similar to that described above by another Morris in part D, that a substantial justification for *respondeat superior* liability is that it provides an incentive for masters to exercise their "considerable measure of control over [the] lives of their workmen" and to discipline them for misconduct. This incentive is not present when the behavior of the servant is nonfaulty. Morris argues that this fact, combined with the fact that the master's risk bearing capacity is sometimes not superior to that of the injured third person (see note 5, below), supplies a reason for hesitating to extend liability to such circumstances.

5. Do the entrepreneur, deep pocket, general deterrence and specific deterrence theories all reach the same result all the time and therefore what we are really saying is make the rich man pay? Keep this question in mind as you go through these materials. And consider the following fact situation, adapted from the Morris article: Jones, a delivery man for the nearly insolvent Ace Printing Company, negligently runs into a properly parked Standard Oil truck while on route delivering some goods, causing substantial damage which exceeds the modest insurance limits of the printing company. Standard Oil sues Ace Printing on *respondeat superior* grounds. Will Ace have to pay for its servant's negligence? Will it if the judgment would bankrupt it, and yet would represent only a tiny fraction of one day's income to Standard Oil? Would your response vary if the person negligently driving into the Standard Oil truck had been a babysitter driving the car of her employer (the mother of a lower middle income family) while on a route prescribed by the mother?

Consider also, with respect to the deep pocket approach, the following reaction of Glanville Williams in *Vicarious Liability and the Master's Indemnity*, 20 Mod. L. Rev. 220, 232 (1957):

> What other theory is there? Well, there is the purely cynical theory that the master is liable because he has a purse worth opening. The master is frequently rich, and he is usually insured—two arguments that might be used by any burglar, if he ever troubled to justify his thefts. The strange thing is to find them put forward by judges of eminence.

Chapter 3

THE INDEPENDENT CONTRACTOR EXCEPTION

A. THE CONCEPT

At the beginning of the first chapter the point was made that the existence of an employment relationship does not automatically mean vicarious liability for the employer in all cases. As you will recall, the Restatement of Agency definitions quoted from drew a distinction between kinds of employees. This chapter will develop that distinction, using the Restatement terminology, which is widely accepted. Those definitions should be reviewed at this time.

Also, as you read through this material, note that two different groups or categories of tortfeasors are involved in the independent contractor exception to vicarious liability. One was mentioned earlier and is the subject of the main case to follow shortly: the nonservant employee. The other category is mentioned immediately below and appears again in the notes following the main cases.

As the material already covered makes clear, you are liable if you hire a neighborhood boy to mow your yard and he negligently injures someone while throwing some object off of your yard during the mowing job. Suppose, however, that the same negligent act takes place but the person doing it was an employee of Ace Lawn Service, a large company which specializes in lawn care but also installs fences, removes trees, and so forth. Can you think of any reason why you would not be held liable for the harm caused by Ace Lawn Service? Would it make any difference in your answer if instead of lawn service you had contracted with the Smith Electric Company to fix a neon sign on a building you owned and, in doing so, one of the electricians had negligently caused a short circuit which resulted in a fire injuring other persons and property?

You might ask yourself whether the above category (which we can call the "separate business" category for lack of a better term) presents any vicarious liability problems at all. It takes a good bit of stretching, after all, to describe the Ace Lawn Service or Smith Electric relationship with the owner as an "employer-employee" relationship. And if it's not an employment relationship, how would you describe it?

One further point to bear in mind: the injured party always can sue the servant, the nonservant agent, or the separate business, and collect directly from him (or it). Ask yourself as you go through these materials whether this fact plays—or should play—an important role in distinguishing the categories.

STOCKWELL v. MORRIS
Supreme Court of Wyoming
46 Wyo. 1, 22 P.2d 189 (1933)
Noted in 32 Mich. L. Rev. 276 (1933)

BLUME, Justice. In this case Morris, salesman for the Maytag Inter-mountain Company, was driving his automobile from Hudson to Lander and collided with the automobile of plaintiff. The latter sued the salesman, as well as his principal, for damages caused by the collision. The court directed a verdict for the company, and the sole question herein is—assuming the agent to have been negligent—as to whether or not the court's action was right. The testimony herein is uncontradicted.

Morris was a salesman for the company in selling washing machines, and had been working for it for some years. That was his only occupation. He received a commission on all sales made, and no further compensation. He made no collections, but occasionally seems to have delivered washing machines sold. He drove his own automobile in the performance of his work, and paid his own expenses. He appointed and discharged sub-salesmen under him, receiving a commission on their sales, and he took them out from time to time to show them how to sell washing machines. He was assigned the central portion of the state as his territory, which, perhaps, was somewhat changed from time to time. In any event, there is some correspondence in the record with the company's manager in Denver as to some change to be made therein. The company furnished him with no rules or regulations as to his work, except as to the terms of the contracts to be made for the sale of washing machines. The details of the work were left to him. Contracts for sales, blank forms for which were furnished by the company, were, by the subsalesmen, delivered in triplicate to a girl in charge of an office, which the company kept at Casper, but Morris apparently sent contracts made by him to the Company at Salt Lake. He seems not to have had anything to do with the office at Casper, though apparently he made that his headquarters. On May 27, 1930, the date of the collision above mentioned, Morris, in company with his wife, drove his automobile to Lander to see a Mr. Tyler, a salesman under him, to see if he could help him in his work. After reaching Lander, he, at the suggestion of Tyler, and in company with him, drove to Hudson, to see Mrs. Radovitch, who had a Maytag washing machine which was out of repair, though repairs of machines were ordinarily made by a special representative of the company. Tyler discovered the trouble, fixed the machine, gratuitously, and he and Morris then drove back to Lander, and the collision occurred while doing so. Morris wrote the Maytag Company as to that fact.

Counsel for appellant argue that the Maytag Inter-mountain Company was the principal and Morris was its agent, and that the former is, accordingly, liable herein, and they say that the cases which hold contrary to their contention deal with the relationship of master and servant, and that such cases have no application here. But an attorney is an agent. If, then, in attempting to manage his client's case, he, without specific directions, travels in an automobile to see a man who, in his opinion, might become an important witness in his case, is his client responsible? So we have "Ford agencies," "Buick agencies," and other similar "agencies," handling products of automobile manufacturers. While today the managers of these agencies, ordinarily, perhaps, buy such products, they might handle them tomorrow on commission. They are agents, in the broad sense of that term, but should the manufacturer be held responsible for all the torts that the former might commit in disposing of these products? The Curtis Publishing Company, located at Philadelphia, every week sends its Saturday Evening Posts throughout the country. If a boy in Cheyenne, while on the errand of soliciting subscriptions for the magazine, or delivering it, negligently runs into another with his bicycle, should the company be held responsible? The citation to these examples, which might be multiplied many times, shows that the solution of the problem before us is not as easy as counsel for appellant seem to think, and in view of the fact that the case before us is one of first impression here, we have deemed it expedient to give it more attention than counsel for appellant apparently have thought it necessary.

Prior to the latter part of the seventeenth century, a master was not responsible for the torts of his servants, unless committed by his express command or subsequent assent. But in the case of Jones v. Hart, 2 Salk. 441, 91 Eng. Repr. 382, decided in 1699, it was held that if a servant driving a cart negligently runs into another cart, the master is liable. And from about that time commenced to be developed the modern doctrine that a master is responsible for the torts of his servant committed within the scope of his employment. . . . Shaw, C. J., said in Farwell v. Railroad Corporation, 4 Metc. 49, 38 Am. Dec. 339, that the "rule is obviously founded on the great principle of social duty, that every man, in the management of his own affairs, whether by himself or by his agents or servants, shall so conduct them as not to injure another." The doctrine was carried to its logical conclusion. Independent agents or contractors were treated the same as servants. It was not until the second quarter of the nineteenth century that it was doubted that the doctrine of respondeat superior should be applied in all cases in which one man was employed to perform an act for another. . . . Two decisions rendered in 1840, namely, Milligan v. Wedge, 12 A. & E. 737, and Quarman v. Burnett, 6 M. & W. 497, took a definite departure from the then generally accepted rule, and by the middle of that century it came to be recognized that there are many cases in which a man should not be held responsible for the acts of a representative, if the latter is not under his immediate control, direction or supervision. Such representative has generally been called an independent contractor, a phrase that has acquired almost a technical meaning, originally, of course, applied to one who actually performed services under an independent contract. It is not altogether appropriate to apply the term in all cases, or in the case at bar, and various other terms have been sought to be substituted, such as entrepreneur or enterpriser.

. . . . The rules governing principal and agent are a later development in our law than those governing master and servant, and have branched off from the latter. And it is insisted in the restatement of the law of agency by the American Law Institute that it is important that the distinction be observed. A servant is defined as a person employed to perform personal service for another in his affairs, and who, in respect to his physical movements in the performance of the service is subject to the other's control or right to control, while an agent is defined as a person who represents another in contractual negotiations or transactions akin thereto. The reason assigned for the importance of making the distinction is that an agent who is not at the same time acting as servant cannot ordinarily make his principal liable for incidental negligence in connection with the means incidentally employed to accomplish the work entrusted to his care. Draft 1, p. 8; draft 5, p. 30-31; pp. 99-100. . . . We think that the distinction mentioned may be drawn with profit. The control, or right of control, over physical movements generally exists when a person performs personal service for another, unless he is an independent contractor. That is not true, or not nearly as true, in the case of an agent. Moreover, actual control is ordinarily more immediate in the case of a servant than in the case of an agent. There can be no doubt that a salesman, such as Morris was, is an agent. . . . Of course, an agent may, as to some work performed for his principal, be a servant. But no personal service, not even the delivery of washing machines, is involved in this case, unless the driving of the automobile may be called such. And the gist of the controversy herein is as to whether the principal is liable for its agent's negligence while engaged in a more or less necessary physical act which is incidental to the performance of his general duties, or, if we must use a special term, whether or not the agent, while engaged in that physical act, must be regarded in the nature of an independent contractor. The test which courts have generally adopted is that already heretofore stated. . . .

. . . .

In Natchez Coca-Cola Bottling Co. v. Watson, 160 Miss. 173, 133 So. 677, the company engaged a truck driver to drive its truck over a designated route for the purpose of selling coca-cola along the route, being paid on a commission basis. The company was held liable for negligence of the driver. A similar case is Dunbaden v. Castles Ice Cream Company, 103 N. J. L. 427, 135 Atl. 886. These cases may be distinguished from the case at bar, whether logically or not we need not say, by the fact that the route to be driven was fixed and definite, showing, perhaps, more detailed control over the physical movements of the person employed. . . .

There are, however, a number of cases which are hard to distinguish from the case at bar. Several of them were decided under the workman's compensation laws, and there is, perhaps, in such cases manifest a tendency toward a liberal construction in favor of a claimant under such laws. . . . And while it seems, at first blush, that there should, perhaps, be no difference of construction in workmen's compensation cases and damage cases, as held by at least some of the authorities, those from Massachusetts, for instance, still the former involve a principle of public policy different from that involved in this case, namely, that each industry should bear its own burdens, and since it is not necessary to decide the point herein, we refrain from doing so. . . .

In this view, then, that the right of control of the physical movements—the automobile—is the decisive inquiry, it becomes important what the record discloses in that regard. The evidence shows that the Maytag Company furnished Morris no rules or regulations to govern him in the performance of the work but that the means and manner thereof was left to him. That, perhaps, does not definitely show that the right of control was not in

the company. The fact that the company did not exercise control
does not show that it did not have the right of control, though it
may be some evidence thereof. It has been held that in the
absence of a stipulation the existence or non-existence of the right
must be determined by reasonable inferences shown by the evidence. . . . Among the points frequently taken into consideration is the fact of the right of discharge. . . . But we take it that
that right exists in the vast majority of cases of the character
under consideration. And it has been said that it is not, by the
later cases, considered any decisive test. . . .

In the case at bar there was no express reservation of control,
and none can be implied. In fact it would seem that in view of
the fact that actual control of an automobile driven hundreds of
miles away from the place of the employer can at best be theoretical only, even though actual control has been reserved, the
right of such control should, in a case of this character, be able to
be implied only from reasonably clear evidence showing it.

We think, accordingly, that the employer in this case ought
not to be held liable. Whether we should hold the same in a
case similar to the instant one, but where the agent uses the
automobile of his principal, in accordance with what seems to be
the rule recognized in Premier Motor Company v. Tilford, 61
Ind. App. 164, 111 N. E. 645, we need not say. Some criticism
has been leveled at courts for their disagreement on this subject
and for not finding a more decisive and clear-cut test. But it
must be remembered that the rule that a master is liable for the
negligence of his servant committed in the course of his employment—which is at the basis of the cases holding the employer
in cases of this character liable—is founded not upon a rule of
logic, but upon a rule of public policy, and hence the digression,
not constituting an abrogation of the rule, must necessarily also
involve the question as to how far public policy requires the digression to be made, and it is not to be wondered at that one
court answers the question one way, another another way. It is
suggested in 28 Mich. L. R. 378 that the "independent calling"
test is easier of application. We are not certain of that, unless we
limit independent callings to those definitely known as such in
the past. But why should we? If a factor is an independent agent,
for whose negligence in his physical movements his principal is
not liable, why should liability lie in a case like that at bar? The
difference between a factor and a man traveling to sell washing
machines, or an insurance agent soliciting insurance, is not vital.
The latter's calling may, in this age of commercial activity, well
be considered as independent as that of a factor.

Every rule should, of course, have a reason. Why should we depart from the ordinary rule applicable in the case of master and servant? Is that departure, in the case at bar, based on reason? We think it is. We have, it may be noted, laid some emphasis on the fact of the ownership of the automobile in question. It has been said that when a plaintiff has suffered injury from the negligent management of a vehicle, it is sufficient prima facie evidence that the negligence was imputable to the owner thereof, though driven by another. . . . The converse of that proposition should, of course, be true. Nay more, it has often been said that ordinarily a person who is not the owner and is not in control of certain property is not liable for negligence in respect to such property. . . . And surely, that is in accordance with the plain dictates of justice, unless a counter-vailing reason appears in a particular case. A number of cases are found in notes to 57 A. L. R. 739 and 60 A. L. R. 1163, in which it was held that the fact that an employee drove his own car or other vehicle did not relieve the employer from liability for the negligence of the employee in driving such car. But generally speaking that ought to be limited, we think, to those cases in which the driver is a servant, as distinguished from an agent, or in which it clearly appears that the right of control is reserved to the principal, and it has, we think, been generally so limited except in the class of cases already heretofore mentioned. And if a departure from the doctrine of respondeat superior is at all justifiable in any case, as we think it is, and we resort to a consideration of broad public policy, reasons for the limitation mentioned are not altogether absent. Practically, in a case of the character before us, the agent has the sole power of control of his automobile. He, as owner, can distribute the risk of driving it by taking out insurance better than, or at least as well as, his principal. If he alone is held responsible for his negligence, that has a tendency to cause him to exercise care to prevent accidents. To put a man upon his own responsibility generally has that effect. And that prevention of automobile accidents is a matter of considerable, nay vital, importance today is, of course, attested by daily experience. And while this reason cannot be held to be controlling, or perhaps should not be even considered in some cases, it furnishes at least some basis in the application of public policy.

The judgment of the trial court is, accordingly, affirmed.

Affirmed.

KIMBALL, Ch. J., and RINER, J., concur.

HUNTER v. R. G. WATKINS & SON, INC.
Supreme Court of New Hampshire
110 N.H. 243, 265 A.2d 15 (1970)

GRIFFITH, J. These are actions for wrongful death, personal injuries and property damage brought as a result of an accident on Route 4A in Enfield, New Hampshire, on August 6, 1965, involving motor vehicles operated by Edgar H. Hunter, Ralph F. Davis, Jr., and Chester D. Abbott.

Ralph F. Davis, Jr. was an employee of R. G. Watkins & Son, Inc. driving his own automobile at the time of the accident. All parties have agreed that it is desirable to have certain legal issues relating to the chargeability of R. G. Watkins & Son, Inc. for the acts of Ralph F. Davis, Jr. determined in advance of trial. These issues were reserved and transferred by *Keller*, J. without ruling, on an agreed statement of facts.

On August 6, 1965 Ralph F. Davis, Jr. was an employee of R. G. Watkins & Son, Inc. operating an L. V. truck on a road construction project in Lyme, New Hampshire. The truck operated by Davis broke down and a replacement part needed to repair it was located in Lawrence, Massachusetts. Davis was instructed to pick up the part and bring it back to the job site the next morning. He left about noon in his own car, stopping in Lebanon, New Hampshire at his apartment on the way down and in Salem, New Hampshire on the way back for personal errands.

The accident happened about 5:00 P.M. in Enfield, New Hampshire when Davis was on his way back to his apartment in Lebanon. His normal work day was from 7:30 A.M. until 5:00 P.M. and he was kept on the payroll until 5:00 P.M. on August 6, 1965 to compensate him for his time and gasoline in getting the part. It is agreed for the purpose of this transfer only that he was acting within the scope of his employment at the time of the accident. The defendant reserves the right to contest this issue at trial.

The questions presented on these agreed facts are:

1. Is R. G. Watkins & Son, Inc. liable for the negligence of its employee, Davis, in the operation of a motor vehicle owned by Davis and operated while on company business within the scope of his employment?

2. If it is necessary to show control or right to control by R. G. Watkins & Son, Inc. what constitutes "control" or "right to control" within the meaning of New Hampshire decisions on this general subject?

Counsel for both the plaintiffs and the defendant expect us to re-examine the rule of *McCarthy* v. *Souther*, 83 N.H. 29, 137

A. 445 in answering the transferred questions. *McCarthy* v. *Souther, id.,* and its descendant *Hutchins v. Insurance Co.,* 89 N.H. 79, 192 A. 498 both involved salesmen operating their own cars on business of their employers. Recovery against the employers was denied on the ground that there was no evidence from which it could be found the employers had any control over the employees in the "management and operation of the latter's automobile." *McCarthy* v. *Souther, supra* at 37. In following this rule it is apparent that we belong to a dwindling minority. *Konick* v. *Berke Moore Company,* 245 N.E. 2d 750 (Mass. 1969), overrules Massachusetts' previous acceptance of the rule and its citations indicate our lonely situation. *See also,* cases cited in Annot., 53 A.L.R.2d 631. . . .

The vicarious liability of a master for the wrongs of a servant acting on the master's business has been firmly established in our law from earliest times. *See* Prosser, Torts 471 (3d ed. 1964).

The simple statement of the rule of respondeat superior, unchanged over the years, has not resulted in simple application. . . .

Restatement, Second, Agency retained without change the definition of a servant contained in section 220 of the first Restatement. In order to put into proper perspective the control test of *McCarthy* v. *Souther, supra,* this definition must be considered.

The facts listed by the Restatement as relevant in determining whether an employer-employee relationship exists require consideration of many factors unless control is decisive. . . . Where other facts indicate the nonexistence of an employer-employee relationship, control may be a decisive factor as in *Paro* v. *Trust Co.,* 77 N.H. 394, 92 A. 331 and *Winslow* v. *Wellington,* 79 N.H. 500, 111 A. 631, dealing with employees of an otherwise independent contractor, and *Currier* v. *Abbott,* 104 N.H. 299, 185 A.2d 263, dealing with a borrowed employee.

Generally the control factor has been overemphasized in judicial reasoning (2 Harper & James, Torts 1400 (1956)) and we are usually concerned with whether on all the facts the community would consider the person an employee. Prosser, Torts 472 (3d ed. 1964). The fact that the employer in this case lacked control of the method by which the employee operated his car does not make the employee an independent contractor. The same may be said of the fact that the employee owned the automobile. In some cases this could be very material but in the present case it is not a controlling factor. *Hinson* v. *United States,* 257 F.2d 178.

"We are of opinion that we should no longer follow our cases
to the extent that they indicate that a master-servant relationship
does not exist unless the employer has a right to control the
manner and means (the details, in other words) of operating the
car." *Konick* v. *Berke Moore Co., Inc.,* 245 N.E. 2d 750, 753
(Mass. 1969). Thus in this case where it is agreed that a regular
employee is sent upon a specific errand, using his own car with
the knowledge and permission of the employer, and it is agreed
he was acting within the scope of his employment at the time of
the accident, the employer is liable for his acts whether it had
control of his detailed operation of the motor vehicle or not. We
answer the first question transferred in the affirmative and the
second question then requires no answer.

          . . . .

                                                  Remanded.

All concurred.

_____

NOTES

1.   Although, as indicated in the *Hunter* case, a trend away
from the result in *Stockwell* when the employee works full time
for his employer seems fairly clearly defined today, *but see* W.
SEAVEY, LAW OF AGENCY 143 (1964), Justice Blume's opinion
nevertheless stands as a monument to the careful use of legal
terminology, to an unusually thoughtful use of analogies and
exploration of the reasons behind the decisions in this area, and
to the exhaustive analysis of relevant authorities (the original
opinion is over twice as long as that contained here). And a good
many of Justice Blume's questions remain relevant. The following notes will deal with some of them.

2.   Justice Blume stated that if the driver "alone is held
responsible for his negligence, that has a tendency to cause him
to exercise care to prevent accidents." Ask yourself why the driver
would not be even more likely to exercise care if his employer was
also subject to liability for his negligent driving. The driver
would remain subject to the risk that he would have to pay, of
course, yet the additional sanction of employer instructions and
discipline would come into play. Also, what effect on Justice
Blume's statement does the existence of automobile liability insurance have?

3.   What if the accident had happened while Morris was delivering a refrigerator? If a different decision was possible, can
you explain why?

4.   Suppose instead that Morris, while delivering or repairing
a refrigerator, had dropped it and injured the owner's foot. Now
how would you advise Maytag as to its exposure to liability?

5. The facts that Morris owned his own car and chose his own route (within bounds) obviously were important to the *Stockwell* decision, as was the lack of control over Morris's physical conduct. These factors have not proved impressive to some courts subsequently deciding the question, even when the tortfeasor was not otherwise clearly a servant. The following language from Peterson v. Brinn & Jensen Co., 134 Neb. 909, 911-12, 280 N.W. 171, 172 (1938), a case involving a traveling salesman who worked full time for the defendant and drove his own automobile, is illustrative:

> The defendant contends that Porter was an independent contractor and that there is no liability on the part of the employer where the employer has no control over the physical movements of the automobile being used by its salesman. Defendant cites the cases of *Pyyny v. Loose-Wiles Biscuit Co.,* 253 Mass. 574, 149 N. E. 541; *Stockwell v. Morris,* 46 Wyo. 1, 22 Pac. (2d) 189; *Wescott v. Henshaw Motor Co.,* 275 Mass. 82, 175 N. E. 153; and *McCarthy v. Souther,* 83 N. H. 29, 137 Atl. 445. A reading of these cases discloses that they are based on the proposition that, unless the employer has the right to direct the manner in which the car was to be operated, there is no liability. We cannot accept this theory of the law. It seems to us that the control of the operation of the automobile is not the dominant feature. It is a question of the control of the driver of the automobile by the employer, as distinguished from the physical control of the car, that to us seems the more important factor. We believe the proper rule to be as follows: Where an employer expressly or impliedly authorizes the use of an automobile owned by an employee in the pursuit of his duties, the employer is liable to innocent third persons for injuries resulting from its negligent use by the employee in the business of his employer.

The recent case of Dow v. Connell, 448 F.2d 763 (10th Cir. 1971), in classifying a traveling salesman as an independent contractor (on much easier facts, however; he worked for several firms), placed emphasis on the absence of liability insurance, workmen's compensation insurance, and unemployment insurance coverage on the salesman by the defendants. The court also observed that none of the defendants deducted social security or federal or state income tax from his compensation. These factors can be important in establishing an employment relationship, from which the courts presumably will more readily draw an inference of right of control. They are not conclusive, however. See Throop v. F. E. Young and Co., 94 Ariz. 146, 382 P.2d

560 (1963), where a traveling salesman was classified as an independent contractor as a matter of law despite being carried on
personnel records of the defendant as an employee, with withholding and unemployment compensation taxes deducted from
his income.

6. RESTATEMENT OF AGENCY § 220, which is frequently cited
by the courts when trying to classify a relationship as independent contractor or servant, reads as follows:

§ 220. Definition of Servant.

(1)   A servant is a person employed to perform services in
the affairs of another and who with respect to the physical conduct in the performance of the services is subject to the other's
control or right to control.

(2)   In determining whether one acting for another is a
servant or an independent contractor, the following matters of
fact, among others, are considered:

(a)   the extent of control which, by the agreement, the
master may exercise over the details of the work;

(b)   whether or not the one employed is engaged in a distinct occupation or business;

(c)   the kind of occupation, with reference to whether, in
the locality, the work is usually done under the direction of
the employer or by a specialist without supervision;

(d)   the skill required in the particular occupation;

(e)   whether the employer or the workman supplies the
instrumentalities, tools, and the place of work for the person
doing the work;

(f)   the length of time for which the person is employed;

(g)   the method of payment, whether by the time or by the
job;

(h)   whether or not the work is a part of the regular business
of the employer;

(i)   whether or not the parties believe they are creating the
relation of master and servant; and

(j)   whether the principal is or is not in business.

Note that the Restatement lists a number of factors in this
section yet in § 2, which deals with the same topic (*see* p. 8 *supra*),
it mentions without qualification in the black letter text only
control over the physical conduct of the employee. (Comment a
to § 2 mentions that this was done only for brevity, and cross-
refers the reader to § 220.) It seems clear that a decision could
vary depending on which section the judge chose to rely upon.

Stockwell v. *Morris* fits under the main text of § 2 very nicely, for example. Does it fit so comfortably under § 220?

7. Note that control over the details of the work of the negligent party is a factor in § 220 (part (2) (a)) to be used in determining the existence of vicarious liability. Such control was of paramount significance to Justice Blume and appears to assume primary significance in § 2 of the Restatement. Why do you suppose it is so important?

8. It is well known that some prominent chefs are notoriously touchy about control over their preparation of food and running of the kitchen. Apparently there frequently is an understanding with the employer-restaurant owner that he shall not exercise control in these areas. Suppose a chef at a famous restaurant, having retained such control, to the extent of even excluding the owner from the kitchen when fixing meals, negligently prepares and serves some bad food. The ill patrons sue the owner. Would he be liable vicariously for the chef's negligence? RESTATEMENT § 220, comment *d,* indicates there is liability. How can this be so?

9. Nearly all states today have some form of incentive for automobile drivers to carry liability insurance, either in the form of financial responsibility laws or variants thereof, or compulsory liability insurance (in a few jurisdictions). Does this fact plus ownership of the vehicle by the employee have a bearing on the correctness of the *Stockwell* decision? Recall Justice Blume's discussion at the end of the *Stockwell* opinion of the risk here being one of driving.

In order to answer the above question we have to have some idea of the goals the law is furthering. If the goal is to ensure solvent defendants, the presence of financially responsible drivers would call for supporting the *Stockwell* decision, would it not? If, on the other hand, the goal is to place the costs of doing business onto an enterprise, then which line of authority is correct? Or if the goal is to deter bad driving, which authority should be followed? One complication which arises in answering these questions is that the law may be attempting to accomplish a mixture of goals; another is that even when a goal is identified the decision which must be made by a court is not always obvious.

10. Justice Blume considered and rejected the "independent calling" test advanced in Leidy, *Salesmen as Independent Contractors,* 28 MICH. L. REV. 365, 370 (1930), which is the article cited by Blume in his opinion. This test was defined as follows:

> [The term independent contractor] has come to be used with special reference to one who, in *pursuit of an independent busi-*

ness, undertakes to do a specific piece of work for other persons, using his own means and methods, without submitting to their control in respect of all its details, . . . [T]he true test of a "contractor" would seem to be that he renders the services in the course of an independent occupation, representing the will of his employer only as to the result of the work and not as to the means by which it is accomplished.

Query whether such a test is not more important than Blume thought it was. What rationale lies behind it? The search for a solvent defendant? Or the effort, most clearly put forth by Calabresi, to properly allocate costs to different enterprises? Deterrence? Has RESTATEMENT § 220 adopted this test? Would the test resolve all cases, including the questions raised in the first two paragraphs of the following note?

Consider whether your reaction to the independent calling test varies if the Ace Lawn Service referred to on page 57 consists of a large and well-financed tree trimming and lawn service with 14 employees, or if it consists of one man in business for himself, possessing as the tools of his trade one old pickup truck, a ladder, a power saw and a lawn mower.

11.   The questions raised by Blume at the beginning of his opinion about attorneys and "Ford agencies" pose some interesting problems. If a lawyer negligently causes a car accident while driving to his client's plant on business, would the client be liable? Why or why not? Would your answer vary if the lawyer was a partner in a local law firm which had a general practice? Or a partner in a firm that spends 90% of its time on this one client? If the attorney was an associate rather than a partner? If the attorney was a full-time employee ("house counsel") of the company owning the plant? If his office was in the plant and he was returning in the early afternoon from representing his employer in court, and had work waiting for him in his office?

If none of the above variations satisfy you that the company should be liable for the lawyer's negligent driving, can you think of any situations where a company *would* be vicariously liable for the tort of one of its attorneys? What situation? What tort?

The reference to "Ford agencies" raises drafting and counseling problems for the lawyers of automobile manufacturers, oil companies, and so forth. As you can appreciate, the client would like control over the retail distributors of its product, but at the same time would not want to be held vicariously liable for the inevitable contract and tort liabilities of its many distributors.

The lawyer is therefore anxious to make the distributors independent contractors for the above reasons as well as for reasons involving state taxation, state licensing and regulation of business, susceptibility to service of process, and so forth. Would he succeed by describing them as such in the contractual agreement between distributor and manufacturer? As you might anticipate, this has influenced some courts and not others. *See* Miami Herald Pub. Co. v. Kendall, 88 So. 2d 276 (Fla. 1956), where the court unanimously reversed a trial court judgment against a newspaper won by a person hit and injured by a news carrier. The court held newsboys to be independent contractors as a matter of law despite a very high degree of actual control by the employer (including routing the boys out of bed when they overslept, prohibiting folding the newspaper in "biscuits," accompanying the newsboy to a customer's home for a conference in the event of a serious complaint, and so forth), relying in part on contractual language ("the NEWSDEALER is a separate, independent contractor and not subject to the exercise of any control by the PUBLISHER . . .").

For a different view, see Frank v. Sinclair Refining Co., 363 Mo. 1054, 256 S.W.2d 793 (1953), where the appellate court reversed a lower court dismissal of a complaint alleging *respondeat superior* liability against the Sinclair Refining Company for the negligent driving of its bulk plant wholesale distributor. Although the distributor owned his own truck, and the contract described him as an independent contractor, the Missouri Supreme Court held that the question could not be determined as a matter of law in view of the conflicting inferences from the factors of control involved in the case, and thus it should be resolved by the trier of the facts. Some of the factors looked at by the court included nonassignability of the contract; the contract was terminable by either party at any time, with or without cause; the distributor could sell only Sinclair products within a limited territory at prices specified by Sinclair, and he could not sell on credit except to customers approved by Sinclair's credit department.

What doubts would you have about inserting a clause in the contract with the distributor which gives your client the power to terminate the contract at will? What risks would you run by inserting clauses requiring your "independent contractor" to make periodic reports and account to the manufacturer or "to keep the premises in a clean and safe condition to the reasonable satisfaction of the company" (a clause particularly relevant to the oil business)? How important would the form of the relationship (lease, franchise, etc.) be? What provisions would you write into the contract to protect your client, at least from the consequences of vicarious tort liability, in view of the risk of losing on independent contractor status?

12. Finally, ask yourself if the independent contractor classification should play any role when the tortfeasor has committed a nonphysical tort, like misrepresentation. Assume, for example, that a power company contracts with a separate business to survey and acquire easements across private land for power lines. The individual representatives of the separate business commit fraud while negotiating with the landowners. Would the independent contractor classification be of use to you in exploring the likelihood of liability of the power company to the landowners in a tort action for deceit? If not, how would you analyze the problem?

B. COMMENTS

1. The following excerpt is taken from Calabresi, *Some Thoughts on Risk Distribution and the Law of Torts,* 70 YALE L. J. 499, 545-46 (1961):

> *Independent Contractor.* An employer is not liable for the torts committed by independent contractors in his hire. This doctrine is justified in terms of our analysis if an independent contractor is defined as a party who would, *a priori,* be more likely to consider the risk in his market decisions than would his employer. Thus, a taxi driver is better suited to bear the risk of taxi accidents than the man who hires a cab. For the rider will almost certainly not carry insurance; and even if he does, he will not be influenced in his use of taxis by the fact that part of the cost of his general liability insurance stems from taking taxis. The taxi driver, on the other hand, will make his insurance cost part of the cost of riding cabs. Similarly, though a home owner who hires a tree surgeon to chop down a tree is about as good a risk spreader as his independent contractor, he is less good at allocating costs. The owner probably carries general home owner's liability insurance, and this policy probably covers injuries caused if the tree falls on his neighbor's head. Thus, the danger of these accidents will be properly allocated as a cost of home ownership. But unless the tree surgeon bears the initial cost, and makes his insurance a part of his price for chopping trees, the injury will not be counted as a cost of *that* activity. The independent contractor makes the danger a cost of both the tree business and the house business, while the owner can not; therefore, the contractor is in a more crucial position to accomplish proper resource allocation.
>
> Of course, if both parties are equally likely to consider the true cost of liability in making their market decisions, alloca-

tion of resources is indifferent as to who should be liable; and if both parties are equally likely to insure, or to bear the loss without causing harmful secondary effects, loss spreading is indifferent as to who should bear the loss. In such cases initial liability will not matter at all since the ultimate burden will generally rest on exactly the same persons no matter who is initially liable.

While originally the independent contractor exception to respondeat superior was considerably broader than would be justified by risk-distribution theories, its scope has been considerably narrowed in recent times. Employees who used to be considered independent contractors are now treated as servants for the purposes of respondeat superior. Thus, newspaper boys, local service stations—if sufficiently controlled by their parent oil companies—and others who are inadequate risk bearers have been excluded from the category of independent contractors. The technical definitions of independent contractors have remained about the same, but courts have tended to apply the definitions in ways more consonant with risk-distribution theories than they did in the past.

Ask yourself whether this analysis satisfactorily resolves the questions raised in note 10 above. And how would an advocate of the resource allocation (or general deterrence) approach respond to the *Stockwell* decision? To RESTATEMENT § 2? § 220? Recall the language in *Stockwell,* used in distinguishing the independent contractor cases from the workman's compensation cases, that in the latter "each industry shall bear its own burden," and this is a "principle of public policy different from that involved" in the independent contractor cases. How do you think the resource allocation advocate would respond to such language?

2. C. Morris in *The Torts of an Independent Contractor,* 29 ILL. L. REV. 339 (1934), takes the position that the problem of the financially irresponsible independent contractor should be resolved by, with some exceptions, holding the party hiring the independent contractor liable for the harms occasioned by him. He notes that the hiring party (the "contractee") could protect himself by employing contractors who are known to be responsible or by demanding an indemnity bond, which would not be available to the financially irresponsible independent contractor and thus theoretically would drive him out of business, a result which Morris thinks is probably desirable in the long run. The parties could contract among themselves as to who would bear the ultimate loss; it almost always would be the independent contractor, of course. In the absence of a contract the law doubt-

less would provide for indemnification of the contractee by the independent contractor.

At the same time one important function of tort law—compensation for innocent, injured persons if their loss was occasioned as a result of someone else's activity—would be realized. Morris notes several exceptions to this thesis: (1) where "it is unreasonable to expect him [the contractee] to exercise his power of selection so as to avoid the employment of judgment proof contractors" (p. 354), such as a person hiring a taxi in a city, or someone acting in an emergency situation; (2) where "there is so little likelihood of tortious injuries that the value of enhanced opportunity overbalances the need for financially responsible contractors" (p. 354), such as when a secretary whom the contractee hires for a day negligently drops her typewriter on the toe of a ballet dancer in the lobby of the hotel where the contractee is staying.

C. THE EXCEPTIONS TO THE EXCEPTION

The independent contractor exception to vicarious liability for the negligent acts of others acting on a person's behalf carries its own exceptions. Sections 410-429 of 2 RESTATEMENT (SECOND) OF TORTS (1965) catalogue the numerous exceptions, following the declaration in § 409 of the general principle that the employer of an independent contractor is not liable for physical harm caused to another by an act or omission of the contractor or his servants. As will be noted briefly below, the rationale and sometimes the consistency of the Restatement exceptions can be hard to follow. An explanation for this may be supplied, at least in part, by reference to the report of a study of all of the independent contractor cases in one major jurisdiction. After studying more than 600 cases with the goal of ascertaining the rule or rules of liability in each of the many fact situations in which the cases fall, the authors of the report resolved that, ". . . in many of the fact situations, the cases are conflicting, the grounds of decision inconsistent and contradictory, so as to make it impossible to state what the law is." REPORT OF NEW YORK LAW REVISION COM'N 422 (1939). Also, ". . . the courts in reaching their decisions have not closely followed fact lines. In support of their decisions in particular cases, the courts have habitually cited and relied upon the general rule or exceptional propositions enunciated in cases involving fact situations quite different from those in the cases before them." *Id.* 422-423.

The introductory note to the Restatement of Torts treatment of this subject observes that the exceptions to the general principle of nonliability stated in § 409 ". . . are so numerous, and they have so eroded the 'general rule,' that it can now be said to be 'general' only in the sense that it is applied where no good reason is found for departing from it." The Restatement quotes with approval a statement from one opinion that, " 'Indeed, it would be proper to say that the rule is now primarily important as a preamble to the catalog of its exceptions.' " (Comment b to § 409).

Some caution would be advisable in literally accepting the above statements, however, and perhaps also in literally accepting the breadth of the examples and illustrations set forth in §§ 410-429 of the Restatement. As some evidence of the need for caution, one should note that nearly one-half of the hundreds of cases surveyed by the New York Law Revision Commission held the employer of an independent contractor not liable for the negligence of the independent contractor in the case before them. See 2 F. HARPER AND F. JAMES, THE LAW OF TORTS § 26.-11, n. 29 (1956). Also, the language quoted above from the Law Revision Report concerning the difficulty of generalizing encourages skepticism in formulating propositions in this area. Finally, for an articulate and forceful dissent from the policy of broad exceptions to the independent contractor doctrine, see Glanville Williams, *Liability for Independent Contractors*, [1956] CAMB. L. J. 180; and *Some Reforms in the Law of Tort*, 24 MOD. L. REV. 101, 112-115 (1961). For other general treatment of the law of independent contractor, see 2 F. HARPER & F. JAMES, THE LAW OF TORTS § 26.11 (1956) (updated in 1968 by a supplemental volume) and Prosser at 468-475.

As set forth by the Restatement, the exceptions seem to fall generally into three very broad categories:

1. *Negligence of the employer in selecting, instructing, or supervising the contractor.* If the party engaging or employing an independent contractor does so under circumstances where risk of injury to others through negligence of the contractor is foreseeable, he will be directly (not vicariously) liable for his own negligence by, for example, not using reasonable care in giving directions to the contractor. Also, the employer must use reasonable care to employ a contractor who is careful and competent. Section 411 of the Restatement states that this duty of care can include the requirement of affirmative and extremely detailed inquiry into reputation, work habits, and so forth, before hiring the contractor, depending on the degree of danger posed by the work to be done. And under some circumstances the employer must inspect the work after it is done, again with the

thoroughness of the inspection depending on the amount of danger involved. This duty seems to be imposed most frequently on landowners and to run in favor of invitees on the land, including employees of subcontractors working on the land.

2. *Inherently dangerous activities.* Many courts have held that a person is vicariously liable for injuries caused during the commission of inherently dangerous activities regardless of the fact that the work was being done by an independent contractor. For example, the installation of high tension wires cannot be contracted out by a power company with the expectation that the company will avoid vicarious liability.

3. *Nondelegable duties of the employer, arising out of some relation toward the public or the particular plaintiff.* This vague category includes duties imposed by statute, by franchise or charter, by contract or by the common law. It involves, for example, the duty of a carrier to transport its passengers in safety, the duty of a railroad to fence its tracks properly and of a landlord to maintain common passageways. Again, this exception can be interpreted in a highly elastic manner. Take the situation of a department store contracting with a large and well known detective agency to handle the policing of shoplifters. Suppose one of the detectives physically restrains a customer outside of the store for suspected shoplifting and it turns out that he was wrong and his conduct unprivileged. Can the store successfully rely on the independent contractor doctrine in order to escape liability for assault, battery and false imprisonment? See 92 A.L.R.2d 15, 61-65 (1963), collecting cases holding a store owner under similar circumstances liable, some of them on the ground that the store's duty of care toward its customers was nondelegable. See also, Adams v. F. W. Woolworth Co., 144 Misc. 27, 257 N.Y. Supp. 776 (1932). As to the criterion for determining what duties are nondelegable, Prosser at 471 acknowledges that it is difficult to suggest any ". . . other than the conclusion of the courts that the responsibility is so important to the community that the employer should not be permitted to transfer it to another."

The above exceptions are qualified by a vague distinction usually labelled "collateral negligence." One example of this is that the employer is held liable only for risks inherent in the work and not, for example, for risks created by an abnormal departure by the servants of the contractor from the usual method of doing the work. See §§ 426-427 of the Restatement of Torts; Prosser at 474-475.

One who plans to read the above sections from the Restatement of Torts should be forewarned to expect some inconsistencies, some puzzling and unexplained distinctions, and an apparent lack of supporting authority for some propositions or illustrations. As mentioned earlier, perhaps a good deal of the explanation for this lies in the complexity of the area itself. The complexities and inconsistencies do not necessarily mean that the common law has done an incompetent job and that legislation is necessary, however. This question was before the New York Law Revision Commission which, after thoroughly reviewing the extensive law of New York, resolved that it would do more harm than good to legislate in the area. "In conclusion, . . . it seems that the present tendency of the courts is to apply the recognized grounds of decision as to achieve a 'just' result in a particular fact situation. The general rule and the exceptions thereto, it must be remembered, are very broad and flexible. . . . It may be more desirable, therefore, to leave the entire situation as it exists today in the hands of the courts." (p. 642)

In the event a person is held vicariously liable for the tortious conduct of an independent contractor, does the party held liable have a right of indemnity against the independent contractor? Is the right of indemnity between master and servant described on pp. 50-52, *supra*, analogous? If not, what other argument could you make for indemnification by the independent contractor?

D. SOCIAL LEGISLATION

The independent contractor exception has considerable relevance beyond the question of who pays a tort judgment. A substantial part of the social legislation at the state and federal level involves defining whether an employment relationship exists between A and B in order to determine, for example, whether A must contribute tax or insurance dollars to funds established for B or respond to labor legislation establishing rights for B.

The best known example of social legislation concerning the employment relationship is workmen's compensation, which swept the state legislatures of this country in the early 1900's. This legislation came about in response to the low level of compensation received by workers for on-the-job injuries under the common law.

The Common Law

The common law imposes on the master a general duty of care toward his employees. The duty extends to providing a safe place to work for his employees, providing safe appliances to work with, to hiring careful and competent fellow employees, to warn and instruct inexperienced employees with respect to dangers which are not apparent, and to promulgate rules of conduct for his employees in order to make the work safe.

The above rules call into play a standard of due care, not one of strict liability. The master is held only to the standard of a reasonable, prudent man acting in the same or similar circumstances. If, therefore, one employee injures another and the master has taken care in hiring the negligent employee, he is not liable for the resulting damage. This is the fellow servant rule mentioned briefly in Chapter 2. It operated in conjunction with the standard common-law tort defenses of assumption of risk and contributory negligence to hold down recoveries for on-the-job injuries.

The latter two defenses operate, of course, only in the event of the employer's negligence. If, for example, a piece of moving machinery becomes dangerous due to an unexpected mechanical defect and injures a careful employee, but the employer had no idea that it was dangerous and a reasonable, prudent man would not inspect for defects any oftener than he did, he is not liable to his employee under the common law. Further, if the machine *is* negligently maintained and is dangerous in such condition, but an employee knows of this and continues to work around it (and was not a seaman or convict, who have been held to have no choice in continuing to work), in the event of injury he doubtless would have to be held to have assumed the risk of his employer's negligence. This would be true even if, from the employer's perspective, it is entirely predictable that someone working around the machine all day long will allow his attention to lapse and will suffer injury. The upshot of all this is, depending on one's choice of statistics, that anywhere from 70 per cent to 94 per cent of industrial accidents went uncompensated under the common-law system. *See* Prosser at 530 n.32.

The study of the above common-law rules is not entirely a matter of history, despite the legislation mentioned briefly below. Millions of workers remain only under the common law for compensation for injuries on the job as a result of exemptions or gaps in the coverage of most workmen's compensation laws, such as the lack of coverage for farm workers, casual and domestic employees, and exemptions for employers who have less than a minimum number (which varies from state to state) of employees. *See* Skolnik, *New Benchmarks in Workmen's Compensation*, 25 Soc. Sec. Bull. No. 6, at 3-18 (June 1962).

Workmen's Compensation

Although there is a great deal of diversity among the different states with respect to detail, workmen's compensation everywhere requires employers to pay premiums for insurance (or set aside reserves) for compensating employees according to a detailed schedule of recoveries for injuries happening in the course of employment. An administrative agency acting under statutory authority promulgates regulations for the system and adjudicates contested cases. Medical care is paid for, and cash payments to the employee reflecting income loss for disability or death are calculated as a percentage of the employee's weekly earnings at the time of his injury, subject both to a percentage maximum (usually 66⅔ per cent) and a dollar limitation. The schedule of recoveries for permanent partial disabilities are very precisely defined. For example, for loss of the second finger an employee in Colorado would get 18 weeks of salary compensation, subject to the above maximum limitations.

An employee is entitled to compensation even if the injury was not caused by the fault of the employer and even though it was caused by the fault of a fellow employee or, more controversial, by the negligence of the employee himself. Employees who are covered by workmen's compensation do not retain their common-law actions against their employer, with the result that a crude trade-off takes place, involving a more certain recovery for less damages (usually) as against the opposite condition under the common law.

Problems of interpretation and thus of litigation remain, of course, through the need to apply terms which have so long disturbed the common law, like who is an "employee," was the employee working within the "course of employment," and so forth, to a vast array of accident situations. An example of a recent case involving this is Bohy v. Pfister Hybrid Co., 179 Neb. 337, 138 N.W.2d 23 (1965). Bohy sold hybrid corn seed for the defendant in the Scottsbluff area of Nebraska pursuant to a "Dealer's Agreement" which specifically provided that Bohy was not an employee of defendant and not entitled to workmen's compensation benefits, that Bohy was to sell the seed on consignment pursuant to prices and terms of sale specified by defendant, the proceeds were to be transmitted to defendant in the form received by Bohy, that orders and a report of completed deliveries were to be sent to defendant weekly, that the contract could be terminated by either party at any time by written notice and that Bohy could not handle any other hybrid seed corn while the contract was in force. The court did not mention whether the work was full time for Bohy, although his widow testified that he "left to go to work" on the day of the accident.

Bohy was killed in a car accident and his widow filed a workmen's compensation claim, which was denied by the Compensation Board. The court upheld the denial of the claim on the ground that Bohy was not subject to the control of his employer because he had "contracted to do a particular piece of work according to his own method." *See also* IA, A. LARSON, WORK-MEN'S COMPENSATION LAW §§ 43-46 (1967), noting that precedents can be found in borderline cases on both sides of almost every situation. Larson rejects the control of the details of work test applied in the *Bohy* case, which he would leave to vicarious liability, and urges adoption of the "relative-nature-of-work" test, meaning basically that if the injured person performs a regular and continuous part of the work of the defendant, and does not have an independent business through which his own costs of industrial accident can be channeled, then the defendant should be deemed his "employer" under workmen's compensation regardless of control over details of the work. Larson states that courts are shifting to this test, citing Gordon v. New York Life Ins. Co., 300 N.Y. 652, 90 N.E.2d 898 (1950), a case strikingly similar to the *Bohy* case (including the existence of a contractual provision specifically denying employee status to the insurance salesmen) except in *Gordon* the case came up in the context of a board grant of compensation, and the Court of Appeals held (4-3) that it was for the Board to choose between conflicting inferences.

Larson criticizes the control of details test on the ground that it is "seldom a demonstrable fact" but rather depends on inferences drawn from other facts. Further, it does not depend on the actual exercise of control but "is, and must be, based on the right, not the exercise," which further increases the vagueness of the test. *Id.* at 640.

Larson also supports his relative-nature test by noting that many businesses have been making an increasing effort to avoid the cost and inconvenience of complying with social legislation by subcontracting portions of their production and distribution process, an effort which can prove successful if the control of details test is used. The incentive to do this is described by Larson on page 693 (footnote 23) as follows:

> Among the employments in which this has been most frequently resorted to are obtaining of logs and hewn material in southern logging areas, because of the inconvenience of employment deductions, premiums and reports to the characteristically small wood products operations of the south; filling station operators because, among other things, of the effort to avoid progressive chain store taxes based on number of outlets of the oil company; and quarry and stone-cutting busi-

nesses, because of high workmen's compensation premiums encountered when silicosis became compensable.

Larson indicates that the subcontracting arrangements are usually drawn with a careful eye on the control test. He notes that the courts have begun to respond to this by using the relative-nature test and, outside the field of workmen's compensation, that Congress has adopted this approach legislatively by adding a specific list of covered employments to the Social Security Act, in addition to its broad category of "employee," defined by "the usual common law rules." *Id.* at 694. Included in the specific list are agent-drivers or commission-drivers engaged in distributing meat, vegetable, fruit and bakery products, beverages (other than milk) or laundry, traveling salesmen who solicit (full-time) orders from commercial establishments, and full-time life insurance salesmen. These provisions in the Act do not apply if the person performing services has a "substantial investment" in his own facilities or if his services are "in the nature of a single transaction not part of a continuing relationship with the person for whom the services are performed." *See* 42 U.S.C. § 410(j).

Other Legislation

Other examples of legislation affecting the employer-employee relationship are: (1) unemployment compensation laws, which require the employer to pay premiums for insurance to partially cover the loss of wages for up to 26 weeks when a worker is involuntarily unemployed for such nonfault reasons as reduction in the work available. These programs are state run, but are federally inspired and financed by virtue of a tax levied upon all employers of more than four employees. The employer receives a 90 per cent credit on the tax if he pays it into an approved state unemployment compensation system; (2) laws requiring employers to rehire returning veterans; (3) the 1964 Civil Rights Act fair employment provisions, forbidding employers of 25 or more employees to discriminate on the basis of race, color, religion, sex or national origin; (4) minimum wage laws; (5) laws regulating the relationship between management and labor; and (6) employee safety legislation, such as the recent federal Occupational Safety and Health Act of 1970 and similar legislation on the state level. For further explanation of some of these legislative changes, see B. AARON, THE EMPLOYMENT RELATION AND THE LAW (1957), and S. RIESENFELD & R. MAXWELL, MODERN SOCIAL LEGISLATION (1950).

As one would expect, the litigation concerning such legislation has been fairly active, a large share of it by employers wishing to avoid paying taxes or being unionized. The opinion in

United States v. W. M. Webb, Inc., 397 U.S. 179 (1970), summarizes the judicial and legislative experience in this area since the 1930's. *See also,* Sears, *A Reappraisal of the Employment Status in Social Legislation,* 23 ROCKY MTN. L. REV. 392 (1951).

PROBLEMS

1. Augustus Juilliard was the owner of a six-story mercantile building in Manhattan, the various floors of which he rented to separate tenants. He furnished these tenants with passenger and freight elevator service. He did not, however, operate and maintain the elevators by his own employees, but had a yearly contract with the Edward Engineering Company to do this work. Edward Engineering furnished an elevator attendant in uniform to operate the passenger elevator, one freight elevator attendant to operate that elevator, plus maintenance and cleaning service. The contract had been renewed from year to year for some four years at the time of the accident explained below.

The Department of Labor of New York City directed Juilliard to provide properly constructed sliding doors at all openings in the freight elevator shaft. Juilliard contracted with the Smith Company to do this work. Smith Company in turn sublet the contract to the National Sash & Door Company. Soon thereafter two employees of National Door began to install the sliding doors. In doing this it was necessary at times for the workmen to enter a portion of the freight elevator shaft. The work proceeded for about two weeks, during which time the freight elevator was used by the various tenants. An arrangement was made, therefore, with the operator of the elevator to stop his car before reaching the place where the men were at work, or to give notice of its descent.

On the day of the accident Besner, one of the workmen, was leaning over into the shaft at the same time the operator was taking a shipment of 500 paper boxes from one of the tenants down in the elevator. The operator lowered the elevator without warning and knocked Besner into the shaft, killing him. His widow sued Juilliard for wrongful death. What result? As attorney for Mrs. Besner, what authority contained in the preceding materials would you rely upon in arguing on her behalf? What authority would you anticipate the defendant using? How do you think a resource allocation advocate would decide this case, assuming all parties involved were before the court?

2. Sunshine Biscuit is in the business of baking and manufacturing food products. Miss Mrachek, a woman 42 years of age,

applied for a position at the New York City factory of the company. She was required to submit to a physical examination and to a blood test for the purpose of determining whether she was suffering from a communicable disease. Such testing was required by the regulations of the Board of Health of New York City. Sunshine Biscuit maintained for this purpose a pre-employment room for examinations, where it kept medical equipment for the use of its employees and where it also had available nurses and a physician. The nurses and the physician were employees of the company. They were carried on its payroll and were covered under the workmen's compensation law.

The physician proceeded to take a blood test, with gruesome results from Miss Mrachek. He attempted again and again to obtain blood from Miss Mrachek's left arm, unsuccessfully. Apparently her veins were not discernible in the left arm and were in her right arm, where he ultimately took the sample. Miss Mrachek is able to prove that as a result of negligent insertion of the needle she suffered severe and painful damage to the median and ulna nerves of the left arm, resulting in a permanent "claw-hand."

a. Make a case on her behalf, using the authority contained in the preceding materials. Then defend against it as the lawyer for the Company. What result would you predict? Would it make any difference if instead Miss Mrachek had been injured on the plant premises, and her injury was aggravated by negligent treatment by the physician?

b. Would it change your analysis if the physician involved had his own practice and dropped over to Sunshine's plant three afternoons a week? If so, why? Would it change anything from the perspective of Miss Mrachek?

c. Would it make any difference if the physician maintained his own office (which, together with many other offices, was near the plant) and Sunshine Biscuit always sent its applicants over to his office for testing? Again, if so, why, and from whose perspective? *See*, with respect to the first set of facts, Mrachek v. Sunshine Biscuit, Inc., 283 App. Div. 105, 126 N.Y. Supp. 2d 383 (1953), *aff'd*, 308 N.Y. 116, 123 N.E.2d 801 (1954), *noted in* 3 BUFF. L. REV. 311 (1954).

3. Mrs. Maloney was seriously injured when her car was struck from behind by a car driven by Mrs. Rath. The brakes on Mrs. Rath's car had failed due to a mechanical defect. Mrs. Rath disclaimed any liability by pointing to the fact that she had had the brakes on her car thoroughly overhauled by a garage mechanic just a short time before the accident. The mechanic

had done a negligent job on the brakes. This was unknown to Mrs. Rath, who had no warning before the brakes failed. The jurisdiction in which the parties live has a statute providing that every motor vehicle "shall be equipped with brakes adequate to control the movement of the vehicle and to stop and hold the vehicle." What arguments can be made on behalf of Mrs. Maloney, and what defense will Mrs. Rath assert? *See* Maloney v. Rath, 69 Cal. 2d 442, 71 Cal. Rptr. 897, 445 P.2d 513, 40 A.L.R.3d 1 (1968), *noted in* 14 VILL. L. REV. 560 (1969) and 6 SAN DIEGO L. REV. 330 (1969).

4. Paul's Trucking Service is a transportation broker, with its office in Chicago. It contracts with individual truckers to deliver commodities for its customers. It does not own and operate any trucks. On several occasions Paul's had used the services of one Hoefle, who owned his own tractor-trailer. Paul's was the chief (but not only) source of Hoefle's work during the last several months before the accident described below.

Hoefle's arrangement with Paul's was that, if a job was available when Hoefle checked at the office, Paul's would determine a flat fee for the trip, give some money to Hoefle as an advance, and pay the balance due when Hoefle reported for his next trip. Paul's did not carry Hoefle on its payroll and did not deduct withholding tax, insurance payments, etc., from its payments to him. Hoefle would sign a bill of lading, receipting on behalf of Paul's for goods picked up at a warehouse. The bill of lading bore the proviso that ". . . the truck operator is an independent contractor and does not expect [Paul's] to furnish any . . . insurance covering said truck operator."

On February 21, 1969, Hoefle called at Paul's office at 10:30 a.m., received a job and drove to a warehouse where his van was loaded with cans of frozen eggs. Since the refrigerating equipment on the trailer was out of order, a Paul's employee put fifteen blocks of dry ice with the load to maintain the temperature. The load's destination was Portland, Maine, but since Hoefle lacked the necessary license plates to enter Maine, his instructions were to arrive at a terminal in Fall River, Massachusetts, the next day by 4:00 or 5:00 p.m. so that transshipment to Maine could be made that night. The distance between Chicago and Fall River was 1050 miles. Hoefle was driving alone, as he always did.

At about 2:00 p.m. the next day, having driven almost all the previous night, Hoefle fell asleep at the wheel of his truck while driving on the Massachusetts Turnpike. His truck collided with an automobile parked on the breakdown lane and seriously injured Joe Petersen.

You have been retained by Petersen, and have discovered that Hoefle's rig is heavily mortgaged as are all his other assets. Can you put together a claim against Paul's? What arguments would you make? What defenses would you anticipate having to rebut? Would you advise the plaintiff that he has a good chance of winning a law suit against Paul's?

Court held that this accident could be imputed to Paul's. Paul's had duty not to send an independent contractor out on such an errand under the circumstances

Chapter 4

BORROWED SERVANTS

As we have seen, the relationship between an independent contractor and his contractee is not one upon which the law imposes vicarious liability, although the contractee can incur liability under several exceptions to this doctrine. Suppose, however, it is conceded that the tortfeasor, the operator of a bulldozer, is employed and paid on a full-time basis by a separate business (sometimes called the "general employer") which specializes in renting operators and equipment, but he has been working in his capacity as operator of a bulldozer for several months for a party (sometimes called the "special employer") paying the independent contractor for his employee's time and for the use of his equipment. The operator reports to work to the special employer every day and takes all his orders from the foreman of the special employer. One day he negligently damages something or someone with the bulldozer, and the special employer is sued on vicarious liability grounds. Does the resolution of the question "servant or independent contractor" end the inquiry?

Perhaps it should. As you will see, however, the law in this area has specialized to some extent, with its own terminology, and poses a hard question concerning the shifting between employers of exposure to vicarious liability on vaguely defined occasions.

CHARLES v. BARRETT
New York Court of Appeals
233 N.Y. 127, 135 N.E. 199 (1922)

CARDOZO, J. One Steinhauser was in the trucking business. He supplied the Adams Express Company, the defendant, with a motor van and a chauffeur at the rate of $2 an hour. The defendant did the work of loading at its station and unloading at the railroad terminal. It sealed the van at the point of departure and unsealed at the point of destination. Between departure and destination, the truck remained without interference or supervision in charge of the chauffeur. While so engaged, it struck and killed the plaintiff's son. Negligence is not disputed. The question is whether the defendant shall answer for the wrong. The trial judge ruled as a matter of law that it must; the Appellate Division, holding the contrary, dismissed the complaint.

We think that truck and driver were in the service of the general employer. There was no such change of masters as would relieve Steinhauser of liability if the driver of the van had broken the seals, and stolen the contents. By the same token, there was no such change as to relieve of liability for other torts committed in the conduct of the enterprise. Where to go and when might be determined for the driver by the commands of the defendant. The duty of going carefully, for the safety of the van as well as for that of wayfarers, remained a duty to the master at whose hands he had received possession. Neither the contract nor its performance shows a change of control so radical as to disturb that duty or its incidence. The plaintiff refers to precedents which may not unreasonably be interpreted as pointing in a different direction. Minute analysis will show that distinguishing features are not lacking. Thus, in *Hartell* v. *Simonson & Son Co.* (218 N. Y. 345) the special employer used his own truck. The submission to a new "sovereign" was more intimate and general (*Driscoll* v. *Towle*, 181 Mass. 416, 418). We do not say that in every case the line of division has been accurately drawn. The principle declared by the decisions remains unquestioned. At most the application is corrected. The rule now is that as long as the employee is furthering the business of his general employer by the service rendered to another, there will be no inference of a new relation unless command has been surrendered, and no inference of its surrender from the mere fact of its division.

The judgment should be affirmed with costs.

HISCOCK, Ch. J., POUND, MCLAUGHLIN, CRANE and ANDREWS, JJ., concur; HOGAN, J., not voting.

Judgment affirmed.

GORDON v. S. M. BYERS MOTOR CAR CO.
309 Pa. 453, 164 Atl. 334 (1932)
Noted in 37 Dick. L. Rev. 267 (1933) *and*
8 Temp. L.Q. 267 (1934)

[The Byers Company was in the business of selling trucks. Hazlett was in the retail and wholesale gasoline business. Hazlett negotiated with Byers for the purchase of a used truck. It was agreed that Byers would furnish Hazlett with a truck and driver (Lewis) for a week so Hazlett could determine if the truck would fit his needs. If Hazlett did not buy the truck, he agreed to pay

Byers $10 a day for the use of it. The truck was operated under the Byers Company's license plates and owner's card.

While delivering gas pursuant to the order of Hazlett, Lewis negligently caused an explosion by allowing the gas to overflow. The plaintiff's husband, a bystander, was killed by the explosion. She sued both Hazlett and the Byers Company on vicarious liability grounds. The jury rendered a verdict against both defendants as joint tortfeasors, but the trial judge, on motion, entered judgment for Hazlett and granted a new trial to the Byers Company because he thought he had misled the jury in submitting the case to them as against both defendants. Plaintiff appealed.]

LINN, J.

. . . Lewis, thus in the sales service of Byers Company as demonstrator, was transferred to the service of Hazlett, also to do his work as directed by him. The employment involved a double service (a) to Byers Company (b) to Hazlett. Hazlett testified that he had "direction and control" over Lewis, limited "only for the gasoline;" "just for the delivery of gasoline." While demonstrating the truck, Lewis was assisting in making a sale of the truck for the Byers Company. "The control of the work reserved to the employer which makes the employee a mere servant is a control, not only of the result of the work, but also of the means and manner of the performance thereof:" Simonton v. Morton, 275 Pa. 562, 569, 119 A. 732. And it means a power of control, not necessarily the exercise of the power. Lewis was not merely performing a service that was sold or loaned by his general employer to Hazlett within the rule applied in Puhlman v. Excelsior Co., 259 Pa. 393, 103 A. 218, and kindred cases; he was at the same time assisting the Byers Company in selling the truck: (citations omitted). He was acting for both parties in accord with their common understanding, the power of control as to one part of this work being in Byers Company, and, as to the other part, in Hazlett.

The next question, then, is, were the acts of Lewis, that resulted in the explosion, performed on behalf of both? Was he then acting pursuant to directions from each? He was promoting the interest of Byers Company in manipulating the machinery on the truck, to cause the gasoline to flow, for, obviously, if the mechanism on the tank would not discharge the load, Hazlett would hardly wish to purchase the truck. Asked "And it was to be demonstrated to you in your business of delivering gasoline to customers, wasn't it?" Hazlett replied "Yes." Lewis was also complying with specific instructions in delivering the gasoline. The conduct, which the jury doubtless found to be negligent, was an act or acts done on behalf of both; . . . .

The Byers Company controlled Lewis as demonstrator for the purpose of selling the truck, and Hazlett controlled him in delivering the gasoline. While breach of Lewis's duty to either alone, would not have involved the other in responsibility for damage, he was negligent in doing an act for the account of both; they are jointfeasors.

[Record remitted, with instructions to enter judgment on the verdict for plaintiff against both defendants.]

NEPSTAD v. LAMBERT
235 Minn. 1, 50 N.W.2d 614 (1951)
Noted in 36 Minn. L. Rev. 290 (1952)

[Plaintiff was a laborer working for the L. G. Arnold Company, a general contractor, on a construction site. He was severely injured when a crane used to install prefabricated steel trusses each weighing four tons made contact with a high voltage power line. Plaintiff was helping guide one of the trusses at the time. The crane together with an operator and an oiler was rented for $12 an hour from the Truck Crane Service Company, owned by J. M. Lambert, apparently as a sole proprietorship. The operator of the crane was August Pasma, a regular employee of the Crane Company. Pasma was operating the crane pursuant to hand and arm signals from Morris, the foreman on the job and an employee of L. G. Arnold Company.

At the trial of the lawsuit brought by plaintiff against J. M. Lambert, the Crane Company and Pasma, the jury found that Pasma was not a loaned servant in the employ of the Arnold Company, with the result that J. M. Lambert and the Truck Crane Service Company were held liable to plaintiff on respondeat superior grounds. This decision was reversed on appeal on the ground that Pasma was a loaned servant as a matter of law. The plaintiff thus was left with a judgment against Pasma on negligence grounds and a workmen's compensation recovery against the Arnold Company, his regular employer. The reasoning of the court is reflected in the following passages from its opinion.]

CHRISTIANSON, JUSTICE. . . .

Though well established, the loaned-servant principle has proved troublesome in its application to individual fact situations. The criteria for determining when a worker becomes a loaned servant are not precise; as a result, the state of the law on this subject is chaotic.[5] Respectable authority for almost any position

---

[5] Cardozo, *A Ministry of Justice,* 35 HARV. L. REV. 113, 121 (1921).

can be found, for even within a single jurisdiction the decisions
are in conflict. . . .

. . . .

In the main, courts have relied on two tests in determining
when a worker becomes a loaned servant. The first of these is
the "whose business" test. It asks: At the time of the negligent act,
which employer's business was being done or furthered? The
answer to the question names the responsible employer. This test
is practically valueless where, as in the instant case, the general
employer's business consists of furnishing men to perform work
for the special employer, because by doing his job the worker is
necessarily furthering and doing the business of both employers.
If the test is meant to determine whether or not the worker's
status was that of a servant of an independent contractor at the
time of the negligent act, then it only begs the question and must
depend for its answer on the "control" test, which we shall discuss
next.

The so-called "right of control or direction" test assumes to
place the responsibility for the servant's negligence upon the
employer having the right to control his actions at the time the
negligent act occurs. The theoretical basis for this test is probably
the desire to impose the liability upon the employer who was in
the best position to prevent the injury. Although this may be
considered inconsistent with the liability-without-fault nature of
respondeat superior, the control test has received widespread approval from the courts.

One danger in using control as a test lies in failing to define
sufficiently the scope and the meaning of the term. In a general
sense, both employers frequently have powers over the employe
which may be considered elements of control.[12] The control
possessed by the general employer may be more remote than that
of the special employer, but nevertheless it has real force behind
it. An example may be found in the instant case. Among other
things, Lambert selected Pasma, could discharge him, paid his
wages, and administered such matters as social security, workmen's
compensation, and income tax withholding. He also unquestionably had the exclusive right to direct how the truck crane
should be cared for. All these may properly be considered elements of control. On the other hand, as we shall see, the Arnold
company exercised detailed on-the-spot control over the actual
construction work done by Pasma.

Cases which require a complete surrender of control by the
general employer as a condition precedent to finding the worker

---

[12] Smith, *Scope of the Business: The Borrowed Servant Problem,* 38 MICH.
L. REV. 1222.

a loaned servant fail to recognize that it is the fact that dual control exists which often causes the loaned-servant problem. . . .

Since both employers may each have some control, there is nothing logically inconsistent, when using this test, in finding that a given worker is the servant of one employer for certain acts and the servant of another for other acts. Excellent examples of this are the cases which hold a machine operator performing work for another to be the servant of the machine owner in the care and maintenance of the machine, but the servant of the borrower in the operation of it. The crucial question is which employer had the right to control the particular act giving rise to the injury. In this connection, Restatement, Agency, § 227, comment a (2), states:

"* * * Since the question of liability is always raised because of some specific act done, the important question is not whether or not he remains the servant of the general employer as to matters generally, but whether or not, *as to the act in question,* he is acting in the business of and under the direction of one or the other." (Italics supplied.)

But, even after limiting the inquiry to the particular act giving rise to the injury, the task of defining the meaning of control remains. Detailed authoritative control must be distinguished from mere designation of work or suggestions made incident to encouraging cooperation between related activities on large projects.

The orders of the borrowing employer must be commands and not requests if the worker is to be found to be a loaned servant.[14] However, it is not necessary, as plaintiff contends, that the penalty for disobedience be discharge or discipline. The right to discharge is one element in measuring the authoritativeness of the order, but it should not be made decisive. Despite the contrary holding in a similar case,[16] where the safety of other workers and the efficiency of the operation depend upon absolute obedience to the orders of the hirer, it seems to flaunt reality to consider such orders mere requests aimed at getting coöperation among the workers.

Authority to designate only the result to be reached is not sufficient under the control test. There must be the authority to exercise detailed authoritative control over the manner in which the work is to be done. The line of cases known as the "carriage cases" will illustrate this distinction amply for our purposes. These cases hold that where a person hires an automobile and

---

[14] Standard Oil Co. v. Anderson, 212 U. S. 215, 29 S. Ct. 252, 53 L. ed. 480. *See, also,* Charles v. Barrett, 233 N. Y. 127, 135 N. E. 199.
[16] Standard Oil Co. v. Anderson, *supra,* footnote 14.

driver and merely designates the destination he wishes to reach, the route to be taken, or even the approximate speed he wishes to travel, the driver does not become a loaned servant for purposes of *respondeat superior.* Unless there is detailed control over the manner in which the driver guides the car over the road, no responsibility devolves upon the hirer.

The application of these principles to the instant case compels the conclusion that Pasma, the **crane** operator, was under the detailed authoritative control of the Arnold company exclusively with respect to the act which caused the injury. Every movement of the crane while it was being used on the job was directed through hand signals by an Arnold company employe. Signals were given indicating when and how far to swing the boom of the crane, when to stop the movement, when and how far to raise or lower the boom, and when and how far to slacken or tighten the hoisting cable. Without these signals, Pasma lacked the knowledge or authority to make a move, because only Morris, the Arnold company's steel foreman, with the aid of his blueprints, knew the pattern and progress the work was to take. More detailed control can hardly be conceived. The crane operator was virtually an automatic eye which caused the machinery of the crane to respond to signals given by the Arnold company's employes.

There can be no doubt that these signals carried the force of command. The work of the crane involved moving heavy pieces of steel to within inches of workmen standing on narrow platforms 10 or 20 feet above the ground. A hesitant response or disobedience to a signal jeopardized their lives, and Pasma was fully aware of it. In such a situation, the orders given, viewed realistically, must be considered authoritative. . . .

It is not material for the purposes of this case whether or not the negligent movement of the crane was actually made in response to a signal by an Arnold company employe. If the Arnold company had the exclusive right to direct all movements of the crane, then Lambert did not; and, when he was moving the crane, Pasma was a loaned servant of the Arnold company. The absence of actual control at the time of the negligent act does not alter its liability. It is to be remembered that the ultimate basis for imposing liability upon either employer is *respondeat superior,* which requires no fault on the part of the responsible employer. The right to control is the basis for imposing this responsibility, and the actual control exercised is merely evidence of which employer held that right. Actual control becomes material only when an attempt is made to hold an employer personally liable as procurer of the negligent act.

After a careful review of the record and in light of the numerous cases and authorities examined, we are of the opinion that as a matter of law Pasma was a loaned servant in the employ of his special employer, the Arnold company, with respect to the negligent act causing plaintiff's injury. It follows from the cases heretofore cited that Lambert, the general employer, is not liable for plaintiff's injury, and judgment must be entered in Lambert's favor.

. . . .

Reversed as to appellants J. M. Lambert and Truck Crane Service Company, with directions to enter judgment in their favor. Affirmed as to appellant August Pasma.

NOTE

McCollum v. Smith, 339 F.2d 348 (9th Cir. 1964), is a recent case involving negligent crane operation under circumstances similar to the *Nepstad* case. A large crane, together with an operator and an oiler, were rented by a construction company from the defendants for $70 an hour to be used for hoisting prefabricated concrete beams into place. The appellate court affirmed a directed verdict against the plaintiff, an injured worker, in his suit against the crane renting company based on the negligence of the operator, citing the *Nepstad* opinion. *See,* however, Nakagawa v. Apana, 52 Hawaii 379, 477 P.2d 611 (1970), another recent crane accident case, where the court affirmed a jury award of $190,000 to a worker in his suit against a crane rental company. The court distinguished the case before it from *Nepstad* and *McCollum* primarily on the grounds that (i) the crane operator in those cases was retained on the job for a period of time, while the crane job in the case before it was a "one-day pour" of concrete on the fourth floor of a building, (ii) the crane work being done "was not the precision placement of concrete beams, but rather the dumping of ready-mixed concrete in an area for hand spreading," and (iii) the signalman also was an employee of the crane rental company. *See also* Chartier v. Winslow Crane Co., 142 Colo. 294, 350 P.2d 1044 (1960), upholding a judgment against a crane rental company on facts similar to the *Nepstad* and *McCollum* cases, including the giving of signals by the foreman of the special employer. The court cited to RESTATEMENT § 227, Comment *b*, which expressly adopts the approach used by Cardozo in the *Charles* case. It also quoted Comment *c* to § 227, "*Factors to be considered.* . . . Upon this question, the fact that the general employer is in the business of renting machines and men is relevant, since in such case there is more likely to be an intent to retain control over the instrumentality."

COMMENTS

1. Professor Calabresi has, in a different context, set forth some factors to weigh in locating the superior risk bearer when attempting to allocate losses among several activities which are related to each other in a bargaining situation. *See* Calabresi, *Fault, Accidents and the Wonderful World of Blum and Kalven,* 75 YALE L. J. 216, 230-31 (1965). Although he did not consider the borrowed servant problem, it nevertheless does involve allocating losses among contractually related activities, and thus the following factors he mentions may prove useful. The factors are as follows:

> In other words, in theory it makes no difference, for *general deterrence,* which of two parties to a bargain bears the accident costs which may result. In practice it might also make no difference (usually when the bargainers are of approximately equal size, number, expertise and wealth). But it may make a great deal of difference. Among the factors which operate to determine who is the better loss bearer from a general deterrence point of view are: (1) which of the parties can better evaluate the risk involved; (2) which of the parties can better evaluate the accident proneness of potential parties on the other side; (3) which of the parties can better let this knowledge, when significant, be reflected in the prices it can command; (4) which of the parties can more cheaply insure against the liability; and (5) placing liability on which of the two parties is less likely to cause the loss to be removed from both, for compensation or other reasons.

Factor number 5 does not bear on our problem. Calabresi is there talking about avoiding a tax financed social insurance solution to problems of inadequate or nonexistent compensation of victims which might occur as a result of political pressure if, for example, our tort system required pedestrians to absorb all losses caused to them by automobile drivers. The other four factors possibly can be of use to us, however. Try working them against the common borrowed servant fact situations raised above in the *Charles, Gordon* and *Nepstad* cases. Can it intelligibly be done? Do you reach a different or a more secure result than the courts did? *See* Strait v. Hale Constr. Co., 103 Cal. Rptr. 487, 26 Cal. App. 3d 941 (1972), where the court rejected the control test and talked in enterprise liability language, asking which employer could best insure and guard against the risk and which could most accurately predict the cost of the risk and allocate it to its consumers. The court placed the loss on both employers, one of whom was a farmer who had leased the equipment involved in the accident (a tractor) on a short term basis to the defendant construction company together with an employee for $18 an hour. The farmer had never before leased the equipment.

2. Note that Calabresi's factors do not include the "risk prevention" (or, in Calabresi's terminology, "specific deterrence") concept which focuses on the accident reduction effect of placing a loss on an enterprise which, because of its control of an activity, can reduce losses to it and thus the level of losses generally through increased safety measures. This concept is treated at length in Douglas, *Vicarious Liability and Administration of Risk*, 38 YALE L. J. 584, 595-602 (1929). Can it usefully be applied to this area? Consider the rented crane and operator problem. Would accident reduction take place if the loss were always put back onto the company in the crane renting business? If, on the other hand, the loss were always put onto the so-called special employer, the construction company in this instance? One can argue, along the lines advanced by Douglas in the article cited above, that placing the loss on the crane company would increase the economic pressure on it to hire the most competent operators, to supervise their work records, and to fire those who have bad work records. They are in control of that end of the business, and obviously have more knowledge about an employee's work record than do the various special employers. Ask yourself, however, whether this goal would not be accomplished just as effectively under the *Gordon v. Byers* approach.

3. A Comment, *Borrowed Servants and the Theory of Enterprise Liability*, 76 YALE L. J. 807 (1967), makes an effort to apply the enterprise liability-superior risk bearer analysis to this area. The thesis there advanced is that accident costs normally should be placed on the general employer on the theory that he is better able to evaluate the risk of accidents. A crane company, for example, "has a better statistical background for estimating the likelihood of crane accidents, and thus can make more accurate insurance and pricing decisions." The builder, on the other hand, would "probably lump all the potential accident costs of his project together and use a broad insurance policy. He is unlikely to isolate the cost of accidents involving cranes, for the purpose either of demanding safer practices from the crane company or of considering safer and cheaper substitutes." (p. 817.) The crane company is thus the "more efficient risk bearer."

If the party primarily liable were judgment-proof, however, the notewriter would allow recovery against the other party in order to ensure compensation of victims and to ensure that the price of the final product (the building, apparently) bore the full accident cost of its production.

The above priority of liabilities would be reversed if the special employer was a better predictor of accidents (if, for example, he rents a machine and operator to perform the same services that a whole fleet of his own machines and employees perform regularly) or if the injury arises from activities outside the scope of the contract. The example given is where a building contractor uses a crane for some particularly exotic and dangerous purpose which he did not disclose to the crane company.

4. An underlying aspect of many borrowed servant cases is the effort by an injured worker to avoid being left with solely a workmen's compensation claim against his employer. Most workers injured on the job have that remedy available. But this leaves the worker with a flat recovery based upon a legislatively set schedule of benefits.

As you can imagine, the schedule of benefits lags several steps behind inflation in many states; also, it does not include the common-law damages elements of pain and suffering. For example, in Colorado, which is representative, the maximum amount recoverable under workmen's compensation for a temporary partial disability is two-thirds of the workman's weekly pay check or $64.75 per week, whichever is less, and cannot exceed the aggregate sum of $8,417.50. The aggregate sum is $16,835 for a permanent partial disability. 12 COLO. REV. STAT. §§ 81-12-3, 81-12-9 (1971 Cum. Supp.). The employer also must pay medical expenses up to a maximum of $7,500. *Id.* at § 81-10-1. There are no social security benefits available to supplement this amount unless the worker is totally disabled (defined as inability to engage in "any substantial gainful work which exists in the national economy . . ."), as contrasted with suffering partial (whether permanent or temporary) disability. *See* 42 U.S.C.A. § 423(d) (1969) and King v. Finch, 428 F.2d 709 (5th Cir. 1970) (interpreting the 1967 amendments to the social security acts tightening up on the disability definitions). A common law tort damages recovery, on the other hand, would allow full recovery for all lost wages and impairment of future earning capacity and, as mentioned earlier, would also allow the trier of fact to establish a dollar amount designed to compensate the plaintiff for his pain and suffering.

An example of why workers are anxious to pursue common-law tort remedies whenever possible is provided by *Chartier v.*

Winslow Crane Co., p. 94 *supra,* where a construction worker injured by the negligence of a crane operator had recovered to the date of his suit $643.50 from his employer under workmen's compensation. He sued the crane company and won on the theory that the operator was not a borrowed servant of the general contractor, recovering common-law damages of $50,531. This example is incomplete, since we do not know how much **Chartier** eventually would have recovered under workmen's compensation, although his recovery would have been subject to limitations in total amount even less than those described above. It nevertheless does reflect a substantial disparity between potential recoveries under the two systems. *See also,* with respect to the coverage of losses by benefits under workmen's compensation, Skolnik, *New Benchmarks in Workmen's Compensation,* 25 Soc. Sec. Bull. 3 (June 1962).

QUESTIONS

1. Suppose the crane operator is injured by the negligence of one of the laborers on the job site. What legal posture would *he* want to take?

2. The following hypothetical is from § 227, illustration 3, of the Restatement of Agency:

> P, a master carpenter, by agreement with B, sends A, a skilled cabinetmaker, to work with B's servants for a week, under the direction of B's foreman, in the reconstruction of a stairway. For this B is to pay P an agreed amount. A acts as the servant of B in building the stairway.

Can you explain this result?

3. A doctor left at a hospital a post-operative order that his patient was to be given an injection of tetracycline every 12 hours. The nurse on duty, acting under this order, negligently injected the prescribed dosage into the patient's sciatic nerve, causing permanent foot paralysis. Both the doctor and the hospital are sued.

    a. Which party will be held responsible for the acts of the nurse? Approach your analysis of this problem from two perspectives: (i) using the law and commentary in the preceding materials, argue seriatim the case for the hospital, the doctor and the plaintiff (who will be proceeding against both, presumably); (ii) using the law and commentary, and acting as judge, to which party would you allocate the loss?

[handwritten in margin: Court held no case against the doctor]

[handwritten: 443 P2d 708]

b. Would your analysis change if the nurse had committed the same act pursuant to the same instructions during the course of the operation? Immediately after it?

[handwritten: Doctor would have control over nurse.]

4. Suppose a company in the crane rental business had its customers sign a billing order containing the following terms:

It is distinctly understood and agreed that the sole function of Owner is to furnish equipment and/or operators for the use of Customer and that such equipment and operators shall be under the exclusive direction, supervision, and control of Customer during performance of this Work Order.

[handwritten: gives facts comparable to the Neptad]

Describe the effect you think this would have on a law suit by an injured worker against the crane rental company following the negligence of one of its crane operators on the site of a job. *See* Welborn v. Dalzell Rigging Co., 181 Cal. App. 2d 268, 5 Cal. Rptr. 195 (1960).

[handwritten: to the Neptad close, accept, new operator, was aware of danger to π.]

5. A delivery truck operator for the Evening Star Newspaper is commandeered while driving on his route by a municipal policeman to chase an escaping convict and, driving negligently (measured even by the emergency conditions), the operator causes an accident. Is the newspaper liable? Is the municipality, assuming no sovereign immunity problems? *See* Balinovic v. Evening Star Newspaper Co., 113 F.2d 505 (D.C. Cir. 1940), *noted in* 29 CALIF. L. REV. 223, 41 COLUM. L. REV. 136, 25 MINN. L. REV. 244, *and* 26 WASH. U.L.Q. 123 (among others). In what manner, if at all, would your response vary if the operator had been commandeered at gun point by an escaping criminal and had caused the same accident?

[handwritten: 2 to 1 in favor of the newspaper
dissent - everyone is suppose to find criminals

majority - only police had power of control at the time of the accident]

Chapter 5

THE SCOPE OF EMPLOYMENT LIMITATION

As was stated in *Jones v. Hart,* p. 6 *supra,* a master is vicariously liable for the negligence of his servant when the servant "runs his cart over a boy." As we have seen, this concept of vicarious liability won overwhelming approval in the common law, with the only serious questions which remain centering on the scope of the concept and its underlying rationale, and with the answers to those questions seemingly dependent on each other.

Suppose, however, that the servant had "run his cart over a boy" while returning from a ten block sidetrip (off an 18 block route) to the office of a competitor of his master to look for another job at a higher wage. Or suppose he had injured someone while taking a load of personal goods home in the cart after work. Or suppose he had intentionally run his cart into a personal enemy while directly on his route making a delivery.

Should the above variations be treated differently than when the servant negligently runs over a boy while delivering his master's goods pursuant to orders and while on the shortest route from the master's to the customer's places of business? If so, why? It remains true, does it not, that the boy would not have been injured if the master had not put the servant in custody of the cart?

Pause at this point and try to work out your own answers to the above questions. Then, as you read through this chapter, test your answers against those that various judges and writers have advanced. Have you or have they come up with a rationale that would satisfy you as a judge in making decisions on the myriad fact situations which can arise in this area?

A.   NEGLIGENT ACTS

JOEL v. MORISON
England, Nisi Prius (Exchequer)
6 Car. & P. 501, 172 Eng. Rep. 1338 (1834)

The declaration stated, that, on the 18th of April, 1833, the plaintiff was proceeding on foot across a certain public and common highway, and that the defendant was possessed of a cart and horse, which were under the care, government, and direction of a servant of his, who was driving the same along the said highway, and that the defendant by his said servant so carelessly, negligently, and improperly drove, governed, and directed the said horse and cart, that, by the carelessness, negligence, and improper conduct of the defendant by his servant, the cart and horse were driven against the plaintiff, and struck him, whereby he was thrown down and the bone of one of his legs was fractured, and he was ill in consequence, and prevented from transacting his business, and obliged to incur a great expense in and about the setting the said bone, &c., and a further great expense in retaining and employing divers persons to superintend and look after his business for six calendar months. Plea—Not guilty.

From the evidence on the part of the plaintiff it appeared that he was in Bishops-gate-street, when he was knocked down by a cart and horse coming in the direction from Shoreditch, which were sworn to have been driven at the time by a person who was the servant of the defendant, another of his servants being in the cart with him. The injury was a fracture of the fibula.

On the part of the defendant witnesses were called, who swore that his cart was for weeks before and after the time sworn to by the plaintiff's witnesses only in the habit of being driven between Burton Crescent Mews and Finchley, and did not go into the City at all.

Thesiger, for the plaintiff, in reply, suggested that either the defendant's servants might in coming from Finchley have gone out of their way for their own purposes, or might have taken the cart at a time when it was not wanted for the purpose of business, and have gone to pay a visit to some friend. He was observing that, under these circumstances, the defendant was liable for the acts of his servants.

Parke, B.—He is not liable if, as you suggest, these young men took the cart without leave; he is liable if they were going *extra viam* in going from Burton Crescent Mews to Finchley; but if they chose to go of their own accord to see a friend, when they were not on their master's business, he is not liable.

His Lordship afterwards, in summing up, said—This is an action to recover damages for an injury sustained by the plaintiff, in consequence of the negligence of the defendant's servant. There is no doubt that the plaintiff has suffered the injury, and there is no doubt that the driver of the cart was guilty of negligence, and there is no doubt also that the master, if that person was driving the cart on his master's business, is responsible. If the servants, being on their master's business, took a detour to call upon a friend, the master will be responsible. If you think the servants lent the cart to a person who was driving without the defendant's knowledge, he will not be responsible. Or, if you think that the young man who was driving took the cart surreptitiously, and was not at the time employed on his master's business, the defendant will not be liable. The master is only liable where the servant is acting in the course of his employment. If he was going out of his way, against his master's implied commands, when driving on his master's business, he will make his master liable; but if he was going on a frolic of his own, without being at all on his master's business, the master will not be liable. As to the damages, the master is not guilty of any offence, he is only responsible in law, therefore the amount should be reasonable.

Verdict for the plaintiff—damages, £30.

NOTES

1. We are unable to ascertain from the opinion the distance which defendant's servants deviated from their direct route. A look at the literal language of the opinion leaves the conclusion, however, that the extent of the deviation was immaterial, so long as the servant was "at all" on his master's business. Also, the intent of the servant to serve his master at the time of the accident does not seem important to the court. As you read through the remaining materials, recall the breadth of the court's language, written before liability insurance was available (Liability insurance apparently was not generally available until the latter part of the 19th century. *See* Douglas, *Vicarious Liability and Administration of Risk I*, 38 YALE L. J. 584, 591 (1929).)

It nevertheless is true that words frequently draw a great deal of their meaning from their context, and this is particularly true of words describing standards of liability. It is also simply a matter of interest as to what the distances actually were. The following superb detective work on the facts of the *Joel* case is thus of importance to us; it is taken from a letter written by Professor Frederic Kirgis of the Colorado Law School (on leave for a year in London) to the author, dated November 11, 1970. Bear in mind when reading the distances that this all took place before the invention of the internal combustion engine.

Herewith my report on the geography in *Joel v. Morison*. Bishops-gate and Shoreditch are major streets which run into each other at the northeastern corner of the City. (The reference to the City in the report, of course, is to the old City rather than to London generally. See map below.) Finchley is a London suburb just a few miles north of [the city]. So far, no problem. But Burton Crescent Mews is another matter.

Careful perusal of a detailed current map of London, and its index, reveals 3 Burton Roads, one Burton Grove, one Burton Street, one Burton Hole Lane and one Burton's Road. No Burton Crescent Mews. However, a little sleuthing has turned up a reproduction of an 1851 map of London on which there is a Burton Crescent (now called Cartwright Gardens), but still no Burton Crescent Mews. It is very near Burton Street, not too far from the City, and in fact lies between Finchley and Bishops-gate-Shoreditch.

On the spot inspection of what is now Cartwright Gardens, and surrounding area, failed to disclose any Burton Cresent Mews, and the local shopkeepers hadn't heard of it. There was a South Crescent Mews, and there were some rather new (i.e. 20th Century) apartment buildings which might very well stand where Burton Crescent Mews once was. The old map does show some unnamed alleyways which appear to lie about where some of these buildings now are. I think it's virtually certain that Burton Crescent Mews was within a one- or two-block radius of Burton Crescent and that you'd be perfectly safe to treat the distance and direction from the old Burton Crescent to Bishops-gate-Shoreditch as the measure of the servant's frolic and detour.

(NOT IN SCALE)

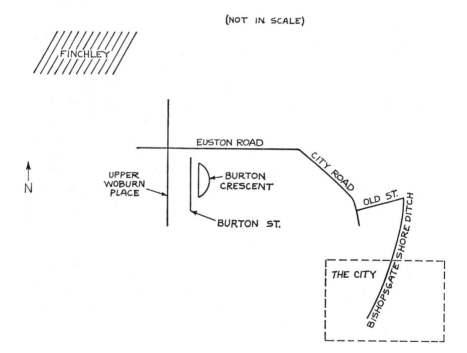

The old map I used is the B. R. Davies map of London (1851), reproduced in E. Jones and D. Sinclair, Atlas of London and the London Region, plate 6 (Pergamon Press, 1968).

Approximate distances:

Finchley-Burton Cresent: 6 miles

Burton Crescent-Bishops-gate: 2-1/4 miles as the crow flies; 3-1/8 miles via main streets shown.

2. The *Joel* case introduced the language of "frolic" and "detour" into this area of the law. As the opinion notes, when a servant is on a frolic, he is outside of the scope of his employment and his master is no longer vicariously liable for his actions. A detour is an "acceptable" deviation within the scope of employment.

3. Defendant sent a truckload of its merchandise from Manhattan to Staten Island, instructing its driver to bring the truck back to its garage at 23rd Street and 11th Avenue, on the west side of Manhattan. After making the delivery (most likely by ferry from the Battery), the driver instead drove to Hamilton Street on the east side of Manhattan to visit his mother. A neighborhood carnival was in progress. The driver took a group of boys in fantastic costumes on a tour of the district, stopping at a pool room on Catherine Street to say a word to a friend. He then drove off, with some of the merry-makers still on the truck. He stated at the trial that his purpose was to return to the garage. An eleven year old boy was injured as he drove off.

Once again we are given no clear idea of the distances involved. A glance at a current New York City map does not resolve this, since Hamilton Street has disappeared. A street map from the early 1920's indicates that Hamilton Street was perpendicular to Catherine Street and was between Monroe and Cherry Streets (see the map on p. 106 infra). Hamilton Street was enveloped in 1934 by a massive (1584 units), state assisted middle income housing project called Knickerbocker Village.

The approximate driving distance from the garage at 23rd and 11th to the intersection of Catherine and Hamilton was 2-1/2 to 3 miles, and from the Battery to the intersection was slightly over one mile. The distance from the Battery to the garage was approximately three miles. Catherine Street runs for only about eight blocks.

Upon the above facts a jury found that the driver was in the course of his employment and the defendant was held liable at the trial level. See Fiocco v. Carver, 234 N.Y. 219, 137 N.E. 309 (1922). What would be your decision on appeal? At this point you have before you only the *Joel* case, the previous material in

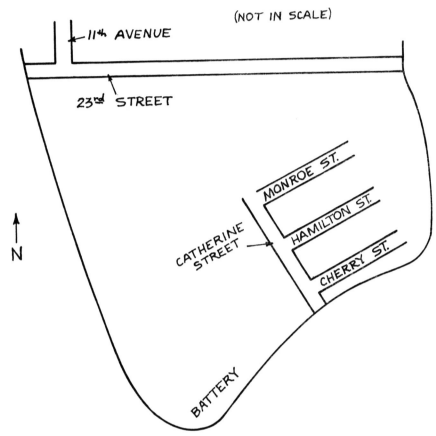

(NOT IN SCALE)

11ᵗʰ AVENUE

23ʳᵈ STREET

N

MONROE ST.

HAMILTON ST.

CATHERINE STREET

CHERRY ST.

BATTERY

this book reflecting decision making in the vicarious liability area, and the summaries of the main theories attempting to rationalize the allocation of loss made nearly 300 years ago in *Jones v. Hart.*

Do the following quotes from the Restatement and three New York cases affect the decision you reached?

SCOPE OF EMPLOYMENT

§ 228. General Statement.

(1) Conduct of a servant is within the scope of employment if, but only if:

(a) it is of the kind he is employed to perform;

(b) it occurs substantially within the authorized time and space limits;

(c) it is actuated, at least in part, by a purpose to serve the master, and

(d) if force is intentionally used by the servant against another, the use of force is not unexpectable by the master.

(2)   Conduct of a servant is not within the scope of employment if it is different in kind from that authorized, far beyond the authorized time or space limits, or too little actuated by a purpose to serve the master.

§ 229.   Kind of Conduct within Scope of Employment.

(1)   To be within the scope of the employment, conduct must be of the same general nature as that authorized, or incidental to the conduct authorized.

(2)   In determining whether or not the conduct, although not authorized, is nevertheless so similar to or incidental to the conduct authorized as to be within the scope of employment, the following matters of fact are to be considered:

(a)   whether or not the act is one commonly done by such servants;

(b)   the time, place and purpose of the act;

(c)   the previous relations between the master and the servant;

(d)   the extent to which the business of the master is apportioned between different servants;

(e)   whether or not the act is outside the enterprise of the master or, if within the enterprise, has not been entrusted to any servant;

(f)   whether or not the master has reason to expect that such an act will be done;

(g)   the similarity in quality of the act done to the act authorized;

(h)   whether or not the instrumentality by which the harm is done has been furnished by the master to the servant;

(i)   the extent of departure from the normal method of accomplishing an authorized result; and

(j)   whether or not the act is seriously criminal.

The succeeding twenty sections of the Restatement treat in more detail the general standards set forth above. Section 237 deals with the subject of "re-entry" after a frolic, stating that a servant does not re-enter the scope of employment "until he is again reasonably near the authorized space and time limits and is acting with the intention of serving his master's business." Ask yourself if the above standards, in particular the concern with the servant's state of mind, are consistent with the underlying reasons for vicarious liability.

In Riley v. Standard Oil Co. of N. Y., 231 N.Y. 301, 308, 132 N.E. 97, 99 (1921), *noted in* 31 YALE L. J. 99 (1921), *and* 20 MICH. L. REV. 98 (1921), a driver for the defendant was instructed to

obtain some paint from the Long Island Railroad freight yards
2 and ½ miles away from defendant's mill and to return at
once. After the truck was loaded at the freight yards, the driver
picked up some waste pieces of wood and left the yards in the
opposite direction from the mill to go to his sister's house four
blocks away and leave the wood. This accomplished, he started
back to the mill. His course would have led him directly past the
freight yards, but he negligently caused an accident after he had
driven only a short distance from his sister's house.

The court, in a 4-3 decision, held that the servant was within
the scope of employment, apparently as a matter of law (the
exact holding of the court is unclear, since a new trial was directed with no explanation of what issue was left to be tried). The
majority opinion did note that a question of fact would have
been raised for the jury had the accident occurred between
leaving the yards and arriving at the sister's house. The dissent,
per McLaughlin, J., stated that the driver's act was not a "mere
deviation," he was doing an independent act of his own, and he
could not as a matter of law re-enter the employment "until he
had again reached the yard. . . . I cannot believe that the liability of the defendant here is to be determined by the way in
which the truck was headed. Rights of property do not rest
upon such a slender thread."

In Clawson v. Pierce-Arrow Motor Car Co., 231 N.Y. 273,
275, 277, 131 N.E. 914, 915 (1921), a servant of defendant drove
the manager of defendant's sales department home in one of
defendant's demonstrator cars. He was then directed to drive a
seamstress personally employed by the manager to her home (5
miles away) and then return the car to the defendant's repair
shop (4 miles away and on the same route). It was clear that the
manager had no authority to direct that the defendant's car be
used to take the seamstress home.* The accident occurred after
the driver had proceeded but a short distance away from the
manager's home, and was at a point which the car would have
passed on its way to the repair shop even if the seamstress had
not been in it.

The plaintiff, who was injured by the servant's negligent driving, sued and won a verdict in the trial court. The trial court
judgment was reversed by the Appellate Division, on the ground
that "the car on its path to the garage was withdrawn from the

---

* Indeed, one could argue that the entire trip was unauthorized, from the
company's perspective. The manager was an invalid, however, and for several years had been driven home by one of the salesmen in a demonstrator
car, apparently with the knowledge of higher officials in the company. Does
this resolve the broader question for you?

defendant's service by the dual purpose of the errand." In a 5-2 *held for plaintiff*
decision, the Court of Appeals reversed the Appellate Division.
The opinion was written by Judge Cardozo and read in part as
follows: "How the case would stand if the collision had occurred
in the course of deviation from the route, we need not now
inquire. Deviation there never was. The unfulfilled intention of
passing the repair shop and returning did not transform the trip
in its entirety, and vitiate that part of the service which was
legitimate and useful." The dissent, per McLaughlin, J., stated
that, "The fact that the defendant had the repair shop on the
route is of no importance, since it played no part in the object
of the journey. . . ."

And finally, consider Marks' Dependents v. Gray, 251 N.Y. 90,
93, 94, 167 N.E. 181, 182-83 (1929), *noted in* 9 B.U.L. REV. 310
(1929), a workmen's compensation case. Marks was a plumber's
helper who worked at Clifton Springs, New York, and one day
was going to Shortsville, New York, after work to pick up his
wife. Marks' employer heard of this proposed journey and asked
him to take his tools and fix some faucets at a house in Shortsville.
The job was a small one, calling for 15 or 20 minutes of work.
Although nothing was said about paying Marks for the job, the
expectation was that he would be paid at the usual rate for
overtime work. Marks used his own car rather than the employer's truck, and was killed in an automobile accident about a
mile out of Clifton Springs, while on the way to Shortsville.*

Marks' dependents received an award by the State Industrial
Board under the workmen's compensation law, on the theory
that the accident was one "arising out of and in the course of
the employment." The award was unanimously affirmed by the
Appellate Division. It was reversed on appeal by the Court of
Appeals.

The 5-2 decision of the Court of Appeals was written by Judge
Cardozo. The basis of the decision in this interesting case was
explained as follows:

Unquestionably injury through collision is a risk of travel
on a highway. What concerns us here is whether the risks of
travel are also risks of the employment. In that view the de-

---

* Again, the distances involved are not described in the opinion. Are
we to conclude from this that distance, as contrasted with direction and
intent of the employee, is not important? That is one inference which
can be drawn, and in some cases it will be correct (but obviously not in
all or even most cases). There is another, more logical explanation, though,
isn't there? What is it?
   In any event, the distance between the two small communities is approximately seven miles by the shortest route. They are located in upstate New
York, north of the finger lakes.

cisive test must be whether it is the employment or something
else that has sent the traveler forth upon the journey or brought
exposure to its perils. A servant in New York informs his
master that he is going to spend a holiday in Philadelphia,
or perhaps at a distant place, at San Francisco or at Paris. The
master asks him while he is there to visit a delinquent debtor
and demand payment of a debt. The trip to Philadelphia, the
journey to San Francisco or to Paris, is not a part of the employment. A different question would arise if performance
of the service were to occasion a detour, and in the course of
such detour the injuries were suffered. So here, a different
question would arise if Marks after making the trip to Shortsville had met with some accident while repairing the defective
faucets (Grieb v. Hammerle, 222 N. Y. 382). The collision
occurred while he was still upon the highway, a mile or less
from home.

In such circumstances we think the perils of the highway
were unrelated to the service. We do not say that service to
the employer must be the sole cause of the journey, but at
least it must be a concurrent cause. To establish liability, the
inference must be permissible that the trip would have been
made though the private errand had been canceled. We cannot draw that inference from the record now before us. On the
contrary, the evidence is that a special trip would have been
refused since the pay would be inadequate. The test in brief is
this: If the work of the employee creates the necessity for travel,
he is in the course of his employment, though he is serving at
the same time some purpose of his own (Clawson v. Pierce-
Arrow Co., 231 N. Y. 273). If, however, the work has had no
part in creating the necessity for travel, if the journey would
have gone forward though the business errand had been
dropped, and would have been canceled upon failure of the
private purpose though the business errand was undone, the
travel is then personal, and personal the risk.

Although the *Marks* case involved a decision under the New
York workmen's compensation law, Cardozo cited a vicarious
liability case (*Clawson v. Pierce-Arrow*) as authority for his major premise; also, the *Marks* case subsequently has been cited
and relied upon by vicarious liability cases in New York. Is there
any reason why the scope of employment tests in the two fields
should be interpreted differently? For a discussion of this question,
see the *Luth* case, p. 115 *infra*.

Has the material in this note affected your earlier conclusion
with respect to vicarious liability for the acts of the carnival-

loving employee? In addition to reaching your own conclusion, speculate as to the conclusion you think the Court of Appeals reached in view of the case authority it had before it (which did not include the *Marks* case). The opinion on these facts is contained immediately below.

FIOCCO v. CARVER
New York Court of Appeals
234 N.Y. 219, 137 N.E. 309 (1922)

CARDOZO, J. [The facts have been summarized earlier.] Upon these facts a jury has been permitted to find that [the driver] was in the course of his employment. The ruling was upheld at the Appellate Division by a divided court.

We think the judgment may not stand.

The plaintiff argues that the jury, if it discredited the driver's narrative of the accident, was free to discredit his testimony that there had been a departure from the course of duty. With this out of the case, there is left the conceded fact that a truck belonging to the defendant was in the custody of the defendant's servant. We are reminded that this without more sustains a presumption that the custodian was using it in the course of his employment. But the difficulty with the argument is that in this case there *is* more, though credit be accorded to the plaintiff's witnesses exclusively. The presumption disappears when the surrounding circumstances are such that its recognition is unreasonable. We draw the inference of regularity, in default of evidence rebutting it, presuming, until otherwise advised, that the servant will discharge his duty. We refuse to rest upon presumption, and put the plaintiff to his proof, when the departure from regularity is so obvious that charity can no longer infer an adherence to the course of duty.

Such a departure is here shown, apart altogether from the narrative put before us by the driver. The plaintiff's testimony, confirmed by the testimony of his witnesses, breaks the force of the presumption that might otherwise be indulged, and leaves his case unproved unless something is in the record, in addition to the presumption, to show that the defendant's servant was in the course of the employment. The wagon was an electric truck intended for the transportation of merchandise in connection with the defendants' business. At the time of the accident it was crowded with boys, "packed as thick as sardines," whom the driver was taking on a frolic. They filled, not only its body, but also the roof and sides and box. Plainly on proof of these facts the

presumption vanishes that the driver was discharging his duty to
the master. The character of the transaction is so extraordinary,
the occupation of the truck by the revellers so dominant and
exclusive, as to rebut the inference that the driver was serving his
employer at the same time that he was promoting the pleasure of
his friends. The dual function, if it existed, can no longer rest
upon presumption. Regularity will no longer be taken for granted
when irregularity is written over the whole surface of the picture.
We will no longer presume anything. What the plaintiff wishes
us to find for him, that he must prove.

We turn, then, to the driver's testimony to see whether anything there, whether read by itself or in conjunction with the
plaintiff's narrative, gives support for the conclusion that the
truck was engaged at the moment of the accident in the business
of the master. All that we can find there, when we view it most
favorably to the plaintiff, is a suggestion that after a temporary
excursion in streets remote from the homeward journey, the
servant had at last made up his mind to put an end to his wander-
ings and return to the garage. He was still far away from the point
at which he had first strayed from the path of duty, but his
thoughts were homeward bound. Is this enough, in view of all
the circumstances, to terminate the temporary abandonment and
put him back into the sphere of service? We have refused to limit
ourselves by tests that are merely mechanical or formal (Riley
v. Standard Oil Co. of N. Y., 231 N. Y. 301). Location in time
and space are circumstances that may guide the judgment, but
will not be suffered to control it, divorced from other circumstances that may characterize the intent of the transaction. The
dominant purpose must be proved to be the performance of the
master's business. Till then there can be no resumption of a
relation which has been broken and suspended.

We think the servant's purpose to return to the garage was
insufficient to bring him back within the ambit of his duty. He
was indisputably beyond the ambit while making the tour of the
neighborhood which ended when he stopped at Catherine street
upon a visit to a pool room. Neither the tour nor the stop was
incidental to his service. Duty was resumed, if at all, when, ending the tour, he had embarked upon his homeward journey. It
was in the very act of starting that the injury was done. The
plaintiff had climbed upon the truck while it was at rest in
front of the pool room, still engaged upon an errand unrelated
to the business. The negligence complained of is the setting
of the truck in motion without giving the intruder an opportunity to reach the ground. The self-same act that was the
cause of the disaster is supposed to have ended the abandon-

ment and re-established a relation which till then had been suspended. Act and disaster would alike have been avoided if the relation had not been broken. Even then, however, the delinquent servant did not purge himself of wrong. The field of duty once forsaken, is not to be re-entered by acts evincing a divided loyalty and thus continuing the offense. Many of the illicit incidents of the tour about the neighborhood persisted. The company of merrymakers was still swarming about the truck. The servant was still using the property of the master to entertain his friends and help the merriment of the carnival. The presence of these merrymakers was the very circumstance that had prompted the little boy to jump upon the truck, and make himself a party to all the fun and frolic. Add to this that the truck was still far away from the route which it would have traveled if the servant had followed the line of duty from the beginning. We do not need to separate these circumstances and to insist that any one of them alone would be strong enough to shape the judgment. Our concern is with the aggregate. We are not dealing with a case where in the course of a continuing relation, business and private ends have been co-incidently served. We are dealing with a departure so manifest as to constitute an abandonment of duty, exempting the master from liability till duty is resumed. Viewing the circumstances collectively, we are constrained to the conclusion that at the moment of the wrong complained of, the forces set in motion by the abandonment of duty were still alive and operative. Whether we have regard to circumstances of space or of time or of causal or logical relation, the homeward trip was bound up with the effects of the excursion, the parts interpenetrated and commingled beyond hope of separation. Division more substantial must be shown before a relation, once ignored and abandoned, will be renewed and re-established.

The judgment of the Appellate Division and that of the Trial Term should be reversed, and the complaint dismissed, with costs in all courts.

HISCOCK, Ch. J., HOGAN, POUND, McLAUGHLIN, CRANE and ANDREWS, JJ., concur.

Judgments reversed, etc.

NOTES

1. The decision in *Joel v. Morison* placed heavy stress on the fact that the servant took proper possession of the master's cart in order to further the master's business. The fact that the servant

is in possession of the cart under such circumstances when he causes the accident would not be conclusive evidence of operation within the scope of employment, however. Several of the above cases are authority to the contrary; and consider the situation of a driver in the midst of a local delivery route in New York City who stops delivering and drives off in the employer's vehicle toward a relative's home in South Carolina, negligently causing a severe accident in Delaware. Even though the driver started out in proper possession of the delivery vehicle, do you think any courts would hesitate to hold as a matter of law that he was outside of the scope of employment at the time of the accident?*

Should, however, the fact that the servant is in possession of his master's vehicle in itself be of any legal significance? The opinion in *Fiocco* states that, since the truck was in the custody of the defendant's servant, "[T]his without more sustains a presumption that the custodian was using it in the course of his employment." This procedural effect is obviously important to a plaintiff's lawyer, although *Fiocco* proves that it will not safely get his client to the jury in all cases.

2. Although it may not seem like it so far, the scope of employment issue does involve something more than automobile accidents. You will see an example of this in the next note. The remaining material and the problems at the end of this chapter also will include some nonvehicular situations. It is true, nevertheless, that a large bulk of the cases are automobile accidents and, of course, the principles established in deciding them apply collaterally to a host of situations.

3. What effect does disobedience by a servant of his master's express instructions have on the matter of scope of employment? Can a master successfully argue that such disobedience always takes the servant outside of the scope of employment? What if the instruction violated is to "drive carefully"? Or suppose the owner of a sporting goods store directs his salesmen never to insert a cartridge while exhibiting a gun for sale. A salesman does so anyway, and someone is injured as a result. Is the salesman's act within the scope of his employment? Does it make any difference whether the salesman violated the instructions forgetfully? Deliberately? See RESTATEMENT § 230, illustration 1, for

---

* What, however, would Morris (Subsection B, *infra*) do with this situation? And would you be troubled by the above common sense response if the vehicle the employee was driving was large and powerful, and the damage was substantially increased because of the size and power of the **vehicle?**

the statement that such an act is within the scope of employment, and drawing no distinction based on the salesman's intent.

LUTH v. ROGERS & BABLER CONSTR. CO.
Supreme Court of Alaska
507 P.2d 761 (1973)

Before Rabinowitz, C.J., Connor and Boochever, JJ.

Rabinowitz, Chief Justice. Anthony and Jeannette Luth were driving south on the Seward Highway when their car collided with another driven by Wayne Jack and owned by John and Freida Knox. The accident occurred approximately two miles north of Twenty Mile Creek when Jack attempted to pass another vehicle going north. On the day of the accident, and for the previous six weeks, Wayne Jack was employed by Rogers and Babler Construction Company as a flagman on a road construction project. At the time of the accident, he was returning home to Anchorage from his jobsite at Twenty Mile Creek, having completed a 7 a. m. to 5:30 p. m. workday. Since he did not live near the jobsite, Jack commuted approximately 25 miles to work by car everyday. The Master Union Agreement under which Jack worked provided for payment of $8.50 daily additional remuneration, since the jobsite was located a considerable distance from Anchorage. However, all of Rogers' employees on this particular construction project received the $8.50 additional remuneration whether they commuted from Anchorage or lived near the jobsite.

At trial, Rogers moved for a directed verdict, arguing that it could not be liable on the basis of *respondeat superior*, since Jack was not acting within the scope of his employment at the time of the accident. In regard to this motion, Rogers conceded that Jack's negligent driving caused the collision with the Luths' vehicle. The trial court denied Rogers' motion and in turn granted Luths' motion for directed verdict, ruling as a matter of law that Rogers was liable under the *respondeat superior* doctrine.

. . .

Under the doctrine of *respondeat superior,* an employer is liable for negligent acts or omissions of his employee committed in the scope of his employment. However, Rogers attempts to avoid liability for Jack's negligence by relying on the so-called "going and coming" rule. Under this rule, an employee is ordinarily considered outside the scope of his employment while going to and from work. Some courts justify this rule by reasoning that ordinarily the employment relationship is suspended and thus

the employer has no right to control the employee from the time
the employee leaves his work until he returns. Others reason that
while commuting the employee is not rendering service growing
out of, or incidental to, his employment.

The Luths attempt to circumvent the going-and-coming rule
by urging this court to obliterate the distinction between the tort
concept "in the scope of employment" and the workmen's compensation concept "arising out of and in the course of employment." As part of their argument, the Luths emphasize that
workmen's compensation law recognizes an exception to the going-and-coming rule for employees who receive travel allowances
for commuting to and from remote jobsites and who are injured
while so commuting.[4]

Until recently, this court maintained that *respondeat superior*
issues would be resolved by applying the "right to control" test
and other factors delineated in the Second Restatement of Agency. Then, in Fruit v. Schreiner,[6] we adopted a modified "enterprise theory" of *respondeat superior*, without rejecting Restatement criteria. In *Fruit*, we noted the similarity between Alaska
workmen's compensation policy and the enterprise theory of
vicarious tort liability. But we did not equate the tort concept
"in the scope of employment" with the workmen's compensation
concept "arising out of and in the course of employment." Nor
have other decisions of this court used these concepts inter-
changeably. Moreover, we do not discern a trend in other jurisdictions to equate these two concepts.[8]

While workmen's compensation law and *respondeat superior*
doctrine both involve allocations of costs regarding industrial
accidents, they differ in scope. Workmen's compensation benefits
turn solely upon whether the employee was injured while performing an activity related to his job—and "relatedness" is
usually a function of benefit to the employer. In contrast, *respondeat superior* subjects employers to liability for injuries

------

[4] *See* 1 Larson, Workmen's Compensation §§ 16.20, 16.30 (1965); *e. g.*,
State, Dep't of Highways v. Johns, 422 P.2d 855, 860 (Alaska 1967).

[6] 502 P.2d 133, 138-142 (Alaska 1972); Although not usually enunciated as
a basis for liability, in essence the enterprise may be regarded as a unit for
tort as opposed to contract liability purposes. Employees' acts sufficiently connected with the enterprise are in effect considered as deeds of the enterprise
itself. Where through negligence such acts cause injury to others it is appropriate that the enterprise bear the loss incurred. *Id.* at 141.

[8] *See, e. g.*, . . . Lundberg v. State, 25 N.Y.2d 467, 306 N.Y.S.2d 947, 255
N.E.2d 177 (1969). Even the California cases on which the Luths rely have
not completely assimilated workmen's compensation and *respondeat superior*
concepts. *See* Huntsinger v. Fell, 22 Cal.App.3d 803, 99 Cal.Rptr. 666, 668-
669 (1972).

suffered by an indefinite number of third persons. To limit this burden of liability, the narrower concept, "scope of employment," has long been tied to the employer's right to control the employee's activity at the time of his tortious conduct. We do not consider the right to control as being a prerequisite to a holding of liability, but it is a factor that may be considered in determining whether the employee's activity is sufficiently related to his employer's enterprise. While the employer's benefit from the employee's activity is relevant to the existence of vicarious liability, benefit is not its sole determinant. We therefore reject the Luths' argument that workmen's compensation law be applied in this tort case.

By rejecting the Luths' primary argument made in support of the trial court's directed verdict, however, we do not necessarily hold that Rogers cannot be vicariously liable for Jack's negligence. Fruit v. Schreiner holds that resolution of scope of employment questions will "depend primarily on the findings of fact in each case" and that the "factual determination generally is left to the jury." . . . .[13] Moreover, the Restatement recognizes that scope of employment questions are jury issues where conflicting inferences can be drawn from undisputed facts.[14]

While in the case at bar the facts were undisputed, the jury, applying Restatement criteria, could have reasonably drawn conflicting inferences as to whether Jack was acting in the scope of his employment with Rogers at the time of the accident. Rogers did not expressly require its Anchorage-based employees to commute by automobile to the Twenty Mile Creek jobsite. On the other hand, Jack's employment at this jobsite some 25 miles from his home in Anchorage necessitated his driving to work, since Rogers did not establish a work camp or provide transportation facilities for its employees. Thus, a jury might reasonably infer that Rogers implicitly authorized its employees to commute by automobile and that such commuting was within the scope of Jack's employment. The jury could have reasoned that the ad-

---

[13] . . . See also Gossett v. Simonson, 243 Or. 16, 411 P.2d 277, 280 (1966), where the court stated that

the trial court should decide the issue of scope of employment as a matter of law only when no more than one reasonable inference could be drawn from the facts. If the facts are in dispute, the jury must determine what the facts are. When conflicting inferences reasonably can be drawn from undisputed facts, it is also for the jury to decide whether the servant was working within or outside the scope of [his employment].

[14] Restatement (Second) of Agency § 228, comment d (1958). We think the factors mentioned in Restatement (Second) of Agency §§ 228, 229 for the most part provide the basis for proper instructions. . . .

ditional $8.50 remuneration induced Anchorage-based laborers to commute to Rogers' out-of-town construction project, thus benefitting Rogers. Since the accident occurred during one of these commuting trips, it would not be unfair to require Rogers to pay for the Luths' resulting injuries.[17] On the other hand, the record discloses that Rogers paid its employees the additional $8.50 regardless of whether they commuted to work. Thus, the jury might reasonably infer that the $8.50 was merely a mileage or inconvenience allowance, and that Jack was not on company time while driving home from work. Since Rogers had no right to control Jack's actions after he completed his workday, a jury could have concluded that Jack was not acting within the scope of his employment.

Since there is substantial evidence from which the jury might have found either that Jack was, or was not, acting within the scope of his employment, we conclude that the trial court erred in directing a verdict for the Luths on the *respondeat superior* liability issue.

. . .

Reversed and remanded for a new trial in accordance with the foregoing.

CONNOR, Justice (concurring in part and dissenting in part). I disagree with the holding of the majority opinion that the employer can be held liable on a *respondeat superior* basis for the torts of its employee.

The majority opinion concludes that when conflicting inferences can be drawn from the facts, here undisputed, the question of whether a tortfeasor was acting within the scope of his employment by an employer will be left to jury determination. With that principle I have no quarrel. However, I am not satisfied that the case before us is an appropriate one for the application of that principle.

The problem presented is whether under any view of, or inferences to be drawn from, the undisputed facts of this case, *respondeat superior* liability can be imposed.

The "going and coming" rule, widely accepted in our law, normally absolves the employer of liability for torts committed by his employee while going to or from the place of work. Judicial decision has developed various exceptions to the rule, most of them covering situations clearly distinguishable from the case before us.

---

[17] *Cf.* Hinman v. Westinghouse Elec. Co., 2 Cal.3d 956, 88 Cal.Rptr. 188, 471 P.2d 988, 992 (1970) (relying on employer's payment for travel time as basis for vicarious liability).

The majority opinion relies on Balise v. Underwood, 71 Wash. 2d 331, 428 P.2d 573, 577 (1967), and Hinman v. Westinghouse Electric Co., 2 Cal.3d 956, 88 Cal. Rptr. 188, 471 P.2d 988, 992 (1970). . . .

In the *Hinman* case the employee traveled directly from his own home to the jobsite. Under a contract with the employee's labor union, the employer paid one and one-half hours pay for round-trip travel time, plus $1.30 travel expense. The court held that the employer was liable for automobile injuries caused by the employee while traveling from work.

When one discards the discussion in the *Hinman* case of the traditional "going and coming" rule and its exceptions, the rationale of decision is rather simple. The court reasoned that the employer benefits by being able to reach out into a broad labor market and, through paying for travel time and expense, to induce persons to work for him. By deciding that it is desirable for his enterprise to go beyond the "normal" labor market, the employer should bear and pay for the risks inherent in his decision.

The difficulty with the *Hinman* doctrine is that it seems boundless. One is left in doubt as to what amount of commuting should be considered "normal" in a particular labor market. The travel allowance dealt with in the *Hinman* case arose from a collective bargaining agreement. The amount of the allowance varied by a fixed standard: the distance from the city hall in Los Angeles, California, to the jobsite. How this standard can have any relationship to reaching outside the "normal" labor market, or to increasing risk of injury to highway users, is never explained. In my opinion, the *Hinman* doctrine so drastically alters the normal "coming and going" rule as to virtually do away with any reliable guide to judicial decision. The rule is based on the employer's surrender of control over his employee once the work day has ended. To say that an exception will be drawn in all instances in which an employee receives a travel allowance, notwithstanding that the employer has no control over the employee during his travel to and from work, is to defeat the very purpose of the rule.

I find more persuasive the reasoning of Lundberg v. State, 25 N.Y.2d 467, 306 N.Y.S.2d 947, 255 N.E.2d 177 (1969). There the employee lived at the jobsite during the work week, with his living expenses being paid for by the employer. On weekends the employee traveled 80 miles to his home to visit his family. He was paid mileage by his employer for such travel. The court held, as a matter of law, that the employee while traveling was not within the scope of his employment. Accordingly the employer could not be held liable upon a *respondeat superior* basis. The factors emphasized by the court were that the employee was not driving to satisfy any obligation owed to his employer, that the employer had no control over the movements or activities of the employee, and that the payment of a mileage allowance bestowed no right of control upon the employer. If anything, the facts in *Lundberg* were stronger than those in the case at bar for finding *respondeat superior* liability.

The difficulty with the majority opinion is that it drastically increases the tort liability of employers without providing any coherent or rationalizing principle by which to keep such liability within reasonably predictable bounds.

The activities of the employee, Jack, seem no different from those of commuting employees generally. Jack was not on any special errand for his employer. As a flagman, driving an automobile was not part of the work he was employed to perform. The accident took place outside working hours and several miles away from the jobsite.

The employer's failure to provide a work camp or to provide transportation for its employees can hardly give rise to liability.[1] The jobsite apparently was not of the remote type where lodging would be furnished, and it was within commuting distance from Anchorage, the main population center of Alaska.

The main support for the majority opinion is that the payment of $8.50 per day extra remuneration somehow induced Anchorage-based workers to accept employment, thus benefiting the employer. I consider this a very fragile basis for imposing liability. The workers were paid their $8.50 regardless of whether they lived close to or far from the jobsite. The payment of the $8.50 resulted from the terms of the employer's labor agreement, which required payment upon a uniform basis having nothing to do with where employees actually lived or how far they might commute. I find it most difficult, then, to regard the extra payment as a commuting inducement.

Resting liability on this basis suffers from all of the difficulties mentioned in connection with the *Hinman* case, *supra*. If an exception is to be carved out of the "going and coming" rule because the employer has reached beyond a "normal" labor market,

---

[1] The situation here is distinguishable from "remote site" cases where employees are required to live on the premises of the employer, relatively isolated from civilization. See Anderson v. Employers Liability Assur. Corp., 498 P.2d 288 (Alaska 1972), which deals with workmen's compensation for recreational injuries sustained at a remote work site.

how can the relevant market ever be determined? Should it rest upon the size, location, and nature of the employer's business? Should it be gauged by the kind of employees one would expect to find in such businesses? Must we rely on sociological and traffic engineering studies to determine what constitutes a normal method of getting to work, as contrasted with means so unusual that the employer must be deemed to have induced his workers to commute from a "broad" job market?

Not only do these questions point to the unworkability of the principle, they also highlight the total dearth of information in the record of this case tending to answer such questions.

It is noteworthy that in large industries most labor agreements are negotiated between an organization representing a number of business enterprises and the union. An entrepreneur who belongs to such a management organization has little choice but to accept the labor agreement negotiated on his behalf. Ordinarily, to reject the agreement is simply to go out of business. Hence it is unrealistic to denominate a travel allowance in a collective bargaining agreement an "inducement" for commuting. The existence of a travel allowance in a collective bargaining agreement is often a matter of pure accident. Finally, workers who receive a higher wage scale—but no travel allowance—may be just as induced to commute as workers who receive a travel allowance but lower hourly wages. In short, basing liability on the presence of a travel allowance would be utterly arbitrary.

Denying the employer's liability in this case does not conflict with our holding in Fruit v. Schreiner, 502 P.2d 133 (Alaska 1972). There we dealt with the activities of an insurance salesman attending a company-sponsored conference where the salesmen were encouraged to have social contacts at places other than the conference headquarters. While returning from the pursuit of such activities to the conference headquarters, one of the salesmen negligently injured the plaintiff. Our holding that the company was liable concerns a factual setting which is obviously distinguishable.

I would hold as a matter of law that Jack was not within the scope of his employment with Rogers & Babler at the time of the accident. . . .

B. COMMENTARY

1. In defining where the outer limits of the scope of employment limitation should be drawn, some followers of the entrepreneur theory urge that liability be confined to the zones

of risk which the entrepreneurs could foresee were incident to their businesses. See Smith, *Frolic and Detour*, 23 Colum. L. Rev. 444, 716 (1923); 2 F. Harper & F. James, The Law of Torts 1375-78 (1956). The reasoning is that since the law requires an entrepreneur to insure the risks of his enterprise at his peril, then the law must take care to limit liability to those risks which the entrepreneur can reasonably be expected to foresee and thus insure against. Enterprise liability therefore should be limited to that zone of risk which the entrepreneur can anticipate, and *this* is the question courts should be exploring. Review the above decisions with this "zone of risk" test in mind.

This theory, which sounds good and does seem to supply a more workable standard than the largely haphazard test of "frolic" or "detour," is challenged by C. Robert Morris, Jr., *Enterprise Liability and the Actuarial Process—The Insignificance of Foresight*, 70 Yale L. J. 554, 576-78 (1961):

> The zone-of-risk analysis of the frolic and detour problem suffers from the same difficulty. Dean Smith hypothesized a business near Wall Street in Manhattan with customers in the Times Square area and a truck for making deliveries to them. Though the entrepreneur orders his truck driver to stay on Broadway and to avoid personal errands, he can foresee that the truck will occasionally return south by way of Seventh Avenue for reasons personal to the driver. He can even foresee that the driver may deviate as far north as Columbus Circle. He cannot foresee a trip to the Bronx or to Staten Island, so the zone-of-risk does not include upper Manhattan, the Bronx, or Staten Island. The entrepreneur, then, should not be liable for accidents in those places.

> But, again, the entrepreneur's *personal* estimate of his zone of risk is irrelevant. The rate territory for commercial vehicles in lower Manhattan includes all of Manhattan, plus the Bronx and Brooklyn. In other words, the Wall Street entrepreneur pays his share of the total risk incurred by trucks garaged in those three boroughs. Even Manhattan enterprises which qualify for experience-rating pay part of that risk, unless they are so large that their experience is completely credible.* Assume

---

* By "credible" Morris means that the very large enterprises have sufficient claims experience that an actuary can estimate from the claims data of one enterprise alone the amount of risk involved per unit of exposure, and thus, for example, estimate the amount of reserves necessary to be set aside by the enterprise to meet claims. "In the automobile liability field, for example, it is considered necessary to have experience involving at least 1084 losses [per year] before the experience can be judged completely credible." (p. 563.)

that each entrepreneur within the rating territory has formulated an idea of his enterprise's zone of risk. Occasionally a truck will stray beyond its zone and have an accident. Will this happen so infrequently that liability in such cases will not affect insurance rates? If so, the zone-of-risk concept is irrelevant. If, on the other hand, it happens frequently enough to affect insurance rates this extra-zone risk is insurable. Each entrepreneur will be surprised when he sees the report of an extra-zone accident, for, by definition, it happened beyond the zone of his expectation. But the actuary, if he were informed about the circumstances of all accidents in the experience he was studying, would not be surprised. He would know that accidents occurred with some regularity beyond the zone of normal business activity. Of course, an occasional accident would surprise even him. He might be blasé about a Wall Street-based truck piling up in Yonkers, but he would be somewhat surprised if the accident occurred in Albany. Yet, the same factors which made the accident surprising would make it ineffective in the rate making process. It would represent a miniscule part of the experience.

In short, an entrepreneur's a priori concept of his own zone of risk should not be a determining factor in the frolic and detour problem; this is so because his vehicle and those of his fellow entrepreneurs in the same rating territory are probably involved in accidents just beyond the boundaries of their respective a priori zones with sufficient frequency to make those accidents "foreseeable and insurable" from an actuarial standpoint. This concept requires a sophisticated approach to each enterprise's zone of risk—an understanding that each zone includes these accidents. However, even this sophisticated notion of the zone of risk may not be significant, for the number of accidents occurring beyond this extended zone will be so small in relation to the total number of claims against the enterprises grouped in the rating territory that these extra-zone claims, if honored, will have no appreciable effect upon insurance rates. Their effect will probably be obscured by the practice of rounding off the rates, so no entrepreneur could claim his insurance rate was unfairly increased by the payment of such claims.[49]

---

[49] This is true even if the entrepreneur qualifies for experience rating and the outlandish claim was against him. This would clearly be true if his rate were set entirely upon his own experience, that is, if his experience had 100% credibility. Then the analysis in the text would apply with very little change, except that the entrepreneur himself would soon have a sophisticated idea of his zone of risk. After a couple of years he would realize that "the

The same point could be made concerning the other uses to which the zone-of-risk analysis has been put. The risk of a producer's liability under foreign strict-liability products-liability law, as well as the risk of an automobile owner's liability under foreign owners' liability statutes, is either frequent enough to be "foreseen and insured," or is infrequent enough to have only a small, random effect upon rates. Either the risk is "foreseeable and insurable," or it is *de minimus.*

Morris would thus consider the limitation of foreseeability to be irrelevant to a vicarious liability standard (at least with respect to activities where liability insurance is available) and apparently would hold a business enterprise liable for all losses, whether or not fault is involved, which have any relation to the enterprise, even though extraordinary in nature, on the theory that the extraordinary and unforeseeable accident is rarely if ever reflected in an insurance premium and that humanitarian and moral (but not economic) reasons dictate that the enterprise bear such losses. Morris recognizes that moral and humanitarian reasons are not relevant to all losses (as, for example, where the plaintiff is itself a large enterprise), but they are relevant in a large enough percentage of cases to justify application of the general principle to all cases in order to promote efficiency and consistency. As noted previously in Chapter 2, Morris also takes note of the specific deterrent feature of putting losses back onto enterprises; this would act as an incentive for the enterprise to promote safety standards in order to minimize its losses, which would reduce losses generally.

2. Calabresi argues for allocating to an enterprise "all costs that are within the scope of that enterprise." 70 YALE L. J. at 514. He urges that "scope of employment" should be read as broadly as the "arising out of and in the course of employment" test of workmen's compensation. *Id.* at 544. This still leaves us with difficult questions of decision-making, of course. How would Calabresi advise the court in the *Marks* case, p. 109, *supra?*

---

damnedest things happen in this business." The few claims which were so farflung as to still shock him would represent such a small part of his experience that they would not materially change his rate. If, however, the enterprise had experience of less credibility, the entrepreneur might still retain a relatively naive concept of the zone of foreseeable risk. He might still be surprised at accidents which, taking the rating territory as a whole, did not involve unforeseeable deviations. However, since the credibility assigned to the enterprise's experience would be low, the effect that experience would have upon the rate charged would be small, and hence the effect of a frolic claim would be similarly decreased.

C. INTENTIONAL TORTS

The shift we are making here is a major one. As we have seen, there has been surprisingly little controversy about holding a master liable for his servant's unintentional torts, although there is dispute about the limits to be drawn.

What happens, however, when the servant commits an intentional tort? Does this so completely shift the ground that the doctrine of vicarious liability should not apply? Or should it make no difference at all, so long as the conduct was "expectable"? Would you anticipate that courts dealing with responsibility for intentional torts would give extra weight to the requirement in RESTATEMENT § 228(1) (c), p. 106 *supra*, that such conduct be "actuated, at least in part, by a purpose to serve the master"? And the relevance of § 228(1) (d) is clear, isn't it?

Suppose, for example, that a seaman who worked on a vessel which was being overhauled in a floating drydock got drunk one night while on shore leave. Upon returning to the vessel late at night, he turned some wheels on the drydock wall. In doing this he opened some valves, which resulted in flooding the tanks on one side of the drydock and caused a listing of the ship and damage to the drydock. The drydock owner sued the ship owner. The defense, of course, was that the seaman was acting completely outside of his scope of employment. How would you argue against that as the plaintiff's lawyer? How would you decide the issue as a judge? Would your answer change if the seaman had been cold sober and did the act out of hostility, planning to quit the next day anyway? What if he had been fired earlier that day, and then did the act (i) while drunk or (ii) while sober?

A delivery man for the New York Tribune negligently ran into Smith while on route. Both drivers stopped. The delivery man refused to identify himself to Smith and gave Smith a shove. After regaining his balance, Smith kneeled down to look at the license plate of the delivery truck. The driver kicked him in the face. Smith sues the New York Tribune on *respondeat superior* grounds. The defense is obvious. What result would you reach if you were the judge in the case?

Finally, suppose a bartender while on duty has a patron call to his attention the fact that a car engine is boiling over in the parking lot of the bar. The bartender goes out to the lot and turns off the engine. The owner of the car, a drunk bar patron who was sitting in the car, resents this. Words are exchanged and the bartender savagely beats the patron up while still out in the parking lot. The bar owner is sued by the injured patron. What result?

BREMEN STATE BANK v. HARTFORD ACC. & INDEM. CO.
United States Court of Appeals, Seventh Circuit
427 F.2d 425 (1970)

SWYGERT, Chief Judge. Plaintiff, Bremen State Bank, brought this diversity action in the district court to recover $10,342.03, which sum was lost during a move by the bank from one location to another within the village of Tinley Park, Illinois. On the day before the move the bank instructed its tellers to put their money at the end of the day in canvas bags on the floor of the vault rather than in metal lockers inside the vault, the usual practice. One teller, Mrs. Laucke, did not receive these instructions and thus put her cash drawer money, $10,342.03, in her metal locker instead of on the vault floor.

Arrangements had been made for the Tinley Park police to move the bank's money and for defendant, Bekins Van & Storage Company, to move the office equipment, including the metal lockers, inside the vault. After the police, under guard, had moved the money from the vault floor to the new location, Bekins' employees entered the bank and began their job. While removing some of the metal lockers from the vault, one of Bekins' employees, Danny Francis, noticed that something was inside one of the lockers. After placing them in a van, he opened the locker used by Mrs. Laucke and discovered the money. Francis finished working that day and later absconded with the $10,342.03, none of which was ever recovered.

Plaintiff's complaint . . . sought recovery . . . against Bekins on the theory of *respondeat superior*. The district court granted summary judgment against the bank. . . .

The bank's claim against Bekins rests on the theory that since Francis stole the money during the performance of his employment by Bekins the latter is civilly liable for the loss occasioned by the criminal act of its employee. We think the bank has misinterpreted the applicable Illinois law. Our reading of the cases leads us to conclude that the rule in Illinois is that the employer is liable for the negligent, wilful, malicious, or criminal acts of its employees when such acts are committed during the course of employment and in furtherance of the business of the employer; but when the act is committed solely for the benefit of the employee, the employer is not liable to the injured third party.

Thus, an employer was not liable for the criminal act of its employee-watchman in setting fire to the building which he had been employed to guard, Apex Smelting Co. v. Burns, 175 F.2d 978 (7th Cir. 1949), or for the shooting of a trespasser who was leaving the employer's premises by a guard who was armed without the knowledge or permission of the employer, Belt Railway Co. v. Banicki, *supra,* or where the employee engaged in a fist-fight for purposes unrelated to his job, Horecker v. Pere Marquette R. Co. 238 Ill.App. 278 (1925), or where the employee-driver deviated from the route leading to the destination assigned by the employer, Boehmer v. Norton, 328 Ill.App. 17, 65 N.E.2d 212 (1946). On the other hand, the employer was held liable where an employee-brakeman who had been instructed to remove unauthorized riders on railroad cars wilfully and maliciously pulled a boy off a moving train, crushing the latter's foot in the process, Illinois Central R. Co. v. King, 179 Ill. 91, 53 N.E. 552 (1899), and where the employee mistakenly injured the plaintiff in defending the employer's property against robbers, Metzler v. Layton, 298 Ill.App. 529, 19 N.E.2d 130, *aff'd* 373 Ill. 88, 25 N.E.2d 60 (1939).

In the instant case, there is no contention that Francis stole the money in furtherance of the business of his employer. In fact, the money came into his hands by inadvertence and without the knowledge or permission of either his employer or the bank. Under Illinois law, therefore, the employer was not liable for Francis' act and the granting of summary judgment in favor of Bekins was correct.

IRA S. BUSHEY & SONS, INC. v. UNITED STATES
United States Court of Appeals, Second Circuit
398 F.2d 167 (1968)
Noted in 82 HARV. L. REV. 1568 (1969)

Before WATERMAN, FRIENDLY and KAUFMAN, Circuit Judges.

FRIENDLY, Circuit Judge. While the United States Coast Guard vessel Tamaroa was being overhauled in a floating drydock located in Brooklyn's Gowanus Canal, a seaman returning from shore leave late at night, in the condition for which seaman are famed, turned some wheels on the drydock wall. He thus opened valves that controlled the flooding of the tanks on one side of the drydock. Soon the ship listed, slid off the blocks and fell against the wall. Parts of the drydock sank, and the ship partially did— fortunately without loss of life or personal injury. The drydock owner sought and was granted compensation by the District Court for the Eastern District of New York in an amount to be determined, 276 F.Supp. 518; the United States appeals.

. . .

The Tamaroa had gone into drydock on February 28, 1963; her keel rested on blocks permitting her drive shaft to be removed and repairs to be made to her hull. The contract between the Government and Bushey provided in part:

(o) The work shall, whenever practical, be performed in such manner as not to interfere with the berthing and messing of personnel attached to the vessel undergoing repair, and provision shall be made so that personnel assigned shall have access to the vessel at all times, it being understood that such personnel will not interfere with the work or the contractor's workmen.

Access from shore to ship was provided by a route past the security guard at the gate, through the yard, up a ladder to the top of one drydock wall and along the wall to a gangway leading to the fantail deck, where men returning from leave reported at a quartermaster's shack.

Seaman Lane, whose prior record was unblemished, returned from shore leave a little after midnight on March 14. He had been drinking heavily; the quartermaster made mental note that he was "loose." For reasons not apparent to us or very likely to Lane,[4] he took it into his head, while progressing along the gangway wall, to turn each of three large wheels some twenty times; unhappily, as previously stated, these wheels controlled the water intake valves. After boarding ship at 12:11 A.M., Lane mumbled to an off-duty seaman that he had "turned some valves" and also muttered something about "valves" to another who was standing the engineering watch. Neither did anything; apparently Lane's condition was not such as to encourage proximity. At 12:20 A.M. a crew member discovered water coming into the drydock. By 12:30 A.M. the ship began to list, the alarm was sounded and the crew were ordered ashore. Ten minutes later the vessel and dock were listing over 20 degrees; in another ten minutes the ship slid off the blocks and fell against the drydock wall.

The Government attacks imposition of liability on the ground that Lane's acts were not within the scope of his employment. It relies heavily on § 228(1) of the Restatement of Agency 2d which says that "conduct of a servant is within the scope of employment if, but only if: * * * (c) it is actuated, at least in part by a purpose to serve the master." Courts have gone to considerable lengths to find such a purpose, as witness a well-known opinion in which Judge Learned Hand concluded that a drunken boatswain who routed the plaintiff out of his bunk with a blow, saying "Get up, you big son of a bitch, and turn to," and then continued to fight, might have thought he was acting in the in-

---

[4] Lane disappeared after completing the sentence imposed by a court-martial and being discharged from the Coast Guard.

terest of the ship. Nelson v. American-West African Line, 86 F.2d 730 (2 Cir. 1936), cert. denied, 300 U.S. 665, 57 S.Ct. 509, 81 L.Ed. 873 (1937). It would be going too far to find such a purpose here; while Lane's return to the Tamaroa was to serve his employer, no one has suggested how he could have thought turning the wheels to be, even if—which is by no means clear—he was unaware of the consequences.

In light of the highly artificial way in which the motive test has been applied, the district judge believed himself obliged to test the doctrine's continuing vitality by referring to the larger purposes *respondeat superior* is supposed to serve. He concluded that the old formulation failed this test. We do not find his analysis so compelling, however, as to constitute a sufficient basis in itself for discarding the old doctrine. It is not at all clear, as the court below suggested, that expansion of liability in the manner here suggested will lead to a more efficient allocation of resources. As the most astute exponent of this theory has emphasized, a more efficient allocation can only be expected if there is some reason to believe that imposing a particular cost on the enterprise will lead it to consider whether steps should be taken to prevent a recurrence of the accident. Calabresi, The Decision for Accidents: An Approach to Non-fault Allocation of Costs, 78 Harv.L.Rev. 713, 725-34 (1965). And the suggestion that imposition of liability here will lead to more intensive screening of employees rests on highly questionable premises, see Comment, Assessment of Punitive Damages Against an Entrepreneur for the Malicious Torts of His Employees, 70 Yale L.J. 1296, 1301-04 (1961).[5] The unsatisfactory quality of the allocation of resource rationale is especially striking on the facts of this case. It could well be that application of the traditional rule might induce drydock owners, prodded by their insurance companies, to install locks on their valves to avoid similar incidents in the future,[6] while placing the burden on shipowners is much less likely to lead to accident prevention.[7] It is true, of course, that in many cases the plaintiff will not be in a position to insure, and so expansion of liability will, at the very least, serve *respondeat superior's* loss spreading function. See Smith, Frolic and Detour, 23 Colum.L.Rev. 444, 456 (1923). But the fact that the defendant is better able to afford

---

[5] We are not here speaking of cases in which the enterprise has negligently hired an employee whose undesirable propensities are known or should have been.

[6] The record reveals that most modern drydocks have automatic locks to guard against unauthorized use of valves.

[7] Although it is theoretically possible that shipowners would demand that drydock owners take appropriate action, *see* Coase, *The Problem of Social Cost*, 3 J.L. & Econ. 1 (1960), this would seem unlikely to occur in real life.

damages is not alone sufficient to justify legal responsibility, see
Blum & Kalven, Public Law Perspectives on a Private Law
Problem (1965), and this overarching principle must be taken
into account in deciding whether to expand the reach of *respondeat superior.*

A policy analysis thus is not sufficient to justify this proposed
expansion of vicarious liability. This is not surprising since
respondeat superior, even within its traditional limits, rests not
so much on policy grounds consistent with the governing principles of tort law as in a deeply rooted sentiment that a business
enterprise cannot justly disclaim responsibility for accidents
which may fairly be said to be characteristic of its activities. It
is in this light that the inadequacy of the motive test becomes
apparent. Whatever may have been the case in the past, a doctrine
that would create such drastically different consequences for the
actions of the drunken boatswain in *Nelson* and those of the
drunken seaman here reflects a wholly unrealistic attitude
toward the risks characteristically attendant upon the operation
of a ship. We concur in the statement of Mr. Justice Rutledge in
a case involving violence injuring a fellow-worker, in this instance
in the context of workmen's compensation:

> "Men do not discard their personal qualities when they go to
> work. Into the job they carry their intelligence, skill, habits of
> care and rectitude. Just as inevitably they take along also their
> tendencies to carelessness and camaraderie, as well as emo-
> tional make-up. In bringing men together, work brings these
> qualities together, causes frictions between them, creates oc-
> casions for lapses into carelessness, and for fun-making and
> emotional flare-up. . . . These expressions of human nature
> are incidents inseparable from working together. They involve
> risks of injury and these risks are inherent in the working
> environment."

. . .

Put another way, Lane's conduct was not so "unforeseeable" as
to make it unfair to charge the Government with responsibility.
We agree with a leading treatise that "what is reasonably foreseeable in this context [of *respondeat superior*] . . . is quite a
different thing from the foreseeably unreasonable risk of harm
that spells negligence. . . . The foresight that should impel the
prudent man to take precautions is not the same measure as that
by which he should perceive the harm likely to flow from his
long-run activity in spite of all reasonable precautions on his own
part. The proper test here bears far more resemblance to that
which limits liability for workmen's compensation than to the

test for negligence. The employer should be held to expect risks, to the public also, which arise 'out of and in the course of' his employment of labor." 2 Harper & James, The Law of Torts 1377-78 (1956). See also Calabresi, Some Thoughts on Risk Distribution and the Law of Torts, 70 Yale L.J. 499, 544 (1961). Here it was foreseeable that crew members crossing the drydock might do damage, negligently or even intentionally, such as pushing a Bushey employee or kicking property into the water. Moreover, the proclivity of seamen to find solace for solitude by copious resort to the bottle while ashore has been noted in opinions too numerous to warrant citation. Once all this is granted, it is immaterial that Lane's precise action was not to be foreseen. . . .

Consequently, we can no longer accept our past decisions that have refused to move beyond the *Nelson* rule, since they do not accord with modern understanding as to when it is fair for an enterprise to disclaim the actions of its employees.

One can readily think of cases that fall on the other side of the line. If Lane had set fire to the bar where he had been imbibing or had caused an accident on the street while returning to the drydock, the Government would not be liable; the activities of the "enterprise" do not reach into areas where the servant does not create risks different from those attendant on the activities of the community in general.

We agree with the district judge that if the seaman "upon returning to the drydock, recognized the Bushey security guard as his wife's lover and shot him," 276 F.Supp. at 530, vicarious liability would not follow; the incident would have related to the seaman's domestic life, not to his seafaring activity, and it would have been the most unlikely happenstance that the confrontation with the paramour occurred on a drydock rather than at the traditional spot. Here Lane had come within the closed-off area where his ship lay, to occupy a berth to which the Government insisted he have access, cf. Restatement, Agency 2d, § 267, and while his act is not readily explicable, at least it was not shown to be due entirely to facets of his personal life. The risk that seamen going and coming from the Tamaroa might cause damage to the drydock is enough to make it fair that the enterprise bear the loss. It is not a fatal objection that the rule we lay down lacks sharp contours; in the end, as Judge Andrews said in a related context, "it is all a question [of expediency,] . . . of fair judgment, always keeping in mind the fact that we endeavor to make a rule in each case that will be practical and in keeping with the general understanding of mankind."

Affirmed.

NOTES

1. Return for a moment to the variations posed in the notes immediately before this case. Assume you are the attorney for the drydock owner and are arguing for liability where the seaman was sober, or had quit earlier and turned the valves while drunk or sober. What langauge, if any, in the opinion would you use in presenting the case for your client?

2. In a thoughtful case note in 82 HARV. L. REV. 1568 (1969) the absolute spatial limitation set by the court under its "characteristic" risk formula for torts of off-duty employees is questioned. The author prefers a presumption against vicarious liability under such circumstances because such actions are "less likely to be predominantly related to the conditions of the employment," but the presumption could be rebutted if certain onshore conduct turned out to be a "characteristic" risk of the enterprise having a causal connection between the tort and the employment. The author also observes that the characteristic risk formula and the principle of fairness used by the court are difficult to fit into the doctrinal shoe of *respondeat superior*. Do you agree with this observation? What reasoning do you think underlies it?

3. Did the court reject Calabresi's allocation of resources analysis? Was Calabresi's thesis correctly described by the court? It is argued in the *Harvard* note that the rationale behind resource allocation thesis would not apply in the factual context of the *Bushey* case, at least, since the tortfeasor's victim was also a business organization, able to take safety measures and to spread costs. "The broad purposes purportedly served by respondeat superior might then be best served by refusing to impose vicarious liability and leaving losses where they lie. . . . If respondeat superior is simply a means of social engineering—not founded in notions of the employer's causation of or responsibility for the injury—the doctrine might be applied only when it best serves the purposes of cost-spreading and long-run injury prevention." (p. 1570.) Do you agree?

4. The bus driver and bartender hypotheticals raised at the beginning of this section are drawn from actual cases. *See* Sauter v. New York Tribune, 305 N.Y. 442, 113 N.E.2d 790 (1953), *noted in* 39 CORN. L. Q. 505 (1954), *and* Maddex v. Ricca, 258 F. Supp. 352 (D. Ariz. 1966), *noted in* 9 ARIZ. L. REV. 110 (1967). In both cases the plaintiff lost on the ground that the employee did not intend to serve, even in part, the interests of his employer. How would the court in the *Bushey* case have resolved these cases?

5. The vicarious liability of a principal for the intentional torts of his agents extends beyond personal injury and property damage to include liability for fraud and deceit. The law concerning fraud is intimately bound up with the authority or appearance of authority of the agent and the reasonable reliance of the injured party, however, and thus will be covered in Chapter 7.

6. Can an employer be held liable in punitive damages for the fraud, malice or gross negligence of his employees acting within their scope of employment? Should the answer to such question depend on whether the employer authorized or ratified the act? *See* Toole v. Richardson-Merrell, Inc., 251 Cal. App. 2d 689, 60 Cal. Rptr. 398, 29 A.L.R.3d 988 (1967) (upholding a $250,000 punitive damages award against defendant drug company for injuries caused by "MER/29," noting that there was ample evidence to show that high-level management knew of the wrong-doing—primarily falsification of data—of its employees). *Contra,* Roginsky v. Richardson-Merrell, Inc., 378 F.2d 832 (2d Cir. 1967). *See also* Note, *The Assessment of Punitive Damages Against an Entrepreneur for the Malicious Torts of his Employees,* 70 YALE L.J. 1296 (1961), noting two divergent lines of authority. One group of opinions permits assessment of punitive damages in any case where the employer would be liable for compensatory damages under *respondeat superior.* The other rule, applied in about an equal number of states, allows the imposition of punitive damages on the employer only if he or his responsible representatives were culpable, such as authorizing the tortious behavior. The notewriter urges the adoption of a third rule, allowing the imposition of punitive damages only against individuals, on any level of employment, who expressly or impliedly authorized or participated in the tortious behavior, and not against the employer.

7. Could an employer be held criminally liable for the crimes of his employees? It is not reasonable to argue that an innocent employer would be criminally liable for an aggravated assault of his employee, is it? But suppose the crime consisted of price-fixing? Or selling liquor in a tavern to a minor? Or selling short weight? With respect to the last example, *see* Ex parte Marley, 29 Cal. 2d 525, 175 P.2d 832 (1946) (owner, absent from the store at the time, was convicted under the short weight statute for the unauthorized actions of his employee and sentenced to 90 days in jail). *See also,* P. MECHEM, OUTLINES OF THE LAW OF AGENCY, §§ 407-411 (4th ed. 1952).

D. WRONGFUL ACTS IN THE "ORDINARY COURSE OF THE BUSINESS" OF A PARTNERSHIP

1. As noted in Chapter 1, the "ordinary course of the business" language comes from § 13 of the UPA and is directed toward a partner's vicarious liability for the torts of his partners. Vicarious liability of the partnership and of individual partners as principals for the torts of their employees is like that of any other employer, of course.

You would not be surprised, would you, to discover that the above language dealing with torts by partners is interpreted by the courts in a manner similar to the interpretation of "scope of employment"? Can you think of any reason, legitimate or otherwise, why it might be interpreted more narrowly? More broadly? Does the rationale behind vicarious liability for masters also underlie this aspect of the doctrine?

2. With respect to the questions raised above, the following passage from Iron v. Sauve, 27 Wash. 2d 562, 568, 179 P.2d 327, 330 (1947), is typical:

> " 'In truth, "the law as to partnership is undoubtedly a branch of the law of principal and agent; and it would tend to simplify and make more easy of solution the questions which arise on this subject, if this true principle were more constantly kept in view." Lord Wensleydale, in *Cox v. Hickman,* 8 House of Lords' Cases 268, . . . "All questions between partners are no more than illustrations of the same questions as between principal and agent." Parke, B., in *Beckham v. Drake,* 9 M. & W. 79, p. 98 . . . The real and ultimate question in all cases like the present is one of agency.' *Eastman v. Clark,* 53 N. H. 276, 289 [16 Am. Rep. 192].
>
> It is not enough for appellants to establish an agency relationship; it must be established that [the tortfeasor] was doing something in furtherance of the purpose for which the relationship was created. In other words, it must be within the scope of the partnership.

See generally, 1 R. ROWLEY, ROWLEY ON PARTNERSHIP § 13.1 (2d ed. 1960), describing specific torts and concluding in general that "the law of agency" applies. The term "scope of business" can be narrowly applied, however, as in Gwynn v. Duffield, 66 Iowa 708, 24 N.W. 523, 55 Am. Rep. 286 (1885), where a partner in a firm of druggists was held not liable for the negligence of his copartner in giving plaintiff a poison instead of the drug requested, on the ground that giving away medicine was not within the scope of the partnership business. *See also,* A. BROMBERG, CRANE AND BROMBERG ON PARTNERSHIP § 54 (1968).

PROBLEMS

1. Smith, a delivery man for the Jones Drug Company, while waiting for receipts to be signed at the warehouse of a customer, negligently flips his cigarette onto the floor, causing a fire. Is Jones Drug liable? Would your answer change if instead Smith, while driving on route with a delivery, had taken both hands off the wheel in order to light the cigarette and had caused an accident? For a discussion of these questions, *see* P. MECHEM, OUTLINES OF THE LAW OF AGENCY §§ 375-377 (4th ed. 1952) *and* 20 A.L.R.3d 893 (1968).

2. White, a truck driver for Ace Trucking Company, while on a direct route to a delivery, negligently parked his truck on the side of the road while coming to the aid of a stranded motorist. An accident results. Is Ace Trucking liable? Would your answer change if the motorist had offered to pay White for the assistance, and White had accepted?

3. A deliveryman, who was forbidden by his employer to pick up riders, did so anyway. While driving on his route, he causes an accident through his gross negligence, severely injuring the rider. Would you advise the rider that a suit against the driver's employer would have a good chance of success? Would it make any difference if the prohibition against riders was posted on the side of the truck? If so, why? In what manner, if at all, would it affect your response if the rider was a small child?

4. Suppose, in problem 3, above, that there was no employer rule against riders, but the injured rider was a member of the driver's family. Suppose further that the jurisdiction in which the accident took place still applied the intra-family immunity rule. What problems do you see in suing the employer? *See* 1 A.L.R.3d 677 (1965); W. SEAVEY, LAW OF AGENCY § 93, part A (1964); Schubert v. August Schubert Wagon Co., 249 N.Y. 253, 164 N.E. 42, 64 A.L.R. 293 (1928).

5. At 8 P.M. one evening, Moody, a Philadelphia police officer on duty at the time, entered the store of Fred Ashley. Ashley was seated in a swivel chair behind a small desk in the office portion of his store, to the right of the front door. His arms were folded across his chest and he was talking to his step-son. Moody entered the office, made a complete turn and faced Ashley while at the same time drawing his revolver. The gun discharged. A bullet struck Ashley in the head, killing him instantly.

Assess the impact, if any, the following facts might have on this case: Moody and Ashley had been friends for several years and on various occasions in the spirit of horse-play had engaged in mock "quick draw" contests in which each would pretend to draw his revolver and shoot the other. Ashley had never actually drawn his revolver; Moody had drawn his at least once in the dozen or so contests.

Could you, as counsel for Ashley's survivors, put together a successful case against the city of Philadelphia on *respondeat superior* grounds (assume that sovereign immunity does not apply)? How would you do so and what problems would you face? Assume the counsel for the city has cited to you a Pennsylvania case holding that a railroad was not liable as a matter of law to an injured child when one of its engineers, "solely in a spirit of mischief," discharged steam on the child, on the ground that the act was "solely a personal one of the engineer, outside the scope of his duty." What argument would you make in attempting to persuade the court not to apply this precedent? Are there any other factual inquiries you would want to make? *See* Frankel v. Moody, 393 F.2d 279 (3d Cir. 1968).

6.   Charles A. Tribbey was the bookkeeper and cashier of the White Oak Coal Company. His duties were to keep the books, take off balances, render bills and take care of the office. One day, while the general manager was gone, Tribbey noticed that the deliveries of coal to customers were falling far behind the daily schedule. He resolved to aid his employer and, leaving the office, drove a loaded truck in the yard off to deliver coal to several long term customers of the company. He had not driven a coal truck before and negligently caused an accident while on route to a customer's place of business. The person he injured has come to you for advice. Assume that Tribbey has insufficient assets to pay the judgment. Can a good case be made against White Oak Coal Company? What problems would you face?

A CONCLUDING QUESTION

This material essentially concludes our inquiry into questions of vicarious liability in tort under agency principles. Can you describe to your own satisfaction the paramount criterion for determining when one person or entity may be liable vicariously for the torts of another? Is it satisfactory? If you think it is not, what criterion for deciding the cases would you suggest?

Part III

*CONTRACTUAL ASPECTS OF
THE AGENCY RELATIONSHIP*

Chapter 6

THE UNDISCLOSED, PARTIALLY DISCLOSED AND DISCLOSED PRINCIPAL DISTINCTIONS; THE AGENT'S LIABILITY

The materials in this chapter deal with contractual rights and liabilities flowing from authorized transactions, for the most part. The problems created by unauthorized transactions are the subject of Chapter 7. The two exceptions to this are part B, ii of this chapter on the agent's warranty of authority, which is included here in order to centralize the coverage of the agent's liabilities arising from contractual matters, and the materials on misapplied payments and set-off on pages 152-154, *infra*.

A. CONTRACTUAL RIGHTS AND LIABILITIES OF THE PRINCIPAL

Assume that Mr. Jones, a wealthy individual who lives in Chicago, arranges with a resident of a resort community to have the resident purchase in his own name but actually on behalf of Jones substantial tracts of land in his community, such as a wealthy industrialist from Chicago is reported to have had done for him in Aspen, Colorado after World War II. Jones is an "undisclosed principal" under this arrangement. After a number of contracts have been made, Jones wants to step in and enforce them against the owners in his own name. Should he be able to do so? What, if anything, would give you pause before answering yes, assuming that no misrepresentations have taken place?

Would your answer change or be easier to reach if the agent had disclosed to the contracting parties that he was acting on behalf "of someone," but refused to disclose his principal's identity? The principal under this circumstance is referred to as a "partially disclosed principal," a term coined apparently by the Restatement of Agency, or as an "unidentified principal."

Would you have any problem with the initial question where the agent expressly disclosed that he was acting on behalf of Jones, the out-of-town principal?

Under which of the above situations, if any, would the agent personally be liable on the contract?

i. *Rights of the Undisclosed Principal*

Restatement of Agency § 302:

A person who makes a contract with an agent of an undisclosed principal, intended by the agent to be on account of his principal and within the power of such agent to bind his principal, is liable to the principal as if the principal himself had made the contract with him.

The Restatement states the following with respect to this in another but related section: "The rules with reference to undisclosed principals appear to violate one of the basic theories of contract." [§ 186] What theory?

SCRIMSHIRE v. ALDERTON
King's Bench Division
2 Strange 1182, 93 Eng. Rep. 1114 (1743)

Where goods are sold by a factor who has agreed to take the risk of the debts, the vendee is answerable for the amount to the owner, if he has received notice from him to pay him and not the factor, previous to his having paid the latter (1).

The plaintiff, who was a farmer in the isle of Ely, sent up oats to Bear-Key, consigned to one Hunt as his factor. The custom of the trade appeared to be, that formerly the factor had 4d. per quarter for selling them, and they gave immediate notice to the farmer of the name of the buyer, and the price: but this being inconvenient to farmers at a distance, it had for many years past been customary for the farmer to allow 2d. per quarter more, upon the factor's taking the risque of the debts: since which they had ceased to inform the farmers of the buyers. The goods in the present case were sold; but the factor failing, the plaintiff (before actual payment) gave notice to the defendant (the buyer) not to pay the factor, which he did notwithstanding: and thereupon this action was brought.

The Chief Justice was of opinion, that this new method had not deprived the farmer of his remedy against the buyer, provided there was no payment to the factor. And the only reason of advancing 2d. per quarter was, to have both at stake: and here being notice before actual payment, there could be no harm done. And therefore he directed the jury in favour of the plaintiff. They went out and found for the defendant; were sent out a second, and a third time to re-consider it, and still adhered to their verdict; and being asked man by man, they separately declared they found for the defendant. Upon this a new trial was moved for, and no cause being shewn was accordingly granted. And at the sittings after this term it came on again before a special jury; when the Chief Justice declared, that a factor's sale does by the general rule of law create a contract between the owner and buyer. But notwithstanding this, the jury found for the defendant; and being asked their reason, declared, that they thought from the circumstances no credit was given as between the owner and buyer, and that the latter was answerable to the factor only, and he only to the owner.

(1) Mr. J. Buller, in his Law of Nisi Prius, p. 130, seems to be of opinion with the jury, that the particular circumstances of this case discharged the operation of the general rule of law, "that the sale of the factor creates a contract between the owner and the buyer," for that from the agreement to take the risque of the debts upon him, the factor himself was to be considered as the debtor to the owner.

See also Darling-Singer Lumber Co. v. Commonwealth, 290 Mass. 488, 195 N.E. 723 (1935). In this case the defendant, a contractor, ordered a large amount of lumber from one A. C. Place, to be shipped from the west coast to defendant's job site. Place was in fact acting for the plaintiff lumber company, although he ran his own business and defendant thought he was dealing directly with Place. The lumber arrived with an invoice on the letterhead of plaintiff company accompanying the bill of lading. Also accompanying the invoice and bill of lading was a notice from a F. P. Gram Co., reading, "We enclose herewith duly assigned to us invoice and bill of lading covering cars containing lumber sold and shipped to you by Darling-Singer Lumber Company . . . We are entitled to the proceeds under this assignment and look to you for payment of the same. Please remit directly to us." On the invoice was typed what purported to be an assignment of the account by Darling-Singer Co. to F. P. Gram Co. Both companies were located in Portland, Oregon.

Defendant had never heard of either company. He paid Place in full and in good faith, having been told at the time he ordered the lumber that the lumber was being shipped from Place's western office in Portland or from his mill. He did not understand the legal significance of the documents mailed to him, and regarded Place as the only one with whom he had contracted and the only one to whom he owed any obligation of payment.

Place failed to remit to plaintiff. Thereafter F. P. Gram Co. reassigned the account to plaintiff and plaintiff sued defendant for the full contract price. Plaintiff prevailed against defendant.

a.   Parol Evidence Rule

What effect does the parol evidence rule, which does not allow variations from or additions to an integrated contract, have on this doctrine? The response of courts has been to submerge contract law in this instance and to allow rights and liabilities to be established between the third party and the undisclosed principal regardless of the absence of any reference to the principal in the contract, unless by its terms the contract excludes the principal as a party. There really was no choice about this once the undisclosed principal doctrine was accepted, was there? The parol evidence rule also is overridden in such cases where a partially disclosed principal is involved. *See* §§ 149 and 190 of the Restatement.

---

b.   Sealed Contracts

Suppose that a contract bears a seal. At common law this had certain definite legal consequences. The authority of an agent signing a sealed instrument had to be under seal. Also, the agent's principal could not sue or be sued unless his name appeared on the instrument. RESTATEMENT § 191. The latter rule affected the undisclosed principal doctrine, of course. A number of states have passed legislation abolishing the legal effect of the seal. *See* P. MECHEM, OUTLINES OF THE LAW OF AGENCY §§ 25, 318 (4th ed. 1952), *and* UNIFORM COMMERCIAL CODE § 2-203 (1962 Official Text) (abolishing the legal effect of seals insofar as contracts for sale of or offers to buy or sell goods are concerned) .

---

c.   Exceptions

The rule stated above in § 302 of the Restatement, like other legal rules, is not without its exceptions. Suppose, for example, that the undisclosed principal knows that the party he wants to contract with will not deal with him due to personal enmity. He therefore hires an agent to enter into the transaction on his behalf but with instructions not to disclose the fact that he is doing so. Can the undisclosed principal step in after the contract is made and enforce it? Would your answer vary if the undisclosed principal merely suspected that the third party would not deal with him personally? An example of this would be where the undisclosed principal and the other party are competitors, and the principal is afraid that the other party will not deal with him. The following case applies some of the law related to these questions.

KELLY ASPHALT BLOCK CO. v. BARBER ASPHALT PAVING CO.
Court of Appeals of New York
211 N.Y. 68, 105 N.E. 88 (1914)

APPEAL from a judgment of the Appellate Division of the Supreme Court in the second judicial department, entered November 6, 1912, affirming a judgment in favor of plaintiff entered upon a verdict.

The nature of the action and the facts, so far as material, are stated in the opinion.

CARDOZO, J. The plaintiff sues to recover damages for breach of an implied warranty. The contract was made between the defendant and one Booth. The plaintiff says that Booth was in truth its agent, and it sues as undisclosed principal. The question is whether it has the right to do so.

The general rule is not disputed. A contract not under seal, made in the name of an agent as ostensible principal, may be sued on by the real principal at the latter's election. The defendant says that we should establish an exception to that rule, where the identity of the principal has been concealed because of the belief that, if it were disclosed, the contract would not be made. We are asked to say that the reality of the defendant's consent is thereby destroyed, and the contract vitiated for mistake.

The plaintiff and the defendant were competitors in business. The plaintiff's president suspected that the defendant might refuse to name him a price. The suspicion was not based upon any previous refusal, for there had been none; it had no other origin than their relation as competitors. Because of this doubt the plaintiff availed itself of the services of Booth, who, though interested to the defendant's knowledge in the plaintiff's business, was also engaged in a like business for another corporation. Booth asked the defendant for a price and received a quotation, and the asphalt blocks required for the plaintiff's pavement were ordered in his name. The order was accepted by the defendant, the blocks were delivered, and payment was made by Booth with money furnished by the plaintiff. The paving blocks were unmerchantable, and the defendant, retaining the price, contests its liability for damages on the ground that if it had known that the plaintiff was the principal, it would have refused to make the sale.

We are satisfied that upon the facts before us the defense cannot prevail. A contract involves a meeting of the minds of the contracting parties. If "one of the supposed parties is wanting," there is an absence of "one of the formal constituents of a legal transaction." (Rodliff v. Dallinger, 141 Mass. 1, 6.) In such a

situation there is no contract. A number of cases are reported
where A has ordered merchandise of B, and C has surreptitiously
filled the order. The question has been much discussed whether
C, having thrust himself without consent into the position of a
creditor, is entitled to recover the value of his wares. That
question is not before us, and we express no opinion concerning
it. We state it merely to accentuate the distinction between the
cases which involve it and the case at hand. Neither of the
supposed parties was wanting in this case. The apparent meeting of the minds between determinate contracting parties was
not unreal or illusory. The defendant was contracting with the
precise person with whom it intended to contract. It was contracting with Booth. It gained whatever benefit it may have
contemplated from his character and substance. An agent who
contracts in his own name for an undisclosed principal does not
cease to be a party because of his agency. Indeed, such an agent,
having made himself personally liable, may enforce the contract
though the principal has renounced it. As between himself and
the other party, he is liable as principal to the same extent as
if he had not been acting for another. It is impossible in such
circumstances to hold that the contract collapses for want of parties to sustain it. The contractual tie cannot exist where there are
not persons to be bound, but here persons were bound, and those
the very persons intended. If Booth had given the order in his
own right and for his own benefit, but with the expectation of
later assigning it to the plaintiff, that undisclosed expectation
would not have nullified the contract. His undisclosed intention
to act for a principal who was unknown to the defendant, was
equally ineffective to destroy the contract in its inception.

If, therefore, the contract did not fail for want of parties to
sustain it, the unsuspected existence of an undisclosed principal
can supply no ground for the avoidance of a contract unless
fraud is proved. We must distinguish between mistake such as
we have been discussing, which renders the contract void
ab initio, because the contractual tie has never been completely formed, and fraud, which renders it voidable at the
election of the defrauded party. (Rodliff v. Dallinger, 141 Mass.
1, 6.) In the language of HOLMES, J., in the case cited: "Fraud
only becomes important, as such, when a sale or contract is
complete in its formal elements, and therefore valid unless
repudiated, but the right is claimed to rescind it." If one who
is in reality an agent denies his agency when questioned, and
falsely asserts that his principal has no interest in the transaction, the contract, it may be, becomes voidable, not because there
is a want of parties, but because it has been fraudulently pro-

cured. That was substantially the situation in Winchester v. Howard (97 Mass. 303). When such a case arises, we shall have to consider whether a misrepresentation of that kind is always so material as to justify rescission after the contract has been executed. But no such situation is disclosed in the case at hand. Booth made no misrepresentation to the defendant. He was not asked anything, nor did he say anything, about the plaintiff's interest in the transaction. Indeed, neither he nor the plaintiff's officers knew whether the defendant would refuse to deal with the plaintiff directly. They suspected hostility, but none had been expressed. The validity of the contract turns thus, according to the defendant, not on any overt act of either the plaintiff or its agent, but on the presence or absence of a mental state. We are asked to hold that a contract complete in form, becomes a nullity in fact because of a secret belief in the mind of the undisclosed principal that the disclosure of his name would be prejudicial to the completion of the bargain. We cannot go so far. It is unnecessary, therefore, to consider whether, even if fraud were shown, the defendant, after the contract was executed, could be permitted to rescind without restoring the difference between the price received for the defective blocks and their reasonable value. It is also unnecessary to analyze the evidence for the purpose of showing that the defendant, after notice of the plaintiff's interest in the transaction, continued to make delivery, and thereby waived the objection that the contract was invalid.

Other rulings complained of by the defendant have been considered, but no error has been found in them.

The judgment should be affirmed, with costs.

WILLARD BARTLETT, Ch. J., WERNER, CHASE, COLLIN, CUDDEBACK and HOGAN, JJ., concur.

Judgment affirmed.

NOTES

1. As indicated above, the law is clear that a third party is not bound if an agent falsely states that he is not acting for a principal and if the third party would not have dealt with the principal as a party to the contract (thereby making the misrepresentation material to the contract). RESTATEMENT § 304. The comments to § 304 would also apply this limitation to the situation where no express misrepresentation was made but the undisclosed principal and his agent knew that the third party would not deal with the principal and the agent failed to disclose the existence of the principal and, in addition, to such situation

where the agent was innocent. "A fraudulent principal cannot obtain rights by intentionally employing an innocent agent." *Id.*, Comment *a.* There also is authority stating that if the contract expressly refers to the agent as principal, or if the language of the contract indicates an intent to treat the agent as a sole contracting party, the undisclosed principal cannot enforce it in his name, or be held liable in such capacity. *See* §§ 150, 189 of the Restatement.

What is the effect of the law allowing assignments of contracts on this? Could the principal avoid these limitations on the undisclosed principal doctrine by having his agent contract directly with the third party and then assign the contract to him? See, with respect to some aspects of the law of assignments of contracts, 4 A. CORBIN, CONTRACTS §§ 866-870 (1951). As you read through this material, ask yourself in what respects, if any, the undisclosed principal doctrine is distinguishable from the law concerning assignments of contracts. A different way to pose this question is to ask yourself whether, if somehow the law recognizing the undisclosed principal were abolishd tomorrow, would it make any practical difference to whomever takes, or would like to take, advantage of it? See also, Comment *b* to § 304 of the Restatement, observing that the question posed at the beginning of this paragraph is outside of the scope of the Restatement.

2. Assume that the agent of Jones, the wealthy Chicagoan mentioned at the beginning of this chapter, transfers the land he has purchased for Jones to someone else. Can Jones assert any rights against that party? See § 307A of the Restatement.

BIRMINGHAM MATINEE CLUB v. McCARTY
Supreme Court of Alabama
152 Ala. 571, 44 So. 642 (1907)

Action by the Birmingham Matinee Club against M. F. McCarty to recover $5,000 as damages for the breach of an agreement entered into by him on Dec. 3, 1904, in substance as follows: Plaintiff sold to defendant for $16,000 cash property known as "Trotwood Park," located near East Lake, Ala., containing 100 acres, said sale being subject to an abstract and warranty deed of good title conveying the property to defendant unincumbered, and defendant agreed to buy said property at said price on said terms; and plaintiff alleges that, although it had complied with all the provisions of said contract on its part, defendant has failed to pay any part of said purchase money, except said sum of $500, which he paid on the 3d day of December, 1904. . . . The third count was further amended by inserting after the words "for the breach of an agreement entered into by him" where they occur in said count, the words, "with plaintiff in the name of W. C. Agee, who was agent and president of plaintiff's corporation."

. . .

It seems from the evidence that this trade was made by Mr. Agee, as president of the association, and others, with M. P. Messer, a real estate agent, who said that he thought he had a client who would buy it and asked the price of it; that some time afterwards Mr. Messer said he thought he had a man who would give $19,000 for the property, and a short time after that conversation Mr. Messer came back and said that his client would not give $19,000, but that, if he would take $15,500 cash, he could close the trade, and it was agreed to take it. It was then that Mr. Messer came up with a check from Mr. McCarty and that was the first time they knew Mr. McCarty as a party to the trade. The note or memorandum of sale is as follows:

"State of Alabama Jefferson County. This is to certify that I have this day sold to M. F. McCarty for $16,000 cash property known as 'Trotwood Park,' located near East Lake, Ala., containing 100 acres, and I herewith acknowledge receipt of $500, being part of purchase money to bind the sale, said sale being subject to an abstract and warranty deed of good title conveying the property to the purchaser unincumbered. (Signed) W. C. Agee.

"Accepted. (Signed) M. F. McCarty."

On motion of defendant this was excluded. There was judgment for defendant, and plaintiff appeals.

McCLELLAN, J.—On this appeal, in our view, the vital and decisive question is: May an undisclosed principal enforce, in breach of performance, a contract made by an agent fully authorized thereunto, in his own name, for the sale to and purchase by another of lands of the principal wherein it is stipulated that the ostensible seller (the agent in reality) will grant by warranty deed an unincumbered title? As a general rule, the principal, though undisclosed, is invested by the authorized act of the agent, for the benefit and advantage of the principal, with every right and burdened with every liability arising out of or pertaining to the contract as perfectly as if the principal had, in his own name and person, made the contract.—Mechem on Agency, § 768 et seq; Story on Agency, §§ 160-162. But this rule is subject to an important exception, viz., that if the contract involves elements of personal trust and confidence, as a consideration moving from the agent (of the undisclosed principal), contracting in his own name, to the other party to the contract, the principal, while it remains executory, cannot, against the resistance of the other party, enforce it, either to compel performance by the other party or in damages for a breach.—Mechem on Agency, § 770; Boston Ice Co. v. Potter, 25 Am. Rep. 9, 123 Mass. 28; . . . Story's Agency, §§ 160, et seq. and notes. The reason for this exception is manifest. If the party contracting without knowledge of the agency, were bound to take the service or conveyance or property from the undisclosed principal, the well-recognized rule that one may determine for himself with whom he will deal, with whom he will contract would be directly infracted; and the elements of the contract reasonably attributable to personal confidence and trust, including the financial responsibility of the agent, with whom he alone deals as principal, would be stricken of force to which under all principles of substantial justice and right the relying party is entitled to the benefit. Of course, it follows that for a failure or refusal, by the party dealing with the agent, to perform the contract, which was in reality, but unknown to be, the undertaking of an undisclosed principal, and not the undertaking of the individual with whom made, the recalcitrant party, cannot be mulcted in damages by the developed principal.

Applying this principle to the case at bar, the appellant is without right to and cannot recover; and the judgment to that effect was well rendered. . . . The sum paid by the defendant was recoverable, the record affirmatively showing that the sum paid was received by the plaintiff. The ratification of the contract as urged, by the plaintiff wrought by the receipt of the sum paid by the defendant to Agee could not avail or compel the latter to accept the former as a *substitute* for Agee with whom he dealt and whose warranty of title, only, he engaged to take.

There is no reversible error in the record and the judgment is affirmed.

Affirmed.

Tyson, C. J., and Dowdell and Anderson, J.J., concurring.

NOTES

1. The court cited Boston Ice Co. v. Potter, 123 Mass. 28, 25 Am. Rep. 9 (1877), as support for the exception to the undisclosed principal doctrine discussed in the opinion. Briefly, the facts of that case were that the Boston Ice Company had fur-

nished defendant with ice at an earlier time but the defendant had become dissatisfied and terminated the contract, contracting instead with the Citizens' Ice Company. Thereafter Citizens' Ice sold its business to Boston Ice, which began delivering ice to the defendant without notifying him of the change of ownership. After delivering ice to defendant for one year, the Boston Ice Company sued him for the market price of the ice, which apparently was used by defendant without complaint. While noting that it was not called upon to determine what other remedy the plaintiff might have had, or what would be the rights of the parties if the ice were still in existence, the court held that an action on account for ice sold and delivered could not be maintained against defendant. The following language from the opinion has been quoted frequently since its publication, and apparently was the language which drew the attention of the court in the *Birmingham Matinee* case.

> A party has a right to select and determine with whom he will contract, and cannot have another person thrust upon him without his consent. It may be of importance to him who performs the contract, as when he contracts with another to paint a picture, or write a book, or furnish articles of a particular kind, or when he relies upon the character or qualities of an individual, or has, as in this case, reasons why he does not wish to deal with a particular party. In all these cases, as he may contract with whom he pleases, the sufficiency of his reasons for so doing cannot be inquired into. If the defendant, before receiving the ice, or during its delivery, had received notice of the change, and that the Citizens' Ice Company could no longer perform its contract with him, it would then have been his undoubted right to have rescinded the contract and to decline to have it executed by the plaintiff. But this he was unable to do, because the plaintiff failed to inform him of that which he had a right to know. If he had received notice and continued to take the ice as delivered, a contract would be implied.

Regardless of your reaction to the substantive merit of the decision in the *Boston Ice* case, ask yourself in what respect, if at all, the case relates to the problems presently before us.

2. The court in *Birmingham Matinee* observes that an undisclosed principal cannot enforce a contract if it involves elements of personal trust and confidence. Is it necessary for the third party to prove that he actually relied on such elements when contracting with the agent? Do you see any language directed to this point in the opinion of the court? What do you think the rule should be?

3. Can you think of a different way the undisclosed principal in the *Birmingham Matinee* case could have handled—or tried to handle—the transfer once the deal was struck by the agent?

---

ii. *Liabilities of the Undisclosed Principal*

It is clear that in the typical situation an undisclosed principal can sue the party contracting with his agent. Should the third party be able to sue the principal, if he discovers his existence? One might ask why he should be able to if he was satisfied, as was obviously the case, with the name and credit of the agent at the time he entered into the contract. Since he did so enter the contract, would failure to allow him to sue the principal result in any loss or upset of his reasonable expectations?

RESTATEMENT OF AGENCY § 186 states the general rule, which is that the principal is bound by the contract and can be sued by the party contracting with his agent. The theory behind this rule, as stated in Comment *a* to § 186, is that since the principal "is the one who initiated the activities of the agent and has a right to control them" he is liable "in accordance with the ordinary principles of agency."* In other words, the principal becomes a party to the contract by operation of agency law, not via the ordinary principles of the law of contracts.

An example of the above concept is supplied by illustration three of § 186, which reads as follows: "P writes to A authorizing him to buy Blackacre. A does not reply, but contracts to buy Blackacre in his own name. Whether P is liable on the contract depends upon whether A intended to act for himself or for P." Do you understand the rationale which underlies this illustration? Does it make sense to you?

Remedies of the Third Party

The third party has the customary contractual remedies against the agent, of course. The agent signed the agreement as sole contracting party. The fact that, unknown to the third party, he was acting on behalf of an undisclosed principal does not somehow reduce or destroy his contractual liability. And, as noted above, the undisclosed principal is liable to the third party in accordance with (and as a result of) principles of agency law.

---

*This is clearly the case when actually authorized contracts have been entered into. The complex problems created when the agent departs from his authority are covered primarily in Chapter 7 *infra*.

Can the third person under this circumstance sue both the principal and the agent in one suit? If so, can he get judgments against both? And if so, can he execute against the assets of either or both until he receives full satisfaction for the amount owing him? (No one contends that he should get more than that, of course.) Suppose he sues the agent first, obtains judgment, fails to get satisfaction, and then discovers the principal. Does he still have a valid cause of action against the principal? Can he sue the principal first, change his mind and thereafter successfully sue the agent?

Comment *a* to § 186 of the Restatement states the following with respect to the above questions:

> The American decisions are illogical, but more equitable [than the English decisions which hold that the third person has only one right which can be exercised in the alternative against the principal or the agent, but not against both, regardless of his knowledge. *Ed.*], in holding that if the third person with knowledge of the facts obtains judgment against either one, he cannot have judgment against the other, although if he obtains judgment against the agent with no knowledge of the identity of the principal, he can later get judgment against the principal. Neither the American nor English courts give reasons, aside from authority, why the third person should not have a right to two judgments, one based on the agreement itself, the other based on the contract created by law upon the agreement.

The American rule thus does not allow the third party to sue both the agent and his principal, obtain judgments against them, and execute on the judgments until he receives satisfaction. Although it is possible procedurally for him to join both the agent and the principal in his suit, he is forced to choose from whom he wishes to obtain judgment. Why should this be so when the law has created for him a right to proceed directly against the undisclosed principal, in addition to his contractual rights against the agent?

Section 210 of the Restatement, Comment *b*, notes that the hardship created by the above rule is ameliorated in several respects. In some states judgment can be entered against both defendants unless they move during the proceedings to require the third party to elect. They are otherwise held to have waived their right to object to the judgments. Also, "if the agent is entitled to exoneration or indemnity from the principal,* the

---

* See W. SEAVEY, LAW OF AGENCY § 168, at 265-70 (1964), discussing the agent's right to exoneration and indemnity and observing that, subject to

defendant is entitled to reach this asset of the agent as in the
other situations in which a defendant is a secondary obligor."

---

iii.   *Payment and Set-off*

a.   Payment By the Third Party

Suppose the third party pays an agent the amount owed under
a contract and the agent fails to remit to his undisclosed principal, who at this stage remains unknown to the third party. Can
the principal successfully sue the third party for the amount he
should have received? There is no doubt about the answer to this
question, at least if the agent was authorized to conceal the
existence of his principal, is there?

---

b.   Payment To the Third Party

Suppose a payment is owed to the third party under a contract entered into by an agent acting for an undisclosed principal.
The principal gives to the agent the amount necessary to make
the payment, and the agent fails to transmit it to the third party.
Can the third party, upon discovering the principal, thereafter
successfully sue him for the amount owing?

Section 208 of the Restatement states with respect to this
problem:

> An undisclosed principal is not discharged from liability to
> the other party to a transaction conducted by an agent by
> payment to, or settlement of accounts with, the agent, unless
> he does so in reasonable reliance upon conduct of the other
> party which is not induced by the agent's misrepresentations
> and which indicates that the agent has settled the account.

This makes sense, doesn't it? Suppose, however, that the undisclosed principal had authorized his agent to buy only for cash,
and supplied him with the cash in advance, and then the agent
had bought on credit. Should the principal be liable under this
circumstance? See RESTATEMENT § 194, Comment *c*, which says
no. Can you support this position?

[handwritten margin note: 3rd party is relying on agent's credit rating + not the principal]

---

their agreement, ". . . a principal has a duty to indemnify an agent for authorized payments or liabilities incurred because of authorized and lawful
acts and transactions, for losses suffered because of the principal's failure
to perform his duties, and for the value of benefits conferred upon him un-
officiously by the agent." *Id.* at 265.

And with respect to the point first raised above, can a rational distinction be drawn between payments by the principal to the agent after the contract is made but before the third party knows of the principal, and payments after he knows of the principal? The Reporter's Notes to § 208 acknowledge that the cases involving the finality of payment by the undisclosed principal to his agent are in conflict and that a number of cases protect the principal even in the absence of reliance upon the conduct of the other party. The Note justifies the Restatement position in the following language:

> The result to be reached is not clear cut. On the one hand it may be said that the third person gets more than he has reason to expect if allowed to hold the principal, since he relied exclusively upon the credit of the agent, and that it is rather extraordinary to hold the undisclosed principal, since he is not in fact a contracting party. This is true, but the whole theory of agency supports the doctrine of undisclosed principal. He is the initiator. He is the one who trusts the agent and if he has authorized the agent to purchase goods he must know that he is responsible for purchases so that, unless the rules are changed in his favor, he cannot escape liability by paying his own man. It is true that the third person gets the liability of a person of whom he knew nothing, but his claim against the agent is less valuable than he had reason to believe. An agent receiving support from the principal is a different kind of person from an independent trader who by hypothesis the third person believes to be the owner of the business. Further, the principal has ample means to protect himself. He can demand evidence from his agent that payment has been made and it is not unfair that he should lose if he relies solely upon the unsupported statement of his own fiduciary. The other party should not lose because the principal has chosen to rely upon his agent's honesty rather than upon his own investigation.

---

c. Set-Off

At first glance, it would seem clear that the third party should be able to set-off against the undisclosed principal the claims that he has against the agent. He would reasonably expect such to be the case when he dealt with the agent and, indeed, the factor of the availability of set-off may have induced him to contract with the agent in the first place by, for example, reducing the amount of cash he would have to put into the purchase. (Would it change things if the third party had loaned money or sold goods to the agent *after* the original contract where he had bought on credit?) Section 306 of the Restatement contains an interesting subtlety on this point, however:

§ 306. Rights Between Other Party and Agent.

(1) If the agent has been authorized to conceal the existence of the principal, the liability to an undisclosed principal of a person dealing with the agent within his power to bind the principal is diminished by any claim which such person may have against the agent at the time of making the contract and until the existence of the principal becomes known to him, if he could set off such claim in an action against the agent.

(2) If the agent is authorized only to contract in the principal's name, the other party does not have set-off for a claim due him from the agent unless the agent has been entrusted with the possession of chattels which he disposes of as directed or unless the principal has otherwise misled the third person into extending credit to the agent.

Can you rationalize this distinction? *See* P. Mechem, Outlines of the Law of Agency §§ 177-83 (4th ed. 1952).

B. LIABILITY OF THE AGENT

i. *On the Contract*

Is an agent who acts on behalf of a partially disclosed principal in negotiating a contract and who signs the contract in his (the agent's) name liable on the contract? *See* § 321 of the Restatement, stating yes. Is the partially disclosed principal a party to the contract? Section 147 of the Restatement says yes. If the third party obtains judgment against one of the two parties to the contract knowing of the existence of both, is he thereafter barred from suing the other party, as in the undisclosed principal situation? Section 336 of the Restatement contains a confusing discussion of this question. The section states that generally an agent is not relieved from liability by the fact that the third party gets a judgment against his principal. The other party "has the same opportunity to select his debtors as where the principal is wholly disclosed." A judgment against one party does destroy the cause of action against the other, says the Restatement, if they are "joint contractors," but does not if they are "joint and several contractors." No attempt is made to define or further develop these terms, other than by a reference to § 119 of the

Restatement of Contracts, and four sections of the Restatement of Judgments.

The questions above have assumed that the agent understood that he was to be a party to the contract. Suppose, however, that such is not the case, and the agent has no desire whatsoever to be personally liable on the transaction. Suppose further that he signs the contract "A, agent," without setting forth the name of the principal, thinking that the indication of agency alone plus the clear oral understanding of the parties would be enough. Are you able to advise him that such a signature is safe? Or suppose an agent acting on behalf of a business with a trade name signs merely the trade name. Does he run any risks in doing so? What form of signature for the agent should be specified to protect him? Does it make any difference whether he's representing a disclosed or a partially disclosed principal?

SACO DAIRY CO. v. NORTON

Supreme Court of Maine

140 Maine 204, 35 A.2d 857, 150 A.L.R. 1299 (1944)

CHAPMAN, J. The above cause comes to this Court on exceptions by the defendant to the findings of the Justice of the Superior Court sitting without a jury.

The case was submitted to the Justice upon an agreed statement set forth in the bill of exceptions as follows:

"The plaintiff, Saco Dairy Company, is a Maine corporation engaged in the delivery of dairy products. The defendant, Thompson Norton, during the years 1941 and 1942, was manager of a summer hotel at Kennebunkport known as Breakwater Court. Breakwater Court is a large hotel containing about 150 rooms. It was owned during 1941 and 1942 by Kate F. Norton, the defendant's mother, in her individual right. During the summer of 1941 the plaintiff, through one of its officers Gordon F. Ilsley, had a number of interviews with the defendant and as a result sold a substantial amount of dairy products for use in the hotel. At no time was there any discussion between Ilsley and the defendant as to who owned Breakwater Court and Ilsley never charged defendant with personal liability. All bills were rendered by the plaintiff in the name Breakwater Court and the total bill for 1941 was paid by a check signed Kate F. Norton by R. T. Norton, Atty. During 1942 more dairy products were sold to the hotel and billed to Breakwater Court as before. No discussion was had between any representatives of the plaintiff and the defendant as to who was owner of Breakwater Court. The bills for 1942 were not paid and are the subject of this suit. Kate F. Norton was not at any time during the events described above, registered as owner of Breakwater Court as required by R. S. Chapter 44, Section 5."

We are justified in assuming from the treatment of the subject in the respective briefs that the ownership of the hotel by the defendant's mother, as set forth in the agreed statement, included proprietorship of the business conducted therein.

The sole issue raised between the parties was whether the agency of the defendant was disclosed to the plaintiff. It was not in dispute that the goods were purchased by the defendant for the benefit of a third party, but the plaintiff claims that no disclosure of his agency was made by the defendant at the time of the transaction. The presiding Justice found for the plaintiff.

The defendant contends that "the fact that the particular entity of a trade name is unknown, i.e., whether it is a corporation, partnership or individual does not justify the application of the doctrine of undisclosed principal." In other words, that the use of the name "Breakwater Court" in the purchase of the supplies was a sufficient disclosure of agency by the defendant to avoid personal liability for the payment thereof.

If an agent who negotiates a contract in behalf of his principal would avoid personal liability, the burden is upon him to disclose his agency to the other contracting party. And his disclosure must include not only the fact that he is an agent, but also the identity of his principal. Amans v. Campbell, 70 Minn., 493, 73 N. W., 506, 68 Am. St. Rep., 547; Ye Seng Co. v. Corbitt and Macleay, 9 Fed., 423; Meyer, et al. v. Barker, 6 Binn. (Pa.) 228; Cobb v. Knapp, 71 N. Y., 348, 27 Am. Rep., 51; Nelson v. Andrews, 44 N. Y. S., 384; Danforth and Carter v. Timmerman, 65 S. C., 259, 43 S. E., 678; Kelly v. Guess, 157 Miss., 157, 127 So., 274.

The fact that a contract is negotiated by an agent, under a trade name, is not of itself a sufficient disclosure of his agency. In the *Amans* v. *Campbell* case, one Campbell, who was the manager of a business belonging to his wife, in making a contract in relation to the business, signed "Campbell & Co." without indicating in any way that he did so as agent. It was held that the mere use of the name "Campbell & Co." did not amount to a disclosure of his agency for his wife, Delia Campbell, doing business under the name of "Campbell & Co."

In *Ye Seng Co.* v. *Corbitt and Macleay,* the defendants executed a contract as "Agent for owners of the American Bark Garibaldi of Portland, Oregon." It was held that the identity of the principal was not disclosed.

In *Meyer, et al.* v. *Barker,* the defendant executed a charter party as "Agent for and in behalf of the American Ship Diana, Samuel Holmes, Master." It was held that this was not a disclosure of the principal.

In *Nelson* v. *Andrews,* it was held that the use of the name "Bradford Estate" was not a disclosure of the identity of the principal.

In *Cobb* v. *Knapp,* it was held that the use of the name "Blissville Distillery" was not conclusive as a disclosure of the principal. The Court in that case said: "It is not sufficient that the seller may have the means of ascertaining the name of the principal. If so, the neglect to inquire might be deemed sufficient. He must have actual knowledge. There is no hardship in the rule of liability against agents. They always have it in their own power to relieve themselves, and when they do not, it must be presumed that they intend to be liable."

While the facts set forth in the cases enumerated are not identical with those of the instant case, each of those cases maintains the principle that the use of a trade name is not in itself a sufficient disclosure.

The fact that the defendant was operating the business of a hotel under the name of "Breakwater Court" was at least as consistent with the fact that he was the proprietor as that he was the manager for another. It is common knowledge that a business may be conducted in either of these ways.

Whether a disclosure of agency has been made depends upon the facts and circumstances surrounding the transaction, and, unless only one inference can legally be drawn from the facts, the question is to be decided upon the judgment of the trier of facts, which in this case was the presiding Justice. . . .

It is not to be questioned that a trade name may be used under such circumstances that agency will be sufficiently disclosed, and counsel for the defendant suggests transactions with attendant circumstances that would have a tendency to impart knowledge of agency, but in such case a question of fact would be raised which would be determined by the fact-finding tribunal. Counsel also cites the case of Hess v. Kennedy, 171 N. Y. S. 51, in which it was held that the failure of a clerk or superintendent in a retail clothing store to disclose to a customer that she was not the proprietor, did not render her liable for the price of a garment returned. The decision in no manner disaffirms the principles that we apply in the instant case. The conclusion arrived at in the cited case necessarily resulted from the universally recognized limitations of authority and responsibility of sales clerks in a shop that invites the public to become its customers with the intent on the part of both shop and customer that they will be responsible, each to the other, for the fulfillment of their respective obligations.

The defendant further claims that by reason of the payment of goods furnished during the previous year by a check signed "Kate F. Norton, by R. T. Norton, Atty." the plaintiff knew of the agency and identity of the principal. This was not, as a matter of law, a disclosure of the agency, nor was it evidence of such probative force that the Justice was bound to consider it conclusive of itself or in connection with other facts submitted. The statement of facts does not disclose that the check came to the knowledge of the official who negotiated the sale of the supplies to the defendant, nor is it disclosed that it ever came to the attention of any official or employee of the plaintiff corporation, the knowledge of whom would bind the corporation. It might well be that the check was received in such routine manner that it had little or no significance on the question of knowledge of the plaintiff. In Baldwin, et al. v. Leonard, 39 Vt., 260, 94 Am. Dec., 324, a sale was made by a partnership to an agent whose agency was known by one partner, but not by the one making the sale. It was held that the partnership was not chargeable with knowledge of the agency. Nor would use of such a check be at all conclusive of proprietorship of "Kate F. Norton." It is not uncommon for a person to have a power of attorney to draw upon funds for his own benefit and for purposes in which the owner of the deposit has no interest. It would be entirely consistent with the loaning of money to be drawn as needed by the loanee in carrying on his own business.

The use of the name "Breakwater Court" was not, as a matter of law, a disclosure of the agency of the defendant, and it cannot be said that upon all of the facts presented the Justice was not warranted in finding that there was no such disclosure. The entry must be

Exceptions overruled.

NOTES

1. Would it make any difference in the *Saco Dairy Co.* case if the true ownership of Breakwater Court was ascertainable by

checking public records? (The facts in the opinion indicate that Maine had adopted a statute requiring businesses operating under an assumed or fictitious name to designate their ownership by filing a certificate in a public office; many jurisdictions do have such a statute.) Does the answer to this question depend on the agent's conduct or lack of conduct at the time of signing?

2. As a variant on the above, suppose the agent signed in a manner clearly indicating his agency status ("Transworld Marine Transport Corp., As Agents for Owners of the good ship Theotokos") but the signature left the identity of the principal undisclosed. Again, assume that the identity of the principal can be discovered through public registration procedures. Is the agent nevertheless personally liable on the contract? Courts have split on this. One line of authority is indicated by some of the cases cited in the above opinion and is also reflected in the case of Mayer v. Buchanan, 50 A.2d 595 (D.C. Mun. App. 1946), where a rental agent signed a lease "A, as agent for the owner only." The agent tried to avoid personal liability for collecting rent in excess of rent control ceilings by arguing that the identity of the owner was a matter of public record under the address of the building. The court held the agent liable. The other line of authority is reflected in Instituto Cubano v. The S. S. Theotokos, 155 F. Supp. 945 (S.D.N.Y. 1957), involving the "Transworld Marine" signature noted above. The court relied on the fact that the name of the owner of the ship could be learned by checking a Shipping Index. With which line of authority do you agree? *See* § 4, comment *f* of the Restatement; 2 S. WILLISTON, CONTRACTS § 288 (3d ed. 1959).

3. With respect to the question raised above immediately before the *Saco Dairy Co.* case where *A* signed "A, Agent," and also involved above in note 2, can the agent introduce parol evidence to show that the parties did not intend him to be bound personally? *See* § 323 of the Restatement, stating yes, on the ground that the contract is ambiguous. (It is not clear whether the Restatement requires that the identity of the principal must have been disclosed in the bargaining process.) As you know from the above material, however, there is authority holding the agent personally liable under this form of signature. The equitable remedy of reformation of the contract, assuming the contract departs from the understanding of both parties, should also be kept in mind.

4. The questions involving the form of signatures also are of major importance in the laws involving negotiable instruments. See the following excerpt from the UNIFORM COMMERCIAL CODE

§ 3-403 (1962 Official Text) for a description of the standards set forth in Article 3 of the Code.

Section 3—403. Signature by Authorized Representative.

(1) A signature may be made by an agent or other representative, and his authority to make it may be established as in other cases of representation. No particular form of appointment is necessary to establish such authority.

(2) An authorized representative who signs his own name to an instrument

    (a) is personally obligated if the instrument neither names the person represented nor shows that the representative signed in a representative capacity;

    (b) except as otherwise established between the immediate parties, is personally obligated if the instrument names the person represented but does not show that the representative signed in a representative capacity, or if the instrument does not name the person represented but does show that the representative signed in a representative capacity.

(3) Except as otherwise established the name of an organization preceded or followed by the name and office of an authorized individual is a signature made in a representative capacity.

Comment

Prior Uniform Statutory Provision: Sections 19, 20 and 21, Uniform Negotiable Instruments Law.

Changes: Combined and reworded; original Section 21 omitted.

Purposes of Changes:

1. The definition of "representative" in this Act (Section 1-201) includes an officer of a corporation or association, a trustee, an executor or administrator of an estate, or any person empowered to act for another. It is not intended to mean that a trust or an estate is necessarily a legal entity with the capacity to issue negotiable instruments, but merely that if it can issue them they may be signed by the representative.

The power to sign for another may be an express authority, or it may be implied in law or in fact, or it may rest merely upon apparent authority. It may be established as in other cases of representation, and when relevant parol evidence is admissible to prove or to deny it.

2.   Subsection (2) applies only to the signature of a representative whose authority to sign for another is established. If he is not authorized his signature has the effect of an unauthorized signature (Section 3-404). Even though he is authorized the principal is not liable on the instrument, under the provisions (Section 3-401) relating to signatures, unless the instrument names him and clearly shows that the signature is made on his behalf.

3.   Assuming that Peter Pringle is a principal and Arthur Adams is his agent, an instrument might, for example, bear the following signatures affixed by the agent—

   (a)   "Peter Pringle", or
   (b)   "Arthur Adams", or
   (c)   "Peter Pringle by Arthur Adams, Agent", or
   (d)   "Arthur Adams, Agent", or
   (e)   "Peter Pringle Arthur Adams", or
   *(f)   "Peter Pringle Corporation Arthur Adams".

A signature in form (a) does not bind Adams if authorized (Sections 3-401 and 3-404).

A signature as in (b) personally obligates the agent and parol evidence is inadmissible under subsection (2) (a) to disestablish his obligation.

The unambiguous way to make the representation clear is to sign as in (c). Any other definite indication is sufficient, as where the instrument reads "Peter Pringle promises to pay" and it is signed "Arthur Adams, Agent." Adams is not bound if he is authorized (Section 3-404).

Subsection 2(b) adopts the New York (minority) rule of Megowan v. Peterson, 173 N.Y. 1 (1902), in such a case as (d); and adopts the majority rule in such a case as (e). In both cases the section admits parol evidence in litigation between the immediate parties to prove signature by the agent in his representative capacity. Case (f) is subject to the same rule.*

4.   The original Section 21, covering signatures by "procuration," is omitted. It was based on English practice under which the words "per procuration" added to any signature are under-

---

* Clause (f) was deleted in the 1966 amendments to the 1962 Official Text of the *Code*. Apparently this recognizes that Adams will be allowed to introduce parol evidence to prove that his signature was in a representative capacity in litigation both between the immediate parties and in litigation brought by a subsequent holder of the instrument. The reason for this change apparently is that it is recognized that corporations can only act through agents and the customary corporate signature is made by setting forth the name of the corporation followed by the signature of its authorized representative; hence even a stranger to the note would understand that Adams is probably signing in a representative capacity.

stood to mean that the signer is acting under a power of attorney which the holder is free to examine. The holder is thus put on notice of the limited authority, and there can be no apparent authority extending beyond the power of attorney. This meaning of "per procuration" is almost unknown in the United States, and the words are understood by the ordinary banker or attorney to be merely the equivalent of "by." The omission is not intended to suggest that a signature "by procuration" can no longer have the effect which it had under the original Section 21, in any case where a party chooses to use the expression.

---

ii. *The Agent's Warranty of Authority*

This brief section focuses on the liability of the agent when the third party, who contracted in reliance on the agent's authority to bind his principal, is unable to hold the principal liable because the agent was unauthorized to make the contract. The liability of the agent in such circumstance has never been in doubt, although the theoretical basis for it has varied at different times and in different jurisdictions.

P. MECHEM, OUTLINES OF AGENCY §§ 322-31 (4th ed. 1952) states that the early cases held the agent liable as a party to the contract. Another basis of liability, made by some courts in recognition that it was illogical to hold the agent on a promise he never made, is in tort for misrepresentation. This works until the situation arises where the agent makes an innocent misstatement as to his authority, raising problems as to the vaguely defined limits of the tort of misrepresentation. As a result, most jurisdictions have adopted the implied warranty of authority theory, apparently first set forth in Collen v. Wright, 8 E. & B. 647, 120 Eng. Rep. 241 (Ex. 1857), where an agent in good faith made an agreement with plaintiff to execute a 12-year lease on behalf of his principal. His authority did not extend to executing that long a lease, and he was held liable to the plaintiff. J. Willes of the court stated in part, "[The agent's] moral innocence, so far as the person whom he has induced to contract is concerned, in no way aids such person or alleviates the inconvenience and damage which he sustains." This view is adopted by RESTATEMENT § 329.

Such liability does not come into effect where the third party knows or has reason to know that the agent lacks authority, of course. Also an agent could avoid the liability by expressly disclaiming it or by fully laying all the facts concerning his authority before the other party and letting him decide for himself.

The agent does not, in the absence of an express agreement, warrant his principal's honesty or solvency. Suppose, however, the principal is nonexistent, such as a corporation not fully organized, although the agent thought it was, or a social or political club which does not, to the ignorance of the agent, legally exist. MECHEM in §§ 327-330 notes that the agent is held liable if his principal is completely lacking in capacity, but not if the principal merely "lacks full contractual capacity," like an infant. *See also,* W. SEAVEY, LAW OF AGENCY § 124(b) (1964), supporting this distinction and explaining that one purporting to act as an agent normally represents that he has an existing principal.

The measure of damages for breach of the warranty is "the amount [by] which T would have been better off if the agent had been authorized." MECHEM at 226. This leaves the possibility that the third party may recover very little, or nothing, if the principal is insolvent or the contract would have been unenforceable anyway due, for example, to Statute of Frauds problems.

As another aspect of the agent's liability, see MECHEM §§ 332-342, and RESTATEMENT §§ 339-342, discussing the liability of the agent for money had and received. Generally, the agent is required to return funds received (or their equivalent) which were paid by the third party by mistake or as a result of the fraud of the principal, if he has not already transferred the funds to the principal. The defense of a good faith transfer to the principal would not be available to the agent if his principal was undisclosed.

PROBLEMS

1. As we have seen, § 302 of the Restatement states that the third party "is liable to the principal as if the principal himself had made the contract with him." Suppose that the Jones Corporation in Massachusetts sold some of its shares to a trust company. The shares were not registered under the "blue-sky" laws of Massachusetts and therefore were not available for sale and distribution to the public. The sale appeared proper on its face, since sales to trust companies are not within the provisions of the blue-sky law, the theory being that they are able to look out for themselves. It turns out, however, that the trust company was buying the shares for an elderly lady, Mrs. Means. Upon receiving the shares, Mrs. Means discovered they were unregistered and, tendering back the shares, sued the Jones Corporation to recover the purchase price plus interest.

Analyze the rights of the parties. *See* Howell v. First of Boston Int'l Corp., 309 Mass. 194, 34 N.E.2d 633 (1941).

2. *A* dealt with *T* on behalf of *P*, a fully disclosed principal. In signing the contract, which stated, "We have this day sold you 1000 tons of bar iron," *A* mistakenly signed only his name. Later *T* brought suit against *A* on the contract. *A* seeks to introduce evidence which clearly shows that the buying party was actually *P* and that *T* had known this at the time the contract was signed. Will he be able to? *See* Higgins v. Senior, 8 M. & W. 834, 151 Eng. Rep. 1278 (1841).

Suppose, on the above facts, that *T* instead is seeking to hold *P* to the contract. *T* attempts to introduce the same evidence that *A* sought to introduce. Will he be able to do so? *See* Calder v. Dobell, L. R. 6 C. P. 486 (1871).

3. Mary Hammon, desiring to engage in stock transactions but not in her own name, turned her 5000 shares of Ventura Corporation over to one John Cuniff on the understanding that he was to use the shares as margins on a trading account for her. Cuniff proceeded to do this, employing the partnership of Paine, Webber & Co. as his brokers. The identity of Mrs. Hammon was not disclosed to them, by her knowledge and consent. Cuniff already had five different accounts of his own with Paine, Webber, numbered consecutively from 1 to 5. This was unknown to Mrs. Hammon. The account carried for Mrs. Hammon was entered on the books of Paine, Webber as account number 6.

Several years later, on March 12, 1970, Mrs. Hammon directed Cuniff to deliver the stock and cash in her account to a certain bank in Boston for her. Cuniff was unable to comply fully because his account number 5 showed a debit balance and Paine, Webber claimed the right to apply the credit balance in number 6 to the debit balance in number 5. Cuniff did, however, obtain the $19,461 cash balance and 2500 shares of stock, which he transferred to the Boston bank. Paine, Webber retained 1,955 shares of stock.

On August 10, 1970, Mrs. Hammon sent notice of her interest in account number 6 by telegram to Paine, Webber. On August 12, 1970, upon receipt of the telegram, Paine, Webber transferred the 1,955 shares of stock and accumulated dividends from account 6 to account 5 and, on August 15, 1970, sold the stock and applied the proceeds to reduce the debit balance in number 5.

Mrs. Hammon has come to you in a state of outrage. Can you advise her that there is something you can do to help her? *See* Hammon v. Paine, 56 F.2d 19 (1st Cir. 1932).

4. A lease was entered into by J. E. Turner as lessee with Sarah Belove, the lessor. Turner was acting on behalf of an un-

disclosed principal. The lease contained a clause that it would be binding on "the heirs, assigns and legal representatives" of the parties, and that it could not be assigned or transferred by the lessee without the written consent of the lessor. The lease did not purport to be binding on "successors."

A fire destroyed the building during the term of the lease. At this stage The Heart of America Lumber Company appeared and, as undisclosed principal, sued the lessor for breach of a covenant to repair. Could the lessor successfully assert a defense against the Lumber Company, other than a defense based on interpretation of the repair clause? If so, how would you evaluate the defense?

Would it affect your analysis if the lease contained an endorsement by the Lumber Company guaranteeing "the performance by J. E. Turner of each and all of the terms, conditions and provisions in said lease contained, including the prompt payment of the monthly rental therein provided," and the endorsement was signed on behalf of the Company by J. E. Turner, Treasurer? If so, why?

5. A bank foreclosed its mortgage on a theatre and placed the title to the building in a nominee, the George Brothers Realty Company. The bank instructed George Brothers to hire a manager, which they did, hiring one Francis McKnight. McKnight managed the theatre for 18 months. During that time he did not know of the interest of the bank in the building. George Brothers got into financial difficulties and stopped paying McKnight's salary. McKnight quit, and, upon discovering the interest of the bank, sued it for his accrued salary. What result?

a. Suppose that McKnight had been a regular employee of George Brothers, and managed several buildings for them. Assuming the above facts otherwise remained the same, would this variation change your legal analysis? If so, why?

b. Suppose the title to the building had remained in the name of the bank. Would that affect your answer under the main facts in part a, above?

Chapter 7

THE WONDERLAND OF AUTHORITY

"[T]he merchant [is] answerable for the deceit of his factor, . . .; for it is more reason, that he, that puts a trust and confidence in the deceiver, should be a loser, than a stranger." Hern v. Nichols, 1 Salk. 289, 90 Eng. Rep. 1154 (1709), per Holt, C. J.

"That portion of the field of law that is classified and described as the law of contracts attempts the realization of reasonable expectations that have been induced by the making of a promise." 1 A. CORBIN, CONTRACTS 2 (1963).

When many students and, one suspects, a good many teachers look back upon their agency courses, the one thing that probably sticks most in mind is the overwhelming confusion caused by inquiries into actual authority, implied authority, apparent authority, inherent agency power and agency by estoppel, among others. Part of the confusion doubtless results from the unclear and overlapping definitions of these terms and from the inconsistency of courts and authors in the use of what terminology we do have, but part of it probably also results from the fact that this area of agency law does not seem to have adopted a clear set of underlying principles. In one respect the legal questions raised reflect the tension involved in choosing between a subjective and an objective approach to the resolution of the myriad problems that can arise in the contractual context. A subjective approach adopts as a starting premise the principle that a person should not be bound to a contract beyond his consent. A literal application of the meeting of the minds principle represents the extreme in that approach. The objective approach, reflected in the above quotation from Corbin, stresses realization of the reasonable expectations of contracting parties. In reading through these materials, assess for yourself how successfully the law of agency has resolved this tension. Also, ask yourself whether in some respects the law has gone beyond even the objective approach and, if so, where are the boundary lines drawn and on the basis of what principles?

The following material will attempt a common definition of
terms through extensive quotation from the definition sections
of the Restatement of Agency. The definitions will be preceded
by a series of questions designed to encourage you first to formu-
late your own approach to this area, and then test it against the
Restatement's approach and the cases which follow it. A few
problems, framed primarily from cases and involving questions
based on the foregoing, will conclude a long and difficult chapter.

A. QUESTIONS

1. Susan Zidek, who had received personal injuries in an automobile accident with an employee of the West Penn Power
Company, retained Elery Mahaffey, an attorney, to represent her
in her claim against the Company. She signed a power of attorney (a formal written instrument which delineates the extent
of authority of an agent, frequently executed on a printed form)
authorizing Mahaffey to:

> either settle, adjust, enter suit, pursue said suit in the proper
> courts, or otherwise dispose of her claim against the West Penn
> Power Company . . . [Mahaffey was also given the power
> generally] to do all and every act and acts, thing and things,
> device and devices whatsoever needful and necessary to be done
> in and about the premises, for her and in her name to do, exe-
> cute, and perform as large and amply, to all intents and pur-
> poses, as she might do or could do, if personally present.

Thereafter Mahaffey made a settlement with the West Penn
Power Company for $500. The Company gave Mahaffey its
check payable to the order of Elery Mahaffey, attorney at law,
and Susan Zidek.

Mahaffey endorsed the check, signing both his name and
Miss Zidek's name, without her knowledge or consent. He cashed
the check at a restaurant and absconded with the proceeds. The
check was deposited by the restaurant to its bank account with
the Forbes Bank for collection. The check was paid by the drawee
bank and the proceeds received by the Forbes Bank, which
credited the amount to the restaurant's bank account.

Miss Zidek sued Forbes Bank in assumpsit for conversion.
The court viewed the matter of the bank's liability as turning
on the question whether the power of attorney authorized
Mahaffey to endorse Miss Zidek's name on the check. What result?

2. (a) P wrote to A directing A to act as his agent to contract
for the sale of a valuable oil painting owned by him. P sent a

copy of the letter to T, a prospective purchaser. The next day P sent a short note to A instructing him not to sell until he (P) had approved the price. T did not receive a copy of this note. One week later A sold the painting to T, without communication to P about the price. P is dissatisfied with the price and wants to avoid the sale. T wants to enforce the bargain he struck with A. Can T do so?

(b) Would your answer change if a copy of the original letter had never been sent to T? If so, why?

(c) Suppose, under the facts as modified in (b), that A had displayed to T the letter sent to him. Would this strengthen T's claim against P?

(d) What effect would it have on your answer under (c) if P had instructed A not to show his letter to anyone?

(e) Would your answer to (a) above change if A, with no relationship to P, had himself typed a letter identical to that in (a) above, forged P's signature, and sent it to T, who contracted in reliance on it? The expectations of T would be identical to the expectations created in (a) above, would they not?

3. Defendant company employed a managing agent to supervise the erecting and dismantling of its oil well derricks in the east Texas area. It instructed the agent not to make any purchases without the issuance of a "field order" on a form countersigned by an officer of the company. Plaintiff, unaware of this limitation, supplied materials used in this work at the request of the agent. The agent did not use a field order in making the purchases. Plaintiff was not paid and sued the company, alleging that a contractual obligation had been entered into on the company's behalf by its agent. What result?

4. P hired A, a real estate broker, to represent him in the sale of his home, including permission to sign on his behalf a contract of sale. P directed A to sell subject to retention of possession by P for three months. A soon thereafter sold P's home, but contracted with the buyer that he could have immediate possession of it. Is P bound by this term?

5. The owner of an expensive television, phonograph and record player console delivered it to a warehouse for storage while he was out of the country. The warehouseman sold it to an innocent third party and transferred possession to him. The owner, upon returning from his trip, somehow discovered the identity of the purchaser and sued to get the console back. The purchaser contends that he should be entitled to keep it, since he bought it from someone in possession. What result?

a. Would your answer change if the owner had delivered the console for repair and storage to a large retail appliance store and the same thing had happened? If so, why?

b. Would your answer change if the owner had delivered it to the appliance store with instructions to obtain offers to purchase from persons but not to sell without his approval, and the store employees had sold it in violation of his instructions?

c. Would it change your answers given above if the item involved was an ancient and unique clock that had been in the owner's family for generations and was of great sentimental value to the owner?

6. Adams was a freight agent for the defendant railroad. His duties included receiving and forwarding goods over the railroad and giving bills of lading for such goods. (Bills of lading are written documents issued by a carrier in which the carrier acknowledges receipt of goods and undertakes to deliver them at a designated place to or at the direction of a named person.) In conspiracy with Williams, Adams fraudulently issued to Williams some bills of lading of his carrier employer, without having received any goods. On the basis of the fraudulent documents, Williams obtained money from a bank, which took the bills of lading (without notice of the fraud) to secure its payment to Williams. The bank had no contact with Adams. When the fraud was discovered, the bank sued the railroad for nondelivery of the goods described in the bills. The railroad defended on the ground that the issuance of the bills by Adams was wholly without authority and was with no intent to serve it. What result?

7. *P,* owner of a retail business, permitted his agents to run the store in their own names without disclosing their agency relationship with him. The agents were instructed not to purchase a certain line of goods that is normally stocked in the business. However, they did so anyway, buying from someone who did not know of the existence of *P.* Is *P* liable to the seller in the event his identity is discovered and he is sued? Would he be liable if he also had instructed his agents never to buy on credit, and they had done so in the transactions upon which the suit is based?

8. Plaintiff entered the office of defendant's cartage business and saw a man apparently in charge of the office. Plaintiff gave him a railroad luggage check for his trunk and asked him to arrange for its delivery from the train station to his rooming house. The man agreed and accepted payment for the service. Plaintiff's trunk was picked up from the railroad by a man displaying the luggage check and both the luggage and the man whom plaintiff believed in charge of the office disappeared. Plain-

tiff sued the defendant for his loss. Defendant asserted that there was no relationship at all between him and the imposter and thus he could not be held liable for the fraud and conversion which took place. What result?

B. DEFINITIONS

The following material contains quotations from Sections 7 and 8 of the Restatement. These sections reflect a major effort to organize and clarify the use of terminology in this area. As you read through the definitions, ask yourself whether the questions posed earlier can be answered from these definitions and, if so, do the answers agree with the conclusions you arrived at independently?

§ 7. Authority.

Authority is the power of the agent to affect the legal relations of the principal by acts done in accordance with the principal's manifestations of consent to him.

Comment:

. . . .

It should be noted that the term "authority" has been used by the courts in a variety of ways. Sometimes it has been used to denote the factual giving of consent by the principal, without reference to the creation of a legal power; sometimes it has been used broadly to indicate the power which an agent has when there is apparent authority, estoppel or other basis for making the principal a party to the transactions.

b. Manifestation of consent. The word "manifestation" as herein used means the expression of the will to another as distinguished from the undisclosed purpose or intention. Manifestation of consent means conduct from which, in light of the circumstances, it is reasonable for another to infer consent. The giving of consent to the performance of an act may be the only reasonable inference, or it may be one of several reasonable inferences. The agent's conduct is authorized if he is reasonable* in drawing an inference that the principal intended him so to act although that was not the principal's intent (see § 44), and

---

*Does the comment mean that the agent must actually draw such an inference, or only that such an inference could be drawn by a reasonable person in the position of the agent? Which interpretation would best serve the purposes underlying the recognition of the agency relation? *Cf.* RESTATEMENT § 34, Comment *a.*

although as to a third person such a manifestation might not bind the principal. See § 8.

c. Express and implied authority. The manifestation may be made by words or other conduct, including acquiescence. Sections 26-31 state the manner in which it may be made. The rules for the interpretation of the manifestation are stated in Sections 32-81.

It is possible for a principal to specify minutely what the agent is to do. To the extent that he does this, the agent may be said to have express authority. But most authority is created by implication. Thus, in the authorization to "sell my automobile," the only fully expressed power is to transfer title in exchange for money or a promise to give money. In fact, under some circumstances (see § 53), "sell" may not mean "convey," and there may or may not be power to take or give possession of the automobile or to extend credit or to accept something in partial exchange. These powers are all implied or inferred from the words used, from customs and from the relations of the parties. They are described as "implied authority." Although frequently used, the phrase "express authority" is usually not adequate to describe the agent's authority, and the use of the adjective "implied" is unnecessary. Both adjectives are to be distinguished sharply from "apparent" as it is used in Section 8, since the latter is distinct in conception, although not in effect as between a principal and third parties. Implied authority as here used is also to be differentiated from a phrase, frequently misused, namely, "authority implied in law," which refers to situations in which a person has power to bind another although not his agent, for example, the power of a wife to bind her husband to pay for necessaries. See § 14 I.

d. Knowledge of third person. The fact that the third person with whom the agent deals on account of the principal has no knowledge of the manifestations of the principal, or even of the principal's existence, does not prevent the agent from having authority to make the principal a party to the transaction in accordance with his instructions. This is true even though the agent acts in accordance with instructions given in error or acts after the principal has withdrawn his consent, if neither the agent nor the third person has notice of such error or withdrawal. If, however, the third person has notice of such error or withdrawal, the agent has no power to bind the principal to him, although the agent, if without notice, is privileged to deal with him.

§ 8. Apparent Authority.

Apparent authority is the power to affect the legal relations. of another person by transactions with third persons, professedly as agent for the other, arising from and in accordance with the other's manifestations to such third persons.

See Reporter's Notes.

Comment:

a. Apparent authority results from a manifestation by a person that another is his agent, the manifestation being made to a third person and not, as when authority is created, to the agent. It is entirely distinct from authority, either express or implied. The power to deal with third persons which results from it may, however, be identical with the power created by authority as it is where the principal's statements to the third person are the same as to the agent and are similarly interpreted. On the other hand, the power may be greater or smaller than that resulting from authority. If it exists, the third person has the same rights with reference to the principal as where the agent is authorized. In the relation between principal and agent, however, apparent authority differs from authority, in that the one having it may not be a fiduciary, may have no privilege to exercise it and may not even know he has it. Although normally it results from a prior relation of principal and agent, this is not necessarily the case. Further, one who is authorized to act for the principal makes the latter a party to the transaction whether or not the third person believes the agent to be authorized or is even aware of the existence of the principal. See §§ 144 and 186. On the other hand, apparent authority exists only with regard to those who believe and have reason to believe that there is authority; there can be no apparent authority created by an undisclosed principal. The rules of interpretation of apparent authority are, however, the same as those for authority, substituting the manifestation to the third person in place of that to the agent. See §§ 27 and 49.

. . . .

b. The manifestation of the principal may be made directly to a third person, or may be made to the community, by signs, by advertising, by authorizing the agent to state that he is authorized,* or by continuously employing the agent. See Sections

---

* Consider the implications and the definitional consistency of this clause. *Ed.*

27 and 49 for further statements as to its creation and interpretation.

. . . .

c. Belief by third person. Apparent authority exists only to the extent that it is reasonable for the third person dealing with the agent to believe that the agent is authorized. Further, the third person must believe the agent to be authorized. In this respect apparent authority differs from authority since an agent who is authorized can bind the principal to a transaction with a third person who does not believe the agent to be authorized.

d. Apparent authority distinguished from estoppel. Apparent authority is based upon the principle which has led to the objective theory of contracts, namely, that in contractual relations one should ordinarily be bound by what he says rather than by what he intends, so that the contract which results from the acceptance of an offer is that which the offeree reasonably understands, rather than what the offeror means. It follows, therefore, that when one tells a third person that another is authorized to make a contract of a certain sort, and the other, on behalf of the principal, enters into such a contract with the third person, the principal becomes immediately a contracting party, with both rights and liabilities to the third person, irrespective of the fact that he did not intend to contract or that he had directed the "agent" not to contract, and without reference to any change of position by the third party.

Estoppel on the other hand, as stated in § 8 B, is essentially a principle in the law of torts developed in order to prevent loss to an innocent person. See §§ 872 and 894 of the Restatement of Torts. Like apparent authority, it is based on the idea that one should be bound by what he manifests irrespective of fault; but it operates only to compensate for loss to those relying upon the words and not to create rights in the speaker. It follows, therefore, that one basing his claim upon the rules of estoppel must show not merely reliance, which is required when the claim is based upon apparent authority, but also such a change of position that it would be unjust for the speaker to deny the truth of his words. Estoppel is dealt with as a form of deceit, in which the remedy is to hold the speaker to the truth of his statements instead of creating a tort action for misrepresentation. The one estopped is given no rights thereby.

In the usual agency case, however, little turns upon the distinction. In fact, the elements of estoppel are so frequently present that the courts have repeatedly stated that apparent authority is based upon estoppel. It would be more accurate to say that both are based upon an underlying principle that one should be bound by his words. In the agency cases, the apparent principal can usually ratify in any event; furthermore, it is not irrational to hold that merely entering into a contract is a change of position which would enable the third person to bring an action against the principal. However, it is useful to preserve the distinction. Thus, when a writing is required to authorize an agent to sell land and the agent was authorized only orally, but the principal tells the third person that the agent was authorized, there is no apparent authority, but the principal would be estopped from denying it. See § 31. Further, where a purported principal has not affirmatively misled the third person but has merely carelessly failed to take affirmative steps to deny that another was his agent, the imposition of liability is so extraordinary that it is doubtful whether he should be made liable to a third person who has made a contract with the pretended agent but has not otherwise changed his position.

. . . .

e. Authority—apparent, ostensible, inferred, implied. As pointed out in Comment *c* to Section 7, apparent authority has an entirely different meaning from inferred or implied authority. The latter terms are merely descriptive of the way in which authority is created, whereas apparent authority is not necessarily coincidental with authority. In fact, apparent authority is generally inferred or implied from manifestations of the principal to third persons, and hence it is correct to speak of implied or inferred apparent authority in most of the situations where apparent authority exists. Ostensible authority is merely a synonym for apparent authority and is so used by many courts. Apparent authority may coexist with authority either with the same limits, or with larger or smaller limits. When the acts of an agent in dealing with a third person are within the limits of either authority or apparent authority, the principal becomes a party to the transaction. In non-consensual transactions entered into by the agent where there has been no reliance by a third person upon the existence of authority, the presence or absence of an appearance of authority is immaterial. Compare Section 267, which states the liability for acts of apparent servants.

. . . .

f. Use by the courts. The term "apparent authority" has been broadly used by the courts to describe the power which agents have in creating liability against their principals, although without authority. Thus, it has been used as a basis for imposing liability upon an undisclosed principal (see § 195), as well as in a variety of other situations dealt with in Chapter 6, where policy considerations require that the principal should be liable for unauthorized conduct. It is believed that the results reached in such cases are sound and that the only objection to the use of apparent authority is its indefiniteness. In its proper setting, the term enables the courts to exercise a kind of business equity as they have been enabled to do by the use of the term "scope of employment." In the law of torts, "proximate cause" is similarly used to indicate liability. In the Restatement of this Subject, however, apparent authority is used in the restricted sense, as defined in this Section.

. . . .

§ 8 A.   Inherent Agency Power.

Inherent agency power is a term used in the restatement of this subject to indicate the power of an agent which is derived not from authority, apparent authority or estoppel, but solely from the agency relation and exists for the protection of persons harmed by or dealing with a servant or other agent.

See Reporter's Notes.

Comment:

a.   Rationale. The power of an agent to bind his principal is the distinctive feature of the Anglo-American agency relation. In many situations, however, its existence and extent can be based upon other legal principles. Thus, the liability of a principal for the authorized acts and contracts of an agent is responsive to the tort rule that one is liable for what he intentionally causes, and to the rule in contracts that one who manifests assent to another is bound by the resulting transaction. Contractual liability based upon apparent authority, or its close relation, estoppel, can equally be referred to tort or to contract principles. Likewise restitutional principles may require a principal to surrender property by which he has been unjustly enriched.

However there are situations in which the principal is made liable because of an act done or a transaction entered into by an agent even though there is no tort, contract or restitutional theory upon which the liability can be rested. A principle which will explain such cases can be found if it is assumed that a power can exist purely as a product of the agency relation. Because such a power is derived solely from the agency relation and is not based upon principles of contracts or torts, the term inherent agency power is used to distinguish it from other powers of an agent which are sustained upon contract or tort theories.

The principles of agency have made it possible for persons to utilize the services of others in accomplishing far more than could be done by their unaided efforts. Although the agency relation may exist without reference to mercantile affairs, as in the case of domestic servants, its primary function in modern life is to make possible the commercial enterprises which could not exist otherwise. The common law has properly been responsive to the needs of commerce, permitting what older systems of law denied, namely a direct relation between the principal and a third person with whom the agent deals, even when the principal is undisclosed. Partnerships and corporations, through which most of the work of the world is done today, depend for their existence upon agency principles. The rules designed to promote the interests of these enterprises are necessarily accompanied by rules to police them. It is inevitable that in doing their work, either through negligence or excess of zeal, agents will harm third persons or will deal with them in unauthorized ways. It would be unfair for an enterprise to have the benefit of the work of its agents without making it responsible to some extent for their excesses and failures to act carefully. The answer of the common law has been the creation of special agency powers or, to phrase it otherwise, the imposition of liability upon the principal because of unauthorized or negligent acts of his servants and other agents. These powers or liabilities are created by the courts primarily for the protection of third persons, either those who are harmed by the agent or those who deal with the agent. In the long run, however, they enure to the benefit of the business world and hence to the advantage of employers as a class, the members of which are plaintiffs as well as defendants in actions brought upon unauthorized transactions conducted by agents.

b. Situations creating inherent agency powers. Inherent agency powers fall into two groups. The first and most familiar is the power of a servant to subject his employer to liability for faulty conduct in performing his master's business. The liability of the master in such cases cannot be based upon any ordinary tort theory, since in many cases the employment is not a causative factor in any accepted sense. The liability results purely from the relation. Its existence depends in most cases upon the fact that the servant is acting in his employer's business and intends so to act; it does not depend upon a connection between the principal's conduct and the harm done.

The other type of inherent power subjects the principal to contractual liability or to the loss of his property when an agent has acted improperly in entering into contracts or making conveyances. Here the power is based neither upon the consent of the principal nor upon his manifestations. There are three types of situations in which this type of power exists. First is that in which a general agent does something similar to what he is authorized to do, but in violation of orders. In this case the principal may become liable as a party to the transaction, even though he is undisclosed. As to such cases, see Sections 161 and 194. Second is the situation in which an agent acts purely for his own purposes in entering into a transaction which would be authorized if he were actuated by a proper motive. See §§ 165 and 262. The third type is that in which an agent is authorized to dispose of goods and departs from the authorized method of disposal. See §§ 175 and 201.

In many of the cases involving these situations the courts have rested liability upon the ground of "apparent authority," a phrase which has been used by the courts loosely. If the meaning of the term is restricted, as is done in Section 8, to those situations in which the principal has manifested the existence of authority to third persons, the term does not apply to the above situations. No theory of torts, contract or estoppel is sufficient to allow recovery in these cases. But because agents are fiduciaries acting generally in the principal's interests, and are trusted and controlled by him, it is fairer that the risk of loss caused by disobedience of agents should fall upon the principal rather than upon third persons.*

c. Rights of the principal. Although the execution of this inherent power ordinarily operates to create liability against the principal or to cause the loss of his things, it may give the principal rights against the other party to the transaction. Thus, when the agent makes an unauthorized purchase, for which the principal is liable, the seller is bound to the principal in accordance with the terms of the agreement.

§ 8 B.   Estoppel—Change of Position.

(1) A person who is not otherwise liable as a party to a transaction purported to be done on his account, is nevertheless

---

* Ask yourself if it is so clear that apparent authority would not apply to the three types of situations described in the above two paragraphs. *Ed.*

subject to liability to persons who have changed their positions because of their belief that the transaction was entered into by or for him, if,

(a) he intentionally or carelessly caused such belief, or

(b) knowing of such belief and that others might change their positions because of it, he did not take reasonable steps to notify them of the facts.

(2) An owner of property who represents to third persons that another is the owner of the property or who permits the other so to represent, or who realizes that third persons believe that another is the owner of the property, and that he could easily inform the third persons of the facts, is subject to the loss of the property if the other disposes of it to third persons who, in ignorance of the facts, purchase the property or otherwise change their position with reference to it.

(3) Change of position, as the phrase is used in the restatement of this subject, indicates payment of money, expenditure of labor, suffering a loss or subjection to legal liability.

.   .   .   .

Comment:

.   .   .   .

c. Estoppel by silence. In many situations one may be deprived of a right of action, be subject to an action or even lose his property by failing to reveal the truth if he knows that another is acting or will act under a misapprehension. Thus, the owner of land who learns that another believes himself to be the owner and because of that belief is making improvements on it, may be required to surrender the land or to pay for the improvements. See the Restatement of Restitution, §§ 40 and 53. So also one who knows that another is purporting to sell his property may be barred from recovery from a bona fide purchaser of it. See the Restatement of Torts, § 894(2). There may even be liability based on a failure to speak, as where one knows that another is purporting or has purported to contract as his agent or to receive money on a forged instrument, and fails to reveal the facts. See § 1031. In some situations in which silence is maintained, authority (§ 43), or ratification (§ 94) results, and, if so, liability can be based upon ordinary agency principles. In situations in which neither authority nor ratification can be found, there may be liability based upon estoppel if the other party has changed his position.

The theory by which estoppel exists where there is a misrepresentation is consistent with tort principles, even when its application results in strict liability. The effect of estoppel which denies the owner of property the right to get it back from an innocent purchaser from a thief, if the owner had remained silent although knowing of the prospective sale, can be justified as based upon a duty placed upon the owner of property. But when a person is subjected to liability because he remained silent with knowledge that another was purporting to contract on his behalf, the normal tort rule denying a duty to prevent another from being harmed is not enforced. This imposition of liability for failure to prevent a fraud is not, however, unjustified. The laissez-faire common law rule which imposes no duty to aid others has probably been retained in its extreme form because of the difficulty in fixing limits and in the agency situation, not only is the purported principal in the best position to prevent the harm, but also it is usually not difficult to ascertain what it was reasonable for him to do. Another departure from strict tort principles, also justifiable, is found in the ratification of a tort. See § 82, Comment *d*.

d. Extent of duty to give information. When one realizes that another is or may come under a misapprehension as to the authority of his agent or the ownership of his property,—a misapprehension for which he is not at fault,—his duty to give information is a duty of due care. It is proportioned to the likelihood of harm and to its extent. If only a specific third person is involved, the duty of the purported principal can frequently be discharged by an inexpensive letter or telephone message. In situations in which one learns that another is purporting to act as his agent in a continuous series of transactions with various persons, the expense of adequate protection may be prohibitive and, if so, it would seem that the duty might be performed by notifying the public authorities. The problem is unlike that involved in the termination of apparent authority, for in that case the relation has been created by the conduct of the purported principal. See §§ 125-133. All that can be stated is that the action required is that which would be taken by a reasonably prudent business man, with the normal regard for the interests of others and his own reputation.

. . . .

f. The rules applicable to governmental officers are not within the scope of the Restatement of this Subject. [The normal rules of apparent authority, estoppel and so forth do not apply to the actions of federal government employees. Court decisions have placed the risk of correctly ascertaining a government employee's authority on the party contracting with him. "In dealings with the government, unlike those with private parties, one is charged with knowledge of the extent of the actual authority of the government's contracting agent since no agent of the government can hold out to have an authority not sanctioned by law." Blake Constr. Co. v. United States, 296 F.2d 393, 396 (D.C. Cir. 1961); *accord,* Federal Crop Ins. Corp. v. Merrill, 332 U.S. 380 (1947), *noted in,* 16 Chi. L. Rev. 128 (1948); 1 Vand. L. Rev. 302 (1948), and 34 Va. L. Rev. 477 (1948). *See,* however, Giglio v. United States, 405 U.S. 150 (1971) (dealing with the unauthorized representations of an assistant United States attorney in a criminal case). *Ed.*]

§ 8 C. Restitution.

A person who has been unjustly enriched at the expense of another is required to make restitution to the other.

Comment:

a. This statement of the basic principle of restitution is made here in order to indicate that in many of the situations involving agency the result is reached not primarily by principles of agency but upon restitutional principles. Thus when a person who has no authority or apparent authority to act for another, purports to act as the agent of another in the acquisition of property, the purported principal may be liable for its value, not because of any agency principle but because he has been unjustly enriched. Again, an agent who properly receives property from a third person on account of the principal may be under a duty of restitution to the transferor if later it is found that the transaction with the principal under which he received the property is voidable by the third person. Between principal and agent the right of the principal to recover profits improperly made by an agent is a restitutional right. Similarly, the duty of the principal to indemnify the agent and, in other situations, the duty of an agent to indemnify the principal, is created by the rules of restitution. Illustrations of restitutional rights and duties are in the statement of the rule, or in the Comments, in Sections 104, 141, 151, 263, 274, 282, 339-341, 388-419, 438-440, among others. In fact, a large proportion of the rules stated in the Restatement of Restitution are applicable to agency situations.

C. PARTNERSHIP AUTHORITY

Uniform Partnership Act (UPA) § 9, which is contained in Appendix A, deals with the authority of a partner to bind the partnership. Note the broad language used in subsections (1) and (2) of § 9. Much of the decision making under § 9 necessarily makes use of general agency principles. The UPA recognizes this in § 4(2) and (3), stating that the "law of estoppel and the law of agency shall apply under this act." Observe, however, the specific statutory restrictions imposed by § 9(3) on authority (and apparent authority?) of partners with respect to certain kinds of acts. Section 9(4) should be read in conjunction with § 18(e) and (h).

D. SOME CASES

As you read through the following cases and the notes and questions following them, ask yourself whether the approach of the cases is consistent with the approach you took when answering the initial series of questions posed at the beginning of this chapter. And if it is not consistent, do not assume, at least without thinking it through carefully, that you are the one who is wrong.

i. *Genuine Authority and its Limits*

VON WEDEL v. McGRATH
United States Court of Appeals, Third Circuit
180 F.2d 716 (1950)
Noted in 24 So. Calif. L. Rev. 124 (1950)

McLAUGHLIN, Circuit Judge. This is an equity action under the provisions of Section 9(a) of the Trading with the Enemy Act, 40 Stat. 411, 50 U.S.C.A. Appendix, § 9(a). It sought the recovery of certain personal property vested in the Attorney General as successor to the Alien Property Custodian. The complaint was dismissed below on the ground that it appears on its face "that the plaintiff has no interest, right or title in the property within the meaning of Section 9(a) of the Act."

The complaint alleges: that plaintiff is a citizen of the United States, the wife of a German national; that on July 5, 1939, she and her husband left this country for a visit to Europe; that prior to departure, the husband, apprehensive that war might break out in Europe prior to their return to this country and that such condition might prevent him coming back to the United States, executed and delivered at New York City a general power of attorney (copy of which is attached to the complaint) to his friend and lawyer Pieter J. Kooiman; that an "express primary object of the giving of the power of attorney was to enable the donee to dispose of all or part of the donor's property in the

United States by gift to the plaintiff herein or otherwise, as the attorney in fact might deem best under all the circumstances"; that on September 1, 1939, while plaintiff and her husband were traveling in Germany, World War II started and the husband since then has been prevented, by causes beyond his control, from returning to the United States; that in 1940 Kooiman, as attorney in fact for the husband, transferred to plaintiff by way of absolute gift, property listed in a schedule attached to the complaint; that the property became vested in the Attorney General as successor to the Alien Property Custodian and that plaintiff filed notice of claim for its return. The complaint prays for a decree awarding her the property and for an accounting.

The all important question in the case is whether the power of attorney upon its face authorized a gift of the principal's property. The initial general language of the power appoints Kooiman ". . . to do any and all acts which I could do if personally present, hereby intending to give him the fullest power and not intending by anything hereinafter contained to limit or cut down such full power. . . ." Specific powers are then stated, namely, "giving and granting unto him full power to demand, sue for, recover and receive all manner of goods, chattels, . . ." and various other enumerated routine business powers. The instrument concludes by giving the attorney in fact "power and authority to do, execute and perform for me and in my name all and singular those things which he shall judge expedient or necessary in and about the premises, as fully as I, . . ., could do if personally present. . . ."[1] There is no real dispute about this last broad language as appellant in her reply brief concedes that its function is merely to round out the specified powers given by the document.

---

[1] The complete power of attorney, with the exception of the witness clause, reads:

"Know All Men by These Presents:

"That I, Carl J. R. H. von Wedel, being about to depart from the United States for an indefinite period of time, by these presents make, constitute and appoint my friend, Pieter J. Kooiman, of 81 North Hillside Place, Ridgewood, New Jersey, my true and lawful attorney, for me and in my name, place and stead, to do any and all acts which I could do if personally present, hereby intending to give him the fullest power and not intending by anything hereinafter contained to limit or cut down such full power, giving and granting unto him full power to demand, sue for, recover and receive all manner of goods, chattels, debts, rents, interest, sums of money and demands whatsoever, due or hereafter to become due and owing or belonging to me on any account, and to make, give and execute acquittances, receipts, releases and other discharges for the same, and to make, execute, endorse, accept and deliver, in my name or in the name of my said attorney, all checks, notes, drafts, warrants, acknowledgments, agree-

Among the carefully stated ordinary business powers set out in the instrument there is nothing which even implies that the attorney in fact is authorized to give his principal's property away. The authority within the instrument is to handle von Wedel's usual affairs. Under the settled law, that authority does not go beyond the specific subject ". . . even though it contains words in the most general terms extending the agent's authority." Brassert v. Clark, 2 Cir., 162 F.2d 967, 973. Restatement on Agency, Section 37, says: "(1) Unless otherwise agreed, general expressions used in authorizing an agent are limited in application to acts done in connection with the act or business to which the authority primarily relates. (2) The specific authorization of particular acts tends to show that a more general authority is not intended."

The language of Judge Woolley, speaking for this Court, in Lanahan v. Clark Car Co., 3 Cir., 11 F.2d 820, 824, is very much in point. He said:

"We construe the general and specific provisions of the power of attorney in the light of the familiar principle of law that general powers in such instruments are limited by the specific powers therein granted. As we read the writing we gather that the donor intended to give, and did give, his attorney in fact every power incident to the management of his business, even, conceivably, the power to sell and convey property if in the management of his business that should become necessary. But in a power to conduct a business there is no implication of a power to dispose of it and this is particularly true of the instrument under consideration where if any such power can be found it is among the general powers. As these are limited by the specific powers and as the specific powers quite clearly relate

---

ments and all other instruments in writing of whatsoever nature, as to my said attorney may seem necessary or proper.

"With full power and authority to sell, transfer or do any other act concerning any stocks or bonds which I may have or possess, and to transfer the same in any manner required by any corporation or law; with full power and authority to commence and prosecute any suits or actions or other legal proceedings for any goods, chattels, debts, cause or thing whatsoever, and to prosecute or discontinue the same; and also for me and in my name and stead to appear, answer and defend in all actions and suits whatsoever which may be commenced against me; and also for me and in my name to compromise, settle and adjust with each and every person or persons all actions, accounts, dues and demands, in such manner as my said attorney shall think proper; hereby giving to my said attorney power and authority to do, execute and perform for me and in my name all and singular those things which he shall judge expedient or necessary in and about the premises, as fully as I, the said Carl J. R. H. von Wedel, could do if personally present, hereby ratifying and confirming whatever my said attorney shall do or cause to be done in, about or concerning the premises, or any part thereof."

not to the ending of the business but to its continuance, we find the power too narrow to authorize the transaction of sale entered into and concluded under its supposed authority."

It is contended for appellant that in the instance before us the specific powers do not control because after the initial broad power, is the phrase ". . . and not intending by anything herein-after contained to limit or cut down such full power. . . ." Williams v. Dugan, 217 Mass. 526, 105 N.E. 615, L.R.A. 1916C, 110, presented a quite similar situation. Concerning the power of attorney in that suit, the Court said, 217 Mass. at page 529, 105 N.E. at page 616, "The general power of attorney is couched in comprehensive terms." After the general power came a statement of specific powers and then the language, "It is understood that the foregoing enumeration of specific powers does not in any way control, limit, or cut down the general powers herein granted, or which should have been granted in order to carry out the purposes hereinbefore expressed." The Court said, regarding this language: "But these words are used with reference to the powers expressly granted and do not enlarge those powers beyond their fair scope. They fall short of conferring the right to borrow money on the principal's account. These are the general words in substance commonly found in printed blank powers of attorney. See Crocker's Notes on Common Forms, 416, where are shorter but equally comprehensive forms. They relate to matters incidental to the main subject, for which the agency is created, and do not confer new or alien powers."

  . . . .

In the absence of ambiguity or incompleteness, we must deal with the intent as actually expressed in the document itself. The power of attorney before us is neither ambiguous nor incomplete. Under the settled law, the specific language governs. That language refers solely to von Wedel's ordinary business affairs. It contains nothing that can be reasonably construed as authority for the attorney in fact to make gifts of von Wedel's property. The principle of ejusdem generis squarely applies and the command of the specific language must be pursued with legal strictness.

The judgment of the District Court will be affirmed.

GOODRICH, Circuit Judge (concurring). I go along with the result because I think it is supported by authority and the subject is not one on which to try to start a revolution. But it seems to me that the whole thing is incongruous. A man has said, in effect, that he gives another the power to do everything for him. Then he enumerates certain specific things which the other

may do, carefully saying, however, that he does not mean to alter
the general power by stating specific powers. Then he ends up by
saying that he means his language to be as broad as he stated it.
Yet the rule seems to be that he is held to mean something much
less than indicated by the language he used. Perhaps the law
cannot quite say that white is black. But in this instance it
certainly can make white look a pretty dark grey.

NOTES

1.   Whose interest is the court protecting in this case?

2.   Would a power of attorney saying only that *A* can "do and
perform all and every act and thing" that *P* himself could do if he
were present, and containing no specific recitals, be effective? *See*
Davis v. Dunnet, 239 N.Y. 338, 146 N.E. 620 (1925), holding no.
Why not?

3.   Based on the above, does the inclusion of general language
serve any purpose? If not, would you in drafting a power of
attorney feel free to leave it out of the document?

4.   *Implied Authority.* This term is defined in RESTATEMENT
§ 7, Comment *c,* as quoted above in the Definitions section. The
extent of an agent's implied authority is determined by his
reasonable interpretation of the instructions given him by the
principal, which can include taking into account the customary
practices of the locality where he operates. His principal is bound
by this although he may not have intended the actual authority
to carry so far. The concept of implied authority thus is based on
the objective theory of contracts. The principal is held on the
basis of a reasonable construction of his manifestation, and not
on the basis of his subjective and unmanifested intention.

Consider the following example of implied authority adapted
from RESTATEMENT § 33, illustration 2. *P,* the owner of a factory
running on half time for lack of orders, before leaving for his one-
month vacation, directs his purchasing agent to "put in our
usual monthly coal supply of 1000 tons." *P* leaves on his vacation,
at a place where he cannot be reached. The following day a
large order comes in which will immediately put the factory on
full running time. Assuming *P* has a sufficient bank balance, it
"may be found" that the agent is authorized to purchase the
additional coal necessary to keep the factory running full time.
This would be true even if *P* subjectively had intended that
1000 tons was all the coal the agent could buy regardless of
conditions, at least as long as that intention remained unex-
pressed.

Implied authority can extend to appointing a subagent. A "subagent" is defined in RESTATEMENT § 5 as "a person appointed by an agent empowered to do so, to perform functions undertaken by the agent for the principal, but for whose conduct the agent agrees with the principal to be primarily responsible." This latter agreement can be implied. An example of this is where *P,* having a claim against *T* in a distant state, hires an attorney, *A,* to take steps for its collection. *A* is authorized to employ an attorney in *T*'s state to initiate proceedings for collection. This is true even if *P* had no idea how attorneys collect debts and expected *A* to handle it by himself.

Normally an agent owes his principal a duty to personally discharge his employment and thus is unable to delegate his authority unless his principal so consents, or the particular circumstances of the case indicate that the principal's consent could reasonably be implied, such as the collection illustration immediately above. The Latin phrase *delegatus non potest delegare* (a delegate cannot delegate) reflects the general rule that an agent's powers cannot be delegated by him in the absence of authority to do so and carries particular weight when the agent's undertaking calls for judgment or discretion. In part this hesitancy to freely legitimate delegation of authority probably reflects the underlying premise of agency law that an agency relationship is a consensual relationship. Since the party to whom authority has been delegated would be exercising powers on behalf of the principal, normally one would expect that the principal would consent to his exercise of such powers. See F. MECHEM, THE LAW OF AGENCY §§ 302-342 (2d ed. 1914).

Two situations should be distinguished in dealing with delegation of authority by an agent. One situation is that described above, where the agent is either delegating some of his own authority or procuring assistance in the exercise of the powers conferred upon him. The other, and distinct, situation is where an agent employed to hire (or "appoint") other agents for his principal, and this is his job. In this latter situation the agent is not delegating his authority, but instead simply exercising it.

5. *Emergency Situations.* If an unforeseen situation arises for which the terms of the authorization make no provision and it is impracticable for the agent to contact the principal, the agent is authorized to do what he reasonably believes to be necessary in order to prevent loss to his principal. For example, assume that *P* employs *A* as a truck driver to carry a load of perishable fruit to a distant town. En route, *A* becomes ill and is unable to drive. Being unable to communicate with *P,* he em-

ploys *B,* a competent driver, to take his place for the trip. *See*
RESTATEMENT § 79, illustration 5, concluding that it "may be
found that A was authorized to employ B as P's servant." If,
incidentally, *B* negligently caused a loss while driving, would
both *A* and *P* be held liable on *respondeat superior* grounds?
If so, *B* would be classified as a "subservant" of *P* and a servant of
A. See RESTATEMENT § 5, stating that situations involving a subservant relationship are relatively rare, and giving no indication
that the trucking hypothetical would fit into that category.

---

ii. *Apparent Authority as an Articulated Ground of Decision*

WALKER v. PACIFIC MOBILE HOMES, INC.
Supreme Court of Washington
68 Wash. 2d 347, 413 P.2d 3 (1966)

HALE, J.—Plaintiff left his trailer to be sold on consignment.
One of the defendant's salesmen sold it and absconded. Defendant, disclaiming responsibility for the consignment, appeals
the $1,290.51 judgment.

The case turns on whether the court properly found from conflicting evidence that defendant's salesmen acted within their
apparent or ostensible authority. Plaintiff Walker owned a 25-
foot, 1953 Mainliner trailer in Seattle. Deciding to sell it and
return to his former home in Oregon, he went to several trailer
lots to see if the dealers would handle it on consignment. He
found no dealers interested in a consignment until he met Robert
Stewart at the lot of defendant Pacific Mobile Homes at South
140th and Pacific Highway.

At the trailer lot where plaintiff first talked to Stewart, he
noticed a large sign designating it as Pacific Mobile Homes,
Inc., an office, a number of trailers on display, and observed that
Mr. Stewart appeared to be the sole employee in attendance.
Behind the lot was a large trailer park known as "Southgate
Trailer Park." Plaintiff told Stewart he would sell on consignment if he could get a net price of $1,500, and Stewart told him
that he was too busy moving the trailers around at the moment to
complete the deal but would pick up the trailer in a few days.

A few days later, Stewart came with a truck to plaintiff's
residence and towed the trailer to the Pacific Mobile Homes
lot where plaintiff on several occasions saw it among the other
trailers displayed there. May 27, 1959, plaintiff stopped at the
trailer lot where he again found Stewart alone in the office,
and suggested that, since he intended to go to Oregon for a while,

some sort of writing should be made out. Thereupon, plaintiff says, Stewart got a blank form having the legend "Trailer Consignment Agreement" in bold-faced type across the top, filled it out in ink, but, in barely legible handwriting, designated thereon Southgate Trailers as consignee. Plaintiff signed the consignment agreement, stating at the trial that, being primarily concerned at the time with the provisions as to net price and the avoidance of storage charges if the trailer was not sold, he did not notice the name of the consignee.

About one month later, a Robert Henderson telephoned plaintiff in Oregon, asking if plaintiff had left his trailer on consignment with Stewart at Pacific Mobile Homes and explained that Stewart was no longer with the firm but that he, Henderson, was the new manager. Henderson then told plaintiff they still had the trailer and had lined up a possible buyer. A few weeks later, plaintiff returned to Seattle from Oregon and talked to Henderson at the trailer lot. Plaintiff saw his trailer on this occasion still on display among the others and testified that Henderson, like Stewart before him, was there alone at the office and trailer lot.

Henderson again told him that he had a likely deal pending, and plaintiff went back to Oregon to have the deal confirmed by mail. He received a letter on the business stationery of Pacific Mobile Homes, Inc., giving the corporation's main office address at Edmonds and the branch office at 140th and Pacific Highway South, and containing also an installment note signed by one Korsmoe as maker. The letter, handwritten by Bob Henderson, dated July 25, 1959, explained that, after four payments, the enclosed note would be discounted and balance thereof paid in cash. Each month for the next three months, plaintiff received a monthly payment in the form of a check signed by Henderson, and when these ceased he returned to the trailer lot to inquire about the unpaid balance.

He found that Henderson had actually sold the trailer not to Korsmoe but to one Anderson for $1,500 cash, and, save for the three payments totaling $209.41, had absconded with the balance. After more than a year spent in tracing him, plaintiff located Henderson in the penitentiary at Walla Walla.

Henry M. Shelly, president of Pacific Mobile Homes, testified that his company maintained a small one-room office on the South 140th street trailer lot; that the lot had a sign 28 feet high and 14 feet long with "Pacific Mobile Homes, Inc." on it; that he visited the lot to check it about three times a week. He said that Stewart worked at the lot from April to July, 1959, and

Henderson started to work there in June, but ordinarily there would be only one salesman on duty at any one time.

He said that neither had authority to complete a sale without approval of himself or the company sales manager and that all sales documents had to be signed by himself personally. He said too that the company forbade its salesmen to take trailers on consignment; that neither he nor the company had any record or knowledge of either the plaintiff's trailer, the consignment arrangement, or any other phases of the transaction; that he had never, during his periodic inspections, seen plaintiff's trailer on the lot. Only on a few occasions, he said, had his company taken trailers for sale on consignment and that all salesmen were well acquainted with this company policy.

Although the agent's authority must be established through proof of the principal's conduct, representations or actions, and cannot be proved by the admissions of the agent, the trial court, in the present case, had before it substantial evidence from which to find apparent authority.

We believe the evidence warranted findings and conclusions that Pacific Mobile Homes had clothed Stewart and later Henderson with apparent or ostensible authority to take the trailer on to the lot for sale on consignment and to collect the purchase money therefor. The salesman's solitary presence in the company office and about the lot on several occasions, among numerous trailers on display, beneath a sign conspicuously proclaiming the whole to be an enterprise of Pacific Mobile Homes, Inc., and his towing plaintiff's trailer to the trailer lot and putting it on display there, allowed a person of ordinary business prudence to reasonably assume that the salesman had authority from Pacific Mobile Homes, Inc., to buy, sell, receive and deliver trailers for cash, on credit, consignment, or in exchange. Then, too, the salesman's untrammeled access to and use of his principal's letterhead, stationery and business forms, and his seeming control of the office and lot, fortify the idea of apparent authority.

Authority to perform particular services for a principal carries with it the implied authority to perform the usual and necessary acts essential to carry out the authorized services.

One dealing in good faith with an agent who appears to be acting within the scope of his authority is not bound by undisclosed limitations on the agent's power.

Our decision in Lamb v. General Associates, Inc., 60 Wn.2d 623, 374 P.2d 677 (1962), succinctly declares the principles which govern the instant case:

It is a general rule, and the rule in this state, that a corporation may be bound by the contracts or agreements of its agent if within the apparent scope of the agent's authority, although the contract may be beyond the scope of his actual authority. [Citing cases.]

It is also the well-established rule that the apparent or ostensible authority of an agent can be inferred only from acts and conduct of the principal. [Citing cases.] The extent of an agent's authority cannot be established by his own acts and declarations. [Citing cases.]

The burden of establishing agency rests upon the one who asserts it. Facts and circumstances are sufficient to establish apparent authority only when a person exercising ordinary prudence, acting in good faith and conversant with business practices and customs, would be misled thereby, and such person has given due regard to such other circumstances as would cause a person of ordinary prudence to make further inquiry. [Citing case.]

A principal may be estopped to deny that his agent possesses the authority he assumes to exercise, where the principal knowingly causes or permits him so to act as to justify a third person of ordinarily careful and prudent business habits to believe that he possesses the authority exercised, and avails himself of the benefit of the agent's acts. [Citing case.]

Applying the foregoing principles to the proofs presented on behalf of both the plaintiff and the defendant compels an affirmance.

Affirmed.

ROSELLINI, C. J., OTT and HUNTER, JJ., concur.

HILL, J. (dissenting)—I dissent. To me it is clear that the plaintiff knew that he was not doing business with Pacific Mobile Homes, Inc., and that he knew he was doing business with Robert Stewart, and later Bob Henderson. This action is somebody's afterthought, which has certainly paid off well.

Not only did the consignment form, which the plaintiff received when he delivered his trailer to Robert Stewart, contain no reference to Pacific Mobile Homes, Inc., but the checks he received in payment on his trailer were the personal checks of Bob Henderson. It was only after he finally located, in the penitentiary, the man who had defrauded him and realized that there was no balm in Gilead there, that the idea that Pacific Homes, Inc., ought to share its wealth with him, was evolved.

I will assume with the majority that the evidence warranted a finding that Pacific Mobile Homes had clothed Stewart, and later

Henderson, with apparent or ostensible authority to take a trailer for sale on consignment.

Where the plaintiff's case breaks down, is that there is no evidence to establish that he relied on that apparent or ostensible authority. Instead it establishes that he at all times believed he was dealing with Stewart or Henderson. For more than a year, he ignored Pacific Mobile Homes, Inc.—all the time transacting business at the same locations, all the time readily available—and instead devoted his time and energies to locating Henderson.

For this hiatus in proof, I would set aside the judgment and dismiss the action.

NOTES

1. What is the policy the court is trying to effectuate in its decision?

2. The majority assume without discussion that the power to buy and sell includes the power to take goods on consignment. Do you agree? In order to see this case in the context of the personal experience of most persons, assume that a new and used car lot was involved.

3. The point made by the dissent was ignored in the majority opinion. Do you think it deserved to be?

4. The following quotation contains, according to the index, the entire treatment by Corbin of the question of apparent authority in his eight volume treatise on contracts. 1 A. CORBIN, CONTRACTS § 33, at 133 (1963). Note the wonderfully vague footnote 78, and also note the allocation of burden of proof in apparent authority cases.

> When a transaction is negotiated by a representative, it is always necessary for the other party to establish the fact that the representative had power to bind his principal. It is possible to establish this in many ways, by various kinds of evidence.[78]

5. Is the determination whether an agent is apparently authorized a question of law or of fact? The decision of this question in the *Walker* case was made by the court, and the opinions contained no reference to a fact finding at the trial level. The determination thus apparently was viewed by the court as a question of law. *See,* however, W. SEAVEY, LAW OF AGENCY § 16B

---

[78] See works on **Agency.**

(1964) (indicating such questions are usually for the jury "unless the facts are undisputed or clear") ; Joseph Greenspon's Sons Iron & Steel Co. v. Pecos Valley Gas Co., 34 Del. 567, 156 A. 350 (1931); and the *Gizzi* case p. 194 *infra*.

6. The appointment of an agent to a certain position can have apparent authority ramifications. *See* RESTATEMENT § 27, Comment *a:* "Likewise, as in the case of authority, apparent authority can be created by appointing a person to a position, such as that of manager or treasurer, which carries with it generally recognized duties; to those who know of the appointment there is apparent authority to do the things ordinarily entrusted to one occupying such a position, regardless of unknown limitations which are imposed upon the particular agent."

7. RESTATEMENT § 27, Comment *c* expands on the phrase in Comment *b* to § 8 that a manifestation from a principal sufficient to create apparent authority in his agent may be made "by authorizing the agent to state that he is authorized." The relevant language in Comment *c* is as follows:

> *c.* *Representation of authority by the agent.* Unless directed not to do so, the agent is authorized to represent the extent of his authority, and he has apparent authority to the extent that he reveals his authority. Thus, a person sent to borrow $1,000 has authority to state the extent of his authority; and if he does state this, he has both authority to borrow and apparent authority to borrow. In such a case there is no substantial legal problem involved. However, it should be noted that if, before borrowing, the agent had decided that after borrowing the money, he would embezzle it, he would not be authorized to represent that he could borrow, since authority can exist only to the extent that the agent intends to carry out his principal's purposes. In such a case, however, whatever the technique used, the courts impose liability upon the principal for the money thus borrowed. See § 165 [stating that such liability results from inherent agency power; see notes after the *Watteau* case, *infra. Ed.*].

Is this aspect of apparent authority consistent with the point made in Comment *c* to § 8, quoted at p. 174, *supra,* that an essential element of apparent authority is that the third person dealing with the agent have a reasonable belief that he is authorized?

GIZZI v. TEXACO
United States Court of Appeals, Third Circuit
437 F.2d 308 (1971)
Noted in 50 N. Car. L. Rev. 647 (1972);
23 S. Car. L. Rev. 826 (1971)

GERALD MCLAUGHLIN, Circuit Judge. The question posed on this appeal is whether the trial judge properly granted appellee Texaco's motion for a directed verdict in this personal injury action. Jurisdiction in the district court was based on diversity of citizenship and requisite amount in controversy.

Appellant Augustine Gizzi was a steady patron of a Texaco service station located on Route 130 and Chestnut Street, Westville, New Jersey. The real estate upon which the station was situated was owned by a third party and was leased to the operator of the station, Russell Hinman. Texaco owned certain pieces of equipment and also supplied the operator with the normal insignia to indicate that Texaco products were being sold there.

In June of 1965, the station operator, Hinman, interested Gizzi in a 1958 Volkswagen van, which Hinman offered to put in good working order and sell for $400. Gizzi agreed to make the purchase and Hinman commenced his work on the vehicle. The work took about two weeks and included the installation of a new master braking cylinder and a complete examination and testing of the entire braking system. On June 18, 1965 Gizzi came to the station and paid the $400. He was given a receipt for the payment and was told that the car would be ready that evening. Gizzi returned at about six o'clock, accompanied by appellant Anthony Giaccio. They took the van and then departed for Philadelphia, Pennsylvania, to pick up and deliver some air-conditioning equipment. While driving on the Schuylkill Expressway, Gizzi attempted to stop the vehicle by applying the brakes. He discovered that the brakes did not work and, as a result, the vehicle collided with the rear end of a tractor trailer causing serious injuries to both Gizzi and Giaccio.

Texaco, Inc. was the only defendant named in the complaint and at trial, the testimony was all directed to the corporation's liability, the court having asked for an offer of proof on that question.

With regard to the sale of this vehicle, no actual agency existed between Texaco and Hinman. Although most of the negotiations involved in the transaction took place at the Texaco station, the record indicates that Hinman was selling the van on his own behalf, and not on behalf of Texaco. Texaco received no portion of the proceeds. The corporation was not designated the seller on the bill of sale, title to the vehicle being listed in the name of a company located in Atlantic City, New Jersey. Gizzi did receive a Texaco credit invoice as a receipt for the cash he paid. It would seem that this was an available convenience utilized by Hinman to record the transaction.

The repair work performed by Hinman was incidental to the sale of the vehicle. He offered to put the vehicle into good working order to further induce Gizzi to purchase it. Some work was done on the van after the money had been paid on June 18 and all work on the braking system was completed prior to that date.

The theory of liability advanced by appellants below was that Texaco had clothed Hinman with apparent authority to make the necessary repairs and sell the vehicle on its behalf and that Gizzi reasonably assumed that Texaco would be responsible for any defects, especially defects in those portions of the van which were repaired or replaced by Hinman. It was further contended that Gizzi entered into the transaction relying on this apparent authority, thereby creating a situation in which Texaco was estopped from denying that an agency did in fact exist.

The concepts of apparent authority, and agency by estoppel are closely related. Both depend on manifestations by the alleged principal to a third person, and reasonable belief by the third person that the alleged agent is authorized to bind the principal. The manifestations of the principal may be made directly to the third person, or may be made to the community, by signs or advertising. Restatement (Second), Agency §§ 8, 8B, 27 (1957). In order for the third person to recover against the principal, he must have relied on the indicia of authority originated by the principal, Bowman v. Home Life Ins. Co. of America, 260 F.2d 521 (3 Cir. 1958); Restatement (Second), Agency § 267 and such reliance must have been reasonable under the circumstances.

In support of their theory of liability, appellants introduced evidence to show that Texaco exercised control over the activities of the service station in question. They showed that Texaco insignia and the slogan "Trust your car to the man who wears the star" were prominently displayed. It was further established that Texaco engaged in substantial national advertising, the purpose of which was to convey the impression that Texaco dealers are skilled in automotive servicing, as well as to promote Texaco products, and that this advertising was not limited to certain services or products. The record reveals that approximately 30 per cent of the Texaco dealers in the country engage in the selling of used cars and that this activity is known to and acquiesced in by the corporation. Actually Texaco had a regional office located directly opposite the service station in question and Texaco personnel working in this office were aware of the fact that used vehicles were being sold from the station. It was further established that there were signs displayed indicating that an "Expert foreign car mechanic" was on the premises.

Appellant Gizzi testified that he was aware of the advertising engaged in by Texaco and that it had instilled in him a certain sense of confidence in the corporation and its products.

In granting Texaco's motion for a directed verdict the court stated:

> "I am convinced that as a matter of law there could not be any apparent authority on the basis of what I heard so far or what I have had the slightest glimmer that you could show, no apparent authority on the part of this operator to bind Texaco in connection with the sale of this used Volkswagon bus. . . .
>
> "In short, nobody could reasonably interpret any of these slogans or representations or indicia of control as dealing with anything more than the servicing of automobiles, and to the extent of putting gas in them and the ordinary things that are done at service stations.
>
> "That 'Trust your car to the man who wears the star' could not possibly be construed to apply to installing new brake systems or selling used cars."

We are of the opinion that the court below erred in granting the motion. Questions of apparent authority are questions of fact, and are therefore for the jury to determine.

On a motion for a directed verdict, and on appeal from the granting of such a motion, all evidence and testimony must be viewed in a light most favorable to the party against whom such motion is made and that party is entitled to all reasonable inferences that could be drawn from the evidence.

While the evidence on behalf of appellants by no means amounted to an overwhelming case of liability, we are of the opinion that reasonable men could differ regarding it and that the issue should have been determined by the jury, after proper instructions from the court.

For the reasons stated herein, the order of the district court will be vacated and the case remanded for further proceedings consistent with this opinion. We do not pass on the merits of any other claims advanced on this appeal, but leave them for the consideration of the district court on the remand.

SEITZ, Circuit Judge (dissenting). I would affirm the order of the district court.

The two plaintiffs in this case each seek to recover damages for their personal injuries, claiming that Texaco is liable under the following four theories: (1) breach of warranty with respect to the sale of the delivery van; (2) breach of warranty with respect to the repairs which were made on the van before the sale; (3) vicarious liability for Hinman's negligence in repairing the van; and (4) negligence in permitting an unqualified person such as Hinman to perform repairs at its service station. Although this diversity action was brought in the Eastern District of Pennsylvania, where the accident occurred, it is not disputed that the issue of Texaco's liability is governed by the substantive law of New Jersey.

Plaintiffs first claim that Hinman warranted that the van was in good running condition and had no mechanical defects; at trial, they presented evidence which indicated that Hinman expressly told them that the van was "in A-1 shape" and that the brakes in particular were in good working order. I agree with the majority that no actual agency relationship existed between Texaco and Hinman with respect to the sale of used vehicles, but I disagree that the district court erred in granting Texaco a directed verdict on the issues of apparent agency and agency by estoppel. The following statement of New Jersey law is pertinent to the disposition of this case:

> "One who represents that another is his agent and thereby causes a third person justifiably to rely upon the care or skill of such apparent agent is subject to liability to the third person for harm caused by the lack of care or skill of the one appearing to be servant as if he were such. Restatement, Agency, par. 267. . . . This rule normally applies where the plaintiff has submitted himself to the care or protection of an apparent servant in response to an apparent invitation from the defendant to enter into such relations with such servant. A manifestation of authority constitutes an invitation to deal with such servant and to enter into relations with him *which are consistent with the apparent authority.*"

Assuming that a person of ordinary prudence would be entitled to believe that Hinman was Texaco's agent in the sale of gasoline, oil, tires, and other items which are ordinarily sold at a filling station, it does not follow that a reasonable man would believe that Hinman's apparent authority extended to the sale of used cars. Such a belief would, in my view, be unreasonable. Moreover, in the absence of an appearance of agency, Texaco's mere acquiescence in the sale cannot be said to create an agency by estoppel. Where the evidence permits only one reasonable conclusion on the issue of agency, that issue must be decided by the trial court, not the jury.

I believe that a directed verdict was equally proper on plaintiffs' second and third theories of liability, involving the repairs which Hinman performed on the van. In Wallach v. Williams, 52 N.J. 504, 246 A.2d 713 (1968), the Supreme Court of New Jersey expressly reserved decision on whether an oil company which creates the impression by signs and advertising that it operates a service station can be held liable for the negligence of an independent contractor who operates the station. The facts of the present case also make it unnecessary to decide this issue. As both the majority and the district court have indicated, the repair work was purely incidental to the sale of the vehicle. Gizzi quoted Hinman as offering not only to sell the van for $400 but also to replace the master cylinder and muffler, repair the engine, repaint the vehicle, and generally "put it in A-1 shape" at no extra charge. I agree with the district judge that, considering plaintiffs' evidence in its most favorable light, the sale was strictly a personal transaction and Hinman made the repairs in his individual capacity simply to induce the sale. Particularly since the cost of the repairs was absorbed into the overall sales price, which was payable directly to Hinman, in my view, no reasonable man could conclude that Hinman was acting as a servant or agent of Texaco.

Finally, I believe that a directed verdict was proper on plaintiffs' claim that Texaco negligently permitted Hinman to perform automobile repairs even though he was unqualified and incompetent to do such work. Plaintiffs' only evidence was that Texaco itself did not give Hinman any specialized training. They produced no evidence to show either Hinman's incompetence or Texaco's negligence.

JENNINGS v. PITTSBURGH MERCANTILE CO.
Supreme Court of Pennsylvania
414 Pa. 641, 202 A.2d 51 (1964)

OPINION BY MR. JUSTICE COHEN, July 1, 1964:

Appellees, Dan R. Jennings, a Pittsburgh real estate broker, and his associate, Daniel B. Cantor, a New York real estate investment counselor and attorney, instituted this action of assumpsit against Pittsburgh Mercantile Company (Mercantile) to recover a real estate brokerage commission for the alleged consummation of a sale and leaseback of all of Mercantile's real property. Mercantile appeals from the lower court's denial of its motion for judgment n.o.v. after jury verdict for appellees.

The principal issue in this appeal is whether there was sufficient evidence upon which the jury could conclude that Mercantile clothed its agent with the apparent authority to accept an offer for the sale and leaseback thereby binding it to the payment of the brokerage commission, the agent having had, admittedly, no actual authority to so do.

Mercantile is a publicly-held corporation with over 400 shareholders. It is managed by a nine-member board of directors. An executive committee, consisting of the three major officers, functions between the board's quarterly meetings.

The facts in issue viewed in a light most favorable to appellees are as follows: In April, 1958, Frederick A. Egmore, Mercantile's vice-president and treasurer-comptroller, and Walter P. Stern, its financial consultant, met with Jennings, explained Mercantile's desire to raise cash for store modernization and provided Jennings with information concerning Mercantile's finances. Jennings was asked to solicit offers for a sale and leaseback.

At this meeting Egmore made the following representations: (1) the executive committee, of which Egmore was a member, controlled Mercantile and (2) would be responsible for determining whether the company would accept any of the offers produced by Jennings; (3) subsequent board of directors' approval of the acceptance would be automatic. Egmore promised the payment of a commission if Jennings succeeded in bringing in an offer on terms as to amount realized, annual rental, and lease duration acceptable to the executive committee. Egmore outlined preliminarily the terms of an acceptable offer.[1]

In July and August, 1958, Jennings brought Egmore three offers, none of which met the originally specified terms. The first two were quickly rejected by Egmore. The third offer came close to the original terms. On November 4, 1958, Jennings was informed by Stern that the executive committee had "agreed to the deal." However, within a week Egmore informed Jennings that the third offer had been rejected. Mercantile refused to pay Jennings' bill for commission of $32,000 and suit was thereafter instituted.

At the outset, we note that for Mercantile this proposed sale and leaseback was not a transaction in the ordinary course of business. Rather, it was unusual and unprecedented. The trans-

---

[1] Although the evidence at various points refers to the actions of other members of the executive committee and to Stern, it is abundantly clear that Egmore was the principal actor with regard to the sale and leaseback. Our reasoning here regarding Egmore's apparent authority applies with equal force to the actions of other executive committee members and to Stern.

action envisaged Mercantile's relinquishment of ownership of all its real property, worth approximately $1.5 million, for a period of 30 years. Hence, the apparent authority which appellees seek to establish is the apparent authority to accept an offer for an extraordinary transaction.

Apparent authority is defined as that authority which, although not actually granted, the principal (1) knowingly permits the agent to exercise or (2) holds him out as possessing. Simon v. H. K. Porter Company, 407 Pa. 359, 364, 180 A. 2d 227, 230 (1962). See 2 Fletcher Cyclopedia Corporations §§ 449, 451 (1954).

Jennings strongly contends that Egmore's representations gave rise to the apparent authority asserted. We do not agree. Without regard to the extraordinary nature of a transaction, a disclosed or partially disclosed principal cannot be bound on the doctrine of apparent authority by virtue of the extra-judicial representations of an agent as to the existence or extent of his authority or the facts upon which it depends. Restatement (2d), Agency § 168 (1958). See Annot. 3 A.L.R. 2d 598, 602-607 (1949). An agent cannot, simply by his own words, invest himself with apparent authority. Such authority emanates from the actions of the principal and not the agent. Therefore, the representations upon which Jennings relies so heavily do not support his contention.

Jennings further argues that apparent authority arose by virtue of (1) certain prior dealings of Egmore and (2) the corporate offices held by Egmore. However, the evidence advanced in support of this argument is insufficient to permit a reasonable inference of the existence of apparent authority in Egmore to accept Jennings' offer.

Focusing on the first of these factors, in order for a reasonable inference of the existence of apparent authority to be drawn from prior dealings, these dealings must have (1) a measure of similarity to the act for which the principal is sought to be bound, and, granting this similarity, (2) a degree of repetitiveness. See, e.g., Brientnall v. Peters, 317 Pa. 356, 176 Atl. 240 (1935); Colonial Trust Co. v. Davis, 274 Pa. 363, 118 Atl. 312 (1922). See Restatement (2d), Agency § 43(2) and comment b thereto (1958). Although the required degree of repetitiveness might have been present here, the prior acts relied upon consisted solely of Egmore's provision of financial information to Jennings and other brokers with regard to the sale and leaseback, and Egmore's solicitation of offers through them. The dissimilarities between these acts and the act of accepting the offer in issue are self-evident, and apparent authority to do the latter act cannot be inferred from the doing of the former.

As to the second of the above factors, the corporate offices of vice-president and treasurer-comptroller, which Egmore held, do not provide the basis for a reasonable inference that Mercantile held out Egmore as having the apparent authority to accept the offers produced by Jennings. See Gabriel v. Auf Der Heide-Aragona, Inc., 14 N.J. Super. 558, 82 A. 2d 644 (1951); Miller v. Wick Bldg. Co., 154 Ohio St. 93, 93 N.E. 2d 467 (1950); Mosell Realty Corporation v. Schofield, 183 Va. 782, 33 S.E.2d 774 (1945). Each of these cases involved a suit against a corporation for a brokerage commission for securing a purchaser for all of the corporation's realty. The principal issue in each was the apparent authority possessed virtute officii to consummate an extraordinary transaction. On facts stronger than those present here,[3] the claims of apparent authority were rejected. We hold likewise on the present facts, for any other conclusion would improperly extend the usual scope of authority which attaches to the holding of various corporate offices, and would greatly undercut the proper role of the board of directors in corporate decision-making by thrusting upon them determinations on critical matters which they have never had the opportunity to consider.

The case of *Simon v. H. K. Porter,* supra, strongly relied upon by the lower court is not controlling. There, defendant Porter's offer of parcels of excess property were relatively small in comparison to its overall size and therefore did not contemplate a transaction of an extraordinary nature. Furthermore, Porter had definitely decided to sell, and in pursuance of this decision, it formulated an offer on rather definite terms and authorized its agent to seek acceptance thereof. In the case at bar, Jennings was merely authorized to solicit offers which Mercantile would then consider in deciding whether to sell, and if it did decide to sell, on what terms. While a reasonable inference of apparent authority to bind a principal to a contract may be drawn from the authority of the offeror's agent to seek acceptances, as in *Porter,* the same inference cannot be drawn from the authority of an offeree's agent merely to solicit offers, as here. Further, the authority of Porter's agent was communicated to the public via an advertisement in the Wall Street Journal. Additionally, Porter clothed its agent with apparent authority by permitting him to accept deposit checks and deposit same, sign deeds to the property, fully negotiate terms and consummate eight prior sales. The consummation of these sales was a major function of

---

[3] These cases involved closely held corporations in which the alleged agent was also a dominant stockholder.

the agent and was in the usual course of his business responsibilities.[5] Porter is therefore clearly distinguishable.

Finally, the extraordinary nature of this transaction placed appellees on notice to inquire as to Egmore's actual authority, particularly since appellees were an experienced real estate broker and investment counselor-attorney team. See cases collected in 2 Fletcher Cyclopedia Corporations, § 461, p. 405, n.96 (1954). Had inquiry been made, appellees would have discovered that the board never considered any of the proposals and obviously did not delegate actual authority to accept offers.

Appellees having failed to produce sufficient evidence upon which the jury could reasonably have found the existence of apparent authority to accept an offer for the sale and leaseback of all of Mercantile's real property, appellant is entitled to judgment n.o.v.

Judgment reversed and entered for appellant.

Mr. Justice ROBERTS concurs in the result.

SEELY v. HAGEN
Court of Appeals of Arizona
— Ariz. App. —, 508 P.2d 343 (1973)

KRUCKER, Judge. This appeal arises from a controversy concerning the ownership of thirty head of cattle. Appellant, plaintiff below, filed suit against appellees, defendants below, alleging that he was the owner of and entitled to the possession of said cattle which the defendants had allegedly converted to their own use; and that by reason of said wrongful conversion and detention he had sustained damages in the amount of $4,035. The defendants denied the material allegations of the complaint and asserted various affirmative defenses. The case was tried to the court resulting in a judgment in favor of the defendants that plaintiff take nothing by his complaint. The judgment contains the following recitation as to the court's reasons for its decision:

> "Where one of two innocent parties must suffer because of the action of a third person, loss should fall upon the one, who by his conduct, created the circumstances which enabled the third party to perpetrate the wrong or caused the loss."

The evidence most favorable to sustaining the judgment is as follows. In June, 1971, the plaintiff consigned a load of cattle to Arlington Cattle Company in Arizona. After the cattle had

---

[5] These facts are contained in part in the lower court's opinion, Court of Common Pleas of Philadelphia County.

been shipped, he learned that Arlington would prefer not to receive the cattle. When his truckdriver called him from Tucson, as he had been instructed, the plaintiff directed him to deliver the cattle to a cattle rest near Eloy. A health certificate issued by Texas inspection authorities was in the possession of the truckdriver who was transporting the cattle. Between the time that the plaintiff had been informed that Arlington did not want the cattle and the call from his trucker, the plaintiff contacted a Mr. Buchanan in Eloy. Buchanan was a cattle broker with whom the plaintiff had previous dealings concerning the sale of his cattle. The plaintiff instructed Buchanan to sell the cattle for him.

According to the plaintiff his previous dealings with Buchanan in cattle transactions were successful. He directed his trucker to unload the cattle at Eloy when Buchanan informed him that there were several farms in the Eloy area that would buy the cattle. Therefore he told Buchanan to try to sell the cattle in small lots and to go ahead and buy the feed and do everything necessary to keep the cattle. Buchanan followed his instructions and took charge of the cattle which were delivered to the cattle rest in Eloy. He arranged for the sale of all the cattle, including a sale of thirty head to Mr. Hagen, defendant in this lawsuit. Buchanan also arranged for a health inspection of the cattle, as required by law, and delivery of the cattle to the Hagen farm. The information on the certificate was supplied to the health inspector by Buchanan. According to the testimony of Hagen and an employee of the cattle rest, Buchanan indicated to Hagen that Seely was his partner. The livestock inspection certificate contained the name George Seely in the space designated "Signature of Seller or Owner" and on the next line in the space designated "By" the name Herman Buchanan was written.

The certificate was delivered to Hagen when he paid Buchanan by means of two checks payable to Herman Buchanan. No payment was forwarded to the plaintiff by Buchanan and after several weeks had elapsed he decided to investigate. He came to Arizona and learned of the sale to Hagen. An attempt to stop payment on Hagen's check was unsuccessful and on July 30, 1971, the plaintiff filed a criminal complaint against Buchanan. This complaint, signed by Seely, alleged that Herman Buchanan was entrusted with property belonging to Seely for the sale or transfer thereof and that Buchanan fraudulently converted proceeds thereof to his own use.

There is no conflict in the evidence as to Buchanan's authority to sell the subject cattle. The plaintiff admitted at trial that he had expressly authorized Buchanan to do so. This is further supported by the allegations of the criminal complaint. Thus we see that there is sufficient evidence to support a finding that Buchanan had authority to bind the plaintiff to a sale of the cattle. Aetna Loan Co. v. Apache Trailer Sales, 1 Ariz.App. 322, 402 P.2d 580 (1965). The next question to be resolved is whether Buchanan had authority to receive or collect payment for the cattle. It is true the general rule is that an agent authorized to sell commodities has no implied authority to receive or collect payment therefor. This rule, however, is subject to certain well-established exceptions. One such exception is if there is an apparent authority on the part of the agent to receive payment. Where the principal has entrusted the agent with possession of the goods to be sold, a purchaser may rightfully assume his authority to collect the purchase money. Daly v. Williams, 78 Ariz. 382, 280 P.2d 701 (1955); Ronald A. Coco, Inc. v. St. Paul's Methodist Church, 78 N.M. 97, 428 P.2d 636 (1967); 3 Am.Jur.2d Agency § 106. Plaintiff Seely was therefore bound by the payment to Buchanan and such payment operated to discharge the indebtedness despite Buchanan's failure to turn the money over to Seely. 3 Am.Jur.2d Agency § 265.

We agree with the lower court's disposition of this case. It is truly unfortunate that the plaintiff's trust and confidence in Buchanan were misplaced. However, it was he who created the circumstances which enabled Buchanan to cause the loss and therefore the law leaves him to his remedy against Buchanan.

Judgment affirmed.

HATHAWAY, C. J., and HOWARD, J., concur.

---

iii. *Beyond Apparent Authority*

The following cases are occasionally cited as examples of the liability of a principal beyond the bounds of apparent authority. In reading them, ask yourself if you agree with this classification of these cases and, if so, which of the other Restatement categories, if any, would you put them under? Also, how safe are we in generalizing from these cases and, for that matter, how do we go about generalizing from them?

KIDD v. THOMAS A. EDISON, INC.
District Court for the Southern District of New York
239 F. 405 (1917), *aff'd,* 242 F. 923 (2d Cir. 1917)

This is a motion by the defendant to set aside a verdict for the plaintiff on exceptions. The action was in contract, and depended upon the authority of one Fuller to make a contract with the plaintiff, engaging her without condition to sing for the defendant in a series of "tone test" recitals, designed to show the accuracy with which her voice was reproduced by the defendant's records. The defendant contended that Fuller's only authority was to engage the plaintiff for such recitals as he could later persuade dealers in the records to book her for all over the United States. The dealers, the defendant said, were to agree to pay her for the recitals, and the defendant would then guarantee her the dealers' performance. The plaintiff said the contract was an unconditional engagement for a singing tour, and the jury so found.

The sole exception of consequence was whether there was either any question of fact involved in Fuller's authority, or a fortiori whether there was no evidence of any authority. In either event the charge was erroneous, and the defendant's exception was good. The pertinent testimony was that of Maxwell, and was as follows: He intrusted to Fuller particularly the matters connected with the arranging of these "tone test" recitals. He told him to learn from the artists what fees they would expect, and to tell them that the defendant would pay the railroad fares and expenses. He also told Fuller to explain to them that the defendant would book them, and act as booking agent for them, and would see that the money was paid by the dealers; in fact, the defendant would itself pay it. He told him to prepare a form of contract suitable for such an arrangement with such artists as he succeeded in getting to go into it, and that he (Maxwell) would prepare a form of booking contract with the dealers. He told him to prepare a written contract with the artists and submit it to him (Maxwell), which he did. He told him that he was himself to make the contracts with the artists by which they were to be booked, that he was not to bring them to him (Maxwell), but that he should learn what fees they would demand, and then confirm the oral agreement by a letter, which would serve as a contract.

This is all the relevant testimony.

LEARNED HAND, District Judge (after stating the facts as above). The point involved is the scope of Fuller's "apparent authority," as distinct from the actual authority limited by the instructions which Maxwell gave him. The phrase "apparent authority," though it occurs repeatedly in the Reports, has been often criticized (Mechem, Law of Agency, §§ 720-726), and its use is by no means free from ambiguity. The scope of any authority must, of course, in the first place, be measured, not alone by the words in which it is created, but by the whole setting in which those words are used, including the customary powers of such agents.

This is, however, no more than to regard the whole of the communication between the principal and agent before assigning its meaning, and does not differ in method from any other interpretation of verbal acts. In considering what was Fuller's actual implied authority by custom, while it is fair to remember that the "tone test" recitals were new, in the sense that no one had ever before employed singers for just this purpose of comparing their voices with their mechanical reproduction, they were not new merely as musical recitals; for it was, of course, a common thing to engage singers for such recitals. When, therefore, an agent is selected, as was Fuller, to engage singers for musical recitals, the customary implication would seem to have been that his authority was without limitation of the kind here imposed, which was unheard of in the circumstances. The mere fact that the purpose of the recitals was advertisement, instead of entrance fees, gave no intimation to a singer dealing with him that the defendant's promise would be conditional upon so unusual a condition as that actually imposed. Being concerned to sell its records, the venture might rightly be regarded as undertaken on its own account, and, like similar enterprises, at its own cost. The natural surmise would certainly be that such an undertaking was a part of the advertising expenses of the business, and that therefore Fuller might engage singers upon similar terms to those upon which singers for recitals are generally engaged, where the manager expects a profit, direct or indirect.

Therefore it is enough for the decision to say that the customary extent of such an authority as was actually conferred comprised such a contract. If estoppel be, therefore, the basis of all "apparent authority," it existed here. Yet the argument involves a misunderstanding of the true significance of the doctrine, both historically (Responsibility for Tortious Acts: Its History, Wigmore, 7 Harv. L. Rev. 315, 383) and actually. The responsibility of a master for his servant's act is not at bottom a matter of consent to the express act, or of an estoppel to deny that consent, but it is a survival from ideas of status, and the imputed responsibility congenial to earlier times, preserved now from motives of policy. While we have substituted for the archaic status a test based upon consent, i.e., the general scope of the business, within that sphere the master is held by principles quite independent of his actual consent, and indeed in the face of his own instructions. Of federal cases the following are illustrative: [citations]. These were, it is true, all cases in which the third person took some action upon the faith of the agent's authority, and it is possible to speak of them as though they were cases of estoppel, but in truth they are not. It is only a fiction to say that the principal is estopped, when he has not communicated with the third person and thus misled him. There are, indeed, the cases of customary authority, which perhaps come within the range of a true estoppel; but in other cases the principal may properly say that the authority which he delegated must be judged by his directions, taken together, and that it is unfair to charge him with misleading the public, because his agent, in executing that authority, has neither observed, nor communicated, an important part of them. Certainly it begs the question to assume that the principal has authorized his agent to communicate a part of his authority and not to disclose the rest. Hence, even in contract, there are many cases in which the principle of estoppel is a factitious effort to impose the rationale of a later time upon archaic ideas, which, it is true, owe their survival to convenience, but to a very different [sic] from the putative convenience attributed to them.

However it may be of contracts, all color of plausibility falls away in the case of torts, where indeed the doctrine first arose, and where it still thrives. It makes no difference that the agent may be disregarding his principal's directions, secret or otherwise, so long as he continues in that larger field measured by the general scope of the business intrusted to his care.

The considerations which have made the rule survive are apparent. If a man select another to act for him with some discretion, he has by that fact vouched to some extent for his reliability. While it may not be fair to impose upon him the results of a total departure from the general subject of his confidence, the detailed execution of his mandate stands on a different footing. The very purpose of delegated authority is to avoid constant recourse by third persons to the principal, which would be a corollary of denying the agent any latitude beyond his exact instructions. Once a third person has assured himself widely of the character of the agent's mandate, the very purpose of the relation demands the possibility of the principal's being bound through the agent's minor deviations. Thus, as so often happens, archaic ideas continue to serve good, though novel, purposes.

In the case at bar there was no question of fact for the jury touching the scope of Fuller's authority. His general business covered the whole tone test recitals; upon him was charged the duty of doing everything necessary in the premises, without recourse to Maxwell or any one else. It would certainly have been quite contrary to the expectations of the defendant, if any of the prospective performers at the recitals had insisted upon verifying directly with Maxwell the terms of her contract. It was precisely to delegate such negotiations to a competent substitute that they chose Fuller at all.

The exception is without merit; the motion is denied.

WATTEAU v. FENWICK
Queen's Bench Division
[1892] 1 Q.B. 346

APPEAL from the decision of the county court judge of Middlesborough.

From the evidence it appeared that one Humble had carried on business at a beerhouse called the Victoria Hotel, at Stockton-on-Tees, which business he had transferred to the defendants, a firm of brewers, some years before the present action. After the transfer of the business, Humble remained as defendants' manager; but the license was always taken out in Humble's name, and his name was painted over the door. Under the terms of the agreement made between Humble and the defendants, the former had no authority to buy any goods for the business except bottled ales and mineral waters; all other goods required were to be supplied by the defendants themselves. The action was brought to recover the price of goods delivered at the Victoria Hotel over some years, for which it was admitted that the plaintiff gave credit to Humble only: they consisted of cigars, bovril, and other articles. The learned judge allowed the claim for the cigars and bovril only, and gave judgment for the plaintiff for 22l. 12s. 6d. The defendants appealed.

1892. Nov. 19. *Finlay*, *Q.C.* (*Scott Fox*, with him), for the defendants. The decision of the county court judge was wrong. The liability of a principal for the acts of his agent, done contrary to his secret instructions, depends upon his holding him out as his agent—that is, upon the agent being clothed with an apparent authority to act for his principal. Where, therefore, a man carries on business in his own name through a manager, he holds out his own credit, and would be liable for goods supplied even where the manager exceeded his authority. But where, as in the present case, there is no holding out by the principal, but the business is carried on in the agent's name and the goods are supplied on his credit, a person wishing to go behind the agent and make the principal liable must shew an agency in fact.

[LORD COLERIDGE, C.J. Cannot you, in such a case, sue the undisclosed principal on discovering him?]

Only where the act done by the agent is within the scope of his agency; not where there has been an excess of authority. Where any one has been held out by the principal as his agent, there is a contract with the principal by estoppel, however much the agent may have exceeded his authority; where there has been no holding out, proof must be given of an agency in fact in order to make the principal liable.

Boydell Houghton, for the plaintiff. The defendants are liable in the present action. They are in fact undisclosed principals, who instead of carrying on the business in their own names employed a manager to carry it on for them, and clothed him with authority to do what was necessary to carry on the business. The case depends upon the same principles as *Edmunds v. Bushell*,[1] where the manager of a business which was carried on in his own name with the addition "and Co." accepted a bill of exchange, notwithstanding a stipulation in the agreement with his principal that he should not accept bills; and the Court held that the principal was liable to an indorsee who took the bill without any knowledge of the relations between the principal and agent. In that case there was no holding out of the manager as an agent; it was the simple case of an agent being allowed to act as the ostensible principal without any disclosure to the world of there being any one behind him. Here the defendants have so conducted themselves as to enable their agent to hold himself out to the world as the proprietor of their business, and they are clearly undisclosed principals: *Ramazotti v. Bowring*. All that the plaintiff has to do, therefore, in order to charge the principals, is to shew that the goods supplied were such as were ordinarily used in the business—that is to say, that they were within the reasonable scope of the agent's authority.

Dec. 12. LORD COLERIDGE, C.J. The judgment which I am about to read has been written by my brother Wills, and I entirely concur in it.

WILLS, J. The plaintiff sues the defendants for the price of cigars supplied to the Victoria Hotel, Stockton-upon-Tees. The house was kept, not by the defendants, but by a person named Humble, whose name was over the door. The plaintiff gave credit to Humble, and to him alone, and had never heard of the defendants. The business, however, was really the defendants', and they had put Humble into it to manage it for them, and had forbidden him to buy cigars on credit. The cigars, however,

---

[1] Law Rep. 1 Q. B. 97.

were such as would usually be supplied to and dealt in at such an establishment. The learned county court judge held that the defendants were liable. I am of opinion that he was right.

There seems to be less of direct authority on the subject than one would expect. But I think that the Lord Chief Justice during the argument laid down the correct principle, viz., once it is established that the defendant was the real principal, the ordinary doctrine as to principal and agent applies—that the principal is liable for all the acts of the agent which are within the authority usually confided to an agent of that character, notwithstanding limitations, as between the principal and the agent, put upon that authority. It is said that it is only so where there has been a holding out of authority—which cannot be said of a case where the person supplying the goods knew nothing of the existence of a principal. But I do not think so. Otherwise, in every case of undisclosed principal, or at least in every case where the fact of there being a principal was undisclosed, the secret limitation of authority would prevail and defeat the action of the person dealing with the agent and then discovering that he was an agent and had a principal.

But in the case of a dormant partner it is clear law that no limitation of authority as between the dormant and active partner will avail the dormant partner as to things within the ordinary authority of a partner. The law of partnership is, on such a question, nothing but a branch of the general law of principal and agent, and it appears to me to be undisputed and conclusive on the point now under discussion.

The principle laid down by the Lord Chief Justice, and acted upon by the learned county court judge, appears to be identical with that enunciated in the judgments of Cockburn, C.J., and Mellor, J., in *Edmunds v. Bushell,* the circumstances of which case, though not identical with those of the present, come very near to them. There was no holding out, as the plaintiff knew nothing of the defendant. I appreciate the distinction drawn by Mr. Finlay in his argument, but the principle laid down in the judgments referred to, if correct, abundantly covers the present case. I cannot find that any doubt has ever been expressed that it is correct, and I think it is right, and that very mischievous consequences would often result if that principle were not upheld.

In my opinion this appeal ought to be dismissed with costs.

Appeal dismissed.

NOTES

1.   The Restatement sections on inherent agency power adopt the rationale of this case. See Sections 194 and 195, dealing with the undisclosed principal, holding the principal to liability in terms strikingly similar to those used in the *Watteau* case.

2.   The distinction between general agents and special agents plays a major role in the inherent agency concept of the Restatement. A general agent is defined by Section 3 of the Restatement as, "[A]n agent authorized to conduct a series of transactions involving a continuity of service," such as "the manager of a business or the agent in charge of a construction project." One "who is an integral part of a business organization and does not require fresh authorization for each transaction is a general agent."

A special agent is defined in the same section as, "[A]n agent authorized to conduct a single transaction or a series of transactions not involving continuity of service," such as a real estate agent. "[A] person employed only to deliver a promissory note on specified terms is . . . clearly a special agent."

Sections 161 and 161A of the Restatement, dealing with the liability of disclosed or partially disclosed principals, have as their subject the inherent agency power ramifications of the above distinctions. Section 161 states that a general agent can bind his principal to contracts where there is neither authority nor apparent authority and where the general agent is acting disobediently, so long as he "does something which is usually done in connection with the transactions he is employed to conduct." Two illustrations of this power are given below in note 3. Section 161A states that special agents do not have this power, and defines the powers of a special agent more narrowly.

The comments to Section 161 note that this liability of the principal of a general agent "exists solely because of his relation to the agent." The rationale behind this power is reflected by the following passage in Comment *a*:

> Commercial convenience requires that the principal should not escape liability where there have been deviations from the usually granted authority by persons who are . . . essential parts of his business enterprise. In the long run it is of advantage to business, and hence to employers as a class, that third persons should not be required to scrutinize too carefully the mandates of permanent or semi-permanent agents who do no more than what is usually done by agents in similar positions.

What duty is left on the third party to inquire into the authority of the agent? Does he have to know that the general agent is a "permanent or semi-permanent" agent of the defendant? The only limitation stated in Section 161 is that the third party must "reasonably believe" that the agent is authorized. Ask yourself what the Restatement meant by this limitation, particularly in light of the two illustrations contained immediately below.

3. RESTATEMENT § 161 contains the following two illustrations in its comments. Can you understand them?

> Illustration 1. P appoints A as his general wheat-selling agent for Philadelphia, instructing A not to give the usual market warranties with wheat sold. T, a stranger in Philadelphia and not familiar with the customs of the Philadelphia market, buys P's wheat from A, who gives him the ordinary market warranty although representing to T that such warranty is not customary. P is bound by the warranty.

> Illustration 3. P employs A as the general manager of his foundry, instructing A to purchase his alloys from a certain firm. A, finding the alloys to be unsatisfactory, and without consultation with P, purchases alloys from another firm, T, writing to T upon personal stationery and signing the letter only "A, agent of P." P is bound upon this transaction.

Ask yourself what interest the law is protecting here. Also, what difference would it make, if any, if the wheat-selling agent in Illustration 1 above had been a special agent rather than a general agent? Would *P* in Illustration 3 above have been bound to the transaction if *A* had signed the letter just "A"?

4. As the quotation from Section 27 on page 193 makes clear, the disclosed or partially disclosed principal is liable to the third party even if his agent acts for his own or other improper purposes, unless the other party has notice that the agent is not acting for the principal's benefit. Is this also true with respect to the undisclosed principal? See Section 199, saying no, because there is no reliance by the other party upon the fact of an agency relationship. "The fact that the existence of the agency suggested or created the opportunity for the act is not sufficient. The only basis for the principal's liability [when he is undisclosed] is the intent of the agent to act in the principal's business." The motive of the agent can be improper and still bind the undisclosed principal, however, "if the act is performed as part of [but not necessarily in furtherance of] the principal's business." The example given is an agent deliberately ordering and selling substandard goods because he disliked his principal and wanted to give the *P*'s store a **bad** reputation.

5. *P* delivers a diamond ring to *A*, a dealer in rings, instructing him to see if a purchaser can be found and if so, to report back to *P* the price offered. Instead, *A* sells the ring. *P* is bound by the sale.

P delivers a diamond to *A*, a dealer in diamonds, to be sold. *A* exchanges it for another diamond. In the absence of a statute, or a custom permitting this, *P* is not bound by the transaction.

The above two paragraphs are taken from RESTATEMENT § 175, Illustrations 5 and 1, respectively. Do they make any sense to you? Does the difference in result follow a consistent theory? There clearly was not actual authority in either case. Was there apparent authority? Estoppel? Inherent agency power? With regard to the latter, is the agent involved a general agent or a special agent? If a special agent, then Section 161A is applicable, which does have a subsection applying the inherent agency power rule to agents in possession of goods or commercial documents with authority to deal with them. Note that this language would resolve the bill of lading problem raised on page 170 *supra*.

UNIFORM COMMERCIAL CODE § 2-403(2) (1962 Official Text) reads as follows: "Any entrusting of possession of goods to a merchant who deals in goods of that kind gives him power to transfer all rights of the entruster to a buyer in ordinary course of business." How does this bear on the problem raised in Section 175, above?

6. As the above materials demonstrate, the potential liability of a principal for the actions of his contracting agent is very broad. Can the principal make effective use of disclaimer or exculpatory clauses to reduce his potential liability in situations where written contracts are involved? This question raises two separate issues: (1) The validity of clauses aimed at limiting the authority of agents to bind the principal contractually to matters outside of the written agreement, which is usually a form contract. Such clauses usually are upheld, on the reasoning that the other party can no longer reasonably believe in the broad authority of the agent. (2) The validity of clauses exculpating the principal from his agent's frauds. Again, according to Section 260 of the Restatement, such clauses are upheld and relieve an innocent principal of tort liability. He may be subject to a claim for rescission by the other party, however, assuming he has not changed position in reliance on a contract or conveyance obtained by his agent. The policy behind this is that the principal should not in fairness benefit from his agent's fraud.

7. The articles in this area include Hetherington, *Trends in Enterprise Liability: Law and the Unauthorized Agent*, 19 STAN.

L. Rev. 76 (1966); Mearns, *Vicarious Liability for Agency Contracts,* 48 Va. L. Rev. 50 (1962); Seavey, *Agency Powers,* 1 Okla. L. Rev. 3 (1948), reprinted in W. Seavey, Studies in Agency 181-202 (1949).

PROBLEMS

1. Bangor Mills is a large user of nylon yarn in its manufacturing business. The demand for nylon yarn has vastly exceeded the supply for some time. Bangor's heavy need and strong economic position are well known, leading it to attempt to deal through an intermediary in order to reduce the cost which it would otherwise have to pay for yarn. It therefore arranged with one Shetzline, an ordinary hosiery jobber, to make purchases for Bangor under his own name when Bangor so requested. Bangor established a bank account in both its name and Shetzline's, with authority for Shetzline to draw funds without using Bangor's name, but not to spend more than $10 per pound nor overdraw the bank account.

Assume that you are the lawyer for Bangor and that the vice-president in charge of purchasing has just presented this plan to you and asked you for your advice. Do you see any legal problems in the arrangement? If so, what problems, and what mode of proceeding would you suggest? (Clients are no more happy with a "no" answer than anyone else is, and they're in a good position to do something about it.)

Assume that what you probably feared would happen did happen: Shetzline buys some yarn for more than $10 per pound and overdraws the account. Assume further that the seller of the yarn, who holds a check returned for insufficient funds, uncovers the involvement of Bangor in the transaction and wants to hold Bangor liable because Shetzline is insolvent, or nearly so. Will Bangor be held liable? Should it be? Does the previous material help you provide an answer?

Try to figure out the answer for yourself. Then *see* Senor v. Bangor Mills, Inc., 211 F.2d 685 (3d Cir. 1954). *See also* the comment by Warren Seavey on this case in 1 Howard L. J. 79 (1955).

2. Templeton and Sheets went into partnership to establish a stock farm. They acquired a herd of brood mares for that purpose. Without the knowledge or consent of Sheets, Templeton undertook to sell the entire herd to Lowman. Sheets refused to surrender them and Lowman brought replevin. What result? Lowman v. Sheets, 124 Ind. 416, 24 N.E. 351 (1890), and *In re* Messenger, 32 F. Supp. 490 (E.D. Pa. 1940) (where a member of a

partnership engaged in the plumbing business sold the firm's truck without the consent of his co-partner). What other authority would you want to consult?

3. Parker had a claim against Thomas and wanted to settle it. He hired Adams, an attorney, to contact Thomas and negotiate an offer of settlement from him. In order to increase the chance that Thomas would take negotiating with Adams seriously, Parker authorized Adams to represent that he was authorized to settle the claim. At the same time, however, Parker said to Adams, "Now don't *actually* settle. Just bring an offer back to me."

Adams contacted Thomas and represented that he was authorized to negotiate and settle the claim. Thereafter, without checking back with Parker, Adams settled with Thomas. Parker doesn't like the deal. Is he bound by it?

4. A leather dealer named Beecher by written instrument appointed one Pierce to carry on a business for him (apparently a branch shop) in Andover, including "to do and perform such matters and things as are necessary and proper for the carrying on and conducting said business. Provided, however, that said Pierce shall not make purchases or incur debts exceeding in amount at any one time the sum of $2000. . . ." Pierce showed this document to one Mussey, who asked Pierce if a sale on credit to him for $1000 would mean that his indebtedness would exceed $2000. No, said Pierce, misrepresenting the fact that he was already considerably over the $2000 limit. Mussey made the sale. Upon being unable to collect his money, he sued Beecher for the full amount. What arguments could be advanced by Mussey and Beecher?

The following language is drawn from the opinion of one of the judges in the case.

But an agent cannot enlarge his authority any more by his declarations, than by his other acts; and the rule is clear, that the acts of an agent, not within the scope of his authority, do not bind the principal. . . . But it is urged, that, upon this construction, no one could safely deal with the agent. This objection . . . is answered by the consideration, that no one is bound to deal with the agent. . . . It is he himself [the seller of goods to the agent on credit], and not the principal, who trusts the agent beyond the expressed limits of the power; and, therefore, the maxim, that where one of two innocent persons must suffer, he who reposed confidence in the wrongdoer must bear the loss, operates in favor of the constituent, and not in favor of the seller of the goods.

Another judge hearing the case viewed the matter as follows:

[I]f [Mussey] might not rely on the representations of the agent, the consequence would be, that no sale could safely be made on credit under the power. But the power was given to be used for the benefit of the defendant, and if given in such a form as to enable the agent to perpetrate a fraud, by obtaining credit by false representations, and credit was so obtained, and a loss occurred, it should be sustained by the defendant, and not by the plaintiff, who dealt with the agent in good faith, without knowing, or having any means of knowing, that he was exceeding his authority.

Which judge do you agree with and why? Are there any other arguments that could be made? *See* Mussey v. Beecher, 57 Mass. (3 Cush.) 511 (1849). *See also,* RESTATEMENT § 171. Would it change your analysis if Mussey had not seen the power of attorney?

5. The Smith & Samson partnership, in which there are two partners, is engaged in the newspaper business. Samson, one of the partners, suffered a heart attack and has spent the last 18 months at home convalescing. During the time he was gone Smith, the other partner, ordered pianos from plaintiff on stationery using the partnership letterhead, which was a plain letterhead setting forth just the name and address of the firm. Several months went by. Smith then ordered some more pianos, again using the partnership letterhead and stating in his letter, "We have a prospect of selling two or three more if we have them." The plaintiff shipped the pianos but was not paid. He sues Smith and Samson. As the lawyer for Samson, what defense would you make on his behalf? And as the lawyer for plaintiff, how would you rebut it? *Cf.* Boardman v. Adams, 5 Iowa 224 (1857). Would it affect your analysis if the letterhead used had also contained the following language directly underneath the names: "50 years in the newspaper business"?

6. On a previous visit to the Koos Bros. store, a spacious furniture store in Rahway, New Jersey, Mrs. Hoddeson had looked over some bedroom furniture. After obtaining sufficient funds, she returned to the store with her aunt to buy the furniture. Upon entering, she was greeted "by a tall man with dark hair frosted at the temples and clad in a light blue suit. He inquired if he could be of assistance, and she informed him specifically of her mission." He immediately guided her to the appropriate furniture, withdrew from his pocket a small pad of paper upon which he recorded her order, and calculated the total purchase price. Mrs. Hoddeson handed him the sum in

cash, failing to take a receipt. He informed her that the items, other than those on display, were not in stock, and that similar items would be sent to her soon.

Mrs. Hoddeson did not receive the items. She returned to the store and related the above facts to the manager. Upon checking, he could find no record of the sale or receipt of payment. Also, Mrs. Hoddeson and her aunt were unable to identify any of the store salesmen as the one she dealt with, and all of the salesmen denied dealing with her.

Mrs. Hoddeson has described the above situation to you. Does she have a valid claim against the store? What legal analysis would you undertake in evaluating her claim? *See* Hoddeson v. Koos Bros., 47 N. J. Super. 224, 135 A.2d 702 (1957).

Suppose Mrs. Hoddeson had agreed to the sale as a result of the salesman's representation that the items were marked down 40% on that day. If she succeeded in holding the store liable, would she be able to collect as damages the benefit of this bargain? Or would she be limited to getting her money back?

7. Parsons, who lives in New York, bought a ranch in Montana. He hired Able to manage it, instructing Able not to sell any cattle for six months. Unknown to Parsons, ranch managers in the area where the ranch is located have the customary power to sell cattle. One month later Able sold some cattle to Treece, who knew that Able was the manager of the ranch but did not know of the local custom. Can Parsons disaffirm the sale? Would it change your analysis if Treece had not even known that Able was the manager?

8. Louis Jacobs is a tobacco merchant in Miami, Florida. He appointed his brother, Leslie Jacobs, to be the New York agent of his business. A power of attorney was executed, reading in part as follows:

Leslie Jacobs is attorney in and throughout the State of New York for me and in my name to purchase and to make and enter into, sign and execute any contract or agreement with any persons, firm, company or companies for the purchase of any goods or merchandise in connection with the business carried on by me as aforesaid . . . and to make such purchase either for cash or for credit, as my attorney shall in his discretion think advisable. . . . And for me and on my behalf, and where necessary in connection with any purchases made on my behalf as aforesaid or in connection with my said business, to make, draw, sign, accept or indorse any bill or bills of exchange, promissory note or promissory notes, . . . and to sign my name or my trading name to any checks or orders for payment of money on my banking account in Miami, Florida.

Soon thereafter Leslie Jacobs, purporting to act on behalf of his principal, applied to Messrs. Morris, a firm of cigar importers in New York, for a loan of $50,000. Jacobs represented that he was authorized to borrow by the power of attorney, which he had with him, and that his principal contemplated manufacturing cigarettes. Jacobs stated he wanted cash for machinery for this purpose and for buying leaf tobacco. Without looking at the power of attorney, Messrs. Morris granted the loan, upon condition that Jacob's firm would push the sale of Morris cigars. Leslie Jacobs applied the money "to his own purposes."

The loan by Messrs. Morris was not repaid and they are asserting a claim against Louis Jacobs. Analyze this situation from two perspectives: (1) what would you as an attorney advise Messrs. Morris to do assuming you were called in for advice just before the loan was granted (and not knowing, of course, of Leslie's intent to convert the funds). (2) Describe what arguments you would make against Louis Jacobs if you were retained on Morris's behalf after the true facts were discovered and the money lost. *See* Jacobs v. Morris, [1901] 1 Ch. 261. Would it have made any difference if Messrs. Morris had looked at the power of attorney, and then loaned the money?

9.   Rudolph, Zamsky & Co. is a partnership engaged in the accounting practice with their principal office in Klamath Falls, Oregon, and a branch office in Medford, Oregon. LaVern Watrud was in charge of the Medford office.

Mrs. Croisant owned a sawmill, timberlands and other property in Oregon. She had engaged the partnership to advise her on tax matters and to prepare her tax returns. These services were performed by Watrud.

In 1956 Mrs. Croisant sold her sawmill. Thereafter her business activities consisted of making collections under the sale contract and on the sale of timber from her lands. In 1957 she moved to California. Before leaving Oregon she arranged with Watrud to make the collections, to make certain disbursements, to keep her financial books and records, and to prepare her tax returns.

In 1958 Mrs. Croisant discovered that Watrud had made unauthorized payments to her husband. She instructed Watrud to the contrary, but he violated these instructions. Also, Watrud diverted money to his own account. He soon thereafter died.

Mrs. Croisant filed a suit for an accounting against the partnership. Assume that uncontradicted testimony was introduced at the trial that accountants do not normally perform fund handling services.

You are the attorney for Mrs. Croisant. The trial judge has asked you to write a memorandum of law explaining the basis of your law suit. What arguments would you make, and citing to what authority?

Now switch hats and defend the partnership. *See* Croisant v. Watrud, 248 Ore. 234, 432 P.2d 799 (1967).

10. A group of housewives in a low income housing project have come to you, an attorney for a legal aid clinic, with the following problem. It appears that a pleasant, well-dressed individual appeared at their respective doors during the last three weeks selling subscriptions to popular magazines at a good rate. With each solicitation he displayed a card indicating that he was an authorized representative of Ace Wholesale Magazines, Inc. He also had with him a large pad of order forms and some colorful advertising flyers. Each housewife who bought some subscriptions from him gave him a check for the first six months of the subscriptions (which usually ran around $15 to $25 and covered a number of magazines) made out to "John Smith, Agent for Ace Wholesaler, Inc." No magazines ever arrived. It turns out that the person selling the subscriptions had stolen the card, order forms and flyers from a magazine salesman in Portland, Oregon, and was working his way around the country with considerable success. Can you bring a successful suit against Ace? Against the magazine publishers whose magazines were prominently displayed in the sales literature and on the order pad?

Would it make any difference to your case if the salesman had picked up the card in a garbage can where it had been discarded? If he actually had been a salesman for Ace but had quit six months ago and kept his materials?

Chapter 8

TERMINATION OF AUTHORITY

As we have seen, the problems surrounding the definition and scope of the power of an agent to bind his principal contractually can be unusually complex. One would expect, however, that the law concerning the termination of this power would be fairly straightforward. And to a considerable extent it is. But the law contains some surprises and uncertainties here, as the following materials will note.

As with all other matters concerning agency and partnership, one must observe the legal problems from two perspectives: those between principal and agent, and those concerning outsiders. This chapter will approach the questions of termination in that manner.

A. TERMINATION BETWEEN THE PARTIES TO AN AGENCY RELATIONSHIP

i. *Termination by Will*

a. Between Principal and Agent

The normal rules of contract law apply to the principal-agent relationship. The basic operating premise is that the relationship is a personal one, which means that each party has the *power* at any time to sever the relationship. It is undisputed that one person cannot be forced to work for another, and that a person is always entitled to decide who will represent him. This is to be distinguished from the issue of the legal *right* of one party to sever his relationship from the other without incurring damages in doing so. Suppose, for example, an owner of a home signs an exclusive sale contract with a real estate broker. Assume that the broker finds a person ready, willing and able to buy, but the owner in bad faith refuses to conclude the sale through the broker and sells the property directly to the purchaser. It is clear that the owner has the power to do this, but it is equally clear that the law will hold him to the commission.

Another example is where a principal contracts for an agent's services over a definite period of time. The principal thereafter discovers another person he likes better and fires his agent. Again, the principal has the power to do this, on the theory that no one should be forced to have someone else represent him, but not the right to do so without liability because a contractual agreement has been broken.

Termination can be accomplished without conflict between the parties, of course, as where the object of the agency is accomplished or where the term of the contract between principal and agent runs out as agreed.

QUESTIONS

1. By an instrument in writing and under seal, P authorizes A to sell Blackacre at any time during the next month. One week later P sees A on the street and says, "Don't sell." Has A's authority been terminated? Would your answer change if in the sealed instrument there was language saying the revocation of the arrangement "shall be effective only if made under seal"? Suppose that P had told A nothing, but had said to a friend that he was going to terminate A's authority as soon as he ran across him, and the friend had mentioned that to A. Is A's authority terminated?

2. P authorizes A to sell Blackacre for $1000. Subsequently A observes that P has built an expensive house on Blackacre. Is A's authority terminated?

3. A wrote a letter to P, his principal, saying that he will no longer work for him. After mailing the letter but before P received it, A closed a deal in accordance with his original authority. Was A's authority terminated at that time? (Ignore for the moment questions of apparent authority in the eyes of the third party that A was dealing with.) See § 119 of the Restatement, from which the above questions were drawn, stating that the agent's authority was terminated in numbers 1 and 2 above, and not terminated in number 3. Can you explain why?

4. Suppose a contract between P and A explicitly states that it shall be irrevocable for a certain period of time. Is this language binding on the parties? If P decides he wants his business to be represented by someone else, has he bound himself to the contrary? See P. MECHEM, OUTLINES OF AGENCY 176 (4th ed. 1952), stating that the language of irrevocability is not binding, on the ground that it should always be in the power of the principal to

manage his own business. *See also,* RESTATEMENT § 118. Consider in this regard the statutes in all states that make the Secretary of State of the particular state the agent for service of process of a nonresident motorist driving in the state for accidents arising out of his driving. Suppose a motorist expressly revokes this appointment. Courts everywhere have said that the motorist-principal cannot do this. Why can't this be done?

5. *P* authorizes *A,* in return for some services *A* had rendered on *P's* behalf, to sell Blackacre (part of *P's* land) and pay himself out of the proceeds, returning the surplus to *P.* Or suppose *P* borrows money from *A* and as part of the deal gives *A* the power to sell *P's* land in the event the loan is not repaid. *P* revokes before *A* can sell. Is the revocation effective? MECHEM, *id.* at 176-77 states that revocation is not possible here, since this is "not in reality a case of agency at all. In a genuine agency case the power is given to the agent to enable him to do something for the principal; here it is given him to enable him to do something for himself." *See also,* RESTATEMENT § 139. Authority for the proposition advanced by Mechem may be supplied by some cognovit note cases which hold that the maker of such a note cannot later revoke the power contained in the note. *See* 44 A.L.R. 1310. (A cognovit note grants the holder of the note the power to confess judgment against the maker without service of process; some jurisdictions refuse to enforce these notes.)

---

b. Between Partners

Do the above principles relating to termination by will of an agency relationship, based on its consensual nature, apply to the partnership relationship? It also is an agency relationship and is consensual in nature. Suppose that one partner of a two-man partnership strongly objects to any further purchases by the partnership of goods from a particular distributor. He so informs both his fellow partner and the distributor involved. It is clear under the normal principal-agent relationship that the objecting party would no longer be liable for such purchases. Is the same thing true in partnership law?

An immediate point of reference for questions on partnership law is the UPA, which is set forth in Appendix A. The relevant sections there seem to be 9 and 18. Is there any language in those sections which would answer the above question? If not, our next point of reference must be case law.

NATIONAL BISCUIT CO. v. STROUD
Supreme Court of North Carolina
249 N.C. 467, 106 S.E.2d 692 (1959)
Noted in 1960 Duke L. J. 150

APPEAL by defendant Stroud from *Parker (Joseph W.), J.,* June Civil Term, 1958, of CARTERET.

The case was heard in the Superior Court upon the following agreed statements of fact:

On 13 September 1956 the National Biscuit Company had a Justice of the Peace to issue summons against C. N. Stroud and Earl Freeman, a partnership trading as Stroud's Food Center, for the nonpayment of $171.04 for goods sold and delivered. After a hearing the Justice of the Peace rendered judgment for plaintiff against both defendants for $171.04 with interest and costs. Stroud appealed to the Superior Court: Freeman did not.

In March 1953 C. N. Stroud and Earl Freeman entered into a general partnership to sell groceries under the name of Stroud's Food Center. Thereafter plaintiff sold bread regularly to the partnership. Several months prior to February 1956 the defendant Stroud advised an agent of plaintiff that he personally would not be responsible for any additional bread sold by plaintiff to Stroud's Food Center. From 6 February 1956 to 25 February 1956 plaintiff through this same agent, at the request of the defendant Freeman, sold and delivered bread in the amount of $171.04 to Stroud's Food Center. Stroud and Freeman by agreement dissolved the partnership at the close of business on 25 February 1956, and notice of such dissolution was published in a newspaper in Carteret County 6-27 March 1956.

The relevant parts of the dissolution agreement are these: All partnership assets, except an automobile truck, an electric adding machine, a rotisserie, which were assigned to defendant Freeman, and except funds necessary to pay the employees for their work the week before the dissolution and necessary to pay for certain supplies purchased the week of dissolution, were assigned to Stroud. Freeman assumed the outstanding liens against the truck. Paragraph five of the dissolution agreement is as follows: "From and after the aforesaid February 25, 1956, Stroud will be responsible for the liquidation of the partnership assets and the discharge of partnership liabilities without demand upon Freeman for any contribution in the discharge of said obligations." The dissolution agreement was made in reliance on Freeman's representations that the indebtedness of the partnership was about $7,800.00 and its accounts receivable were about $8,000.00. The accounts receivable at the close of business actually amounted to $4,897.41.

Stroud has paid all of the partnership obligations amounting to $12,014.45, except the amount of $171.04 claimed by plaintiff. To pay such obligations Stroud exhausted all the partnership assets he could reduce to money amounting to $4,307.08, of which $2,028.64 was derived from accounts receivable and $2,278.44 from a sale of merchandise and fixtures, and used over $7,700.00 of his personal money. Stroud has left of the partnership assets only uncollected accounts in the sum of $2,868.77, practically all of which are considered uncollectible.

Stroud has not attempted to rescind the dissolution agreement, and has tendered plaintiff, and still tenders it, one-half of the $171.04 claimed by it.

From a judgment that plaintiff recover from the defendants $171.04 with interest and costs, Stroud appeals to the Supreme Court.

PARKER, J. C. N. Stroud and Earl Freeman entered into a general partnership to sell groceries under the firm name of Stroud's Food Center. There is nothing in the agreed statement of facts to indicate or suggest that Freeman's power and authority as a general partner were in any way restricted or limited by the articles of partnership in respect to the ordinary and legitimate business of the partnership. Certainly, the purchase and sale of bread were ordinary and legitimate business of Stroud's Food Center during its continuance as a going concern.

Several months prior to February 1956 Stroud advised plaintiff that he personally would not be responsible for any additional bread sold by plaintiff to Stroud's Food Center. After such notice to plaintiff, it from 6 February 1956 to 25 February 1956, at the request of Freeman, sold and delivered bread in the amount of $171.04 to Stroud's Food Center.

In Johnson v. Bernheim, 76 N.C. 139, this Court said: "A and B are general partners to do some given business; the partnership is, by operation of law, a power to each to bind the partnership in any manner legitimate to the business. If one partner go to a third person to buy an article on time for the partnership, the other partner cannot prevent it by writing to the third person not to sell to him on time; or, if one party attempt to buy for cash, the other has no right to require that it shall be on time. And what is true in regard to buying is true in regard to selling. What either partner does with a third person is binding on the partnership. It is otherwise where the partnership is not general, but is upon special terms, as that purchases and sales must be with and for cash. There the power to each is special, in regard to all dealings with third persons at least who have notice of the terms." There is contrary authority: 68 C.J.S., Partnership, pp.

578-579. However, this text of C.J.S. does not mention the effect of the provisions of the Uniform Partnership Act.

The General Assembly of North Carolina in 1941 enacted a Uniform Partnership Act, which became effective 15 March 1941. G.S. Ch. 59, Partnership, Art. 2.

G.S. 59-39* is entitled PARTNER AGENT OF PARTNERSHIP AS TO PARTNERSHIP BUSINESS, and subsection (1) reads: "Every partner is an agent of the partnership for the purpose of its business, and the act of every partner, including the execution in the partnership name of any instrument, for apparently carrying on in the usual way the business of the partnership of which he is a member binds the partnership, unless the partner so acting has in fact no authority to act for the partnership in the particular matter, and the person with whom he is dealing has knowledge of the fact that he has no such authority." G.S. 59-39(4) states: "No act of a partner in contravention of a restriction on authority shall bind the partnership to persons having knowledge of the restriction."

G.S. 59-45 provides that "all partners are jointly and severally liable for the acts and obligations of the partnership."

G.S. 59-48 is captioned RULES DETERMINING RIGHTS AND DUTIES OF PARTNERS. Subsection (e) thereof reads: "All partners have equal rights in the management and conduct of the partnership business." Subsection (h) thereof is as follows: "Any difference arising as to ordinary matters connected with the partnership business may be decided by a majority of the partners; but no act in contravention of any agreement between the partners may be done rightfully without the consent of all the partners."

Freeman as a general partner with Stroud, with no restrictions on his authority to act within the scope of the partnership business so far as the agreed statement of facts shows, had under the Uniform Partnership Act "equal rights in the management and conduct of the partnership business." Under G.S. 59-48(h) Stroud, his co-partner, could not restrict the power and authority of Freeman to buy bread for the partnership as a going concern, for such a purchase was an "ordinary matter connected with the partnership business," for the purpose of its business and within its scope, because in the very nature of things Stroud was not, and could not be, a majority of the partners. Therefore, Freeman's purchases of bread from plaintiff for Stroud's Food Center as a

---

* Subtract 30 from the last two numerals in order to locate the citation in the UPA.—*Ed.*

going concern bound the partnership and his co-partner Stroud. The quoted provisions of our Uniform Partnership Act, in respect to the particular facts here, are in accord with the principle of law stated in *Johnson v. Bernheim, supra;* same case 86 N.C. 339.

In Crane on Partnership, 2nd Ed., p. 277, it is said: "In cases of an even division of the partners as to whether or not an act within the scope of the business should be done, of which disagreement a third person has knowledge, it seems that logically no restriction can be placed upon the power to act. The partnership being a going concern, activities within the scope of the business should not be limited, save by the expressed will of the majority deciding a disputed question; half of the members are not a majority."

Sladen v. Lance, 151 N.C. 492, 66 S.E. 449, is distinguishable. That was a case where the terms of the partnership imposed special restrictions on the power of the partner who made the contract.

At the close of business on 25 February 1956 Stroud and Freeman by agreement dissolved the partnership. By their dissolution agreement all of the partnership assets, including cash on hand, bank deposits and all accounts receivable, with a few exceptions, were assigned to Stroud, who bound himself by such written dissolution agreement to liquidate the firm's assets and discharge its liabilities. It would seem a fair inference from the agreed statement of facts that the partnership got the benefit of the bread sold and delivered by plaintiff to Stroud's Food Center, at Freeman's request, from 6 February 1956 to 25 February 1956. See Guano Co. v. Ball, 201 N.C. 534, 160 S.E. 769. But whether it did or not, Freeman's acts, as stated above, bound the partnership and Stroud.

The judgment of the court below is

Affirmed.

RODMAN, J., dissents.

NOTES

1. The *Stroud* case represents an example of an inherent agency power which is very unusual. In this instance the party who was bound expressly disapproved *and* communicated his disapproval to the third party. Do you think the special nature of this agency relationship logically leads to such a result? If so, why?

2. What alternatives are open to a partner who finds himself in the situation faced by Stroud? Apparently only dissolution

under § 32 of the UPA remains open to him and this comes at the price of no longer continuing in the business.

3. There is authority opposed to the *Stroud* case. *See* A. BROMBERG, CRANE AND BROMBERG ON PARTNERSHIP 305 (1968).

4. Suppose a partnership has three members. One partner dissents to the terms of a proposed contract and notifies the third party he will not be bound. He does not, however, intend to dissolve the partnership. The contract is entered into anyway. Is the dissenter bound? *See* CRANE & BROMBERG, *id.* at 304-305, stating that the minority "may not hamper the majority in carrying on the business in accordance with the articles or other partnership agreement." The dissenter thus would not possess the power to terminate the majority's authority in the absence of forcing a dissolution.

---

ii. *Termination by Operation of Law*

a. Between Principal and Agent

I. *Death*

One might ask what justifies a separate heading for this topic, since one can logically assume that the same distinctions as those drawn above on revocability would apply here, with the added qualification that death of the principal or agent should normally result in automatic termination of the relationship due to its consensual nature. While this rational supposition is largely borne out, there are some interesting distinctions that have been drawn by the courts, as will be seen below. For a starter, think back to the questions raised in number 5 to part a, above. Should the fact that death, rather than the principal's will, is the intervening factor make a difference? Draw your own conclusion, and then consider the answer given below in a case which has troubled courts and commentators for 150 years.

HUNT v. ROUSMANIER'S ADMINISTRATORS
Supreme Court of the United States
21 U. S. (8 Wheaton) 174 (1823)

APPEAL from the Circuit Court of Rhode Island.

The original bill, filed by the appellant, Hunt, stated, that Lewis Rousmanier, the intestate of the defendants, applied to the plaintiff, in January, 1820, for the loan of 1450 dollars, offering to give, in addition to his notes, a bill of sale, or a mortgage of his interest in the brig Nereus, then at sea, as collateral security for the repayment of the money. The sum requested was lent; and, on the 11th of January, the said Rousmanier executed two notes for the amount; and, on the 15th of the same month, he executed a power of attorney, authorizing the plaintiff to make and execute a bill of sale of three fourths of the said vessel to himself, or to any other person; and, in the event of the said vessel, or her freight, being lost, to collect the money which should become due on a policy by which the vessel and freight were insured. This instrument contained, also, a proviso, reciting, that the power was given for collateral security for the payment of the notes already mentioned, and was to be void on their payment; on the failure to do which, the plaintiff was to pay the amount thereof, and all expenses, out of the proceeds of the said property, and to return the residue to the said Rousmanier.

The bill further stated, that on the 21st of March, 1820, the plaintiff lent to the said Rousmanier the additional sum of 700 dollars, taking his note for payment, and a similar power to dispose of his interest in the schooner Industry, then also at sea. The bill then charged, that on the 6th of May, 1820, the said Rousmanier died insolvent, having paid only 200 dollars on the said notes. The plaintiff gave notice of his claim; and, on the return of the Nereus and Industry, took possession of them, and offered the intestate's interest in them for sale. The defendants forbade the sale; and this bill was brought to compel them to join in it.

The defendants demurred generally, and the Court sustained the demurrer; but gave the plaintiff leave to amend his bill.

The amended bill stated, that it was expressly agreed between the parties, that Rousmanier was to give specific security on the Nereus and Industry; and that he offered to execute a mortgage on them. That counsel was consulted on the subject, who advised, that a power of attorney, such as was actually executed, should be taken in preference to a mortgage, because it was equally valid and effectual as a security, and would prevent the necessity of changing the papers of the vessels, or of taking possession of them on their arrival in port. The powers were, accordingly, executed, with the full belief that they would, and with the intention that they should, give the plaintiff as full and perfect security as would be given by a deed of mortgage. The bill prayed, that the defendants might be decreed to join in a sale of the interest of their intestate in the Nereus and Industry, or to sell the same themselves, and pay out of the proceeds the debt due to the plaintiff. To this amended bill, also, the defendants demurred, and on argument the demurrer was sustained, ...

Mr. Chief Justice MARSHALL delivered the opinion of the Court. The counsel for the appellant objects to the decree of the Circuit Court on two grounds. He contends,

1. That this power of attorney does, by its own operation, entitle the plaintiff, for the satisfaction of his debt, to the interest of Rousmanier in the Nereus and the Industry.

2. Or, if this be not so, that a Court of Chancery will, the conveyance being defective, lend its aid to carry the contract into execution, according to the intention of the parties.

We will consider, 1. The effect of the power of attorney.

This instrument contains no words of conveyance or of assignment, but is a simple power to sell and convey. As the power of one man to act for another, depends on the will and license of that other, the power ceases when the will, or this permission, is withdrawn. The general rule, therefore, is, that a letter of attorney may, at any time, be revoked by the party who makes it; and is revoked by his death. But this general rule, which results from the nature of the act, has sustained some modification. Where a letter of attorney forms a part of a contract, and is a security for money, or for the performance of any act which is deemed valuable, it is generally made irrevocable in terms, or if not so, is deemed irrevocable in law. Although a letter of attorney depends, from its nature, on the will of the person making it, and may, in general, be recalled at his will; yet, if he binds himself for a consideration, in terms, or by the nature of his contract, not to change his will, the law will not permit him to change it. Rousmanier, therefore, could not, during his life, by any act of his own, have revoked this letter of attorney. But does it retain its efficacy after his death? We think it does not. We think it well settled, that a power of attorney, though irrevocable during the life of the party, becomes extinct by his death.

This principle is asserted in *Littleton*, (sec. 66.) by Lord Coke, in his commentary on that section, (52 b.) and in *Willes' Reports*, (105. note, and 565). The legal reason of the rule is a plain one. It seems founded on the presumption, that the substitute acts by virtue of the authority of his principal, existing at the time the act is performed; and on the manner in which he must execute his authority, as stated in *Coombes' case*. In that case it was resolved, that "when any has authority as attorney to do any act, he ought to do it in his name who gave the authority." The reason of this resolution is obvious. The title can, regularly, pass out of the person in whom it is vested, only by a conveyance in his own name; and this cannot be executed by another for him, when it could not, in law, be executed by himself. A conveyance in the name of a person who was dead at the time, would be a manifest absurdity.

This general doctrine, that a power must be executed in the name of a person who gives it, a doctrine founded on the nature of the transaction, is most usually engrafted in the power itself. Its usual language is, that the substitute shall do that which he is empowered to do *in the name of his principal.* He is put in the place and stead of his principal, and is to act in his name. This accustomed form is observed in the instrument under consideration. Hunt is constituted the attorney, and is authorized to make, and execute, a regular bill of sale in the name of Rousmanier. Now, as an authority must be pursued, in order to make the act of the substitute the act of the principal, it is necessary that this bill of sale should be in the name of Rousmanier; and it would be a gross absurdity, that a deed should purport to be executed by him, even by attorney, after his death; for, the attorney is in the place of the principal, capable of doing that alone which the principal might do.

This general rule, that a power ceases with the life of the person giving it, admits of one exception. If a power be coupled with an "interest," it survives the person giving it, and may be executed after his death.

As this proposition is laid down too positively in the books to be controverted, it becomes necessary to inquire what is meant by the expression, "a power coupled with an interest?" Is it an interest in the subject on which the power is to be exercised, or is it an interest in that which is produced by the exercise of the power? We hold it to be clear, that the interest which can protect a power after the death of a person who creates it, must be an interest in the thing itself. In other words, the power must be engrafted on an estate in the thing.

The words themselves would seem to import this meaning. "A power coupled with an interest," is a power which accompanies, or is connected with, an interest. The power and the interest are united in the same person. But if we are to understand by the word "interest," an interest in that which is to be produced by the exercise of the power, then they are never united. The power, to produce the interest, must be exercised, and by its exercise, is extinguished. The power ceases when the interest commences, and, therefore, cannot, in accurate law language, be said to be "coupled" with it.

But the substantial basis of the opinion of the Court on this point, is found in the legal reason of the principle. The interest or title in the thing being vested in the person who gives the power, remains in him, unless it be conveyed with the power, and can pass out of him only by a regular act in his own name. The act of the substitute, therefore, which, in such a case, is the act of the principal, to be legally effectual, must be in his name, must be such an act as the principal himself would be capable of performing, and which would be valid if performed by him. Such a power necessarily ceases with the life of the person making it. But if the interest, or estate, passes with the power, and vests in the person by whom the power is to be exercised, such person acts in his own name. The estate, being in him, passes from him by a conveyance in his own name. He is no longer a substitute, acting in the place and name of another, but is a principal acting in his own name, in pursuance of powers which limit his estate. The legal reason which limits a power to the life of the person giving it, exists no longer, and the rule ceases with the reason on which it is founded. The intention of the instrument may be effected without violating any legal principle.

. . . .

It is, then, deemed perfectly clear, that the power given in this case, is a naked power, not coupled with an interest, which, though irrevocable by Rousmanier himself, expired on his death.

. . . .

NOTES

1. One argument made by plaintiff's counsel was an appeal to the equity powers of the court to reform the instruments due to a mistake being made by the parties to the transaction. The court, however, drew a distinction between mistakes of law and mistakes of fact, holding that this constituted a mistake of law and thus was irremediable. Hunt v. Rousmanier's Admin., 26 U. S. (1 Peters) 1 (1828).

2. The distinction drawn by Chief Justice Marshall between powers coupled with a security and powers coupled with an interest has resulted in endless problems of classification. Suppose, for example, that Jones is given authority by Smith to collect certain rents normally payable to Smith until the principal and interest of a loan from Jones to Smith is paid off. Smith dies two months later, while the payments have another year to go. Is the authority given to Jones revoked?

Consider also the effect of death of a policyholder on the following power typically given an insurance company under a liability policy: that the "sole right of settlement and defense" is in the hands of the insurance carrier. Cf. MacDonald v. Gough, 326 Mass. 93, 93 N.E.2d 260 (1950), noted in 49 MICH. L. REV.

755 (1951); Hayes v. Gessner, 315 Mass. 366, 52 N.E.2d 968 (1944) (the power is coupled with an interest; the principal cannot revoke nor control the exercise of the power). Should the same result follow if a contract gives an agent as compensation a specified per cent of the property secured by his services? *See* Bowman v. Ledbetter, 173 Okla. 345, 48 P.2d 334 (1935) (power revoked by the principal's death).

The cognovit note reference in number 5 to part a above, dealt only with revocation by the maker during his lifetime providing, you will recall, that the maker has no power to revoke. The event of death calls for a different result before some courts, however. A fairly substantial number of jurisdictions hold that such a note is revoked by death (although not by insanity or other incapacity). *See* 44 A.L.R. 1310. The decisions are based primarily on the *Rousmanier* doctrine. MECHEM, at 182-83, attempts to rationalize this result, stating that the rights given by the power are procedural rather than substantive in nature. The purpose is to eliminate the necessity of litigation. When the maker dies the procedural convenience is lost anyway by the requirement that the note holder—or judgment creditor, if he obtains a judgment under the confession clause—has to submit the claim for payment under the estate procedures.

One final example: some mortgages provide that the mortgagee shall have a power of sale in the event of default by the mortgagor. Is this power terminated by the death of the mortgagor? Clearly not in title theory states, where the theory is that title is actually conveyed to the mortgagee, subject to a condition subsequent of payment of the mortgage debt, as that satisfies even the test of the *Rousmanier* case. Although a different result might obtain where the mortgage constitutes only a lien, the courts have been unaffected by such doctrinal distinctions. *See* G. OSBORNE, MORTGAGES § 338 (2d ed. 1970), arguing that the mortgagee's power of sale is *sui generis* and should be treated as independent of agency concepts, and citing to cases treating the power as irrevocable. *See also,* 56 A.L.R. 224.

3. Sections 138 and 139 of the Restatement of Agency are addressed to the *Rousmanier* problem, and handle it in the following manner:

TOPIC 5. TERMINATION OF POWERS GIVEN AS SECURITY

§ 138. Definition.

A power given as security is a power to affect the legal relations of another, created in the form of an agency authority, but held for the benefit of the power holder or a third person

and given to secure the performance of a duty or to protect a
title, either legal or equitable, such power being given when
the duty or title is created or given for consideration.

§ 139.   Termination of Powers Given as Security.

(1)   Unless otherwise agreed, a power given as security is not
terminated by:

(a)   revocation by the creator of the power;

(b)   surrender by the holder of the power, if he holds for
the benefit of another;

(c)   the loss of capacity during the lifetime of either the
creator of the power or the holder of the power; or

(d)   the death of the holder of the power, or, if the power
is given as security for a duty which does not terminate at the
death of the creator of the power, by his death.

(2)   A power given as security is terminated by its surrender
by the beneficiary, if of full capacity; or by the happening of
events which, by its terms, discharges the obligations secured
by it, or which makes its execution illegal or impossible.

See Seavey, *Termination by Death of Proprietary Powers of
Attorney*, 31 YALE L.J. 283 (1922), *reprinted* in W. SEAVEY,
STUDIES IN AGENCY 109-127 (1949) .

II.   Insanity

It is commonly held that insanity of either the agent or the
principal will terminate the relationship. This is for basically
the same reasons mentioned above in the discussion of death.
RESTATEMENT § 122; MECHEM, at 186.

III.   Bankruptcy

This event terminates the power of the agent to deal with
the assets of his bankrupt principal at once and irrespective of
notice. RESTATEMENT § 114, Comment *c*. The agent's authority
to bind the principal personally, however, is terminated only
upon notice to the agent. *Id.*

IV.   War

The effect of the outbreak of war has occasioned differing
judicial responses. Several courts have held that such an event
automatically terminates the agency where the principal and

agent are residents or nationals of the two countries at war. *See* Mutzenbecher v. Ballard, 266 N.Y. 574, 195 N.E. 206 (1935), *noted in* 3 U. CHI. L. REV. 137 (1935). *See also* Note, 31 HARV. L. REV. 637 (1918). Other courts have held that automatic revocation depends on whether the agency involves communication with the enemy; if not, and if it is in "the manifest interest of the principal that the agency, constituted before the war, should continue, the assent of the principal will be presumed." Aldridge v. Franco-Wyoming Sec. Corp., 27 Del. Ch. 80, 89, 31 A.2d 246, 251 (1943) (the question in this case was whether a proxy to vote stock in a Delaware corporation was revoked by the fact that the principals subsequently became alien enemies).

---

b.   *Between Partners*

Termination by operation of law with respect to partnerships is codified in the UPA, §§ 31, 32. Note the automatic nature of the termination under § 31, relating to certain clearly definable events (death, bankruptcy) and the necessity of obtaining a court decree under § 32, relating to the insanity of a partner, bad conduct of a partner, and so forth. Note also that "termination" is used loosely here. Sections 31 and 32 describe events of dissolution; termination is generally used to describe the time when all partnership affairs are wound up.

Our topic, however, is termination of *authority* between partners. What bearing does dissolution under §§ 31 and 32 have on that? See §§ 33-35, which relate to this question. Note the distinction between "knowledge" and "knowledge or notice" in § 34(a) and (b). These terms are defined in § 3 of the UPA. What do you think is the reasoning underlying the distinction drawn between subsections (a) and (b) of § 34?

B.   NOTICE OF TERMINATION TO THIRD PARTIES

i.   *Termination by Will*

Once again we return to the questions surrounding the expectations of third parties, and again it takes not one look, but two, in order to resolve—perhaps put in focus is more accurate language—the problems which arise from the agency relationship.

The more subtle questions arise in this area. If you tell someone that Mr. *A* is authorized to act on your behalf in some sort of continuing relationship, it seems obvious that you would make an effort to inform that person when your agent's authority is terminated. Problems of effectuating the notice to third parties can be substantial, however, and they increase with the size of an organization and the extent to which it delegates authority.

Assume, for example, that a door to door saleswoman for Cleanway Products (a nationwide distributor of soap and detergents), who operates on a franchise basis and thus takes checks in her own name and turns over a percentage to Cleanway, violates a provision of the franchise agreement and loses her franchise. Cleanway soon thereafter assigns a different person for that area, but it will take her a while to become familiar with the territory. Assume that the embittered former saleswoman quickly returns to her old customers and makes "one last sale" and leaves the territory. Is Cleanway bound by the sales? How would you advise Cleanway to anticipate and guard against such an event? Is there anything you could do in the drafting of the franchise agreement? Before it? After it? How does a newspaper protect itself when newsboys (who collect cash) change or leave routes?

Assume that the owner of a sole proprietorship business which buys a substantial amount on credit sells the business to his manager or to a group of former employees with the right to continue using the name of the business. How does the seller protect himself from claims of former creditors of his who may unknowingly give credit to the new owner, believing that the new owner is still the agent of the former owner? An immediate and obvious answer would be to write all the creditors and inform them of the sale, which you would undoubtedly advise any client selling a business to do. Suppose, however, that some of your client's creditors are town to town drummers who simply walk up to the store and sell merchandise on credit. How do you inform these people? Would a notice in the local newspaper be enough? Should it be? *See* Courtney v. G. A. Linaker Co., 173 Ark. 777, 293 S.W. 723 (1927), where the seller did put a notice in the newspaper. This was held insufficient by the court to terminate the authority of the buyers, who apparently had worked in the business before the sale. The court does not mention whether the name and address of the plaintiff creditor was on the books of the business. Apparently, however, the plaintiff had previously extended credit to the former owner. This fact would be crucial, wouldn't it? See page 241 *infra*.

Suppose the new owners continue to use the firm name but move the business to a new location in town. Now would notice be necessary? Is there any other way you can advise the seller to protect himself? Would the seller have to concern himself with these questions if he sold the business to a stranger?

You are familiar with the basic approach of the law with respect to third-party expectations from Chapter 7 on authority.

As you read through the following materials, try to resolve the tension you will observe between a common law presumption and the approach toward third-party expectations indicated earlier.

MONTANA RESERVOIR & IRRIGATION CO. v. UTAH JUNK CO.
Supreme Court of Utah
64 Utah 60, 228 P. 201 (1924)
Noted in 23 Mich. L. Rev. 285 (1925)

Action by the Montana Reservoir & Irrigation Company against the Utah Junk Company and others. From a judgment for plaintiff, defendants appeal.

GIDEON, J. Plaintiff had judgment and defendants appeal. The amended complaint presents two causes of action. In the first cause of action plaintiff seeks to recover the balance of the purchase price for ten car loads of junk alleged to have been sold by plaintiff to the Utah Junk Company through its agent, one Aaron Rosenblatt. The second cause of action presents the same agreement of sale claimed to have been entered into between plaintiff and Rosenblatt on behalf of the Utah Junk Company. It is further alleged that prior to the sale Rosenblatt had been the agent of the junk company and that the junk company had represented to plaintiff and to its officers and directors acting as officers and directors of associated corporations that said Rosenblatt was its agent. It is further alleged that, if Rosenblatt was not the agent of the junk company, plaintiff dealt with him as such and no notice had been given plaintiff or the associated companies of the termination of such agency.

The answer denies that plaintiff sold the metal junk to the junk company; denies any agreement of the sale with any one for the material in behalf of the junk company. The answer admits that certain cars of junk were shipped to the junk company from Yellowstone station in Montana between the dates mentioned in the complaint, but it is alleged that said material was shipped to the junk company by Rosenblatt as an independent trader, and that the junk company fully paid and accounted to Rosenblatt for said material. It is also admitted in the answer that Rosenblatt had, prior to May 31, 1917, been in the employ of the junk company as its traveling representative, but it is denied that the junk company held him out and represented to plaintiff that he was its agent.

The court found that plaintiff on July 11, 1917, sold to the junk company the goods and merchandise mentioned in the complaint. The court also found that an agreement was entered into between plaintiff and Rosenblatt acting on behalf of the junk company; that Rosenblatt had for a long time prior to the date of the sale been the agent of the junk company for the purpose of buying metal junk, and that during all of said time the junk company held out and represented said Rosenblatt to plaintiff and to the individual officers and directors of its associate corporations as the agent of the junk company authorized and empowered by it to purchase metal junk for and on account of said junk company. The court further found that plaintiff dealt with Rosenblatt, believing him to be the agent of the junk company, and that no notice had been given of the termination of the relationship of agency between the junk company and Rosenblatt. As a further finding of fact the court found that Rosenblatt was the agent at the time of the sale and that the junk company ought to be estopped from denying such agency.

These findings are assailed as not having support in the evidence. It is without dispute that between August 11th and September 23, 1917, ten cars of junk, the property of plaintiff, was loaded on cars near Yellowstone, Mont., and shipped to the Utah Junk Company. The junk company was named both as consignor and consignee in that shipment. It is also without dispute that the company received the consignment. The first writing evidencing the sale is a letter dated August 11, 1917, and it is signed by Rosenblatt personally, and addressed to one W. T. Jackson, purchasing agent for plaintiff. The letter is a confirmation of the purchase made under the oral agreement between Rosenblatt and the representative of plaintiff. It also appears that the junk company had purchased from the Montana Power Company certain cars of junk. These purchases were made as early as April, 1917.

There is no question, nor is there any claim to the contrary, that Rosenblatt acted for and in behalf of the junk company in making those purchases. The Montana Power Company is a New Jersey corporation. Plaintiff is a Montana corporation. It is a subsidiary company of the Montana Power Company. The Montana Power Company holds all the stock of plaintiff, with the exception of nine shares, which are designated as directors' shares. The material purchased by Rosenblatt acting for the Utah Junk Company from the Montana Power Company was shipped from different places. Purchases were also made from two other companies, which companies were also subsidiary companies of the Montana Power Company. The general offices of the Montana Power Company in the state of Montana were, at the time of the trial, located at Butte, Montana. Plaintiff occupied the same offices. The president of the plaintiff company was vice-president and general manager of the Montana Power Company. The treasurer of plaintiff was assistant treasurer of the Montana Power Company, and there were other officers interlocking between these two companies. It is without dispute that Rosenblatt, at the time of making the purchase in question, represented himself to be the agent of the junk company. It appears from the books of the junk company, as well as from the testimony of its officers that the agency of Rosenblatt had been terminated in May of that year. There is a dispute as to whether any notice had been given to the Montana Power Company of the termination of such agency. The president of the junk company testified positively that he mailed such notice. The officers of the Montana Power Company testified that no such notice, to their knowledge, had ever been received by that company. The court found that no such notice had been given.

There is no controversy, nor can there be, as to the general rule of law that one who has dealt with an agent in a matter within the agent's authority has the right to assume, if not otherwise informed, that such authority continues, and unless notice of revocation of such agency is brought to his knowledge, the principal is bound, if the dealings continue after the authority is actually revoked. No citation is necessary in support of that general proposition. Clearly, under that, if the purchase in this instance had been from the Montana Power Company, in the absence of any notice of the revocation of Rosenblatt's agency, the junk company would be liable, assuming as the proof in this case shows, that Rosenblatt represented himself to be such agent, and the power company acted in good faith in dealing with him as such. As above stated, the officers of the Montana Power Company were likewise officers of the plaintiff. The agent, in transacting business with the plaintiff, was dealing with the same individuals that he had dealt with in making the purchase from the Montana Power Company. The Montana Power Company and the plaintiff company are two distinct legal entities. It does not appear that the plaintiff had ever dealt with the junk company through the agency of Rosenblatt. On the contrary, it appears that no such relationship existed.

The concrete question presented may be stated: Did the officers of the Montana Reservoir & Irrigation Company have the legal right to rely upon their knowledge gained while acting as officers of the Montana Power Company that Rosenblatt had been the agent of the junk company, and then representing himself to be such agent, and thereby bind the junk company?

I have found no case dealing with a like situation. The authorities cited by counsel do not aid in the solution of the problem here presented. Corporations act, and can act, only through and by their officers or agents designated by such officers. Knowledge imparted to the officers is generally held to be knowledge of the corporation. If the Utah Junk Company, by its acts and conduct, is estopped to deny the agency of Rosenblatt while dealing with the officers of the Montana Power Company, it would be illogical to hold that it would not be estopped while dealing with the same individuals as the officers of another or different corporation, especially so when, as shown here, the two corporations have the same ownership. The author, in 1 Mechem on Agency (2d Ed.) § 628, says:

"Where a general authority is once shown to have existed, it may be presumed to continue until it is shown to have been revoked, and persons who have dealt with the agent as such, or who have had knowledge of his authority, and are therefore likely to deal with him, may very properly expect that if the authority be withdrawn, reasonable and timely notice of the fact will be given and they may therefore lawfully presume, in the absence of such notice, that the authority still continued."

We are of the opinion, and so hold, that the findings of the court are supported by substantial competent testimony.

Errors are assigned respecting the admission of certain testimony. That testimony was offered to show the good faith of the plaintiff in dealing with Rosenblatt as the agent of the junk company, and was properly admitted for that purpose, and in no way was prejudicial to any substantial right of the junk company.

The judgment of the district court is affirmed, with costs.

WEBER, C. J., did not participate herein.

NOTE

Does the distinction drawn in Chapter 7 between general and special agents have any relevance here? Can one argue logically that notice of revocation to the third party is always unnecessary when the third party was dealing with a special agent, and is always necessary when the agent was a general agent? And should it make any difference whether the revocation was by will rather than by operation of law?

In general, the rule seems to be that no notice of revocation is necessary in the case of a special agent since the third party could not be relying on any custom of dealing with the agent as such, and there was no appearance of continuing authority. One can, however, posit situations where this generalization will not stand up. Suppose, for example, that a principal has given his special agent a power of attorney or other indicium of authority. Does the special agent "rule" stand without exception in the face of this circumstance? Incidentally, what happens if *P,* desiring to revoke, cannot locate the power of attorney or the agent? Upon whom would the risk of loss lie if in this situation the agent negotiated a contract after revocation: the third party or the principal? *See* Morgan v. Harper, 236 S.W. 71 (Tex. Com'n of App. 1922), where Harper had given one Simmons a power of attorney to sell his land "at the price and upon the terms above named . . . from this date to 12/1/17." The price of the land advanced sharply soon thereafter, so Harper sent his son to Simmons' office to orally revoke the authority. This was done, but Simmons thereafter sold the land to plaintiff (who was suing for specific performance) before December 1, 1917.

The appellate court held it was error to exclude plaintiff's testimony that he knew of the power of attorney and contracted with reference to it and remanded for a new trial. The court said that Harper should have demanded return of the written authority and, if "Simmons had refused to give it up, Harper was under the duty to give notice of his revocation of the purported authority. . . ." How would you advise someone in this position to "give notice"? Is there any other remedy available?

Would it change your analysis of the rights involved if the buyer had never seen the power of attorney, relying instead on the statements of Simmons? If so, why?

With regard to general agents, the law requires that *P* give notice of termination of the agent's authority in order to protect those who relied on the agent's authority in the past or who may rely on his appearance of continuing authority. Does this mean, however, that the principal must give each party who falls in those categories personal notice or take the risk that the agent may bind him to contracts beyond the date of revocation? One could argue that he should be under just such an obligation, but the current status of the law does not carry liability so far. So far as they are ascertainable, the rules in this area are very similar to § 35 of the Uniform Partnership Act. They provide that the principal must give actual notice to those who in the past had given or received credit from him (presumably their names and addresses would be on the books of the business), and give public notice to the others, which is usually done by advertising in a local newspaper. With respect to many persons this latter requirement will of course be fictional in terms of their actually receiving notice. It serves, however, as a convenient, mildly satisfying cut off point for the law. Is there a better way to resolve the conflicting interests?

ii. *Termination by Operation of Law*

As has been indicated above, it is everywhere agreed that death of either of the parties to an agency relationship automatically terminates the relationship, for the reason that it is based on mutual consent. Thus, the actual authority of an agent to act on behalf of his principal terminates on death. Is the same true with respect to the agent's apparent authority? Should it be true, if it is not?

The decision of a clear majority of the courts which have been faced with this question is that, outside of the area of power coupled with an interest, termination of *all* authority is automatic upon death. No notice to third parties relying in good faith on the apparent authority of the agent is required. RESTATEMENT § 120.

This rule was described by Warren Seavey when Reporter for the first Restatement of Agency as "shocking" but the Restatement in § 120 restated it anyway on the theory that its function was to restate, not reform, the law. 11 ALI PROCEEDINGS 85 (1932-1934). One example among many of this rule is that a debtor can pay an agent in good faith without notice of the death of the principal and be liable again to the estate of the deceased principal. Also, an agent while acting in good faith can incur liability under his warranty of authority. (Could an agent protect himself in advance by obtaining his principal's agreement that his estate will assume the risk of the agent acting in good faith and without knowledge of the principal's death?) The rule constitutes a major exception to the principle of realization of reasonable expectations that seems to underlie most of the law in the contractual area of agency.

A few jurisdictions have changed the common-law rule by decision or by statute. And in every state there are statutes protecting banks against liabilities for cashing checks or forwarding checks for collection after the unknown death of a depositor. *See* UCC § 4-405(1).

The New York Law Revision Commission considered the problem of automatic termination of authority on death in 1939 and came to the following conclusion:

> Upon completion of a study of the question, transmitted herewith, the Commission has concluded that a remedial statute changing the law would not be desirable, for several reasons. The instances of injustice under the present law are extremely rare and there is consequently little demand for a change. The New York rule is in accord with the majority of jurisdictions.

A changed rule would give rise to the possibility of fraud or collusion between the agent and a third person and there would be danger of injustice in holding the principal's estate on contracts made by agents who, unknown to the representative of the estate, have authority outstanding and whose authority cannot be disproved by the representative. Any extension of the time during which an agent's authority is valid as to third persons without notice, for a period after death, would not necessarily eliminate the possibility of injustice, but would merely extend the period and set another arbitrary date after which injustice might also be done. Furthermore, there are procedural difficulties to be considered, such as delay in the settlement of estates and in the final accountings of executors and administrators, difficulties in proof, conflict in jurisdiction between the Supreme Court and the Surrogate's Court. N. Y. LAW REVISION COMM'N REPORT 687 (1939).

P. MECHEM, OUTLINES OF AGENCY § 288 n.65 (4th ed. 1952), has the following comment to make on the Law Revision Commission's statement: "With all respect to the learned Commission it would seem to the present writer that they have both underestimated the real dangers of the present rule and gone out of their way to imagine unlikely dangers in a different one."

As mentioned above, there is common-law authority on the other side of this question. See the following statement against the automatic revocation rule contained in Cassiday v. McKenzie, 4 Watts & S. 282, 285, 39 Am. Dec. 76, 79 (Pa. 1842):

Thus, if a man is the notorious agent for another to collect debts, it is but reasonable that debtors should be protected in payments to the agent until they are informed that the agency has terminated. But this, it is said, is only true of an agency terminated by express revocation, and does not hold, of an implied revocation by the death of the principal. It would puzzle the most acute man to give any reason why it should be a mispayment when revoked by death, and a good payment when expressly revoked by the party in his lifetime.

Are the other instances of termination by operation of law (insanity, bankruptcy and war) also terminable without notice? There is little case authority on this question. Ask yourself whether the same issues are raised in each of these instances. There is some case authority to the effect that termination does not operate without notice. *See* MECHEM, *id.* at 195 n.73.

With respect to partnership law and notice to third parties, see the provisions of UPA §§ 33-35, to which reference has already been made. Notice the statutory exceptions contained in those sections to the above rules concerning automatic termination of authority on death. Also, it is important to distinguish between acts by partners and acts by employees or other agents of the partnership. Do §§ 33-35 speak to the latter situation? *See* § 4(3) ("The law of agency shall apply under this act").

PROBLEMS

1. Defendant opened a charge account for his wife at an expensive department store in town, expressly authorizing her to buy on credit. He later became dissatisfied with her extravagance and notified the bookkeeper at the department store that she was to be extended no further credit. He did not, however, inform his wife of this. She continued charging items, and the store sued defendant for the amount of the bills. What result? *See* Robert Simpson Co. v. Godson [Can. 1937] 1 D.L.R. 454, *noted in* 15 CAN. B. REV. 196 (1937).

2. *P* has secured by entry the right to register a corporation in a certain name. *A* desires to organize a corporation and to use the same name. *A* proposes to *P* that if *P* will consent to the withdrawal of his entry, so that *A* can properly use the name, *A* will pay to *P* $1000 in cash and give him 10 shares in the corporation. *P* agrees. *A* pays him the money and executes an agreement for the shares, and *P* gives *A* a power of attorney, irrevocable in terms, authorizing *A* to execute and file in *P*'s name a relinquishment of *P*'s entry. *A* spends time and money in completing his organization and is ready to file his papers when *P* informs *A* that he revokes the power of attorney. *P* then dies. Is the power of attorney to *A* still valid? Analyze this problem from the perspectives both of the *Rousmanier* case and the Restatement. *See* RESTATEMENT § 138, upon which this example is based.

    a. Would your analysis change if *A* had agreed to pay *P* the cash and give the stock but had not done so at the time of *P*'s death?

    b. Would it affect your analysis if *P* had given *A* the power of attorney gratuitously, saying "I don't need that name anymore," and then changed his mind or died, or both, before *A* had effected the transfer?

    c. How would you as *A*'s lawyer advise him to cast this transaction, assuming your advice was sought in the beginning stages?

3. A patient in a hospital is dying of tuberculosis. He is totally disabled, but is not incompetent mentally. The attorney for the hospital is called upon to arrange payment of the accumulated bills, which are substantial, from the patient's life insurance policy. He was pressured for time, so he dictated a power of attorney for the patient to sign, authorizing the hospital to collect the insurance and apply it to the hospital bill. The patient dies soon thereafter. Will the hospital be able to make effective use of the power of attorney?

a. Suppose the policy contained both death benefits and total disability benefits. Would that fact strengthen the case for the hospital? If so, why?

b. Can you think of a better way the attorney could have cast the form of the document?

4. Martin Gough died intestate on July 27, 1968. He was survived by Margaret, a woman who lived with him for 25 years and claimed to be his widow, and three brothers, Luke, Frank and James. The three brothers were concerned about the disposition of Martin's assets to his widow, so they entered into a written agreement on August 16, 1968, "in consideration of the covenants hereinafter set forth" appointing Luke to negotiate with Margaret "to settle any claim she has against the estate of Martin Gough and to act as administrator of said estate, and as trustee of a proposed trust for the benefit of said Margaret," and agreeing "that we will approve any settlement made by him for our benefit." This was the substance of the agreement.

Luke thereafter negotiated a settlement with Margaret, providing her $195 monthly for the remainder of her life in consideration of her relinquishment of all claims against the estate. The money would be paid by Luke, who was to become trustee under a trust established with the assets of Martin's estate.

Two instruments were prepared, dated August 18, 1968, one a contract setting forth the above agreement with Margaret and the other an indenture of trust. They were signed by Luke, Frank and Margaret. James did not sign either instrument. Luke, at some later time, signed both instruments as attorney for James. On August 23, 1968, Luke's attorney received a letter from the attorney of James revoking the August 16 power of attorney.

Luke filed a petition for the administration of Martin's estate. James filed a similar petition and objected to the allowance of the petition filed by Luke. Luke then filed a bill in equity to obtain specific performance of the August 18 contract and indenture of trust.

What arguments would you make as attorney for Luke, using the material contained in this chapter? What defense would you anticipate James making? What difference does it make, if any, whether Luke signed James's name before or after August 23, 1968?

5. A partnership doing business as the Canadian Hay & Grain Co., Limited, of which Brown and Cressey were the partners, employed Rose in June, 1968, as an agent to buy hay for them in the New York State area. Brown subsequently withdrew from the business, effective January 1, 1969. Rose was not notified of this until July 22, 1969. On May 2, 1969, pursuant to the order of Cressey, Rose had purchased hay from the plaintiff, purporting to act wholly on his own account and on his own credit, but actually acting on behalf of his employer, Canadian Hay.

Rose died in August, 1969. Prior to his death he told the plaintiff that he had purchased the hay as agent for Canadian Hay & Grain Co.

Plaintiff, who did not get paid for his hay, initiated suit against Brown, the only solvent person left in the picture. Assume that the partnership, as undisclosed principal, would have been liable for this contract under normal circumstances. Brown defends on the ground that he had withdrawn from the partnership prior to the purchase of the hay. How would you analyze the rights between the parties? See Morris v. Brown, 115 Conn. 389, 162 A. 1 (1932), and RESTATEMENT OF AGENCY § 7, Comment d; § 110, Comment c, and § 119. In what respect, if at all, is the Restatement doctrine affected by the fact that the principal in this case is a partnership?

a. Would it change your analysis if Brown had been an inactive partner who had not participated in the business and was unknown to Rose?

b. Suppose the purchase made by Rose had been a routine, ordinary one made at that time of year, with no specific order from Cressey. What difference, if any, would that make in your analysis of the main problem?

c. Would it affect your response if Rose initially had told plaintiff he was acting on behalf of Canadian Hay & Grain Co., and this was the first time he had dealt with plaintiff?

Chapter 9

NOTICE AND NOTIFICATION; IMPUTED KNOWLEDGE

A. INTRODUCTION

When is the knowledge of an agent concerning a transaction in which he is involved imputed to his principal, and vice versa? Does "notice" differ from "knowledge"? Does the word "notification" have a meaning distinct from knowledge and notice and, if so, is the distinction defensible?

This chapter involves some surprisingly difficult problems of analysis. In part this is a result of semantic confusion. The Restatement definitions of the above words in Sections 9 through 11 are unusually hard to grasp, even after several readings, and the court opinions frequently talk in language that is conclusory and question-begging.

The major articles in this area include Seavey, *Notice Through an Agent*, 65 U. PA. L. REV. 1 (1916), *reprinted in* W. SEAVEY, STUDIES IN AGENCY 29-64 (1949); Merrill, *The Anatomy of Notice*, 3 U. CHI. L. REV. 417 (1936), and Merrill, *Unforgettable Knowledge*, 34 MICH. L. REV. 474 (1936). They are not easy reading. Finally, and perhaps this serves to underscore the point made above, there exists a three volume treatise on the general subject of notice. *See* M. MERRILL ON NOTICE (3 vols. 1952).

This chapter will draw the conventional distinctions made concerning this subject. You will be asked, as usual, to test critically what is being said and done and to try to figure out for yourself what is going on and why.

The following summary from W. SEAVEY, LAW OF AGENCY 17-18 (1964) may prove helpful in understanding the use by the Restatement and many courts of the words notice, notification and knowledge:

> . . . [N]otice will be herein used only to indicate the legal consequence which follows when a person has received a notification or has acquired relevant knowledge. . . .
>
> A notification is an act intended to give information to another, which for most purposes has the same legal effect as if the other had received the information. . . . There may be a notification of an action brought against an individual,

effected by leaving the required document at his last legal abode. . . .

Knowledge, on the other hand, is subjective, although the evidence to prove it is objective. It is entirely factual. . . .

B. NOTIFICATION

Notification involves a deliberate effort to bring some fact to the attention of a person or group of persons or, for that matter, of all present or future persons who may have or claim any interest in the subject matter (made through a valid recording, for example). The major question to be explored in this section is under what circumstances will notification to an agent be effective? As with most legal problems, common sense can take us a long way toward answering this. Consider and answer the following questions (some, as you will see, are drawn from actual cases or Restatement illustrations), and then try to figure out the principles upon which you based your answers.

1. *P* tells *A*, a cashier, to do no business between the hours of twelve and one, and to direct all customers to cashier *B*. In *P*'s absence, *T* enters between twelve and one o'clock and, for the purpose of notifying the bank of a default by the maker of a negotiable instrument upon which the bank is an indorser, hands to *A* a letter indicating the facts. *A* puts the letter into his pocket and later loses it. Has *P* been "notified"? What analysis would you go through in answering this question? Would you look to any law that we have already covered? This hypothetical is drawn from RESTATEMENT § 268, illustration 1.

2. Mr. Wing was insured for disability under a group insurance policy issued to his employer by John Hancock Insurance Company. The employer took care of all details involved in procuring coverage for its employees. Both Wing and the employer contributed to the premiums. The insurance company issued one master policy to the employer and gave it individual certificates to give to the employees. Each certificate was headed by the name of the insurance company and contained the terms and conditions of the policy. One of the terms was that written notice of disability had to be received "by the [insurance] Company" within a specified period of time. After suffering a heart attack, Wing gave his employer a doctor's certificate as to his disability. No notice was given directly to the insurance company. The time period for notice elapsed, and the company refused to honor Wing's claim. Wing sued for benefits under the policy. What result? *See* Wing v. John Hancock Mut. Life Ins. Co., 314

Mass. 269, 49 N.E.2d 905 (1943) (holding the notice ineffective, and citing three other cases in agreement, on the ground that the employer was not the agent of the Company with regard to receiving notice). Could you make an effective argument against this result?

3. In a pending action, T "serves notice" of a motion upon P's attorney, A. Intending to injure P, A does not inform him of the motion and does not appear against it. Is P bound by the notification?

The above hypothetical, taken from RESTATEMENT § 271, illustration 3, includes an element different from the hypotheticals given in the preceding notes. What element? And how would you resolve the question?

For a case somewhat related to the above, *see* Freeman v. Superior Court, 44 Cal. 2d 533, 537-38, 282 P.2d 857, 860 (1955). In this case the court unanimously upheld a criminal contempt conviction of the petitioner before them, who had failed to pay counsel fees and court costs in a divorce action after being ordered to do so. Petitioner testified that he had not known of the order. He had been represented in court, however, by counsel at the time the order was made. The court held that the presence of petitioner's attorney created a rebuttable presumption that he had received knowledge, and this could support the finding of fact of knowledge "even though the accused may give uncontradicted evidence to the contrary." The court stated that the presumption would be conclusive in civil actions.

The reasoning of the court is as follows:

The general rule of agency, that notice to or knowledge possessed by an agent is imputable to the principal, applies for certain purposes in the relation of attorney and client. The rule rests on the premise that the agent has acquired knowledge which it was his duty to communicate to his principal, and the presumption is that he had performed that duty.

Are you satisfied that the analysis should stop at this point? What policy considerations are involved in holding a client to the consequences of his attorney's failure to transmit information received by him in his capacity as attorney? Do these considerations extend to criminal liability?

4. Plaintiff owns a toll bridge across the Missouri River at St. Charles, Missouri. Defendant is an electric utility, located in St. Louis. By agreement with plaintiff, defendant transmits electricity to St. Charles through uninsulated high tension wires strung on spans above the superstructure of the bridge. It was

agreed that defendant would indemnify plaintiff from liability resulting from the presence of the wires. It was further agreed that:

"Eighth. It is necessary and may from time to time become necessary during the term of this contract for said Bridge Company to paint said bridge and add to, alter and repair the same, in which event, and when it becomes necessary for it to do so in the opinion of said Bridge Company, the said Electric Company in order to secure the safety of the persons making said repairs, additions, alterations or painting of said bridge shall, upon notice by the Bridge Company, arrange to have a representative in attendance during such repairing or construction for the purpose of instructing the workmen to maintain a safe distance between the wires and themselves, and the Electric Company, in the event the same becomes necessary, will at its own expense so adjust the wires on said bridge as to render the condition of the workmen of the Bridge Company reasonably safe from danger."

Subsequently a workman, who was painting the bridge, was severely injured by contact with the wires. There was no representative of the electric company there at the time. The bridge company settled with the injured employee and brought suit against the defendant for reimbursement. The defense was that no notice of the repair and maintenance work was ever received by the defendant. This was denied by the plaintiff. The following facts were before the court:

It was shown that Jones was a new manager [for defendant] at St. Charles, having been appointed to that position shortly before the commencement of the painting of the bridge.

The evidence for the plaintiff shows that shortly after the painting of the bridge was commenced and while the work was in progress the plaintiff's president, Charles D. Bolin, casually met the new local manager at a restaurant in St. Charles, being introduced to him by some citizen of that city; that the two gentlemen had lunch together, engaged in social conversation, and incidentally discussed a business matter. Concerning this Mr. Bolin testified:

"I told Mr. Jones that we were going to double the bridge toll houses, that the tolls had all been collected at the St. Charles side, that we were going to build a toll house on the east side, and we had no way to get light on the east side, and that I would like to have arrangements made for wires to run down to light the toll house on the east side. Mr. Jones said that those were high-power wires on the bridge and that the wire for the light would have to be run back across the bridge from St. Charles. He said it would be an expensive proposition to bring the light wire off from the high-power wires on the east side, and that he would get the necessary information from Mr. Stokes and take the matter up with me later. I told him we were painting the bridge and expected to paint the bridge from one end to the other. We walked out in front of the restaurant and I pointed to the painters painting the bridge and said that we were going to commence at this end and paint from one end to the other, and that I would like to get the wires put in on the east side in the toll house. He said to come back in a few days and he would let me know what could be done and what would be the cost. I went back afterwards and he told me it would be necessary to bring the wires from St. Charles back across the bridge. I said, 'Here are the workmen painting the bridge and we won't do anything about wiring until we are through painting the bridge, that we didn't want them stringing wires while the painters were working.' At the time I had these conversations with Mr. Jones I was not familiar with the contract in question and was not intending to give any notice under the contract. These conversations occurred some time before Corder was injured."

 . . . .

  It is this testimony of the plaintiff's president that counsel rely on in support of their insistence that defendant had sufficient notice and knowledge of the painting of the bridge to meet the requirements of the contract.

What result, and why? Explain the distinction between this question and the questions asked previously. And try slight variations of the facts to see if you come out with different results and, if you do, can you explain them? For example, would the result be different if the same language were used, but Bolin's mood was very serious when he told Jones "[W]e [are] painting the bridge and expect to paint the bridge from one end to the other"; or if the same conversation had taken place in the office of the new manager?

Does it make any difference that Jones was new on the job? Would it make any difference if Bolin *was* "intending to give . . . notice" under the contract?

The above quotation is taken from St. Louis & St. Charles Bridge Co. v. Union Electric Light & Power Co., 216 Mo. App. 385, 268 S.W. 404 (1925). The decision unanimously adopted by the court is contained in the following passage:

The law is well settled in this State and elsewhere that knowledge which comes to an officer or agent of a corporation through his private transactions, and beyond the range of his duties as such officer or agent is not notice to the corporation. The rule that notice to an officer or agent is notice to the corporation applies only where the matter with reference to which notice is given or acquired is within the scope of his authority and has some direct connection with his agency, and the notice or knowledge comes to, or is possessed by, him in his official or representative capacity, and where the officer or agent in the line of his duty ought, and could reasonably be expected, to act upon or communicate the knowledge to the corporation.

Under these well-established principles it is clear that the evidence relied on is insufficient to show any such notice to the defendant corporation of the painting of the plaintiff's bridge as was required to meet the condition of the contract. The notice or knowledge which the defendant's local manager obtained concerning the painting of the bridge was not obtained in his official or representative capacity, nor within the scope of his authority, and was therefore not imputable to the corporation. The knowledge was obtained by him through mere casual remarks of the plaintiff's president while the parties were engaged in a discussion of a business proposition relating to a matter having not the remotest connection with the respective rights and obligations of the plaintiff and the defendant under the provisions of the contract in question. In the casual notice thus given to the defendant's local manager there was no suggestion or intimation that it was given under the contract or that any action was desired or expected to be taken thereunder. In fact the president conceded that the notice or information given by him was not intended as a notice under the contract. It does not appear that this local manager in the line of his duty as such ought to have communicated to his principal the knowledge he thus obtained, or that he could reasonably have been expected to do so.

5. The drawer of a check on defendant bank, issued Saturday night, called the cashier of the bank at his home on Sunday and told him to stop payment. The cashier said he would do so, but arrived to work late on Monday, and the check had already been paid. Is the bank liable to the drawer? The court deciding this question held that notice to the cashier was notice to the bank and thus the bank was held liable. Hewitt v. First Nat. Bank of San Angelo, 113 Tex. 100, 252 S.W. 161 (1923). The

court stated that the drawer had the right to expect the cashier to "diligently execute the promise he had given." Would you expect the case to come out the same today? *See* UCC § 4-403(1), stating that the customer's order "must be received at such time and in such manner as to afford the bank a reasonable opportunity to act. . . ."

Suppose the same facts except the cashier had said, "I'll do my best, sir. If I remember, I'll let the right people know." Would you advise your client that he could safely rely on that? Or suppose the cashier had said, "Don't bother me at home. Call me Monday." Suppose, finally, that Hewitt had called the cashier on Monday during working hours (having, say, issued the check just minutes before) and the cashier had said, "Don't bother me now. I'm very busy. Call back a little later." The check cleared between calls. Would you predict different results for the above variations, and if so, why?

6. Another problem along these lines involves notice of dishonor of a negotiable instrument to an indorser, who agrees that in the event of dishonor (involving nonpayment by the maker upon due presentment) he will pay it, if he is given "due notice" of the dishonor. Suppose that the holder sends written notice of dishonor to the indorser's correct address, but it miscarries in the mail. Who bears the risk of nondelivery under these circumstances? *See* UCC § 3-508(4), which states, "Written notice is given when sent although it is not received." Is it safe to generalize from this? *See* RESTATEMENT § 11, Comment *b*.

7. Finally, suppose the maker makes his stop payment order, or a holder orally gives his notice of dishonor, to one branch of a huge bank with dozens of branches. Another branch pays the item or claims it failed to receive "due notice" of the dishonor before the information from the first branch reaches it. Is the notice (or "notification") effective? Do these facts call for different answers? *See* UCC § 4-106 and comments, indicating that this is not an easy problem to resolve, but generally opting to treat branches as separate banks for purposes of receipt of notice. Suppose, however, that although the maker gives his stop payment order to the wrong branch, four days elapse before his check is presented for payment at the proper branch, and no effort was made at all with respect to intra-bank communication. What result, and on what principle? *See* UCC § 1-201(27), requiring "due diligence" in communicating information within an organization, assuming that the communication is "part of the regular duties" of the employee first receiving the information, or that he "has reason to know of the transaction." Due

diligence is defined as "reasonable routines for communicating significant information to the person conducting the transaction."

8. You represent a client who owns an unrecorded equitable interest in some land in midtown Manhattan. He has heard that General Motors Corporation is about to buy the land and place an office building on it. You want to effectively notify GM of the equitable interest, and your time is very limited. How would you go about doing so?

9. Section 268 of the Restatement, setting forth the general rule as to notification to or by agents, reads as follows:

§ 268.   General Rule.

(1)   Unless the notifier has notice that the agent has an interest adverse to the principal, a notification given to an agent is notice to the principal if it is given:

(a)   to an agent authorized to receive it;

(b)   to an agent apparently authorized to receive it;

(c)   to an agent authorized to conduct a transaction, with respect to matters connected with it as to which notice is usually given to such an agent, unless the one giving the notification has notice that the agent is not authorized to receive it;

(d)   to an agent to whom by the terms of a contract notification is to be given, with reference to matters in connection with the contract; or

(e)   to the agent of an unidentified or undisclosed principal with reference to transactions entered into by such agent within his powers, until discovery of the identity of the principal; thereafter as in the case of a disclosed principal.

(2)   The rules as to the giving of notification to an agent apply to the giving of notification by an agent.

10. The following quotation from the Restatement, Introductory Note to Chapter 8, will serve as a conclusion to the material on notification and as an introduction to the material on imputation of knowledge.

As stated in Section 9, "notice" may result from an act, as in the case of notification given to an endorser of a negotiable instrument, or may result from knowledge or reason to know, as where a person has "notice" of a defect in his premises because he knows of it, or is aware of facts which should lead him to inquire whether the defect exists. The distinction becomes important in determining whether the principal is affected by the notice which the agent has. By and large, the rules relating to notification correspond to those determining the principal's

rights and liabilities with reference to contracts and conveyances made by an agent or purported agent, and these are
largely dependent upon the rules of contracts. The rules relating to the liability of a principal because of the knowledge
which an agent has are generally consistent with those defining the principal's liability for torts.

A notification is intended to affect the relations between the
parties, and it has that effect only if given to or by an agent
who has power to bind the principal under the rules relating
to consensual transactions between the principal and third persons. As in the case of contracts and conveyances, one with apparent authority to give or to receive a notification can bind
the principal, and it is unimportant, unless known to the other
party, that the agent does not intend to act for the principal's
business. On the other hand, where the knowledge of the agent
is the basis of the principal's liability, and where there is no
element of reliance upon the appearance of agency, the principal is liable only because his agent failed to act or acted improperly in light of the knowledge which he had. The principal is not liable unless the agent was authorized and intended
to act in part, at least, for the principal's benefit, or unless the
principal in some way benefited from the transaction. For these
reasons it is necessary to deal with the two situations separately.

C. IMPUTED KNOWLEDGE

Suppose that Baker, an attorney, represented Peters in obtaining a mortgage on the Johnson farm to secure a loan from
Peters to Johnson. Through mistake, Baker failed to record the
mortgage. Six months later Baker represents Smith, who is in
the process of buying the Johnson farm. Baker says nothing to
Smith about the outstanding mortgage in favor of Peters, and
Smith buys in good faith thinking there are no liens against the
farm. Is the knowledge of Baker imputed to Smith? Does it make
any difference whether Baker remembered the Peters' lien and
deliberately said nothing, or he simply had forgotten about the
lien? Would it change your answer if he had represented the
mortgagor rather than the mortgagee? If the time period between
transactions was six years rather than six months? What legal
principle would you resort to in order to decide these questions?

Assume that a cashier at the Reliable Bank is involved in a
conspiracy with one partner to defraud the other partner of a
two-man partnership by accepting checks drawn on the partnership account by the defrauding partner which he knows are

drawn without the actual authority of the innocent partner, although it is within the apparent authority of the defrauding partner to write the checks. Reliable Bank, the payee of the checks, seeks to collect against the innocent partner. The cashier has left town with the defrauding partner, having embezzled other bank funds as well. Is the knowledge of the cashier imputed to the bank? Would your answer vary if the cashier was still an employee of the bank? For that matter, can the bank successfully argue that the knowledge of the defrauding partner is imputed to his innocent partner? How would you resolve this? Would you be able to make use of the principles you used in resolving the first hypothetical?

The treasurer of Merrill Corporation, acting pursuant to a resolution of the Board of Directors, negotiates and signs an employee fidelity bond with a bonding company. The application states that Merrill Corporation has no knowledge that any of its officers or employees are dishonest. It is a condition of coverage that all statements made in the application are true. Unfortunately, the treasurer himself has been embezzling funds from the corporation. He leaves town suddenly. The corporation demands payment under the bond. The bonding company refuses and is sued by the corporation. The defense of the bonding company is that the knowledge of the treasurer that the application contained a false statement is imputed to the corporation with the result that the bond is void. What result?

The following case is one of the famous ones in this area. Is it of help to you in resolving some of the above questions?

CONSTANT v. UNIVERSITY OF ROCHESTER
Court of Appeals of New York
111 N.Y. 604, 19 N.E. 631 (1889)

[Plaintiff Constant sued to foreclose a mortgage executed by Mrs. Meehan to plaintiff's testator on February 17, 1883. The defendant University had acquired title to the land in question through purchase at a foreclosure sale on a mortgage executed to it by Mrs. Meehan dated January 10, 1884, and recorded the next day. Plaintiff's mortgage had not been recorded at the time that defendant took its mortgage nor at the time of sale. Defendant denied any notice or knowledge of the existence of plaintiff's mortgage until the commencement of this action, and thus asserts that its title, having been purchased in good faith and without notice, is not subject to plaintiff's lien. Plaintiff won below, and defendant appealed.]

PECKHAM, J. In taking the mortgage of January, 1884, we think the university occupied the position of mortgagee for a valuable consideration. . . . If the university be not chargeable with notice of the prior mortgage to Constant, which was unrecorded, then its own mortgage is the prior lien as between the two. The first important question arising is, did Deane, who acted in the transaction as the attorney and agent for the university at the time of the existence of the mortgage to the university, have knowledge of the existence of the prior mortgage to Constant, executed in February, 1883, and which he then took as agent for Constant? In other words, is there any proof that he in January, 1884, had that fact present in his mind and recollection, so that it can be said from the evidence that he then had knowledge of its existence as an unpaid, outstanding obligation? The transaction out of which the mortgage to the university arose occurred eleven months subsequent to the transaction out of which the mortgage in suit arose; and the former mortgage was neither a part of the same transaction as the latter, nor had it the least connection therewith. Under the law, as decided by the older cases in England, such fact would have been an absolute defense to the claim that there was any constructive notice to the defendant arising out of notice to its agent, because such notice was in another and entirely separate transaction. In Warrick v. Warrick, decided by Lord Chancellor Hardwicke in 1745 (3 Atk. 291, 294), that able judge assumed it as unquestioned law that notice to the agent, in order to bind his principal by constructive notice, should be in the same transaction. He said: "This rule ought to be adhered to, otherwise it would make purchasers' and mortgagees' title depend altogether on the memory of their counselors and agents, and oblige them to apply to persons of less eminence as counsel, as not being so likely to have notice of former transactions." Cases were continually arising subsequent to that case wherein the principle was assumed as the law of England, although the cases did not in their facts absolutely call for a decision on that point.

But in Mountford v. Scott, 1 Turn. & R. Ch. 274, upon an appeal from a decision of the vice-chancellor, Lord Chancellor Eldon said that the vice-chancellor proceeded upon the notion that notice to a man in one transaction is not to be taken as notice to him in another transaction. The lord chancellor continued: "In that view of the case it might fall to be considered whether one transaction might not follow so close upon the other as to render it impossible to give a man credit for having forgotten it." He further said that he would be unwilling to go so far as to say that if an attorney has notice of a transaction in the morning he shall be held in a court of equity to have forgotten it in the evening; that it must, in all cases, depend upon the circumstances.

. . . .

In Nixon v. Hamilton, 2 Dru. & Wal. Irish Ch. 364, decided in 1838, Lord Chancellor Plunket adverted to the rule as to the necessity of notice in the same transaction, and stated, if it were notice acquired in the same transaction, necessarily the principal was to be charged with the knowledge of the agent; but if it were notice received by him in another transaction, then such notice was not to affect the principal unless he actually had the knowledge at the time of the second transaction. . . .

This modification of the old English rule is recognized in the comparatively late case of The Distilled Spirits, 11 Wall. 356. Mr. Justice Bradley, in delivering the opinion of the Supreme Court of the United States, stated that the doctrine in England seems to be established that, if the agent at the time of effecting a purchase has knowledge of any prior lien, trust or fraud affecting the property, no matter when he acquired such knowledge, his principal is affected thereby. If he acquire the knowledge when he effects the purchase, no question can arise as to his having it at that time. If he acquired it previous to the purchase, the presumption that he still retains it and has it present to his mind will depend upon facts and other circumstances. Clear and satisfactory proof that it was so present seems to be the only restriction required by the English rule as now understood.

. . . .

From all these various cases it will be seen that the farthest that has been gone in the way of holding a principal chargeable with knowledge of facts communicated to his agent, where the notice was not received, or the knowledge obtained, in the very transaction in question, has been to hold the principal chargeable upon clear proof that the knowledge which the agent once had, and which he had obtained in another transaction, at another time and for another principal, was present to his mind at the very time of the transaction in question. Upon a careful review of the testimony in this case, we have been unable to find any such proof. . . .

The other facts in the case uncontradicted are that, for some years prior to January, 1884, Deane and the plaintiffs' decedent were acting together, and that the plaintiffs' decedent was, weekly and even almost daily, in the habit of investing large amounts of money upon mortgages of this nature, and that the dealings of plaintiffs' decedent in these various building mortgages, through

Deane's office, had amounted, at the time of the mortgage to the university, in the aggregate, to three millions of dollars, if not more; that the mortgages were of all sizes, from six up to forty thousand dollars. It also appears that this very mortgage in suit was found after the execution of the university mortgage in a pigeon-hole in which satisfied mortgages were kept, and was found by the assignee of Deane after the assignment was made.

There is no proof in the case showing that Deane made any pretense of remembering, at the time of the execution of the mortgage to the university, that, eleven months before, he had taken a mortgage on the same property for the plaintiffs' decedent, which was not recorded. Taking into consideration the enormous amount of business done by Deane for Constant of this same general nature, and the length of time that elapsed since the taking of the Constant mortgage by him, and the fact that it was never taken from the office by the mortgagee, and that it remained there and was found in a pigeon-hole appropriated to satisfied mortgages . . . ; all these facts would tend to show very strongly that Deane had no recollection whatever of the existence of the Constant mortgage as an existing lien at the time he took the mortgage to the university.

.   .   .   .

The plaintiffs are bound to show by clear and satisfactory evidence that when this mortgage to the university was taken by Deane, he then had knowledge, and the fact was then present to his mind, not only that he had taken a mortgage to Constant eleven months prior thereto on the same premises, which had not been recorded, but that such mortgage was an existing and valid lien upon the premises, which had not been in any manner satisfied, if he recollected that there had been such a mortgage, but honestly believed that it was or had been satisfied, then, although mistaken upon that point, the university could not be charged with knowledge of the existence of such mortgage.

Quite a strong reason for not imputing knowledge to the agent in this case, unless upon evidence clear and satisfactory, is that, if he had such knowledge, and thus knowingly took an utterly worthless security for his principal, he acted in the most improper and dishonest manner, and willfully caused a loss to his principal of substantially, the whole amount of the money represented by the mortgage which he took as a second lien. While this consideration is not controlling, if the evidence justified the assumption, it is yet of considerable weight, and adds to the propriety of the rule requiring clear proof of such knowledge at the very time of taking the mortgage to the university.

One other question has been argued before us which has been the subject of a good deal of thought. It is this: Assuming that Deane had knowledge of the existence of the Constant mortgage at the time of the execution of the mortgage to the university, is his knowledge to be imputed to the university, considering the position Deane occupied to both mortgagees?

. . . .

At the time of the execution of the latter mortgage, therefore, he owed conflicting duties to Constant and to the university, the duty in each case being to make the mortgage to each principal a first lien on the property. Owing these conflicting duties to two different principals, in two separate transactions, can it be properly said that any knowledge coming to him in the course of either transaction should be imputed to his principal? Can any agent occupying such a position bind either principal by constructive notice? It has been stated that in such a case where an agent thus owes conflicting duties, the security which is taken or the act which is performed by the agent may be repudiated by his principal, when he becomes aware of the position occupied by such agent. Story Agency, § 210.

The reason for this rule is, that the principal has the right to the best efforts of his agent in the transaction of the business connected with his agency, and where the agent owes contracting [sic] duties he can not give that which the principal has the right to demand, and which he has impliedly contracted to give. Ought the university to be charged with notice of the existence of this prior mortgage when it was the duty of its agent to procure for it a first lien, while, at the same time, in his capacity as agent for Constant, it was equally his duty to give to him the prior lien? Which principal should he serve? There have been cases where, in the sale and purchase of the same real estate, both parties have employed the same agent, and it has been held under such circumstances that the knowledge of the agent was to be imputed to both of his principals. If, with a full knowledge of the facts that his own agent was the agent of the other, each principal retained him in his employment, we can see that there would be propriety in so holding; for each then notes the position which the agent has with regard to the other, and each takes the risk of having imputed to him whatever knowledge the agent may have on the subject.

. . . .

I have found no case precisely in point where the subject has been discussed and decided either way. I have very grave doubts as to the propriety of holding in the case of an agent, situated as I have stated, that his principal in the second mortgage should be charged with knowledge which such agent acquired in another transaction at a different time while in the employment of a different principal, and where his duties to such principal still existed and conflicted with his duty to his second principal. We do not deem it, however, necessary to decide the question in this case.

For the reasons already given the judgment should be reversed and a new trial ordered, with costs to abide the event.

GRAY, J. (dissenting.) The question presented by this appeal seems to possess sufficient interest to call for a brief statement of the grounds, upon which we dissent from the views entertained by a majority of the court.

. . . .

The trial judge found that Deane had knowledge of the Constant mortgage at the time of the transaction of the university loan, and I think the evidence supports such a finding in the proof of the circumstances attending it.

The general rule is not open to dispute that notice to the agent is notice to the principal. If the agent has knowledge of a fact, while he is acting for the principal, in the course of the very transaction which becomes the subject of the suit, this operates as constructive notice to the principal himself. For, upon general principles of policy, it must be taken for granted that the principal knows what the agent knows.

"To constitute constructive notice, it is not indispensable that it should be brought home to the party himself. It is sufficient if it is brought home to the agent, attorney or counsel of the party; for in such cases the law presumes notice in the principal, since it would be a breach of trust in the former not to communicate the knowledge to the latter." Story's Eq. Jur. § 408. These rules are well recognized as underlying the law of principal and agent.

. . . .

Lord Plunket, in Nixon v. Hamilton, said: "If, from the circumstances of the case, it satisfactorily appeared that the attorney, at the time of the second transaction, had full knowledge and recollection of the first transaction, it was fraudulent in him to conceal it from his principal, and, if so, the principal should not be at liberty to derive a benefit from the fraud of his attorney. . . . However acquired, if it (knowledge) existed at the time of the second transaction, it was fraud to conceal it, and this fraud of the attorney should be visited on the principal."

. . . .

All concur with PECKHAM, J., for reversal, except ANDREWS and GRAY, JJ., dissenting.

Judgment reversed.

NOTES

1. The terminology in the *Constant* opinion is not always consistent with the distinctions we have drawn. For example, the statement in the first paragraph of the opinion that "such fact would have been an absolute defense to the claim that there was any constructive notice to the defendant arising out of notice to its agent, . . ." talks of "notice" to the agent, when the Restatement would talk of the agent's knowledge. The court also mentions "constructive notice" to the principal rather than imputed knowledge, which is the term more frequently used today.

2. What is involved here is an allocation of the risk of loss between two innocent persons. Neither Constant nor the University of Rochester had the slightest idea that the other had any interest in the property. As the lower court opinion which was reversed makes clear (54 N.Y. Super. 515), both mortgagees had largely turned over their mortgage investment business to Deane. Do the opinions give you some reasons for the principles of law they set forth? Do such statements as the following supply the reasons? "Notice to the agent is notice to the principal." "The principal knows what the agent knows." "For in such cases [if knowledge is brought home to the agent] the law presumes notice in the principal, since it would be a breach of trust in the former not to communicate the knowledge to the latter."

Why isn't the rule of *Warrick v. Warrick*, mentioned in the first paragraph of the opinion, perfectly correct? The court there at least supplies a reason behind its decision, namely that a rule of imputation of nonimmediate knowledge would make purchaser's titles "depend altogether on the memory of their counselors and oblige them to apply to persons of less eminence as counsel. . . ."

Perhaps one way to approach this problem is by taking the simplest case first. Apparently all courts agree that the knowledge acquired by the agent *during* the transaction at issue is imputed to his principal. Why is this so? Assume, for example, that Deane had learned of Constant's unrecorded interest from a banker while talking about interest rates on the University of Rochester loan, and negligently (or intentionally) failed to tell his principal. Why is it so clear that the University should be held to his knowledge? (Contrast "notification" being given to Deane which he fails to convey. There the reasonable expectations argument underlying apparent authority comes into play. But that argument doesn't apply here, does it?) If you can answer this question, are you then on the way to answering the nontransaction knowledge question posed by the *Constant* case?

We do see one more example in the opinion of reference to the reasoning behind a principle. It is contained in the dissent, where *Nixon v. Hamilton* is quoted from, saying if the agent had knowledge, "[I]t was fraudulent in him to conceal it from his principal [fraudulent with respect to whom?] and, if so, the principal should not be at liberty to derive a benefit from the fraud of his attorney." What principles of law are involved?

3. The discussion in the majority opinion about the doubts raised because Deane represented two principals in a circumstance of conflict between their interests without either knowing of the other is interesting and thoughtful. The language quoted from Story, however, that "[I]n such a case . . . the security which is taken . . . may be repudiated by his principal. . . ." doesn't make any practical sense in the context of this case, does it?

4. Note the relatively high burden of proof set by the court in *Constant* and upon whom it is imposed. The fact to be proved (the state of mind of the agent) will in many cases be impossible to present independent evidence on. The burden of proof thus is crucial, isn't it?

5. The principle of law established in the *Constant* case is widely accepted in this country. *See* RESTATEMENT § 272. *See also,* Comments *a* and *b* of § 274, stating that "The rule stated in this section [dealing with an agent acquiring property for his principal] is not primarily a rule of agency, but of restitution. The prima facie liability of the principal exists because of unjust enrichment." Deane did not receive property for the University of Rochester, but does the rationale in the Comments serve to explain the principle involved in the *Constant* case?

6. To consider a different illustration, suppose a bank officer discounts a promissory note held as payee by a business customer of the bank. The maker of the note has a personal defense to it. The bank officer is also an officer of the business customer and knows of the defense. Would his knowledge be imputed to the bank and thus destroy its holder in due course status? Would it if the officer had not had anything to do with the actual discounting of the note? What arguments would you make on behalf of the bank? What arguments against the bank? Would the following case be of any assistance to you? In Poole v. Newark Trust Co., 40 Del. 163, 8 A.2d 10 (1939), one of defendant's depositors became insane. Defendant's trust officer, one of its directors,

learned of this in the course of his private affairs. Thereafter the depositor drew out most of his account. The bank was not held to the knowledge of its officer, who had no duties in connection with the banking details and no knowledge of the existence of the deposit.

7. During prohibition times the defendant's salesmen collaborated with bootleggers in diverting the denatured alcohol that defendant manufactured to alcoholic beverage purposes, thus increasing sales for the company and commissions for the salesmen. Defendant was sued by the federal government to recover the high taxes due upon alcohol withdrawn and distributed in violation of regulations. Defendant argued that the knowledge of its salesmen should not be attributed to it because they were acting contrary to the company's interests, and for their own gain. What result? Consider, in formulating your answer, RESTATEMENT § 282, stating in part that, "A principal is not affected by the knowledge of an agent in a transaction in which the agent secretly is acting adversely to the principal and entirely for his own or another's purposes. . . ."

The above facts, modified slightly, were drawn from *In re* Mifflin Chem. Corp., 123 F.2d 311, 315-16 (3d Cir. 1941). The decision of Judge Goodrich reads in part as follows:

> The scheme for the illegal diversion of this alcohol was carried out by salesmen for Mifflin in New York and Philadelphia. There is no dispute that these men had full knowledge of the transactions. Mifflin argues, however, that such knowledge is not to be attributed to it because in carrying out the unlawful plans its agents were acting contrary to the company's interests; therefore, their knowledge is not attributable to the employer. The evidence on this point is somewhat equivocal. But for the purpose of the discussion it may be assumed that the salesmen did not tell their superiors for fear of disapproval of the scheme. Added to that is another piece of evidence to the effect that one of them received a commission or gift from one of the bootleggers for help given.
>
> Even then, we believe unquestionably that Mifflin is charged with responsibility for the knowledge of its employees. As Judge Holly puts the legal proposition: "It is elementary law that the knowledge of an agent or employee obtained within the sphere of his agency or employment will be imputed to the corporation." The very job these salesmen were employed to do was to sell alcohol and selling alcohol they were, although in an improper way. Of course they were doing it to make money; the difference between doing it in a proper and an

improper way was that doubtless they made more by the latter course. But: "The mere fact that the agent's primary interests are not coincident with those of the principal does not prevent the latter from being affected by the knowledge of the agent if the agent is acting for the principal's interests." Restatement, Agency § 282, Comment b.

Counsel for Mifflin have cited authorities where courts have held that when an agent departs from his employment and acts adversely to his principal the latter is no longer responsible for facts known to the wrongdoing employee. But in these cases the agent was found either to be actively cheating or defrauding his principal or acting adversely as the other party to the same transaction in which he was serving as his principal's agent.

Zito v. United States, 7 Cir., 1933, 64 F.2d 772 is a case presenting facts not dissimilar in this respect to the case at bar. The knowledge of the agent in that case was sufficient to charge the company with criminal responsibility. In the instant case the question is not that of punishment or penalty, but simply that of the payment of a tax because the conditions on which non-liability was conditioned have not been complied with. One need not talk about actual knowledge by Mifflin or a presumption that the employer knows everything that the employee knows. It has been conceded that these employees were violating instructions and that they concealed from their superiors in the Mifflin organization the knowledge of their activities in promoting illegal diversion of the alcohol. That does not, on principles of agency, ipso facto relieve the employer of liability. Responsibility of an employer for things his agent does is not imposed on the basis of knowledge in fact, but under the general rule of respondeat superior. No reliance need be made on any fictional attributing of knowledge to Mifflin. The employers are responsible for the knowledge of the facts had by their agents in doing the very business for which they were employed. The learned trial judge correctly concluded that the tax was due and payable.

8. Suppose no single one of the employees of a bank has knowledge of a breach of trust affecting a customer of the bank with respect to which the bank is handling documents, but if all the facts known to the different employees were pieced together, the breach of trust would become apparent. Should the bank be held to the composite knowledge of its agents? *Compare* Colby v. Riggs Nat'l Bank, 92 F.2d 183 at 195 (1937) with Neal v. Cincinnati Union Stock Yards Co., 25 Ohio Cir. Ct. 299, 1 Ohio C.C.R. (n.s.) 13 (1903).

9. The Reliable Bank (defrauding cashier) hypothetical at the beginning of this section was based on the case of Matanuska Valley Bank v. Arnold, 116 F. Supp. 32, 35-36 (D. Ala. 1953). The court decided that the knowledge of the cashier was imputed to the bank, destroying its cause of action against the innocent partner. The following language reflects the basis of decision:

2. Imputed Knowledge Doctrine

The well-established principle that the knowledge of the agent is the knowledge of the principal as to acts done by the agent within the scope of his authority and in furtherance of the principal's business is of course applicable to banking corporations and their agents. The knowledge of a bank officer which will be imputed to the bank is knowledge concerning matters within the scope of his authority that he is under a duty to communicate to the bank.

The exception to this rule, known as the "adverse agent doctrine," does not seem applicable to this case. The gist of this exception is that the knowledge of the agent will not be imputed to the principal if the agent is engaged in fraudulent activities which it is necessary to conceal in the perpetration of the fraud. But even if the adverse agent exception would seem to be applicable to a situation of this kind, the sole actor qualification prohibits the application of the exception where, as here, only one agent of the bank deals with the third party. The apparent basis of the qualification is estoppel. The Courts refuse to permit a bank to recognize the agency of its officer for the purpose of accepting the benefit of a note obtained through him and at the same time deny the knowledge the officer had when the note was made. The same result may be reached on the theory of ratification. The bank cannot sue on the notes and then attempt to escape the imputed knowledge rule by setting up the fraudulent scheme of its officer.

In order to avoid the imputed knowledge rule, the agent's interest must be so adverse to that of his principal as to virtually destroy the agency relation. In the case at bar, since it cannot be said that such a condition existed, Maze's knowledge of Davis' lack of authority to make notes on behalf of the firm is imputable to the bank.

We will take up the concept of ratification in the next chapter. The sole actor rule is an interesting and somewhat vague qualification of the adverse interest exception. Basically, it holds that the knowledge of an agent can be imputed to a principal, even if the agent is otherwise clearly within the adverse interest exception, when he occupies an important and sole position as agent for his principal in the transaction, such as a general agent in charge of all affairs of his principal in a particular state, and he is the only such agent in the state. *See*, however, Note, *Notice to an Agent Acting Adversely—"Sole Actor,"* 19 ILL. L. REV. 174 (1924) (authored by Floyd Mechem and challenging the validity of any such distinction). See also, Annot., 111 A.L.R. 657 (1936).

10. The question raised in the Merrill Corporation (fraudulent treasurer) hypothetical at the beginning of this section has been the subject of a fair amount of litigation. *See* Gordon v. Continental Cas. Co., 319 Pa. 555, 181 A. 574, 104 A.L.R. 1238 (1935), holding that the knowledge of the treasurer was imputed to his principal. Can you articulate why the court would do this? Can you frame an argument against the result in the *Gordon* case? *See also,* W. SEAVEY, LAW OF AGENCY 187 (1964) (stating the present tendency is to allow recovery on the bond).

11. Section 12 of the UPA contains language of the above problems which is generally reflective of the common law. *See* Appendix A *infra.*

12. For a discussion of when a person has "reason to know" or "should know" (by inquiry after hearing something suspicious or unusual, for example) a fact, see § 9 of the Restatement and the Reporter's Notes thereto.

PROBLEMS

1. Bunn and Richardson were attorneys at law. On August 11, 1919, they entered into a contract with John Garand, the inventor of the "M-1" rifle, under the terms of which Garand contracted to compensate each of the attorneys, who were to use their best efforts to secure patents on his inventions and to promote their sale, to the extent of five per cent of any proceeds up to $100,000 and 33⅓ per cent of proceeds above $100,000 on sales of patents on automatic firearms. The attorneys thereafter negotiated on their own and on Garand's behalf with the War Department for the sale of an automatic weapon that Garand had perfected at that time and, in the process of doing so, left copies of the contract with two officers, a Major and a Colonel, in the Office of the Chief of Staff of the United States Army. Somehow the submission of the contracts, with the description of their interest in the sale proceeds, served the function of explaining why the attorneys were unwilling to entertain the Government's offer for the purchase of Garand's rights in the patents. Apparently nothing further was said or done after the negotiations had failed.

Subsequently, on January 20, 1936, Garand, without the knowledge or consent of either Bunn or Richardson, executed an assignment to the United States of all of his interest in his inventions and patents "by reason of the character of my employment by the Government of the United States." The assignment was taken by the officers of the Ordinance branch of the War Department in ignorance of the attorneys' rights.

An executor of the attorneys sued the Government to recover "just compensation" for the alleged taking of their interest in the patents. What result? Frame in your own mind the arguments that you as counsel for the two attorneys would make in prosecuting their case for them. Then do the same for the Government. *See* Burke v. United States, 107 Ct. Cl. 106, 67 F. Supp. 827 (1946), for the court decision on this question.

2. Assume that you represent a client who enjoys the contract rights owned by Bunn and Richardson in problem 1, above. You are, of course, concerned with protecting his interests, including avoiding the kind of problem that Garand created for his attorneys. How would you do so? Would you feel safe in addressing a notification of your client's interest as follows:

> United States Government
> Defense Department
> Washington, D. C.

3. Plaintiff sold land to Galt, receiving a note secured by a "crop payment" plan, under which he was entitled to have applied to the obligation the proceeds of the sale of one-half of all crops grown on the land until the note and interest were paid in full, including "the grain at the nearest elevator and the other products at the nearest market, and the then market price of same shall be credited on said note." Galt thereafter delivered a large amount of wheat to the Dimmitt Elevator Company and received full payment. Plaintiff, upon discovering this, demanded payment of one-half from the elevator company. This was refused, so he sued the Company, alleging that he had informed them of his interest by making a statement to that effect to one Caudle, the bookkeeper for the Company, before the wheat had been delivered and paid for. The Company claimed bona fide purchaser status, arguing that it had no effective notice of plaintiff's interest. What result? Again, consider the arguments from both points of view; then consult Dimmitt Elevator Co. v. Carter, 70 S.W.2d 615 (Tex. Ct. Civ. App. 1934). Evaluate for yourself the soundness of the opinion on this question. Also, the court said that at the trial, "[T]he general manager of the elevator, Boothe, should have been permitted to testify as to the authority

of the defendant's bookkeeper, Caudle." Would this be relevant to the decision?

4. In September, 1966, Poynor, a contract-writing agent for the Gulf Insurance Company, executed a one-year policy insuring against fire loss a fraternity house in Norman, Oklahoma. The local chapter of the fraternity that rented the house had become inactive in September, 1965, and the house was unoccupied thereafter. Poynor knew it was unoccupied. The insurance policy contained a standard clause saying the Company was not liable for any loss occurring while "a described building . . . is vacant or unoccupied beyond a period of 60 consecutive days."

At all pertinent times Poynor was a member of the fraternity owning the house and of its local Alumni Control Board. Poynor had agreed with the Board after the house became vacant to look after it, protect it from vandalism, keep it insured, and so forth. Also, the property was listed with him for sale.

On October 31, 1966, the house was destroyed by fire. A claim under the fire policy was made by the fraternity. Gulf Insurance Company refused to pay the claim, pointing to the fact that the house was vacant for more than 60 days.

What argument would you make on the fraternity's behalf? What defense would you expect from the Company?

5. Charles Munroe loaned some of his securities to Joseph A. Harriman to be used by Harriman as he saw fit to secure personal loans. The loan from Munroe was procured by fraud. Harriman promptly pledged the securities to the Harriman National Bank & Trust Company, of which he was president, as collateral for a loan of $380,000 by the bank to the M. H. O. Company, one of Harriman's dummy corporations.

None of the officers or employees of the bank who took part in the making of the loan, other than Harriman, were aware that the pledged securities had been procured from Munroe by fraud. The loan was formally approved by the loan committee of the bank but actually it was put through on Harriman's instructions before it was brought to the attention of the committee members. Subsequently the executive committee and board of directors confirmed the loan, all of them acting pursuant to the instructions of Harriman.

Munroe wants to rescind the transaction and get his securities back. The securities are still in the possession of the bank, which is now in liquidation and under the control of a receiver. It is clear that Harriman did not act as the bank's agent in borrowing the securities.

How would you assess Munroe's chances of getting his securities back? What legal obstacle does he have to overcome, and what arguments will he make in trying to do so? *See* Munroe v. Harriman, 85 F.2d 493 (2d Cir. 1936), commented on in the Reporter's Notes to Section 274 of the Restatement (Appendix, at 459-460); W. SEAVEY, STUDIES IN AGENCY 179-180 (1949); 35 MICH. L. REV. 686 (1937).

6. Clare Childers's husband, Hal Childers, was killed in a plane crash on December 19, 1967. Mrs. Childers employed the law firm of Brown, Kronzer, Abraham, Watkins and Steely to represent her in a suit against the Federal Aviation Administration (FAA) for the alleged negligence of their employees in causing her husband's death. The case was assigned to Robert Steely, a partner of the firm, because of his expertise in aircraft litigation.

On July 23, 1968, Steely filed a claim with the FAA. In response to the FAA's request for a statement of authority, Mrs. Childers stated in a written document that she had employed the above law firm and Mr. Steely as her attorneys to represent her in the claim.

On February 6, 1969, Steely was killed in a plane crash. On February 18, 1969, the FAA denied Mrs. Childers's tort claim by certified letter, return receipt requested, addressed to Steely at the law firm's address. In the confusion following Steely's death, the letter, which was receipted for by the receptionist of the firm, was placed in the "evidence" file of the case without any member of the firm seeing it. Federal regulations provide that final denial can be sent to the claimant's legal representative.

On August 18, 1969, the six month statute of limitations under 28 U.S.C.A. § 2401 for appeal from denial of a FAA claim expired. Mrs. Childers has discovered the above facts and has come to you for help. Can you, by promptly filing suit, save her claim? What arguments on her behalf would you make?

7. Farr entered into an agreement, evidenced by a memorandum, to purchase certain real property from the Newmans for $3000. After the making of this agreement, Hardy, who knew nothing about it, took a conveyance to the same property from the Newmans, paying $4000. Hardy's attorney had knowledge of the Farr-Newman agreement, however. He had been informed directly by Farr of his interest, but believed in good faith that Farr's interest was unenforceable under the Statute of Frauds. He did not tell Hardy about this.

Farr has brought suit against Hardy to compel Hardy to convey the property to him upon payment of $3000. At that stage, how would you assess the claim of Farr?

Suppose the attorney for Hardy had also represented the Newmans in the sale to Hardy. Would this additional fact change your analysis? If so, why? *See* Farr v. Newman, 14 N.Y.2d 183, 199 N.E.2d 369, 4 A.L.R. 3d 215 (1964) (a 4-3 decision).

8.   An agent, Clarke, acting on behalf of the owner, rented a house to Fowke. While discussing the transaction with Clarke, Fowke asked, "Pray, sir, is there anything objectionable about the house?" Clarke replied, in good faith, "Nothing whatever." He was unaware that the adjoining house was a "brothel of the worst description." His principal, however, was fully aware of that fact. Fowke, upon discovering the facts, refused to stay in the place and pay rent, with the result that he was sued by the principal for breach of contract. He based his defense on fraud and misrepresentation. The principal's response was that he did not authorize his agent to make any such statement and he did not intend that he make it. Should the defense succeed? *See* Cornfoot v. Fowke, 6 M. & W. 358, 151 Eng. Rep. 450 (1840).

a.   Would it vary your analysis of the rights of the parties if Clarke had said the same thing knowing of the brothel? If so, why?

b.   Would your analysis vary if Fowke had taken the initiative and sued the owner for breach of contract? Is there any other remedy that might have been available to Fowke?

Chapter 10

THE DOCTRINE OF RATIFICATION

The *Matanuska* case, described in the previous chapter on page 266, gave as one of the grounds for its decision "the theory of ratification," explaining that, "The bank cannot sue on the notes and then attempt to escape . . . . the fraudulent scheme of its officers. . . ." What does this mean?

"Ratify" is defined in Webster's International Dictionary, Second Edition, as meaning to approve, to sanction, to confirm. And ratification is defined in its legal context by the RESTATE-MENT OF AGENCY § 82, as follows:

§ 82. Ratification.

Ratification is the affirmance by a person of a prior act which did not bind him but which was done or professedly done on his account, whereby the act, as to some or all persons, is given effect as if originally authorized by him.

The Restatement explains and gives its justifications for the unusual features of this concept in a useful essay contained in the following Comments *c* and *d* to the above section:

c. A unique concept. The concept of ratification is not a legal fiction, but denotes the legal consequences which result from a series of events beginning with a transaction inoperative as to the principal, and ending in an act of validation. The statement that there is a relation back to the time of the original act is fictitious in form, but in effect, it is a statement of liabilities. The concept is unique. It does not conform to the rules of contracts, since it can be accomplished without consideration to or manifestation by the purported principal and without fresh consent by the other party. Further, it operates as if the transaction were complete at the time and place of the first event, rather than the last, as in the normal case of offer and acceptance. It does not conform to the rules of torts, since the ratifier may become responsible for a harm which was not caused by him, his property or his agent. It can not be justified on a theory of restitution, since the ratifier may not have received a benefit, nor the third person a deprivation. Nor is ratification dependent upon a doctrine of estoppel, since there may be ratification although neither the agent nor the other party suffer a loss resulting from a statement of affirmance or a failure to disavow. However, in some cases in which ratification is claimed, the principal's liability can be based upon unjust enrichment or estoppel, either in addition to or as alternative to his liability based on ratification. See §§ 103, 104.

d. *Justification.* That the doctrine of ratification may at times operate unfairly must be admitted, since it gives to the purported principal an election to blow hot or cold upon a transaction to which, in contract cases, the other party normally believes himself to be bound. But this hardship is minimized by denying a power to ratify when it would obviously be unfair. See §§ 88-90. Further, if the transaction is not ratified normally the pseudo-agent is responsible; if not, it is because the third party knew, or agreed to take the risk, of lack of authority by the agent. In many cases, the third person is a distinct gainer as where the purported principal ratifies a tort or a loan for which he was not liable and for which he receives nothing. This result is not, however, unjust, since although the creation of liability against the ratifier may run counter to established tort or contract principles, the liability is self-imposed. Even one who ratifies to protect his business reputation or who retains unwanted goods rather than defend a law suit, chooses ratification as preferable to the alternative. Further, the sometimes-derided doctrine of relation back not only is one used in other parts of the law, but it tends to give the parties what they wanted or said they wanted. If it sometimes happens that a mistaken or over-zealous agent is relieved from liability to the third person, the net result causes no harm to anyone. However, perhaps the best defense of ratification is pragmatic; that it is needed in the prosecution of business. It operates normally to cure minor defects in an agent's authority, minimizing technical defenses and preventing unnecessary law suits. In this aspect, it is a beneficial doctrine, which has been adopted in most systems of law.

A. WHAT CONSTITUTES RATIFICATION?

Under what circumstances will a principal against whom a claim is being asserted on the ground of ratification be held to have ratified the actions taken on his behalf? The most obvious case, which resolves the question of intent to ratify at least, is where the principal says, "I'll agree to that" or "I'll ratify that."

Suppose, however, that the principal is informed of the act and says nothing at all. And he is aware, in addition, that the third party is relying on the "agent's" acts to his clear detriment. Would these facts make out a case for ratification? For example, in one well known case the defendant's name was signed to a guaranty of payment, in reliance on which plaintiff sold several bills of goods. Plaintiff notified defendant by registered mail of the guaranty and that he was selling goods in reliance thereon. Defendant gave no answer, and later was sued on the guaranty. What result? How would you, as the attorney for the plaintiff, argue that ratification had taken place? Recall the language in the Comments to § 82 that ratification ". . . can be accomplished without . . . manifestation by the purported principal. . . ." Of what relevance is the underlying principle of tort law that no affirmative duty to aid others is placed on persons, the well known illustration of that being the no duty to rescue cases? Would § 16 of the UPA (see Appendix A) be of aid to you, by way of analogy, in framing an argument? Would the contract doctrine of acceptance by silence be more in point here?

Would you want to inquire into the relationship, if any, between defendant and the person who signed his name? Into the surrounding circumstances at the time of the signing of defendant's name? If so, why? *Cf.* Furst v. Carrico, 167 Md. 465, 175 A. 442, 96 A.L.R. 375 (1934), holding the defendant not liable under the guaranty, but with the special fact that defendant's name was forged by the person buying the goods. The court in its opinion does not disclose whether or not there was any prior relationship between defendant and the purchaser, nor does it describe the circumstances surrounding the execution of the forgery. The court found it significant that the failure to answer was with respect to an inquiry by letter rather than a failure to respond to an oral statement, since "men use the tongue much more readily than the pen." P. MECHEM, OUT-LINES OF AGENCY (4th ed. 1952), notes at 146 n.44, that other cases involving the same factual background have reached the opposite conclusion. On what reasoning, do you think? Whatever the reasoning may be, in what manner, if at all, does it relate to the law of agency?

Suppose the case was altered to make the transaction a sale to X of a piece of property, and X signed his wife's name as well as his to the note. The signing of the wife's name was done without her consent. Assume that the wife later found out about this and said nothing to the salesman, but also received no direct communication from him. Would the *Furst* case be harder or easier to overcome under this variation? Could you successfully argue under this variation, at least, that the plaintiff salesman should bear the risk of loss? He did act without knowledge that the additional signature was authorized, and there is no apparent authority in the case or it would be unnecessary to worry about ratification. (Of course, both grounds may be pursued in the alternative in a close case.) Would it affect your analysis if the property is soon thereafter sold by *X*, so the salesman will be unable effectively to rescind the sale by him? *See* Myers v. Cook, 87 W. Va. 265, 104 S.E. 593 (1920), holding no ratification, on the ground that the wife's silence after being informed by her husband of his use of her name was not sufficient evidence of ratification in the absence of a pre-existing agency relationship or of receipt and retention of benefits. *See* Restatement § 94, agreeing with the *Myers* case and requiring circumstances "which reasonably justify an inference of consent" before there is ratification by silence. *See also,* Seavey, *Ratification by Silence,* 103 U. Pa. L. Rev. 30 (1954).

The Comments to Section 82 of the Restatement state that tortious actions can be ratified. The same problem of determining from the facts whether there was under § 82 ". . . the affirmance by a person of a prior act . . . done . . . on his account . . ." exists in this setting, of course. Suppose a bartender savagely beats up a customer for purely personal reasons. (The customer had been married to the bartender's wife. The wife was present at the time, and the beating followed this statement by the customer to his wife: "Well, I don't suppose you bought another man a bathrobe and I had to pay for it.") Assume that thereafter the bar owner, who was not present at the time, failed to discharge the bartender after learning of the incident. Could you, as the attorney for the injured patron, successfully argue that the continued employment constituted ratification of the tort? Assume you are in a jurisdiction—of which there are still many—that takes a narrow view toward vicarious liability for intentional torts, and thus an argument based on ratification would be important to your case. If so, the employer would incur liability for the damages. (Would it, incidentally, be vicarious liability?) Would it make any difference to your case if, in retaining the bartender, the employer had said nothing about the incident to him, as contrasted with issuing specific instructions to "never do that again"?

Suppose, in addition to retaining the bartender, the owner had filed a criminal complaint against the patron. Now how would you assess your case? Or suppose he later billed the patron for his drinks. Finally, suppose upon next seeing the patron, the owner had said to him, "What's the matter with you, Gouldsberry? Are you crazy? If I had been there, I would have broken your . . . neck."

If you succeed on your ratification theory, would your chances of recovering punitive damages against the employer be enhanced? *See* Novick v. Gouldsberry, 173 F.2d 496 (9th Cir. 1949), upholding liability, including $1000 punitive damages, of the employer, who had done everything noted above except express disapproval to his employee and send a bill. Is it possible to argue logically, regardless of the factual variations above, that the act of the bartender ". . . was done or professedly done on [his employer's] account . . ." (§ 82)?

B.   IS PARTIAL RATIFICATION POSSIBLE?

Suppose a principal knows of the transaction and elects to ratify, but does not want the whole deal. Can he ratify only as to part? What is your common sense reaction to this? *See* Section 96 of the Restatement, stating, "A contract or other single transaction must be affirmed in its entirety in order to effect its ratification." The Restatement continues in the comments to flatly state that the purported principal ". . . cannot affirm a sale and disavow unauthorized representations or warranties which the purported agent made to induce it. He cannot affirm a contract and disavow unauthorized terms which the purported agent included."

Does the above rule establish a principle which we can rely upon to resolve all cases in which the question arises? Consider the following fact situation: Nicholson was a special agent of Standard Pecan Company, with authority to sell its stock for cash at the rate of $10 per share. He was equipped with blank certificates, signed by the president and the secretary, with authority to fill in the name of the purchaser and deliver them for sale. He had no authority to enter into any agreements for repurchase or to vary the transaction in any way.

Nicholson sold 100 shares to Mrs. Murray, and wrote on the back of the certificate that, "It is hereby agreed that the Standard Pecan Co. shall at the end of three years from date repurchase this stock at $11 per share upon 30 days notice." The certificate was delivered to Mrs. Murray. She gave Nicholson $1000 which he paid to the Company. The Company did not know of the endorsement until three years later, when the heirs of Mrs.

Murray demanded a repurchase of the stock. The Company refused to repurchase and repudiated the agreement of Nicholson. Counsel for Mrs. Murray's heirs argued the "no partial ratification" rule set forth above in RESTATEMENT § 96. Should this argument prevail? What arguments would you make on behalf of the Company in rebuttal?

The court rejected the argument based on § 96, stating that it devolved upon Mrs. Murray to acquaint herself with the extent of the agent's authority, and limiting the rule of § 96 to executory contracts. See Murray v. Standard Pecan Co., 309 Ill. 226, 140 N.E. 834, 31 A.L.R. 604 (1923).

Would it make any difference if Mrs. Murray had paid for the stock with a promissory note and the procedural context of the suit was switched, with the corporation as plaintiff suing for the purchase price? See Independent Harvester Co. v. Malzohn, 147 Minn. 145, 179 N.W. 727 (1920). In this case the court invoked the rule of no partial ratification where a corporation was suing for the purchase price on a stock subscription agreement. The defense was that the agent as part of the sale promised the stock buyer a job, a promise the corporation repudiated. Judgment was rendered in favor of the defendant. Also, would it make any difference if the plaintiffs in the *Murray* case had pleaded in the alternative for rescission and restitution? See Seifert v. Union Brass & Metal Mfg. Co., 191 Minn. 362, 254 N.W. 273 (1934), holding that it does. Does this set of facts lend itself to application of the doctrine of restitution? Normally one sees restitution as placing the parties back in their original position, without loss to either party. Would that be likely under the facts of these cases?

C. THE KNOWLEDGE REQUIREMENT

One of the conventional rules of ratification is that the principal must have knowledge of all the material facts before he can be held to ratify. See RESTATEMENT § 91, stating, "If, at the time of affirmance, the purported principal is ignorant of material facts involved in the original transaction, and is unaware of his ignorance, he can thereafter avoid the effect of the affirmance."

Would the following illustration fall within the above rule? *P*'s agent in this country advanced *P*'s money to a mutual friend to enable the friend to save stock that she was carrying on a margin account. This was done without authority. *P*, in Europe, on being informed of *A*'s action, expressly approved. Later, however, he attempted to disavow the ratification on the ground that he had no idea what a critical condition her account was in. Can he escape under the general principle that one must have knowledge of all material facts before he is held to a ratification? *See* Currie v. Land Title Bank & Trust Co., 333 Pa. 310, 5 A.2d 168 (1939) (holding no). Why not? *See* W. SEAVEY, LAW OF AGENCY 66 (1964).

LEWIS v. CABLE
United States District Court, Western District of Pennsylvania
107 F. Supp. 196 (1952)

MARSH, District Judge. This action was instituted by plaintiffs to recover from defendant 20¢ for each ton of coal produced by defendant for use or sale during the life of the National Bituminous Coal Wage Agreement of 1948 and to recover 30¢ for each ton of coal produced by defendant for use or sale during the life of the National Bituminous Coal Wage Agreement of 1950. Plaintiffs allege that said Agreements were signed on behalf of defendant by the Somerset County Coal Operators Association of Pennsylvania (Association) of which defendant is a member.

Plaintiffs filed a motion for summary judgment. In support of their motion, they contend that the Association had apparent authority to execute the contracts on behalf of the defendant; or, if the Association did not have apparent authority then defendant ratified the contracts by making payments thereunder.

Defendant made payments on the production of coal up to April 30, 1949. These payments were 20¢ for each ton of coal produced for use or sale. On October 10, 1949, counsel for plaintiffs sent defendant a letter demanding payment for coal produced "due and owing in accordance with and pursuant to the terms and provisions of the National Bituminous Coal Wage Agreement of 1948. . . . If the aforesaid debt is not paid within a reasonable time, it will be necessary for the Trustees of the United Mine Workers of America Welfare and Retirement Fund to take the legal steps necessary to compel compliance of your contractual obligations." Defendant, on October 12, 1949, replied: "In reference to your letter of Oct. 10, 1949, regarding the Welfare fund I owe the U. M. W. A. Right now I'm in no position to pay anything on this debt. But just as soon as we go back to work my broker will advance the money on the output for the first two days, this will be sent to you at once to apply on the welfare fund."

In opposition to plaintiffs' motion, defendant filed an affidavit in which he states that "The payments made as aforesaid were made by me under the influence of fear of strike and repercussions which I was convinced would inevitably result if such payments had not been made and which would entail irreparable loss to me in my business, and were in nowise made pursuant to any legal obligation known by me to exist at that time and, on the contrary, I was not cognizant of any legal obligation incurred by me at any time for making such payments."

Defendant's defense, therefore, appears to be that subjectively he did not intend to ratify the 1948 Agreement. But the court is of the opinion that it is the manifestation and not the undisclosed intention of the alleged principal which controls. See Restatement of the Law of Agency, § 26 Comment a, § 27 Comment a. See also Restatement of the Law of Contracts, §§ 20, 71. In fact, we are of the opinion that proof of his subjective intent is not material and would not be admissible in evidence.[1] Defendant cannot by his acts and declarations pretend to be bound by the Agreement so as to prevent strikes and repercussions and then, when full liability under said Agreement is asserted, seek to disaffirm it. See Restatement of the Law of Agency, § 96. And his uncommunicated motives in making payments cannot now alter the legal effect of his manifested acts and declarations.

Defendant further urges, however, that he did not ratify the 1948 Agreement because it is not shown that he had full knowledge of all the material facts concerning the Agreement. We do not agree with this contention. If he did not have full knowledge of all the material facts, the payments and the above letter of defendant indicate to the court a willingness on the part of defendant to ratify the contracts without complete knowledge. See Restatement of the Law of Agency, § 91. He paid over $9,000 under the 1948 Agreement. If he thought this was sheer extortion, he would not have paid it. The same is true of the promise in his letter of October 12, 1949, to continue payments after he returned to work. If he did not believe he owed the money, he should not have acknowledged the debt. Under these facts, defendant was under a duty to repudiate liability under the Agreement before making payments or acknowledging liability. See Restatement of the Law of Agency, §§ 93, 94. From defendant's acts and declarations, we find, as a matter of law, that he did ratify the 1948 Agreement.

---

[1] See RESTATEMENT OF THE LAW OF CONTRACTS, § 71, Comment a, which states "If the words or other acts of one of the parties have but one reasonable meaning, his intention is material only in the exceptional case, stated in Clause (c), that an unreasonable meaning which he attaches to his manifestations is known to the other party." In the case sub judice, the undisclosed intention of defendant was not known to plaintiffs and the payments and letter have but one reasonable meaning. Therefore, any attempt by defendant to prove his undisclosed intention would be immaterial and inadmissible at the trial of this case.

Although defendant did not make payments under the 1950 Agreement, we find that the ratification of the 1948 Agreement created apparent authority in the Association to enter into the later Agreement on defendant's behalf. The ratification of the prior Agreement appears to the court to be such "conduct of the principal which, reasonably interpreted, causes a third person to believe that the principal consents to have the act done on his behalf by the person purporting to act for him." Restatement of the Law of Agency, § 27.

It further appears to the court that the motion for summary judgment should be granted because the defendant is estopped from denying the authority of the Association to act on his behalf. Defendant's affidavit indicates that he made payments under the 1948 Agreement in order to circumvent strikes and other repercussions. Obviously this course of action was taken to insure continued production at defendant's mines by inducing the employees and their union to believe that defendant had a contract with the union. The success of this deception is demonstrated by the fact that the 1950 Agreement was entered into in the same manner as the 1948 Agreement. As a result, the employees and their union did not undertake to enter into a separate contract with defendant although they have the right to insist that defendant bargain collectively. Defendant's action and declarations caused the employees and their union to forego this valued right of labor. If we were to sustain defendant's contention, the employees and their union would be prejudiced after they had relied on the only reasonable inference to be drawn from defendant's course of conduct. Thus, the elements of estoppel are present. See Restatement of the Law of Agency, § 103.

The motion, therefore, will be granted and summary judgment will be entered for the amount shown to be due by the number of tons admittedly produced by defendant.

D. CHANGED CIRCUMSTANCES

Suppose the third party decides he wants out of the transaction before the principal has ratified. Should he be able to repudiate at that time? Should it make any difference what his reasons are? As you might expect, courts have reacted differently to this. A conventional application of the relation-back rule would supply the answer, of course. But would it do so satisfactorily? The following case discusses this issue in an interesting context.

KLINE BROS. & CO. v. ROYAL INS. CO.
United States District Court, Southern District of New York
192 F. 378 (1911)
Noted in, 25 Harv. L. Rev. 729 (1912)

[McIntosh, the president of the plaintiff corporation, contracted with defendant for fire insurance. It was clear under the corporation's by-laws that he was not authorized to do so. The by-laws provided that "the business of the corporation shall be managed by the board of directors" and that "all contracts shall be made by the board." The court also held that McIntosh had no apparent authority to make the contract. The board of directors attempted to ratify his acts and tendered the premium, after a fire loss.]

L. Hand, J. . . . Thus there seems to be no escape from the conclusion that by his contract with the defendants McIntosh did not bind the corporation to pay the premium. Furthermore, the board of directors never learned of the policies until after the fire, and did not therefore ratify them up to that time. At least, there is no evidence upon that question, and the burden rests with the plaintiff. As I view it, no subsequent ratification was possible. After the fire McIntosh tendered the premium, and after that the defendants repudiated any liability.

The facts, therefore, raise two questions: First, whether a third party who has made a contract with an unauthorized agent on behalf of his principal is bound before the principal has ratified; and second, if not, whether the occurrence of a fire before the unauthorized application for the policy has been ratified prevents its future ratification so as to bind the company. Upon the first question, there is no doubt some division of authority. In England the law now is that the third party may not withdraw, provided the principal ratifies the contract in season. Bolton Partners v. Lambert, 41 Ch. D. 295; Re Tiedemann (1899) 2 Q. B. D. 66. I do not regard Hagedorn v. Oliverson, 2 M. & S. 485, as authoritative, because the policy was there taken out for whom it might concern and the premium had been paid before capture. So, also, in Lucena v. Crawford, 1 Taunt. 325, and Routh v. Thompson, 13 East, 274, the premium appears to have been paid, though the facts are not quite clear. The case at bar is not, however, one in which the premium had been paid and accepted, and it is governed by quite different considerations, because in such cases the insured has received the consideration, and cannot be compelled to return it whether or not the principal ratifies. On the other hand, in Wisconsin (Dodge v. Hopkins, 14 Wis. 630; Atlee v. Bartholomew et al., 69 Wis. 43, 33 N. W. 110, 5 Am. St. Rep. 103), and apparently in Illinois (Cowan v. Curran,

216 Ill. 598, 75 N. E. 322), the whole unauthorized contract seems to amount only to an offer by the third person, which must be accepted de novo by the principal, a rule certainly at variance with the well-established law that an uncommunicated ratification by the principal will bind him. The English case proceeds on the civil law maxim, "Omnis ratihabitio retrotrahitur," though it by no means follows, because a ratification relates back when once a valid contract is made, that the third party is bound meanwhile, and may not withdraw while the principal remains unbound. Now, relation back is in the sense here used a fiction, and certainly should not be extended to cover unjust cases, of which this is one, as I shall show. In so far as by the maxim it is only meant to say that a ratification carries with it by implication the intention of the principal that the contract shall in fact date from the time when it was made between the agent and the third party, it is unobjectionable in principle, and accords with the facts; but, if taken in the sense that the law will regard both parties as bound from the date of the contract, it merely misstates the facts, because, by hypothesis, the principal is not bound before ratification. All that the law can do is to hold the third party bound from the outset, and that by the mere force of authority. It certainly serves no useful purpose to cloak that authority in a phrase which misstates the truth in Latin, unless it accords with the principles of the law of contracts, or at least produces just results at the expense of those principles.

Upon principle the doctrine does not appear to be correct, and it has been criticised by text-writers. Wambaugh, 9 Harv. L. R. 60; 31 Cyc. 1291. The contract of insurance is bilateral, and, until the principal ratifies, he is by hypothesis under no obligation to pay the premium. If so, there is until then no consideration to support the counter promise of the third person, for a consideration implies a legal obligation, and his promise ought not in principle to bind him, being indeed nudum pactum. Second. The result is unfair to the third party, since it permits the principal to speculate on the value of the contract, while he himself remains unbound. If it proves advantageous, he may ratify. If not, he may repudiate. There is no just ground for giving him such an advantage over the third party merely because of an unknown defect in the agent's powers. In view of the dearth of authority in this country and especially of any decisions binding upon me, I do not think that I should follow the rule in Bolton v. Lambert, supra, but rather what I cannot but believe to be the result necessary under the principles of the laws of contract.

The question should be clearly distinguished from those cases in which a factor or other agent takes out a policy, like those in suit, for goods held on commission or in trust, and in which the principals may come in later and assume the benefit. In such cases the agent binds himself to pay the premium, and a valid bilateral contract at once results. He is in such case acting in fact as a trustee for his principals, and they may come in and assume the valid chose in action so created, either before or after the loss. This is the meaning I think of the cases cited by the plaintiff, as it is of Hagedorn v. Oliverson, Lucena v. Crawford, supra, and Routh v. Thompson, supra. In the case at bar McIntosh certainly did not intend to bind himself, and he had no authority to bind the company. Therefore, the insurer got no valid promise at all. Nor should this case be confused with those in which a ratification is used against the principal when he is sued. These two situations exhaust all the plaintiffs' citations.

The next question is whether, if the contract was not binding upon either party until McIntosh tendered the premium, the occurrence of the fire terminated that possibility. I may assume under Hagedorn v. Oliverson, supra, Routh v. Thompson, supra, and Lucena v. Crawford, supra, that the tender was sufficient, even though there is no evidence that even at that time McIntosh had been authorized to make it by the other two directors. If, however, the fire, which was known to both the insured and the insurer, terminated the possibility of binding the bargain by either ratification or tender, it was a nullity. An insurer's undertaking is a promise to pay upon a given event which either must happen in futuro, or if it have already happened must be still unknown. Were it not so, the promise would be merely to pay a large sum of money in consideration of a small one, which is an absurd intention to ascribe to any one. In the case at bar, since the loss had happened before the policy became binding, the promise could only be to pay for an existing loss. Such promises are common enough in marine insurance when the policy reads, "lost or not lost," and they have been held to be binding in the case of fire insurance when the policy was antedated and the loss occurred between the date and delivery of the policy. Commercial Ins. Co. v. Hallock, 27 N. J. Law, 645, 72 Am. Dec. 379. In all such cases, however, the policy at its inception must be construed as an insurance of a risk, not as a certain agreement to pay, for otherwise, as I have said, the contract becomes absurd. Thus in a marine policy, though the loss may have in fact occurred, the fact is unknown, and there is the same aleatory element in the promise, as though it might occur in the future. When that element disappears, the character of the contract goes with it, so that it may be said with accuracy that the element of some chance is a condition to the promise of the insurer, and, if that element does not exist, his promise is made under a mistake of existing fact. It is of no consequence whether that fact be the actual loss, in a case where the insurance is of future loss, or of the insured's knowledge of the loss, in a case where the insurance is of an existing loss. In either case there must be some uncertainty as to the loss, or else the presupposition upon which the promise is made does not exist.

In the case of Com. Ins. Co. v. Hallock, supra, the loss occurred only two hours before the policy took effect (see the report of cause in 26 N. J. Law, 271), and it did not appear when the insured learnt of it. Certainly the insured had no opportunity to withdraw the application before it was accepted. The court held that the antedating of the policy made it equivalent to an insurance, "lost or not lost," and noted that there was no question raised of either fraud or concealment. If, however, the insured had known of the loss before making application, the contract would, of course, be fraudulent. But the same thing is true, even though when the application was made the risk is as supposed, provided that the insured learns of the change before the policy becomes binding. Wales v. N. Y. Bowery Fire Ins. Co., 37 Minn. 106, 33 N. W. 322. In Canning v. Farquhar, L. R. 16 Q. B. D. 727, although the insured informed the insurer at the time of making tender of the change in risk, the company had not withdrawn the offer to insure before the tender. The basis in the case of the judgment for the defendant was not that the offer was not outstanding when accepted, but that the character of the risk had changed before the policy went into effect, and that the insured knew of the change when he accepted it. The same rule was enforced in Equitable Life Ass'n Soc. v. McElroy, 83 Fed. 631, 28 C. C. A. 365 (C. C. A. 8th Cir.), in which the assured accepted after the risk had changed to his knowledge, but in which because he had not disclosed the change the court assimilated the facts to a case where there was fraud in the application itself.

There is no difference of judicial opinion so far as I can find upon the proposition that the insurer is not bound, where the insured at the time of the binding of the bargain had learned that the loss has happened or the risk has changed since the original application. The only difference between those cases and the case at bar is this: That here the insurer likewise knew that the loss had occurred, and nevertheless did not withdraw from the contract. This fact would perhaps be irrelevant in any case, even if the insurer did not formally withdraw his offer upon learning of the loss, for it might be held that to withdraw it after a loss has occurred would be an idle ceremony; but that question is not up at present, because the defendants had no knowledge that McIntosh had not bound the plaintiff to pay the premium, and that their own undertaking had therefore been without consideration from the outset. They certainly dealt with him in good faith, and were not called upon to disaffirm a contract which, so far as they knew, was binding upon them. If, however, it be once admitted that it was not binding upon them until ratified, it could not be ratified or accepted by paying a premium after the risk had ceased and the fundamental condition of the promise no longer existed. This would be quite obvious had the offer never been accepted at all, before the loss, but, if the policy was not binding while unratified, the situation was the same as though the offer had never been accepted.

[Judgment was entered for the defendant.]

NOTES

1. P. MECHEM, OUTLINES OF AGENCY (4th ed. 1952), states in § 252 that the prevailing American view is that the principal can ratify in the insurance situation if he does so before the insurance company withdraws. Although the result of this is that the principal is able to insure lost property, Mechem argues that this is not so anomalous since the premium will have been paid or must be accounted for and "the transaction from the standpoint of the insurance company will be completely routine." See also, Marqusee v. Hartford Fire Ins. Co., 198 F. 475, 1023 (holding, in litigation arising from the same facts as in the Kline case, that the principal can ratify even after the insured property is destroyed); Robinson, Ratification After Loss in Fire Insurance, 18 CORN. L. Q. 161 (1933). But see RESTATEMENT § 89.

2. The factor of changed circumstances has relevance beyond disputes between the immediate parties. See Section 101 of the Restatement, stating that ratification ". . . is not effective . . . (c) in diminution of the rights or other interests of persons not parties to the transaction which were acquired in the subject matter before affirmance." See also, Section 90 of the Restatement: "If an act to be effective in creating a right against another or to deprive him of a right must be performed before a specific time, an affirmance is not effective against the other unless made before such time."

E. OTHER QUESTIONS

1.   Can a forgery be ratified? What conceptual problems, if any, do you see in the way of an affirmative answer? The common law split on this question. The Negotiable Instruments Law § 23 said ratification was not possible. The UNIFORM COMMERCIAL CODE § 3-404, allows ratification of an "unauthorized signature," which includes both a forgery and a signature made by an agent exceeding his actual or apparent authority.

2.   Can an undisclosed principal ratify? Again, what conceptual problems are involved? *See* Section 85 of the Restatement, stating, "Ratification does not result from the affirmance of a transaction with a third person unless the one acting purported to be acting for the ratifier."

3.   Should ratification be effective if the agent admits to the third party at the time of the agreement that he is not authorized to act? *See* RESTATEMENT § 85, stating in Comments *a* and *e* that this does not affect the power of the principal to ratify. Why not? The third party has no reasonable expectations that are realized by the ratification, does he?

4.   Can a nonexistent or incompetent principal (who later comes into existence or becomes competent) ratify a contract made on his behalf? For example, suppose a promoter for a corporation not yet formed enters into several contracts on its behalf. The corporation thereafter is formed and the Board of Directors at its first meeting seeks to ratify the promoter's contracts. Can it do so? Again, what conceptual difficulties are involved? *See* Section 84(2) of the Restatement, stating, "An act which, when done, the purported or intended principal could not have authorized, he cannot ratify. . . ." This conceptual problem was resolved by courts holding that the corporation can "adopt" the promoter's contracts, with the problems surrounding adoption sounding very similar to those surrounding ratification.

5.   Can ratification create genuine or apparent authority in an agent to conduct further transactions? Under what circumstances would you expect this to happen? *See* W. SEAVEY, LAW OF AGENCY 59 (1964).

PROBLEMS

1. A member of the household of the defendant, who had no authority to work in the defendant's business, filled a customer's order for coal. In delivering it, he broke the customer's window. The defendant sent a bill to the customer for coal. Does this act constitute ratification? Would it make any difference whether the

defendant knew or did not know about the accident at the time of sending the bill? *See* Dempsey v. Chambers, 154 Mass. 330, 28 N.E. 279 (1891).

In Jones v. Mutual Creamery Co., 81 Utah 223, 17 P.2d 256, 85 A.L.R. 908 (1932), Sager, an employee of the defendant Creamery Company who as part of his duties gathered eggs from farmers for the Company using his own truck, was informed one day while at work that a customer had some eggs to sell to the Company. Sager's friend Mecham was with him at the time. Sager told Mecham that he would be unable to pick up the eggs, complete the other work he had to do, and still go "to a show" with Mecham, as previously planned. Mecham then volunteered to get the eggs. Sager agreed and let Mecham use his truck. Mecham negligently injured the plaintiff while en route to the farm. Thereafter he picked up the eggs and brought them back to the Company. The eggs were used and paid for by the Company.

Frame an argument for the plaintiff in her suit against the Company. Then change hats and defend the Company against the claim. What material distinctions are there, if any, between this case and the *Dempsey* case? Finally, decide the case.

2. John Kreggenwinkel died, leaving no estate other than certain insurance policies, of which his father was the beneficiary. The father was in a convalescent home. Deceased's mother, who was divorced from the father, went to the funeral home of Hirzel, arranged for the burial and charged the account to the father. At the time she had in her possession the policies of insurance naming the father as beneficiary. She left "stating in substance that she would talk to the father at the convalescent home; that she was on friendly terms with him." Hirzel then sent a bill to the father, who signed a document saying he authorized payment of the bill out of the proceeds of the insurance policies. (Whether he signed the document before or after the funeral is not clear from the opinion. Does it make any difference?) The document, which was introduced into evidence in court, never came into Hirzel's possession and the bill was not paid. The father died, and his estate is being sued for the bill. What result? *See* Hirzel Funeral Homes, Inc. v. Equitable Trust Co., 46 Del. 334, 83 A.2d 700 (1951), *commented on in* 56 Dick. L. Rev. 263 (1952) *and* 21 Chi. L. Rev. 248 (1954). The latter comment was authored by Warren Seavey.

3. Miss Blanche Watson was in severe financial straits. The Farmers' Supply Company was about to attach some of her property for a feed bill, so she wired Holman, her agent, to sell a filly,

Easter by name, for $300. On October 16, Holman wired Miss Watson the following: "We are lucky. Sold Kadiak for two thousand dollars. Took up draft Farmers' Supply Company." Miss Watson received this telegram and said nothing. On December 26 of the same year she sued the purchaser of Kadiak for return of the horse. What result?

a. Would it affect your answer to know that Kadiak ran in six races between October 15 and December 26 and won four times?

b. Suppose Miss Watson had been away on a trip from October 15 to December 15 and could not be contacted. This fact was unknown to her agent. Would that affect the result? In answering this, look at it from the purchaser's perspective too.

4. Leibsohn, Sr., was authorized in writing by his son-in-law, Schurman, "to list it [a hotel Schurman owned in Leibsohn's town] for sale, if you want to." Leibsohn then contracted with one Estes, a real estate agent, on the following terms:

> I hereby grant you the sole and exclusive right to sell the property described on the reverse side hereof and I hereby relinquish my right to sell the said property. Should said property be sold or exchanged . . . by you, or by myself, or by any other person, . . . I agree to pay you the commission. This contract shall terminate on 25 September 1950.

On September 18, 1950, Leibsohn's son, Sidney, acting without knowledge of his father's agreement and without authority from Schurman negotiated a sale of the hotel to an out-of-state investor. Sidney thereafter called Schurman's attention to the purported sale and on September 28 Schurman ratified the sale by Sidney. The deed was executed on October 28.

Upon discovering this, Estes sued Leibsohn, Sr., who knew nothing about the sale by Sidney, for his commission. What argument can be made on behalf of Estes? What defense, if any, is available to Leibsohn, Sr.?

Would your analysis change if Leibsohn, Sr., had been the owner of the property and had himself ratified the sale on September 28, not having heard of the sale by Sidney before that day? Assume all the other facts remained the same.

5. While employed by the Lion Coal Company at Wattis, Utah, Janko Taslich sustained injuries from which he died on April 13, 1923. The Utah compensation statute requires that, "Any claim for compensation must be filed with the commission within one year from the death of the deceased." On February 15, 1924, an application for compensation was filed on behalf of Tas-

lich's widow, who was living in Europe, by one Milka Skrinarich, her friend and country-woman. The application was filed voluntarily and without authority from Mrs. Taslich.

The Lion Coal Company soon thereafter discovered the lack of authority and objected to the power of the commission to grant an award. Thereafter a formally executed power of attorney was presented to the commission, signed by Mrs. Taslich and ratifying and confirming the previous act of Milka Skrinarich. The document was executed on May 29, 1924 and filed with the commission on August 16, 1924. Assume that the communication of the need for authorization, and the response thereto, was done as rapidly as the passage of mail would permit in those days before airmail delivery was possible.

You are the attorney for Mrs. Taslich. What arguments would you make on her behalf, and what do you anticipate would be the defense of the coal company? How would you assess the chances of her succeeding on her claim? Would it make any difference to your case if the power of attorney had been executed on May 29, 1926, and filed August 16, 1926? *See* Taslich v. Industrial Comm'n, 71 Utah 33, 262 P. 281 (1927).

6.   In July 1955, Hlobil was the owner of a 50 per cent interest in a certain patent which he claimed was being infringed by the Boeing Aircraft Corporation. By a letter dated July 20, 1955, he gave T. O. Toon complete authority to act as his agent to negotiate a settlement of his claim against Boeing. In order to provide funds for the expenses to be involved, Hlobil authorized Toon to sell up to seven per cent of his interest in the claim.

On July 26, 1955, Toon received from Maud Volandri $3000 in return for a contract assigning to her three per cent of Hlobil's interest in the claim and a promissory note promising to pay her $3000 one year from date. The note was signed by Toon, who also signed Hlobil's name to it. This was done without the knowledge or consent of Hlobil.

Miss Volandri sought payment of the note on July 26, 1956, the due date, from Toon. When this failed, she wrote to Hlobil, stating she held a promissory note by him and demanding payment. Hlobil, not understanding the transaction, and thinking this was part of Toon's sale of an interest in the claim, replied asking Miss Volandri to be patient while the final settlement was concluded. Six months later Miss Volandri wrote again, making the same demand and receiving the same reply. Two months later she learned from her attorney that Hlobil denied execution of the note. She promptly filed suit against him.

What legal claim would she have against Hlobil? As his attorney, frame a defense on his behalf. Do you think it will succeed?

7. On February 19, 1962, Audrey Navrides was injured on the premises of one Crancer who was insured by Zurich Insurance Company. She employed an attorney, Robert S. Forsyth, who filed an action for damages on her behalf. Forsyth negotiated a settlement of the claim with Zurich for $9000. Miss Navrides rejected the settlement but Forsyth represented to Zurich that she had approved it. Zurich then delivered to Forsyth for signature a release of all claims and a request for the dismissal of the pending action. It also delivered to Forsyth a check dated September 22, 1964 in the sum of $9000 payable to "Audrey R. Navrides and Robert S. Forsyth, her attorney." Forsyth retained the check and returned to Zurich the other documents with the forged signature of Miss Navrides. The request for dismissal was filed and the action dismissed.

On September 25, 1964, the check, bearing the forged endorsement of Miss Navrides and Forsyth's endorsement, was cashed by Forsyth. One year later Miss Navrides discovered the facts and comes to you as an attorney. What course of action would you recommend for her?

What her second attorney did was to sue Zurich, alleging that Zurich had for a valuable consideration drawn, executed and delivered a check to Miss Navrides, that the check was wrongfully paid on a forged endorsement, that Zurich "has not paid said check, or any part thereof, to plaintiff, and that by reason of said fact there has been a failure of consideration" and that defendant owed plaintiff the sum of $9000. What arguments would be made in Zurich's defense? What arguments would plaintiff's attorney make? How should the case be decided? Do you think the effective date of the adoption of the UCC in California might possibly affect the outcome? *See* Navrides v. Zurich Ins. Co., 97 Cal. Rptr. 309, 488 P.2d 637 (1971).

8. The charter of the City of San Francisco states that the city can sell city property only at public auction after appropriate notice in the public journals. Some city property is sold informally by an employee acting on the city's behalf to a private person at a price which was very advantageous to the city. The matter comes up before the city council for approval. You are the city attorney. What would you advise? *See* Zottman v. San Francisco, 20 Cal. 96, 81 Am. Dec. 96 (1862).

9. Dockery is a salesman for the New Home Sewing Machine Company. His authority extends merely to soliciting orders for the Company, subject to acceptance and approval by the head office. He uses order blanks containing the following sentence immediately above the signature line:

It is understood that no conditions agreed to by any salesman or agent and not embodied herein will be binding on The New Home Sewing Machine Company, and it is understood and agreed that The New Home Sewing Machine Company shall not be in any way liable under any separate agreement made between the undersigned and its salesman.

Babbitt, on being solicited by Dockery, said he would buy a carload of machines only if the seller would furnish experienced salesmen to sell them and would guarantee their resale within a reasonable time. Dockery, to induce the purchase, agreed to these terms in a separate piece of writing. He sent in the signed order but not the separate agreement. The machines were sent to Babbitt and he was billed for the contract price of $9096.60. Later Babbitt called the Company's attention to the separate agreement, but they disclaimed the unauthorized terms. Babbitt refused to pay and is now being sued by the Company. What arguments would you make as the lawyer for the Company? As the lawyer for Babbitt? And what decision of this case would you make as judge? *See* Babbitt Bros. Trading Co. v. New Home Sewing Machine Co., 62 F.2d 530 (9th Cir. 1932).

Would it make any difference in your analysis if Babbitt actually had read the above limitation on Dockery's authority? If he had not done so? Is there any room in this case for an argument based on imputed knowledge? Can you think of any other remedy for Babbitt to pursue?

Chapter 11

THE FIDUCIARY OBLIGATION

You will recall from Chapter 1 that an agent is described as a "fiduciary" of his principal. That term is applied by the Restatement (§ 13) to one who "has a duty, created by his undertaking, to act primarily for the benefit of another in matters connected with his undertaking." Some of the responsibilities attached to this status are described as follows in W. SEAVEY, THE LAW OF AGENCY 236 (1964):

> He has a duty to account for money or property received on account of the principal. In his dealing with the principal, he has the duty of full disclosure [a common example of this is that the agent cannot represent the other party in the absence of full disclosure to his principal—*Ed.*]; in acting for the principal he must not prefer his own [or others] interests, he cannot compete with the principal nor, without disclosure of his interest, sell his own property to the principal. In carrying out the directions of the principal, he has the duty to use normal care. . . .

A. THE DUTY OF LOYALTY

As mentioned above, the agent owes his principal a duty to transact the business with which he is entrusted with due care and to be loyal to his principal. Due care is fairly understandable, in the abstract at least. But what does "loyalty" mean? We can all agree that an agent has violated his duties to his principal, and is subject to reimburse him for losses, if, for example, he steals from his principal or if, pursuant to an offer of a bribe from a third party, he commits the principal to a transaction he doesn't want and the agent knows it. But suppose the agent negotiates a transaction his principal *does* want and, in addition, takes a little "gratuity" that the third party has offered him in order to hurry the deal through. The principal, satisfied with the transaction, pays the agent his commission and then discovers the facts.

Has the agent violated his fiduciary duty? What considerations are most influential in deciding the case? What incentive is there for the law to act, since the principal got what he wanted at no extra cost to him?

If you decide a violation did occur, what remedy would you grant the principal? Would you recommend that a mandatory injunction be issued, requiring the agent "to give it back" to the third party? What would *that* accomplish? Or would you require the agent to pay the "gratuity" over to the principal? Would you, in addition, require that the agent return his regular commission to the principal?

Finally, could the principal successfully sue the third party and collect the amount of the gratuity from him, even if he had already paid it to the agent? If so, could the third party then collect over against the agent? (Remember the *in pari delicto* rule from contracts.) *See* Tarnowski v. Resop, 236 Minn. 33, 51 N.W.2d 801 (1952) in which a principal recovered the agent's secret commission, even though he had rescinded the contract and recovered that with which he had parted; he also recovered attorney's fees, all expenses, and loss of time devoted to the operation, *and* Boston Deep Sea Fishing & Ice Co. v. Ansell, 39 Ch. D. 339 (1888), where the agent had to pay to his principal a one per cent commission he had received for placing a ship-building contract with the third party. The principal was also absolved from paying his agent's current salary. *See also* Donemar, Inc. v. Molloy, 252 N.Y. 360, 169 N.E. 610 (1930) where a third party was ordered to pay the $4555 "gratuity" over to the principal, even though he had already paid it to the agent.

The duty not to make secret profits from the relationship extends beyond clandestine arrangements with the party on the other side. *See,* for example, Diamond v. Oreamuno, 24 N.Y.2d 494, 301 N.Y.S.2d 78, 248 N.E.2d 910 (1969), a unanimous decision of the New York Court of Appeals holding under the facts alleged that a corporation can recover from its president and chairman of the board profits they made on the sale of shares of stock of the corporation which they had held for more than six months. The complaint alleged that these profits were made as a result of inside information known by the defendants by virtue of their positions with the corporation. The defendants had sold 56,500 shares prior to the release of information showing a sharp decline in net earnings of the corporation.

The defendants were required to account for their profits despite the absence of any loss to the corporation due to their actions. The opinion stated in part as follows:

It is well established, as a general proposition, that a person who acquires special knowledge or information by virtue of a confidential or fiduciary relationship with another, is not free to exploit that knowledge or information for his own personal benefit but must account to his principal for any profits derived therefrom. This, in turn, is merely a corollary of the broader principle, inherent in the nature of the fiduciary relationship, that prohibits a trustee or agent from exacting secret profits from his position of trust.

The opinion notes that the defendants can protect themselves from double liability by impleading all possible claimants, which in this case would be the purchasers of the stock they sold, assuming they can be identified.

___

B. COMPETITION WITH THE PRINCIPAL

As mentioned above, the fiduciary duty includes a duty not to compete with the principal. Again, it is easy to pose an obvious situation: the agent cannot, while acting for his principal, be outbidding him on the same transaction. But can an agent, after learning a particular skill, quit his principal's business and set up a competing business? Again, it depends on the facts, does it not? One situation might be where the principal runs an urban grocery store and his agent, having learned the grocery business, quits and sets up his own store two blocks away. Another might be where the principal runs a printing shop with one major client: printing the yellow pages of the telephone directory for the telephone company. His shop foreman quits and takes the customer away. Would you decide these two situations differently? If so, how would you rationalize the distinction?

___

TOWN & COUNTRY HOUSE & HOME SERVICE v. NEWBERY
New York Court of Appeals
3 N.Y.2d 554, 147 N.E.2d 724 (1958)

VAN VOORHIS, J. This action was brought for an injunction and damages against appellants on the theory of unfair competition. The complaint asks to restrain them from engaging in the same business as plaintiff, from soliciting its customers, and for an accounting and damages. The individual appellants were in plaintiff's employ for about three years before they severed their relationships and organized the corporate appellant through which they have been operating. The theory of the complaint is that plaintiff's enterprise "was unique, personal and confidential," and that appellants cannot engage in business at all without breach of the confidential relationship in which they learned its trade secrets, including the names and individual needs and tastes of its customers.

The nature of the enterprise is house and home cleaning by contract with individual householders. Its "unique" quality consists in superseding the drudgery of ordinary house cleaning by mass production methods. The house cleaning is performed by a crew of men who descend upon a home at stated intervals of time, and do the work in a hurry after the manner of an assembly line in a factory. They have been instructed by the housewife but work without her supervision. The householder is supplied with liability insurance, the secrets of the home are kept inviolate, the tastes of the customer are served and each team of workmen is selected as suited to the home to which it is sent. The complaint says that the customer relationship is "impregnated" with a "personal and confidential aspect."

The complaint was dismissed at Special Term on the ground that the individual appellants were not subjected to negative covenants under any contract with plaintiff, and that the methods and techniques used by plaintiff in conducting its business are not confidential or secret as in the case of a scientific formula; that house cleaning and housekeeping "are old and necessary chores which accompany orderly living" and that no violation of duty was involved in soliciting plaintiff's customers by appellants after resigning from plaintiff's employ. The contacts and acquaintances with customers were held not to have been the result of a confidential relationship between plaintiff and defendants or the result of the disclosure of secret or confidential material.

By a divided vote the Appellate Division reversed, but on a somewhat different ground, namely, that while in plaintiff's employ, appellants conspired to terminate their employment, form a business of their own in competition with plaintiff and solicit plaintiff's customers for their business. The overt acts under this conspiracy were found by the Appellate Division to have been that, in pursuance of this plan, they formed the corporate appellant and bought equipment and supplies for their operations— not on plaintiff's time—but during off hours, before they had severed their relations as employees of plaintiff. The Appellate Division concluded that "it is our opinion that their agreement and encouragement to each other to carry out the course of conduct thus planned by them, and their consummation of the plan, particularly their termination of employment virtually en masse, were inimical to, and violative of, the obligations owed by them to appellant as its employees; and that therefore appellant was entitled to relief. (Cf. Duane Jones Co. v. Burke, 306 N. Y. 172.)"

The *Duane Jones* case involved unusual facts. There the defendants appropriated overnight upwards of 50% of the business of their previous employer, and 90% of its skilled employees as well as a majority of the entire working force. There the findings were in favor of the plaintiff in the trial court, whereas in this case the findings of the trial court were in favor of defendants, and those of its findings which remain untouched by the Appellate Division stand in favor of defendants. The dominating purpose in the *Duane Jones* case was to damage and paralyze the plaintiff corporation to enable the defendants to seize it or force a sale to them on their own terms. There the employees were all executives, whereas in this simpler organization (although Newbery is called a key man) the formation and supervision of teams for house cleaning was not complicated and could be done by others. Moreover in *Duane Jones* there had been solicitation of the customers of plaintiff while the defendants were still employed; there was an attempt to panic and break the morale of the employees, again with the over-all purpose of paralyzing the plaintiff in order to seize it. Here, although these three employees and their wives left at the same time, there was no abrupt departure of most of the key men and nothing in reference to the interruption or paralysis of plaintiff's business. In fact, at the time of the trial, Mrs. Rossmoore testified that they had 280 customers and 8 crews, which were 40 more customers and 1 more crew than at the time when appellants departed.

Although the Appellate Division implied more relief than we consider to have been warranted, we think that the trial court erred in dismissing the complaint altogether. The only trade secret which could be involved in this business is plaintiff's list of customers. Concerning that, even where a solicitor of business does not operate fraudulently under the banner of his former employer, he still may not solicit the latter's customers who are not openly engaged in business in advertised locations or whose availability as patrons cannot readily be ascertained but "whose trade and patronage have been secured by years of business effort and advertising, and the expenditure of time and money, constituting a part of the good-will of a business which enterprise and foresight have built up" (Witkop & Holmes Co. v. Boyce, 61 Misc. 126, 131, affd. 131 App. Div. 922, followed in People's Coat, Apron & Towel Supply Co. v. Light, 171 App. Div. 671, 673, affd. 224 N. Y. 727). In the latter case it was pointed out by the Appellate Division that although there was no evidence that the former employee had a written customers list, "There was in his head what was equivalent. They were on routes, in streets and at numbers revealed to him through his service with plaintiff. Their faces were familiar to him, and their identity known because of such employment."

The testimony in the instant record shows that the customers of plaintiff were not and could not be obtained merely by looking up their names in the telephone or city directory or by going to any advertised locations, but had to be screened from among many other housewives who did not wish services such as respondent and appellants were equipped to render, but preferred to do their own housework. In most instances housewives do their own house cleaning. The only appeal which plaintiff could have was to those whose cleaning had been done by servants regularly or occasionally employed, except in the still rarer instances where the housewife was on the verge of abandoning doing her own work by hiring some outside agency. In the beginning, prospective customers of plaintiff were discovered by Dorothy Rossmoore, wife of plaintiff's president, by telephoning at random in "sections of Nassau that we thought would be interested in this type of cleaning, and from that we got directories, town directories, and we marked the streets that we had passed down, and I personally called, right down the list." In other words, after selecting a neighborhood which they felt was fertile for their kind of business, they would telephone to all of the residents of a street in the hope of discovering likely prospects. On the first day Mrs. Rossmoore called 52 homes. If she enlisted their interest, an appointment would be made for a personal call in order to sell them the service. At the end of the first year, only 40 to 50 customers had thus been secured. Two hundred to three hundred telephone calls netted 8 to 12 customers. Moreover, during the first year it was not possible to know how much to charge these customers with accuracy, inasmuch as the cleaning requirements of each differed from the others, so that special prices had to be set. In the beginning the customer usually suggested the price which was paid until some kind of cost accounting could demonstrate whether it should be raised or lowered. These costs were entered on cards for every customer, and this represented an accumulated body of experience of considerable value. After three years of operation, and by August, 1952, when the individual appellants resigned their employment by plaintiff, the number of customers amounted to about 240. By that time plaintiff had 7 or 8 crews doing this cleaning work, consisting of 3 men each.

Although appellants did not solicit plaintiff's customers until they were out of plaintiff's employ, nevertheless plaintiff's customers were the only ones they did solicit. Appellants solicited 20 or 25 of plaintiff's customers who refused to do business with appellants and about 13 more of plaintiff's customers who transferred their patronage to appellants. These were all the people that appellants' firm solicited. It would be different if these customers had been equally available to appellants and respondent, but, as has been related, these customers had been screened by respondent at considerable effort and expense, without which their receptivity and willingness to do business with this kind of a service organization could not be known. So there appears to be no question that plaintiff is entitled to enjoin defendants from further solicitation of its customers, or that some profits or damage should be paid to plaintiff by reason of these customers whom they enticed away.

For more than this appellants are not liable.

. . . .

Inasmuch as the complaint asks that appellants be enjoined, severally and jointly, from engaging directly or indirectly in the business of house and home cleaning in any manner, shape or form adopted by the plaintiff, it is necessary for us to point out that plaintiff is not entitled to that much relief. The business of plaintiff has not been found to be unique either by Special Term or the Appellate Division and the evidence demonstrates that it is not so. No trade secrets are involved, as has been stated, except the customers list. The theory on which the Appellate Division implied that such relief should be granted is that of *Duane Jones Co. v. Burke (supra)*. The alleged similarity to the *Duane Jones* case stems from the circumstance that appellant Percy Newbery was second in command of plaintiff's business under president Howard Rossmoore, that he had worked there for three years during which time he had been assigned important duties by Rossmoore; that in June, 1952 (about three years after plaintiff went into business), appellants Newbery, Colagrande, Bordini, and their wives conferred about starting a new competing business after Rossmoore had declined to increase their remuneration or to give them greater security in the business (it does not appear how much their wages were except that the two who were highest paid received about $1,700 during half a year); that while still on plaintiff's payroll but outside of business hours, they met upon a number of occasions to plan the organization of a company of their own, and purchased some equipment for that purpose (Bordini was to buy a truck, Newbery to get supplies and Colagrande to buy a vacuum cleaner, and someone was to get a waxing machine for their projected operations). The appellant corporation was organized August 19, 1952; Newbery quit on August 29, 1952, and the others, including their wives, at about the same time. They went to work on the night shift at Fairchild

Engineering Company at Farmingdale, Long Island, after leaving plaintiff, and started operating their small personal service corporation during the daytime. That forms an insufficient basis on which to invoke the relief that was granted in *Duane Jones Co. v. Burke* (306 N. Y. 172, *supra*).

It would have been courteous of appellants to have given Rossmoore advance notice that they were going to leave plaintiff's employ and engage in a competing business, but their employment was at will, which legally required no notice to be given, and rendered the employments terminable at any time at the option of either party. Plaintiff is entitled to enjoin appellants from soliciting its former customers, and to recover such damages or loss of profits as may be established to have resulted from those that have been solicited to date. Further than that the complaint is dismissed.

. . . .

Chief Judge CONWAY and Judges DESMOND, DYE, FULD, FROESSEL and BURKE concur.

NOTES

1. Suppose that three restaurants also were customers of the employer, having been solicited from approximately 15 businesses in the vicinity, and the business of these customers was also obtained by the defendants after quitting their employer. Would the court grant relief with respect to this part of the business?

2. The litigation on the issue involved in the principal case is substantial. See the 278 page annotation in 28 A.L.R.3d 7 (1969), dealing solely with the use of customer lists by former employees, and the annotation in 30 A.L.R.3d 631 (1970), dealing with the use or disclosure by former employees of special skills or techniques acquired in the earlier employment.

3. The *Newbery* opinion mentioned several times the term "trade secret." As you can imagine, defining what is or is not a trade secret, and the scope of protection to be granted to one, can be a complex task. And the problems of enforcing this aspect of the fiduciary relationship are compounded by the presence of conflicting interests: protecting the property interests of the employer and discouraging unethical conduct by employees versus encouraging competition and allowing a person to derive maximum benefit from his knowledge and skills.

A trade secret is defined in the RESTATEMENT OF TORTS § 757, as "any formula, pattern, device or compilation of information which is used in one business, and which gives him an opportunity to obtain an advantage over competitors who do not know or use it." The standards for determining what is a protected trade secret are not so strict as those for determining what is patentable. The distinction is drawn in the following quote from 2 CALLMAN, UNFAIR COMPETITION, TRADEMARKS AND MONOPOLIES § 52.1 (3d ed. 1968):

> As distinguished from a patent, a trade secret need not be essentially new, novel or unique; therefore, prior art is a less effective defense in a trade secret case than it is in a patent infringement case. The idea need not be complicated; it may be intrinsically simple and nevertheless qualify as a secret, unless it is in common knowledge and, therefore, within the public domain.

Consider, for example, the case of Donald Wohlgemuth, a graduate in chemistry, who worked for eight years for B. F. Goodrich Company in its pressure space suit department, rising to manager of the department. He then quit to work for International Latex Corporation, which competes with Goodrich in the pressure space equipment field and had five months earlier been awarded the space suit part of the NASA Apollo contract. Goodrich sued to enjoin Wohlgemuth from "performing any work for any corporation relating to the design, manufacture and/or sale of high-altitude pressure suits." What result? See Goodrich v. Wohlgemuth, 117 Ohio App. 493, 192 N.E.2d 99 (1963), resolving—without going into specifics—that trade secrets were known by Wohlgemuth, and granting an injunction. Ask yourself, in evaluating this result, what Wohlgemuth can do with the eight years of experience he accumulated, other than work for Goodrich. Also, would it make any difference to you if he had entered into a contract with Goodrich in 1954 "to keep confidential all information of which I have knowledge because of my employment with the Company"? (He had, but the court indicated it would have reached the same result even in the absence of contractual agreement.)

Does the law of trade secrets survive the federal pre-emption under the Patent Act reflected in the decisions of Sears, Roebuck & Co. v. Stiffel Co., 376 U.S. 225 (1964) and Compco Corp. v. Day-Brite Lighting, Inc., 376 U.S. 234 (1964), which struck down provisions of the Illinois law of unfair competition invoked to prevent competitors from copying unpatentable products of the plaintiffs, on the ground that the state could not grant an unlimited monopoly to something that did not qualify for the protection of the federal patent law? See the discussion of this question in Doerfer, *The Limits on Trade Secret Law Imposed by*

Federal Patent and Antitrust Supremacy, 80 Harv. L. Rev. 1432 (1967).

4. Another aspect of the above is the "shop rights" doctrine. This doctrine "shortly stated, is that where a servant, during his hours of employment, with his master's materials and appliances, conceives and perfects an invention for which he obtains a patent, he must accord his master a non-exclusive right to practice the invention." United States v. Dubilier Condenser Corp., 289 U. S. 178 (1933). This doctrine is based on general equitable principles and operates when the employer has made no contractual arrangements on this matter and where the employee is hired in a noninventive capacity. It is to be distinguished from the circumstances where an employee is employed specifically to invent, where the courts, in the absence of an express agreement, will imply an agreement of the employee to assign his invention to the employer.

For a case involving an aspect of the shop rights doctrine, *see* Kinkade v. New York Shipbuilding Corp., 21 N.J. 362, 122 A.2d 360, 61 A.L.R.2d 348 (1956). Kinkade was employed as a tinsmith by defendant, which was converting three passenger liners to troop ships under government contracts. Kinkade worked on a crew installing sleeping bunks, which was a complicated proceeding. One night at home he conceived of a simple idea of rearranging the hooks, which reduced by 75% the number of clips which were required. The next day he told the shop supervisor. It took only several minutes to make the device and it was promptly put to use. The result: Kinkade took a substantial cut in pay, since defendant's labor costs were reduced. He then asked defendant for compensation for the device. This was refused, so he sued for unjust enrichment and lost, the court citing to the shop rights doctrine (and indicating, as well, that the device need not be patentable for the doctrine to apply).

Suppose that Kinkade, after this series of disappointments, decides to quit and work for a competitor. Could the defendant complete the circle by enjoining him under the trade secret doctrine?

5. Another aspect of the *Newbery* case involved the absence of any covenant not to compete. Such covenants are quite common and aid the employer's case a great deal. Their enforceability depends on the breadth of their terms and on the attitude of the jurisdiction toward them. *See,* for example, Lynch v. Bailey, 275 App. Div. 527, 90 N.Y.S.2d 359 (1949), *aff'd,* 300 N.Y. 615, 90 N.E.2d 484 (1949), where the court held invalid a covenant in the partnership agreement of a large accounting firm which pro-

vided that if a partner withdrew voluntarily from the firm he could not for four years thereafter, either individually or as a member or employee of another firm, practice accountancy within 100 miles of any city in which the partnership was located at the time of withdrawal. The firm had offices in ten major cities. The court observed that this covenant did not relate to the sale of a business and did not involve protecting the firm from the disclosure of trade secrets, and thus, in view of its restriction on the partner's means of procuring a livelihood, it should be subjected to a strict test of reasonableness. The court found the covenant "unreasonably broad in its scope, resulting in undue hardship to plaintiff wholly disproportionate to any proper need for defendants' protection." For a liberal construction of such covenants, see Zeff, Farrington & Associates, Inc. v. Farrington, 168 Colo. 18, 449 P.2d 813 (1969), enforcing by injunction an employment contract stating that defendant ex-employee, a soil engineer, will not engage in soil engineering for three years after terminating his employment with plaintiff (a Denver firm) within a 200 mile radius of Denver, Colorado. Defendant had worked for plaintiff for seven months.

C. PRE-EMPTING OPPORTUNITIES INCIDENT TO THE RELATIONSHIP

MEINHARD v. SALMON
New York Court of Appeals
249 N.Y. 458, 164 N.E. 545, 62 A.L.R. 1 (1928)
Noted in 29 Colum. L. Rev. 367; 42 Harv. L. Rev. 953; 13 Minn. L. Rev. 711; 38 Yale L.J. 782 (all in 1929)

CARDOZO, Ch. J. On April 10, 1902, Louisa M. Gerry leased to the defendant Walter J. Salmon the premises known as the Hotel Bristol at the northwest corner of Forty-second street and Fifth avenue in the city of New York. The lease was for a term of twenty years, commencing May 1, 1902, and ending April 30, 1922. The lessee undertook to change the hotel building for use as shops and offices at a cost of $200,000. Alterations and additions were to be accretions to the land.

Salmon, while in course of treaty with the lessor as to the execution of the lease, was in course of treaty with Meinhard, the plaintiff, for the necessary funds. The result was a joint venture with terms embodied in a writing. Meinhard was to pay to Salmon half of the moneys requisite to reconstruct, alter, manage and operate the property. Salmon was to pay to Meinhard 40 per cent of the net profits for the first five years of the lease and

50 per cent for the years thereafter. If there were losses, each party was to bear them equally. Salmon, however, was to have sole power to "manage, lease, underlet and operate" the building. There were to be certain pre-emptive rights for each in the contingency of death.

The two were coadventurers, subject to fiduciary duties akin to those of partners (King v. Barnes, 109 N. Y. 267). As to this we are all agreed. The heavier weight of duty rested, however, upon Salmon. He was a coadventurer with Meinhard, but he was manager as well. During the early years of the enterprise, the building, reconstructed, was operated at a loss. If the relation had then ended, Meinhard as well as Salmon would have carried a heavy burden. Later the profits became large with the result that for each of the investors there came a rich return. For each, the venture had its phases of fair weather and of foul. The two were in it jointly, for better or for worse.

When the lease was near its end, Elbridge T. Gerry had become the owner of the reversion. He owned much other property in the neighborhood, one lot adjoining the Bristol Building on Fifth avenue and four lots on Forty-second street. He had a plan to lease the entire tract for a long term to some one who would destroy the buildings then existing, and put up another in their place. In the latter part of 1921, he submitted such a project to several capitalists and dealers. He was unable to carry it through with any of them. Then, in January, 1922, with less than four months of the lease to run, he approached the defendant Salmon. The result was a new lease to the Midpoint Realty Company, which is owned and controlled by Salmon, a lease covering the whole tract, and involving a huge outlay. The term is to be twenty years, but successive covenants for renewal will extend it to a maximum of eighty years at the will of either party. The existing buildings may remain unchanged for seven years. They are then to be torn down, and a new building to cost $3,000,000 is to be placed upon the site. The rental, which under the Bristol lease was only $55,000, is to be from $350,000 to $475,000 for the properties so combined. Salmon personally guaranteed the performance by the lessee of the covenants of the new lease until such time as the new building had been completed and fully paid for.

The lease between Gerry and the Midpoint Realty Company was signed and delivered on January 25, 1922. Salmon had not told Meinhard anything about it. Whatever his motive may have been, he had kept the negotiations to himself. Meinhard was not informed even of the bare existence of a project. The first that he knew of it was in February when the lease was an accomplished fact. He then made demand on the defendants that the lease be held in trust as an asset of the venture, making offer upon the trial to share the personal obligations incidental to the guaranty. The demand was followed by refusal, and later by this suit. A referee gave judgment for the plaintiff, limiting the plaintiff's interest in the lease, however, to 25 per cent. The limitation was on the theory that the plaintiff's equity was to be restricted to one-half of so much of the value of the lease as was contributed or represented by the occupation of the Bristol site. Upon cross-appeals to the Appellate Division, the judgment was modified so as to enlarge the equitable interest to one-half of the whole lease. With this enlargement of plaintiff's interest, there went, of course, a corresponding enlargement of his attendant obligations. The case is now here on an appeal by the defendants.

Joint adventurers, like copartners, owe to one another, while the enterprise continues, the duty of the finest loyalty. Many forms of conduct permissible in a workaday world for those acting at arm's length, are forbidden to those bound by fiduciary ties. A trustee is held to something stricter than the morals of the market place. Not honesty alone, but the punctilio of an honor the most sensitive, is then the standard of behavior. As to this there has developed a tradition that is unbending and inveterate. Uncompromising rigidity has been the attitude of courts of equity when petitioned to undermine the rule of undivided loyalty by the "disintegrating erosion" of particular exceptions (Wendt v. Fischer, 243 N. Y. 439, 444). Only thus has the level of conduct for fiduciaries been kept at a level higher than that trodden by the crowd. It will not consciously be lowered by any judgment of this court.

The owner of the reversion, Mr. Gerry, had vainly striven to find a tenant who would favor his ambitious scheme of demolition and construction. Baffled in the search, he turned to the defendant Salmon in possession of the Bristol, the keystone of the project. He figured to himself beyond a doubt that the man in possession would prove a likely customer. To the eye of an observer, Salmon held the lease as owner in his own right, for himself and no one else. In fact he held it as a fiduciary, for himself and another, sharers in a common venture. If this fact had been proclaimed, if the lease by its terms had run in favor of a partnership, Mr. Gerry, we may fairly assume, would have laid before the partners, and not merely before one of them, his plan of reconstruction. The pre-emptive privilege, or, better, the preemptive opportunity, that was thus an incident of the enterprise, Salmon appropriated to himself in secrecy and silence. He might have warned Meinhard that the plan had been submitted, and that either would be free to compete for the award. If he had done this, we do not need to say whether he would have been under a duty, if successful in the competition, to hold the lease so acquired for the benefit of a venture then about to end, and thus prolong by indirection its responsibilities and duties. The trouble about his conduct is that he excluded his coadventurer from any chance to compete, from any chance to enjoy the opportunity for benefit that had come to him alone by virtue of his agency. This chance, if nothing more, he was under a duty to concede. The price of its denial is an extension of the trust at the option and for the benefit of the one whom he excluded.

No answer is it to say that the chance would have been of little value even if seasonably offered. Such a calculus of probabilities is beyond the science of the chancery. . . . The very fact that Salmon was in control with exclusive powers of direction charged him the more obviously with the duty of disclosure, since only through disclosure could opportunity be equalized. If he might cut off renewal by a purchase for his own benefit when four months were to pass before the lease would have an end, he might do so with equal right while there remained as many years (cf. Mitchell v. Reed, 61 N. Y. 123, 127). He might steal a march on his comrade under cover of the darkness, and then hold the captured ground. Loyalty and comradeship are not so easily abjured.

Little profit will come from a dissection of the precedents. None precisely similar is cited in the briefs of counsel. What is similar in many, or so it seems to us, is the animating principle. Authority is, of course, abundant that one partner may not appropriate to his own use a renewal of a lease, though its term is to begin at the expiration of the partnership (Mitchell v. Reed, 61 N. Y. 123; 84 N. Y. 556). The lease at hand with its many changes is not strictly a renewal. Even so, the standard of loyalty for those in trust relations is without the fixed divisions of a graduated scale. There is indeed a dictum in one of our decisions that a partner, though he may not renew a lease, may purchase the reversion if he acts openly and fairly (Anderson v. Lemon, 8 N. Y. 236; cf. White & Tudor, Leading Cases in Equity [9th ed.], vol. 2, p. 642; Bevan v. Webb, 1905, 1 Ch. 620; Griffith v. Owen, 1907, 1 Ch. 195, 204, 205). It is a dictum, and no more, for on the ground that he had acted slyly he was charged as a trustee. The holding is thus in favor of the conclusion that a purchase as well as a lease will succumb to the infection of secrecy and silence. . . . To say that a partner is free without restriction to buy in the reversion of the property where the busi-

ness is conducted is to say in effect that he may strip the good
will of its chief element of value, since good will is largely dependent upon continuity of possession (Matter of Brown, 242
N. Y. 1, 7). . . .

We have no thought to hold that Salmon was guilty of a conscious purpose to defraud. Very likely he assumed in all good
faith that with the approaching end of the venture he might
ignore his coadventurer and take the extension for himself. He
had given to the enterprise time and labor as well as money. He
had made it a success. Meinhard, who had given money, but
neither time nor labor, had already been richly paid. There
might seem to be something grasping in his insistence upon more.
Such recriminations are not unusual when coadventurers fall out.
They are not without their force if conduct is to be judged by the
common standards of competitors. That is not to say that they
have pertinency here. Salmon had put himself in a position in
which thought of self was to be renounced, however hard the
abnegation. He was much more than a coadventurer. He was a
managing coadventurer. For him and for those like him, the
rule of undivided loyalty is relentless and supreme. A different
question would be here if there were lacking any nexus of relation between the business conducted by the manager and the opportunity brought to him as an incident of management. For
this problem, as for most, there are distinctions of degree. If
Salmon had received from Gerry a proposition to lease a building at a location far removed, he might have held for himself the
privilege thus acquired, or so we shall assume. Here the subject-
matter of the new lease was an extension and enlargement of
the subject-matter of the old one. A managing coadventurer ap-
propriating the benefit of such a lease without warning to his
partner might fairly expect to be reproached with conduct that
was underhand, or lacking, to say the least, in reasonable candor,
if the partner were to surprise him in the act of signing the new
instrument. Conduct subject to that reproach does not receive
from equity a healing benediction.

A question remains as to the form and extent of the equitable
interest to be allotted to the plaintiff. The trust as declared has
been held to attach to the lease which was in the name of the
defendant corporation. We think it ought to attach at the option
of the defendant Salmon to the shares of stock which were owned
by him or were under his control. The difference may be important if the lessee shall wish to execute an assignment of the
lease, as it ought to be free to do with the consent of the lessor.
On the other hand, an equal division of the shares might lead
to other hardships. It might take away from Salmon the power

of control and management which under the plan of the joint venture he was to have from first to last. The number of shares to be allotted to the plaintiff should, therefore, be reduced to such an extent as may be necessary to preserve to the defendant Salmon the expected measure of dominion. To that end an extra share should be added to his half.

. . . .

ANDREWS, J. (dissenting). . . . I am of the opinion that the issue here is simple. Was the transaction in view of all the circumstances surrounding it unfair and inequitable? I reach this conclusion for two reasons. There was no general partnership, merely a joint venture for a limited object, to end at a fixed time. The new lease, covering additional property, containing many new and unusual terms and conditions, with a possible duration of eighty years, was more nearly the purchase of the reversion than the ordinary renewal with which the authorities are concerned.

. . . .

Were this a general partnership between Mr. Salmon and Mr. Meinhard I should have little doubt as to the correctness of this result assuming the new lease to be an offshoot of the old. Such a situation involves questions of trust and confidence to a high degree; it involves questions of good will; many other considerations. As has been said, rarely if ever may one partner without the knowledge of the other acquire for himself the renewal of a lease held by the firm, even if the new lease is to begin after the firm is dissolved. Warning of such an intent, if he is managing partner, may not be sufficient to prevent the application of this rule.

We have here a different situation governed by less drastic principles. . . .

It seems to me that the venture so inaugurated had in view a limited object and was to end at a limited time. There was no intent to expand it into a far greater undertaking lasting for many years. The design was to exploit a particular lease. Doubtless in it Mr. Meinhard had an equitable interest, but in it alone. This interest terminated when the joint adventure terminated. There was no intent that for the benefit of both any advantage should be taken of the chance of renewal—that the adventure should be continued beyond that date. Mr. Salmon has done all he promised to do in return for Mr. Meinhard's undertaking when he distributed profits up to May 1, 1922. Suppose this lease, non-assignable without the consent of the lessor, had contained a renewal option. Could Mr. Meinhard have exercised it? Could he have insisted that Mr. Salmon do so? Had Mr. Salmon done so could he insist that the agreement to share losses still existed or could Mr. Meinhard have claimed that the joint adventure was still to continue for twenty or eighty years? I do not think so. The adventure by its express terms ended on May 1, 1922. The contract by its language and by its whole import excluded the idea that the tenant's expectancy was to subsist for the benefit of the plaintiff. On that date whatever there was left of value in the lease reverted to Mr. Salmon, as it would had the lease been for thirty years instead of twenty. Any equity which Mr. Meinhard possessed was in the particular lease itself, not in any possibility of renewal. There was nothing unfair in Mr. Salmon's conduct.

I might go further were it necessary. Under the circumstances here presented had the lease run to both the parties I doubt whether the taking by one of a renewal without the knowledge of the other would cause interference by a court of equity. An illustration may clarify my thought. A and B enter into a joint venture to resurface a highway between Albany and Schenectady. They rent a parcel of land for the storage of materials. A, unknown to B, agrees with the lessor to rent that parcel and one adjoining it after the venture is finished, for an iron foundry. Is the act unfair? Would any general statements, scattered here and there through opinions dealing with other circumstance, be thought applicable? In other words, the mere fact that the joint venturers rent property together does not call for the strict rule that applies to general partners. Many things may excuse what is there forbidden. Nor here does any possibility of renewal exist as part of the venture. The nature of the undertaking excludes such an idea.

So far I have treated the new lease as if it were a renewal of the old. As already indicated, I do not take that view. Such a renewal could not be obtained. Any expectancy that it might be had vanished. What Mr. Salmon obtained was not a graft springing from the Bristol lease, but something distinct and different— as distinct as if for a building across Fifth avenue. I think also that in the absence of some fraudulent or unfair act the secret purchase of the reversion even by one partner is rightful. Substantially this is such a purchase. Because of the mere label of a transaction we do not place it on one side of the line or the other. Here is involved the possession of a large and most valuable unit of property for eighty years, the destruction of all existing structures and the erection of a new and expensive building covering the whole. No fraud, no deceit, no calculated secrecy is found.

Simply that the arrangement was made without the knowledge of Mr. Meinhard. I think this not enough. . . .

POUND, CRANE and LEHMAN, JJ., concur with CARDOZO, Ch. J., for modification of the judgment appealed from and affirmance as modified; ANDREWS, J., dissents in opinion in which KELLOGG and O'BRIEN, JJ., concur.

NOTES

1. Suppose that in 1917 Meinhard had assigned all his "right, title and interest in and to" the agreement. Would this affect the decision reached above? Would it if the assignee was Meinhard's wife, and it was done for income tax reasons?

2. Suppose that the other "capitalists and dealers" had accepted Gerry's plan and Gerry, nevertheless impressed by Salmon's management abilities, had offered him a rental arrangement on a building Gerry owned directly across the street. Could Meinhard make a successful argument that he is entitled to a share of this arrangement? Why or why not?

PROBLEMS

1. The real estate branch of Harrods Limited, a large company which deals with real estate, building construction, and so forth, was employed by Mrs. Kent Lemon as real estate agents to find a purchaser for her property known as "Blythswood," located at Ascot. On July 3, Harrods arranged for the sale of the property to one Mrs. Campbell, "subject to contract and a surveyor's report" (the latter meaning a building inspection). On July 8, Mrs. Campbell, who had had previous business dealings with the building department of Harrods (which was situated in a separate building from that of the real estate department) called upon the manager of the building department, told him she had contracted for a house at Ascot, and asked him to inspect it. He did so and suggested that the drains be put in repair, which was a fairly expensive proposition. On July 16, the solicitor for Mrs. Campbell wrote the solicitor for Mrs. Lemon calling this defect to their attention and specifying either that it be repaired before the sale or that the cost of repair be deducted from the purchase price. Soon thereafter the relationship between the two branches was discovered, and the solicitors for Mrs. Lemon complained of this. Harrods replied, offering to advise Mrs. Campbell to have an independent firm test the drains. Noth-

ing further was done by Mrs. Lemon and the contract was signed on July 31, with a discount for the cost of repairing the drains. Mrs. Lemon thereafter refused to pay the real estate department their commission. Harrods sued for the commission. What result? See Harrods Limited v. Lemon, [1931] 2 K.B. 157, noted in 4 CAMB. L. J. 373 (1932) and 44 HARV. L. REV. 1294 (1931).

Would it change your analysis if the sale had been completed, with a discount from the purchase price, and then for the first time Mrs. Lemon and Harrods discovered the involvement of both departments? If so, why?

Suppose the discovery of the involvement of both departments had resulted in the entire transaction being called off. How would you assess the rights between the parties?

2. After foreclosure proceedings against the mortgagor of the Half Moon Hotel in Coney Island, a trustee was appointed for the benefit of the holders of the first mortgage certificates. The attorneys for the trustee bought some of the certificates for themselves. They bought in their own name from brokers and dealers only, and not directly from certificate holders; they alleged that they did not act upon any inside or secret information, and they consistently advised the certificate holders to keep their certificates rather than sell them. The average cost per certificate to the attorneys was less than 16 cents on the dollar. Distributions on the certificates amounted to nearly 56 cents on the dollar up to the time that the attorneys, who made a $22,000 profit on the certificates, requested in the final accounting a legal fee of $25,000, having previously received a legal fee of $10,000. The fee was objected to by the present certificate holders. On what grounds, do you think? Do you think the holders were successful? Why? What remedy (assuming they were successful) do you think the holders would get?

Would it change your analysis of the above facts if the attorneys had taken steps to ensure full disclosure of their purchases to all parties, including existing certificate holders and, assuming the market was small enough to make it possible, all purchasers and sellers of certificates?

3. Paul Chalupiak purchased a tract of land assessed as "land of James Moore Heirs" at a tax sale. He employed an engineer to make a survey and a lawyer to have the title examined. Both mistakenly reported to him that the tract included 30 acres that it did not actually include. Chalupiak thereafter went to Stahlman, who was employed in a mill in the area and was also the tax collector and a justice of the peace, and asked him to prepare a deed for part of the tract which he was subdividing. Stahlman

asked Chalupiak, "Are you sure that you own this ground?" (referring to the area Chalupiak was intending to deed, which was in the mistakenly included 30 acres). Stahlman showed Chalupiak on the borough map that the descriptions didn't match and informed him that the land to which title was in question was being advertised for sale by the County Commissioners. Chalupiak then took his request for a deed to a lawyer, who drew it. Stahlman later did draw four deeds for Chalupiak which conveyed land in the disputed area. He received $18 total consideration for doing this. Approximately one year later Stahlman bought the land in question at the county sale, acting as agent for his sister. Chalupiak sued in equity to compel conveyance of the land purchased by Stahlman to him. What result? *See* Chalupiak v. Stahlman, 368 Pa. 83, 81 A.2d 577 (1951) (*commented on in* 100 U. PENN. L. REV. 448 (1951), 13 U. PITT. L. REV. 162 (1951), *and* 56 DICK. L. REV. 357 (1952)).

Would it affect your analysis if Stahlman had not drawn the four deeds for Chalupiak? If so, how and why?

4. John Smith became employed by a medium size law firm as an associate attorney seven years ago. During that time he came to work almost exclusively with the Acme Corporation, a substantial client of the firm. The work nominally was done under the supervision of one of the senior partners of the firm, who signed the opinion letters, attended the closings, and so forth, but actually was done by Smith, and the officers of Acme knew this.

About three months ago Smith inquired subtlely about partnership status for himself, and was curtly informed that, "We don't respond to associates' requests about such matters." Offended, Smith decided to quit. Before quitting, he telephoned several of the key officers of Acme with whom he had worked extensively, told them he was leaving to enter his own practice, and said, "I would be delighted, of course, to continue handling your work." The officers decided to keep their business with him and accordingly withdrew their account from the firm.

One of the partners of the firm has come to you for advice as to what, if anything, they can do about this. What is your advice?

a. What difference would it make if Smith had first left the firm and then made his telephone call to the Acme officers? Should it make a difference?

b. Suppose Smith had quit first, set up his own office, and then sent Acme a copy of the card he had printed which announced the opening of his office. Thereafter Acme transfers its legal business to Smith. Would this variation affect your legal analysis of the above facts? If so, how? And why?

c.   Finally, suppose Smith quits and sets up his office, making no effort to contact Acme, and Acme transfers its business to him anyway. What advice would you give the partner as to his rights against Smith?

d.   Would it affect your analysis of the above facts and variations if Smith had brought the client into the firm in the first place? Would it if, instead of only one person, the above facts involved three young associates who quit together and established their own practice, the other facts and variations remaining the same?

5.   The Capitol Fixture and Supply Company acquired a lease in a building at 1430 Larimer Street, Denver, Colorado on July 7, 1944, which by its terms expired September 30, 1947. The Company was a partnership consisting of three members (Lerner, Schwartz and Stone) each of which had an undivided one-third interest in the Company. At the time the lease was executed there were some negotiations for the purchase of the building. Lerner and Stone were in favor of purchasing but nothing further was done because Schwartz objected to it.

On August 11, 1945, Lerner sold his interest to the other two partners. In May, 1946, Stone bought Schwartz's half interest and continued the business first as sole proprietor and then under corporate form.

In June 1946 Lerner's wife and sister-in-law purchased the building at 1430 Larimer Street. They later transferred the property to Lerner and his brother. On July 27, 1947, the Lerners served notice upon Stone to vacate after the termination of the lease on September 30, 1947. Stone refused to do so and the Lerners brought a forcible entry and detainer action (a statutory procedure where the holder of legal title asserts his right to possession of real estate).

Describe the defense which Stone would assert to this suit. Do you think it will succeed? What problems are there in granting relief to Stone, assuming he is entitled to relief? *See* Stone v. Lerner, 118 Colo. 455, 195 P.2d 964 (1948), *noted in* 47 MICH. L. REV. 591 (1949) *and* 21 ROCKY MT. L. REV. 346 (1949).

6.   F. W. Enwright was a part-time reporter for the Lynn Publishing Company, which published a daily newspaper. The Company leased the basement and first floor of a building in the town of Lynn. It had substantial amounts of heavy equipment in the basement, including a press embedded in concrete which would take two weeks to move at a considerable expense.

Enwright was given an assignment to write a story on the rental market in Lynn. In the process of researching the story, he talked to an officer of the International Trust Company, the lessor of the building, and learned that the newspaper's lease was about to expire. The newspaper was in economic trouble, and was behind on its rent. Enwright persuaded the lessor to grant a new lease to him. Upon obtaining the lease, he gave the publishers notice to quit.

The publishers do not intend to leave. They have come to you for advice. What arguments would you make in their behalf? Would you advise your clients that you have a good chance of succeeding? *See* Essex Trust v. Enwright, 214 Mass. 507, 102 N.E. 441 (1913).

a.   Would it change your analysis if Enwright had learned of the imminent expiration of the lease by seeing a sign on the main entrance to the building saying "For Lease" while going to work one day? If he had seen a sign saying "Premises for Lease" (and specifying the building in question) in a window of the International Trust Company while taking a Sunday stroll? If so, why?

b.   Would it affect your analysis if Enwright had been a trustee for the newspaper rather than a part-time reporter? If he had been the janitor for the paper and had discovered the facts (i) by overhearing a conversation between an officer of the lessor and the office manager of the newspaper, or (ii) by seeing the sign on the main entrance door?

PART IV

THE PARTNERSHIP FORM OF DOING BUSINESS

Chapter 12

THE PARTNERSHIP RELATION

A. INTRODUCTION

A general partnership is easy to form and operate. By definition it consists of an association of two or more persons to carry on as co-owners a business for profit (UPA § 6). A partnership can be created by oral agreement alone and can be run with considerable informality. As we shall see later in this chapter, persons can create a partnership relationship between themselves without even realizing they are doing so, sometimes with unfortunate consequences. (With respect to corporations, the other widely adopted vehicle for doing business when there is more than one owner involved, statutory law in all states requires that formal documents be filed with a designated officer of the state, and other procedures, including the payment of fees, be complied with before a corporation can even come into existence; and thereafter most states require that meetings of shareholders must be held annually, that books, records, and minutes must be kept, annual reports filed with the secretary of state of the state of incorporation, and so forth.) Despite the informality which is possible in the partnership form of doing business, however, thoughtful and imaginative legal advice is helpful to even the simplest partnership, as the following materials presumably will demonstrate.

A preliminary question one might ask is whether the partnership form of doing business is used very much anymore. One may have the impression that only a few service enterprises—such as lawyers and doctors—use this form, and that many of them are incorporating as fast as possible in order to take advantage of the favorable income tax treatment of retirement plans accorded to the corporate form of doing business (*see* Section B, *infra*). This impression is dispelled by reference to the U.S. Bureau of the Census, Statistical Abstract of the United States 469-471 [Charts 744-749] (1972). The most recent figures available are as of 1969. In that year there were 921,000 active partnerships in this country (the statistics show a net increase of three thousand active partnerships between 1968 and 1969), with total receipts of 84 billion dollars and net profits of over 10 billion dollars. This included substantial numbers of partnerships in every category of industry included by the *Abstract,* with the bulk of them in retail trade, finance, insurance, real estate and services. And the total number of partnerships increased to that level from 271,000 in 1939 and 627,000 in 1945, although it has remained fairly constant since 1960.

The above statistics do not distinguish between general partnerships and limited partnerships (see discussion below). And the corporate form of doing business has continued to grow in absolute numbers in the 1960's, increasing from over 1,100,000 in 1960 to over 1,600,000 in 1969. The statistics on partnerships nevertheless make it clear that you need not fear that you are studying a vanishing form of doing business. The tax law summary in Section B, *infra,* which briefly summarizes nonretirement tax advantages, plus the informality involved in the creation and operation of a partnership, may serve in part to explain the continuing vitality of this form of doing business when multiple ownership is involved.

---

i. *The Uniform Partnership Act—Background Information*

The matrix of partnership law in 43 states plus the District of Columbia is the Uniform Partnership Act (UPA), which is set forth in full in Appendix A. The UPA serves a dual function. It establishes certain basic principles of law which operate regardless of any agreement between the partners, such as Sections 11-15 (defining when a partnership is bound by admissions of or notice to a partner, the nature of a partner's liability, and so forth). And similar to, for example, the statutes of intestacy, it defines certain principles which function only in the absence of agreement between the partners, such as Section 18 (rules determining rights and duties of partners in relation to the partnership).

It is a useful and necessary exercise at this stage to read the UPA completely through several times. You benefit by observing the full scope of the statute and how the various sections complement each other.

The literature on the drafting and scope of the UPA is substantial. In addition to a number of articles by people involved in the drafting of the Act,* which was promulgated by the Commissioners on Uniform State Laws in 1914, there exists an ex-

---

* See Lewis, *The Uniform Partnership Act,* 24 Yale L. J. 617 (1915); Williston, *The Uniform Partnership Act, with Some Remarks on Other Uniform Commercial Laws,* 63 U. Pa. L. Rev. 196 (1915): Lewis, *The Desirability of Expressing the Law of Partnership in Statutory Form,* 60 U. Pa. L. Rev. 93 (1911).

change between William Draper Lewis, who completed drafting
the Act after the death of Dean James Barr Ames, the initial
draftsman, and Judson Crane, a professor at George Washington
Law School at the time who later wrote a hornbook on partnership law. *See* Crane, *The Uniform Partnership Act—A Criticism,*
28 HARV. L. REV. 762 (1915); Lewis, *The Uniform Partnership
Act—A Reply to Mr. Crane's Criticism,* 29 HARV. L. REV. 158, 291
(1915); and Crane, *The Uniform Partnership Act and Legal Persons,* 29 HARV. L. REV. 838 (1916).

The essence of Crane's criticism was that the Act did not fully
adopt the theory, widely accepted by the civil law, that the partnership was itself a distinct legal entity. Instead, the Act was
drawn largely on the "aggregate" theory, with some modifications
of traditional doctrine which will be covered in the materials to
follow. The aggregate theory is that a partnership is merely an
aggregate of persons—which can include individuals, corporations, other partnerships—acting with a common purpose, sharing profits and losses, and holding partnership assets in some
form of joint ownership.

Crane argued that there existed many decisions at common
law and some statutes which were impossible to reconcile with
the aggregate theory and which had to be rationalized on the
theory that a partnership was itself a legal "person." The authorities were not unanimous, however, and Crane wanted the UPA,
by adopting the legal entity theory, to resolve the doubts completely. As examples supporting his thesis, Crane cited the
following:

(1) Legislation treating the partnership as a separate entity.
One example given by Crane was legislation permitting the partnership to sue or be sued in the firm name. The common law
rule (which retains vitality even today in some states), reflecting
the aggregate theory, is that suit cannot be brought by or against
a partnership in the firm name; only the individual partners can
sue or be sued. This raises procedural problems of considerable
magnitude. *See* Section C, *infra.*

(2) Many common-law decisions were described by Crane as
irreconcilable with any other than the legal entity theory, although that theory was not expressly referred to as the basis of
the decisions. Crane's point apparently was that it would be
best to adopt the entity theory in the UPA and thus provide
a rational basis for the decisions and avoid the possibility of
inconsistent decisions. As examples, Crane cited cases drawing a
distinction between creditors of individual partners and those of
the partnership (*see* Chapter 14, *infra*); giving partnership cred-

itors priority as to partnership assets; classifying a partnership which signs a note as co-maker as one person for purposes of contribution; recognizing that a bill bearing the names of two firms engaged in two distinct activities but composed of the same partners is signed by two different persons; and cases upholding the validity of a contract between a firm and one of its members or between two firms having a common member. (In using these cases to support his entity thesis, Crane relies on the "rule of law . . . that one person cannot be both a party obligor and a party obligee to a joint contract," citing a half-dozen cases as subscribing to such a rule including several cases holding such contracts invalid under the aggregate theory. *The Uniform Partnership Act and Legal Persons*, 29 HARV. L. REV. 843, notes (1916).)

(3) Crane argued that many decisions expressly declared a partnership to be a legal person as such and reached their result on that theory. These cases are described in detail by Lewis in his rebuttal article in 29 HARV. L. REV. at 175-182. They include cases upholding a suit against a partnership for a slander uttered by an agent of the firm; giving legal validity to a transfer of property from one firm to another, both containing the same partners; recognizing that an assignment for the benefit of partnership creditors of partnership assets was valid as against the individual creditors of a partner; and so forth. All of the opinions expressly stated that a partnership was a separate legal entity.

Lewis responded to Crane's thesis at great length in the articles cited above. He defined the issue as follows:

> The issue is whether the group of activities carried on by the partners should be regarded as being carried on by them— which is the actual fact—or as being carried on by a legal personality distinct from the legal personalities of the partners. Thus under the aggregate theory the partners own in common the partnership property, and they are all joint principals in partnership transactions. Under the legal person theory the partnership legal person owns the partnership property, and the partners are merely its agents. 29 HARV. L. REV. at 162.

Lewis noted on the same page that the Commissioners initially had drafted the act on the entity theory. The incentive to do so was the "almost hopeless confusion" that existed at the common law on the rights of a partner in partnership property, including the rights of those claiming derivatively from the partner such as assignees, creditors and heirs.

The confusion began in 1693 with the case of Heydon v. Heydon, 1 Salk. 392, 91 Eng. Rep. 340 (1693), per Lord Holt, where partners were classified as co-owners of partnership property holding as joint tenants. A traditional common-law concept was thus applied to the partnership relationship, which is understandable, but it had bizarre consequences. Execution of judgments at common law could reach only tangible physical assets. The method for executing on an individual partner's interest, therefore, once the joint tenant nature of partnership property was established, was by physically seizing specific partnership property. A separate creditor of a partner thus was able to levy on partnership property and have the sheriff sell the debtor partner's interest. The purchaser then became a tenant in common with the other partners, to their disadvantage. Also, the remaining partners lost possession of the property while the process of levy and execution was taking place.

As will be developed in Chapter 14, courts responded to this problem in a variety of conflicting ways, supplying an incentive for uniform legislation. Similar problems arose when a partner voluntarily assigned his interest in the partnership.

Lewis acknowledged that the entity theory of partnership would have resolved the above problems, since a separate creditor of a partner would be left with an equitable claim against "the interest" of that partner in the partnership rather than a legal claim to title in partnership property. Also, voluntary assignment by one partner would not assign title to property of the firm, but rather would secure to the assignee "the beneficial interest" of the partner in the firm. The commissioners thus were convinced by Dean Ames to base the act on the entity theory, and the first two drafts of the Act were drawn on that basis.

As mentioned, Lewis became draftsman on the death of Dean Ames. He convinced the commissioners and their advisers to change their approach to the aggregate theory for two reasons. First, he argued that existing theory would be changed, since persons would no longer be dealing with partners as principals. Under the entity theory, and under the first two drafts of the Act, partners would be regarded as contributors to the firm but not as co-principals of the firm. In other words, the persons dealing with the firm would deal with the entity itself, and not the partners as such. In order to realize on firm obligations, therefore, the creditors would first have to sue the firm, exhaust firm assets, and then proceed "by legal or equitable process" to levy on the separate property of the partners.

Second, if the legal entity theory was adopted, it would be necessary to have some efficient system for the registration of all partnerships. "If a partnership is a legal person it should only be sued under its name. To ascertain beyond possibility of dispute what the name is, every partnership doing business in the state should register its name in a public office." Lewis, *Id.* at 167. Lewis noted that universal registration would be difficult to enforce. One method of enforcement would be a statutory requirement that registration of a partnership would be necessary before it could bring suit. This would mean in many suits that the admittedly difficult questions surrounding the determination of the existence of a partnership (*see* Section E, i, *infra*) would be vulnerable to litigation by the opposing side to a suit. Also, Lewis argued that the registration system would destroy the secret or dormant partner status available at the common law. He notes that the common law did not object to this status, pointing to the undisclosed principal status as an analogy.

The above reasons induced Lewis to draft an act which was based mainly on the aggregate theory. The act created a "tenancy in partnership" as a response to the property ownership problems. *See* Sections 24-28 of the UPA, discussed in Chapters 13 and 14, *infra*. Lewis's draft was discussed at a meeting of a committee of the uniform law commissioners, law teachers and practitioners, where the shift in theory was unanimously approved.

One question you should ask yourself as you go through these materials is what difference, as a practical matter, does it make what theory the act adopted? Some of the later materials will return to this question, as well as sketch out what ambiguities in the common law the act did resolve, and those that were not resolved. *See also,* Jensen, *Is a Partnership Under the Uniform Partnership Act an Aggregate or an Entity?* 16 Vand. L. Rev. 377 (1963); Mersky, *The Literature of Partnership Law,* 16 Vand. L. Rev. 389 (1963).

---

ii. *The Uniform Limited Partnership Act*

The Uniform Limited Partnership Act (ULPA), which is adopted in 47 states plus the District of Columbia, is set forth in full in Appendix B. It is a unique device which allows the capital investor the best of two worlds: participation in profits plus enjoyment of the income tax advantages of the partnership form, and yet freedom from unlimited liability (recall Section 15 of the UPA, defining the all-encompassing personal liability of the general partner). As will be seen later, one has to exercise considerable care when creating and operating under this form. For commentary by the draftsman of the ULPA, which was promulgated by the Commissioners on Uniform State Laws in 1916, see Lewis, *The Uniform Limited Partnership Act,* 65 U. Pa. L.

Rev. 715 (1917). Again, it is helpful at this stage to read the act completely through several times.

---

iii. *Preliminary Questions about Partnerships*

One way to approach the legal problems involved in operating through the partnership form is to look at a typical arrangement and, using a little imagination, our knowledge of agency principles and a few general principles from the UPA, to ask some questions. Take three recent law school graduates who plan to form a partnership in order to practice law. They think it advisable to draft an agreement. Using common sense, what would one expect the agreement to cover? The division of net income comes immediately to mind. How would this be done in a service enterprise dependent on individual efforts (and luck)? Suppose one of the partners has an exceptional year, and then almost nothing in the next year. Obviously the typical set percentage arrangement in, for example, a manufacturing partnership would need some modification.

The problem of losses is not so apparent as in a manufacturing or underwriting business. But losses nevertheless can occur, from minor ones like unpaid rent, salaries of supporting personnel, and so forth, to the lawyer's nightmare of a major malpractice judgment which exceeds insurance coverage. How are the losses to be shared? How are losses treated by the law if nothing is said about them in the agreement?

Questions of authority must be settled. Are all partners to have equal authority to make lease arrangements, write checks for firm expenses, order office equipment, and so forth? If this is not covered in the partnership agreement, what does the law, assuming it is ascertainable in the particular jurisdiction, say about this? Also, how are disputes among partners to be resolved?

When the partnership acquires property, what is the nature of each partner's interest in it? Suppose, for example, the law firm decides to buy a building. What sort of interest does each partner have in the building? In what form can title be taken and how does the partnership convey it to a future purchaser?

What are the rights of creditors of the partnership and of individual partners? Suppose one partner gets himself into serious personal financial difficulties. Can his creditors attach and sell his share of the partnership assets, regardless of the adverse effect on the business? Do partnership creditors have a claim on a partner's personal assets equal to his personal creditors?

Under UPA § 31 death or retirement or expulsion of a partner, among other events, automatically "dissolves" the partnership. What does this mean? Can the business be continued by the remaining partners? Questions both as to the power to continue the business and the disposition of the interest of the ex-partner should be resolved. Is the widow of a deceased partner to be allowed to continue to take a share of the profits? If so, how is this arranged? Can it be done if this contingency is not covered in the partnership agreement? And, if not, how is the deceased partner's interest to be valued—and paid for?

What other aspects of such an arrangement should be considered? Do the drafting problems vary a great deal if the partnership will be mercantile in nature? Financial? If the partnership is one of the classic money man, service man arrangements?

---

iv. *Partnerships Revisited*

a.   Relations Among Partners

I.   *The Authority of Partners*

The power of one or more partners to bind the other partners of a partnership to contractual obligations is the subject of Sections 9 and (subject to variation in the partnership agreement) 18(e) and (h) of the UPA. This topic was raised at pages 181-182 of Chapter 7, *supra*, and in problems 2, 5 and 9 at the end of that chapter. The questions concerning termination of such power were raised at pages 223-228, 235, 241, 243-244 and problem 5 in Chapter 8, *supra*.

II.   *Fiduciary Duties*

As noted in Section 21 of the UPA, partners are fiduciaries of each other. Some of the questions involving the definition and limits of fiduciary obligations were covered in Chapter 11, *supra*. *See also,* problems 4 and 5 at the end of that chapter, and Sections 19-22 of the UPA.

---

b.   Vicarious Tort Liability

A partnership as employer is liable under *respondeat superior* for the torts of its nonpartner employees committed in the scope of their employment as is any other employer. It is also liable for the torts committed by partners acting in the ordinary course of the business of the partnership. *See* Sections 13 and 15 of the

UPA, page 21 of Chapter 1, and page 134 of Chapter 5, *supra.* Although the use of the word "partnership" in this paragraph sounds like a reference to an entity, it is actually used as a convenient reference to the association of persons involved as co-owners in the business, who are jointly and severally liable for such torts. The UPA frequently uses "partnership" in such a sense.

B. INCOME TAX CONSIDERATIONS—A BRIEF SUMMARY

Unlike corporations, partnerships do not pay federal income tax on the income generated by partnership business. Instead, each individual partner is taxed directly on his share of the partnership's taxable income. He also takes losses directly into his return. INT. REV. CODE § 701. In this important respect the Code adopts the aggregate theory of partnership law. This can create desirable tax consequences, since the income which is passed through directly to the partners retains its original character (as tax exempt, for example); the same is true with losses, including losses generated solely on paper, such as depreciation.

The partnership does play a role as an entity under federal tax laws, however. It is required to file a tax return, setting forth its income and losses. INT. REV. CODE § 6031. The return serves informational purposes and also is the vehicle through which elections affecting the computation of taxable income derived by a partner from the partnership are made. This includes methods of accounting, computation of depreciation, deduction of intangible drilling and development costs, and so forth. If a partnership fails to make a favorable tax election, the individual partners are powerless to change that by taking action in their individual returns.

The treatment of a partnership as an entity under the federal income tax laws for some purposes thus can have an impact on the individual partner's tax liability. See Bibart, *Partnership Taxation*, 40 U. CIN. L. REV. 456 (1971), for a useful summary of the tax questions involved in operating through the partnership form. Bibart discusses, among other things, the limitations set by the Code and Regulations on special allocations by partnership agreement of gains and losses among partners as well as the considerations involved in the calculation of the basis of a partner's interest in the partnership, in making contributions of depreciated property, in transactions by a partner with the partnership, the sale or exchange of partnership interests, transfers at death, and so forth, all of which have substantial tax consequences and are beyond the scope of this brief treatment.

Profit Sharing and Retirement Plan Tax Benefits

As mentioned in the Introduction, many partnerships today, including partnerships of professional persons, are incorporating in order to take advantage of profit sharing and pension plan tax benefits not as fully available to self-employed persons. "Professional service associations" is the label customarily used to describe this type of corporation. Legislation permitting doctors, dentists and lawyers to incorporate has been enacted in nearly all states.

The tax advantage is that the professional person can be "employed" by the corporation and thus take advantage of the income tax deductions allowed corporate profit sharing plans and contributions to the retirement plans of its employees. If both a pension and profit sharing plan are used, the corporation may deduct from its current income up to 25% of the compensation of its employees covered by the plan, which must include all full-time employees of the corporation. INT. REV. CODE § 404(a)(7). In addition, the corporate form allows deductions for medical and substantially all life insurance premiums under group plans. *Id.* §§ 79(a) and 106. Equivalent income tax advantages are not available to the partner, who is a self-employed person and is limited to a retirement deduction of $2,500 or 10% of earnings, whichever is less, per year and who cannot deduct his medical or life insurance premiums. *Id.* § 404(e). Thus if 25% of total employee compensation would exceed $2,500 per year for each of the owners of the business, a greater deduction would be allowed the owners under the corporate form, with correspondingly higher ultimate retirement benefits financed from pre-tax income. The disadvantages of incurring the double form of taxation to which corporations are subject is substantially mitigated by paying out nearly all the income to the professional employees in salary form, leaving very little, if any, net income to the corporation which it would report on its tax return. The corporate status of professional service associations has, after a brief battle, been recognized by the Internal Revenue Service. *See* T.I.R. 1019 (1969).

The alert reader doubtless caught the 1969 date on the Internal Revenue Service's recognition of the professional service association and thus may ask whether the statistics described above in the Introduction as to the widespread adoption of the partnership form of doing business, which were as of 1969, are outdated. There are, however, tax considerations on the other side, in addition to the obvious point that not *all* partnerships are interested in retirement plans. Consider the retirement plan concerns of a partnership engaged in a real estate development, for example.

As mentioned above, if a large share of the enterprise's income will be tax exempt, the partnership form is advisable since it will be treated as though directly received by each partner, while dividends from a corporation would be fully taxable regardless of the character of the income received by the corporation. Also, if the enterprise is planned to function only for a limited period of time, the partnership form may be preferable in order to avoid taxable gain upon dissolution of a corporation. And, as mentioned, operating losses may be carried over against a partner's other income, while failure of a corporate business usually results merely in a capital loss for worthless stock. Other disadvantages (and advantages) are summarized in Capouano, *Tax Advantages and Disadvantages of Professional Corporations*, 58 A.B.A.J. 758 (1972) and K. STRONG and K. HOLDSWORTH, PROFESSIONAL CORPORATIONS (1970). *See also* Note, *Professional Corporations and Associations*, 75 HARV. L. REV. 776 (1962).

These tax considerations have been affected somewhat by the option granted under Subchapter S (INT. REV. CODE §§ 1371-1377) to certain corporations to be taxed as though they were partnerships. A corporation qualifying under Subchapter S must have not more than 10 stockholders, however, and is subject to restrictions as to kinds of income (income from rents, dividends and interest generally cannot be more than 20% of the corporation's gross receipts), plus limitations on passing through income; also, the calculation of basis for determining losses is more restricted than for a partnership. In addition, the 1969 Tax Reform Act provides that the stockholders of a Subchapter S corporation are subject to the retirement deduction limitations of self-employed persons. *See* A. ARONSOHN, PARTNERSHIPS AND INCOME TAXES 196-207 (1970). *See also,* on partnership taxation generally, J. PENNELL & J. O'BYRNE, FEDERAL INCOME TAXATION OF PARTNERS AND PARTNERSHIPS (1971); A. WILLIS, PARTNERSHIP TAXATION (1971); Sullivan, *Conflicts Between State Partnership Laws and the Internal Revenue Code*, 15 TAX L. REV. 105, 229 (1959-60); Jackson, et al., *The Internal Revenue Code of 1954: Partnerships*, 54 COLUM. L. REV. 1183 (1954).

C. THE NATURE OF PARTNERSHIP LIABILITY; SERVICE OF PROCESS

i. *Joint and Several Liability Versus Joint Liability of Partners*

Read Sections 13, 14 and 15 of the UPA which deal with this subject. They are set forth in Appendix A. The distinction between "joint and several" obligations under Section 15(a) and

"joint" obligations under Section 15(b) raises procedural and substantive problems that have troubled partnership law for some
time. Note that the UPA simply declares the general nature of
a partner's liability, leaving the procedural effect of this declaration up to local law. *See* the Commissioner's Notes to Section 15,
6 Unif. Laws Annot., Master Ed., at 175.

Ask yourself what the consequences would be if Jones, a tort
claimant (injured by the deceit of a partner committed while
acting within the ordinary course of the partnership's business),
sued only one of three partners in a partnership. Could he successfully do so? If so, and he obtains a judgment against the
partner and executes, receiving only one-half the amount of the
judgment, can he then successfully sue the other two partners
and execute against their assets? If so, would he have to reliti-
gate the question of liability or would the first judgment be res
judicata in the subsequent suits? (Questions as to the existence
of separate partnership assets, and whether Jones can proceed
against the partnership assets simultaneously with his subsequent
suits against the other two partners, will be covered in Chapter
14.)

An obvious starting point in answering the above questions is
to locate where you are in the UPA. The clear impression from
the language is that tort claims fall under Section 15(a). The
argument that an unliquidated tort claim was a "debt" under
Section 15(b) and thus only joint liability was involved was litigated and lost in Soberg v. Sanders, 243 Mich. 429, 220 N.W. 781
(1928).

Assuming, therefore, that joint and several liability applies, the
normal procedural rules come into play and presumably give us
the answers to the questions asked above. *See* 1 R. Rowley, Rowley on Partnership 390-94 (2d ed. 1960) [cited hereafter as Row-
ley], indicating that the other partners remain liable for the
satisfaction of the claim and that res judicata does not apply to
the subsequent suits. To the same effect is A. Bromberg, Crane
and Bromberg on Partnership 339, 361-63 (1968) [cited hereafter as Crane & Bromberg on Partnership].

The procedural consequences of pursuing a joint obligation
under Section 15(b) are more complex. Assume that you want to
sue a partnership of five people on a contractual obligation. The
partnership is located in New York and three of the five partners
reside there. Two reside out of state. Assume that you could get
service of process over them under the New York long arm statute, but you prefer not to incur the time delay and expense in
doing so. You are satisfied that the three in New York are financially responsible and, since each person bound by a joint obliga-

tion is bound for the whole obligation, are not concerned about the other two. Realizing this, can you successfully sue merely the three in New York? The answer of the common law in some jurisdictions was a decisive no. The three partners could plead "in abatement" and the action would be dismissed. The theory was that at common law all joint obligors must be sued jointly, subject to an exception where jurisdiction over all could not be obtained. See BROMBERG at 335. If they did not plead in abatement the defense was deemed waived and the suit could continue to judgment, although many jurisdictions held that the cause of action merged with the judgment, with the result that the plaintiff could no longer recover against the two not joined.

Could you avoid the abatement plea by suing the partnership as an entity and executing against the partnership assets? The answer in many states was no because a partnership was not a legal entity. Suits affecting partnership matters had to be brought against or by all the members of the firm.

In addition, the release of one joint obligor released all at common law. Further, the death of a partner shifted liability to the remaining partners when a joint obligation was involved. Equity intervened against application of this latter rule when the surviving partner or partners were insolvent.

The response to this obviously unsatisfactory situation varied greatly in the different states. The Bromberg book discusses the various legislative responses at pages 342-51. One form of legislation, known as the joint debtor act, allowed actions against joint debtors to proceed against less than all the debtors if all the debtors were named as defendants, with the judgment enforceable against the joint property of all and the separate property of the debtors actually served. A different response was legislation, known as common name statutes, permitting suit against a partnership in its own name, again with the judgment binding the joint property of the partners and the individual property of the partners actually served, although questions concerning necessary parties, the susceptibility of partnership property to execution and so forth, sometimes were not clearly resolved. Another response was legislation declaring that all contracts joint at common law were to be regarded as joint and several. Also, Section 36(4) of the UPA makes the individual property of a deceased partner liable for partnership obligations incurred while he was a partner, whether or not the other partners are insolvent.

Assuming that the three partners served with process were able to and did pay the ensuing judgment, do they have a right of contribution against the other partners not joined? Does it make any difference whether the liability is joint or is joint and several? See Section 18(b) of the UPA and, if the partnership is unable to indemnify, Sections 40(d) and 40(b)(II).

---

ii.   *Suits Against the Partnership*

As mentioned above, a partnership is viewed as an aggregate of persons by the common law, and thus is not suable in its own name since only legal persons may be named as parties to litigation. Suits affecting partnership matters have to be brought against the members of the firm. This raises the joint obligor problems mentioned above when the claim is based on contractual grounds. If the suit is based on tort liability, there was no need to serve all partners. But in neither event could the firm itself be sued. As noted, this has been changed by statute in some jurisdictions. Approximately 30 jurisdictions allow suit against a partnership as such, leaving some 20 jurisdictions where the common law rule is still in effect. The UPA does not have a provision on this matter, on the ground that it is procedural in nature.

---

iii.   *Suits by the Partnership*

The common law, consistent with the aggregate theory, also does not allow suit by the partnership in the firm name. With some exceptions, suits to enforce partnership rights have to be brought in the names of all the partners, since only legal persons may be named as parties to litigation. Some 21 states have provided by statute that actions may be brought in the partnership name. The majority of states thus still follow the common law rule. Again, the UPA does not have a provision on this.

D. LIABILITY AS A GENERAL PARTNER THROUGH ESTOPPEL

Assume that Mr. Bardon, a prominent and wealthy banker in a community of 100,000 people, has just been sued for the unpaid indebtedness of the World Investment Association, an investment banking partnership in the community which specialized in speculative ventures until several miscarried and it became insolvent. Mr. Bardon feels particularly incensed by this suit because he had expressly refused to join the World partnership when it was formed due to his distrust of some of the people involved in it. The reason he has been sued is that the World people have used his name in their advertising for the past six months. Now the creditors are referring to the old ads and claiming that they relied on the good name of Mr. Bardon in loaning money to the firm.

a.   Assume that Mr. Bardon knew that World was using his name but refused "to dignify their atrocious act with a denial." He retains you to defend him. Will you be able to assert a successful defense? Would you want to know any other facts? Where is the first place you would go to locate authority on this question?

b.   Assume that one creditor will admit that he did not see the old ads, but he intends to sue Bardon anyway. In what manner, if at all, would this affect your defense?

c.   Suppose Mr. Bardon had not known about the use of his name until he was sued. Would that make a difference in your case? Why?

d.   Would it make any difference if one of the creditors had come up to your client prior to extending credit and said, "Bardon, I'm going to loan some money to that no good World firm of yours." And your client, irritated at the creditor's over-familiar manner, had walked away without comment.

The UPA

Section 16 of the UPA deals with the question of estoppel to deny partnership liability. It reads as follows:

§ 16.   Partner by Estoppel.

(1) When a person, by words spoken or written or by conduct, represents himself, or consents to another representing him to any one, as a partner in an existing partnership or with one or more persons not actual partners, he is liable to any such person to whom such representation has been made, who has, on the faith of such representation, given credit to the actual or apparent partnership, and if he has made such representation or consented to its being made in a public manner he is liable to such person, whether the representation has or has not been made or communicated to such person so giving credit by or with the knowledge of the apparent partner making the representation or consenting to its being made.

(a) When a partnership liability results, he is liable as though he were an actual member of the partnership.

(b) When no partnership liability results, he is liable jointly with the other persons, if any, so consenting to the contract or representation as to incur liability, otherwise separately.

(2) When a person has been thus represented to be a partner in an existing partnership, or with one or more persons not

actual partners, he is an agent of the persons consenting to such representation to bind them to the same extent and in the same manner as though he were a partner in fact, with respect to persons who rely upon the representation. Where all the members of the existing partnership consent to the representation, a partnership act or obligation results; but in all other cases it is the joint act or obligation of the person acting and the persons consenting to the representation.

BROWN & BIGELOW v. ROY
Court of Appeals of Ohio
132 N.E.2d 755 (Ohio App. 1955)
Noted in 45 Ky. L. J. 553 (1957)

MILLER, Presiding Judge. This is a law appeal from the judgment of the Municipal Court rendered in favor of the plaintiff-appellee for the sum of $413.66 and interest and costs. The action was one on an account for goods and merchandise sold and delivered to the F. & M. Truck Stop, an alleged partnership consisting of Clarence F. Roy, the appellant, and H. Fay Lucas, who was not a party to the action.

The answer was a general denial. Upon request being made the court filed separate findings and conclusions of law and fact. Those pertinent to the issues presented are:

(1) The merchandise was "purchased by the partnership, and sold to it."

(2) That the defendant-appellant "held himself out or permitted himself to be held out as a partner in the F. & M. Truck Stop."

(3) That the defendant-appellant is estopped from denying such partnership; and

(4) That no notice or publication pertaining to termination or dissolution of said partnership was made by the defendant.

All of the errors assigned relate to the sufficiency of the evidence to sustain the judgment, the appellant urging that his motion to dismiss at the close of plaintiff's case and again at the conclusion of all of the evidence, should have been sustained.

No direct proof of a partnership was offered, but the same was based upon the conduct of the appellant at the place of business; that a sum of money was advanced by the appellant which he testified was a loan to the other alleged partner and upon the further fact that a vendor's license was secured from the State of Ohio in the name of "Henry F. Lucas and Clarence F. Roy, DBA F. & M. Truck Stop." The application for this license was signed by both of the alleged partners and the license issued in response thereto was posted at the place of business of the alleged partnership. It is urged that the evidence does not disclose that the appellee had any knowledge of the information contained in the license and therefore there could have been no reliance placed on the statements it contained; that the doctrine of estoppel has no application. We concur with counsel for the appellant upon his factual conclusion and are of the opinion that his views as to the law would be correct were it not for the fact that our statutory law modifies the common-law rule. Section 1775.15 of the Revised Code provides:

. . . . [the court quotes Section 16(1) of the UPA]

Clearly the defendant represented that he was a partner in the business when he signed the application for a vendor's license and the posting of the license at the place of business was notice to the public of the nature of the business being conducted on the premises. The Court did not err in holding that the defendant was a partner.

. . . .

[Judgment affirmed, with a modification in the amount of interest.]

NOTES

1. Which variation on the Bardon hypothetical at the start of this section does this case affect?

2. The opinion is vague on its construction of Section 16(1) of the UPA. Can you articulate the construction which the court must have placed on the language in order to arrive at its conclusion? Do you agree with it, either as a matter of statutory construction or as the way you think the issue should have been decided as a matter of policy?

3. The court's construction is disputed in Painter, *Partnership by Estoppel*, 16 VAND. L. REV. 327 (1963) and in CRANE AND BROMBERG ON PARTNERSHIP at 198 n.22.

STANDARD OIL CO. OF N.Y. v. HENDERSON
Supreme Judicial Court of Massachusetts
265 Mass. 322, 163 N.E. 743 (1928)

Writ in the Third District Court of Bristol dated April 20, 1926.

The plaintiff's first, third and fourth requests were as follows:

"1. If the place of business to which the plaintiff sold and delivered its gasoline and oil was conducted under the name of

Thomas Henderson & Son with the knowledge of the defendant Thomas Henderson, Sr., he would be liable to the plaintiff."

"3. If the plaintiff was honestly misled by the fact that the name of the defendant Thomas Henderson, Sr., was used as owner of the business and gave credit to the apparent partnership the defendant would be liable for the indebtedness as if he had been a partner in fact.

"4. The plaintiff and its agents were justified to interpret the appearance of the defendants' place of business as being owned and conducted by the defendants as copartners."

Findings and rulings by the trial judge are stated in the opinion. He found for the defendant and reported the action to the Appellate Division for the Southeastern District. The report was ordered dismissed. The plaintiff appealed.

PIERCE, J. This case is before this court on the appeal of the plaintiff from an order "Report Dismissed" of the Appellate Division for the Southeastern District. The report of the special justice of the Third District Court of Bristol to the Appellate Division "contains all the evidence material to the questions reported," which are: should the special justice have ruled, and should he have refused to rule, as requested by the plaintiff?

The pertinent facts disclosed in the report in substance are as follows: About November 13, 1924, one Thomas Henderson, Jr., opened a gasoline station at 660 Brock Avenue, New Bedford, and put on the window of the station the words "Henderson & Son." This "was the only name which appeared on the premises." On November 13, 1924, the plaintiff and Thomas Henderson, Jr., executed an "equipment loan agreement" for the installation of a tank, pump and accessories for the gasoline station. The agreement recites that it is made between the Standard Oil Company of New York and "Henderson & Son of 688 Brock Avenue, New Bedford"; and it was signed "Standard Oil Company of New York. By J. E. Winter. Henderson & Son by Thomas Henderson, Jr." The business was conducted by Thomas Henderson, Jr., the son of the defendant. The defendant was a loom fixer employed in one of the local mills. His wife and daughter conducted a grocery store within a short distance of the gasoline station. Thomas Henderson, Jr., at the time the action was commenced and at the time of the trial was in the State of California.

On the evidence the trial judge found that the plaintiff sold and delivered the items referred to in the plaintiff's declaration; that they were charged to Henderson & Son; that the delivery slips were signed by Thomas Henderson, Jr. "The plaintiff's

evidence did not show that the defendant was a partner in fact."
For the purposes of this case we assume the defendant was not a
partner of Thomas Henderson, Jr. The record contains no direct
evidence that the defendant had knowledge or notice that he was
held out as a partner in the business of his son, and no circumstantial evidence to warrant a finding of such knowledge and
notice, other than can logically be deduced from the evidence
that he "walked past the gasoline station almost every day; . . .
[that] he saw the name 'Henderson & Son'" on a window of the
premises, and knew that the business was conducted under that
name; that he made no inquiries as to whether any credit was
being extended by the plaintiff or any other person or concern
relying on the fact that his name was used in connection with the
business, and he did not tell any one that he was not connected
with the business or ask his son to remove his name. The trial
judge specifically found "that . . . [the defendant] was not asked
by the plaintiff concerning his responsibility." He stated that he
was "unable to find . . . that the defendant ever visited the place
of business of the plaintiff." Other than is above stated there is
no evidence reported to warrant an inference that the defendant
consented to the use of the sign "Henderson & Son" on the
window of the station, and there is no affirmative evidence reported that the plaintiff gave credit to "Henderson & Son" on the
faith that Thomas Henderson, Sr., the defendant, was a partner
in the business carried on by the son under the sign name "Henderson & Son."

St. 1922, c. 486, § 16(1) [of the UPA] provides that. . . . On
the evidence the issues which were presented at the trial were
(1) As matter of fact did the defendant consent to his being held
out as a partner in a public manner? and (2) Did the plaintiff
give credit to the apparent partnership on the faith that there was
a partnership and that the defendant was a member of it? The
statutory rule is an expression of the common law as recognized
in this Commonwealth.

The first request of the plaintiff was denied rightly. The evidence presented an issue of fact, and did not warrant the requested ruling of law that the defendant was a partner by estoppel
in the business carried on under the style of "Henderson & Son."
Bartlett v. Raymond, 139 Mass. 275, relied on by the plaintiff,
decided merely that the evidence in that case warranted a finding
for the plaintiffs. The third request was also denied rightly. There
is no evidence reported to warrant a finding that the plaintiff
gave credit to the apparent partnership on the faith that the defendant was a partner in the partnership.

The fourth request was properly denied. The second request, which was given, reads: "If the defendant permitted himself to be held out as a partner in the gasoline and oil business conducted at 660 Brock Avenue, New Bedford, he is liable to the plaintiff as a partner whether actually a partner or not."

This request did not require that the judge should have entered judgment for the plaintiff; there remained open the issue whether the defendant consented to the holding out and whether the plaintiff gave the credit on the faith of the membership of the defendant.

The fifth request of the defendant, "The plaintiff cannot recover on the ground that the defendant Thomas Henderson, Sr. is liable as a partner for estoppel unless he proves by a fair preponderance of the evidence: (a) That Thomas Henderson, Sr. held himself out as a partner; (b) That such holding out was by Thomas Henderson, Sr. or his authority; (c) That the plaintiff had knowledge of such holding out; (d) That the plaintiff acted on the strength of such holding out to his prejudice," correctly stated the law applicable to the evidence before the court. We find no error. The entry must be order of Appellate Division dismissing report affirmed.

So ordered.

NOTES

1.   Which, if any, of the variations on the Bardon hypothetical posed at the start of this section does the *Henderson* case affect?

2.   Once again, the relevant language of Section 16(1) is not isolated and analyzed by the court. The entire section is quoted without comment. What language *is* relevant?

3.   The Official Comment to Section 16 of the UPA reads in part as follows:

> The section clears several doubts and confusions of our existing case law. It has been held that a person is liable if he has been held out as a partner and knows that he is being held out, unless he prevents such holding out, even if to do so he has to take legal action. . . . On the other hand, the weight of authority is to the effect that to be held as a partner he must consent to the holding and that consent is a matter of fact. The act as drafted follows this weight of authority and better reasoning.

The draftsmen of the Official Comments do not explain what they mean by the "better reasoning."

4. There is authority *contra* to the *Henderson* case, even in a jurisdiction which had adopted the UPA. *See* Brocato v. Serio, 173 Md. 374, 196 A. 125 (1938), *noted in* 3 MD. L. REV. 189 (1939); McBriety v. Phillips, 180 Md. 569, 26 A.2d 400 (1942), *noted in* 6 MD. L. REV. 337 (1942). What reasoning do you think underlies these decisions? For a discussion of this, see Painter, *Partnership by Estoppel,* 16 VAND. L. REV. 327, 330-31 (1963).

5. Does Section 16 cover the problem of vicarious tort liability? Vicarious tort liability is important, of course, but normally it is not a matter of primary concern in the partnership context, as the language of Section 16 would seem to confirm. Probably this is because insurance is easily obtainable and is much more likely to have been taken care of when the relationship is one of a business nature, where losses and gains usually are consciously considered. In addition, vicarious tort liability by estoppel cases are very rare, due to the absence of reliance in most cases. Thus a person held to be a partner by estoppel would be much less likely (assuming he has been "estopped into" a going business) to find a tort loss to be the difficulty that he faces upon assuming that status.

The approach of the draftsmen of the UPA appears to reflect this. The matter of tort liability seems not to have occurred to them. *See,* however, Frye v. Anderson, 248 Minn. 478, 493, 80 N.W.2d 593, 603 (1957). ("It has been held . . . where there was a holding out of a partnership relation . . . such that estoppel applies, it may extend to tort actions as well as matters of credit or contract.") And *see* ROWLEY, § 16.1, E 2.

E. AVOIDING GENERAL PARTNER STATUS WHILE SHARING PROFITS

i. *The Active Creditor*

Assume that an old and respected partnership in investment banking, a high risk enterprise, is about to fail. Some close friends of one of the old time partners decide to try to help but definitely do not want to become partners of the business in its existing critical condition. They will be putting in substantial sums of money and want to make sure that it is not mishandled. They therefore want some control over the business decisions. Also, if they do succeed in saving the business, they want the option to become partners of the old firm. Finally, even if they decide not to become partners after the business has become successful again, they would like to receive the profits attributable to the money they let the firm use.

What risks do they run? Assume they come to you as a lawyer and want you to draft an agreement protecting their interests. How would you go about doing so?

As previously noted, an immediate point of reference in nearly all jurisdictions when dealing with—or avoiding—partnership matters is the UPA. Section 7, setting forth rules for determining the existence of a partnership, is right on point. And you will want to bear Section 16 in mind as well. Consult those sections and the following background material, draw your own conclusions, and then observe below how first a law firm and then a court dealt with a similar problem.

The early common law held that receipt of profits from an enterprise was a conclusive test of partnership status. *See* Waugh v. Carver, 2 H. Bl. 235, 126 Eng. Rep. 525 (1793). In the *Waugh* case two ship agents (apparently persons who employed tradesmen in repairing ships, and then billed the ship owner on a commission basis) at different ports had agreed in an elaborate written instrument to share the profits on their respective commissions and thus not to compete with each other. The agreement provided that neither was responsible for the losses of the other.

One ship agent was sued by a tradesman in assumpsit for work done for the other agent. The defense was that there was no liability in the absence of a partnership relationship, and that relationship did not exist between the ship agents since the parties clearly did not intend it. The defendant argued that a partnership should not be created by law against the express intent of the parties in the absence of an appearance of fraud "by holding out false colours to the world" through using the names of nonpartners, or where one party had authority to contract for the rest or where there was joint capital or stock. The *Waugh* case quite clearly did not fit any of these categories. The court nevertheless held the noncontracting ship agent liable for the contractual debt of the other agent on the ground that

> [H]e who takes a moiety of all the profits indefinitely, shall, by operation of law, be made liable to losses, if losses arise, upon the principle that by taking a part of the profits, he takes from the creditors a part of that fund which is the proper security to them for the payment of their debts. (2 H. Bl. at 247; 126 Eng. Rep. at 532.)

The court reached this decision despite its statement that "[I]t is plain upon the construction of the agreement, if it be construed only between the Carvers and Giesler, that they were not nor ever meant to be partners. They meant each house to carry on trade without risk of each other, and to be at their own loss." *Id.*

The common law moved away from *Waugh* in the well known case of Cox v. Hickman, 8 H.L. 268, 11 Eng. Rep. 431 (1860). In this case the original firm of B. Smith and Son became financially embarrassed and, by agreement, assigned its property to certain of its creditors as trustees for all its creditors who joined in the arrangement. The deed of assignment empowered the trustees to carry on the business under the name of "Stanton Iron Company" and to divide the net income among the creditors in rateable proportions, stipulating, however, that such income was deemed the property of the Smiths. After the debts were discharged, the property was to be retransferred by the trustees to Smith and Sons.

Two of the creditors who were trustees at the outset of the arrangement were sued by Hickman on a bill of exchange executed by some of the other trustees. The basis of the suit was that the Stanton Iron Company was a new partnership created by the creditors. At the trial level a verdict was rendered for the plaintiff. The Exchequer Chamber affirmed the decision by a three to three vote of the judges. The case was appealed to the House of Lords where the judgment was reversed, three judges dissenting.

The basis of the decision is difficult to ascertain in view of the numerous and conflicting opinions. One of the clearest positions is taken in the opinion of Lord Chief Baron Pollock (subsequently the drafter of the English Partnership Act), who stated that the agreement of the parties should govern all cases between them, and that such rule should also apply to third parties (*Waugh* to the contrary) unless the parties had held themselves out as partners to the public, or their conduct operated as a fraud or deceit upon third persons. Does this make sense to you? No mention is made in any of the opinions of the point made in *Waugh* that the persons who share in the profits are held as partners because they, by taking the profits, are diverting assets otherwise available to the creditors.

Section 7 of the UPA reflects the statutory movement away from the *Waugh* case. Can you, at this stage, advise your clients in the problem first posed above that you can draft an agreement that will fulfill their desires and safely avoid the risk of partnership status?

MARTIN v. PEYTON
New York Court of Appeals
246 N.Y. 213, 158 N.E. 77 (1927)
Noted in 2 Ala. L.J. 193 *and* 2 St. John's L. Rev. 51 (1927)

ANDREWS, J. Much ancient learning as to partnership is obsolete. Today only those who are partners between themselves may be charged for partnership debts by others. (Partnership Law [Cons. Laws, ch. 39], sec. 11) [UPA § 7.] There is one exception. Now and then a recovery is allowed where in truth such relationship is absent. This is because the debtor may not deny the claim. (Sec. 27.) [UPA § 16.]

Partnership results from contract, express or implied. If denied it may be proved by the production of some written instrument; by testimony as to some conversation; by circumstantial evidence. If nothing else appears the receipt by the defendant of a share of the profits of the business is enough. (Sec. 11.)

Assuming some written contract between the parties the question may arise whether it creates a partnership. If it be complete; if it expresses in good faith the full understanding and obligation of the parties, then it is for the court to say whether a partnership exists. It may, however, be a mere sham intended to hide the real relationship. Then other results follow. In passing upon it effect is to be given to each provision. Mere words will not blind us to realities. Statements that no partnership is intended are not conclusive. If as a whole a contract contemplates an association of two or more persons to carry on as co-owners a business for profit a partnership there is. (Sec. 10.) On the other hand, if it be less than this no partnership exists. Passing on the contract as a whole, an arrangement for sharing profits is to be considered. It is to be given its due weight. But it is to be weighed in connection with all the rest. It is not decisive. It may be merely the method adopted to pay a debt or wages, as interest on a loan or for other reasons.

An existing contract may be modified later by subsequent agreement, oral or written. A partnership may be so created where there was none before. And again, that the original agreement has been so modified may be proved by circumstantial evidence—by showing the conduct of the parties.

In the case before us the claim that the defendants became partners in the firm of Knauth, Nachod & Kuhne, doing business as bankers and brokers, depends upon the interpretation of certain instruments. There is nothing in their subsequent acts determinative of or indeed material upon this question. And we are relieved of questions that sometimes arise. "The plaintiff's position is not," we are told, "that the agreements of June 4, 1921, were a false expression or incomplete expression of the intention of the parties. We say that they express defendants' intention and that that intention was to create a relationship which as a matter of law constitutes a partnership." Nor may the claim of the plaintiff be rested on any question of estoppel. "The plaintiff's claim," he stipulates, "is a claim of actual partnership, not of partnership by estoppel, and liability is not sought to be predicated upon article 27 of the New York Partnership Law."

Remitted then, as we are, to the documents themselves, we refer to circumstances surrounding their execution only so far as is necessary to make them intelligible. And we are to remember that although the intention of the parties to avoid liability as partners is clear, although in language precise and definite they deny any design to then join the firm of K. N. & K.; although they say their interests in profits should be construed merely as a measure of compensation for loans, not an interest in profits as such; although they provide that they shall not be liable for any losses or treated as partners, the question still remains whether in fact they agree to so associate themselves with the firm as to "carry on as co-owners a business for profit."

In the spring of 1921 the firm of K. N. & K. found itself in financial difficulties. John R. Hall was one of the partners. He was a friend of Mr. Peyton. From him he obtained the loan of almost $500,000 of Liberty bonds, which K. N. & K. might use as collateral to secure bank advances. This, however, was not sufficient. The firm and its members had engaged in unwise speculations, and it was deeply involved. Mr. Hall was also intimately acquainted with George W. Perkins, Jr., and with Edward W. Freeman. He also knew Mrs. Peyton and Mrs. Perkins and Mrs. Freeman. All were anxious to help him. He, therefore, representing K. N. & K., entered into negotiations with them. While they were pending a proposition was made that Mr. Peyton, Mr. Perkins and Mr. Freeman or some of them should become partners. It met a decided refusal. Finally an agreement was reached. It is expressed in three documents, executed on the same day, all a part of the one transaction. They were drawn with care and are unambiguous. We shall refer to them as "the agreement," "the indenture" and "the option."

We have no doubt as to their general purpose. The respondents were to loan K. N. & K. $2,500,000 worth of liquid securities, which were to be returned to them on or before April 15, 1923. *loan of securities for collateral* The firm might hypothecate them to secure loans totalling $2,-000,000, using the proceeds as its business necessities required. To insure respondents against loss K. N. & K. were to turn over

to them a large number of their own securities which may have
been valuable, but which were of so speculative a nature that
they could not be used as collateral for bank loans. In compensation for the loan the respondents were to receive 40 per cent
of the profits of the firm until the return was made, not exceeding, however, $500,000 and not less than $100,000. Merely because the transaction involved the transfer of securities and not
of cash does not prevent its being a loan within the meaning
of section 11. The respondents also were given an option to join
the firm if they or any of them expressed a desire to do so before
June 4, 1923.

Many other detailed agreements are contained in the papers.
Are they such as may be properly inserted to protect the lenders?
Or do they go further? Whatever their purpose, did they in
truth associate the respondents with the firm so that they and
it together thereafter carried on as co-owners a business for
profit? The answer depends upon an analysis of these various
provisions.

As representing the lenders, Mr. Peyton and Mr. Freeman are
called "trustees." The loaned securities when used as collateral
are not to be mingled with other securities of K. N. & K., and
the trustees at all times are to be kept informed of all transactions
affecting them. To them shall be paid all dividends and income
accruing therefrom. They may also substitute for any of the
securities loaned securities of equal value. With their consent
the firm may sell any of its securities held by the respondents, the
proceeds to go, however, to the trustees. In other similar ways the
trustees may deal with these same securities, but the securities
loaned shall always be sufficient in value to permit of their hy-
pothecation for $2,000,000. If they rise in price the excess may
be withdrawn by the defendants. If they fall they shall make
good the deficiency.

So far there is no hint that the transaction is not a loan of
securities with a provision for compensation. Later a somewhat
closer connection with the firm appears. Until the securities are
returned the directing management of the firm is to be in the
hands of John R. Hall, and his life is to be insured for $1,000,000,
and the policies are to be assigned as further collateral security
to the trustees. These requirements are not unnatural. Hall was
the one known and trusted by the defendants. Their acquaintance
with the other members of the firm was of the slightest. These
others had brought an old and established business to the verge
of bankruptcy. As the respondents knew, they also had engaged
in unsafe speculation. The respondents were about to loan $2,500,-
000 of good securities. As collateral they were to receive others of

problematical value. What they required seems but ordinary caution. Nor does it imply an association in the business.

The trustees are to be kept advised as to the conduct of the business and consulted as to important matters. They may inspect the firm books and are entitled to any information they think important. Finally they may veto any business they think highly speculative or injurious. Again we hold this but a proper precaution to safeguard the loan. The trustees may not initiate any transaction as a partner may do. They may not bind the firm by any action of their own. Under the circumstances the safety of the loan depended upon the business success of K. N. & K. This success was likely to be compromised by the inclination of its members to engage in speculation. No longer, if the respondents were to be protected, should it be allowed. The trustees, therefore, might prohibit it, and that their prohibition might be effective, information was to be furnished them. Not dissimilar agreements have been held proper to guard the interests of the lender.

As further security each member of K. N. & K. is to assign to the trustees their interest in the firm. No loan by the firm to any member is permitted and the amount each may draw is fixed. No other distribution of profits is to be made. So that realized profits may be calculated the existing capital is stated to be $700,000, and profits are to be realized as promptly as good business practice will permit. In case the trustees think this is not done, the question is left to them and to Mr. Hall, and if they differ then to an arbitrator. There is no obligation that the firm shall continue the business. It may dissolve at any time. Again we conclude there is nothing here not properly adapted to secure the interest of the respondents as lenders. If their compensation is dependent on a percentage of the profits still provision must be made to define what these profits shall be.

The "indenture" is substantially a mortgage of the collateral delivered by K. N. & K. to the trustees to secure the performance of the "agreement." It certainly does not strengthen the claim that the respondents were partners.

Finally we have the "option." It permits the respondents or any of them or their assignees or nominees to enter the firm at a later date if they desire to do so by buying 50 per cent or less of the interests therein of all or any of the members at a stated price. Or a corporation may, if the respondents and the members agree, be formed in place of the firm. Meanwhile, apparently with the design of protecting the firm business against improper or ill-judged action which might render the option valueless, each member of the firm is to place his resignation in the hands of Mr. Hall. If at any time he and the trustees agree that such resignation should be accepted, that member shall then retire, receiving the value of his interest calculated as of the date of such retirement.

This last provision is somewhat unusual, yet it is not enough in itself to show that on June 4, 1921, a present partnership was created nor taking these various papers as a whole do we reach such a result. It is quite true that even if one or two or three like provisions contained in such a contract do not require this conclusion, yet it is also true that when taken together a point may come where stipulations immaterial separately cover so wide a field that we should hold a partnership exists. As in other branches of the law a question of degree is often the determining factor. Here that point has not been reached.

The judgment appealed from should be affirmed, with costs.

Cardozo, Ch. J., Pound, Crane, Lehman, Kellogg and O'Brien, JJ., concur.

NOTES

1. In a widely cited article, Douglas, *Vicarious Liability and the Administration of Risk*, 38 Yale L.J. 720 (1929), the thesis is advanced that the risk of partnership liability should be placed on those parties in an enterprise who share the power to set prices and to control costs of the enterprise, since such persons can best distribute the risk of loss. Douglas thus isolates control as the key element for consideration, and by this he means more than the power to prevent actions of the enterprise, as was given the creditors in *Martin v. Peyton,* although it would seem that a broad power to veto can in effect mean the power to prescribe terms as well, depending on the type of enterprise involved.

2. Minute Maid Corp. v. United Foods, Inc., 291 F.2d 577 (5th Cir. 1961), *cert. denied,* 368 U.S. 928 (1961), *noted in* 40 N. Car. L. Rev. 355 (1962), is a recent example of an elaborate arrangement between parties which was tested judicially on whether it was a partnership or a creditor-bailee relationship. United Foods, Inc. ("United"), was an authorized direct buyer of frozen food products from Minute Maid Corporation. Minute Maid's terms of sale to direct buyers included discounts based on volume. United did not have the financial ability to enable it to carry a large inventory of frozen food products and thus obtain the maximum discounts. Cold Storage Corportion ("Storage"), which owned and operated a cold storage warehouse in Dallas, did have the financial resources and the storage space.

United and Storage entered in a formal written agreement providing that Storage would loan United up to $300,000 on purchases of frozen foods to be stored in its facilities. Storage received a six per cent note on each loan. The notes were secured by the commodities stored if they were acceptable to Storage. Storage also billed United for warehouse charges and insurance.

The warehouse charges, interest and insurance were all charged to a "Special Account" established on the books of Storage. The Account also accumulated as credits all discounts and other special allowances received by United as a result of being able to buy in larger quantities. The agreement also provided that the Account was to be closed at the end of the calendar year, and

> "a. If there is a credit balance, one-half thereof shall be paid by [Storage] to United, and the remainder shall be retained by [Storage] as its property.
> "b. If there is a debit balance, [Storage] shall so notify United, who will pay [Storage] one-half the amount of such debit balance within 20 days of notification."

Another clause in the agreement provided that "In case of pending price increase, [Storage] and United may agree on the volume to be purchased by United, and [Storage] will loan, upon receipt of product in storage, the cost to United."

Minute Maid found itself with $143,000 of unpaid invoices to United. Apparently United was insolvent, so Minute Maid sought to hold Storage liable for the debt as a partner. It admitted that it did not know of the relationship between United and Storage.

The trial court, sitting without a jury, found that a partnership did not exist and denied Minute Maid's claim. On appeal, the judgment of the trial court was reversed (2 to 1) on the ground that, as a matter of law, a partnership existed. Can you articulate the basis for the court's decision?

---

ii. The Limited Partner

As mentioned in the Introduction, another device for securing a share of the profits without assuming general partner status is utilization of the limited partnership form of doing business. If the certificate completion and filing requirements to be mentioned briefly in the notes following the main case are followed, the resulting insulation from liability is a good bit more secure than the active creditor status involved in the *Peyton* case. It comes at a price, however. Consult the ULPA in Appendix B and determine if you could have satisfied the *Peyton* creditors' requirements by utilizing the limited partnership form.

The first qualification is that the money man is now an investor, not a creditor. The natural consequence of that shift of status is that his money comes out after, not along with, the claims of creditors of the business (§ 16). The second qualification involves control. The creditors in *Peyton* demanded and received a considerable amount of control. See Section 7 of the ULPA for the treatment of this for limited partners. Finally, what are the consequences for the limited partner of technical errors in the form and filing requirements?

RATHKE v. GRIFFITH

Supreme Court of Washington
36 Wash. 2d 394, 218 P.2d 757, 18 A.L.R.2d 1349 (1950)
Noted in, 26 Wash. L. Rev. 222 (1951)

ROBINSON, J. This case involves two actions, consolidated for purposes of trial, in which respondent sought and obtained judgment against appellants Griffith, on account of advances made by respondent to the partnership known as Midfield Packers, a frozen foods concern, in which Mr. Griffith was allegedly a general partner. The amounts of the judgments are not at issue, and the sole question raised on appeal concerns the status of Mr. Griffith in the partnership. If he was, as is asserted, a general partner, he is liable to respondent; on the other hand, he urges that he was a limited partner only, and it is conceded that, if he is correct in this contention, he may not be held responsible for the debts in question. The facts in the case are as follows:

On or about August 14, 1942, Mr. Griffith, in company with several others, executed a writing, denominated "Articles of Limited Copartnership," which provided that the parties thereto were associating under the firm name of Midfield Packers, an organization formed for the purpose of canning and otherwise processing fruits and vegetables. Therein appellant Griffith is described as a limited copartner, and his liability is fixed at one thousand dollars. On December 8, 1942, the articles were filed in the office of the Thurston county auditor. Mr. Griffith's only contribution to the partnership consisted of his assuming the indebtedness of the Midfield Packers on a certain truck. He paid this indebtedness in full, the entire payment amounting to over one thousand dollars.

In 1944, the original agreement was supplemented by another agreement allowing certain of the original parties to withdraw from the concern, and specifying that Mr. Griffith was to remain in the organization as a limited partner. This agreement was likewise filed with the Thurston county auditor on April 3, 1944. No publication of the certificate of partnership, or of the modification thereof, was ever made by the parties in accordance with the requirements of Rem. Rev. Stat., § 9969 [P.P.C. § 768-7], which statute was in force during this period.

The Midfield Packers entered into business, and, in the course of time, contracted the indebtedness which has become the subject of this action. Mr. Griffith testified that, upon learning that creditors of the partnership were claiming that he was a general partner, he immediately executed a bill of sale by the terms of which he conveyed all of his interest in the partnership to the two individuals named as general partners in the original articles and in the later modification. This bill of sale purports to have been executed in November, 1946, and was filed in the office of the Thurston county auditor.

It would appear that, in a number of respects, the parties involved in the organization of the Midfield Packers failed to comply with the strict terms of the limited partnership statutes in force at the time. Their most significant lapse was their failure to publish the certificate of partnership, in accordance with the terms of Rem. Rev. Stat., § 9969 (in effect prior to 1945), which provided that:*

"The partners shall, for four consecutive weeks immediately after the filing of the certificate of partnership, publish a copy of the same in some weekly newspaper published in the county where the principal place of business of the partnership is, or if no such paper be published therein, then in some newspaper in general circulation therein. . . ."

The statute further provided that, until this requirement was complied with, the partnership was to be deemed general. Rem. Rev. Stat., § 9969. Neither of the parties to this action has referred us to any Washington cases interpreting this statute, but it is admitted that, in jurisdictions where similar statutes were in force, it was customary to construe them strictly and literally. In the present case, the trial court took the view that the failure of the parties to comply with this, and with certain other statutory requirements not necessary to be discussed here, had the effect of imposing liability as a general partner upon Mr. Griffith, the alleged limited or special partner. It would appear that the trial court's decision was in accord with the majority of the cases decided in other states under the old type of limited partner-

---

* A publication requirement is not contained in the ULPA—*ed.*

ship laws. The question before us is whether the passage of the uniform limited partnership act in 1945 changed the situation with respect to attempted limited partnerships formed prior to its adoption. In this connection, it is pertinent to consider briefly the history of the concept of the limited partnership in the United States.

This form of association, though common on the continent of Europe since the middle ages, was unknown to the common law of England and the United States, and was originally borrowed from the civil law of France. Clapp v. Lacey, 35 Conn. 463; 3 Kent's Commentaries (14th ed.) 38. Ames v. Downing, 1 Bradford (N. Y.) 321, includes an interesting account of the historical background of the limited partnership; see, also, Jacquin v. Buisson, 11 Howard's Practice Reports (N. Y.) 385. From their earliest inception (in New York and Connecticut in 1822), limited partnership statutes, being in derogation of the common law, were strictly construed by most courts. The view was commonly taken that the special or limited partner was essentially a general partner, with immunity from personal liability only on condition of full and exact compliance with the statutory requirements as to the details of formation of the association. Crane on Partnership 81, § 26, note 15. At a later date some courts began to take a more liberal view, and to hold that "substantial compliance" with the statutory terms was sufficient to free the special partner from liability. Thus, the statutes often provided that, at the time of filing the certificate of partnership, one of the general partners should file an affidavit stating that sums specified in the certificate of partnership to have been contributed by each of the special partners had actually been paid in cash; and they commonly further provided that any false statement in this affidavit would result in the alleged special partners being held liable as general partners. The earlier cases held that a statement that the payment had been made in cash when it had actually been made by check (and the check had not been presented for payment at the time of the filing of the affidavit), was a false statement within the meaning of the latter proviso, and rendered all parties to the transaction liable as general partners. Later cases, in recognition of the fact that payment by check is commonly accepted as payment in cash, relaxed this rule, and, expressing the view that, in the situation described, it would be unreasonable to hold the special partner to general liability, refused to do so.

But such liberality was by no means universal, and in any event did not extend to cases such as the one at bar, for the statutes commonly stated explicitly that, if publication of the certificate was not **made** as specified, the partnership should be treated as general. Even "substantial compliance" demanded that the requirements for publication be satisfied. Smith v. Argall, 6 Hill (N. Y.) 479, affirmed 3 Denio (N. Y.) 435. If they were not, the partnership was deemed general. Davis v. Sanderlin, 119 N. C. 84, 25 S. E. 815. As Rem. Rev. Stat., § 9969, was identical with the New York and North Carolina statutes in this respect, both the persuasive authority of the cases above cited, as well as the express wording of the statute itself, would doubtless compel us, if we held the statute binding, to find in the present case that appellant Griffith, in spite of his expressed intention to become a limited partner, was, as a matter of law, a general partner and liable as such.

But it was coming to be recognized that the strict interpretation being given to the limited partnership statutes by the courts, though it unquestionably carried out the intent of those responsible for the adoption of these statutes, was rendering this form of association commercially impracticable. See, Commmissioners' note to § 1 of the uniform limited partnership act, Vol. 8, Uniform Laws Annotated, p. 2. The limited partnership statutes were quite commonly coming to be regarded as a trap (*In re* Marcuse & Co., 281 Fed. 928); for the fact that any minor deviations from the statutory provisions might have the effect of subjecting the "limited" partners to unlimited liability, naturally rendered the limited partnership a hazardous means of obtaining limited liability, and, therefore, discouraged its employment. Accordingly, in 1916, a uniform limited partnership act was drafted in order to remedy these deficiencies. It has since been adopted by more than half of the states (see Vol. 8, Uniform Laws Annotated, 1949 Supp., p. 6), and has been in effect in Washington since 1945. Rem. Supp. 1945, §§ 9975-1 to 9975-30, inclusive. Mr. William Lewis, the draftsman of the new act, has written of it as follows:

"Practically all the differences between the new Uniform Act and the existing statutes are due to the desire of the Conference to present to the legislatures of the several states an act, under which a person willing to invest his money in a business for a share in the profits, may become a limited partner, with the same sense of security from any possibility of unlimited liability as the subscribers to the shares of a corporation." William D. Lewis, The Uniform Limited Partnership Act, 65 U. Pa. L. Rev. 715, 723.

Representative of these remedial changes is § 11 of the act, upon which appellants here rely. Illustrating the type of situation which § 11 was intended to meet, Mr. Lewis says:

"Again, suppose a person is asked to contribute to the capital of a business conducted by a person or partnership, and that he does so, believing he has become a limited partner, but the certificate required to be filed is not filed, or being filed is so defective that no limited partnership has been formed. Under existing acts a person in the position described runs a danger of becoming a general partner, if he takes a share in the profits, and a still greater danger if he exercises a limited partner's right to look over the books and give advice to his supposed copartners. It is immaterial that he may have thought all things had been done necessary for the formation of the limited partnership, and also that the persons doing business with the partnership may at the time they extended credit believe he was a limited partner. Section 11 of the Uniform Act meets this situation. . . ."

Section 11 provides:

"A person who has contributed to the capital of a business conducted by a person or partnership erroneously believing that he has become a limited partner in a limited partnership, is not, by reason of his exercise of the rights of a limited partner, a general partner with the person or in the partnership carrying on the business, or bound by the obligations of such person or partnership: *Provided*, That on ascertaining the mistake he promptly renounces his interest in the profits of the business, or other compensation by way of income." (Rem. Supp. 1945, § 9975-11.)

It was not long before a case arose to test the efficacy of this section, a case, moreover, like the case at bar, in that it involved a partnership which the associates did not intend to organize under the uniform act. . . .

[T]he court pointed out that, while, under the old act, a false statement would automatically result in the alleged special partners being held as general partners, under the new act, it was requisite that the creditor seeking to hold them as such had relied on the false statement and suffered a loss as a result. It did not appear that any creditor had suffered a loss from reliance on the allegedly false statement, and for that reason nothing in the new act barred the application of § 11.

It would seem from [cases previously cited] that § 11 was to apply to *all* cases where an individual had entered upon a supposed limited partnership with the intent that he should be liable only as a special partner, provided, of course, that no creditors had been misled, to their loss, by any misrepresentations to which he was a party. The broad language employed seems quite adequately to cover those situations where the individual attempted to become a limited partner in a partnership defectively organized under the old acts, as well as under the uniform act; and the persuasive effect of this language would seem to be sufficient in itself to suggest a resolution of any ambiguity in the statute in favor of the contention of such an individual that he should not be held as a general partner in this type of situation. In addition, this solution is plainly in accord with the policy of the uniform act, which, as we have shown earlier in this opinion, was expressly designed to relieve the hardship consequent in holding liable as general partners those who intended in good faith to become limited partners, but were held not to occupy that status by reason of errors in the formation of the partnership for which they were not responsible.

We hold, therefore, that § 11 will apply to relieve all those persons who have erroneously believed they have become limited partners, either in a partnership organized under the old statutes, or in one organized under the uniform act.

Respondent points out, however, that § 11 requires that, in order for a person erroneously believing himself to be a limited partner to escape liability as a general partner, he must, upon discovering his mistake, promptly renounce his interest in the profits of the business. It is the claim of respondent that no proper renunciation was made in this case. But the statute does not specify any particular form which this renunciation should take. It will be recalled that Mr. Griffith never took any profits from this business, and so was not under any obligation to pay them into court. . . . He did, however, execute a bill of sale by the terms of which he conveyed all of his interest in the limited partnership to the general partners in the concern. This appears to have been done as soon as he learned that the creditors of the Midfield Packers were attempting to hold him as a general partner.

We think this relinquishing of all of his claims against the assets of the Midfield Packers was sufficient compliance with the requirements of § 11. . . .

But respondent urges that Mr. Griffith, by reason of his activity in the affairs of the alleged limited partnership, lost his status as a special partner and became a general partner. It is true that among the instruments introduced in evidence was one entitled "BY-LAWS OF MIDFIELD PACKERS, A Limited Co-Partnership," which provided that the affairs of the partnership should be handled by a board of directors composed of three members of the copartnership; and that Mr. Griffith was named therein as one of the directors. However, he testified that he never functioned as such, and, in fact, respondent, in his brief, does not appear to contend, and Mr. Griffith vigorously denies, that he in any sense managed the affairs of the concern or had the power to initiate and control the execution of policy. Respondent's charge of unwarranted participation is largely based upon two warranty deeds in which the grantees are named as "Herbert H. Huber, G. I. Griffith, and Harold A. Schmitt, copartners doing business as Midfield Packers"; and upon a number of documents purportedly executed by Mr. Griffith, together with the admitted general partners, as copartner in the firm of Midfield Packers. These include a power of attorney, purporting to be signed by the general partners, and by Griffith, "d/b/a Midfield Packers"; an agreement with the Peoples National Bank, signed by the general partners and by Griffith, "d/b/a Midfield Packers"; an instrument purporting to be a contract, signed by Griffith for Midfield Packers; and certain leases, signed by the general partners and by Griffith, "Partners doing business under the firm name of Midfield Packers." It does not appear that respondent was acquainted with most of these exhibits, or that he extended credit to the partnership on the faith of Mr. Griffith's apparent status as a general partner. One of the warranty deeds, first mentioned above, was introduced in the *Baumer Foods* case [an earlier case involving substantially the same question which was litigated in the federal courts—*ed.*]; and the following finding of fact was also made by the court therein:

"That the defendant, G. I. Griffith, took no part in the business of the Midfield Packers except that some time in the spring of 1945 he accompanied the managing partner, H. H. Huber, to Seattle to negotiate a loan from the Sun Life Assurance Company with which to construct a building for said partnership, and negotiated with A. G. Homann, a contractor, for the construction of said building."

In spite of this finding, neither the Federal district court nor the circuit court of appeals appears to have had any difficulty in holding that Mr. Griffith remained a limited partner. Although the evidence introduced in this case indicates a greater participation in the business by Mr. Griffith than did the evidence introduced in the *Baumer Foods* case, it does not appear to be different in quality or to indicate that his status in the concern varied in any degree from his status as it appeared to the courts which decided that case. We call attention once more to the fact that it is not alleged that respondent ever relied on Mr. Griffith's position as a general partner, or in fact ever understood that Mr. Griffith was anything other than a limited partner. Under these circumstances, we see no reason for holding Mr. Griffith liable to respondent as a general partner.

. . . It appears to us that, Mr. Griffith not having intended to be, and not having been in fact, a general partner in the Midfield Packers, he should not be held liable for the debts herein involved.

The judgments appealed from are accordingly reversed, and the causes dismissed as to the appellants.

NOTES

1. The problems of interpretation and of setting limits under the control test of Section 7 of the ULPA are explored in a thoughtful article by Feld, *The "Control" Test for Limited Partnerships,* 82 HARV. L. REV. 1471 (1969). Feld raises and discusses different possible constructions of the language in Section 7, as well as highlighting several other problem areas in the ULPA. He observes that there appear to be only three cases which have applied Section 7 to difficult fact situations. The *Rathke* case was one; the other two are Silvola v. Rowlett, 129 Colo. 522, 272 P.2d 287 (1954) (en banc) and Grainger v. Antoyan, 48 Cal. 2d 805, 313 P.2d 848 (1957), *noted in* 56 MICH. L. REV. 285 (1957). Feld notes that these decisions do not attempt to state a general standard for determining when the control test is met nor to articulate the policy underlying the statute.

2. A limited partnership is formed when the certificate required by Section 2 of the ULPA is filed. Note that, among other things, it must disclose the names of all partners, the nature and amount of the limited partners' contributions, and the share of profits or other compensation to be paid to the limited partners. Sections 2(2), 5, 6, and 7 of the ULPA describe circumstances under which a limited partner can lose his exemption from personal liability. These include having his name in the partnership name in violation of the statute, lack of substantial compliance in good faith with the filing requirement, knowing falsehood in the certificate of limited partnership, and control. As Feld points out, all of these events except the control test are sufficiently specific that the limited partner can easily determine whether he has complied.

3. The court in *Rathke* held that a limited partner would lose his exemption from personal liability only if the creditor could show he relied on the apparent status of the limited partner as a general partner. Is this reliance qualification mandated by the language of the Act? Is it for all of the events described

in note 2 above under which a limited partner loses his protection from personal liability? If so, would the protection granted to a secret or dormant partner be roughly equivalent to that of a fully qualified limited partner? Would it be even if he actually exercised control?

4. Section 11 of the ULPA also extends protection to a limited partner who is not fully qualified. Does this apply to all of the events described in note 2 above? What is meant by the phrase "promptly renounces his interest in the profit of the business"? (Note that this language is reminiscent of the reasoning in *Waugh v. Carver*, p. 338 *supra.*) Does this mean he has to return all profits previously paid to him? It would under the *Waugh* rationale, wouldn't it? *See* Gilman Paint & Varnish Co. v. Legum, 197 Md. 665, 80 A.2d 906 (1951), *noted in* 31 BOSTON U. L. REV. 561 (1951) *and* 26 N.Y. U. L. REV. 717 (1951).

5. Section 9 of the ULPA states that control of a limited partnership is vested in the general partners subject, however, to the requirement that the limited partners consent in writing to or ratify certain actions taken by the general partner or partners. The circumstances (there are seven) under which this limitation of authority apply are described in Section 9.

6. All partners, general and limited, must execute any amendments to the certificate (§ 25(1)(b)). The certificate "shall" be amended upon ten contingencies. See Section 24(2), which also describes the contingencies. What are the consequences if the partnership fails to amend the certificate after one of the contingencies occurs, such as a change in the amount or character of the contribution of a limited partner?

7. Limited partners are entitled to have the partnership books kept at the partnership's principal place of business, to inspect and copy the books, to demand information on "all things affecting the partnership," to demand a formal account of partnership affairs "whenever circumstances render it just and reasonable," to have dissolution by judicial decree, to share in the profits and withdraw their contributions from the partnership (all in §§ 10, 15 and 16) and to make loans to the partnership (§ 13) and to assign their interests (§ 19).

8. To what extent can the rights and limitations specified in the above notes be altered by the partnership agreement? Does the ULPA cover this? *See* Section 9(f), which, however, does not cover all situations.

9. The limited partnership form of doing business and investing enjoys considerable use beyond the small business enterprise involved in the *Rathke* case. Because of the flow-through features

of the partnership form under the federal income tax laws, it is an attractive form of enterprise for wealthy investors. Persons in a high tax bracket can purchase units of a limited partnership that is, for example, constructing or buying a building, and take the depreciation allowed directly against their ordinary income, as well as enjoy limited liability. The limited partnership thus has proved an attractive device for raising capital, and pressure has existed to allow limited partnerships to "go public" so that substantial amounts of capital can be generated in one "offering." *See* Hrusoff and Cazares, *Formation of the Public Limited Partnership,* 22 HASTINGS L. J. 87 (1970), describing the experience in California with this device. The authors note that as late as 1961 a California appellate court was saying,

> In *bona fide* limited partnerships, there is the right of *delectus personam,* the right to determine membership. No partner is admitted without unanimous approval of every other partner. . . . [M]emberships are never indiscriminately offered at random to the public at large. [*See* Rivlin v. Levine, 195 Cal. App. 2d 13, 21, 15 Cal. Rptr. 587, 592 (1961).]

In 1968, however, a statute was passed in California making possible the creation of publicly held limited partnerships. *See* CAL. CORP. CODE §§ 25000-804, and the regulations thereunder. CAL. AD. CODE tit. 10, §§ 260.140.110-.115 (1968). Not all jurisdictions have such legislation. And it involves a legislative alteration to the ULPA, thereby affecting uniformity. The Hrusoff article states that this type of limited partnership thus far has been used only in oil and gas explorations, feed lots and real estate ventures.

The California legislation allows any type of business to be conducted by limited partnerships except banking or insurance. Approximately half of the jurisdictions impose some restrictions on the type of business that may be conducted by limited partnerships, usually banking and insurance. *See* the "Action in Adopting Jurisdictions" section under 6 UNIF. LAWS ANNOT., UNIFORM LIMITED PARTNERSHIP ACT § 3, at 578 (1969).

The Hrusoff article discusses the legal problems connected with the formation of a public limited partnership. The fundamental ULPA statutory requisites apply to this specialized entity too. One general partner and one limited partner are always required. (Surprisingly, the general partner can be a corporation in some states, with limited liability thereby being completely achieved. *See* Note, *The Corporate Partner: An Exercise in Semantics,* 35 N.Y.U.L. 548, 552-53 (1960); Armstrong, *Can Corporations Be Partners?,* 20 BUS. LAW 899 (1965).)

In addition, Hrusoff points out that special legal problems are involved in the public limited partnership. One, ironically, is that this entity runs the risk of being classified as an "association" under the Internal Revenue Code and thus being taxed as a corporation. *See* INT. REV. CODE of 1954, § 7701(a)(3). The standards for determining this are continuity of life of the entity, centralized management, limited liability and free transferability of interests. *See* Morrisey v. Commissioner, 296 U. S. 344 (1935). Some large public limited partnerships run perilously close to "qualifying" under those standards, although Hrusoff indicates that competent drafting can avoid this problem today (noting, with a trace of apprehension, that the existing nonaggressive policy of the IRS toward the public limited partnership may change). See Hrusoff, *Id.* at 100-108.

Also, if a limited partnership is large enough, its ownership interests (or "units") will be classified as "securities" and they will, depending on the facts, have to register with the Securities and Exchange Commission or with the state Securities Commissioners. *Id.* at 108-118.

10.   In addition to the literature cited above, *see* F. TROUBAT, THE LAW OF COMMANDATORY AND LIMITED PARTNERSHIP IN THE UNITED STATES (1853); Note, *The Limited Partnership*, 45 YALE L.J. 895 (1936); Crane, *Are Limited Partnerships Necessary—The Return of the Commenda*, 17 MINN. L. REV. 351 (1933); Lewis, *The Uniform Limited Partnership Act*, 65 U. PA. L. REV. 715 (1917).

PROBLEMS

1.   The Tovell Construction Company consists of two general partners, each of whom had contributed $25,000 to the capital, and Legum, a limited partner who had contributed $150,000. A certificate of limited partnership was filed on December 1, 1964 in a state which had adopted the ULPA. It stated that the partnership would exist for two years. Another certificate extending the term for an additional two years was notarized on December 1, 1966, but not filed until July 30, 1970 (a third certificate, extending the term from month to month after January 31, 1968, also was not filed until July 30, 1970).

On December 31, 1966, $13,400 of profits was distributed to Legum. Between that date and January 1, 1970, $7,000 of profits were credited to Legum's partnership account. He paid income taxes on that amount, but did not withdraw it from the firm.

In January, 1970, plaintiff sold $5,000 worth of paint goods to the Company. His bill was not paid. He sued Legum, who pleaded that he was a limited partner. How would you, as counsel for the plaintiff, respond to that defense? Would Legum in turn have an effective response? If you were Legum's attorney, what action, if any, would you advise him to take?

a. In what manner, if at all, would it affect your analysis if Legum's initial capital contribution had consisted of $100,000 cash, a promissory note to the Company of $35,000, and $15,000 which was fairly and reasonably calculated as the value of Legum's work in drafting the necessary papers, obtaining the various licenses required and obtaining a line of credit for the new business at a bank?

b. Would your analysis of the main problem be affected if Legum had been instrumental in obtaining construction contracts for the new business during the first three years of its existence, and then had turned his attention to other matters?

2. For many years Mr. Little and Miss Sheldon had conducted separate insurance businesses in Fair Haven, Vermont. For the last seven years, however, they have operated a consolidated agency under a written agreement. During this period Little acted as sole manager. Miss Sheldon lived in another town and took no part in the enterprise. Little submitted a written report on the business to Miss Sheldon at the end of each year.

Their written agreement provided that the combined agencies should be run as the property of Miss Sheldon and under the name of the Sheldon Agency; that Little would devote his entire working time to the management of the business; that the net profits would be equally divided between the two parties; that no substantial increases in management expenses would be incurred without Miss Sheldon's approval and that she could terminate the arrangement at any time and discharge Little as manager by paying him a sum equal to one-half the earnings for the past year.

Miss Sheldon sued Little in assumpsit to recover balances due during the last five years. Little moved to dismiss on the ground that the parties were partners and thus plaintiff's proper action was in equity for an accounting and not at law in assumpsit. What result? See Sheldon v. Little, 111 Vt. 301, 15 A.2d 574, 137 A.L.R. 1 (1940).

a. Would your answer change if the suit was brought against Miss Sheldon by one Sam Jones, seeking damages for the losses he sustained as a result of certain misrepresentations concerning insurance coverage which Little had made and on which he (Jones) had relied? What if the misrepresentations had instead related to the commercial desirability and zoning of some property on the outskirts of Fair Haven?

b. Would your answer to the main problem change if the suit was brought against Miss Sheldon and Mr. Little by Fred Peters, the owner of the building in which the business was located, for unpaid rent? Would you need to know any additional facts? Would it affect your answer under this variation if instead the suit were brought by a salesman of office equipment for unpaid bills due on new office equipment which Little had ordered?

3. A group of individuals wish to invest capital in an enterprise that will engage in investment activities. The group is divided roughly into two categories: those with money, and those with (or who purport to have) investment skills. The money group decide, on legal advice, to invest through the limited partnership form as limited partners. They have chosen this form because of the limited liability, which is important because some of the investments may expose the partnership to liability, and because of the flow-through feature under the tax laws of losses and gains. The group has rejected electing to be a corporation taxed as a partnership under Subchapter S of the Internal Revenue Code because there are more than ten people in the group and because it is likely that more than twenty per cent of the enterprise's gross receipts will be passive investment income.

The limited partner group will contribute ninety-five per cent of the capital and will receive eighty per cent of the partnership profits and losses. The group with investment skills will contribute five per cent of the capital, will receive twenty per cent of the profits, and will be the general partners. They will manage the enterprise, including making the day to day investment decisions.

The limited partners want to protect their investment and have asked you whether the following protective measures present any legal problems:

a. Although the general partners will manage the ordinary investment activities, it is unlikely as a practical matter that major commitments of capital will be made without informing the limited partners and perhaps obtaining their consent. The limited partners are entirely content with this. What risks, if any, does this create?

b. The limited partners want the power reserved in the agreement:

   (i)   to limit the salaries paid to the general partners;

  (ii) to prevent the general partners from becoming partners or directors in other businesses; and

 (iii) to prevent the general partners from acting as accommodation endorsers or guarantors of the commercial instruments of others.

Again, what risks are run under these circumstances? Does the cumulative effect of reserving all three of the above limitations pose a different problem than each limitation treated alone?

c. Assume that one of the limited partners, Smith, contributes marketable stock of a corporation controlled by him. The partnership will be able to borrow against the stock and make investments, and any gain or loss in the value of the stock will affect only Smith's account. Smith wants to reserve the power to prevent the partnership from selling, otherwise disposing of or unduly encumbering the stock he contributed. What risks does he run, if any, in reserving these powers?

See Feld, The "Control" Test for Limited Partnership, 82 HARV. L. REV. 1471 (1969), from which the above problem is adapted.

4. Hubbard, the manager of a used car business which Cullingworth had sold several years earlier, decided to open his own lot and asked Cullingworth if he would "back" him. Cullingworth replied that he would, provided Hubbard secured a lot, completed it for the conduct of business and would sell the cars promptly.

Hubbard rented a lot, contracted for utility services, obtained liability insurance and filed an application for a license stating that he was the sole owner. The license was granted in the name of Hubbard Used Cars, and was displayed on the wall of his office in the lot. Hubbard opened up a bank account in his name and hired, paid and discharged all the employees.

Cullingworth attended auctions with Hubbard and paid for cars purchased. If Cullingworth did not agree on a vehicle, Hubbard did not buy it since he did not have the immediate cash necessary at an auction. The titles to the cars purchased were put in the name of Hubbard Used Cars, and Cullingworth held the titles as security until the cars were sold. He and Hubbard split the profits on each car financed by Cullingworth. There was no agreement as to losses.

Hubbard did purchase other cars on his own account through credit arrangements. Cullingworth did not share in the profits from the sales of cars that he did not finance.

Cullingworth stayed at the lot about half the time during business hours. He answered telephone calls on occasion and sold several cars.

One of the businesses which had sold Hubbard cars without Cullingworth financing did not receive the balance due. It sued both Hubbard and Cullingworth, claiming that they were partners. This issue was submitted by the trial court to the jury, which found that a partnership existed.

Cullingworth has appealed this decision. What arguments would you make on his behalf? Assume that the UPA is in force in the particular jurisdiction.

5. On April 9, 1969, a document entitled "Amendment of Certificate of Limited Partnership" was executed and filed in the appropriate state office by the Marlbeck Motor Company, reciting that Albert Antoyan was being added as a limited partner to the firm. The document stated that Antoyan had contributed $1000, and that he had loaned the Company $50,000, to be repaid in installments of $750 per month or ten per cent of the profits, whichever was greater. Upon satisfaction of the loan he would continue to get ten per cent of the profits. The loan was secured by a chattel mortgage on the inventory of the Company.

Antoyan was employed by Marlbeck Motor Company from January 1, 1967, to approximately April of 1970. In 1968 he became sales manager. He sold new cars, had an office and had salesmen working under him. He had no authority to hire or fire the people under him nor authority to order new cars without the consent of Mr. Marlbeck. He followed a formula set by Mr. Marlbeck on calculating trade-in allowances to customers purchasing new cars. He had nothing to do with the used car aspect of the business, nor with running the general office.

In April, 1969, Antoyan was authorized to co-sign checks of the Company. He did so only when Mr. Marlbeck was out of town or indisposed. Antoyan never bought anything and paid for it by a check drawn on the Company's account.

In April of 1970, Antoyan left the employ of the Company and never returned to work for them. Soon thereafter the Company went bankrupt and Antoyan was sued by the creditors, who claimed he was liable for the debts of the firm. What result? *See* Grainger v. Antoyan, 48 Cal. 2d 805, 313 P.2d 848 (1957), *noted in* 56 MICH. L. REV. 285 (1957).

Chapter 13

PARTNERSHIP PROPERTY

As you know, a partnership can be created and, more importantly, run with considerable informality. Although this makes things easier in the day to day operation of the business, it does tend toward confusion as to who owns what, particularly in the small businesses. The following materials will deal with the problem of inadequate specification of ownership by the partners. Also, the definition of good will, that intangible which occasionally can be of great value, and whether it normally is considered partnership property, will be briefly covered. Finally, the partnership form historically has had trouble adjusting to real estate law. The historical problems will be summarized, as will be the UPA sections responding to them.

A. WHEN IS PROPERTY OWNED BY THE PARTNERSHIP?

This question arises with some frequency when an informally run partnership is involved, with partners freely commingling their personal and business assets and with the partnership agreement vague as to who contributed what. As the following case will demonstrate, the law has established certain presumptions in an effort to deal fairly when disputes arise concerning the ownership of assets.

QUINN v. LEIDINGER
New Jersey Court of Chancery
107 N.J. Eq. 188, 152 A. 249 (1930),
aff'd, 110 N.J. Eq. 663, 160 A. 537 (1932)

LEWIS, V. C. This matter is before the court on exceptions to the master's report after hearings on bill for an accounting.

In 1925 complainant and one Harry C. Leidinger formed a partnership to conduct a real estate business and to share equally in the profits. Subsequently two corporations were organized by them for convenience in conducting their business. Each of these corporations had a nominal amount of stock which was held

361

equally between them. The business was conducted and the assets
and business of the two corporations were handled substantially as
though the corporations did not exist, the two corporations being
used by the partners apparently as a mere matter of convenience
and the lines between the corporate and individual transactions of
the partners were substantially ignored. On July 18th, 1928, Harry
C. Leidinger died as a result of an accident. At the time of his
death there was an insurance policy payable to his estate in the
sum of $25,000, with a double indemnity clause in case of acci-
dental death. This policy was collected in the sum of $50,000 by
Anna M. Leidinger as administratrix of the estate of Harry C.
Leidinger. After this action was commenced and by stipulation
Anna M. Leidinger was made a party defendant to the action in
her representative capacity as administratrix of her husband's
estate.

The master found there were certain charges and credits as
between the respective partners. The master found as against
the claim of the complainant [and found] that the $50,000, the
proceeds of the insurance policy of Harry C. Leidinger, was not
a partnership asset. The sole ground of exception to the master's
report is based on his failure to find that the complainant is to
be credited with a one-half interest in this insurance policy.

Complainant contends that it was the intention of the partners that this policy should enure to the benefit of the partnership.

The master found that the contention of the complainant
that the policy on the life of Leidinger was impressed with
a trust in favor of the partnership was not sustained because
the complainant's proofs did not measure up to the standard
fixed by law in that they were not sufficiently definite, reliable
and convincing. In my opinion, however, the proofs do show
with sufficient certainty that it was the intention of the parties
that the insurance should be for the benefit of the partnership.
The history of the policy taken out on Leidinger's life as well
as that taken out on complainant's life seems to show this. In
December, 1927, the partners wished to secure a loan for the
financing of a transaction in which they were interested. The
president of the bank, to whom they applied for the loan, said to
them: "How do you stand on your insurance; how are you fixed
as far as your insurance goes? What would happen to the remaining party if one of you fellows died?" The partners then proceeded
to investigate the question of insurance, although before any
insurance was taken out they had secured the loan from the bank
in question. They first saw an insurance broker who testified that
they told him that they discussed with him the form of policy

that could be used to protect business interests of each partner. This broker further testified that complainant said in the presence of Leidinger: "We want this insurance so if anything happens to either one of us, the one of us who is left will have the money to wind up the business or to carry on as he sees fit." The broker told them, erroneously it would seem, that insurance could not be taken out payable to the partnership, and told them it would be necessary for each of them to take out insurance on his own life, payable to the estate of the insured. Up to this point it seems absolutely certain and there is no evidence to the contrary that the two partners intended that each should insure his life for the benefit of the partnership. As a matter of fact, each of them applied for $25,000 of insurance. Complainant's application was accepted and the policy issued to him, but Leidinger's application was rejected because he was found to be overweight. A few months later, namely, April, 1928, Leidinger was accepted as impaired risk in another company. The face of the policy was $25,000, with double indemnity in case of accidental death. This second policy was taken out through another broker who testified he asked Leidinger, "Whom shall we make beneficiary? As long as this is going to be partnership insurance, who is going to be beneficiary?" As Leidinger had already been advised by his broker that the partnership could not be named as beneficiary he naturally answered: "That question has already been thrashed out as to the beneficiary."

The premiums on both the policies were paid from the partnership funds. The Partnership act, laws of 1919, chapter 212, section 8, subdivision 2, provides: "Unless the contrary intention appears, property acquired with partnership funds is partnership property."* The section is perhaps not controlling since it is undisputed that these partners were in the habit of indiscriminately paying individual obligations with partnership funds. There is no evidence whatever that it was the intention of the partners in regard to these two insurance policies that they should not be partnership funds, except such conclusion as can be reached from the fact that the policies were taken out payable to the individual estates. It seems perfectly clear, however, that the naming of individual beneficiaries was based wholly on the statement of the broker that no other course could be pursued. The broker Stowe, who wrote the policy on complainant's life, testified that when the partners discussed the form of policy complainant said: "We want this insurance so if anything happens to either one of us, the one of us who is left will have the money to wind up

---

* UPA § 8 (2).

the business, or to carry on as he sees fit." Such an expression could have no meaning if on the death of one of the partners the proceeds of the insurance on his life were to go to his individual estate. It could only have meaning if the proceeds of the policy were to go to the benefit of the partnership.

The defendant lays stress upon the fact that complainant paid no further premiums and allowed his policy to lapse after the death of Leidinger. I cannot see that this has any bearing, since if the policy on complainant's life was for the benefit of the partnership and since the partnership terminated on Leidinger's death, there would be no occasion to carry insurance any longer for the benefit of the partnership.

From the foregoing it seems clear to me that the partners intended to take out insurance on the lives of both of them so as to protect the partnership in case of the death of either of them. The insurance was taken out on the life of each partner and it is immaterial that the insurance was taken out in the individual names, since the proceeds of each policy would be in trust for the benefit of the partnership. I find ample evidence to sustain the contention of the complainant as to the existence of this agreement and I do not find any evidence inconsistent therewith and accordingly the exceptions to the master's report are sustained. I find that the complainant is entitled on this accounting to a credit for one-half of the insurance policy on the life of Leidinger.

NOTES

1. The opinion in the instant case refers to Section 8(2) of the UPA, which establishes a presumption to aid in resolving the confused ownership cases. Note, however, that it was of little aid in the case since "the partners indiscriminately paid individual obligations with partnership funds." What law does the court then turn to in resolving the case before it? Does Section 8 of the UPA, entitled "Partnership Property," contain any other language which would aid in a confused ownership case?

2. In 1964 Curtis Cyrus wrote his brother Cecil in North Dakota urging him to come to Minnesota to go into partnership in a resort venture. Curtis recently had purchased a 60 acre tract of land in Minnesota with his own funds and in his own name. Cecil, a skilled carpenter, found the idea attractive and moved his family to a rented house near the tract in December, 1965. Cecil soon built a cabin on the tract and moved his family into it. He thereafter built six other cabins which were operated as

a resort. The expense of building the cabins was paid for out of operating earnings. Curtis personally paid the taxes on the land and purchased the boats used in the business. There is a conflict of testimony whether he was reimbursed for these expenditures out of resort earnings. In 1967 an additional 40 acre tract was purchased in Curtis's name. Again, there was a conflict of testimony on whether he was reimbursed out of resort earnings.

Cecil received the living expenses for his family out of resort earnings. He contributed his labor to the project, his wife did all the washing, ironing and cleaning, and their three children, the oldest of whom was 18, helped with the resort work. Curtis remained regularly employed in Minneapolis. He did not contribute any personal work to the operation of the resort "other than to build an occasional cabin shelf while on his vacation." The earnings of the resort were accounted for every fall and Curtis was given his one-half share.

Cecil died in December, 1971. His widow is not interested in remaining at the resort, and would like her share of the business evaluated and paid to her. She wants one-half of the entire value of the resort business, including the fair market value of the land. Curtis objects to this, claiming that the land is his and not property of the partnership. If you were representing the widow, what arguments would you make on her behalf and on what authority? *See* Cyrus v. Cyrus, 242 Minn. 180, 64 N.W.2d 538, 45 A.L.R.2d 1002 (1954).

a. Suppose that soon after Cecil's funeral Curtis had told the widow that he would deed half the place to her, saying, "It's yours as much as mine." Of what legal significance would his statement be, assuming you could prove it?

b. In what manner, if at all, would it alter your analysis made above in the main problem if Cecil had died in June, 1966?

c. Would it affect your analysis of the main problem if Curtis had purchased the 60 acre tract of land already complete with buildings, boats, and so forth, and the arrangement between the parties was otherwise the same?

d. Would it vary your analysis of the main problem if the claim that the land was a partnership asset was being made by a creditor of the partnership?

3. The necessity for clearly spelling out ownership interests in the partnership agreement can be brought more closely home by taking the case of an established lawyer with a fairly substantial library who forms a partnership with a young lawyer. Nothing is said about the library in their informal, oral agree-

ment. They practice together for five years, during which time various supplements and other publications are purchased. The partnership then dissolves, by mutual but acrimonious agreement of the two partners. Does the older lawyer run a serious risk of losing one-half the value of his library to the younger lawyer?

4. See, on the problem of distinguishing partnership property from separate property, CRANE & BROMBERG ON PARTNERSHIP 202-221; 1 ROWLEY ON PARTNERSHIP 183-219.

B. GOOD WILL

IN RE BROWN
Court of Appeals of New York
242 N.Y. 1, 150 N.E. 581, 44 A.L.R. 510 (1926)
Noted in 41 Harv. L. Rev. 803 (1928)

CARDOZO, J. Vernon C. Brown & Company were stockbrokers for many years in the city of New York. Stephen H. Brown, one of the partners, died. The survivors, denying that there was any good will to be accounted for, continued the business at the old stand and in the old name. The executors acquiesced. For so acquiescing they have been held to be at fault, and their accounts have been surcharged accordingly. The question is whether the decree may be sustained.

The Browns, Vernon and Stephen, were brothers. They began business in 1895 with one Watson, under the name of Watson & Brown. In 1901 Watson withdrew, and the brothers went on. "Vernon C. Brown & Company" became the name of the continued partnership. New members were admitted from time to time, but the firm name remained unchanged. Good will was not mentioned in the partnership articles or in any books of account. Incoming members did not pay anything for it. One member, Mr. Schoonmaker, retired while Stephen Brown was alive. If good will was an asset, he was entitled to share in it. The evidence is uncontradicted that nothing was paid him. We may infer that in the thought of the partners nothing was due.

At the outset, Stephen Brown like his brother was active in the business. He had a seat on the Exchange, and represented the firm upon the floor. Falling ill in 1912, he sold his seat, and, though leaving his capital intact, gave no services thereafter. His share of the profits, which before his illness had been thirty-three per cent, was gradually reduced till at his death in July, 1917, it was only fifteen per cent. The business was lucrative, though it was run, one would gather, in a more or less old-fashioned and conservative way, without advertising in newspapers or solicitation of accounts. It had four branches or departments: (1) The general commission business; (2) the so-called "odd lot" business, which proved to be the most lucrative of all; (3) the so-called "two-dollar" business; and (4) speculative business transacted for the firm itself. There is a finding that all the branches of the business except the last had in them an element of good will for which the survivors were accountable. The net profits of the three branches were averaged for a period of three years, allowance being made for interest on capital and for the personal services rendered by the partners. The value of the good will was fixed at two years' purchase price of the profits so computed. On this basis, the value was $103,891.60, of which 15%, $15,-583.74, was the share due to the estate. The surrogate, confirming the report of a referee, held that the accounts of the executors were to be surcharged for failing to collect this amount from the survivors. The Appellate Division unanimously affirmed.

The books abound in definitions of good will (People *ex rel.* Johnson Co. v. Roberts, 159 N. Y. 70, 80; Von Bremen v. Mac-Monnies, 200 N. Y. 41, 47). There is no occasion to repeat them. Men will pay for any privilege that gives a reasonable expectancy of preference in the race of competition (cf. Walton Water Co. v. Village of Walton, 238 N. Y. 46, 50). Such expectancy may come from succession in place or name or otherwise to a business that has won the favor of its customers. It is then known as good will. Many are the degrees of value. At one extreme there are expectancies so strong that the advantage derived from economic opportunity may be said to be a certainty. At the other are expectancies so weak that for any rational mind they may be said to be illusory. We must know the facts in any case.

Good will, when it exists as incidental to the business of a partnership, is presumptively an asset to be accounted for like any other by those who liquidate the business (Slater v. Slater, 175 N. Y. 143; Matter of David & Matthews, 1899, 1 Ch. 378; Witkowsky v. Affeld, 283 Ill. 557). The course of dealing, however, can stamp it with a different quality. Partners may contract that good will, though it exist, shall not "be considered as property or as an asset of the co-partnership" (Douthart v. Logan, 190 Ill. 243, 252; Witkowsky v. Affeld, *supra*). The contract may "be expressly made," or it may "arise by implication, from other contracts and the acts and conduct of the parties" (*Douthart v. Logan, supra*). The implication will be drawn the more readily when the good will, if any, is tenuous or doubtful. Upon this appeal, the form of the findings precludes us from adjudging that the distribution of what would otherwise be an asset has been varied by agreement. We state, however, for the guidance of the trial court, that evidence exists from which such an agreement may be gathered. The trier of the facts might not unreasonably infer from the course of dealing between the partners when new members came in and old ones went out that by tacit understanding there was to be no accounting for good will. No doubt there must be caution before property interests of value are thus excluded by implication. The life of the business must be scrutinized for every relevant circumstance affecting the intention of the partners. The inference is one of fact, to be drawn, if at all, when intention is thus appraised and probabilities are measured.

Assuming for present purposes that the disposition of good will has not been varied by agreement, we reach the question whether there was any good will to be disposed of upon the facts recited in the findings. To answer that question, we must consider at the outset what rights would have passed to a buyer of the good will if the surviving partners had sold it in the course of liquidation. The chief elements of value upon any sale of a good will are, *first*, continuity of place, and, *second*, continuity of name (People *ex rel*. Johnson Co. v. Roberts, 159 N. Y. 70, at p. 83). There may indeed at times be others, *e. g.*, continuity of organization. That element is of value in business of a complex order. Where the business is simple, the benefits of organization are slight and not so easily transmitted. Confining ourselves now to the two chief elements of value, we may assume that the buyer of this good will would have been reasonably assured of continuity of place. The firm offices were the same from the beginning of the business till the death of Stephen Brown and later. There is nothing to show that the survivors, genuinely endeavoring to dispose of the good will, would have been unable to deliver possession to a buyer of the lease. A more difficult question is presented when we ask to what extent there would have been continuity of name. "Vernon C. Brown & Co." was not an arbitrary symbol, like The Snyder Mfg. Co., *e. g.*, in *Snyder Mfg. Co. v. Snyder* (54 Ohio St. 86). It had not gained a secondary meaning supplanting a primary meaning which had been descriptive of a man or men, and instead identifying impersonally an organization or a product. Writ large in this style or title was the name of a living man who had done nothing by word or act to give the name a reality or a significance external to himself. A buyer of the good will would gain no right to the use of any style or title whereby this man would be represented as still a partner in the business. We assume that in conducting the new business he would be privileged to describe himself, subject, however, to the rules of the Exchange, as the "successor" to the old one (Moore v. Rawson, 199 Mass. 493, 497, 499). He would not be suffered to go farther. One who writes his name at large in the style or title of a partnership does not dedicate to the partnership, by force of that act alone without other tokens of intention, the right to sell the name at auction upon every change of membership.

We do not overlook the provisions of the statute (Partnership Law, § 80, subd. 1; formerly Partnership Law, § 20 [Cons. Laws, ch. 39]) whereby partnership names are made capable of transfer to the successors to a business.* The sole effect of that provision is to give the approval of the law to a use that would otherwise be criminal though a transfer were attempted (*Slater v. Slater, supra,* at p. 149; Caswell v. Hazard, 121 N. Y. 484, 496). The statute tells us what the partners are at liberty to assign. It does not tell us what they are under a duty to assign. A case in Wisconsin states their duty in that regard with clarity and precision (Rowell v. Rowell, 122 Wis. 1). A name which in popular thought is solely or predominantly the name of a living man, may not be sold against his protest as it might if it were the impersonal symbol of an organization or a product. The objection is not merely that the partner whose name is thus appropriated may be exposed to the risk of liability for debts of the continued business (Burchell v. Wilde, 1900, 1 Ch. 551; Thynne v. Shove, 45 Ch. D. 577). If that were all, he might be adequately protected by the certificate which his successors must file under the statute (*Slater v. Slater, supra*). He would remain exposed to other perils though this one were averted. Business designed for him might be diverted to some one else. Worse than this, he might suffer in standing or good name "by reason of inferiority of goods or dishonorable business conduct to which he is thereby made ostensibly a party" (*Rowell v. Rowell, supra*). A different situation presents itself when the name is "arbitrary or fancy" (*Rowell v. Rowell, supra*). The like is true when, though it may have once have designated a person, it has "practically become an artificial one, designating nothing but the establishment" (*Rowell v. Rowell, supra,* at p. 20, citing Rogers v. Taintor, 97 Mass. 291; *Slater v. Slater, supra*).

Slater v. Slater (supra), if it stands for more than this, must be limited accordingly. We think that more was not intended. Border cases will at times occur. The *Slater* case was one of them. Even there, however, the court recognized the distinction between names purely personal or individual, and names that had acquired, through the incrustations of time, a veneer of associations artificial and impersonal (*Slater v. Slater, supra,* at p. 148).

---

* There is no corresponding section in the UPA—*Ed.*

This will happen oftener in trading partnerships than in those where the personal relation, even though not exclusive, counts for more. It will happen oftener where the title contains the surnames only of the members than it will when individuals are identified more sharply (Lindley on Partnership, pp. 540, 541). The question in last analysis is one of probable intention. To answer it we must know whether by reasonable intendment as gathered from the nature of the business and the course of dealing, the partner whose name is appropriated by a stranger has given consent to his associates to submit to an impersonation so disturbing and deceptive. In the record before us there is neither finding of consent nor evidence pointing to the conclusion that consent should be implied.

We have said that the members of the old firm might compete without restraint, after a sale of the good will, with the members of the new one. There are distinctions in that regard between voluntary and involuntary sales (Von Bremen v. MacMonnies, 200 N. Y. 41). After a voluntary sale, the seller, though he may compete, may not drum up or circularize the customers of the business. After a sale *in invitum,* he is not subject to a disability so heavy. For the purpose of this distinction, a sale by surviving partners upon a liquidation of the business, is a sale coerced by law (Hutchinson v. Nay, 187 Mass. 262; *Moore v. Rawson, supra*). The survivors may indeed be bound as upon a voluntary sale if they have given the transaction such an aspect in the eyes of the buyer (Caswell v. Hazard, 121 N. Y. 484, 495; Lindley on Partnership, p. 543). The representative of the deceased partner, however, has no cause for complaint if by appropriate recitals or reservations they disclose its involuntary quality and thus limit its effect. Their duty as liquidators is done when they convey what would be conveyed upon a sale by a receiver (*Hutchinson v. Nay, supra*).

We conclude, then, that a buyer of this good will, if it had been put up for sale by the liquidating partners, would have had the benefit at most of continuity of place and of such continuity of name as would belong to a "successor." We have next to consider the relation of these benefits to the several branches or departments in which the business was conducted.

(1) There is a finding, unanimously affirmed, that appurtenant to the general commission branch was an element of good will not incapable of conveyance. We cannot say that this finding is qualified by others to such an extent that as a matter of law it must be disregarded as erroneous. The buyer of the good will would take over the firm records, which would give the names of the old customers. He would be in a position to

notify them that he had succeeded to the business. True the old
partners might send out notices that they were still in business
for themselves. None the less, some customers might wander into
the old place from forgetfulness or habit. Once there, inertia
might lead them to give an order to brokers whom they found
established in possession (Hill v. Fearis, 1905, 1 Ch. 466, stockbrokers; Rutan v. Coolidge, 241 Mass. 584, architects; Witkowsky
v. Affeld, 283 Ill. 557, insurance brokers). The relation is not so
distinctly personal or professional that good will is excluded
either for reasons of public policy or as an inference of law
(Bailly v. Betti, 241 N. Y. 22; Blakely v. Sousa, 197 Penn. St. 305;
Messer v. Fadettes, 168 Mass. 140). We may doubt whether a
privilege so uncertain would be worth a great deal. The surrogate would have been justified in placing the value at a much
lower figure than he did, or even at a nominal amount (*Rutan v.
Coolidge, supra*). The question is not whether the buyer would
be willing to pay much or would be making a wise bargain. The
question is whether a reasonable man would be willing to pay
anything.

(2) The odd lot business stands on a different basis. Its essential characteristics are established by the findings. There is a
rule of the New York Stock Exchange by which the unit of trading on the floor of the Exchange is declared to be one hundred
shares. Dealings in smaller numbers of shares are known as odd
lot transactions. Most stockbrokers do not transact an odd lot
business, but there are some that do, and Vernon C. Brown &
Company was one of them. Orders for odd lots do not come
through the office. They are given on the floor of the Exchange
to the individual member or members of the firm who are its
floor representatives. They come invariably from other brokers
communicating with fellow-members of the Exchange whom they
know as individuals.

A buyer of the good will would gain nothing in respect of
this branch of the business from continuity of place. There was
no relation between such orders and the place where the firm
business was transacted. He would gain nothing from the privilege of announcing himself the successor to the business without
continuity of name. The individual brokers who had been accustomed to receive these orders from fellow-members of the
Exchange would still be on hand to receive them as before. The
findings suggest no reason why business so individual and personal should be diverted or diminished. Very likely the new firm,
when announcing its succession to the business, would advertise
the fact that its board members, if there were any, would buy and
sell odd lots. It might advertise a like readiness though the busi-

ness it was starting had no relation of succession to any that had gone before. The appeal to favor would be hardly stronger in one case than in the other. The situation would be different if the old partners had been about to withdraw from the field of competition. While they remained in the arena, the tie of succession was too attenuated to give to the buyer in transactions so individual and personal a fair promise of advantage. One cannot gain a foothold upon a ledge of opportunity so narrow. Expectancy in such conditions may be said to have reached the vanishing point at which it merges in illusion.

(3) The "two-dollar" or "specialist" business is personal and individual like the department just considered. The specialist is a broker who remains at one post of the Exchange where particular stocks are dealt in and there executes orders received from other brokers. He receives a commission of $2.50 for every 100 shares. Good will does not attach to business of this order for the same reason that none attaches to dealings in odd lots.

Mention should be made in conclusion of a provision of the will of Stephen Brown whereby his executors are relieved of responsibility for mistakes or errors of judgment. This provision may become important upon a rehearing in determining liability for the value of the good will, if any, incidental to the commission business. In the event that the value of such good will shall be found to be doubtful or insignificant, the surrogate may properly conclude that the failure to collect it was an error of judgment and nothing more.

The order of the Appellate Division and the decree of the Surrogate's Court, so far as such decree is appealed from, should be reversed, and a rehearing ordered, with costs to abide the event.

HISCOCK, Ch. J., POUND, McLAUGHLIN, CRANE, ANDREWS and LEHMAN, JJ., concur.

Order reversed, etc.

NOTES

1. As Justice Cardozo stated in the instant case, good will is "presumptively an asset to be accounted for like any other," subject to course of dealing. The recognition of good will as an asset which is normally part of the property of a partnership is reflected in the UPA. See Section 9(3)(b), requiring unanimity for the disposition of the good will of a partnership. The rights to good will thus presumably are the same as other property rights in partnership personalty.

2. Justice Cardozo mentioned later in his opinion that the presumptive recognition of good will as an asset of a partnership does not apply "for reasons of public policy or as an inference of law" if the relation between the partners is "distinctly personal or professional." What does he mean by this? Does this mean that a partnership of doctors or lawyers, or a professional singing group, presumptively does not have good will as an asset which can be sold to a new business, whether the new business consists of complete strangers buying the old partnership out or consists of the remaining partners continuing the business after one partner dies or retires (the former partnership having "dissolved")? Does this mean in addition that the partnership *cannot* contract with respect to good will, either between themselves or with strangers, "for reasons of public policy"? What policy would dictate this restriction? For that matter, what policy prescribes the absence of the usual presumption that good will exists as an asset of the firm, when dealing with personal or professional firms?

The theory apparently is that personal skills and professional qualifications are incapable of transfer (*see* CRANE & BROMBERG at 478) or, stating it another way, "Ability, skill, experience, acquaintanceship, personal clientele, and other personal characteristics do not constitute good will." Stanton v. Commissioner, 189 F.2d 297, 299 (7th Cir. 1951). One might ask why not, if one party is willing to sell and another to buy on this basis? Also, does the quotation from the *Stanton* case square with reality? *See* CRANE & BROMBERG at 479, noting that it is becoming difficult to make the traditional distinction drawn by Cardozo and others between mercantile partnerships and professional partnerships.

Is it possible that another reason for the restrictive attitude toward good will is fear that the public will be defrauded? *See* Crane, *Partnership Good Will*, 18 VA. L. REV. 651 (1932); Laube, *Good Will in Professional Partnerships*, 12 CORN. L. Q. 303 (1927). Would there be available less drastic ways to accomplish protection of the public?

3. Assume that a mercantile partnership is sold by its partners to a group of strangers. Nothing is said in the purchase agreement about competition. Can the selling partners soon thereafter establish a new enterprise engaged in the same business which competes with the purchasers? Would the presence or absence of any mention of good will in the purchase agreement have a bearing on this?

The clearest way to resolve these questions is to draft a clause on competition when negotiating the contract of sale. A covenant not to compete, assuming it is not too broad, resolves the questions posed above.

4. The above materials, including the *Brown* case, highlight the importance of drafting language in the partnership agreement (and, if the business is sold, in the contract of sale) specifying the manner in which good will is to be treated by the firm. This should include providing for the method by which evaluation of this asset will be determined, if it is to be taken into account at all, particularly since it may be years before an event requiring evaluation will arise. Recall the disagreement on this question between the lower and appellate courts in *Brown*. For one example of a clause directed toward good will, see Appendix C at p. 472 *infra,* containing the form of general partnership agreement. Note that the draftsman took the easy way out although, as explained below, this does have favorable tax consequences for the partnership. The Mulder book, from which the form was taken, sets forth on pages 99-105 alternative ways of dealing with good will. After noting that, "The item of good will depends largely upon the nature of the business, the extent to which a well-known name and good reputation attract business, and most important, a high earning record," the text states that when good will is to be considered,

> the amount to be allowed is often determined by multiplying by two, three or some other figure, the average annual earnings of the past few years. Sometimes it is entered as a fixed sum, such as $15,000, or it may be ascertained by a formula sometimes followed by the Internal Revenue Service. Under this formula the normal rate of return upon the capital invested in the business is subtracted from the total net earnings and the difference capitalized at a rate agreed upon by the partners. Another method is to provide that the partners fix the value of good will by agreement. (Pages 99-100.)

The Mulder book follows this discussion with some sample clauses, although they do not encompass all of the above variations. Clauses recognizing and evaluating good will typically are accompanied by covenants not to compete.

5. You should be alert to the fact that the treatment of good will by a partnership in making payments to a retired partner or deceased partner's beneficiary has income tax consequences. If good will is classified in the partnership agreement as property of the firm, payment of it to the ex-partner is treated as a tax-free return of capital to him to the extent of his basis, and capital gain in excess of that. This is also true of the rest of his interest in partnership property, other than unrealized receivables and substantially appreciated inventory (which are treated as ordinary income). Payment of the partner's interest in partnership property is not deductible by the firm. Any other payment is ordinary income to the recipient and deductible by the firm.

If good will is not classified as partnership property, payments representing substantially the same interest are classified as ordinary income to the recipient and are deductible by the partnership. A firm is thus inclined to place a low evaluation on its assets, not treat good will as property, and deduct payments in excess of the assets. The outgoing party in interest probably will be in a lower tax bracket and agreeable to this. See Section 736(a) and (b) of the Internal Revenue Code.

C. REAL ESTATE AND THE PARTNERSHIP

The partnership form of business had great difficulty adjusting to the traditional rules of real estate law. At common law a conveyance of land to the partnership of Smith and Company ran afoul of the rule that a partnership was not an entity (not a "person") and title to real property had to be in a "person." Courts responded in different ways to this, some saying legal title was in Smith, with the equitable title being held for all the partners. And if the partnership name was something like "Denver Supply Co.," some courts held legal title did not pass at all. The partners did have equitable title, but ran the risk of losing this to a subsequent bona fide purchaser, and problems arose when the firm later attempted to convey the property. The result was that conveyances were usually made to all the partners as individuals. This raised problems as to the legal status of the property vis-a-vis the partners and creditors of the partnership. The problems were compounded when the membership of the partnership changed during the period of ownership of the property. Similar problems were not encountered with the ownership of personal property and choses in action.

Problems also arose when a partner died. If he was deemed to hold legal title (depending on the mode of conveyance), his interest went to his heirs; if his interest was deemed personalty, it went to his next-of-kin. Also, the interests of creditors had to be defined within this confusing context. How did they realize payment of their debts from real estate if, under the common law, it descended directly to the heirs of the partners? The response was the creation of the fiction of "equitable conversion." The realty was deemed in equity converted into personalty to facilitate its deposition. It is described briefly in the case below.

Finally, what of conveyances *from* the partnership? In what manner could the partners convey property held in the firm name? As can be expected, the answer at common law varied with the way in which title was taken in the first place.

This is an area in which the UPA has made a substantial and sound change. *See* §§ 8(3), (4) and 10.

CULTRA v. CULTRA

Supreme Court of Tennessee
188 Tenn. 506, 221 S.W.2d 533 (1949)
Noted in 98 U. Pa. L. Rev. 269 (1949) *and* 21 Tenn. L. Rev. 202 (1950)

BURNETT, Justice. This case presents the question of whether or not the real estate owned by a partnership, purchased by said partnership with partnership funds for partnership purposes, and not needed to pay partnership debts, descends to the heirs of a deceased partner or continues to be personalty and subject to the laws of distribution.

The cause was heard below on bill, answer and on a stipulation of facts. It is shown, and was found by the chancellor, that four people (Cultra's) were partners doing business under the trade name "Morning Star Nursery," the interest being ⅓ in one of the four and 2/9 in the other three. These partners for the purpose of the partnership acquired three tracts of land. Two of these tracts of land were acquired in the name of the four partners, "Trading and doing business as Morning Star Nursery," while the third tract was merely acquired in the names of the individuals, the trade name not being inserted in the deed. It is shown though without question that this third tract was acquired by partnership out of partnership funds and for partnership purposes.

Two of the partners have died. The question here is raised by the after-born child of one of these partners. This child through her guardian ad litem takes the position that the property descends as realty to her to the exclusion of the widow, that is, the interest of her deceased father. The chancellor held that this property, all having been acquired with partnership funds and for the use of the partnership, upon the death of the partners, their interest therein was to be disposed of as personalty and that the surviving partners had a right to sell this land and then distribute the proceeds thereof as other partnership property.

Prior to the enactment of the Uniform Partnership Law in 1917, Chapter 140 of the Public Acts of that year and is now carried in the Code as Sections 7841-7882 inclusive, the courts of this State have uniformly held that it is a rule of property that real estate of a partnership is held as personalty for the purposes of the partnership but where not needed for such purposes it descends, as other real estate, to the heirs. Williamson v. Fontain, Ex'r, 66 Tenn. 212.

In thus holding the courts of this State were in line with the majority of the cases in the United States. These cases hold that the real estate, in equity, is regarded as personal property so long as it was necessary to use the real estate in settling and paying debts of the partnership and in adjusting the equities between the partners, but after this was done, any real estate remaining descends as real estate and was subject to laws of descent and distribution. See the full and copious Annotation 25, A.L.R. 389, 414, where cases from practically every state in the Union are cited and many are digested, setting forth the respective rules as adopted by various states.

Since the adoption of the Uniform Partnership Act, above referred to, the courts of this State have not passed upon the question. One case, Marks v. Marks, 1 Tenn. App. 436, apparently held that the passage of this Act did not affect the previous law, but in deciding that case, the court more or less went off on the proposition that the facts of the case did not show that it was the intent of the partnership to use the realty for partnership purposes or in other words, they held that the interested parties failed to carry the burden of showing that that intent appeared. We, therefore, do not consider this case as an authority upon the question here presented. It is true that in the *Marks* case, the court there cited Williamson v. Fontain, *supra*, but in citing it, the court merely said this was the established law in this State.

Courts of other states, in construing the Uniform Partnership Act, adopt the rule of "out and out" conversion, that is, that when the property is acquired by the partnership, from the partnership fund, for partnership purposes, it becomes personalty for all purposes. The most notable of these cases is Wharf v. Wharf, 306 Ill. 79, 137 N.E. 446, 449.

These cases, and the holdings last above referred to, in effect adopt the English rule. This rule is that partnership realty must be regarded as personalty for all purposes, including descent and distribution. Real estate purchased and used for partnership purposes is an "out and out" conversion to personalty so that it will be distributed as such. See 25 A.L.R. at page 405.

In Tiffany Real Property, 3rd Edition, Vol. 2, at section 445, it is said: "A conveyance to the partners for partnership purposes makes them, in England, in accordance with the general rule there prevailing, joint tenants as regards the legal title, with the right of survivorship, and the same view might, it seems, be adopted in those states in which trustees take as joint tenants, since the partners are, in such case, trustees. This appears also to be the purpose and effect of the Uniform Partnership Act."

Those courts that have considered the Uniform Partnership Act in reference to realty, used and purchased for partnership purposes, have considered the same with reference "to the sections of the Act to the effect that: (1) The title to the firm realty vests in the surviving partner and, if there is none, in the personal representative of the deceased partner (Code Section 7864(2) (d)); (2) A partner's interest is only a share in the profits and surpluses, the same being personal property (Code Section 7865); (3) a partner's interest in specific partnership property is not subject to dower, curtesy, or allowance to the next of kin (Code Section 7864(2) (e)); and (4) the debts of the partnership are to be paid and the surplus paid in cash to the partners (Code Section 7877 (1))."* 16 Tenn. Law Review, 886.

The Supreme Court of Illinois in *Wharf v. Wharf, supra,* in commenting on these various sections of the Uniform Partnership Act (the Act of Illinois being identical with that of Tennessee) said: "It seems that the legislative intention was to adopt the English rule that real estate which becomes personal property for the purposes of a partnership remains personal property for the purpose of distribution."

It is true that in the *Wharf* case the partnership was solely for the purpose of dealing in real estate and that the general rule is that real estate partnerships are considered as personalty, and must be distributed as such. See list of cases in 25 A.L.R. at the bottom of page 403. We consider the reasoning in the *Wharf* case, that is, that the rule is changed as to all partnerships, whether real estate or otherwise, by reason of the passage of the Uniform Partnership Act, is the most reasonable rule and is one that we should adopt and do adopt as the applicable rule in this State.

In this construction and application of the Uniform Partnership Act we are meeting and reaching the intent of the Legislature in passing this Act. By so doing the conversion of real estate into personalty for certain purposes and then when those purposes have been met, reconverting the real estate back into realty is done away with by this Act. By this construction when a partnership once acquires real estate, with partnership funds and for partnership purposes, it then becomes personalty for all purposes and can be conveyed according to the terms of the Act as other

---

* These sections are: §§ 25 (2) (d), 26, 25 (e) and 38 (1) of the UPA, respectively.

partnership property. This seems a sound rule to apply and we are applying it here.

From what has been said above, it results that the decree of the Chancellor must be affirmed. The cause will be remanded so that the Chancellor may fix solicitors fees in the case.

All concur.

PROBLEMS

1. Newton, Emmons and Miller each acquired a one-third interest in a parcel of four acres upon which stood a flour mill. Later they orally formed a partnership to engage in the business of milling grain. The business was conducted in the mill upon the land, and new machinery was placed in the mill from partnership funds. There was no agreement as to whether the mill remained the property of the individual partners or was capital of the partnership.

Thereafter, Emmons and Miller mortgaged their interests in the land for personal debts. Later the partnership became heavily indebted to the Robinson Bank and deeded the land, at the Bank's request, to one Woolworth as trustee for the benefit of the Bank. The partnership became insolvent and the Bank brought suit in equity to set aside the individual mortgages, claiming the land was partnership property. What result? What additional matters, if any, should be inquired into?

2. On December 1, 1968, plaintiff and the three defendants entered into a partnership for the purposes of giving musical performances under the firm name of Florzaley Quartet. The agreement contained no provision with respect to good will. The partnership was for a fixed term, to expire June 1, 1972. The Quartet gave performances and made records for three years. The defendants in December 1971 served notice on plaintiff that they would not continue with him after June 1, 1972, and contended his only interest was in some music sheets. Plaintiff sued to dissolve the partnership and demanded an interest based on good will. What result? *See* Bailly v. Betti, 241 N.Y. 22, 148 N.E. 776 (1925) (*noted in* 11 Corn. L. Q. 256, 24 Mich. L. Rev. 515, *and* 35 Yale L. J. 496).

3. McBride was sole proprietor of the McBride Potato Company until September 1, 1939, when he and plaintiff entered into a partnership by the same name. McBride had, prior to that date, entered into contracts for the future delivery of potato bags. The price was determined at the time the contract was entered into. Payment for the bags at the time of delivery was made from partnership funds, at the contract price. The market value of the bags

had increased sharply by that time, and McBride contends that he is entitled to the difference between the contract price and the market value, and to have this credited to his capital interest. What result? *See* Baum v. McBride, 152 Neb. 152, 40 N.W.2d 649 (1950).

4. In an action for a partnership accounting and determination of the amount due plaintiff partner from the sale of the partnership restaurant business, the defendant partners claimed that plaintiff was not entitled to good will because the business had been losing money just before the sale. The business had enjoyed a net income for two consecutive years but suffered an operating loss during the last six months of its existence. What result?

5. After division of the physical assets between themselves, plaintiff and defendant dissolved their partnership for the practice of veterinary medicine. Defendant promised to pay plaintiff a substantial sum for "all of his right, title and interest" in the practice. Defendant failed to pay and plaintiff sued to recover the purchase price. The defense was that good will of a professional partnership is an item that cannot be sold to another partner. What result? *See* Durio v. Johnson, 68 N.M. 82, 358 P.2d 703 (1961).

6. In July, 1965, Able and Baker, both of whom were real estate agents, formed a partnership in order to pool their capital and expertise and purchase land for development. They had known each other for years, were both respected and financially secure members of their community, and trusted each other completely. They thus did not bother to go to a lawyer, and made simply an oral agreement.

During the succeeding six years they bought a large number of parcels of land, some of which they held for speculation and some of which they started developing. Their acquisition of title to the land was done as casually and trustingly as was their entering into the partnership. Some parcels were purchased in Able's name, some in Baker's name, some in the name of the Able and Baker partnership, some in the name of "Able and Baker, as joint tenants," and some in the name of "Able and Baker." All of these purchases were made with partnership funds.

Baker died in August, 1971. Able is very upset by this and is himself getting along in years. He has decided to sell all the land owned by the partnership and retire. If you represented the purchaser of the various parcels of land, to what extent, if any, would you be concerned about Able's attempted conveyance to your client of the land held as follows:

1. Those parcels held in Able's name. *O K*
2. Those parcels held in Baker's name.
3. Those parcels held in the name of the Able and Baker *O K* partnership.
4. Those parcels held in the name of "Able and Baker, as *O K* joint tenants."
5. Those parcels held in the name of "Able and Baker."

Also, what problems would you foresee if Able was unable to clearly establish that some of the above parcels in each of the five categories were purchased with partnership funds (a problem that frequently occurs in a casually run business)?

Chapter 14

RIGHTS OF CREDITORS

A. RIGHTS OF PERSONAL CREDITORS OF A PARTNER

i. *Rights Against the Interest of a Partner in his Partnership*

It is clear that the unpaid unsecured personal creditors of a partner can initiate legal proceedings against his personal assets (bank account, car, home if not mortgaged or if there is existing an equity above the amount of a mortgage on it, and so forth), and so can a secured creditor, who may be seeking to recover a deficiency judgment after exhausting his security. The question which now concerns us is whether such creditors can assert rights against the partner's interest in his partnership, which may constitute a substantial part of his assets.

The common law treatment of the rights of personal creditors of an individual partner to reach his interest in the partnership's assets was briefly referred to on page 321, *supra*. You will recall that partners were treated as co-owners of partnership property and that creditors could physically seize specific partnership property "and sell a moiety thereof undivided, and the vendee will be tenant in common with the other partner." Heydon v. Heydon, 1 Salk. 392, 91 Eng. Rep. 340, 341 (1693). The result was that the partnership lost possession, at least temporarily, and had a relationship with a stranger involuntarily imposed upon it. Equity responded to this by establishing the principle that the co-partner's right to apply partnership property to partnership obligations prevailed against separate creditors and execution purchasers, who were left with a right to proceed in equity to have a partnership accounting.

The UPA avoids the above common-law ambiguities and difficulties by expressly prohibiting attachment or execution against a partner's right in specific partnership property (§ 25(2)(c)). The nature of a partner's right in specific partnership property is defined in Section 25(1) and (2). A partner is declared to be co-owner with his partners of specific partnership property "holding as a tenant in partnership." Among the incidents of this tenancy are an equal right with his partners to possess specific partnership property for partnership purposes; an inability to assign this right "except in connection with the assignment of rights of all partners in the same property"; a survivorship feature, in that upon a partner's death his right in specific partnership property vests in the surviving partner or partners; and, as mentioned, the right is not subject to attachment or execution except on a claim against the partnership.

The property rights of an individual partner are also covered in Sections 24 and 26 of the UPA. An individual partner's interest in the partnership is defined in Section 26 as "his share of the profits and surplus, and the same is personal property." Section 27 defines the limited legal consequences of an assignment by a partner of his interest, including the rights of a partner's assignee in the event of dissolution of the partnership.*

In order to define in more concrete terms the legal rights and interests described in the above several paragraphs, assume that X, Y and Z operate a real estate brokerage business as equal partners. The partnership is described as the X, Y, Z partnership, in which each partner owns a one-third interest. The partnership owns six automobiles, several of which are driven by employees, nine typewriters, and a small office building in which it conducts its business. The net equity of the partnership in all of these

---

* The assignment by an individual partner of his interest, or a portion of his interest, is to be distinguished from "sub-partnership," which involves a relationship between an individual partner and an outsider in which they agree to share the individual partner's profits and losses from the firm business. The individual member of the firm is often referred to as the "common partner," and the third person is usually described as the "sub-partner." As with the assignee of a partner's interest, the sub-partner does not become a partner with the noncommon partners in the firm, since no "association" based on mutual consent has been entered into between them. Although the sub-partner is thus not directly liable to creditors, they may be able to claim rights as third-party creditor beneficiaries of his promise to the common partner to share losses. The sub-partnership form is used very little today. It carries no particular tax significance, and is a risky way of achieving limited liability. See Burnett v. Snyder, 76 N.Y. 344 (1879); CRANE & BROMBERG, § 28.

The sub-partner is to be distinguished from the "dormant" or "secret" partner, who actually is a member of the partnership but whose association with the firm is not generally known. He may or may not be active in the firm. The dormant or secret partner is nevertheless a full partner, subject to all partnership liabilities, with the only legal distinction in his status perhaps being that of lack of need to give full notice required upon retirement or death from the firm in order to avoid liability for obligations incurred by the firm thereafter. Some distinction has been drawn between the secret and dormant partner on the ground that, while the identity of both types of partners are unknown to people outside the partnership, the secret partner is actively engaged in the management of the business, while a dormant partner is totally inactive. The *Rowley* treatise, at Section 6.10, indicates that this distinction has not been consistently followed. "Silent" partners are defined in *Rowley* as actual members of the firm and known to the world as such, who nevertheless take no part in the management of the business. Their liabilities remain the same as those of active partners.

assets, after deducting current and long-term indebtedness, is $36,-000. Each partner contributed $5000 in cash or in goods of equivalent value to the partnership when the business first began three years ago. Define in economic terms the interest that partner X has in his firm.

As was discussed earlier, Section 25 effectively seals specific partnership property against the claims of creditors of individual partners and thus makes a sharp change from the common law. A remedy has been provided for creditors under Section 28, however, in the form of a "charging order" which may be imposed by court order against "the interest" of the debtor partner on due application by a judgment creditor. The interest of a partner in a partnership is defined in Section 26 as "his share of the profits and surplus." The meaning of profits is obvious; "surplus" is not defined in the UPA but usually means the excess of partnership assets over partnership liabilities. Would liabilities in this context include the capital accounts of the firm? See Section 40(b) of the UPA, defining "liabilities" in the context of distribution of assets after dissolution. What arguments can be made for and against the inclusion of capital accounts?

Although Section 28 does not so specify, all payments, like distributions of earnings or withdrawal of capital, which would otherwise go to the debtor partner should go to the creditor and the creditor should ask for language to that effect when obtaining the charging order.

Section 28(2) of the UPA provides that the creditor may foreclose on the charging order, achieving sale of the debtor partner's interest. The purchaser does not buy the privilege to exercise managerial powers, however. The purchaser of the interest does acquire the power to dissolve the partnership under Section 32(2) if it is one at will, or at the termination of the specified term. Presumably this power would encourage the other partners to purchase the interest at the sale or to redeem it before foreclosure, which they can do under Section 28(2). *See* Gose, *The Charging Order Under the Uniform Partnership Act*, 28 Wash. L. Rev. 1 (1953); Hutchison, *Enforceability of Iowa Creditors' Judgments Against Partnership and Partners' Assets*, 44 Iowa L. Rev. 643 (1959).

TUPPER v. KROC
Supreme Court of Nevada
— Nev. —, 494 P.2d 1275 (1972)

Batjer, Justice. These two cases were consolidated for the purpose of appeal because the same legal issues are involved in each.

Lloyd G. Tupper, appellant, and Ray A. Kroc, respondent, entered into three limited partnerships for the purpose of holding title to and leasing parcels of real estate. Tupper was the general partner, Kroc was the limited partner and each held a fifty per cent interest.

Kroc filed an action alleging that Tupper had mismanaged and misappropriated funds from these partnerships and requested that they be dissolved and that a receiver be appointed. Pending the final outcome of that action the trial court appointed a receiver to manage the three business organizations. Prior to the date on which the complaint for dissolution had been filed, Tupper had on several occasions been unable to pay his share of the partnerships' obligations. Kroc on those occasions personally contributed the total amounts owed by the partnerships, and in return accepted interest bearing notes from Tupper in amounts equal to one-half of the partnerships' debts paid by him. Kroc thereafter filed an action against Tupper to recover on those notes and was awarded a summary judgment in the amount of $54,609.02.

In an effort to collect on that judgment, Kroc filed a motion pursuant to NRS 87.280[1] requesting the district court to charge Tupper's interest in the partnerships with payment of the judgment and for the sale of Tupper's interest to satisfy the judgment. On June 12, 1969, a charging order was entered directing the sheriff to sell all of Tupper's "right, title and interest" in the three partnerships and to apply the proceeds against the unsatisfied amount of the judgment. Tupper was served with notice of the sale, but he took no action to redeem his interest. The sale was held on June 27, 1969, and Kroc purchased Tupper's interest for $2,500.

Kroc filed a motion to terminate the receivership on March 12, 1970, contending that he was the sole owner of the partnerships and that the need for a receiver had ceased. On May 18, 1970, the appellants filed an objection to the respondents' motion to terminate the receivership, and a motion to set aside the sale conducted pursuant to the charging order. The trial court denied the appellants' motion to set aside the sale, and granted the respondents' motion to terminate the receivership and discharge the receiver. It is from these two orders that this appeal is taken.

The appellants contend that the trial court erred when it confirmed the sale of Tupper's interest in the three partnerships because (1) Kroc failed to affirmatively show that a sale of Tupper's

---

[1] [This is Section 28 of the UPA, which the court quotes in its entirety. *Ed.*]

interest in the partnerships was necessary; (2) a partner's interest in a partnership is not subject to a sale in satisfaction of a judgment; (3) it was improper to nominate the sheriff to conduct the sale which was irregularly and improperly held; (4) the sheriff's sale was inequitable in that the price paid for Tupper's partnership interest was grossly inadequate; (5) it was impermissible to conduct the sale of Tupper's interest in the partnerships while they were in receivership; and (6) the sale was in violation of the partnerships' agreements. Furthermore, the appellants contend that it was improper to discharge the receiver because Tupper retained such an equity in the partnership business and assets as to compel continuation of the receivership.

The appellant's contention that Kroc was required to affirmatively prove that a sale of Tupper's interest in the partnerships was necessary before a sale could be ordered was not raised in the court below, but raised for the first time in this appeal. Upon the rule announced in Cottonwood Cove Corp. v. Bates, 86 Nev. 751, 476 P.2d 171 (1970) and Clark County v. State, 65 Nev. 490, 199 P.2d 137 (1948), that a party on appeal cannot assume an attitude or accept a theory inconsistent with or different from that at the hearing below, we will not consider that issue. Also, this issue amounts to an attack upon the validity of the charging order and the appellants concede that the charging order is not under attack.

The charging order was properly entered by the district court against Tupper's interest in the three partnerships. NRS 87.280; Balaban v. Bank of Nevada, 86 Nev. 862, 477 P.2d 860 (1970); State v. Elsbury, 63 Nev. 463, 175 P.2d 430 (1946). The district court also was authorized, in aid of the charging order, to make all orders and directions as the case required. NRS 87.280(1). Pursuant to the provisions of this statute the district court was authorized to appoint a receiver to act as a repository for Tupper's share of the profits and surplus for the benefit of Kroc, or as the court did here, order the sale of Tupper's interest. NRS 87.280(1), (2); Frankil v. Frankil, 15 Pa.Dist. & Co. 103 (Phila. Co. 1928); see also 87.320(2).* In Kroc's application for the order charging Tupper's interest in the partnerships he requested an order directing a sale of that interest. Likewise in the notice to Tupper and his attorneys they were advised that Kroc was seeking a sale of Tupper's interest. The application and notice afforded Tupper an opportunity to take whatever steps he deemed necessary to either limit the charging order or prevent the sale.[2] Tupper was

---

* UPA § 32 (2)—*Ed.*

[2] If only a charging order had been entered or had the court in the charging order appointed a receiver under NRS 87.280, to receive Tupper's

allowed 30 days to file an appeal from the order charging his interest in the partnerships and ordering the sale. NRCP 73. He did not appeal from that order, but instead waited nearly a year after the sale was made before filing a motion to set it aside. The appellants are now estopped to question the propriety of the charging order.

Although the appellants concede that the charging order is not under attack they continue a collateral attack by insisting that the sale of Tupper's interest in the partnerships authorized by the charging order was void. One of those contentions of irregularity is based upon the fact that an accounting "to determine the nature and extent of the interest to be sold" was not required by the district court before it entered its order authorizing the sale. In support of this contention the appellants rely upon *Balaban v. Bank of Nevada, supra.* Although we declared the sale in that case to be void and ordered an accounting, it is inapposite to support a claim that the sale in this case is void. In *Balaban* the notice of sale advised that "said sale will include all physical assets." This was impermissible and for that reason we set the sale aside. Furthermore, *Balaban* concerned a dissolution of a partnership by death, its winding up and the interplay of the Uniform Partnership Act (NRS Ch. 87) and the probate code (NRS Chs. 143 and 148). Within those chapters are found special provisions and requirements for an accounting (NRS 143.040; NRS 87.430;* NRS 148.210) which are not found in the statute authorizing the charging order (NRS 87.280). An accounting prior to the sale of Tupper's interest was not compelled in this case.

The appellants also contend that Tupper's interest in the partnership was inadequately described. Anyone reading or relying on the notice of sale was, as a matter of law, deemed to understand that by statute the sale of Tupper's interest in the partnerships consisted of a sale of his share of the profits and surplus and no more. NRS 87.240; NRS 87.260; NRS 87.280.** Any further or more extensive description would have been confusing or redundant. An accounting might have revealed the amount of current profits, if any, or the estimated value of the surplus, if any,

---

share of the partnerships' profits or upon dissolution his share of the surplus instead of ordering a sale, then upon receipt by Kroc of an amount sufficient to satisfy the judgment against Tupper entered on April 30, 1969, Tupper would have been restored to his right to receive his share of the profits or upon dissolution his share of the surplus; however, when his interest in the partnerships was sold he was forever foreclosed from receiving any profits or surplus from the three partnerships.

* UPA § 43—*Ed.*

** UPA §§ 24, 26 and 28, respectively—*Ed.*

but it would not have added anything to the description of Tupper's interest beyond that found in NRS 87.260.

Pursuant to NRS 87.280(1) the district court was authorized to make any order which the circumstances of the case required. The statute authorized the appointment of the sheriff of Clark County to sell Tupper's interest in the partnerships, and authorized Tupper's interest to be sold in accordance with the provisions of NRS 21.130(2)[3] at a time certain on June 27, 1969. Because this was a judicial sale authorized by NRS Ch. 87, and not an execution sale, the district court was not bound to have Tupper's partnership interest sold in strict compliance with NRS 21.130(2) but the court was free, pursuant to NRS 87.280(1), to order any notice procedure that it deemed reasonable. Therefore, it was authorized to modify the notice requirements of NRS 21.130(2) by requiring that Tupper's interest be sold at 9:00 a. m. on June 27, 1969. The fact that the sale was conducted fourteen days after the notice of sale was posted by the sheriff has no effect upon the validity of the sale and can be construed to have inured to the benefit of Tupper.

The appellants' contention that the price paid by Kroc for Tupper's interest in the three partnerships is inadequate, is without merit. The mode for determining the value of Tupper's interest in the partnerships was by a public sale. *See* McMillan v. United Mortgage Co., 82 Nev. 117, 412 P.2d 604 (1966). The fair market value of $2,500 was established by Kroc's bid at the sheriff's sale. The respondents were under no duty or obligation to support or justify that price and the entire burden was upon the appellants to prove its inadequacy. Thus it became a question of fact to be determined by the trial judge who heard the testimony and observed the witnesses.

We will not substitute our judgment for that of the trial judge as to the weight given to evidence.

The appellants seek to enlist the aid of the doctrine of *custodia legis*[4] to support their claim that it was impermissible to conduct the sale of Tupper's interest in the partnerships' assets and busi-

---

3 NRS 21.130 (2): "In case of other personal property, by posting a similar notice in 3 public places of the township or city where the sale is to take place, not less than 5 nor more than 10 days before sale, and, in case of sale on execution issuing out of a district court, by the publication of a copy of the notice in a newspaper, if there be one in the county, at least twice, the first publication being not less than 10 days before date of sale."

4 The phrase "custodia legis" means in the custody of the law. Hopping v. Hopping, 233 Iowa 993, 10 N.W.2d 87 (1943); Stockwell v. Robinson, 9 Hust. 313, 32 A. 528 (Del. 1892).

ness but not the interest of a partner in the partnerships. Tupper's interest in the partnerships, *i. e.* his right and title in the profits and surplus, were his personal property and not partnership property in the custody of the receiver. NRS 87.260.[5]

The appellants contend that the sale amounted to an involuntary assignment of Tupper's interest in the partnerships and is in violation of the partnership agreements which preclude a partner from assigning his interest. We do not agree. A sale made pursuant to a charging order of a partner's interest in a partnership is not an assignment of an interest in a partnership. See NRS 87.270.* Furthermore, the partnership agreements could not divest the district court of its powers provided by statute to charge and sell an interest of a partner in a partnership.

Finally the appellants contend that because Tupper retained an equity in the partnerships' business and assets, the district court erred when it discharged the receiver. Unfortunately for the appellants this is not true. After Kroc bought all of Tupper's interest in the partnerships, *i. e.* all of his right and title to the profits and surplus, Kroc was entitled to all of the profits and all of the surplus. "Surplus" is the excess of assets over liabilities. *Balaban v. Bank of Nevada, supra; State v. Elsbury, supra;* Anderson v. United States, 131 F.Supp. 501 (S.D.Cal.1954). After the sale Tupper had no immediate or future rights to any profits or surplus or any equity whatever in the partnership property, and therefore he had no valid reason to insist on a continuation of the receivership.

Although as a matter of law the respondents were entitled to have the receivership terminated and the receiver discharged, the wisdom of that request, short of the dissolution of the partnerships, is questionable, for as soon as the receiver was discharged Tupper had the authority under NRS Ch. 87, as well as the partnerships' agreements, to assert his right to participate in the management. By purchasing Tupper's interest in the partnerships Kroc did not divest Tupper of his other property rights (NRS 87.240).

The receiver was appointed at the request of Kroc, now Tupper wants the receiver to be reappointed to protect Tupper as a general partner from liability that might be incurred through excessive partnership debts. At a glance it might seem that Tupper's fears have some merit. However, as a matter of law, at the moment the receiver was discharged Tupper's right to participate

---

[5] [Quoting § 26 of the UPA—*Ed.*]

* UPA § 27—*Ed.*

in the management of the partnerships (NRS 87.240) was restored, and as the general partner he would, at least theoretically, be able to prevent the partnerships from incurring liabilities in excess of assets.

The orders of the district court from which these appeals have been taken are affirmed.

ZENOFF, C. J., and MOWBRAY, THOMPSON and GUNDERSON, JJ., concur.

---

ii. *Rights Against the Assets of the Partnership*

Creditors of individual partners have no rights against partnership assets as such. As mentioned above, they can take advantage of a charging order under Section 28. This reaches only the individual partner's interest in the partnership, however, and provides no rights against specific partnership property. Even if the creditor forecloses on his charging order, buys at the sale and eventually forces the partnership into dissolution, he still is able to realize the value of the debtor partner's interest only after the partnership creditors have been fully paid. *See* CRANE & BROMBERG at 248.

B. RIGHTS OF CREDITORS OF THE PARTNERSHIP

i. *Rights against Partnership Assets*

It has never been doubted that partnership creditors have rights against partnership assets. But how does an unpaid, unsecured creditor realize his rights? The expected answer would be that he simply obtain a judgment against the partnership and execute against partnership assets. Does the UPA provide that the partnership can be sued and hold property as a separate entity, so that this remedy is available? Surprisingly, it contains no direct language on this point. As mentioned at page 330, *supra,* many states by statute have authorized suits against a partnership, which presumably would allow a creditor to proceed directly against the partnership, obtain judgment on his debt, and execute against the partnership assets, as well as the individual assets of any partner personally joined and served with process. For those jurisdictions which do not provide for this, a creditor must sue the individual partners, obtain judgment and execute against the partnership assets by exercise of the equity described immediately below.

The *Rowley* treatise (§ 38.0-C) indicates that a creditor's rights are purely derivative from a partner's rights under Section 38 of the UPA to have partnership property paid to discharge liabilities. (This is referred to as a partner's "equity," since this right historically was first recognized in the equity courts.) Thus, if each partner has assigned away his interest, his equity is extinguished and there is no partnership property right to be reached by the partnership creditor. CRANE & BROMBERG, in § 42, acknowledge the above line of authority ("the equities of the creditors can only be worked out through the equities of the partners"), but continue on to state:

> But if the partnership, as a group entity or person, is considered to be the owner of partnership property, and the partner has the power to assign only his interest in surplus after payment of debts, the assignments of all do not affect the partnership ownership in the property and its availability for partnership creditors. The UPA appears to have adopted this latter view. (p. 238.) [There is no citation behind the last sentence, and two cases (decided in 1873 and 1899) are cited behind the first sentence. Can you find support in the UPA for the authors' reading of it?—*Ed.*]

The problem with the rule allowing destruction of creditors' equities is that partners are given the arbitrary power to prefer creditors or, under some of the cases, even to transfer firm property to one of themselves. As mentioned, the UPA did not cover this, but the Uniform Fraudulent Conveyance Act, which is adopted in 25 jurisdictions, does have two sections dealing with this. Section 8 declares conveyances of partnership property when the firm is or will be thereby rendered insolvent to be fraudulent as to partnership creditors if there is no fair consideration given to the partnership. Insolvency is defined in Section 2(1) as the time when "the present fair salable value of [a person's] assets is less than the amount that will be required to pay his probable liability on his existing debts as they become absolute and matured." Insolvency in the partnership context is defined in Section 2(2): "In determining whether a partnership is insolvent there shall be added to the partnership property the present fair salable value of the separate assets of each general partner in excess of the amount probably sufficient to meet the claims of his separate creditors. . . ." 7 UNIF. LAWS ANNOT. 436 (1970). *See* Liebowitz v. Arrow Roofing Co., 259 N.Y. 391, 182 N.E. 58 (1932).

The rights of firm creditors when the partnership sells out or merges into a new partnership are discussed in Chapter 15, *infra*.

ii. *Rights Against the Personal Assets of Individual Partners*

The extent of an individual partner's personal liability to creditors of the partnership was covered at pages 327-330, *supra.* As was there observed, the individual assets of general partners are subject to all partnership liabilities (§ 15). We have reached, therefore, the problem of priority among creditors.

RODGERS v. MERANDA
Supreme Court of Ohio
7 Ohio St. 180 (1857)

THIS is a petition in error to reverse the judgment of the common pleas of Clark county.

The original proceeding was a petition for an order of distribution of the separate or individual assets of an insolvent debtor, as between separate and partnership creditors.

It appears from the record, that about the 13th of June, 1854, Peter Murray, an insolvent debtor, made an assignment of all his estate, real and personal, to the plaintiff, in trust for the payment of his individual creditors, in proportion to the amount of their respective demands. Though possessed of a large and valuable estate, it had been found insufficient to pay his separate debts and liabilities in full. At the date of his failure and assignment, he was a partner with John W. Dever, in a mercantile firm, under the name and style of Dever & Murray, which firm had also become insolvent, and likewise Dever; and the firm had made an assignment of the partnership property and assets, about the same time, to John Meranda, one of the defendants, in trust for the payment of the joint debts or liabilities of the firm.

In this condition of affairs, the partnership creditors, although they have filed their claims with the assignee of the firm for their distributive shares out of the partnership property, claim the right to be admitted to a participation in the dividends of the separate estate of Murray, *pari passu* with his individual creditors; while the latter deny the right, and insist that his separate estate shall be applied to the satisfaction of his individual debts in preference to his partnership debts.

It appears further, that Murray, besides advancing his part of the capital of the firm, also loaned money to the firm to a large amount, for which he held the obligations of the firm; which obligations, by the assignment of Murray, came into the hands of the plaintiff, who has presented the same to the assignee of the firm, and claims to have the same paid out of the assets of the firm, *pari passu* with the other partnership debts. The other creditors resist this, and plaintiff asks an order of distribution to that effect, out of the partnership assets.

Defendants demurred to the petition. The court below sustained the demurrer, and gave judgment in favor of the defendants. And this petition in error is filed to review and reverse that judgment.

BARTLEY, C. J. Two questions are presented for determination in this case. The first is, whether in the distribution of the assets of insolvent partners, where there are both individual and partnership assets, the individual creditors of a partner are entitled to be first paid out of the individual effects of their debtor, before the partnership creditors are entitled to any distribution therefrom. It is well settled that, in the distribution of the assets of insolvent partners, the partnership creditors are entitled to a priority in the partnership effects; so that the partnership debts must be settled before any division of the partnership funds can be made among the individual creditors of the several partners. This is incident to the nature of partnership property. It is the right of a partner to have the partnership property applied to the purposes of the firm; and the separate interest of each partner in the partnership property, is his share of the surplus after the payment of the partnership debts. And this rule, which gives the partnership creditors a preference in the partnership effects, would seem to produce, in equity, a corresponding and correlative rule, giving a preference to the individual creditors of a partner in his separate property; so that partnership creditors can, *in equity,* only look to the surplus of the separate property of a partner, after the payment of his individual debts; and, on the other hand, the individual creditors of a party can, in like manner, only claim distribution from the debtor's interest in the surplus of the joint fund, after the satisfaction of the partnership creditors. The correctness of this rule, however, has been much controverted; and there has not been always a perfect concurrence in the reasons assigned for it by those courts which have adhered to it. By some, it has been said to be an arbitrary rule, established from considerations of convenience; by others, that it rests on the basis that a primary liability attaches to the fund on which the credit was given—that in contracts with a partnership, credit is given on the supposed responsibility of the firm; while in contracts with a partner as an individual, reliance is supposed to be placed on his separate responsibility. 3 Kent Com. 65. And again, others have assigned as a reason for the rule, that the joint estate is supposed to be benefited to the extent of every credit which is given to the firm, and that the separate estate is, in like manner, presumed to be enlarged by the debts contracted by the individual partner; and that there is consequently, a clear equity in confining the creditors, as to preferences, to each estate respectively, which has been thus benefited by their transactions. 1 Har. & Gill, 96. But these reasons are not entirely satisfactory. So important a rule must have a better foundation to stand upon than mere considerations of convenience; and practically it is undeniable, that those who give credit to a partnership, look to the individual responsibility of the partners, as well as that of the firm; and also, those who contract with a partner in his separate capacity, place reliance on his various resources or means, whether individual or joint. And inasmuch as individual debts are often contracted to raise means which are put into the business of a partnership, and also partnership effects often withdrawn from the firm and appropriated to the separate use of the partners, it can not be practically true, that the separate estate has been benefited to the extent of every credit given to each individual partner, nor that the joint estate has retained from the separate estate of each partner, the benefit of every credit given to the firm. Unsatisfactory reasons may weaken confidence in a rule which is well founded.

What then is the true foundation of the rule, which gives the individual creditor a preference over the partnership creditor, in the distribution of the separate estate of a partner? To say that it is a rule of general equity, as has been sometimes said, is not a satisfactory solution of the difficulty; for the very question is, whether it be a rule of equity or not. In the distribution of the assets of insolvents, equality is equity; and to say that the rule which gives the individual creditor a preference over the partnership creditor in the separate estate of a partner, is a rule of equality, does not still rid the subject of difficulty. For, leaving the rule to stand, which gives the preference to the joint creditors in the partnership property, and perfect equality between the joint and individual creditors, is, perhaps, rarely attainable. That it is, however, more equal and just, as a general rule, than any other which can be devised, consistently with the preference to the partnership creditors in the joint estate, can not be successfully controverted. It originated as a consequence of the rule of priority of partnership creditors in the joint estate, and for the purposes of justice, became necessary as a correlative rule. With what semblance of equity could one class of creditors, in preference to the rest, be exclusively entitled to the partnership fund, and, concurrently with the rest, entitled to the separate estate of each partner? The joint creditors are no more meritorious than the separate creditors; and it frequently happens, that the separate debts are contracted to raise means to carry on the partnership business. Independent of this rule, the joint creditors have, as a general thing, a great advantage over the separate creditors. Besides being exclusively entitled to the partnership fund, they take their distributive share in the surplus of the separate estate of each of the several partners, after the payment of the separate creditors of each. It is a rule of equity, that where one creditor is in a situation to have two or more distinct securities or funds to rely on, the court will not allow him, neglecting his other funds, to attach himself to one of the funds to the prejudice of those who have a claim upon that, and no other to depend on. And besides the advantage, which the joint creditors have, arising from the fact that the partnership fund is usually much the largest, as men in trade, in a great majority of cases, embark their all, or the chief part of their property, in it; and besides their distributive rights in the surplus of the separate estate of the other partners, the joint creditors have a degree of security for their debts and facilities for recovering them, which the separate creditors have not; they can sell both the joint and the separate estate on an execution, while the separate creditor can sell only the separate property and the interest in the joint effects that may remain to the partners, after the accounts of the debts and effects of the firm are taken, as between the firm and its creditors, and also as between the partners themselves. With all these advantages in favor of partnership creditors, it would be grossly inequitable to allow them the exclusive benefit of the joint fund, and then a concurrent right with individual creditors to an equal distribution in the separate estate of each partner. What equality and justice is there in allowing partnership creditors, who have been paid eighty per cent on their debts, out of the joint fund, to come in *pari passu* with the individual creditors of one of the partners, whose separate property will not pay twenty per cent to his separate creditors? How could that be said to be an equal distribution of the assets of insolvents among their creditors? It is true, that an occasional case may arise where the joint effects are proportionably less than the separate assets of an insolvent partner. But, as a general thing, a very decided advantage is given to the partnership creditors, notwithstanding this preference of the individual creditors in the separate property. And that advantage, arising out of the nature of a partnership contract, is unavoidable. Some general rule is necessary; and that must rest on the basis of the unalterable preference of the partnership creditors in the joint effects, and their further right to some claim in the separate property of each of the several partners. The preference, therefore, of the individual creditors of a partner in the distribution of his separate estate, results, as a principle of equity, from the preference of partnership creditors in the partnership funds, and their advantages in having different funds to resort to, while the individual creditors have but the one.

. . . .

It is argued, however, that this doctrine was overruled in Ohio, in the case of Grosvenor *v.* Austin, 6 Ohio, 104. It is true, that the reasoning of the court in the opinion, is to that effect; but the case decided falls within one of the acknowledged exceptions to the rule. Where the partnership has become insolvent, and there are no partnership assets for distribution, and no living solvent partner, it has been uniformly conceded, that the principle of the rule does not apply. The case of *Grosvenor v. Austin,* was a bill in equity by the creditors of the firm of Seymour Austin & Calvin Austin, for a distributive share with the individual creditors of Seymour Austin out of the assets of his separate estate in the hands of his administrator. There were no partnership assets, and both parties had died insolvent. This was not a case, therefore, for the application of the principle under consideration. . . .

The remaining matter for determination, in this case, involves the inquiry, whether, in case of an indebtedness for money lent to the partnership by a partner who afterward becomes insolvent, the separate creditors of the latter shall be entitled therefor to a *pro rata* distribution with the partnership creditors, out of the joint fund. It is claimed that the liability of the firm to a partner for money loaned is a partnership debt, and that the individual creditors of that partner are, in equity, entitled to an equal distribution therefor, out of the partnership property. On the other hand, it is claimed, that as each partner is individually liable for the debts of the firm, and as no partner can be allowed to participate with his own creditors in the distribution of a fund, the separate creditors of a partner, as they can only claim through the rights of their debtor, can not be allowed such participation with the joint creditors.

It was at one time held to be the law, on the authority of adjudications by Lord Talbot and Lord Hardwicke, that if a partner has loaned money to the partnership, or the partnership has loaned money to the separate estate of one of the partners, according to the equitable rule of distribution of the assets after insolvency, in the former case, the separate creditors of the partner would be entitled to an equal share out of the joint assets to the extent of the debt created for the money lent; and that, in the latter case, the partnership creditors would be entitled to payment to the same extent, out of the individual estate of the partner. Ex parte Hunter, 1 Atk. 223; Story on Part., sec. 390. But this doctrine has long since been overruled; and the contrary appears now to be well settled. In Ex parte Lodge, 1 Ves. Jr. 166, Lord Thurlow held, that the assignees on behalf of the joint estate could not be entitled to distribution out of the separate estate of Lodge, for money which he had abstracted from the partnership, unless he had taken it with a fraudulent intent to augment his separate estate. And in Ex parte Harris (2 Ves. & Bea. 210, 212), Lord Eldon said: "There has long been an end of the law which prevailed in the time of Lord Hardwicke, whose opinion appears to have been, that if the joint estate lent money to the separate estate of one partner, or if one partner lent to the joint estate, proof might be made by the one or the other, in each case. That has been put an end to, among other principles, upon this certainly, that a partner can not come in competition with separate creditors of his own, nor as to the joint estate with the joint creditors. The consequence is, that if one partner lends £1,000 to the partnership, and they become insolvent in a week, he can not be a creditor of the partnership, though the money was supplied to the joint estate; so, if the partnership lends to an individual partner, there can be no proof for the joint against the separate estate; that is, in each case no proof to affect the creditors, though the individual partners may certainly have the right against each other."

This doctrine proceeds upon the principle, that, in the distribution of the assets of insolvents, the equities of the creditors, whether joint or separate, must be worked out through the medium of the partners; that creditors can only step into the shoes of their immediate debtors in reaching their effects where there are conflicting claims; and that, inasmuch as an individual partner could not himself come in and compete with the partnership creditors, who are in fact his own creditors, in the distribution of the fund, and thereby prejudice those who were not only creditors of the partnership but also of himself; therefore the separate creditors of a partner could not enforce any claim to a distributive share of the joint effects against the partnership creditors, which could not have been enforced by the partner himself for his own benefit. Story on Partnership, sec. 390. The rule, however, that these several funds are to be thus administered as they stood at the time of the insolvency, is to be received with this important limitation, that it does not apply in case either where the effects obtained, creating the debt, were taken from the separate estate to augment the joint estate, or from the joint estate to augment the separate estate, fraudulently, or under circumstances from which fraud may be inferred, or under which it would be implied.

In the case before us, however, it is not pretended that the firm obtained the borrowed money from Murray improperly. The separate creditors of Murray, therefore, are not, on account of this claim for money lent by Murray to the firm, entitled to participate with the partnership creditors in the distribution of the joint effects.

Judgment of the common pleas reversed; and ordered that the separate effects of Peter Murray be distributed *pro rata* first among his individual creditors, before any application thereof be made to the payment of the partnership debts of Dever & Murray; and that the partnership effects be applied first to the payment of the partnership debts, irrespective of the claim of the partner, Peter Murray, for money loaned by him to the firm.

SWAN, BRINKERHOFF, SCOTT, and SUTLIFF, JJ., concurred.

NOTES

1. The rule established in the instant case, that partnership creditors have priority in partnership assets and individual creditors in individual assets, was adopted by the UPA in Section 40(b) and (i). It is known as the "dual priorities" rule or the "jingle" rule. *See* MACLACHLAN, BANKRUPTCY 424 (1956). Section 40(h) applies the dual priorities rule if the assets are in the possession of a court for distribution.

2. Sections 40(a)-(d) and 18(a) require that a partner "contribute towards the losses . . . sustained by the partnership according to his share in the profits." Note, however, that the dual priorities rule would require that individual creditors of the partner be satisfied before such a contribution can be made.

3. The second aspect of the instant case, that individual creditors are not entitled to an equal distribution with partnership creditors on indebtedness owed by the firm to the particular partner, is reflected in Section 40(b) of the UPA. Is this consistent with the dual priorities rule?

C. THE FEDERAL BANKRUPTCY ACT

Section 5 of the Federal Bankruptcy Act, 11 U.S.C.A. § 23 (1966), deals with partnership bankruptcy and reads as follows:

§ 23. Partners.

(a) A partnership, including a limited partnership containing one or more general partners, during the continuation of the partnership business or after its dissolution and before the final settlement thereof, may be adjudged a bankrupt either separately or jointly with one or more or all of its general partners.

(b)   A petition may be filed by one or more or all of the general partners in the separate behalf of a partnership or jointly in behalf of a partnership and of the general partner or partners filing the same: *Provided, however,* That where a petition is filed in behalf of a partnership by less than all of the general partners, the petition shall allege that the partnership is insolvent. A petition may be filed separately against a partnership or jointly against a partnership and one or more or all of its general partners.

(c)   The creditors of the bankrupt partnership shall appoint the trustee, who shall be the trustee of the individual estate of a general partner being administered in the proceeding: *Provided, however,* That the creditors of a general partner adjudged a bankrupt may, upon cause shown, be permitted to appoint their separate trustee for his estate. In other respects, so far as possible, the partnership estate shall be administered as herein provided for other estates.

(d)   The court of bankruptcy which has jurisdiction of one of the general partners may have jurisdiction of all the general partners and of the administration of the partnership and individual property.

(e)   The trustee or trustees shall keep separate accounts of the partnership property and of the property belonging to the individual general partners.

(f)   The expenses shall be paid from the partnership property and the individual property in such proportions as the court shall determine.

(g)   The net proceeds of the partnership property shall be appropriated to the payment of the partnership debts and the net proceeds of the individual estate of each general partner to the payment of his individual debts. Should any surplus remain of the property of any general partner after paying his individual debts, such surplus shall be added to the partnership assets and be applied to the payment of the partnership debts. Should any surplus of the partnership property remain after paying the partnership debts, such surplus shall be distributed among the individual partners, general or limited, or added to the estates of the general partners, as the case may be, in the proportion of their respective interests in the partnership and in the order of distribution provided by the laws of the State applicable thereto.

(h)   The court may permit the proof of the claim of the partnership estate against the individual estates, and vice versa, and may marshal the assets of the partnership estate and individual estates so as to prevent preferences and secure the equitable distribution of the property of the several estates.

(i)   Where all the general partners are adjudged bankrupt, the partnership shall also be adjudged bankrupt. In the event of one or more but not all of the general partners of a partnership being adjudged bankrupt, the partnership property shall not be administered in bankruptcy, unless by consent of the general partner or partners not adjudged bankrupt; but such general partner or partners not adjudged bankrupt shall settle the partnership business as expeditiously as its nature will permit and account for the interest of the general partner or partners adjudged bankrupt.

(j)   The discharge of a partnership shall not discharge the individual general partners thereof from the partnership debts. A general partner adjudged a bankrupt either in a joint or separate proceeding may, pursuant to the provisions of this title, obtain a discharge from both his partnership and individual debts.

(k)   If a limited partnership is adjudged bankrupt, any limited partner who is individually liable under the laws of the United States or of any State for any of the partnership debts shall be deemed a general partner as to such debts and, if he is insolvent, shall be subject to the provisions and entitled to the benefits of this title, as in the case of a general partner.

NOTES

1.   *In re* Ira Haupt & Co., 240 F. Supp. 369 (S.D.N.Y. 1965) is a recent case involving a well known bankruptcy. The question before the court was whether the Trustee in Bankruptcy of the bankrupt partnership had the right and duty to marshal the assets of a general partner, for the purpose of administering them in accordance with Section 5* of the Bankruptcy Act, who had not been individually adjudicated a bankrupt, had a minor interest in the partnership and may have been unaware of the activities which had brought about the bankruptcy of the partnership. The question was answered affirmatively. The story of the involvement of the Haupt firm in the catastrophe spawned by Anthony De Angelis is set forth in N. MILLER, THE GREAT SALAD OIL SWINDLE (1965). It is a graphic illustration of the fi-

---

* 11 U.S.C.A. § 23, quoted above.

nancial hazards one can run as a general partner in certain businesses.

2. Section 5(a) of the Bankruptcy Act adopts the entity theory of partnership law by providing that a partnership may be adjudicated bankrupt without regard to the adjudication of its members as individuals. The aggregate theory is applicable, however, in the determination of the solvency or insolvency of the partnership, since the assets of the partnership include the excess of each partner's individual assets over his individual liabilities. *See* Kaufman-Brown Potato Co. v. Long, 182 F.2d 594 (1950); Francis v. McNeal, 228 U.S. 695 (1913). "Partnership" is not defined in the Act. The existence in fact of a partnership is controlled by state law. Kaufman-Brown Potato Co. v. Long, *supra*.

3. Section 5(g) of the Act adopts the dual priorities rule described in *Rodgers v. Meranda*. Under bankruptcy law, however, the rule applies even when there are no firm assets and no solvent partners. Farmers' & Mechanics' Nat'l Bank v. Ridge Avenue Bank, 240 U.S. 498 (1916).

Chapter 15

DISSOLUTION

This chapter will highlight a few of the innumerable problems that can arise when a firm dissolves without a competent partnership agreement to anticipate and resolve the inevitable conflicts occasioned by the need to receive and disburse money. We will begin with a treatment of some of the causes of dissolution, followed by some of the problems created when a "new" partnership continues the business of the dissolved firm, and concluding with a review of the steps which must be taken when a firm terminates its business and faces payment of its liabilities and distribution of its assets.

Sections 29 and 30 of the UPA draw a distinction between dissolution, winding up and termination. Section 29 defines the legal event of dissolution as "the change in the relation of the partners caused by any partner ceasing to be associated in the carrying on . . . of the business," such as the death or bankruptcy of a partner. Section 30 cautions the reader that the partnership is not thereby terminated "but continues until the winding up of partnership affairs is completed."

"Dissolution" thus designates the point of time when the partners cease to carry on the business together. The partnership, consisting of that particular group of individuals, has technically "dissolved." "Termination" is the point in time when all partnership affairs are wound up: assets are sold or distributed, debts are paid, capital is returned, and so forth. And "winding up" is the process by which one gets from dissolution to termination. It is important to keep this terminology straight when drafting an instrument or briefing a case, but most people in everyday language use "dissolution" to cover the whole process.

The language of Sections 29 and 30 makes the existence of any partnership seem fragile and apt to be drastically disrupted at any time by events beyond the partners' control. Consider a large law firm, for example. One of 15 partners dies or goes bankrupt. Is the partnership, a successful and well known firm of years standing, now "dissolved" and the remaining partners forced to "terminate"? That doesn't make any sense, does it? What reasoning underlies the rigid language of these two sections? *See* Adams

v. Jarvis, 23 Wis. 2d 453, 127 N.W.2d 400 (1964); Bromberg, *Partnership Dissolution—Causes, Consequences and Cures,* 43 Tex. L. Rev. 631 (1965). We will return to the matter of continuing the business and the problems involved in forming a new business in Part B in this chapter.

A.　CAUSES OF DISSOLUTION

The causes of dissolution are set forth in Section 31, as amplified by Section 32, and bear careful reading. These sections largely codify (and clarify) the rules formulated at common law. Ask yourself why the situations described in Section 32 require a court decree before dissolution is effected.

Note that Section 31 is divided into three parts: dissolution caused without violation of the partnership agreement, at the termination of the partnership as agreed upon or at the will of any partner if no term was agreed upon; dissolution caused in violation of the partnership agreement (observe, therefore, that a partner always has the power to terminate a partnership, even though he may not have the contractual right to do so); and, finally, four circumstances where it doesn't seem to make any difference what the partnership agreement provides. One of the four circumstances is dissolution by court decree under Section 32 which, with the exception of clause (e), operates under vague and ill-defined circumstances. Ask yourself whether you could make the language in Section 32 less broad if you were given the job of drafting the statute.

POTTER v. BROWN
Supreme Court of Pennsylvania
328 Pa. 554, 195 A. 901, 118 A.L.R. 1415 (1938)

Opinion by Mr. Justice Barnes:

The dissolution of a partnership is sought in this proceeding where it is charged that the wrongful conduct of three of the ten members of the firm affects prejudicially the carrying on of its business and renders impracticable the continuance of the partnership.

The parties to this litigation have been conducting a general insurance business in Philadelphia since January 1, 1934, under the firm name of Henry W. Brown & Co. This long established business has been a prosperous one. It was founded in 1871 by Henry W. Brown, the father of defendant, Henry I. Brown,

Sr., and has continued through various successor partnerships until the formation of the present firm in 1934. Most of the parties to this litigation have been associated in business for many years. Defendant Brown, Sr., has been actively in control since his father's retirement in 1899. The plaintiffs have been connected with the present and predecessor partnerships for periods varying from twenty-eight years in the case of Potter to nineteen years in the case of Jones. All of the plaintiffs entered the business in minor capacities, and reached their respective positions by their faithful efforts.

The present partnership was formed in 1934, when the parties entered into a written agreement of partnership for a term of five years from January 1, 1934. While the agreement expressly vests in all partners the right to be acquainted with, vote upon and participate in firm business, it confers unlimited control over the business of the firm upon Henry I. Brown, Sr. The partnership articles provide that "The business and capital of the partnership shall be considered as divided into one hundred (100) parts or shares, as a convenient method of determining the rights of the respective partners to profits and as to management"; that Henry I. Brown, Sr., "shall own a majority of the said shares"; the other partners "shall own such shares and receive such salaries or other compensation as may be arranged by each of them individually with the said Henry I. Brown." A few days later the agreement was supplemented with respect to the interests of some of the partners in the event of death, matters which are not here in issue. On November 22, 1934, Henry I. Brown, Sr., by letter fixed the salary and percentage interest of each of the seven plaintiffs in the firm.*

The articles of partnership further provided that "The vote of the majority in interest of the shares shall, however, control any question which may come up for decision unless otherwise provided herein." The only right reserved to the majority in number of the firm members, rather than in interest, was to vote for admission of partners into the firm, or to terminate the interest of any partner other than Henry I. Brown, Sr.

---

* The percentages so agreed upon in so far as the plaintiffs are concerned were as follows: Potter, 7%; Jones, 3½%; Seal, 7%; Booth, 6%; Wise, 5%; Mackerell, one-third of 2½% each year until the end of 1936 when his proprietary interest was to be 2½%. Deacon's interest in the partnership was identical with that of Mackerell.

The interests in the partnership of the defendants Henry R. Ruhl and Henry I. Brown, Jr., do not clearly appear from the record, but such interests are junior ones, while the large majority interest is possessed by Henry I. Brown, Sr.

From the record it appears that the net profits of the business after payment of partners' salaries (other than Henry I. Brown, Sr.) amounted to $80,484.52 for the year 1936, nor did the prosperity of the business decline after the institution of this proceeding, as profits for January and February, 1937, were $26,947.97, compared with a corresponding profit of $20,716.36 for the same months of 1936. The amounts received by the plaintiffs, as salaries, shares of profits and bonuses from the business were substantial, varying from $10,529.72 and $12,133.92, received by Seal in 1934 and 1935, respectively, to $6,023.10 and $6,812.11 paid to Mackerell in the same years. A portion of the payments to the plaintiffs consisting of personal bonuses was distributed by Henry I. Brown, Sr., out of his individual share of the profits. It was also Mr. Brown's practice to pay similar bonuses to employees of the business in recognition of meritorious services. These bonus payments were customarily made at the end of each year.

There are no allegations here of the failure by the partners to attend properly to the partnership business. The parties concede that the prosperity of the business is due to the skill and efforts of all the partners, each in his particular field. However, the operation of a general insurance business, such as this, requires substantial cash balances for working capital. The major portion of this working capital has been furnished by Mr. Brown, Sr. It has been his custom in the past to permit his share of the profits to accumulate, and to be used by the firm as working capital. At the end of 1936 the partnership was availing itself of approximately $65,000 of undrawn profits payable to Mr. Brown. The other partners withdrew the greater portion of their shares of the profits promptly after they were determined, and since it was the practice of the firm to ascertain profits semiannually, at the time of this litigation there were profits payable to the other partners only for the last six months of 1936.

The partnership differences giving rise to the present litigation concerned the proposed admission into the partnership of Charles H. Moore, who had been the accountant for the firm for several years. At the regular monthly partnership meeting held November 30, 1936, Henry I. Brown, Sr., proposed to his associates that new articles of partnership for a ten-year period be executed, giving to him complete control over partnership affairs without any limitation whatsoever, and that Moore be admitted into the firm as a partner. Both proposals were rejected by the plaintiffs. A new partnership agreement was not suggested again, and requires no further consideration. The admission of Moore into the firm was defeated by a vote of seven to three,

all seven plaintiffs voting against the motion, and the three defendants voting in its favor. The plaintiffs deny any animosity
toward Moore, but assert that membership in the firm should
be limited to insurance men.

Thereafter Mr. Brown called a special meeting of partners
which was held on December 8, 1936, to reconsider the vote
taken at the prior meeting, but again the result was the rejection
by the same vote of the motion to admit Moore into the partnership. Then, in order to compel his partners to submit to his
wishes, the senior partner called another special meeting for the
following day for the purpose of acting on a motion to reduce
salaries. He introduced at this meeting and had passed a resolution to reduce the plaintiffs' salaries to an unspecified amount.
On December 15, 1936, the plaintiffs received checks representing a fifty per centum reduction of the amount of the salaries
then due them.

Subsequently Mr. Brown abandoned his intention of coercing
his partners, and while the resolution of December 9, 1936, reducing salaries has not been formally rescinded, checks in the full
amount of their salaries were delivered shortly thereafter to
plaintiffs, and on each due date since that time they were given
checks for all salary due. However, the plaintiffs refused to attend
any meetings of the firm subsequent to December 9, 1936, upon
the ground that Mr. Brown's conduct had breached the partnership agreement.

The present bill was filed by plaintiffs thereafter, praying for
a decree of dissolution of the partnership, and that they be
granted the right to continue the business under the name of
Henry W. Brown & Co. until the expiration date of the partnership agreement. The court below after hearing reached the conclusion that the defendants had wilfully and persistently violated
the partnership agreement and had so conducted themselves that
it was not reasonably practicable to carry on the business in partnership with them. It entered an order dissolving the partnership, enjoining the three defendants from interfering with its
affairs and decreeing that plaintiffs should continue the business
during the remainder of the partnership period under the name
of Henry W. Brown & Co.

As we review the record, we must determine whether the evidence supports the findings made by the chancellor, and whether
his inferences therefrom justify the drastic decree of dissolution
which has been entered in this case. The gravamen of the plaintiffs' complaint is that Henry I. Brown, Sr., by endeavoring first
to persuade and subsequently to coerce them into accepting
Moore as a partner so affected the harmonious operation of the

business that its continuance as now constituted is not feasible from a partnership standpoint. The plaintiffs argue that the measures of compulsion adopted by Mr. Brown in furtherance of his purpose to force Moore as a partner upon them was misconduct of such character as to operate as a repudiation and cancellation of the agreement.

There seems to be no question that the senior partner did endeavor to compel obedience to his wishes by his copartners, and while his conduct undoubtedly was improper and of a character meriting condemnation, the record is nevertheless devoid of any evidence of acts or threatened acts on his part which would cause serious or permanent injury to the partnership business. The increasing profits clearly indicate that the partnership has not materially suffered. Indeed it is undisputed that by permitting his undrawn profits to be used by the partnership for working capital and "good will" purposes Mr. Brown has contributed toward the prosperity of the business far beyond his duties as a partner.

Few, if any, reasons upon which ordinarily the dissolution of a partnership will be decreed are present in this case. There is neither allegation nor proof of fraudulent or dishonest practices and conduct upon which a dissolution would be granted. While it is well settled, as we said in Herman v. Pepper, 311 Pa. 104 (p. 108): that "the exclusion of one partner by another from the management of the partnership business or possession of the partnership property is undoubtedly ground for dissolution by a court of equity," we are of opinion that the plaintiffs have failed to show that they were denied their proper share of participation in the management of the business. The rights of the partners among themselves are regulated by the articles of partnership. Where, as in this case, the partnership articles provide for the vesting of exclusive control in one partner such stipulation will be strictly enforced: Peacock v. Cummings, 46 Pa. 434; Nick v. Craig, 301 Pa. 50. If the plaintiffs are aggrieved because they are unable to exercise the direction over partnership affairs that they feel is their due, the reason is to be found primarily in the partnership agreement of October 12, 1934, rather than because of any misconduct of Mr. Brown.

The ill-advised and almost immediately abandoned attempt to reduce the salaries of the plaintiffs does not, in our opinion, under the particular circumstances, constitute such gross misconduct on the part of Brown, Sr., and the two partners who supported him, as to require their expulsion from the business. It is not apparent from the evidence that the occurrence has in any way interfered with the success of the partnership. The contention of the plaintiffs that the continuance of the partnership with the defendants is impractical is so manifestly inconsistent with the success of the business that the absence of merit therein is obvious. Differences and discord should be settled by the partners themselves by the application of mutual forbearance rather than by bills in equity for dissolution. Equity is not a referee of partnership quarrels. A going and prosperous business will not be dissolved merely because of friction among the partners; it will not interfere to determine which contending faction is more at fault.

Moreover, we are not convinced that plaintiffs have shown such an absence of blame on their part as entitles them to equitable relief. It would appear that they were willing to pick up the gauntlet of partnership conflict and to seize upon incidents, constituting at their gravest import mere technical misconduct of a partner, for the purpose of acquiring as their own a long established and valuable business to the exclusion of the partner who is the owner of the major interest therein.

From our review of the case it follows that the Act of March 26, 1915, P. L. 18, Section 32, subsections (c) and (d) thereof, has no application here. This section provides that whenever "(c) A partner has been guilty of such conduct as tends to affect prejudicially the carrying on of the business," and "(d) A partner wilfully or persistently commits a breach of the partnership agreement, or otherwise so conducts himself in matters relating to the partnership business that it is not reasonably practicable to carry on the business in partnership with him," dissolution will be decreed. The facts here negative the existence of such a state of affairs as makes applicable the provisions of this section of the act, although it is apparent that the present proceeding was founded upon this section.

The case is ruled by the principle as stated in Story On Partnership, Section 287, where it is said: "It is proper to observe that it is not for every trivial departure from duty or violation of the articles of partnership, or for every trifling fault or misconduct that courts of equity will interfere and decree a dissolution."

After careful examination of the record we find that the evidence does not sustain the conclusions reached by the court below. The chancellor's deductions or inferences made from the facts which he has found are erroneous and cannot stand. As was said in Pennsylvania Knitting Mills v. Bayard, 287 Pa. 216, 219: "While it is true that a chancellor's findings of fact, supported by evidence, have the force of a jury's verdict, it is likewise true that, where there is no evidence to support them, or the finding is based on an inference erroneously taken, they will not stand."

In the light of our decision that the acts of Henry I. Brown, Sr., did not justify the decree of dissolution, it is unnecessary to discuss separately the charges against the defendants Henry I. Brown, Jr., and Henry R. Ruhl, and likewise, since the decree of dissolution was in error, we need not consider whether it was proper to order that plaintiffs continue the partnership business for the balance of the term under the firm name.

The assignments of error are sustained; the decree of the court below is reversed, and it is ordered that the bill be dismissed. Appellees to pay the costs.

PAGE v. PAGE
Supreme Court of California
55 Cal. 2d 192,
359 P.2d 41, 10 Cal. Rptr. 643 (1961)

TRAYNOR, J. Plaintiff and defendant are partners in a linen supply business in Santa Maria, California. Plaintiff appeals from a judgment declaring the partnership to be for a term rather than at will.

The partners entered into an oral partnership agreement in 1949. Within the first two years each partner contributed approximately $43,000 for the purchase of land, machinery, and linen needed to begin the business. From 1949 to 1957 the enterprise was unprofitable, losing approximately $62,000. The partnership's major creditor is a corporation, wholly owned by plaintiff, that supplies the linen and machinery necessary for the day-to-day operation of the business. This corporation holds a $47,000 demand note of the partnership. The partnership operations began to improve in 1958. The partnership earned $3,824.41 in that year and $2,282.30 in the first three months of 1959. Despite this improvement plaintiff wishes to terminate the partnership.

The Uniform Partnership Act provides that a partnership may be dissolved "By the express will of any partner when no definite term or particular undertaking is specified." (Corp. Code, § 15031, subd. (1)(b).)* The trial court found that the partnership is for a term, namely, "such reasonable time as is necessary to enable

-----

* § 31 (1) (b) of the UPA. The last two numerals of the statutory citations correspond to the sections of the UPA—*Ed.*

said partnership to repay from partnership profits, indebtedness incurred for the purchase of land, buildings, laundry and delivery equipment and linen for the operation of such business. . . ." Plaintiff correctly contends that this finding is without support in the evidence.

Defendant testified that the terms of the partnership were to be similar to former partnerships of plaintiff and defendant, and that the understanding of these partnerships was that "we went into partnership to start the business and let the business operation pay for itself,—put in so much money, and let the business pay itself out." There was also testimony that one of the former partnership agreements provided in writing that the profits were to be retained until all obligations were paid.

Upon cross-examination defendant admitted that the former partnership in which the earnings were to be retained until the obligations were repaid was substantially different from the present partnership. The former partnership was a limited partnership and provided for a definite term of five years and a partnership at will thereafter. Defendant insists, however, that the method of operation of the former partnership showed an understanding that all obligations were to be repaid from profits. He nevertheless concedes that there was no understanding as to the term of the present partnership in the event of losses. He was asked: "[W]as there any discussion with reference to the continuation of the business in the event of losses?" He replied, "Not that I can remember." He was then asked, "Did you have any understanding with Mr. Page, your brother, the plaintiff in this action, as to how the obligations were to be paid if there were losses?" He replied, "Not that I can remember. I can't remember discussing that at all. We never figured on losing, I guess."

Viewing this evidence most favorable for defendant, it proves only that the partners expected to meet current expenses from current income and to recoup their investment if the business were successful.

Defendant contends that such an expectation is sufficient to create a partnership for a term under the rule of Owen v. Cohen, 19 Cal.2d 147, 150 [119 P.2d 713]. In that case we held that when a partner advances a sum of money to a partnership with the understanding that the amount contributed was to be a loan to the partnership and was to be repaid as soon as feasible from the prospective profits of the business, the partnership is for the term reasonably required to repay the loan. It is true that *Owen v. Cohen, supra,* and other cases hold that partners may impliedly agree to continue in business until a certain sum of money is earned (Mervyn Investment Co. v. Biber, 184 Cal. 637, 641-642 [194 P. 1037]), or one or more partners recoup their investments (Vangel v. Vangel, 116 Cal.App.2d 615, 625 [254 P.2d 919]), or until certain debts are paid (*Owen v. Cohen, supra,* at p. 150), or until certain property could be disposed of on favorable terms (Shannon v. Hudson, 161 Cal.App.2d 44, 48 [325 P.2d 1022]). In each of these cases, however, the implied agreement found support in the evidence.

In *Owen v. Cohen, supra,* the partners borrowed substantial amounts of money to launch the enterprise and there was an understanding that the loans would be repaid from partnership profits. In *Vangel v. Vangel, supra,* one partner loaned his co-partner money to invest in the partnership with the understanding that the money would be repaid from partnership profits. In *Mervyn Investment Co. v. Biber, supra,* one partner contributed all the capital, the other contributed his services, and it was understood that upon the repayment of the contributed capital from partnership profits the partner who contributed his services would receive a one-third interest in the partnership assets. In each of these cases the court properly held that the partners impliedly promised to continue the partnership for a term reasonably required to allow the partnership to earn sufficient money to accomplish the understood objective. In *Shannon v. Hudson, supra,* the parties entered into a joint venture to build and operate a motel until it could be sold upon favorable and mutually satisfactory terms, and the court held that the joint venture was for a reasonable term sufficient to accomplish the purpose of the joint venture.

In the instant case, however, defendant failed to prove any facts from which an agreement to continue the partnership for a term may be implied. The understanding to which defendant testified was no more than a common hope that the partnership earnings would pay for all the necessary expenses. Such a hope does not establish even by implication a "definite term or particular undertaking" as required by section 15031, subdivision (1)(b), of the Corporations Code.

All partnerships are ordinarily entered into with the hope that they will be profitable, but that alone does not make them all partnerships for a term and obligate the partners to continue in the partnerships until all of the losses over a period of many years have been recovered.

Defendant contends that plaintiff is acting in bad faith and is attempting to use his superior financial position to appropriate the now profitable business of the partnership. Defendant has invested $43,000 in the firm, and owing to the long period of losses his interest in the partnership assets is very small. The fact that plaintiff's wholly owned corporation holds a $47,000 demand note of the partnership may make it difficult to sell the business as a going concern. Defendant fears that upon dissolution he will receive very little and that plaintiff, who is the managing partner and knows how to conduct the operations of the partnership, will receive a business that has become very profitable because of the establishment of Vandenberg Air Force Base in its vicinity. Defendant charges that plaintiff has been content to share the losses but now that the business has become profitable he wishes to keep all the gains.

There is no showing in the record of bad faith or that the improved profit situation is more than temporary. In any event these contentions are irrelevant to the issue whether the partnership is for a term or at will. Since, however, this action is for a declaratory judgment and will be the basis for future action by the parties, it is appropriate to point out that defendant is amply protected by the fiduciary duties of copartners.

Even though the Uniform Partnership Act provides that a partnership at will may be dissolved by the express will of any partner (Corp. Code, § 15031, subd. (1) (b)), this power, like any other power held by a fiduciary, must be exercised in good faith.

We have often stated that "Partners are trustees for each other, and in all proceedings connected with the conduct of the partnership every partner is bound to act in the highest good faith to his copartner and may not obtain any advantage over him in the partnership affairs by the slightest misrepresentation, concealment, threat or adverse pressure of any kind." (Corp. Code, § 15021.) Although Civil Code, section 2411, embodying the foregoing language, was repealed upon the adoption of the Uniform Partnership Act, it was not intended by the adoption of that act to diminish the fiduciary duties between partners.

A partner at will is not bound to remain in a partnership, regardless of whether the business is profitable or unprofitable. A partner may not, however, by use of adverse pressure "freeze out" a copartner and appropriate the business to his own use. A partner may not dissolve a partnership to gain the benefits of the business for himself, unless he fully compensates his copartner for his share of the prospective business opportunity. . . .

Likewise in the instant case, plaintiff has the power to dissolve the partnership by express notice to defendant. If, however, it is proved that plaintiff acted in bad faith and violated his fiduciary duties by attempting to appropriate to his own use the new prosperity of the partnership without adequate compensation to his copartner, the dissolution would be wrongful and the plaintiff would be liable as provided by subdivision (2) (a) of Corporations Code, section 15038 (rights of partners upon wrongful dissolution) for violation of the implied agreement not to exclude defendant wrongfully from the partnership business opportunity

The judgment is reversed.

GIBSON, C. J., McCOMB, J., PETERS, J., WHITE, J., DOOLING, J., and WOOD (Parker), J. pro tem., concurred.

B. CONTINUING THE BUSINESS

(i) *Liability of an Incoming Partner*

One could argue that this topic is not directly related to dissolution of a partnership, since apparently under the UPA a partner can come into an existing business without affecting the entity (recall that Section 29 talks in terms of partners *leaving* the business, not of new partners entering it). Consider, however, the discussion of that point in the following case, which also involves an interesting twist on the liability of an incoming partner under Section 17 of the UPA.

ELLINGSON v. WALSH, O'CONNOR & BARNESON
Supreme Court of California
15 Cal. 2d 673, 104 P.2d 507 (1940)
Noted in 29 Calif. L. Rev. 252 (1941)

GIBSON, C. J. This is an action against a partnership and its members for rent due under a written lease. The case was submitted upon an agreed statement of facts. Judgment was rendered against the partnership and all general partners, and from this judgment Lionel T. Barneson, one of the general partners, appeals. Appellant admits his liability for rent, but contends that the obligation therefor arose before his admission to the partnership, and that under section 2411 of the Civil Code this liability must be satisfied only out of partnership property.

On October 4, 1929, the First National Corporation, as lessor, let the premises in question to Walsh, O'Connor & Company, a special partnership, as lessee, for a period of ten years, at a total rental of $66,000, payable in monthly instalments of various amounts. In September, 1930, the original lessor assigned the lease to the First National Bank of Beverly Hills, of which plaintiff is receiver. In December, 1930, the limited partnership of Walsh, O'Connor & Barneson was formed, and all of the rights of the original lessee were assigned to the new partnership, which thereafter occupied the premises and paid rent to the bank as lessor.

On April 21, 1931, H. J. Barneson withdrew as a general partner. On April 28, 1931, appellant Lionel T. Barneson was taken in as a general partner, and ever since has enjoyed all of the rights and privileges and assumed the obligations as a general partner of said partnership. In February, 1932, the partnership, pursuant to written consent obtained from the lessor, sublet the premises to a third party who was in possession all of the time for which rental is sought to be recovered. The sublessee paid rent to the partnership. During the period between April, 1931, and March, 1932, the partnership paid the full rent due under the lease to the lessor. The judgment herein is for rent claimed to be due for the period commencing March 1, 1932, and ending January 25, 1933, in the sum of $2,374.13, after deducting certain credits and payments. The judgment was a general one against all defendants, with no proviso restricting its enforcement or satisfaction against appellant.

The issue in this case is not the liability of the partnership as such, nor the liability of its assets. There is no doubt whatever that the plaintiff may satisfy his claim against the partnership out of any of its properties. The sole question is whether the appellant's liability as an incoming partner may be satisfied by resort to his personal assets.

Section 2411 of the Civil Code (sec. 17 of the Uniform Partnership Act) provides: "A person admitted as a partner into an existing partnership is liable for all the obligations of the partnership arising before his admission as though he had been a partner when such obligations were incurred, except that his liability shall be satisfied only out of partnership property." It is this section upon which appellant relies, and the interpretation urged by appellant is the sole basis of his case. Appellant contends that since the lease was executed before he became a partner, the obligation of the lease arose before his admission, and therefore his liability can only be satisfied out of partnership property.

This contention would be sound if the only obligation of the partnership in this transaction was one which arose prior to appellant's admission to the firm. For example, if a promissory note had been executed by the partnership for a consideration then passing to it, the obligation would have arisen at the time of execution of the note and the case would plainly be within the statute. But appellant's contention overlooks the fact that a tenant of real property is not liable for rent solely by reason of

the contract of lease. Tenancies in property need not necessarily
be created by valid leases. One may become a tenant at will or a
periodic tenant under an invalid lease, or without any lease at all,
by occupancy with consent. Such tenancies carry with them the
incidental obligation of rent, and the liability therefore arises
not from contract but from the relationship of landlord and
tenant. The tenant is liable by operation of law. Where there is a
lease the liability of the tenant arising by operation of law is not
superseded by the contractual obligation. Both liabilities exist
simultaneously. The lease has a dual character; it is a conveyance of an estate for years, and a contract between lessor and
lessee. The result is that dual obligations arise,—contractual
obligations from the terms of the lease, and obligations under the
law from the creation of the tenancy. As it is sometimes expressed,
there are dual obligations arising from "privity of contract" and
"privity of estate." (See Samuels v. Ottinger, 169 Cal. 209, 211
[146 Pac. 638, Ann. Cas. 1916E, 830].)

This dual character of the obligations of a tenant may be
illustrated by an assignment of the tenant's right without any
assumption by the obligations by the assignee. The assignee who
does not assume is not liable on the lease, that is to say, is not
bound by its contractual obligations. But the non-assuming assignee who occupies the premises is liable by reason of his tenancy,
and his obligation, arising out of privity of estate, continues at
least through the period of his occupancy. Likewise, where the
new tenant comes in without even a written assignment, but
takes over the possession of the old lessee with the consent of the
lessor, he is liable for rent. The liability in such case, as in this
case, is not merely for the reasonable value of the use, as would
be the case where the tenancy was one at will. The entry and occupation here is under the lease, and despite the lack of contractual assumption of the obligations of the lease, the successor to
the original lessee is bound by the convenant to pay rent in the
lease, which runs with the land.

Under the above principles, the first partnership, which did
not include appellant as a member, was bound by these dual
obligations; that is, having expressly assumed the obligations of
the lease, it was bound in contract and also by reason of its tenancy. When appellant became a member, the first partnership
was, in legal theory, dissolved and a new partnership came into
being composed of the old members and appellant. This second
partnership did not expressly assume the obligations of the lease,
but it occupied the premises. Whether it was liable contractually
on the lease is immaterial; it became liable for rent as a tenant.
Strangers coming in with consent and occupying the premises

would be liable; tenants would be liable even if there were no lease at all; and this second partnership and all its members were liable regardless of any lack of assumption of the obligations of the lease. If this were not true, then the second partnership could have been ousted despite its asserted right to occupy the premises under the existing lease. No one has suggested that the admission of appellant as a partner would have permitted the lessor to terminate the lease. But if the new partnership could not be ousted, it was a tenant and was liable for rent. And with respect to the liability of a tenant during this period, appellant's position is identical with that of any other member of the new partnership formed when he entered the old association.

The only remaining question is whether the section of the Uniform Partnership Act, quoted above, has changed the rule. Appellant's theory is that he, as a member of the second partnership, may receive the benefits of years of occupancy under the lease, but that his personal assets cannot be reached in satisfaction of liability therefor if the lease was executed before he became a member of the partnership. The statute, however, neither contemplates nor accomplishes any such result. The provision refers simply to "obligations of the partnership arising before his admission." The statute does not determine the nature of any particular obligation, nor the time when it may be deemed to arise. It does not attempt, in other words, to interfere with the general rules of contract or property. Under the general law the obligation of a tenant arising from occupation of the premises is a continuing one; that is, it arises and binds him continually throughout the period of his occupation. This obligation on the part of appellant first arose when the new partnership, of which he was a member, occupied the premises as a tenant. It follows that his obligation as a tenant arose after his admission to the partnership and the immunity given by section 2411 does not apply.

The judgment is affirmed.

SHENK, J., CURTIS, J., CARTER, J., and EDMONDS, J., concurred.

Rehearing denied. HOUSER, J., voted for a rehearing.

NOTE

The Commissioners' Note to Section 17 states that the section "conforms to the actual decisions of the courts which, however, are arrived at by making every effort to impress an assumption of liability on the part of the new partnership, formed as a result of the admission of the new partner, of the debts of the old partnership." Apparently, therefore, the event of dissolution does carry beyond the leaving of a partner.

The common-law rule was that any change in personnel automatically dissolved the old partnership. Also, "the common law was formally stated to the effect that an incoming partner is not liable for debts contracted before his admission." *Id.* The consequence of this at common law was that creditors of the old partnership were left with only claims against the old partners, and were put at a disadvantage to the extent the new partnership became indebted to new creditors.

As stated above in the Commissioners' Note, in response to this the common-law courts worked hard to find assumptions of obligations by the new partnership. *See also,* Annot., 45 A.L.R. 1240 (1926). Sections 17 and 41(1) now resolve this, don't they?

(ii)   *Liability of the Withdrawing Partner*

What is the relationship of the withdrawing partner to the creditors of the old firm? Does he remain indefinitely liable for its obligations, no matter how often extended by the remaining members of the firm (who, let us assume, continue the business)? Can he demand that the creditors promptly seek payment from the remaining partners? What is the effect of an assumption of partnership liabilities by the remaining partners? *See* Section 36 (1)-(3) of the UPA. And *see* Faricy v. J. S. Brown Mercantile Co., 87 Colo. 427, 288 Pac. 639 (1930) where a retired partner informed a creditor of the assumption by the continuing—and still solvent—partner, and told him to collect promptly from that partner. The creditor failed to do so. The court held that the retiring partner could not avoid liability. The *Faricy* case was decided before the UPA was adopted in Colorado. Would the same result be reached today under the UPA?

(iii)   *Liability and Rights of a Deceased Partner's Estate*

BLUT v. KATZ

Supreme Court of New Jersey
13 N.J. 374, 99 A.2d 785 (1953)
Noted in 63 Yale L.J. 709; 9 Rutgers L. Rev. 212;
67 Harv. L. Rev. 1271; 23 Fordham L. Rev. 211;
38 Minn. L. Rev. 553; 29 N.Y.U.L. Rev. 1151 (all in 1954)

The opinion of the court was delivered by

WACHENFELD, J. We granted cross-petitions for certification in this cause, in which the dispute between the widow of a deceased partner and the surviving partners concerns her efforts to be paid for her deceased husband's share in the partnership business and the endeavors of the surviving partners to recover from the widow amounts paid to others to perform the work normally performed by the decedent.

In 1925 five partners executed a partnership agreement under which they conducted the United Shop Cap Company. The term was for a period of one year. Amongst other things, it provided for even distribution of the profits, weekly allowances to the partners, and the paying off of any partner who should voluntarily withdraw.

Before 1940 two partners withdrew, but no further agreement was executed by the remaining partners, and from that date until the death of the decedent they operated the business as equal one-third partners.

In 1946 the plaintiff's husband became ill and thereafter, until his death in 1949, rendered no services to the partnership business. During this time, however, he continued to receive his customary weekly salary and his share of other withdrawals, amounting in all to some $60,000. He also had free access to the books of the business and complete information as to its operation, and apparently approved the various financial reports.

After his death the widow instituted this action as executrix against the two surviving partners, seeking a dissolution of the partnership, an accounting, and the appointment of a receiver. A counterclaim was filed seeking to charge the account of the deceased partner with the cost of providing substitute help during his illness from 1946 to 1949. To avoid the appointment of a receiver, the defendants deposited $25,000 with the court to secure payment of whatever sum might be determined to be due to the plaintiff.

At the trial level, judgment was entered in the amount of $19,153 and interest for the plaintiff to the date of the defendants' deposit into court, and the counterclaim was dismissed. Blut v. Katz, 14 N. J. Super. 121 (Ch. Div. 1951). The sum so arrived at represented the deceased partner's interest in the capital account at the time of his death. Good will was excluded as an asset of the partnership in calculating the deceased partner's interest.

On cross-appeals to the Appellate Division, it was there determined good will should have been included, and the cause was remanded to the Chancery Division to determine the value thereof. Both sides are dissatisfied with the results and each appeals.

The first issue to be decided is the denial by both lower tribunals of the plaintiff's demand for an option to recover the profits earned after the dissolution which might be attributable to the use of her husband's capital by the defendants in continuing the partnership business. The demand was made pursuant to R. S. 42:1-42 and the briefs are replete with discussion of the meaning of the statute.

The Appellate Division reasoned thusly:

"The plaintiff argues that under R. S. 42:1-42 she is entitled to receive the profits attributable to the use of Blut's capital since his death. However, such right accrues where the business is continued after the death of a partner 'with the consent of . . . the representative of the deceased partner.' R. S. 42:1-41.3. The trial court found that in this instance there had been no consent, citing Laterra v. Laterra, 134 N. J. Eq. 162 (E. & A. 1943), which held that participation in the profits of an enterprise rested upon contribution of skill, time and diligence, rather than the mere use of capital. With this view we agree. Phillips v. Reeder and Prior, 18 N. J. Eq. 95 (Ch. 1866)."

The plaintiff asserts this is erroneous because it gives "a novel and unjustifiable interpretation" to the statute, and her consent to the continuation of the business is "immaterial on the question of her right of election."

The statute referred to deals with the liability of persons continuing partnership business without liquidation. It is obviously designed to protect the estate of a deceased partner from the demands of creditors in the event the executors see fit to liquidate. If the executor gives consent to the continuation of the partnership business without liquidation, then the estate's interest in the partnership is subjected to the claims of any new creditors.

It is contended the statutory plan requiring consent as therein outlined consistently provides that the *quid pro quo* is the right to a proportionate share of the profits of the new partnership if the personal representative so chooses, for the assumption of the additional risk of claims of the new creditors. Without the personal representative's consent, it is said, no additional risk is assumed and the Legislature by its enactment, therefore, gave no right to a share of the profits.

R. S. 42:1-42, entitled "Ascertaining value of interest of retired or deceased partner," giving the right to profits, refers to "conditions set forth in paragraph . . . 3 . . . of section 42:1-41 of this title. . . ." Paragraph 3 of R. S. 42:1-41 provides:

"When any partner retires or dies and the business of the dissolved partnership is continued as set forth in paragraphs '1' and

'2' of this section, with the consent of the retired partners or the representative of the deceased partner. . . ."

R. S. 42:1-42 pointedly refers to *paragraph* 3 of R. S. 42:1-41, which, in turn, specifically provides for the consent of the retired partner or the representative of the deceased partner.

This is the manner in which the statute was construed by both lower tribunals, and in that construction we concur, even though research fails to disclose judicial adjudications in other jurisdictions buttressing this interpretation.

The only contrary thoughts we have encountered are expressed in an opinion construing the New York Partnership Act, identical with our own, M. & C. Creditors Corp. v. Pratt, 172 Misc. 695, 17 N. Y. S. 2d 240 (Sup. Ct. 1938), affirmed 255 App. Div. 838, 7 N. Y. S. 2d 662 (1938), app. den. 255 App. Div. 962, 8 N. Y. S. 2d 990 (1938), affirmed, no opinion, 281 N. Y. 804, 24 N. E. 2d 482 (Ct. App. 1939), where the writer, referring to the sections already discussed, says they could not have been intended to limit the rights of the representatives to require payment of the decedent's interest as of the date of death. Also, in Cahill v. Haff, 248 N. Y. 377, 162 N. E. 288 (Ct. App. 1928), the court, although finding consent express or implied by the representative and holding he was therefore entitled to receive the profits attributable to the use of his rights in the property of the dissolved partnership, by way of dictum opined: "Probably the same thing is true if there be no consent."

However, we have concluded in the case *sub judice* that the statutory plan involves the giving of consent to the continuation of the partnership business before a deceased partner's representative can exercise the option to profits. Furthermore, consideration of merely the broad equitable doctrines applicable, without recourse to the statute, brings us to the same end result.

There is much authority sustaining the principle that, where one or more partners of a firm continue the business after the death of one of the partners, the legal representative of the deceased partner is entitled to his share of the profits made, Phillips v. Reeder and Prior, 18 N. J. Eq. 95 (Ch. 1866); Drapkin v. Klebanoff, 5 N. J. Misc. 531 (Ch. 1927), but this principle is not universally applied; it has many limitations and qualifications and is always subject to equitable considerations.

So, where the main success of the firm is due to the skill, time and diligence of the remaining partners, the application of the rule has been withheld upon the ground that it would be inequitable to do otherwise. Profits having been denied, interest on the amounts involved is substituted in its place. *Phillips v. Reeder and Prior, supra;* Laterra v. Laterra, 134 N. J. Eq. 162 (E. & A. 1943).

Here the success of the business, from the record, appears to be due to the personal element and efforts, the plaintiff's husband having made no contribution to its continuance for a long period of time while he was ill. Under the circumstances and the proof, it would be inequitable to permit the plaintiff to participate in the profits made after the dissolution, to which she contributed nothing, as determined by the trial court.

Assuming consent to be a prerequisite to her right to elect to receive profits in lieu of interest, the plaintiff insists the findings of the trial court and the Appellate Division that she did not give consent to the continued operation of the partnership business were erroneous, as "all the evidence on the case is to the contrary."

This lavish assertion, however, finds little support in the record. There is an abundance of evidence sustaining the conclusions arrived at below. Being purely a fact issue, decided adversely to the plaintiff by both lower courts, we will not ordinarily make an independent finding unless a miscarriage of justice is imminent. Midler v. Heinowitz, 10 N. J. 123 (1952). We do not conceive that to be the situation here.

The defendants on their cross-appeal charge error in the holding that they were not entitled to be reimbursed for sums paid to other employees required to perform the deceased partner's work.

The trial court embraced the doctrine of waiver, finding the defendants, in approving the accountant's reports and statements of the partnership business, waived any right they may have had to charge the deceased partner later with the cost of providing substitute help, while the Appellate Division reached a like result, laying emphasis on the fact that no deductions were made from Blut's drawing account nor were his partnership accounts so charged, concluding the payments were gratuitous.

These expenditures were not charged, admit the defendants, against the deceased partner's account while he was alive for fear of its deleterious effect upon his health, but they argue strenuously there is no waiver since there was no consideration. Further, there is said to have been no ground for application of the doctrine of estoppel and no gratuity.

The classification of these expenditures is evidenced by an abundance of irresistible testimony indicating there was no intention to charge these items against the deceased partner. The defendants' whole course of conduct bespeaks otherwise. The expense had been absorbed in the accounts of the company, and financial statements to that effect had been issued with full knowledge of all the circumstances. The defendants' commendable generosity, extended to their ailing partner over the years, was not converted into a demand for reimbursement until they felt they were being imposed upon by the widow's aggressive action and excessive claims.

Defendants next allege error in the Appellate Division's allowing good will to be considered as a partnership asset in determining the value of the deceased partner's interest.

The trial court denied its inclusion, relying upon the original partnership agreement, which provided if any partner voluntarily withdrew, then good will should not be considered in determining the amount due. The Appellate Division, however, logically points out the withdrawal here was not voluntary but was caused by death, and the contingency of death was never considered or contemplated in the partnership agreement as drawn.

Our statutes impliedly recognize good will as a partnership asset, *R. S.* 42:1-9, and there appears to be ample authority for its inclusion as an asset in determining the value for purposes of liquidation, where the partnership agreement does not eliminate it by express terms. In Kanzler v. Smith, 123 N. J. Eq. 602 (E. & A. 1938), the Court of Errors and Appeals said the liquidation of the partnership property in accordance with law does not contemplate more than disposal of the physical assets and an accounting by the surviving partner of the value of the deceased partner's interest, including the value of good will, if any. The same court, in *In re* Westhall's Estate, 125 N. J. Eq. 551 (E. & A. 1939), said:

"It is a commercial corollary that a long established business which can net a profit of $12,000 in less than a year possesses a tangible and substantial good will value."

Here the record indicates the partnership earned approximately $73,000 in 1946, about $47,000 in 1947, and $28,000 in 1948. The facts in the case under consideration make us conclude good will should have been considered, as the Appellate Division decided.

The defendants contend the issue of good will was not embraced in the pretrial order and "the Appellate Division was not warranted in considering the matter and, on the merits, its conclusion was wrong."

The issue was clearly raised at the trial, recognized by the court, and not objected to by the defendants. Rule 3:15-2, now R. R. 4:15-2. The record shows the court granted permission to the plaintiff "to reserve the right to offer evidence of the value of good will." To deny consideration of this issue, under these circumstances, would be inequitable.

Lastly, the defendants urge that when the cash deposit was made in court to secure any judgment recovered, they should not have been required to pay further interest.

The order permitted the filing of a bond, but the defendants decided to deposit cash. Interest after dissolution is normally payable to the date of judgment, *Laterra v. Laterra, supra,* and the deposit as construed by the Appellate Division was in no sense payment to the plaintiff. It was security for payment and made to avoid the appointment of a receiver. We are in accord with the Appellate Division's conclusions.

For the reasons herein cited, the judgment of the Appellate Division is affirmed and the cause remanded to the Chancery Division for disposition not inconsistent with these views.

HEHER, J. (dissenting in part). I agree that the proofs do not sustain the contention that the plaintiff representative of the deceased partner consented to the continuance of the partnership business after his death. But this does not defeat her right, if she so elects, to recover the profits earned after the dissolution of the partnership fairly attributable to the use of the deceased partner's capital in the continuance of the partnership business. If this be the representative's right where such consent is given, and *R. S.* 42:1-41 and *R. S.* 42:1-42 expressly so provide, then *a fortiori* this is so where the business is continued without consent; for it would seem that on the plainest principles of equity and justice the surviving partners should account for the profits ensuing from their unauthorized use of the deceased partner's capital. The principle of unjust enrichment has peculiar application in such circumstances. It is not the capital risk that determines the right, but rather the reaping of a profit from the use of the capital.

The statutory provisions cited *supra* have reference to the rights of creditors where consent is given to continue the partnership business.

I would modify the judgment in this regard also.

For affirmance—Justices OLIPHANT, WACHENFELD, BURLING, JACOBS and BRENNAN—5.

For modification—Chief Justice VANDERBILT and Justice HEHER—2.

NOTES

1. An able Note in 63 YALE L. J. 709 (1954) criticizes the *Katz* case on the ground that it discards the common-law doctrine that a former partner normally receives profits or interest at his option

whether the business is continued with or without his consent, and does this in the absence of a clear legislative mandate. The Note author argues that Section 42 does not constitute such a mandate. Do you arrive at the same conclusion applying Section 42? The policy underlying the common-law approach is explained as the prevention of unjust enrichment of the remaining members of the firm and not allowing them to gain through a breach of their fiduciary duty to wind up partnership affairs. (§ 38(1)). The author observes that all other courts considering Section 42 have construed it to reach the common-law result, citing four opinions.

2. Under the majority construction of Section 42 described above, would the nonconsenting but profit-taking former partner be an "ordinary creditor" under Section 42, and thus in the same position vis-a-vis other creditors of the partnership as a consenting former partner? Does this make sense to you? What position, incidentally, would that be? Assume that a new creditor loans money to the new firm. How would he rank in priority to the consenting and nonconsenting former partners?

3. What are the rights under the UPA, if any, of a partner who has wrongfully caused dissolution to recover profits from the firm? If the nonconsenting former partner is unable to recover profits under the Act, should a partner wrongfully causing dissolution be able to?

4. If an executor consents to leaving the assets in the business (or the deceased partner's will so directs), is the general estate liable for losses occasioned in the business beyond the value of the interest left in the business?

5. Dissolution requires the remaining partners to wind up partnership affairs, unless there has been an effective consent by the former partner or his personal representative to continuation of the business. UPA § 38(1); CRANE & BROMBERG § 86; Dial v. Martin, 37 S.W.2d 166 (Tex. Civ. App. 1931), *rev'd on other grounds,* 57 S.W.2d 75 (1933); Mosher v. Lount, 29 Ariz. 267, 240 P. 1027 (1925). Assume that the executor of a deceased partner's estate refuses to consent to leaving the deceased's interest in the partnership and demands dissolution of the business, sale of its assets and payment of the deceased's share. Assume further that the partnership was formed by oral agreement, with nothing said about dissolution. Can the remaining partners continue the business anyway, and pay the estate its "fair share"? Who determines what is a fair share in the absence of an agreement? Can the surviving partners forfeit their right to be liquidators of the business, file a bill in equity for winding up the business under a receiver, and then buy the business at a receiver's sale? *See*

James v. Wade, 200 Ark. 786, 141 S.W.2d 13 (1940) (holding yes). *But cf.* Note, 47 MICH. L. REV. 430 (1949), indicating that some courts refuse to honor a request by the surviving partners to a court to evaluate the deceased partner's interest and allow the business to continue without liquidation.

6. Obviously one way to avoid the problems of note 5 above is to draw an agreement arranging for continuity and a valuation of a deceased partner's interest. *See* Fuller, *Partnership Agreements for Continuation of an Enterprise After the Death of a Partner,* 50 YALE L. J. 202 (1940). *See also* Note, 71 HARV. L. REV. 687 (1958), describing some of the tax and planning complexities involved in business purchase agreements.

C. WINDING UP AND TERMINATING THE BUSINESS

Part VI of the UPA is relevant here. Note especially the rules for distribution in Section 40.

---

i. *Winding Up*

Section 37 of the UPA substantially codifies the common-law rules on winding up. It establishes a duty on the surviving partner to wind up and account for the interest of the decedent. The process of winding up involves reducing the partnership property, including contributions from partners for the payment of partnership obligations, to cash and distributing the proceeds. If the surviving partner is not acting diligently and in good faith, a court having jurisdiction may appoint a receiver on petition of the representative of the deceased partner's estate. If more than one partner survives, they may agree among themselves that one or more of their number shall act as liquidating partner. Section 18(f) of the UPA provides for compensation for the partner performing these services.

---

ii. *Termination*

The order of distribution of assets is specified by UPA § 40(b). Creditors outside of the partnership are paid first, then the claims of partners other than for capital contributions or profits, then capital is returned and finally the remaining balance, if any, is distributed as profits. If the partnership property is insufficient to repay capital contributions, the loss is to be shared by the solvent partners in the proportions in which they share profits. UPA §§ 18(a), 40(d). The statutory rules of distribution may be varied by agreement of the partners (UPA § 40, first clause), except that the rights of third persons cannot be affected without their consent.

MAHAN v. MAHAN
Supreme Court of Arizona
107 Ariz. 517, 489 P.2d 1197 (1971)

CAMERON, Justice. Plaintiff brought this action individually and as executrix of the estate of her deceased husband. She sought an accounting and division of properties of a partnership in which her husband had been a partner. From a decision of the Superior Court of Coconino County granting her what she considered inadequate relief, she appeals.

We are called upon to consider the following questions:

1. Did the court err in determining that plaintiff's husband's partnership share should be measured by his capital account?
2. Did the court err in accepting the book value as the proper valuation of the property?
3. Did the court err in failing to direct the liquidation and sale of the remaining partnership assets?

Plaintiff is the widow of Terrell B. Mahan, who died 15 July 1966, in Prescott, Arizona. She is suing Gordon Mahan in her own right and as executrix of Terrell Mahan's estate, which is being probated in Yavapai County, Arizona.

When plaintiff married Terrell Mahan in 1948, a construction and agriculture partnership existed between Terrell and his brothers, Gordon and Merwin. (Merwin withdrew from the partnership in 1962 and is not involved in the lawsuit.) The partnership was an equal one in the sense that the profits were divided on an equal basis, first three ways, and then two.

In 1964 the partnership traded one of the partnership properties for a home into which Terrell and his wife moved. The property was taken in the name of Terrell and his wife. The bookkeeper reduced the capital account of Terrell and his wife by $23,000. In short, Terrell and his wife received a house worth $23,000, more or less, in exchange for reducing their capital account to $23,000 less than Gordon's.

At about this time (1964-1965), the partnership became inactive, and it remained inactive through Terrell's death in 1966 and the bringing of the present lawsuit in 1969. Gordon, the surviving partner, did nothing toward settling the affairs of the partnership and accounting to the executrix until Terrell's widow brought this suit.

The principal partnership asset at Terrell's death and the time of the lawsuit was the remainder of a block of Coconino County land bought in 1950 and known as the Red Lake Ranch. In 1960, the partnership sold a portion of the ranch for $80,000, leaving 1,752.34 acres of patented land, plus 1,843 acres of State leased land. In December, 1961, the partnership made an aborted sale of practically the same block owned at Terrell's death. The sale, for $284,200, fell through in 1963, and the Mahan brothers regained the land. In 1963, an appraiser valued the land at $43,-868.44, and in 1965 an accountant, for federal tax purposes, lowered the value on the partnership books to $15,622.61.

The balance sheet of the partnership as of 31 December 1965 showed $33,274.61 worth of assets. The principal components of this amount were $15,622.61 for the Red Lake Ranch, two investments with a total book value of $9,150, but market values of $900 and $0 respectively, and an oil lease listed at $4,000 but actually worthless.

PARTNERSHIP SHARE

The defendant advanced, and the trial court accepted, the contention that since Terrell's capital account was reduced by $23,-000 to $4,005.45 and was one-eighth of the value of the total capital account ($31,308.06), Terrell's widow should receive, in distribution, one-eighth of $33,274.31 or $4,159.29.

To illustrate, the amounts in controversy are as follows:

PARTNERSHIP ASSETS:

Red Lake Ranch	$15,622.61*
Investments	9,150.00**
Oil Lease	4,000.00***
Miscellaneous	4,502.00****
	$33,274.61

* Sold in 1961 for $284,200; appraised for $43,868.44 in 1963; the $15,622.61 was a figure allowed by the I.R.S. for tax purposes after an aborted sale.

** Represents 7,500 shares of Unita Finance Company, which the plaintiff's (and partnership's) accountant testified was worthless, and 180 shares of Arizona Livestock Production Credit Association, which the accountant testified was worth $5.00 per share or $900.

*** Valueless, according to the accountant.

**** Subject to extreme disagreement on several items.

CAPITAL ACCOUNT:

Terrell	$ 4,005.45
Gordon	27,302.61
	$31,308.06

Plaintiff contends that after payment of the partnership debts, she should share with Gordon on a 50-50 basis. We agree with plaintiff as long as it is understood that the capital account, as used by the bookkeeper in this case, represents a debt of the partnership.

Upon liquidation, the rules of payment are governed by § 29-240 A.R.S.,* which decrees that the liabilities of the partnership shall rank in the following order of payment:

"(a) Those owing to creditors other than partners.
(b) Those owing to partners other than for capital and profits.
(c) Those owing to partners in respect of capital.
(d) Those owing to partners in respect of profits."

"The capital of the partnership is the amount specified in the agreement of the partners, which is to be contributed by the partners for the purpose of initiating and operating the partnership business." Barrett & Seago, Partners and Partnerships, Law and Taxation, Vol. I, § 3.1, p. 169. Thus, ordinarily we would look to the initial contributions for a determination of the amounts "owing to partners in respect of capital." While the general rule is that the amount of capital may not be changed absent consent of all the partners, the partners in this case have apparently conceded to adjustments in their capital accounts. See Barrett, supra at 170. Thus, we accept, for purposes of this case, adjustments in plaintiff's and defendant's capital accounts to $4,005.45 and $27,302.61 respectively.

"The distribution of partnership assets in the course of winding up consists, first of all, in the payment of creditors other than partners. Then come the claims of partners other than those for repayment of capital contributions or profits, such as claims for advancements made by partners. . . . After this, *partners are entitled to return of their respective capital contributions.* . . . *Finally, any remaining balance of partnership property is distributable as profits.*" Judson A. Crane, Handbook on the Law of Partnership, 2nd ed., § 90, p. 477. (Emphasis added)

---

* The last two numerals indicate the corresponding section in the UPA— *Ed.*

In accord, Rowley, Modern Law of Partnership, Vol. II, § 673. These theories are supported by § 29-218 A.R.S., which provides as follows:

"Rules determining rights and duties of partners

. . . .

"1.   Each partner shall be repaid his contributions, whether by way of capital or advances to the partnership property and share equally in the profits and surplus remaining after all liabilities, including those to partners, are satisfied. . . ."

Therefore, whether the money left after satisfaction of creditor's claims and recoupment of partnership capital is termed profits or surplus, the clear mandate of the authorities is that, absent agreement to the contrary, it is divided equally as profits.

As mentioned earlier, the defendant in this case has placed reliance on § 29-242 A.R.S., relating to continuation of the business when a partner dies. In the instant case, the business was not continued by the surviving partner. Quite the contrary. The partnership remained dormant and nothing was done until suit was brought by the plaintiff to compel an accounting. Where the efforts of one partner in the production of profits in an active partnership cease, it is apparent that he no longer bears full entitlement to his respective share of the profits. In this case, however, where the partnership has been and continues to be inactive, any appreciation of worth is due to the nature of the partnership property rather than the effort of the surviving partner. Thus, we hold that any profit or surplus resulting shall be shared equally.

This conclusion is buttressed by the situation confronting plaintiff and her husband Terrell when they gave up $23,000 of their capital account for a $23,000 home. They knew that the partnership had few or no debts and owned a piece of property that had sold for $284,200 a few years previous. If the value of the land had stayed reasonably constant in the interim, the partnership would have been worth over $300,000. It is highly unlikely that the plaintiff and her husband intended, when they gave up $23,000 of their capital account for a $23,000 house, that they were actually giving up not $23,000 but well over $100,000.

DID THE COURT ERR IN ACCEPTING THE BOOK VALUE AS THE PROPER VALUATION OF THE PROPERTY?

The answer to the question of whether the court erred in accepting the book value of the assets can be answered by looking at the figures we have reconstructed. Every single component of the $33,274.61 book value has been strongly contested. The Red Lake Ranch, for example, was sold in 1961 for over $280,000, but has an arbitrary book value of $15,622.61. An "investment" valued at $9,150 is made up of two investments, one worthless and the other worth only $900. In short, the book values are completely arbitrary and should not have been used.

A very similar situation confronted the Court of Appeals in Hurst v. Hurst, 1 Ariz.App. 227, 232, 401 P.2d 232, 237 (1965). The court there stated, "The book value[s] assigned to the tangible assets . . . are arbitrary valuations and cannot be applied." Defendant attempts to distinguish Hurst, supra, by arguing that in Hurst no one strongly pushed for using book value while defendant is pushing for that solution here. However, that distinction is not persuasive, for the Court of Appeals in Hurst was faced with the problem of the relative fairness of different methods of asset valuation of partnerships, and concluded that the book value was arbitrary.

Our determination that the trial court erred in accepting book value is in accord not only with the Arizona case of Hurst v. Hurst, supra, but with general principles of partnership accounting. The normal rule is that book value is only used in ascertaining the respective shares when there is an explicit contractual provision to that effect, and even then is not used where the facts of the case make it inequitable to do so. See 47 A.L.R.2d 1425. Here there was no contractual provision mandating the use of book value, and even if there were, the facts show book value in this case to be so disproportionate to possible real values that it would be inequitable for it to be used anyway.

DID THE COURT ERR IN FAILING TO DIRECT THE LIQUIDATION AND SALE OF THE REMAINING PARTNERSHIP ASSETS?

Having decided that book value should not be used in valuing the partnership assets, we are forced to conclude that the trial court should have granted plaintiff's wish to have the assets liquidated. Hurst v. Hurst, supra; Carrasco v. Carrasco, 4 Ariz.App. 580, 422 P.2d 411 (1967); 68 C.J.S. Partnership § 316-b, p. 828.

§ 14-541 A.R.S. also lends support to our position:

"A. The surviving partner of a decedent may continue in possession of the partnership property and settle its affairs, but the interest of decedent in the partnership shall be included in the inventory and appraised as other property.

"B. The surviving partner shall settle the affairs of the partnership without delay, account to the executor or administrator and pay over such balances as may from time to time be payable to him as the personal representative of decedent.

"C.   Upon application of the executor or administrator, the court may order the surviving partner to render an account and if he neglects or refuses may compel such accounting by attachment for contempt. The executor or administrator may maintain against the surviving partner any action which decedent could have maintained."

CONCLUSION

We hold that the partnership assets must be liquidated, and that the general creditors be paid first. If the assets are insufficient for this purpose, the estate and Gordon should be charged equally for the losses. If the assets are more than sufficient then the surviving partner should be paid first up to the amount of $23,297.16 to set off the withdrawal from the capital account by Terrell. Any amount left over should be equally divided between Terrell's estate and the surviving partner, Gordon Mahan.

Reversed and remanded for further proceedings not inconsistent with this opinion.

STRUCKMEYER, C. J., and LOCKWOOD, J., concur.

———————

PROBLEMS

1.   *A* and *B* orally formed a partnership at will, each contributing $1,000 capital. The partnership made a $7,000 net profit the first year, which was not withdrawn by the partners. Then *C* joined the partnership, contributing $1,000. The partnership lost $4,000 in the next year. *A* has decided to leave the business. What return of capital is he entitled to? Assume nothing was said about this matter when the partnership was formed.

2.   *A* and *B* orally formed a partnership for a three-year term. As part of their capital contributions *A* transferred 1,000 shares of *X* corporation stock, and *B* transferred 1,000 shares of *Y* corporation stock, to the partnership. The shares were of approximately equal value. The partnership did not sell any of the stock. The three-year term has come to an end. *A*'s stock has increased five fold in value, and *B*'s has declined by 70 per cent. *A* wants to take his stock back, and *B* wants all stock to be sold and the proceeds divided equally. Assume this matter was not covered in the partnership agreement. Who should prevail?

3.   After two years with the firm Guinand, an employee of the partnership of Walton and Kearns, was granted an interest

in the partnership under the following terms, which were contained in a letter to him:

Dear Mr. Guinand:

This letter is to confirm your ownership of an undivided ten per cent (10%) interest in WALTON-KEARNS, a co-partnership composed of Paul T. Walton and Thomas F. Kearns. This interest includes and is not in addition to the various interests from time to time heretofore acquired by you.

Upon termination of your employment with the partnership for any cause whatsoever your interest in the partnership will be determined and discharged as of said time without resulting in a dissolution of the partnership; and such interest as may have theretofore been vested in you in specific properties shall become your separate property, subject to adjustments incident to your proportionate share of the then partnership indebtedness.

> (Signed by the partners,
> Paul T. Walton and
> Thomas F. Kearns.)

Do you see any problems of interpretation in the above letter? If you were drafting the letter for the partners, in what manner, if at all, would you vary the language? *See* Guinand v. Walton, 25 Utah 2d 253, 480 P.2d 137 (1971).

4. In July, 1968, Mocquot applied for work at the Cotton Gin Company. He was informed that they had no work for him but that one Meadows needed someone to run his gin for him. Mocquot went to Meadows and told him that he had no money but, at the suggestion of Meadows, agreed he would go in partnership with Meadows and run the gin for the season, including buying, receiving, ginning and shipping the cotton, for half the net profit. Meadows agreed to contribute $10,000 capital. Nothing else was spelled out in the agreement. Mocquot worked for the season (approximately eight months), and received nothing for his services because the business lost money due to a severe fluctuation in the cotton market. Meadows paid the resulting loss of $5,000. The partnership has dissolved and Meadows now seeks to recover one-half the loss of his capital from Mocquot. What result?

If no agreement losses are based on how profits are shared

APPENDIX A

UNIFORM PARTNERSHIP ACT

Source: The text contained below is taken from Volume 6 of UNIFORM LAWS ANNOTATED, MASTER ED., UNIFORM PARTNERSHIP ACT (1969) and is reproduced with permission of the publishers. The Master Edition contains the text of the Act, the Official Comments to particular sections (which are notes or comments prepared by the Commissioners on Uniform State Laws in explanation of particular sections of the Act, including sometimes a description of the status of the case law existing at that time and the impact of the Act upon it, the source of the particular section, if drawn from other legislation, and so forth), a listing of the jurisdictions which have made variations from the official text when adopting the Act and a brief description of the nature of the variation, a citation to law review commentaries pertaining to the subject matter of the particular section, and annotations of court decisions construing the particular section. The data contained immediately below on adoptions of the Act is drawn from the 1973 pocket part to Volume 6.

The Act was approved by the National Conference of Commissioners on Uniform State Laws, October 14, 1914, and adopted in the following jurisdictions: Alabama (1972), Alaska (1917), Arizona (1954), Arkansas (1941), California (1949), Colorado (1931), Connecticut (1961), Delaware (1947), District of Columbia (1962), Florida (1973), Guam (no date), Idaho (1920), Illinois (1917), Indiana (1950), Iowa (1971), Kentucky (1954), Maryland (1916), Massachusetts (1923), Michigan (1917), Minnesota (1921), Missouri (1949), Montana (1947), Nebraska (1943), Nevada (1931), New Jersey (1919), New Mexico (1947), New York (1919), North Carolina (1941), North Dakota (1959), Ohio (1949), Oklahoma (1955), Oregon (1939), Pennsylvania (1915), Rhode Island (1957), South Carolina (1950), South Dakota (1923), Tennessee (1917), Texas (1962), Utah (1921), Vermont (1941), Virgin Islands (1957), Virginia (1918), Washington (1955), West Virginia (1953), Wisconsin (1915), and Wyoming (1917).

The states which are not included in the above list are: Georgia, Hawaii, Kansas, Louisiana, Maine, Mississippi, and New Hampshire.

PART I

PRELIMINARY PROVISIONS

§ 1. Name of Act

This act may be cited as Uniform Partnership Act.

§ 2. Definition of Terms

In this act, "Court" includes every court and judge having jurisdiction in the case.

"Business" includes every trade, occupation, or profession.

"Person" includes individuals, partnerships, corporations, and other associations.

"Bankrupt" includes bankrupt under the Federal Bankruptcy Act[1] or insolvent under any state insolvent act.

"Conveyance" includes every assignment, lease, mortgage, or encumbrance.

"Real property" includes land and any interest or estate in land.

§ 3. Interpretation of Knowledge and Notice

(1) A person has "knowledge" of a fact within the meaning of this act not only when he has actual knowledge thereof, but also when he has knowledge of such other facts as in the circumstances shows bad faith.

(2) A person has "notice" of a fact within the meaning of this act when the person who claims the benefit of the notice:

(a) States the fact to such person, or

(b) Delivers through the mail, or by other means of communication, a written statement of the fact to such person or to a proper person at his place of business or residence.

§ 4. Rules of Construction

(1) The rule that statutes in derogation of the common law are to be strictly construed shall have no application to this act.

(2) The law of estoppel shall apply under this act.

(3) The law of agency shall apply under this act.

(4) This act shall be so interpreted and construed as to effect its general purpose to make uniform the law of those states which enact it.

(5) This act shall not be construed so as to impair the obligations of any contract existing when the act goes into effect, nor to affect any action or proceedings begun or right accrued before this act takes effect.

---

[1] 11 U.S.C.A. § 1 et seq.

§ 5. Rules for Cases Not Provided for in This Act

In any case not provided for in this act the rules of law and equity, including the law merchant, shall govern.

PART II

NATURE OF PARTNERSHIP

§ 6. Partnership Defined

(1) A partnership is an association of two or more persons to carry on as co-owners a business for profit.

(2) But any association formed under any other statute of this state, or any statute adopted by authority, other than the authority of this state, is not a partnership under this act, unless such association would have been a partnership in this state prior to the adoption of this act; but this act shall apply to limited partnerships except in so far as the statutes relating to such partnerships are inconsistent herewith.

§ 7. Rules for Determining the Existence of a Partnership

In determining whether a partnership exists, these rules shall apply:

(1) Except as provided by section 16 persons who are not partners as to each other are not partners as to third persons.

(2) Joint tenancy, tenancy in common, tenancy by the entireties, joint property, common property, or part ownership does not of itself establish a partnership, whether such co-owners do or do not share any profits made by the use of the property.

(3) The sharing of gross returns does not of itself establish a partnership, whether or not the persons sharing them have a joint or common right or interest in any property from which the returns are derived.

(4) The receipt by a person of a share of the profits of a business is prima facie evidence that he is a partner in the business, but no such inference shall be drawn if such profits were received in payment:

(a) As a debt by installments or otherwise,

(b) As wages of an employee or rent to a landlord,

(c) As an annuity to a widow or representative of a deceased partner,

(d) As interest on a loan, though the amount of payment vary with the profits of the business,

(e) As the consideration for the sale of a good-will of a business or other property by installments or otherwise.

§ 8. Partnership Property

(1) All property originally brought into the partnership stock or subsequently acquired by purchase or otherwise, on account of the partnership, is partnership property.

(2) Unless the contrary intention appears, property acquired with partnership funds is partnership property.

(3) Any estate in real property may be acquired in the partnership name. Title so acquired can be conveyed only in the partnership name.

(4) A conveyance to a partnership in the partnership name, though without words of inheritance, passes the entire estate of the grantor unless a contrary intent appears.

PART III

RELATIONS OF PARTNERS TO PERSONS DEALING WITH THE PARTNERSHIP

§ 9. Partner Agent of Partnership as to Partnership Business

(1) Every partner is an agent of the partnership for the purpose of its business, and the act of every partner, including the execution in the partnership name of any instrument, for apparently carrying on in the usual way the business of the partnership of which he is a member binds the partnership, unless the partner so acting has in fact no authority to act for the partnership in the particular matter, and the person with whom he is dealing has knowledge of the fact that he has no such authority.

(2) An act of a partner which is not apparently for the carrying on of the business of the partnership in the usual way does not bind the partnership unless authorized by the other partners.

(3) Unless authorized by the other partners or unless they have abandoned the business, one or more but less than all the partners have no authority to:

(a) Assign the partnership property in trust for creditors or on the assignee's promise to pay the debts of the partnership,

(b) Dispose of the good-will of the business,

(c) Do any other act which would make it impossible to carry on the ordinary business of a partnership,

(d) Confess a judgment,

(e) Submit a partnership claim or liability to arbitration or reference.

(4) No act of a partner in contravention of a restriction on authority shall bind the partnership to persons having knowledge of the restriction.

§ 10. Conveyance of Real Property of the Partnership

(1)   Where title to real property is in the partnership name, any partner may convey title to such property by a conveyance executed in the partnership name; but the partnership may recover such property unless the partner's act binds the partnership under the provisions of paragraph (1) of section 9, or unless such property has been conveyed by the grantee or a person claiming through such grantee to a holder for value without knowledge that the partner, in making the conveyance, has exceeded his authority.

(2)   Where title to real property is in the name of the partnership, a conveyance executed by a partner, in his own name, passes the equitable interest of the partnership, provided the act is one within the authority of the partner under the provisions of paragraph (1) of section 9.

(3)   Where title to real property is in the name of one or more but not all the partners, and the record does not disclose the right of the partnership, the partners in whose name the title stands may convey title to such property, but the partnership may recover such property if the partners' act does not bind the partnership under the provisions of paragraph (1) of section 9, unless the purchaser or his assignee, is a holder for value, without knowledge.

(4)   Where the title to real property is in the name of one or more or all the partners, or in a third person in trust for the partnership, a conveyance executed by a partner in the partnership name, or in his own name, passes the equitable interest of the partnership, provided the act is one within the authority of the partner under the provisions of paragraph (1) of section 9.

(5)   Where the title to real property is in the names of all the partners a conveyance executed by all the partners passes all their rights in such property.

§ 11. Partnership Bound by Admission of Partner

An admission or representation made by any partner concerning partnership affairs within the scope of his authority as conferred by this act is evidence against the partnership.

§ 12. Partnership Charged with Knowledge of or Notice to Partner

Notice to any partner of any matter relating to partnership affairs, and the knowledge of the partner acting in the particular matter, acquired while a partner or then present to his mind, and the knowledge of any other partner who reasonably could and should have communicated it to the acting partner, operate as notice to or knowledge of the partnership, except in the case of a fraud on the partnership committed by or with the consent of that partner.

§ 13. Partnership Bound by Partner's Wrongful Act

Where, by any wrongful act or omission of any partner acting in the ordinary course of the business of the partnership or with the authority of his co-partners, loss or injury is caused to any person, not being a partner in the partnership, or any penalty is incurred, the partnership is liable therefor to the same extent as the partner so acting or omitting to act.

§ 14. Partnership Bound by Partner's Breach of Trust

The partnership is bound to make good the loss:

(a) Where one partner acting within the scope of his apparent authority receives money or property of a third person and mis-applies it; and

(b) Where the partnership in the course of its business re-ceives money or property of a third person and the money or property so received is misapplied by any partner while it is in the custody of the partnership.

§ 15. Nature of Partner's Liability

All partners are liable

(a) Jointly and severally for everything chargeable to the partnership under sections 13 and 14.

(b) Jointly for all other debts and obligations of the partner-ship; but any partner may enter into a separate obligation to perform a partnership contract.

§ 16. Partner by Estoppel

(1) When a person, by words spoken or written or by con-duct, represents himself, or consents to another representing him to any one, as a partner in an existing partnership or with one or more persons not actual partners, he is liable to any such person to whom such representation has been made, who has, on the faith of such representation, given credit to the actual or ap-parent partnership, and if he has made such representation or consented to its being made in a public manner he is liable to such person, whether the representation has or has not been made or communicated to such person so giving credit by or with the knowledge of the apparent partner making the representa-tion or consenting to its being made.

(a)   When a partnership liability results, he is liable as though he were an actual member of the partnership.

(b)   When no partnership liability results, he is liable jointly with the other persons, if any, so consenting to the contract or representation as to incur liability, otherwise separately.

(2)   When a person has been thus represented to be a partner in an existing partnership, or with one or more persons not actual partners, he is an agent of the persons consenting to such representation to bind them to the same extent and in the same manner as though he were a partner in fact, with respect to persons who rely upon the representation. Where all the members of the existing partnership consent to the representation, a partnership act or obligation results; but in all other cases it is the joint act or obligation of the person acting and the persons consenting to the representation.

§ 17. Liability of Incoming Partner

A person admitted as a partner into an existing partnership is liable for all the obligations of the partnership arising before his admission as though he had been a partner when such obligations were incurred, except that this liability shall be satisfied only out of partnership property.

PART IV

RELATIONS OF PARTNERS TO ONE ANOTHER

§ 18. Rules Determining Rights and Duties of Partners

The rights and duties of the partners in relation to the partnership shall be determined, subject to any agreement between them, by the following rules:

(a)   Each partner shall be repaid his contributions, whether by way of capital or advances to the partnership property and share equally in the profits and surplus remaining after all liabilities, including those to partners, are satisfied; and must contribute towards the losses, whether of capital or otherwise, sustained by the partnership according to his share in the profits.

(b)   The partnership must indemnify every partner in respect of payments made and personal liabilities reasonably incurred by him in the ordinary and proper conduct of its business, or for the preservation of its business or property.

(c)   A partner, who in aid of the partnership makes any payment or advance beyond the amount of capital which he agreed to contribute, shall be paid interest from the date of the payment or advance.

(d)   A partner shall receive interest on the capital contributed by him only from the date when repayment should be made.

(e)   All partners have equal rights in the management and conduct of the partnership business.

(f)   No partner is entitled to remuneration for acting in the partnership business, except that a surviving partner is entitled to reasonable compensation for his services in winding up the partnership affairs.

(g)   No person can become a member of a partnership without the consent of all the partners.

(h)   Any difference arising as to ordinary matters connected with the partnership business may be decided by a majority of the partners; but no act in contravention of any agreement between the partners may be done rightfully without the consent of all the partners.

§ 19.   Partnership Books

The partnership books shall be kept, subject to any agreement between the partners, at the principal place of business of the partnership, and every partner shall at all times have access to and may inspect and copy any of them.

§ 20.   Duty of Partners to Render Information

Partners shall render on demand true and full information of all things affecting the partnership to any partner or the legal representative of any deceased partner or partner under legal disability.

§ 21.   Partner Accountable as a Fiduciary

(1)   Every partner must account to the partnership for any benefit, and hold as trustee for it any profits derived by him without the consent of the other partners from any transaction connected with the formation, conduct, or liquidation of the partnership or from any use by him of its property.

(2)   This section applies also to the representatives of a deceased partner engaged in the liquidation of the affairs of the partnership as the personal representatives of the last surviving partner.

§ 22.   Right to an Account

Any partner shall have the right to a formal account as to partnership affairs:

(a)   If he is wrongfully excluded from the partnership business or possession of its property by his co-partners,

(b) If the right exists under the terms of any agreement,

(c) As provided by section 21,

(d) Whenever other circumstances render it just and reasonable.

§ 23. Continuation of Partnership Beyond Fixed Term

(1) When a partnership for a fixed term or particular undertaking is continued after the termination of such term or particular undertaking without any express agreement, the rights and duties of the partners remain the same as they were at such termination, so far as is consistent with a partnership at will.

(2) A continuation of the business by the partners or such of them as habitually acted therein during the term, without any settlement or liquidation of the partnership affairs, is prima facie evidence of a continuation of the partnership.

PART V

PROPERTY RIGHTS OF A PARTNER

§ 24. Extent of Property Rights of a Partner

The property rights of a partner are (1) his rights in specific partnership property, (2) his interest in the partnership, and (3) his right to participate in the management.

§ 25. Nature of a Partner's Right in Specific Partnership Property

(1) A partner is co-owner with his partners of specific partnership property holding as a tenant in partnership.

(2) The incidents of this tenancy are such that:

(a) A partner, subject to the provisions of this act and to any agreement between the partners, has an equal right with his partners to possess specific partnership property for partnership purposes; but he has no right to possess such property for any other purpose without the consent of his partners.

(b) A partner's right in specific partnership property is not assignable except in connection with the assignment of rights of all the partners in the same property.

(c) A partner's right in specific partnership property is not subject to attachment or execution, except on a claim against the partnership. When partnership property is attached for a partnership debt the partners, or any of them, or the representatives of a deceased partner, cannot claim any right under the homestead or exemption laws.

(d) On the death of a partner his right in specific partnership property vests in the surviving partner or partners, except where the deceased was the last surviving partner, when his right in such property vests in his legal representative. Such surviving partner or partners, or the legal representative of the last surviving partner, has no right to possess the partnership property for any but a partnership purpose.

(e) A partner's right in specific partnership property is not subject to dower, curtesy, or allowances to widows, heirs, or next of kin.

§ 26. Nature of Partner's Interest in the Partnership

A partner's interest in the partnership is his share of the profits and surplus, and the same is personal property.

§ 27. Assignment of Partner's Interest

(1) A conveyance by a partner of his interest in the partnership does not of itself dissolve the partnership, nor, as against the other partners in the absence of agreement, entitle the assignee, during the continuance of the partnership, to interfere in the management or administration of the partnership business or affairs, or to require any information or account of partnership transactions, or to inspect the partnership books; but it merely entitles the assignee to receive in accordance with his contract the profits to which the assigning partner would otherwise be entitled.

(2) In case of a dissolution of the partnership, the assignee is entitled to receive his assignor's interest and may require an account from the date only of the last account agreed to by all the partners.

§ 28. Partner's Interest Subject to Charging Order

(1) On due application to a competent court by any judgment creditor of a partner, the court which entered the judgment, order, or decree, or any other court, may charge the interest of the debtor partner with payment of the unsatisfied amount of such judgment debt with interest thereon; and may then or later appoint a receiver of his share of the profits, and of any other money due or to fall due to him in respect of the partnership, and make all other orders, directions, accounts and inquiries which the debtor partner might have made, or which the circumstances of the case may require.

(2) The interest charged may be redeemed at any time before foreclosure, or in case of a sale being directed by the court may be purchased without thereby causing a dissolution:

(a)   With separate property, by any one or more of the partners, or

(b)   With partnership property, by any one or more of the
partners with the consent of all the partners whose interests are
not so charged or sold.

(3)   Nothing in this act shall be held to deprive a partner of
his right, if any, under the exemption laws, as regards his interest
in the partnership.

PART VI

DISSOLUTION AND WINDING UP

§ 29.   Dissolution Defined

The dissolution of a partnership is the change in the relation
of the partners caused by any partner ceasing to be associated
in the carrying on as distinguished from the winding up of the
business.

§ 30.   Partnership not Terminated by Dissolution

On dissolution the partnership is not terminated, but continues until the winding up of partnership affairs is completed.

§ 31.   Causes of Dissolution

Dissolution is caused:

(1)   Without violation of the agreement between the partners,

(a)   By the termination of the definite term or particular undertaking specified in the agreement,

(b)   By the express will of any partner when no definite term
or particular undertaking is specified,

(c)   By the express will of all the partners who have not assigned their interests or suffered them to be charged for their
separate debts, either before or after the termination of any
specified term or particular undertaking,

(d)   By the expulsion of any partner from the business bona
fide in accordance with such a power conferred by the agreement
between the partners;

(2)   In contravention of the agreement between the partners,
where the circumstances do not permit a dissolution under any
other provision of this section, by the express will of any partner
at any time;

(3)   By any event which makes it unlawful for the business of
the partnership to be carried on or for the members to carry it
on in partnership;

(4)   By the death of any partner;

(5) By the bankruptcy of any partner or the partnership;

(6) By decree of court under section 32.

§ 32. Dissolution by Decree of Court

(1) On application by or for a partner the court shall decree a dissolution whenever:

(a) A partner has been declared a lunatic in any judicial proceeding or is shown to be of unsound mind,

(b) A partner becomes in any other way incapable of performing his part of the partnership contract,

(c) A partner has been guilty of such conduct as tends to affect prejudicially the carrying on of the business,

(d) A partner wilfully or persistently commits a breach of the partnership agreement, or otherwise so conducts himself in matters relating to the partnership business that it is not reasonably practicable to carry on the business in partnership with him,

(e) The business of the partnership can only be carried on at a loss,

(f) Other circumstances render a dissolution equitable.

(2) On the application of the purchaser of a partner's interest under sections 28 or 29:[1]

(a) After the termination of the specified term or particular undertaking,

(b) At any time if the partnership was a partnership at will when the interest was assigned or when the charging order was issued.

§ 33. General Effect of Dissolution on Authority of Partner

Except so far as may be necessary to wind up partnership affairs or to complete transactions begun but not then finished, dissolution terminates all authority of any partner to act for the partnership,

(1) With respect to the partners,

(a) When the dissolution is not by the act, bankruptcy or death of a partner; or

(b) When the dissolution is by such act, bankruptcy or death of a partner, in cases where section 34 so requires.

---

[1] So in original. Probably should read "sections 27 or 28." [Footnote from 6 UNIF. LAWS ANNOT., MASTER ED., UNIFORM PARTNERSHIP ACT 394 (1969). The original of the UPA apparently was first published, other than in pamphlet form, in the American Bar Association annual reports. XL REPORTS OF THE AMER. BAR ASS'N 441-459 (1915) contains the UPA as Exhibit A to the report of the Committee on Uniform Laws.—*Ed.*]

(2) With respect to persons not partners, as declared in section 35.

§ 34. Right of Partner to Contribution from Co-partners after Dissolution

Where the dissolution is caused by the act, death or bankruptcy of a partner, each partner is liable to his co-partners for his share of any liability created by any partner acting for the partnership as if the partnership had not been dissolved unless

(a) The dissolution being by act of any partner, the partner acting for the partnership had knowledge of the dissolution, or

(b) The dissolution being by the death or bankruptcy of a partner, the partner acting for the partnership had knowledge or notice of the death or bankruptcy.

§ 35. Power of Partner to Bind Partnership to Third Persons after Dissolution

(1) After dissolution a partner can bind the partnership except as provided in Paragraph (3).

(a) By any act appropriate for winding up partnership affairs or completing transactions unfinished at dissolution;

(b) By any transaction which would bind the partnership if dissolution had not taken place, provided the other party to the transaction

(I) Had extended credit to the partnership prior to dissolution and had no knowledge or notice of the dissolution; or

(II) Though he had not so extended credit, had nevertheless known of the partnership prior to dissolution, and, having no knowledge or notice of dissolution, the fact of dissolution had not been advertised in a newspaper of general circulation in the place (or in each place if more than one) at which the partnership business was regularly carried on.

(2) The liability of a partner under Paragraph (1b) shall be satisfied out of partnership assets alone when such partner had been prior to dissolution

(a) Unknown as a partner to the person with whom the contract is made; and

(b) So far unknown and inactive in partnership affairs that the business reputation of the partnership could not be said to have been in any degree due to his connection with it.

(3) The partnership is in no case bound by any act of a partner after dissolution

(a) Where the partnership is dissolved because it is unlawful to carry on the business, unless the act is appropriate for winding up partnership affairs; or

(b)   Where the partner has become bankrupt; or

(c)   Where the partner has no authority to wind up partnership affairs; except by a transaction with one who

(I)   Had extended credit to the partnership prior to dissolution and had no knowledge or notice of his want of authority; or

(II)   Had not extended credit to the partnership prior to dissolution, and, having no knowledge or notice of his want of authority, the fact of his want of authority has not been advertised in the manner provided for advertising the fact of dissolution in Paragraph (1bII).

(4)   Nothing in this section shall affect the liability under Section 16 of any person who after dissolution represents himself or consents to another representing him as a partner in a partnership engaged in carrying on business.

§ 36.   Effect of Dissolution on Partner's Existing Liability

(1)   The dissolution of the partnership does not of itself discharge the existing liability of any partner.

(2)   A partner is discharged from any existing liability upon dissolution of the partnership by an agreement to that effect between himself, the partnership creditor and the person or partnership continuing the business; and such agreement may be inferred from the course of dealing between the creditor having knowledge of the dissolution and the person or partnership continuing the business.

(3)   Where a person agrees to assume the existing obligations of a dissolved partnership, the partners whose obligations have been assumed shall be discharged from any liability to any creditor of the partnership who, knowing of the agreement, consents to a material alteration in the nature or time of payment of such obligations.

(4)   The individual property of a deceased partner shall be liable for all obligations of the partnership incurred while he was a partner but subject to the prior payment of his separate debts.

§ 37.   Right to Wind Up

Unless otherwise agreed the partners who have not wrongfully dissolved the partnership or the legal representative of the last surviving partner, not bankrupt, has the right to wind up the partnership affairs; provided, however, that any partner, his legal representative or his assignee, upon cause shown, may obtain winding up by the court.

§ 38. Rights of Partners to Application of Partnership Property

(1) When dissolution is caused in any way, except in contravention of the partnership agreement, each partner, as against his co-partners and all persons claiming through them in respect of their interests in the partnership, unless otherwise agreed, may have the partnership property applied to discharge its liabilities, and the surplus applied to pay in cash the net amount owing to the respective partners. But if dissolution is caused by expulsion of a partner, bona fide under the partnership agreement and if the expelled partner is discharged from all partnership liabilities, either by payment or agreement under section 36(2), he shall receive in cash only the net amount due him from the partnership.

(2) When dissolution is caused in contravention of the partnership agreement the rights of the partners shall be as follows:

(a) Each partner who has not caused dissolution wrongfully shall have,

I. All the rights specified in paragraph (1) of this section, and

II. The right, as against each partner who has caused the dissolution wrongfully, to damages for breach of the agreement.

(b) The partners who have not caused the dissolution wrongfully, if they all desire to continue the business in the same name, either by themselves or jointly with others, may do so, during the agreed term for the partnership and for that purpose may possess the partnership property, provided they secure the payment by bond approved by the court, or pay to any partner who has caused the dissolution wrongfully, the value of his interest in the partnership at the dissolution, less any damages recoverable under clause (2aII) of this section, and in like manner indemnify him against all present or future partnership liabilities.

(c) A partner who has caused the dissolution wrongfully shall have:

I. If the business is not continued under the provisions of paragraph (2b) all the rights of a partner under paragraph (1), subject to clause (2aII), of this section,

II. If the business is continued under paragraph (2b) of this section the right as against his co-partners and all claiming through them in respect of their interests in the partnership, to have the value of his interest in the partnership, less any damages caused to his co-partners by the dissolution, ascertained and paid to him in cash, or the payment secured by bond approved by the court, and to be released from all existing liabilities of the partnership; but in ascertaining the value of the partner's interest the value of the good-will of the business shall not be considered.

§ 39.   Rights Where Partnership is Dissolved for Fraud or Misrepresentation

Where a partnership contract is rescinded on the ground of the fraud or misrepresentation of one of the parties thereto, the party entitled to rescind is, without prejudice to any other right, entitled,

(a)   To a lien on, or a right of retention of, the surplus of the partnership property after satisfying the partnership liabilities to third persons for any sum of money paid by him for the purchase of an interest in the partnership and for any capital or advances contributed by him; and

(b)   To stand, after all liabilities to third persons have been satisfied, in the place of the creditors of the partnership for any payments made by him in respect of the partnership liabilities; and

(c)   To be indemnified by the person guilty of the fraud or making the representation against all debts and liabilities of the partnership.

§ 40.   Rules for Distribution

In settling accounts between the partners after dissolution, the following rules shall be observed, subject to any agreement to the contrary:

(a)   The assets of the partnership are:

I.   The partnership property,

II.   The contributions of the partners necessary for the payment of all the liabilities specified in clause (b) of this paragraph.

(b)   The liabilities of the partnership shall rank in order of payment, as follows:

I.   Those owing to creditors other than partners,

II.   Those owing to partners other than for capital and profits,

III.   Those owing to partners in respect of capital,

IV.   Those owing to partners in respect of profits.

(c)   The assets shall be applied in order of their declaration in clause (a) of this paragraph to the satisfaction of the liabilities.

(d)   The partners shall contribute, as provided by section 18 (a) the amount necessary to satisfy the liabilities; but if any, but not all, of the partners are insolvent, or, not being subject to process, refuse to contribute, the other partners shall contribute their share of the liabilities, and, in the relative proportions in which they share the profits, the additional amount necessary to pay the liabilities.

(e) An assignee for the benefit of creditors or any person appointed by the court shall have the right to enforce the contributions specified in clause (d) of this paragraph.

(f) Any partner or his legal representative shall have the right to enforce the contributions specified in clause (d) of this paragraph, to the extent of the amount which he has paid in excess of his share of the liability.

(g) The individual property of a deceased partner shall be liable for the contributions specified in clause (d) of this paragraph.

(h) When partnership property and the individual properties of the partners are in possession of a court for distribution, partnership creditors shall have priority on partnership property and separate creditors on individual property, saving the rights of lien or secured creditors as heretofore.

(i) Where a partner has become bankrupt or his estate is insolvent the claims against his separate property shall rank in the following order:

I.   Those owing to separate creditors,

II. Those owing to partnership creditors,

III. Those owing to partners by way of contribution.

§ 41. Liability of Persons Continuing the Business in Certain Cases

(1) When any new partner is admitted into an existing partnership, or when any partner retires and assigns (or the representative of the deceased partner assigns) his rights in partnership property to two or more of the partners, or to one or more of the partners and one or more third persons, if the business is continued without liquidation of the partnership affairs, creditors of the first or dissolved partnership are also creditors of the partnership so continuing the business.

(2) When all but one partner retire and assign (or the representative of a deceased partner assigns) their rights in partnership property to the remaining partner, who continues the business without liquidation of partnership affairs, either alone or with others, creditors of the dissolved partnership are also creditors of the person or partnership so continuing the business.

(3) When any partner retires or dies and the business of the dissolved partnership is continued as set forth in paragraphs (1) and (2) of this section, with the consent of the retired partners

or the representative of the deceased partner, but without any assignment of his right in partnership property, rights of creditors of the dissolved partnership and of the creditors of the person or partnership continuing the business shall be as if such assignment had been made.

(4) When all the partners or their representatives assign their rights in partnership property to one or more third persons who promise to pay the debts and who continue the business of the dissolved partnership, creditors of the dissolved partnership are also creditors of the person or partnership continuing the business.

(5) When any partner wrongfully causes a dissolution and the remaining partners continue the business under the provisions of section 38(2b), either alone or with others, and without liquidation of the partnership affairs, creditors of the dissolved partnership are also creditors of the person or partnership continuing the business.

(6) When a partner is expelled and the remaining partners continue the business either alone or with others, without liquidation of the partnership affairs, creditors of the dissolved partnership are also creditors of the person or partnership continuing the business.

(7) The liability of a third person becoming a partner in the partnership continuing the business, under this section, to the creditors of the dissolved partnership shall be satisfied out of partnership property only.

(8) When the business of a partnership after dissolution is continued under any conditions set forth in this section the creditors of the dissolved partnership, as against the separate creditors of the retiring or deceased partner or the representative of the deceased partner, have a prior right to any claim of the retired partner or the representative of the deceased partner against the person or partnership continuing the business, on account of the retired or deceased partner's interest in the dissolved partnership or on account of any consideration promised for such interest or for his right in partnership property.

(9) Nothing in this section shall be held to modify any right of creditors to set aside any assignment on the ground of fraud.

(10) The use by the person or partnership continuing the business of the partnership name, or the name of a deceased partner as part thereof, shall not of itself make the individual property of the deceased partner liable for any debts contracted by such person or partnership.

§ 42. Rights of Retiring or Estate of Deceased Partner When the Business is Continued

When any partner retires or dies, and the business is continued under any of the conditions set forth in section 41 (1, 2, 3, 5, 6), or section 38(2b) without any settlement of accounts as between him or his estate and the person or partnership continuing the business, unless otherwise agreed, he or his legal representative as against such persons or partnership may have the value of his interest at the date of dissolution ascertained, and shall receive as an ordinary creditor an amount equal to the value of his interest in the dissolved partnership with interest, or, at his option or at the option of his legal representative, in lieu of interest, the profits attributable to the use of his right in the property of the dissolved partnership; provided that the creditors of the dissolved partnership as against the separate creditors, or the representative of the retired or deceased partner, shall have priority on any claim arising under this section, as provided by section 41(8) of this act.

§ 43. Accrual of Actions

The right to an account of his interest shall accrue to any partner, or his legal representative, as against the winding up partners or the surviving partners or the person or partnership continuing the business, at the date of dissolution, in the absence of any agreement to the contrary.

PART VII

MISCELLANEOUS PROVISIONS

§ 44. When Act Takes Effect

This act shall take effect on the . . . . day of . . . . one thousand nine hundred and . . . .

§ 45. Legislation Repealed

All acts or parts of acts inconsistent with this act are hereby repealed.

APPENDIX B

UNIFORM LIMITED PARTNERSHIP ACT

Source: 6 Unif. Laws Annot., Master Ed., Uniform Limited Partnership Act (1969). Reproduced by permission. This edition of the Act is annotated, describes variations in text by the states adopting the Act, and so forth, in the same manner as that described for the UPA in Appendix A. Source of data contained immediately below: *Id.*, 1973 pocket part.

Approved by the National Conference of Commissioners on Uniform State Laws, August 28, 1916, and adopted in the following jurisdictions: Alabama (1972), Alaska (1917), Arizona (1943), Arkansas (1953), California (1949), Colorado (1931), Connecticut (1961), District of Columbia (1962), Florida (1943), Georgia (1952), Hawaii (1943), Idaho (1920), Illinois (1917), Indiana (1949), Iowa (1924), Kansas (1967), Kentucky (1970), Maine (1969), Maryland (1918), Massachusetts (1924), Michigan (1931), Minnesota (1919), Mississippi (1964), Missouri (1947), Montana (1947), Nebraska (1939), Nevada (1931), New Hampshire (1937), New Jersey (1919), New Mexico (1947), New York (1922), North Carolina (1941), North Dakota (1959), Ohio (1957), Oklahoma (1951), Pennsylvania (1917), Rhode Island (1930), South Carolina (1960), South Dakota (1925), Tennessee (1920), Texas (1955), Utah (1921), Vermont (1941), Virgin Islands (1957), Virginia (1918), Washington (1945), West Virginia (1953), Wisconsin (1919), and Wyoming (1971).

The states which are not included in the above list are: Delaware, Louisiana, and Oregon.

§ 1. Limited partnership defined

A limited partnership is a partnership formed by two or more persons under the provisions of Section 2, having as members one or more general partners and one or more limited partners. The limited partners as such shall not be bound by the obligations of the partnership.

Official Comment

The business reason for the adoption of acts making provisions for limited or special partners is that men in business often

455

desire to secure capital from others. There are at least three classes of contracts which can be made with those from whom the capital is secured: One, the ordinary loan on interest; another, the loan where the lender, in lieu of interest, takes a share in the profits of the business; third, those cases in which the person advancing the capital secures, besides a share in the profits, some measure of control over the business.

At first, in the absence of statutes the courts, both in this country and in England, assumed that one who is interested in a business is bound by its obligations, carrying the application of this principle so far, that a contract where the only evidence of interest was a share in the profits made one who supposed himself a lender, and who was probably unknown to the creditors at the times they extended their credits, unlimitedly liable as a partner for the obligations of those actually conducting the business.

Later decisions have much modified the earlier cases. The lender who takes a share in the profits, except possibly in one or two of our jurisdictions, does not by reason of that fact run a risk of being held as a partner. If, however, his contract falls within the third class mentioned, and he has any measure of control over the business, he at once runs serious risk of being held liable for the debts of the business as a partner; the risk increasing as he increases the amount of his control.

The first Limited Partnership Act was adopted by New York in 1822; the other commercial states, during the ensuing 30 years, following her example. Most of the statutes follow the language of the New York statute with little material alteration. These statutes were adopted, and to a considerable degree interpreted by the courts, during that period when it was generally held that any interest in a business should make the person holding the interest liable for its obligations. As a result the courts usually assume in the interpretation of these statutes two principles as fundamental.

First: That a limited (or as he is also called a special) partner is a partner in all respects like any other partner, except that to obtain the privilege of a limitation on his liability, he has conformed to the statutory requirements in respect to filing a certificate and refraining from participation in the conduct of the business.

Second: The limited partner, on any failure to follow the requirements in regard to the certificate or any participation in the conduct of his business, loses his privilege of limited liability and becomes, as far as those dealing with the business are concerned, in all respects a partner.

The courts in thus interpreting the statutes, although they made an American partnership with limited members something very different from the French Societe en Commandite from which the idea of the original statutes was derived, unquestionably carried out the intent of those responsible for their adoption. This is shown by the very wording of the statutes themselves. For instance, all the statutes require that all partners, limited and general, shall sign the certificate, and nearly all state that: "If any false statement be made in such certificate all the persons interested in such partnership shall be liable for all the engagements thereof as general partners."

The practical result of the spirit shown in the language and in the interpretation of existing statutes, coupled with the fact that a man may now lend money to a partnership and take a share in the profits in lieu of interest without running serious danger of becoming bound for partnership obligations, has, to a very great extent, deprived the existing statutory provisions for limited partners of any practical usefulness. Indeed, apparently their use is largely confined to associations in which those who conduct the business have not more than one limited partner.

One of the causes forcing business into the corporate form, in spite of the fact that the corporate form is ill suited to many business conditions, is the failure of the existing limited partnership acts to meet the desire of the owners of a business to secure necessary capital under the existing limited partnership form of business association.

The draft herewith submitted proceeds on the following assumptions:

First: No public policy requires a person who contributes to the capital of a business, acquires an interest in the profits, and some degree of control over the conduct of the business, to become bound for the obligations of the business; provided creditors have no reason to believe at the times their credits were extended that such person was so bound.

Second: That persons in business should be able, while remaining themselves liable without limit for the obligations contracted in its conduct, to associate with themselves others who contribute to the capital and acquire rights of ownership, provided that such contributors do not compete with creditors for the assets of the partnership.

The attempt to carry out these ideas has led to the incorporation into the draft submitted of certain features, not found in, or differing from, existing limited partnership acts.

First: In the draft the person who contributes the capital, though in accordance with custom called a limited partner, is not in any sense a partner. He is, however, a member of the association (see Sec. 1).

Second: As limited partners are not partners securing limited liability by filing a certificate, the association is formed when substantial compliance, in good faith, is had with the requirements for a certificate (Sec. 2(2)). This provision eliminates the difficulties which arise from the recognition of de facto associations, made necessary by the assumption that the association is not formed unless a strict compliance with the requirements of the act is had.

Third: The limited partner not being in any sense a principal in the business, failure to comply with the requirements of the act in respect to the certificate, while it may result in the nonformation of the association, does not make him a partner or liable as such. The exact nature of his ability in such cases is set forth in Sec. 11.

Fourth: The limited partner, while not as such in any sense a partner, may become a partner as any person not a member of the association may become a partner; and, becoming a partner, may nevertheless retain his rights as limited partner; this last provision enabling the entire capital embraced in the business to be divided between the limited partners, all the general partners being also limited partners (Sec. 12).

Fifth: The limited partner is not debarred from loaning money or transacting other business with the partnership as any other non-member; provided he does not, in respect to such transactions, accept from the partnership collateral security, or receive from any partner or the partnership any payment, conveyance, or release from liability, if at the time the assets of the partnership are not sufficient to discharge its obligations to persons not general or limited partners. (Sec. 13).

Sixth: The substitution of a person as limited partner in place of an existing limited partner, or the withdrawal of a limited partner, or the addition of new limited partners, does not necessarily dissolve the association (Secs. 8, 16(2b)); no limited partner, however, can withdraw his contribution until all liabilities to creditors are paid (Sec. 16(1a)).

Seventh: As limited partners are not principals in transactions of the partnership, their liability, except for known false statements in the certificate (Sec. 6), is to the partnership, not to creditors of the partnership (Sec. 17). The general partners cannot, however, waive any liability of the limited partners to the prejudice of such creditors. (Sec. 17(3)).

§ 2. Formation

(1) Two or more persons desiring to form a limited partnership shall

(a) Sign and swear to a certificate, which shall state

I. The name of the partnership,

II. The character of the business,

III. The location of the principal place of business,

IV. The name and place of residence of each member; general and limited partners being respectively designated,

V. The term for which the partnership is to exist,

VI. The amount of cash and a description of and the agreed value of the other property contributed by each limited partner,

VII. The additional contributions, if any, agreed to be made by each limited partner and the times at which or events on the happening of which they shall be made,

VIII. The time, if agreed upon, when the contribution of each limited partner is to be returned,

IX. The share of the profits or the other compensation by way of income which each limited partner shall receive by reason of his contribution,

X. The right, if given, of a limited partner to substitute an assignee as contributor in his place, and the terms and conditions of the substitution,

XI. The right, if given, of the partners to admit additional limited partners,

XII. The right, if given, of one or more of the limited partners to priority over other limited partners, as to contributions or as to compensation by way of income, and the nature of such priority,

XIII. The right, if given, of the remaining general partner or partners to continue the business on the death, retirement or insanity of a general partner, and

XIV. The right, if given, of a limited partner to demand and receive property other than cash in return for his contribution.

(b) File for record the certificate in the office of [here designate the proper office].

(2) A limited partnership is formed if there has been substantial compliance in good faith with the requirements of paragraph (1).

§ 3. Business which may be carried on

A limited partnership may carry on any business which a partnership without limited partners may carry on, except [here designate the business to be prohibited].

§ 4. Character of limited partner's contribution

The contributions of a limited partner may be cash or other property, but not services.

§ 5. A name not to contain surname of limited partner; exceptions

(1) The surname of a limited partner shall not appear in the partnership name, unless

(a) It is also the surname of a general partner, or

(b) Prior to the time when the limited partner became such the business had been carried on under a name in which his surname appeared.

(2) A limited partner whose name appears in a partnership name contrary to the provisions of paragraph (1) is liable as a general partner to partnership creditors who extend credit to the partnership without actual knowledge that he is not a general partner.

§ 6. Liability for false statements in certificate

If the certificate contains a false statement, one who suffers loss by reliance on such statement may hold liable any party to the certificate who knew the statement to be false.

(a) At the time he signed the certificate, or

(b) Subsequently, but within a sufficient time before the statement was relied upon to enable him to cancel or amend the certificate, or to file a petition for its cancellation or amendment as provided in Section 25(3).

§ 7. Limited partner not liable to creditors

A limited partner shall not become liable as a general partner unless, in addition to the exercise of his rights and powers as a limited partner, he takes part in the control of the business.

§ 8. Admission of additional limited partners

After the formation of a limited partnership, additional limited partners may be admitted upon filing an amendment to the original certificate in accordance with the requirements of Section 25.

§ 9. Rights, powers and liabilities of a general partner

(1) A general partner shall have all the rights and powers and be subject to all the restrictions and liabilities of a partner in a partnership without limited partners, except that without the written consent or ratification of the specific act by all the limited partners, a general partner or all of the general partners have no authority to

(a) Do any act in contravention of the certificate,

(b) Do any act which would make it impossible to carry on the ordinary business of the partnership,

(c) Confess a judgment against the partnership,

(d) Possess partnership property, or assign their rights in specific partnership property, for other than a partnership purpose,

(e) Admit a person as a general partner,

(f) Admit a person as a limited partner, unless the right so to do is given in the certificate,

(g) Continue the business with partnership property on the death, retirement or insanity of a general partner, unless the right so to do is given in the certificate.

§ 10. Rights of a limited partner

(1) A limited partner shall have the same rights as a general partner to

(a) Have the partnership books kept at the principal place of business of the partnership, and at all times to inspect and copy any of them.

(b) Have on demand true and full information of all things affecting the partnership, and a formal account of partnership affairs whenever circumstances render it just and reasonable, and

(c) Have dissolution and winding up by decree of court.

(2) A limited partner shall have the right to receive a share of the profits or other compensation by way of income, and to the return of his contribution as provided in Sections 15 and 16.

§ 11. Status of person erroneously believing himself a limited partner

A person who has contributed to the capital of a business conducted by a person or partnership erroneously believing that he has become a limited partner in a limited partnership, is not, by reason of his exercise of the rights of a limited partner, a general partner with the person or in the partnership carrying on the business, or bound by the obligations of such person or partnership; provided that on ascertaining the mistake he promptly renounces his interest in the profits of the business, or other compensation by way of income.

§ 12. One person both general and limited partner

(1) A person may be a general partner and a limited partner in the same partnership at the same time.

(2) A person who is a general, and also at the same time a limited partner, shall have all the rights and powers and be subject to all the restrictions of a general partner; except that, in respect to his contribution, he shall have the rights against the other members which he would have had if he were not also a general partner.

§ 13. Loans and other business transactions with limited partner

(1) A limited partner also may loan money to and transact other business with the partnership, and, unless he is also a general partner, receive on account of resulting claims against the partnership, with general creditors, a pro rata share of the assets. No limited partner shall in respect to any such claim

(a) Receive or hold as collateral security any partnership property, or

(b) Receive from a general partner or the partnership any payment, conveyance, or release from liability, if at the time the assets of the partnership are not sufficient to discharge partnership liabilities to persons not claiming as general or limited partners,

(2) The receiving of collateral security, or a payment, conveyance, or release in violation of the provisions of paragraph (1) is a fraud on the creditors of the partnership.

§ 14. Relation of limited partners inter se

Where there are several limited partners the members may agree that one or more of the limited partners shall have a priority over other limited partners as to the return of their contributions, as to their compensation by way of income, or as to any other matter. If such an agreement is made it shall be stated in the certificate, and in the absence of such a statement all the limited partners shall stand upon equal footing.

§ 15. Compensation of limited partner

A limited partner may receive from the partnership the share of the profits or the compensation by way of income stipulated for in the certificate; provided, that after such payment is made, whether from the property of the partnership or that of a general partner, the partnership assets are in excess of all liabilities of the partnership except liabilities to limited partners on account of their contributions and to general partners.

§16. Withdrawal or reduction of limited partner's contribution

(1) A limited partner shall not receive from a general partner or out of partnership property any part of his contribution until

(a) All liabilities of the partnership, except liabilities to general partners and to limited partners on account of their contributions, have been paid or there remains property of the partnership sufficient to pay them,

(b) The consent of all members is had, unless the return of the contribution may be rightfully demanded under the provisions of paragraph (2), and

(c) The certificate is cancelled or so amended as to set forth the withdrawal or reduction.

(2) Subject to the provisions of paragraph (1) a limited partner may rightfully demand the return of his contribution

(a) On the dissolution of a partnership, or

(b) When the date specified in the certificate for its return has arrived, or

(c) After he has given six months' notice in writing to all other members, if no time is specified in the certificate either for the return of the contribution or for the dissolution of the partnership.

(3) In the absence of any statement in the certificate to the contrary or the consent of all members, a limited partner, irrespective of the nature of his contribution, has only the right to demand and receive cash in return for his contribution.

(4) A limited partner may have the partnership dissolved and its affairs wound up when

(a) He rightfully but unsuccessfully demands the return of his contribution, or

(b) The other liabilities of the partnership have not been paid, or the partnership property is insufficient for their payment as required by paragraph (1a) and the limited partner would otherwise be entitled to the return of his contribution.

§ 17. Liability of limited partner to partnership

(1) A limited partner is liable to the partnership

(a) For the difference between his contribution as actually made and that stated in the certificate as having been made, and

(b) For any unpaid contribution which he agreed in the certificate to make in the future at the time and on the conditions stated in the certificate.

(2) A limited partner holds as trustee for the partnership

(a) Specific property stated in the certificate as contributed by him, but which was not contributed or which has been wrongfully returned, and

(b) Money or other property wrongfully paid or conveyed to him on account of his contribution.

(3) The liabilities of a limited partner as set forth in this section can be waived or compromised only by the consent of all members; but a waiver or compromise shall not affect the right of a creditor of a partnership who extended credit or whose claim arose after the filing and before a cancellation or amendment of the certificate, to enforce such liabilities.

(4) When a contributor has rightfully received the return in whole or in part of the capital of his contribution, he is nevertheless liable to the partnership for any sum, not in excess of such return with interest, necessary to discharge its liabilities to all creditors who extended credit or whose claims arose before such return.

§ 18. Nature of limited partner's interest in partnership

A limited partner's interest in the partnership is personal property.

§ 19. Assignment of limited partner's interest

(1) A limited partner's interest is assignable.

(2) A substituted limited partner is a person admitted to all the rights of a limited partner who has died or has assigned his interest in a partnership.

(3) An assignee, who does not become a substituted limited partner, has no right to require any information or account of the partnership transactions or to inspect the partnership books; he is only entitled to receive the share of the profits or other compensation by way of income, or the return of his contribution, to which his assignor would otherwise be entitled.

(4) An assignee shall have the right to become a substituted limited partner if all the members (except the assignor) consent thereto or if the assignor, being thereunto empowered by the certificate, gives the assignee that right.

(5) An assignee becomes a substituted limited partner when the certificate is appropriately amended in accordance with Section 25.

(6) The substituted limited partner has all the rights and powers, and is subject to all the restrictions and liabilities of his assignor, except those liabilities of which he was ignorant

at the time he became a limited partner and which could not be ascertained from the certificate.

(7)   The substitution of the assignee as a limited partner does not release the assignor from liability to the partnership under Sections 6 and 17.

§ 20.   Effect of retirement, death or insanity of a general partner

The retirement, death or insanity of a general partner dissolves the partnership, unless the business is continued by the remaining general partners
    (a)   Under a right so to do stated in the certificate, or
    (b)   With the consent of all members.

§ 21.   Death of limited partner

(1) On the death of a limited partner his executor or administrator shall have all the rights of a limited partner for the purpose of settling his estate, and such power as the deceased had to constitute his assignee a substituted limited partner.

(2) The estate of a deceased limited partner shall be liable for all his liabilities as a limited partner.

§ 22.   Rights of creditors of limited partner

(1) On due application to a court of competent jurisdiction by any judgment creditor of a limited partner, the court may charge the interest of the indebted limited partner with payment of the unsatisfied amount of the judgment debt; and may appoint a receiver, and make all other orders, directions, and inquiries which the circumstances of the case may require.

(2) The interest may be redeemed with the separate property of any general partner, but may not be redeemed with partnership property.

(3) The remedies conferred by paragraph (1) shall not be deemed exclusive of others which may exist.

(4) Nothing in this act shall be held to deprive a limited partner of his statutory exemption.

§ 23.   Distribution of assets

(1) In settling accounts after dissolution the liabilities of the partnership shall be entitled to payment in the following order:
    (a) Those to creditors, in the order of priority as provided by law, except those to limited partners on account of their contributions, and to general partners,
    (b) Those to limited partners in respect to their share of the profits and other compensation by way of income on their contributions,

(c) Those to limited partners in respect to the capital of their contributions,

(d) Those to general partners other than for capital and profits,

(e) Those to general partners in respect to profits,

(f) Those to general partners in respect to capital.

(2) Subject to any statement in the certificate or to subsequent agreement, limited partners share in the partnership assets in respect to their claims for capital, and in respect to their claims for profits or for compensation by way of income on their contributions respectively, in proportion to the respective amounts of such claims.

§ 24. When certificate shall be cancelled or amended

(1) The certificate shall be cancelled when the partnership is dissolved or all limited partners cease to be such.

(2) A certificate shall be amended when

(a) There is a change in the name of the partnership or in the amount or character of the contribution of any limited partner,

(b) A person is substituted as a limited partner,

(c) An additional limited partner is admitted,

(d) A person is admitted as a general partner,

(e) A general partner retires, dies or becomes insane, and the business is continued under Section 20,

(f) There is a change in the character of the business of the partnership,

(g) There is a false or erroneous statement in the certificate,

(h) There is a change in the time as stated in the certificate for the dissolution of the partnership or for the return of a contribution,

(i) A time is fixed for the dissolution of the partnership, or the return of a contribution, no time having been specified in the certificate, or

(j) The members desire to make a change in any other statement in the certificate in order that it shall accurately represent the agreement between them.

§ 25. Requirements for amendment and for cancellation of certificate

(1) The writing to amend a certificate shall

(a) Conform to the requirements of Section 2(1a) as far as necessary to set forth clearly the change in the certificate which it is desired to make, and

(b) Be signed and sworn to by all members, and an amendment substituting a limited partner or adding a limited or general partner shall be signed also by the member to be substituted or added, and when a limited partner is to be substituted, the amendment shall also be signed by the assigning limited partner.

(2) The writing to cancel a certificate shall be signed by all members.

(3) A person desiring the cancellation or amendment of a certificate, if any person designated in paragraphs (1) and (2) as a person who must execute the writing refuses to do so, may petition the [here designate the proper court] to direct a cancellation or amendment thereof.

(4) If the court finds that the petitioner has a right to have the writing executed by a person who refuses to do so, it shall order the [here designate the responsible official in the office designated in Section 2] in the office where the certificate is recorded to record the cancellation or amendment of the certificate; and where the certificate is to be amended, the court shall also cause to be filed for record in said office a certified copy of its decree setting forth the amendment.

(5) A certificate is amended or cancelled when there is filed for record in the office [here designate the office designated in Section 2] where the certificate is recorded

(a) A writing in accordance with the provisions of paragraph (1), or (2) or

(b) A certified copy of the order of court in accordance with the provisions of paragraph (4).

(6) After the certificate is duly amended in accordance with this section, the amended certificate shall thereafter be for all purposes the certificate provided for by this act.

§ 26. Parties to actions

A contributor, unless he is a general partner, is not a proper party to proceedings by or against a partnership, except where the object is to enforce a limited partner's right against or liability to the partnership.

§ 27. Name of act

This act may be cited as The Uniform Limited Partnership Act.

§ 28. Rules of construction

(1) The rule that statutes in derogation of the common law are to be strictly construed shall have no application to this act.

(2) This act shall be so interpreted and construed as to effect its general purpose to make uniform the law of those states which enact it.

(3) This act shall not be so construed as to impair the obligations of any contract existing when the act goes into effect, nor to affect any action or proceedings begun or right accrued before this act takes effect.

§ 29. Rules for cases not provided for in this act

In any case not provided for in this act the rules of law and equity, including the law merchant, shall govern.

§ 30. Provisions for existing limited partnerships

(1) A limited partnership formed under any statute of this state prior to the adoption of this act, may become a limited partnership under this act by complying with the provisions of Section 2; provided the certificate set forth

(a) The amount of the original contribution of each limited partner, and the time when the contribution was made, and

(b) That the property of the partnership exceeds the amount sufficient to discharge its liabilities to persons not claiming as general or limited partners by an amount greater than the sum of the contributions of its limited partners.

(2) A limited partnership formed under any statute of this state prior to the adoption of this act, until or unless it becomes a limited partnership under this act, shall continue to be governed by the provisions of [here insert proper reference to the existing limited partnership act or acts], except that such partnership shall not be renewed unless so provided in the original agreement.

§ 31. Act (acts) repealed

Except as affecting existing limited partnerships to the extent set forth in Section 30, the act (acts) of [here designate the existing limited partnership act or acts] is (are) hereby repealed.

APPENDIX C

FORM OF GENERAL PARTNERSHIP AGREEMENT

Source: J. MULDER, M. VOLZ & A. BERGER, THE DRAFTING OF PARTNERSHIP AGREEMENTS 32-39 (5th ed. 1967).

GENERAL PARTNERSHIP AGREEMENT

STYLEPROOF HOSIERY COMPANY

THIS AGREEMENT is executed this .... day of September, 1965, by and among JOHN SMITH, HAROLD JONES, and FRANK BROWN, all of ....

RECITALS

1. The parties hereto have been and are conducting business as a general partnership in ...., ..., under the name of STYLEPROOF HOSIERY COMPANY, pursuant to an oral agreement dated February 1, 1963, under which JOHN SMITH, HAROLD JONES, and FRANK BROWN have been sharing the profits or losses in the proportions of 50 per cent, 25 per cent, and 25 per cent respectively.

2. The parties desire to continue the business under the same name, to redefine the terms of their association, and to commit their agreement to writing.

Now, THEREFORE, intending to be legally bound hereby, these parties hereby agree to continue the aforementioned partnership under the laws of the State of ...., under the following terms and conditions:

ARTICLE I

Name and Place of Business

1. The name of the partnership shall be STYLEPROOF HOSIERY COMPANY.

2. The principal place of business of the partnership shall be at .... Street, ..., ..., and at such other localities within or without the State of .... as may be agreed upon by the partners.

Article II
Purposes of the Business

1. The partnership shall engage in the business of manufacturing, selling, and dealing generally in ladies' hosiery of all kinds and in such other business of a similar nature or related as may be agreed upon by the partners.

Article III
Capital Contributions, Accounts, and Withdrawals

1. The capital of the partnership shall consist of the amount shown on the balance sheet of the partnership business as of ...., 1965, a copy of which is attached hereto as Exhibit "A". The capital contributions of each partner shall consist of the capital invested by each partner as shown in the aforementioned balance sheet.

2. An individual capital account shall be maintained for each partner.

3. Except by unanimous agreement of the partners, or upon dissolution, the capital contributions of the partners shall not be subject to withdrawal.

Article IV
Profits and Losses

1. The net profits or net losses of the partnership shall be distributable or chargeable, as the case may be, to each of the partners in equal proportions.

2. An individual income account shall be maintained for each partner. Profits and losses shall be credited or debited to the individual income accounts as soon as practicable after the close of each fiscal year.

3. If there be no balance in the individual income accounts, net losses shall be debited to the individual capital accounts. If the capital account of a partner shall have been depleted by the debiting of losses under this paragraph, future profits of that partner shall not be credited to his income account until the depletion shall have been made good, but shall be credited to his capital account. After the depletion in his capital account shall have been made good, his share of the profit thereafter shall be credited to his income account.

Article V
Management; Salaries

1. Each of the partners shall have an equal voice in the management and conduct of the partnership business. All decisions

shall be by a majority vote, and each partner shall be entitled to one vote. Each partner shall devote his full time and attention to the partnership business. Each partner shall receive such salary as shall from time to time be agreed upon, but the payment of salaries shall be an obligation of the partnership only to the extent that there are partnership assets available for them, and shall not be an obligation of the partners individually. Salaries shall be treated as expenses of the partnership in determining net profits or net losses.

Article VI
Dissolution Because of the Retirement, Death, or Insanity of a Partner

1. Any partner may retire from the partnership upon sixty (60) days' prior notice to the other partners.

2. Retirement, death, or insanity of a partner shall work an immediate dissolution of the partnership.

3. In the event of the dissolution of the partnership by the retirement, death, or insanity of a partner, a proper accounting shall be made of the capital and income accounts of each partner and of the net profit or net loss of the partnership from the date of the last previous accounting to the date of dissolution.

4. In the event of the retirement, death, or insanity of a partner, the remaining partners shall have the right to continue the business of the partnership under its present name by themselves, or in conjunction with any other person or persons they may select, but they shall pay to the retiring partner, or the legal representatives of the deceased or insane partner, as the case may be, the value of his interest in the partnership as provided in the following paragraphs of this Article. If the remaining partners both desire to continue business, but not together, the partnership shall be liquidated in accordance with the provisions of Paragraph 1 of Article VII.

5. The value of the interest of a retiring, deceased, or insane partner, as of the date of dissolution, shall be the sum of:

(a) His capital account;

(b) His income account;

(c) Any earned and unpaid salary due him; and

(d) His proportionate share of accrued net profits.

If a net loss has been incurred to the date of dissolution, his share of such loss shall be deducted.

Inventory for purposes of this Article shall be valued at cost or market value, whichever is lower. Other assets shall be valued at book value.

No value for good will or firm name shall be included in any computations of a partner's interest under this Article.

ARTICLE VII
Voluntary Dissolution

1. Unless dissolved by the retirement, death, or insanity of a partner, the partnership shall continue until dissolved by agreement of the partners. Upon any such voluntary dissolution by agreement, the affairs of the partnership shall be liquidated forthwith. The assets of the partnership shall first be used to pay or provide for all debts of the partnership. Thereafter, all moneys in the income accounts of the partners, and all amounts due for earned or unpaid salaries of the partners, shall be paid to the partners respectively entitled thereto. Then the remaining assets shall be divided according to the proportionate interests of the partners on the basis of their respective capital accounts as they stood upon the date of such dissolution, after crediting or debiting to them the net profit or net loss accrued or incurred, as the case may be, from the date of the last accounting to the date of dissolution.

2. Upon termination of the partnership by agreement of the partners, any two partners shall have the right, in lieu of the liquidation provided for in the preceding paragraph of this Article, to continue the business of the partnership under its present name, by themselves or in conjunction with any person or persons they may select, upon paying in cash forthwith to the withdrawing partner the amounts to which he would be entitled under Paragraph 5 of Article VI, in case of a dissolution under Article VI. If more than one of the partners desires to take advantage of this paragraph, but they do not desire to continue the business of the partnership together, then the affairs of the partnership shall be liquidated in accordance with the preceding paragraph of this Article.

ARTICLE VIII
Partners' Powers and Limitations

1. Checks shall be drawn on the partnership bank account for partnership purposes only and shall be signed by any two partners.

2. No partner may without the consent of the other partner:

(a) Borrow money in the firm name for firm purposes or utilize collateral owned by the partnership as security for such **loans;**

(b) Assign, transfer, pledge, compromise, or release any of the claims of or debts due the partnership except upon payment in full, or arbitrate or consent to the arbitration of any of the disputes or controversies of the partnership;

(c) Make, execute, or deliver any assignment for the benefit of creditors, or any bond, confession of judgment, chattel mortgage, deed, guarantee, indemnity bond, surety bond, or contract to sell or contract of sale of all or substantially all of the property of the partnership;

(d) Lease or mortgage any partnership real estate or any interest therein or enter into any contract for any such purpose;

(e) Pledge or hypothecate or in any manner transfer his interest in the partnership, except to another party to this agreement;

(f) Become a surety, guarantor, or accommodation party to any obligation.

ARTICLE IX
Miscellaneous

1. The partnership shall maintain a bank account or bank accounts in such bank or banks as may be agreed upon by the partners.

2. All notices provided for under this agreement shall be in writing and shall be sufficient if sent by registered mail to the last known address of the party to whom such notice is to be given.

3. Proper and complete books of account shall be kept at all times and shall be open to inspection by any partner or his accredited representative at any reasonable time during business hours. The books of account shall be examined and reviewed as of the close of each fiscal year by an independent certified public accountant agreeable to the partners, who shall make a report thereon.

4. The parties hereto covenant and agree that they will execute any further instruments and that they will perform any acts which are or may become necessary to effectuate and to carry on the partnership created by this agreement.

IN WITNESS WHEREOF, the parties hereto have hereunto set their hands and seals the day and year first above written.

WITNESSED:

....(SEAL)
....(SEAL)
....(SEAL)

APPENDIX D

FORM OF LIMITED PARTNERSHIP AGREEMENT

Source: J. Mulder, M. Volz & A. Berger, The Drafting of Partnership Agreements 44-53 (5th ed. 1967).

AGREEMENT OF LIMITED PARTNERSHIP

Sunnyside Dairy Company

Agreement of Limited Partnership made this . . . . day of September, 1965, by and among John Smith and Harold Jones, both of . . . . (hereinafter sometimes referred to as "General Partners"), and Frank Brown and George Green, both of . . . . (hereinafter sometimes referred to as "Limited Partners").

Recitals

1. John Smith and Harold Jones have been conducting a general partnership business under a written agreement dated February 1, 1963.

2. It is the mutual desire of the parties hereto that the business be continued and that Frank Brown and George Green be admitted as limited partners.

Now, Therefore, intending to be legally bound hereby, the parties hereto hereby agree to operate a limited partnership business under the laws of the State of . . . . , under the following terms and conditions:

Article I

Formation of Limited Partnership

1. The parties hereto form a limited partnership pursuant to the act of the legislature of . . . . , approved on . . . . , and known as the Uniform Limited Partnership Act.

2. The parties hereto shall forthwith execute:
(a) A certificate and an affidavit thereto and cause same to be filed in the office of the Recorder of Deeds of the County of . . . . , in accordance with the provisions of the Uniform Limited Partnership Act of . . . .

(b) A certificate and cause the same to be filed with the Department of State of .... and the Clerk of Court of the County of ...., together with proof of publication as required by the Fictitious Names Act of ...., as amended.

ARTICLE II
Name, Character, Place of Business, and Term of Partnership

1. The business of the partnership shall be conducted under the firm name of "SUNNYSIDE DAIRY COMPANY".

2. The purpose of the partnership shall be to engage in the general dairy business, together with all other business necessary and related to it, including the purchase, processing, manufacture, sale, and distribution of milk, cream, and other products which may conveniently be handled with such products.

3. The principal place of business of the partnership shall be at ...., but additional places of business may be conducted at those locations as may from time to time be agreed upon by the general partners.

4. The partnership shall commence on the 1st day of September, 1965, and shall continue for an indefinite term.

ARTICLE III
Capital Contributions, Accounts, and Withdrawals

1. JOHN SMITH and HAROLD JONES shall be the general partners. FRANK BROWN and GEORGE GREEN shall be the limited partners.

The general partners shall contribute as their shares of the capital the amount credited respectively to them in the balance sheet, dated August 31, 1965, of the general partnership business heretofore conducted by them under the name of Sunnyside Dairy Company, a copy of which is attached hereto as Exhibit "A".

Each of the limited partners shall make the following contributions in cash to the capital of the partnership:

> Frank Brown $10,000
> George Green $10,000

2. Each partner, general or limited, may make additional contributions to the capital of the partnership in such amount as may from time to time be agreed upon by the general partners.

3. Each partner, general or limited, may make such withdrawals from his capital account as may from time to time be agreed upon by the general partners.

4. An individual capital account shall be maintained for each partner, to which shall be credited or debited his contributions or withdrawals, as the case may be.

ARTICLE IV

Duties, Powers, and Salaries of Partners

1. The general partners shall each have an equal voice in the management and conduct of the partnership business.

The general partners shall devote their full time and best efforts to the conduct of the partnership business.

Checks shall be drawn on the partnership bank account or bank accounts and shall be signed by any general partner or partners who may be designated by the general partners.

2. The general partners shall receive such salaries as may from time to time be agreed upon by the general partners. The payment of salaries shall be an obligation of the partnership only to the extent that there are partnership assets available for them, and shall not be an obligation of the individual partners. Each salary payment shall be treated as an expense of the partnership in determining the net profit or loss of the partnership in any fiscal year, as provided in Article V.

3. An individual withdrawal account shall be maintained for each general partner, to which shall be credited his salary. Any general partner may withdraw such portion of his salary as he may desire from time to time, which shall be charged to his withdrawal account.

Any portions of salaries not withdrawn by a general partner at the close of a fiscal year shall forthwith be credited to his capital account.

4. The limited partners shall not take part in the management of the business or transact any business for the partnership, and they shall have no power to sign for or to bind the partnership. No salary shall be paid to any limited partner.

5. Proper and complete books of account of the business of the partnership shall be kept by or under the supervision of the general partners at the principal place of business of the partnership and shall be open to inspection by any of the partners, general or limited, or by their accredited representatives, at any reasonable time during business hours. The books and records of account shall be examined and reviewed as of the close of each fiscal year by an independent certified public accountant, acceptable to the general partners, who shall make a report thereon.

ARTICLE V

Profits and Losses

1. The fiscal year of the partnership shall be the calendar year. The net profit or net loss of the partnership shall be determined in accordance with approved and accepted accounting practice as soon as possible after the close of each fiscal year.

2. The net profits earned by the partnership during each fiscal year shall be credited as of the close thereof to the capital accounts of the partners in the following proportions:

General Partners

| John Smith | 40 per cent |
| Harold Jones | 40 per cent |

Limited Partners

| Frank Brown | 10 per cent |
| George Green | 10 per cent |

3. The net loss incurred by the partnership during any fiscal year shall be debited as of the close thereof to the capital accounts of the partners in the same proportions to which the partners are respectively entitled to share profits pursuant to Paragraph 2 of this Article.

4. No limited partner shall be personally liable for any of the debts of the partnership or any of its losses beyond the amount originally contributed by him to the capital of the partnership, anything to the contrary herein inferable notwithstanding.

ARTICLE VI

Termination of Partnership; Changes in Membership

1. A general partner may retire from the partnership by giving at least ninety (90) days' notice in writing to all of the partners.

2. Retirement, death, or insanity of a general partner shall work an immediate dissolution of the partnership.

3. In the event of the dissolution of the partnership by retirement, death, or insanity of a general partner, a proper accounting shall be made of the capital and withdrawal accounts of each partner and of the net profit or net loss of the partnership from the date of the last previous accounting to the date of dissolution.

4. Upon the dissolution of the partnership business, by agreement of the partners or for any other reason, its liabilities and obligations to creditors shall be paid, and its assets, or the

proceeds of their sale, shall then be distributed in the following order:

(a) To the limited partners in proportion to their share of the profits;

(b) To the limited partners in proportion to their capital contributions;

(c) To the general partners in proportion to their share of the profits;

(d) To the general partners in proportion to their capital contributions.

5. In the event of the retirement, death, or insanity of a general partner, the remaining partners shall have the right to continue the business of the partnership under its present name by themselves, or in conjunction with any other person or persons they may select, but they shall pay to the retiring partner, or to the legal representatives of the deceased or insane partner, as the case may be, the value of his interest in the partnership, as provided in Paragraph 6 of this Article. If the remaining partners exercise the right given them in this paragraph, the provisions of Paragraph 4 of Article VI shall not be applicable.

6. The value of the interest of a retiring, deceased, or insane partner, as of the date of the exercise of the option given in Paragraph 4 of Article VI, shall be the sum of:

(a) His capital account;

(b) His withdrawal account; and

(c) His proportionate share of accrued net profits.

If a net loss has been incurred to the date of dissolution, his share of such loss shall be deducted.

The assets of the partnership shall be valued at book value for purposes of this Paragraph 6. In computing the value of the interest of a retiring, deceased, or insane partner under this Paragraph 6, no value shall be attributed to good will.

Article VII

The General Partners

1. A general partner may not, without the consent of the other partners:

(a) Assign, transfer, or pledge any of the claims of or debts due to the partnership except upon payment in full, or arbitrate or consent to the arbitration of any disputes or controversies of the partnership.

(b) Make, execute, or deliver any assignment for the benefit of creditors or any bond, confession of judgment, chattel mortgage, deed, guarantee, indemnity bond, surety bond, or contract to sell or contract of sale of all or substantially all of the property of the partnership.

(c) Lease or mortgage any partnership real estate or any interest therein or enter into any contract for any such purpose.

(d) Pledge or hypothecate or in any manner transfer his interest in the partnership, except to parties to this agreement.

(e) Become a surety, guarantor, or accommodation party to any obligation except for partnership business.

In Witness Whereof, the parties hereto have hereunto set their hands and seals, on the day and year first above written.

.... (Seal)
　　　　　　　　General Partner

.... (Seal)
　　　　　　　　General Partner

.... (Seal)
　　　　　　　　Limited Partner

.... (Seal)
　　　　　　　　Limited Partner

Signed, sealed, and delivered
　　in the presence of:

....
　　　　Witness

....
　　　　Witness

....
　　　　Witness

....
　　　　Witness

APPENDIX E

FORM OF CERTIFICATE OF FORMATION OF LIMITED PARTNERSHIP

Source: J. Mulder, M. Volz & A. Berger, The Drafting of Partnership Agreements 40-43 (5th ed. 1967).

CERTIFICATE OF FORMATION OF LIMITED PARTNERSHIP UNDER UNIFORM LIMITED PARTNERSHIP ACT

The undersigned, being desirous of forming a limited partnership under the Act of . . . ., entitled "The Uniform Limited Partnership Act", hereby make and sign the following certificate for that purpose:

I.   The name under which the partnership is to be conducted is "Sunnyside Dairy Company".

II.   The purpose of the partnership shall be to engage in the general dairy business, together with all other business necessary and related thereto, including the purchase, processing, manufacture, sale, and distribution of milk, cream, and other products which may conveniently be handled with such products.

III.   The location of the partnership's principal place of business is . . . .

IV.   The names and places of residence of the general and limited partners are:

John Smith	General Partner	(Address)
Harold Jones	General Partner	(Address)
Frank Brown	Limited Partner	(Address)
George Green	Limited Partner	(Address)

V.   The partnership shall continue for an indefinite term.

VI.   The limited partners have contributed the following cash to the partnership:

Frank Brown	$10,000
George Green	$10,000

VII.   Each limited partner may make any additional contributions to the capital of the partnership as may from time to time be agreed upon by the general partners.

VIII.   Each limited partner may make those withdrawals from his capital account as may from time to time be agreed upon by the general partners.

IX. By reason of their contributions the limited partners shall receive the following percentages of the net profits of the partnership:

Frank Brown	10 per cent
George Green	10 per cent

X. In the event of the retirement, death, or insanity of a general partner, the remaining partners shall have the right to continue the business of the partnership under the same name by themselves, or in conjunction with any other person or persons they may select.

IN WITNESS WHEREOF, we have hereunto set our hands and seals this . . . . day of . . . . , 1965.

. . . . (SEAL)

General Partner

. . . . (SEAL)

General Partner

. . . . (SEAL)

Limited Partner

. . . . (SEAL)

Limited Partner

Witnesses:

. . . .

. . . .

. . . .

. . . .

STATE OF . . . . }
COUNTY OF . . . . } ss

JOHN SMITH and HAROLD JONES, being duly sworn according to law, depose and certify that they are the general partners named in the foregoing certificate and that the facts set forth therein are true and correct.

. . . . (SEAL)

. . . . (SEAL)

Jurat

STATE OF . . . . }
COUNTY OF . . . . } ss

FRANK BROWN and GEORGE GREEN, being duly sworn according to law, depose and certify that they are the limited partners named in the foregoing certificate and that the facts set forth therein are true and correct.

. . . . (SEAL)

. . . . (SEAL)

Jurat

Index